VISIONS FOR CHANGE

VISIONS FOR CHANGE

CRIME AND JUSTICE
IN THE TWENTY-FIRST CENTURY

ROSLYN MURASKIN

Long Island University

ALBERT R. ROBERTS

Rutgers University

Prentice Hall
Upper Saddle River, NJ 07458

Library of Congress Cataloging-in-Publication Data

Muraskin, Roslyn.
   Visions for change : crime and justice in the twenty-first century
/ Roslyn Muraskin, Albert R. Roberts.
      p.   cm.
   Includes bibliographical references.
   ISBN 0-13-294604-1 (pbk.)
   1. Criminal justice, Administration of—United States—
Forecasting.   2. Crime forecasting—United States.   I. Roberts,
Albert T.   II. Title.
HV9950.M87   1996   95-36550
364.973—dc20   CIP

Editorial/Production Supervision,
   Interior Design, and Electronic Paging: *Naomi Sysak*
Managing Editor: *Mary Carnis*
Director of Production: *Bruce Johnson*
Manufacturing Buyer: *Ed O'Dougherty*
Acquisitions Editor: *Robin Baliszewski*
Editorial Assistant: *Rosemary Florio*
Cover Designer: *Bruce Kenselaar*

 ©1996 by Prentice-Hall, Inc.
A Simon & Schuster Company
Upper Saddle River, New Jersey 07458

Printed in the United States of America

10   9   8   7   6   5   4   3   2   1

ISBN 0-13-294604-1

Prentice-Hall International (UK) Limited, *London*
Prentice-Hall of Australia Pty. Limited, *Sydney*
Prentice-Hall Canada Inc., *Toronto*
Prentice-Hall Hispanoamericana, S.A., *Mexico*
Prentice-Hall of India Private Limited, *New Delhi*
Prentice-Hall of Japan, Inc., *Tokyo*
Simon & Schuster Asia Pte. Ltd., *Singapore*
Editora Prentice-Hall do Brasil, Ltda., *Rio de Janeiro*

This book is dedicated by Roslyn Muraskin
to her husband Matthew
and Tracy, Seth and Stacy, Craig and Elissavet

This book is dedicated by Albert R. Roberts
to his wife Beverly
and his son Herb

We jointly dedicate this book to the chapter authors and their families.

This comprehensive text would have never been completed
without the understanding of our significant others,
when we all spent long evenings and weekends writing our chapters.

C O N T E N T S

❖

PART III

POLICING NOW AND INTO THE TWENTY-FIRST CENTURY   73

PART IV

THE COURTS AND FUTURE LAW   128

PREFACE

❖

Criminal justice books vary distinctly on at least four dimensions in their focus and the amount of detail in each chapter: the types of contemporary issues discussed; the degree to which different components of the criminal justice process are described; the approach to examining the issues and policies (e.g., Point-Counterpoint, incremental approach of legislative development); and the specific types of crime control and rehabilitation strategies examined.

In *Visions for Change: Crime and Justice in the Twenty-First Century*, the editors have assembled a text which fully examines critical criminal justice policies and practices used by all criminal justice agencies throughout the United States. This is a text that links the past, present, and future of criminal justice as we approach the twenty-first century. Crime remains a problem today; law and order is still something that we strive for; there is the belief that the courts should dispense justice; and, advanced technology is transforming the world into a "global village," changing the dimensions of the crime scene as we have known it.

The future of criminal justice seems to be pessimistic, based on the obvious fact that incarceration has not succeeded in reducing the crime rate. Although the state and federal prison population grew from approximately 400,000 inmates in 1974 to one million inmates at the end of 1994, the rate of Part I offenses has remained the same. According to the FBI Uniform Crime Reports (1990), the rate of all Part I offenses (seven major crimes) reported to the police remained about the same in 1981 compared to 1990 (5,858.2 per 100,000 inhabitants in 1981 and 5,820.3 per 100,000 inhabitants in 1990). A crime bill has been passed, and before it has been implemented changes are being suggested. The populace wants the government to be "tough on crime," to build bigger and better prison facilities, and to emphasize the use of the death penalty. However, with the estimate of five billion dollars needed for prison construction, the question remains whether this is a proper remedy. With the passage of President Clinton's crime bill (which he inherited from President Bush), the prison systems in this country will worsen. It is estimated that during the years 1995-2000, as a result of the crime bill, the federal government will spend an additional nine billion dollars on prisons, including alternative prison facilities. Most promising is the authorization of billions of dollars for more and better educated law enforcement officers on both the state and local levels.

The critical issues that will shape the future of criminal justice can be identified by reviewing the current policies and issues. Debates continue to rage with regard to the benefits of incarceration versus probation; the benefits of punishment versus rehabilitation; the benefits of community policing versus traditional policing; the benefits of computer-based technology on the courts and law enforcement versus the status quo; and the benefits of delivering services to crime victims versus offenders.

These debates have usually been based on rhetoric and political expediency rather than on reasoned empirical studies. We firmly believe it is time to change the "status quo" in law enforcement, corrections, the courts, and the law. This text creates the vision of what is needed based on a review of the past and present. For the student this is not simply rhetoric but a study of how changes can be made based on present day policies.

It is vital to blend research with creativity to shape a vision for the future that moves beyond the status quo. In this book the authors have applied their many years of research as well as years of practical experience to link the past, present and future. Each chapter examines the most promising and reform-oriented policies, programs, and technological advancements for the twenty-first century.

The editors wish to express tremendous thanks to Robin Baliszewski of Prentice Hall for her advice, help, and guidance. She is a very special person. Thanks go also to all our contributors who have reviewed the past and have looked to the future of criminal justice issues.

Roslyn Muraskin, Ph.D.
Long Island University
C.W. Post Campus

Albert R. Roberts, D.S.W.
Rutgers University

VISIONS FOR CHANGE

PART I

CHAPTER 1

OVERVIEW

Roslyn Muraskin, Ph.D. and Albert R. Roberts, D.S.W.

The headlines scream out:

> *Don't Trample Prisoners' Rights!*
>
> *When Does a Young Offender Lose the Right to Privacy?*
>
> *New Standards for Drug Cases Anger Prosecutors!*
>
> *Lawyer in Trade Center Blast Case Says Client was Duped!*
>
> *Appeal in Death Sentence of the Killer of Four Girls!*
>
> *The Bust in Boot Camps (You Just Can't Intervene for a Short Time and Then Cut People Loose)!*
>
> *No More Death Penalty in the Year 2025!*
>
> *Lock 'em Up!...and Throw Away the Key!*
>
> *Crime and Punishment: Is Jail a Deterrent to Criminals?*
>
> *Acts of Terrorism Limit Freedom of American's Citizens!*
>
> *Opponents of Police Merger Doubt Savings!*
>
> *The Penile Plethysnography and Systematic Desensitization Works with Sex Offenders—No Recidivism at Eighteen-Month Follow-up!*

This is a text about the future of the criminal justice system looking to the twenty-first century. Criminal justice is an integral concern of all human beings around the world. Quantum leaps in technology, growing out of basic science research, are transforming societies globally, and consequently the crime scene, criminals and the criminal justice system. As we approach the millenium there are emerging changes that demand more accountability and offer new challenges. In the twenty-first century, a shift in philosophy will probably occur with respect to the disposition of criminal offenders: from a preference for punishment to a preference for treatment.

The argument will emerge that it is not enough to lock people up; something must be done to reduce the likelihood that they will commit crimes as juveniles and become repeat offenders. As a result public sentiment for treatment-oriented reform and prevention strategies will develop.

Since incarceration involves the practice of warehousing criminals (many of whom are violent) in overcrowded and understaffed institutions, it stands to reason that prisons continue to be among the most dangerous places in society. Institutional violence has remained a problem throughout the history of American corrections, and is likely to remain a critical issue in the future.

A major dilemma of criminal justice in a democratic society is how to process suspects and punish law violators in a humane and rational manner. The widespread prevalence of court orders to reform unconstitutional conditions of confinement in American jails and prisons, including unprecedented overcrowding, indicates a significant gap in the courts' current ability to do so and an important opportunity to change. As we head into the next century, we look for a coordinated approach to problem analysis and policy design to deal with the scope of jail overcrowding and court-ordered reform.

The society in which we will live in the early twenty-first century will be different from what it was in the late twentieth century. The age of information will have taken hold. We will be able to communicate visually and orally with anyone in the world instantaneously.

As the impending arrival of the twenty-first century marks a time of significant expectations and advanced preparedness, criminal justice professionals will encounter enormous challenges while experiencing marked changes. Whether or not the technological advancements in criminal justice investigations and crime control significantly reduce rates of violent crime remains to be seen. Technological and social developments as well as policy changes offer much promise for the future. Some of the most promising strategies include the following:

- The increased use of biosensors, lasers, and thermal neutron analysis equipment will greatly assist investigators searching for missing persons or toxic wastes.
- The increased development and use of nonlethal weapons such as laser guns, rubber bullets, and chemical sprays could save thousands of lives each year.
- The use of bionic eyes and eardrums could provide a major aid to police surveillance activities.
- Electronic tracking devices such as subdural implants, bracelets, and anklets could save states millions of dollars by using home detention and electronic monitoring instead of incarceration.
- Day reporting, day fines, intensive probation supervision and restitution could save states and counties millions of dollars with nonviolent offenders provided that each jurisdiction has an adequate accounting and monitoring staff.
- Behavior altering drugs implanted in a sex offender or alcoholic can be automatically activated when the offender approaches an elementary school or a tavern. The implanted microprocessor relays the physiological reactions to a central monitoring station which triggers the release of either a small amount of tranquilizer or a fast acting sleep inducer.

Futurist and criminal justice professor Gene Stephens aptly sums up what the future holds for law enforcement:

> From a crime-and-justice standpoint, the twenty-first century could be either heaven or hell. Police will have new tools that will allow them to better fight crime—or prevent crime from occurring in the first place. These same tools will have the potential for abuse—particularly in the area of

> invasions of privacy....[Nevertheless] in the twenty-first century, technology and new crime management methods will be able to significantly reduce street crime—the theft and violence that frightens citizens most.

In the first quarter of the century, many police departments will be using digital technology for automated fingerprint image capture, storage, retrieval, and transmission. As a result, remote positive identification from any part of the United States will be possible within minutes. Automated Fingerprint Identification Systems (AFIS) and other technologically advanced information systems will provide much faster and more accurate fingerprint card processing than the methods currently available. On-line and efficient access to criminal history and juvenile records will be made available to all police departments within seconds. At the county and city levels a growing number of jurisdictions will establish county-wide criminal justice information networks that link computers from different computer manufacturers and different county agencies into an integrated regional system. This cost-effective strategy to computer networking will allow each authorized operator to transfer information electronically from one agency to another. This system will save local criminal justice agencies hundreds of thousands of dollars each year in time and effort of investigators and computer operators. For example, a county probation officer or deputy prosecutor will only have to retrieve the information from the authorized computer operator, rather than starting from scratch and duplicating information already collected and entered into the system by one of the local police departments.

Crime laboratories will benefit greatly from the technology advancements and innovations. The future successes of law enforcement agencies will be enhanced by futuristic forensic scientists applying deoxyribonucleic acid (DNA) to personal identification, analytical instrumentation, electronic imaging technology, and still video photography. With regard to the detection of drugs and explosives, biosensors, lasers, and thermal neutron analysis equipment will greatly aid investigators searching for missing persons or toxic wastes. In the cases of missing or abducted women, identification will no longer be made through plaster casts and sculpturing (i.e. skin depth measurements, using clay to make a replica of the victim's face). Forensic scientists will be able to do a computer assisted anthropological study by using computer imaging to define what the missing person looks like.

Computer-based technologies and artificial intelligence systems will be used by many criminal justice agencies by the year 2000. Data based management systems (DBM) have already begun to provide important information to jail and court administrators throughout the United States. DBMs will be more widely used in the next century. Court DBM systems manage case dockets, maintain files on offenders, and enter official court decisions when rendered. DBMs can interface with telephone and tele-video computer-based tracking systems (CBTS) to produce closed circuit television systems that make it possible for courts to conduct remote bookings, initial hearings, and preliminary arraignments from hundreds of miles away. In futuristic local jails and state prisons. retinal identification, as well as hand palm and finger print matching will be more widely used to control access to restricted areas of institutions.

The Federal Bureau of Investigation (FBI) uses data-based systems (also known as "expert systems") to analyze criminal behavior patterns among serial killers, rapists, terrorists and other violent criminals. For many years the FBI's National

Criminal Information Center (NCIC) has provided local police departments with criminal history record checks of suspects within seconds. The NCIC-2000 system will enable law enforcement officers to rapidly identify missing persons and fugitives by placing a subject's finger on the fingerprint reader which will be located in patrol cars of the future. The fingerprint reader will then instantly transmit the image to the NCIC 2000 computer at FBI Headquarters, and within a few minutes, the computer will relay a reply to the police officer. Futuristic printers installed in patrol cars will permit officers to quickly obtain copies of a suspect's photograph, signature or tattoos, as well as composite drawings of unknown subjects. The FBI has also shared their crime laboratory resources with local departments investigating homicides (e.g. psychological profiling of serial killers, DNA typing, microscopic fiber analysis, and computer enhancing imaging of the facial features of persons dead for some time).

There is a belief that the justice process will be participatory, a mediation process where victim and defendant come to a satisfactory agreement. There will be increased resources. The population will be wealthier, older and more culturally diverse. There will be a steady increase in the crime rate and the diversity of crime will increase.

The time has come to reshape the future of the criminal justice system, to help redefine its character and method of operation. The time has come to create effective mechanisms for collaboration in solving the problems of the justice system as well as to provide a framework for appropriate channels of communication. As we approach the new century, the time has come to revisit the facilitation, planning, coordination, and implementation of the system as we currently understand it. We need to improve legislation and its procedures. There needs to be a commitment for additional human and financial resources to strengthen the criminal justice system. We need to formulate national policies concerning crime prevention as well as criminal justice strategies in order to contribute to the preservation and reinforcement of democracy and justice based on the rule of law. We need to have programs in place that have the capability to plan, implement, and evaluate crime prevention and criminal justice assistance projects—to sustain national developments, enhance justice and gain respect for human rights. We need to review the role of criminal law in the protection of the environment, crime prevention in urban areas, juvenile and violent criminality, and efficiency, fairness and improvement in the management and administration of criminal justice and related systems.

Compatible information technology will facilitate the administration of criminal justice and strengthen practical cooperation of crime control throughout. Both the private sector and criminal justice professionals should be encouraged to exchange proposals, information on projects, and innovations that enhance the operations of all criminal justice systems. This text is a collection of articles written by those individuals whose expertise in criminal justice systems lends itself to great consideration of what is yet to come. All the authors first look at criminal justice from an historical perspective, then review what is, and finally propose what ought to be.

PART II

INTRODUCTION

LINKING CRIME CHALLENGES IN THE TWENTY-FIRST CENTURY

This text concerns itself with much of the material discussed in the "Overview." We look at areas such as sentencing, prison/jail overcrowding, crimes of violence, gangs, the use of technology, the media, gender, the courts and the law, correctional health issues, legal issues in policing, and the rights of victims. We talk about policies, we talk about new programs, we suggest solutions to complex problems, we review strategies, and we look at the steady increase of crime and its impact on the twenty-first century. The book is divided into eight parts, each dealing with a different aspect of our criminal justice system as we know it.

Part II is titled, "Linking Crime Challenges in the Twenty-First Century." All across the United States, in communities large and small, the fear of teen gangs is growing. Ken Peak, in his chapter "Gangs: Origin, Outlook, and Policy Implications," describes how people have become virtual prisoners in their own homes. The trepidation caused by gang drive-by shootings forces schools to practice "ducking drills" and people to huddle in their darkened homes, hide their children in the bathtubs, and be afraid to let their children play outside in a growing number of areas throughout the United States. Peak takes a futuristic view of our society's changing demographics and the demands of an information-oriented job market, forecasting a larger underclass and fostering an expanded gang culture. He looks at the strategies for addressing the gang problem in the future, which include police responses and community programs.

Edith Flynn, in "Crime and Justice in the Twenty-First Century: International Terrorism and the United States," describes how the future of terrorism needs to be examined and analyzed in terms of international, transnational, domestic, and state terrorist activities. She asks: What are the effective tools to educating the public into the causes, tactics, and players of terrorism? What dangers to the American soil exist with the threat of international terrorism? How does a criminal justice system such as ours deal with such a problem?

In "'Murder and Mayhem' in the Media: Public Perceptions (and Misperceptions) of Crime and Criminality," Charles Field and Robert Jerin ask what the future trends are in the way crime is to be reported in all forms of media, and will such reporting be distorted?

Andrew Karmen, in "The Situation of Crime Victims in the Year 2020," talks of different strategies that can be employed to try to anticipate what the situation facing crime victims will be like in the future. One way is to examine the development of the past twenty-five years to see how much can be accomplished and reformed in this time span. A second way to speculate about what lies just beyond the horizon begins by identifying the driving forces for change. By focusing upon anticipated technological innovations, needed improvements can be predicted.

Jay Albanese takes a look at a different area: "Looking for a New Approach to an Old Problem: The Future of Obscenity and Pornography." Explicit songs, movies, cable television, talk radio and computer services are the latest manifestations of public concern over the proper role of sex and violence in the media and in American life in general. Research needs to be done to propose alternatives in defining and regulating obscenity and pornography. What are the trends in the pornography industry? What are the effects of pornography on behavior? What is the appropriate action to be taken by private citizens? What remedies must be taken by the legislatures and law enforcement to control pornography and obscenity? Who are the victims when we talk about such areas?

CHAPTER 2

GANGS: ORIGIN, OUTLOOK AND POLICY IMPLICATIONS

Kenneth J. Peak, Ph.D.

ABSTRACT

As futurists, criminal justice academicians, and lay persons "peek over the rim" and attempt to forecast what is in store for our society, certainly today's expanding fear of gang behaviors will rank high on their list of causes for future trepidation. In this chapter we examine gangs and their outlook. Specifically, we examine gang origins, composition, and characteristics. The chapter concludes by exploring some strategies for addressing the future gang problem and implications for policy making.

INTRODUCTION

It is no secret that in American communities large and small, the fear wrought by teen gangs has spread rapidly. With gang victimizations reported daily, many people have become virtual prisoners in their own homes. The trepidation caused by gang drive-by shootings causes schools to practice "ducking drills" and people to huddle in their darkened homes, hide their children in the bathtubs, and be afraid to let their children play outside.

This chapter examines gangs and what the future holds for them. Included are two broad areas of discussion: gang origins, composition, and characteristics, followed by an analysis of possible strategies for addressing the gang problem.

GANG ORIGINS, COMPOSITION, CHARACTERISTICS

Early Formation and Research

A youth gang is an association of individuals normally between the ages of fourteen and twenty-four years, which has a gang name and recognizable symbols, a geographic territory, a regular meeting pattern, and an organized, continuous course of criminality (Block and Block, 1993). The formation of youth gangs is not a recent phenomenon. Hispanic youth gang activity was first recognized in the early 1900s in the Southern California area. Thrasher's seminal study of 1,313 gangs in 1927 found that most gangs were small (six to twenty members) and formed spontaneously in poor and socially disorganized neighborhoods, by:

> disintegration of family life, inefficiency of schools, formalism and externality of religion, corruption and indifference in local politics, low wages

and monotony in occupational activities, unemployment, and lack of opportunity for wholesome recreation. Such underlying conditions...must be considered together as a situation complex which forms the matrix of gang development. *Among the groups within which the boy delinquent finds expression, the gang is one of the most vital to the development of his personality* (emphasis his) (Thrasher, 1927: 33, 339, 346).

Thrasher also observed that the gang functions with reference to these conditions in two ways: "It offers a substitute for what society fails to give; and it provides a relief from suppression and distasteful behavior. It fills a gap and affords an escape" (Thrasher, 1927:33).

Cloward and Ohlin (1960) later asserted that gangs emerged from "blocked opportunity" for legitimate success, resulting in one of three outcomes for juveniles: becoming organized or career criminals, committing wanton violence in search of status, or retreating into drug use and dropping out. This typology of gangs has been substantially confirmed by a number of subsequent studies in several different cities (see, for example, Fagan, 1990; Huff, 1989; Taylor, 1990; Yablonsky, 1962).

After this flurry of interest in gangs during the 1950s and 1960s, gang studies and investigations virtually ended. There is little evidence of serious concern about gangs from police or scholars from the mid-1960s to the mid-1970s. In fact, the 1973 National Advisory Commission on Criminal Justice Standards and Goals (p. 33) reported that "youth gang violence is not a major problem in the United States." Concern with gangs has experienced a rebirth since then, and it continues today at a high level. Immigration patterns, economic conditions, and increased violence have been identified as contributing factors to the reemergence of gangs (Albanese, 1993).

Today there are many youth gangs, usually organized along ethnic lines and including Asian, black, Hispanic and white groups. Members usually join the gang either by committing a crime or undergoing an initiation procedure. Gang members use automatic weapons and sawed-off shotguns in violent drive-by shootings, while becoming more sophisticated in their criminal activities and more wealthy. Crack cocaine and other illegal enterprises have provided a level of wealth and a lifestyle they would probably otherwise not have attained. The availability of guns, a violence-prone film and entertainment industry, and the inherent violence of today's youths only serve to exacerbate the problem. Fear of the criminal justice system is largely absent in these young people; they know the juvenile system is backlogged and that relatively few severe penalties are meted out.

Gangs are comprised of three types of members: hardcore (those who commit violent acts and defend the reputation of the gang); associates (members who frequently affiliate with known gang members for status and recognition, but who move in and out on the basis of interest in gang functions); and peripherals, who are not gang members, but associate or identify with gang members for protection—usually the dominant gang in their neighborhood. Most females fall into this category (Witkin, 1991).

Contemporary Ethnic and Racial Gangs

Today gangs are growing like weeds. The "Crips" and the "Bloods" began in Southern California over a quarter century ago and now have affiliations in thirty-two states and more than one hundred cities. In the Los Angeles area, gangs doubled from four hundred with 4,500 members in 1985 to eight hundred with 90 thousand members in 1990. The Los Angeles Police Department's aggressive enforcement in the mid-1980s displaced youth gangs throughout western and midwestern cities. Few police agencies possessed the knowledge or strategies to effectively combat the reign of terror and violence that often ensued after gangs sprung up in a neighborhood (Witkin, 1991).

The expansion of the gangs basically followed the interstate highway system. As an example, they moved from Minneapolis to Chicago almost ten years ago and have been building ever since. They became especially violent in Chicago, where youth gangs have been fighting for control of thriving narcotics, auto theft, gunrunning, and extortion operations. Retailers are expected to pay "seguro," also known as "insurance" or a "street tax," to gang members if they want to carry on their business (Starr, 1985).

Asian gangs include Chinese and Filipino youths. Chinese gangs can be traced back to the latter part of the 19th century with the influx of Chinese immigrants. In 1965 the first Chinese gang was formed in Southern California; it is believed they have continued to flourish because of the exploitation of migrant workers which led to a breakdown in traditional family ties and crime. Throughout the 1980s, gang leaders found that ethnic Chinese from Vietnam were most suited for criminal activities. Today the most powerful Chinese gang (especially in California) appears to be "Suey Sing," which has taken over the extortion and protection of several gambling houses and in 1990 began brutally executing influential members of rival gangs such as the "Wah Ching" (Toy, 1992). Filipino gangs began in the Philippines during World War II, by many hardcore criminals released from prison. Filipino gang members may be identified by their distinctive tattoos. They also display their gang name in graffiti. Filipino gang members are usually older, often in their thirties.

Black gangs of prominence are the Crips and the Bloods. The Crips began in Los Angeles in 1969, reportedly on the campus of Washington High School as *C*ommunity *R*esources for an *I*ndependent *P*eople; one of the school's colors was blue, which is now the color of gang identification. Another popular belief is that their name derived from "crypt," from the "Tales from the Crypt" horror movie. The groups began by robbing, extorting, and assaulting other area youths.

Crips address each other with the nickname "Cuzz." Crip graffiti can be identified by the symbol "B/K," which stands for "Blood Killers." Bloods reportedly formed as a means of protection against the Crips, in and near Compton, California. Bloods identify with the color red, and address each other as "Blood." Gang graffiti frequently uses the terms "BS" for "Bloodstone" or "C/K" for "Crip Killers." Both Crips and Bloods refer to fellow gang members as "homeboys" or "homeys."

Hispanic gangs invariably name their gangs after a geographical area or "turf" which they feel is worth defending. Hispanic gang activity often becomes a family affair, with young males (ten to thirteen) being the "pee wees," the fourteen to twenty-two-year-old being the hardcore, and those living beyond age twenty-two becoming a "vetrano," or veteran. Headgear (knit cap or monickered bandanna), shirts, pants (highly starched khaki or blue jeans), tattoos (of gang identification) and vehicles (often older model Chevrolets, lowered and with extra chrome and fur) are standard fare.

White gangs are also expanding, as growing numbers of young neo-Nazi Skinheads are linking up with old-line hate groups in the United States. This unity has bolstered the morale and criminal activity of the Ku Klux Klan and other white supremacist organizations. Numerous Skinhead groups have aligned with the White Aryan Resistance, which tends to encourage violence for "self-defense." Skinheads have shaved heads and may sport Nazi and/or Satanic insignia or tattoos. They preach violence against blacks, Hispanics, Asians and homosexuals. They range in age from thirteen to twenty-five, and associate with "white power" music. Their preferred mode of dress is military-like in nature, with khaki pants, black leather or tuffy-type jackets, and lace-up black boots.

Graffiti and Hand Signals

All social groups and cultures have self-styled communicative methods; teen gangs are no exception. Nonverbal forms of communication allow gang members to communicate with each other and with rival gangs; graffiti also serves to mark the gang's turf; if a gang's graffiti is untouched or unchallenged for a period of time, the gang's control in that area is reaffirmed.

Within the Chicano gang, there is a nonverbal communicative method that has existed for approximately fifty years. This method, called a "placa," is one that allows the Chicano gang member to express himself, his gang, other gangs and direct challenges to others. These gangs, having existed since the turn of the century, have developed many standard symbols. Hand signals, or "throwing signs," are made by forming letters or numbers with the hands and fingers, depicting the gang symbol or initials. This signalling allows the gang member to show which gang he belongs to and issue challenges to other gangs in the vicinity.

To have any success at all in investigating gang activities, police agencies must develop expertise in gang movements, activities, nonverbal communication, graffiti, tattoos, and dress codes. Police have also developed intelligence files on known or suspected gang members.

Girl Gangs

A study of a Chicago black girl gang by Fishman (1988) found the "Vice Queens" to be loosely knit and composed of about thirty members, nineteen of whom were considered hard core; the girls ranged in age from thirteen to nineteen. The gang did not have a rigid structure like that of their male counterparts, the "Vice Kings"; their main interest lay in the achievements of the Kings, but they also had achievements of their own, including criminal activities. Fishman placed black girl gangs in a larger context:

> There has been little improvement in the economic situation of the black community since 1965. The situation for teenage black girls today is even bleaker.... As black girls are increasingly exposed to the worsening conditions within their low income neighborhood where legitimate opportunities become increasingly restricted...they...increasingly turn to black female auxiliary gangs which provide these girls with the opportunity to learn the skills to make the adaptations to poverty, violence, and racism. In response to the economic crisis within their communities, black female gangs today have become more entrenched, more violent, and more and more oriented to "male" crime...(which) stems from the economic crisis within the black community (26-27).

Campbell (1984) concurred, finding that girls joined gangs because society has little to offer women of color. The possibility of a decent career is practically nonexistent; men still "make decisions that circumscribe the possibilities that are open" to them. And, they share with their male counterparts the general powerlessness of members of the urban underclass. Their lives, Campbell asserted, reflect the burdens of their triple handicaps of race, class, and gender. For them, the gang represents "an idealized collective solution." The lack of recreational opportunities, the long days unfilled by work or school, and the absence of money mean that hours and days are whiled away on street corners. "Doing nothing" means hanging out on the stoop; the hours of "bullshit" are punctuated by trips to the store to buy one can of beer at a time. When an unexpected windfall arrives, marijuana and rum are purchased in bulk and the partying begins. The next day, life returns to normal (Campbell, 1984:176).

STRATEGIES FOR THE FUTURE

Methods of Addressing the Problem

Some authors have maintained that gangs are not inherently evil or totally devoid of any positive attributes: "Gangs offer their members love, companionship, friendship, loyalty, and trust. They also help members and their families with living expenses, such as rent and utility payments, clothing and medicine purchases, and transportation" (Fattah, 1994:106). However, for most Americans, gang activities like drug abuse, prostitution, and other street crimes, are deeply offensive and frightening.

Today, as Thrasher observed in 1927, there are "really only two alternatives" in successfully reforming a youth who has come under the influence of the gang: either remove the individual from the gang and the social world it represents, or reform the gang. Both are very difficult to accomplish. Thrasher asserted that the problem of redirecting the gang turns out to be one of giving life meaning for the youth: "It is a matter of 'definition of the situation,' but this has too often come to mean the process of setting up taboos and prohibitions. We need to make the boy understand what he may not do, but it is more important to lead him to see the meaning of what society wants him to do and its relation to some rational scheme of life." (Thrasher, 1927:356).

Two primary methods have been attempted thus far to control youth gangs: police sweeps or crackdowns, and community programs. Below we discuss what is being done with both methods.

The Police Response

Police sweeps are essentially mass arrests of gang members on minor changes. Taking young people off the streets for a short time has only a temporary effect on gangs. The commanding officer of the Gang Crime Section of the Chicago Police Department observed that "Today, we are arresting more gang members than ever before; we are getting more convictions than ever before; and we are getting longer sentences than ever before. But ironically, we have more gangs than ever before. Arrest and prosecution are not the deterrent we expected them to be" (Bryant, 1989:1).

A review of eighteen case studies of police crackdowns in various cities found similar results: the impact "began to decay after a short period, sometimes despite continued dosage of police presence" (Sherman, 1990). Police understand that enforcement alone provides little relief or solution to the underlying problem, which is vested in social, political, and economic factors. A fundamental question to ask is: How do we as a society replace the gang's social importance and financial benefits (with children "earning" literally hundreds of dollars a day in drug-related activities) with education or work programs that pay minimum wage? This is a complex issue; there are no simple answers. There is a strong consensus, however, that the police should have some authority to intervene.

Some states are attempting to deal with the gang problem by enacting legislation which makes gang membership a crime. These gang/association laws do not appear to be spreading, however; many people fear the law will be overbroad and very difficult to enforce, as well as ineffective for true gang members.

Injunctive relief is also used by the police in some jurisdictions. It can be used to great advantage in a preventive way. For example, in Los Angeles the city attorney's office obtained an injunction ordering members of a drug-dealing street gang not to annoy, harass, or intimidate the residents of the gang's territory. Prosecutors contended that the gang was an "unincorporated association" whose members were individually liable for the actions of its members and, as such, constituted a nuisance (*Wall Street Journal*, 1988).

WHEN POLICE GOALS AND INDIVIDUAL LIFESTYLES COLLIDE

A police department in one western city was recently sued for conducting a "war on gangs" and "routinely harassing" young Hispanics suspected of being gang members—searching, photographing, and sometimes detaining them. The lead plaintiff in the lawsuit, which requested the federal district judge to "include at least five hundred Hispanics as plaintiffs," claimed police stopped him at least thirty-five times, photographed him twice without his permission, subjected him to extensive questioning about alleged gang membership, and that a group of ten or more officers once drew their guns on him. He also claimed that he and his vehicle, including its stereo speakers, were searched without reason and without permission. The suit requested an unspecified amount of damages.

The police, for their part, admitted to having a "war on crime," but categorically denied having a war against gangs. However, gang members who were criminals were police targets, but police actively worked with the community's Gang Alternatives Program and sponsored a Community Action Team to try to head young people away from gang membership. The department did, nevertheless photograph persons suspected of gang membership, including those who displayed gang hand signals. The department had a policy whereby people could have their photos removed from gang files when proving they were not gang members. The plaintiffs' attorney, however, argued that such a policy put citizens in a position of being guilty until they prove themselves innocent.

This case illustrates the "no-win" situation often confronting police when combating gang problems. Left in a defensive, litigious position for all of their efforts, it can only be a frustrating, dispiriting task for them.

APPLYING THE COPPS APPROACH

The primary approach to youth gangs in the 1950s and 1960s was to reach out to youth and prevent gang involvement or intervene with social services. In the 1970s and 1980s a police suppression approach prevailed. There is no clear evidence that either approach was successful (Spergal et al., 1990).

One strategy being implemented across the country is community-oriented policing and problem solving ("COPPS") which brings the community and police together in a partnership to work toward reducing neighborhood disorder and fear of crime (see Goldstein, 1990; Trojanowicz and Bucqueroux, 1990; Peak et al., 1992). Case studies about the COPPS approach to gangs are becoming more commonplace. An excellent example of a "success story" is that of Sacramento County, California, where two deputies, on their own initiative, spearheaded the drive to eliminate gang disorder.

The "Lichen Boys Posse" surfaced in 1982, and over the years the gang grew from a small group of young teens to at least forty members, predominantly white but including some blacks and Hispanics. Crime and graffiti quickly began to flourish in the comfortable, middle-class, north county area. An analysis revealed that approximately half of the assaults and burglaries were gang-related. A sheriff's deputy assigned himself to the Lichen tract and quickly asked residents to let him know when problems occurred; meanwhile, a Neighborhood Watch was organized by another crime prevention specialist in the sheriff's office. More than three hundred residents turned out at the first area meeting; they formed nighttime community patrols, phone trees, and block organizations. They held painting parties of fifty people to eradicate gang graffiti as soon as it appeared. They monitored all traffic in and out of their neighborhoods, recording license plate numbers and descriptions for deputies.

Meanwhile, another sheriff's deputy, working as a bailiff in Sacramento County Juvenile Court, noticed that arrest reports often took up to a month to trickle through the system, so judges often made rulings without full knowledge of a youth's criminal record. Judges often slapped imaginative probation orders on juveniles, such as "no association" clauses that made it illegal for youths on probation to associate with known gang members. However, patrol officers were almost always ignorant of such special orders that would allow them to arrest juvenile troublemakers.

This deputy happened to "moonlight" as a security guard in a Lichen-area shopping center and noticed the increase in gang-related graffiti and activity. He traced down and copied the probation reports for names on a list of suspects, and walked all arrest reports through juvenile court in a matter of days instead of weeks; he made sure deputy district attorneys knew the particulars about the Lichen Boys appearing in court before them. Concurrently, the work of these deputies and the Lichen residents was paying off; about one quarter of the seventy arrests made of gang members was a result of community area patrol (Blattner, 1992).

This illustration shows what the police can accomplish when they leave their patrol vehicles, empower the community to assist in crime-fighting, and engage in proactive problem-solving.

A Program Approach

Clearly, something more than police work alone is needed to break the cycle of gang delinquency. A continuing roadblock to prevention has been the lack of community interest and support of gang reduction initiatives. In too many communities, gang violence is tolerated as long as gang members victimize each other and do not bother the rest of society (Horowitz, 1987). Without community support the contemporary cycle of youth gang activities will continue; even gang members who are imprisoned join branches of their gang behind bars while replacements are found to take their place on the street (Jacobs, 1983; Moore, et al., 1978).

As one observer commented, "if families, schools, and churches don't socialize children to act responsibly, and if the national and local economies don't provide adequate legal opportunity structures, we as a society are in deep trouble" (Huff, 1990:316). Another researcher offered that "community and political institutions, beginning with the family itself, must be better organized and more committed to ameliorating the conditions conducive to gang delinquency" (Albanese, 1993:178).

As noted above, the recent emergence of gangs in middle- and smaller-sized cities is tied up with demographic trends, deindustrialization, the continuing problem of race in our cities, as well as other variables. Many authors (see, for example, Hagedorn, 1988; Moore, et al., 1978; Thrasher, 1963; Suttles, 1959) believe gangs are spontaneous products of local communities, best understood by analyzing local conditions and group process. They feel that those who look to "diffusion" or conspiracy theories of gang development or who hope to find easy "solutions" from outside gang "experts" are mistaken; that most cities have not balanced their law enforcement emphasis with equal resources spent on genuine community programs; and that, while full, meaningful employment will not solve all the problems, it would solve most of them.

Hagedorn (1988:167-169) offered three practical lessons from our experiences in trying to "do something" about gangs for the future:

1. Gang members must participate in any meaningful programs. Gang programs need to train and hire former local gang members as staff, utilize older gang members as consultants in developing new programs, and make sure input from the gang "clients" takes place and is genuine.

2. Emphasis needs to be placed on creating jobs and improving education, not rationalizing the criminal justice system. While "diversion" or other kinds of community-based programs would be welcome, the emphasis needs to be elsewhere. While harsh sanctions should be meted out for serious and violent behavior, the criminal act itself should merit punishment; the gang member should not be punished merely for who he is.

3. Research on gangs is necessary if we are to go beyond the law enforcement paradigm in understanding or policy. Why have gangs formed in some cities and not in others? How do we measure the influence of minority institutions and whether that influence is declining? What are the causes for the extreme variation in rates of homicides among gangs? What role is prison playing in gang development in cities where gangs have emerged within the last ten years?

Which Method Is Best?

Determining the best course of action for dealing with street gangs is not easy. A number of questions about the origin, activities, and future of gangs are still unanswered; several common sense approaches have been offered for addressing the problem. Most experts describe programs in communities with gangs that would include some combination of the following:

- *Fundamental changes in the way schools operate.* Schools should broaden their scope of services and act as community centers involved in teaching, providing services, and serving as locations for activities before and after the school day.

- *Job skills development for youths and young adults accompanied by improvements in the labor market.* Many youths have dropped out of school and do not have the skills to find employment. Attention needs to be focused on ways both to exand the labor market, including the development of indigenous businesses in these communities, and to provide job skills for those in and out of school.

- *Assistance to families.* A range of family services including parent training, child care, health care, and crisis intervention must be made available in communities with gangs.

- *Changes in the way the criminal justice system—particularly policing— responds generally to problems in these communities and specifically to gang problems.* Police agencies need to increase their commitment to understanding the communities they serve and to solving problems. This may require a shift from a strict calls-for-service approach to a proactive COPPS approach.

- *Intervention and control of known gang members.* Illegal gang activity must be controlled by diverting peripheral members from gang involvement and criminal activity. Achieving control may mean making a clear statement—by arresting and incapacitating hard-core gang members—that communities will not tolerate intimidating, violent, and/or criminal gang activity (Conly, et al., 1993:65-66).

Support for such a strategy has by no means been unanimous. Observers like Walter Miller (1990), who has studied gangs for decades, maintain that gang programs have not worked when based on the notion that the solution lies with changing the characteristics of lower-class life (e.g., community conditions). The major assumption that gangs arise out of lower class life is confounded by the fact that there are lower-class communities with no gangs. Miller advocated programs narrowly focused on gang members and those at immediate risk of membership, organized at the community level and involving the provision of educational and employment support to these individuals.

Other writers (e.g., Huff, 1990) counter this position and suggest that certain "ecological areas are generating the highest rates of crime, delinquency, incarceration, mental illness, public assistance, and other indicators of 'social pathology'"; this pathology makes it fiscally responsible to invest in prevention and community-wide coordination to address the broad range of social ills in those communities. Another long-time gang researcher, James Short, also sees considerable promise in recent community attempts at creating "a community of values in which institutions and programs are mutually supportive" (Short, 1990). Finally, David Fattah (1994:105-106), co-founder of the House of Umoja in Philadelphia (providing residential and nonresidential services to juvenile gang members for over a quarter century) also argued that much can be done at the community level. Note that his recommendations appear to favor a COPPS approach:

1. Gangs need to attach themselves to positive aspects of their communities; jobs are an important part of this positive attachment process.

2. Given the national nature of gang networks, a national task force on gangs should be established, designed and managed by neighborhood-based organizations working to reduce gang drug dealing and violence.

3. Police, neighborhood-based organizations, and other concerned parties should be trained in how to recognize and respond to the presence of gangs.

4. Immediate efforts should be taken to contain the spread of drug dealing and violence, by preventing drug use and abuse and preventing gang recruitment by targeting preteens.

5. There should be implementation of a grievance procedure directed toward violence avoidance through counseling, mediation, and conflict resolution training, which has already proven effective with warring gang members.

One way to resolve the "police crackdowns or community programs?" debate is to test both strategies in several different communities with gangs. One program model could target only gang members and those at high risk for membership and include a comprehensive set of prevention, intervention, and suppression strategies. The other model could include a component aimed at gang members, but be more broadly focused on making changes in the way major community institutions relate to each other. Both would require coordination of key leaders, including educators, criminal justice practitioners, labor specialists, private industry representatives, housing specialists, community groups, health and mental health professionals, representatives of the local media, and the residents themselves (Conly, et al., 1993).

Determining which approach to test would depend on the community and its ability to effect major structural changes. Furthermore, the implementation of either scenario requires careful planning and the development of a set of outcome measures that can be monitored and evaluated. Both program packages will also need to be funded sufficiently to allow some degree of institutionalization. Gang programs often fail because they are not sustained long enough to make a difference. One way to maximize the impact of funding is to develop a coordinated federal gang strategy, in which funds now targeted independently on education, substance abuse prevention, gang control, job skills development and employment, and criminal justice reform, among others, are made available in a package to communities with gangs.

SUMMARY AND POLICY IMPLICATIONS

The gang problem is not going to dissipate soon; where poverty and hopelessness are at their worst, and people live in violent surroundings and seek protection in numbers, gangs will thrive as they have for nearly one hundred years. There is room for hope, however. If the advice of experts is heeded and communities will take the initiative toward developing policy, initiating programs, and providing necessary resources, we may be able to stem the growing tide of gang activities.

There are several policy implications for the future. First, while support must be unflagging for police anti-gang activities, the COPPS strategy holds promise for addressing this problem. Intervention strategies to reduce violence must be built on a foundation of current information about the types of street gangs and street gang activities in each neighborhood where gangs flourish. Initiatives for reducing gang violence must also recognize the difference between turf protection and drug trafficking. A strategy to reduce gang involvement in drugs in a community in which gang members are mostly concerned with defense of turf will have little chance of success (Block and Block, 1993).

Another focus of control over gang violence should be on reducing the availability of the most dangerous weapons (e.g., large caliber, automatic, or semiautomatic). Finally, street gang membership, violence and other illegal gang activity must be understood in light of both long-term or chronic social patterns. We must also attempt to understand rapidly changing street-gang problems stemming from the existing economic conditions, weapon availability, drug markets, and the spatial arrangement of street gang territories across a city. The ultimate solution rests on a coordinated criminal-justice response and changes in educational opportunities, racial and ethnic attitudes, and job structure.

We can ill afford to "hurtle into the future without eyes fixed firmly on the rearview mirror" (Postman, 1991:19). The future will not likely witness the diminution of gang activities unless communities resolve to seek solutions and take action.

STUDY QUESTIONS

1. Explain how and why youth gangs are formed and what gangs provide to their members.

2. Describe the three types of gang members

3. Given the demographic predictions for our society, what appears to be the outlook for gangs? Explain.

4. Discuss the major facets of the two primary methods attempted thus far to control youth gangs.

5. In your opinion, who wins the "police response or community programs" debate? Defend your answer.

REFERENCES

Albanese, Jay S. (1993). *Dealing with Delinquency: The Future of Juvenile Justice* (2d ed.). Chicago: Nelson-Hall.

Blattner, Bob. (1992). Community Policing and Gang Intervention. In California Department of Justice, Attorney General's Office, Crime Prevention Center, *COPPS: Community Oriented Policing and Problem Solving*. Sacramento, CA: Author, pp. 167-170.

Block, Carolyn R. and Block, Richard. (1993). *Street Gang Crime in Chicago*. Washington, DC: National Institute of Justice, Research in Brief.

Bryant, Dan. (1989). Communitywide Responses Crucial for Dealing with Gang Problems. *Juvenile Justice Bulletin* (September).

Campbell, A. (1984). *The Girls in the Gang*. Oxford: Basil Blackwell.

Cloward, Richard A., and Ohlin, Lloyd E. (1960). *Delinquency and Opportunity: A Theory of Delinquent Gangs*. New York: The Free Press.

Conly, Catherine H., Kelly, Patricia, Mahanna, Paul, and Warner, Lynn. (1993). *Street Gangs: Current Knowledge and Strategies*. Washington, D.C.: U.S. Department of Justice, National Institute of Justice.

Fagan, Jeffrey A. (1990). Treatment and Reintegration of Violent Juvenile Offenders: Experimental Results. *Justice Quarterly* 7 (June): 233-263.

Fattah, David. (1994). Drugs and Violence in Gangs. In *African-American Perspectives on Crime Causation, Criminal Justice Administration, and Crime Prevention*, edited by Anne T. Sulton, 101-107. Englewood, CO: Sulton Books.

Fishman, L.T. (1988). The Vice Queens: An Ethnographic Study of Black Female Gang Behavior. Paper presented at the annual meeting of the American Society of Criminology.

Goldstein, Herman. (1990). *Problem-Oriented Policing*. New York: McGraw-Hill.

Hagedorn, John M. (1988). *People and Folks: Gangs, Crime and the Underclass in a Rustbelt Society*. Chicago: Lake View Press.

Horowitz, Ruth. (1987). Community Tolerance of Gang Violence. *Social Problems* 34 (December): 437-450.

Huff, C. Ronald. (1990). Denial, Overreaction, and Misidentification: A Postscript on Public Policy. In *Gangs in America*, edited by C. Ronald Huff, 310-317. Newbury Park, CA: Sage.

Huff, C. Ronald. (1989). Youth Gangs and Public Policy. *Crime and Delinquency* 35:525-537.

Jacobs, James B. (1983). *New Perspectives on Prisons and Imprisonment*. Ithaca, NY: Cornell University Press.

Miller, Walter. (1990). Why Has the U.S. Failed to Solve Its Youth Gang Problem? In *Gangs in America*, edited by C. Ronald Huff, 263-287. Newbury Park, CA: Sage.

Moore, Joan W., Garcia, Carlos, Cerda, Luis, and Valencia, Frank. (1978). *Homeboys: Gangs, Drugs, and Prison in the Barrios of Los Angeles*. Philadelphia: Temple University.

National Advisory Commission on Criminal Justice Standards and Goals. (1976). *Report of the Task Force on Juvenile Justice and Delinquency Prevention*. Washington, DC: U.S. Government Printing Office.

Peak, Ken, Bradshaw, Robert V., and Glensor, Ronald W. (1992). Improving Citizen Perceptions of the Police: "Back to the Basics" with a Community Policing Strategy. *Journal of Criminal Justice*, 20:25-40.

Postman, Neil. (1991). Quoted in Osborne, David, and Gaebler, Ted, *Reinventing Government: How the Entrepreneurial Spirit is Transforming the Public Sector*. Reading, MA: Addison-Wesley.

Sherman, Lawrence W. (1990). Police Crackdowns: Initial and Residual Deterrence. In *Crime and Justice: A Review of Research*, Vol. 12, edited by Michael Tonry and Norval Morris. Chicago, IL: University of Chicago Press.

Short, James F. (1990). New Wine in Old Bottles? Change and Continuity in American Gangs. In *Gangs in America*, edited by C. Ronald Huff, 223-239. Newbury Park, CA: Sage.

Spergal, Irving A., Chance, Ronald L., and Curry, G. David. (1990). *National Youth Gang Suppression and Intervention Program*. Washington, DC: U.S. Department of Justice, Office of Juvenile Justice and Delinquency Prevention.

Starr, Mark. (1985). Chicago's Gang Warfare. *Newsweek* (January 28).

Suttles, Gerald D. (1959). *Territoriality, Identity, and Conduct: A Study of an Inner-City Slum with Special Reference to Street Corner Groups*. Unpublished dissertation, Champaign, IL, University of Illinois.

Taylor, Carl S. (1990). Gang Imperialism. In *Gangs in America*, edited by C. Ronald Huff, pp. 103-115. Newbury Park, CA: Sage.

The Wall Street Journal (30 March 1988).

Thrasher, Frederick. (1927). *The Gang*. Chicago: University of Chicago Press.

Toy, Calvin. (1992). "A Short History of Asian Gangs in San Francisco," *Justice Quarterly* 9 (December):647-665.

Trojanowicz, Robert, and Bucqueroux, Bonnie. (1990). *Community Policing: A Contemporary Perspective*. Cincinnati: Anderson.

Witkin, Gordon. (1991). Kids Who Kill. *Newsweek* (April 8):26-32.

Yablonsky, Lewis. (1962). *The Violent Gang*. Baltimore: Penguin Books.

CHAPTER 3

INTERNATIONAL TERRORISM AND THE UNITED STATES

Edith E. Flynn, Ph.D.

ABSTRACT

The scourge of international and national terrorism will continue to challenge the United States well into the twenty-first century. It represents a unique, pervasive, and costly challenge to this country's ideals, principles, and safety. The full dimensions of its threats have yet to be recognized by this nation. This chapter traces the roots of politically motivated terrorism to its earliest manifestations in ancient history. It identifies the changing characteristics of modern terrorism, which have made its contemporary versions more potent, more destructive, and much more lethal. The combination of rapid technological development in weaponry, telecommunications, and mobility has greatly increased the vulnerability of modern, industrialized nations. Nuclear plants, pipelines, powergrids, public transport systems, centralized computer banks storing vital governmental, private, and commercial records, represent countless targets for terrorists, the destruction of which could create great losses and disruptions.

The confluence of these developments means that ever smaller groups of malcontents and extremists will be able to inflict ever greater harm and damage now and into the future. By using global and national examples of terrorist movements and incidents, the defining characteristics of modern terrorism are presented and important distinctions are made between national, international, and transnational terrorism.

INTRODUCTION

America was founded on the principles of individual freedom, the rule of law, liberty, equal justice for all, and an abiding concern for the intrinsic value of human life. Throughout the history of this nation, these principles have survived many serious challenges and threats. They have been severely tested during periods of great national stress, such as the Civil War, the World Wars, Vietnam, and on many occasions during the past forty years, a time period better known as the "Cold War."

Today, the Cold War is over, and the Soviet Union, long perceived as America's chief protagonist in world politics, has ceased to exist. The fall of the Berlin Wall in 1989, coupled with the withering of communism throughout Eastern Europe, signaled the advent of a new era in world politics. It also brought about monumental changes in the international security environment affecting the United States and the rest of the world.[1] But instead of being able to enjoy the fruits of the peace by reallocating scarce resources from armaments to social programs, our nation continues to face unique, pervasive, and costly challenges to its ideals, principles, and safety from a continuing and growing scourge of international and national terrorism.[2]

It is the purpose of this chapter to examine contemporary international terrorism, discuss its origins, and its manifestations. The growing threat of terrorism to this nation's national and international interests and security is analyzed. A probable future course of the threat of international terrorism in the United States is charted. The final segment outlines the inherent dangers of terrorism to civil liberties and discusses the special challenges counterterrorist measures present in the development of governmental and criminal justice system responses.

THE NATURE OF TERRORISM

Logically, any discussion of terrorism should begin with a precise definition of the subject. Regrettably, there is no universally accepted definition of terrorism, in spite of a vast body of historical and sociopolitical research and writing on this topic.[3] There are many reasons for this lack of agreement. Among them is the fact that the term "terrorism" has been promiscuously applied to a variety of violent acts which are not strictly terroristic in nature. For example, guerrilla warfare is often described by the media and some writers as terrorism, in spite of fundamental differences between the goals, objectives, strategies and actions of guerrillas and terrorists.[4] Admittedly, the differences between the two types of groups are sometimes blurred, especially when their tactics and techniques are considered. But on the whole, terrorism is easy to differentiate from guerrilla warfare.[5]

Another example of misusing the word "terrorism" comes from the tendency by some to look upon politically motivated violence in purely relativist terms. In this sense, what is labeled terrorism is contingent upon the user's particular point of view. As such, one man's terrorist becomes another man's "freedom fighter" as if inhumanity and savagery were a matter of individual perception or interpretation.

Finally, "terrorism" carries a pejorative connotation. Terrorism is what bad persons do. In this context, governments can label almost any activity by the opposition as "terrorist," even if it involves legitimate resistance against an oppressive or tyrannical regime.[6]

These brief examples of definition problems with the term terrorism highlight the ongoing debate surrounding this difficult subject. In that light, Laqueur's observation that there will be no agreement on a comprehensive and universally accepted definition of terrorism is probably correct. This is because terrorism has appeared throughout the ages in many forms which includes systematic terror accompanying peasant uprisings, violent disputes, civil wars, revolutionary wars, wars of national liberation, as well as resistance to colonialism or foreign occupation.[7]

The lack of definition clarity and inappropriate use of the word terrorism gives cause for concern. For if the label of terrorism continues to be applied indiscriminately to too many acts of violence, it will lose its utility for academic and public discourse and will quickly become meaningless. Hence, some circumscription of the subject is necessary. To that end we begin with a taxonomy of terrorism.

A TYPOLOGY OF TERRORISM

In an early but incisive analysis of terrorism in the United States, the National Advisory Committee on Criminal Justice Standards and Goals developed a comprehensive typology of terrorism grounded in the underlying motives and purposes of the terrorists:

1. **nonpolitical terrorism**, defined as the deliberate creation of fear for coercive purposes, with an end goal of collective or individual gain. Included here is terrorism engendered by the authentically mentally ill;

2. **quasi-terrorism**, defined as the application of terroristic techniques in situations that do not involve terroristic crimes as such. Examples include the taking of hostages in derailed robberies or prison riots for use as bargaining chips. Also included here are **pseudo-political criminals**, who rationalize their predatory activities as natural responses to governmental oppression;[8]

3. **limited political terrorism**, which involves ideologically or politically motivated terroristic acts, such as assassinations or bombings, but which fall short of seeking to overthrow established governments. Also included in this category are **political extremists**, whose goals may range from nihilism or anarchism, to ill-defined visions of utopian social change;

4. **official or state terrorism**, defined as governmental rule based on fear, oppression and persecution. Examples include ruling juntas, such as the former Somoza regime in Nicaragua, or right-wing terrorists in El Salvador, where thousands of citizens and foreigners, including a number of American Jesuit priests and nuns, have been ruthlessly murdered;

5. **political terrorism**, defined as violent, criminal behavior designed to create fear in a society, or in a substantial segment of it, for political purposes.[9] When fully developed, political terrorism is revolutionary in character and seeks to subvert or overthrow an existing government.

Since the focus of this chapter is on **politically motivated terrorism**, it is important to examine its roots and identify its most salient characteristics.

TERRORISM: HISTORICAL ROOTS

Terrorism is firmly rooted in ancient history. Even though the term "terrorism" is of relatively recent vintage, originating in France during the Reign of Terror of the French Revolution (1793-94)[10], the phenomenon of systematic political violence, such as assassinations, or tyrannicide, is found in the earliest writings of history. Among the earliest "terrorist movements" are the **sicarii** and the **assassins**. The sicarii were a secretive, religious sect, given to unorthodox tactics when attacking and killing their victims. Part of the better known Zealot movement, they were active in Palestine, around 66-73 AD.[11] The assassins[12] were also part of a secret order, encompassed by the Ismaili sect of Islam. Their characteristics included fanatical devotion and absolute obedience to their religious leaders. Murder was seen as a sacred obligation for eliminating one's enemies. The assassins first appeared in the eleventh century in Persia and Syria and inspired terrorism throughout the Muslin world. Invading

Mongols ended the assassins' influence in the thirteenth century. However, scattered groups of this sect are believed to persist through today, especially in the north of Syria.[13]

THE ROOTS OF MODERN TERRORISM AND ITS CHANGING CHARACTERISTICS

While terrorism has afflicted humanity for millennia, its contemporary versions have become ever more potent, destructive, and lethal. The reasons for this development are grounded in technological progress, modernization, and social change. First, today's terrorist can strike anywhere around the globe and leave the scene of carnage long before the dust settles thanks to the unprecedented mobility provided by **jet air travel**.[14]

Second, technological developments have provided terrorists with a wide range of **high-technology weaponry**, including those capable of mass destruction. Among them are (1) powerful explosives, of which minute amounts can wreak havoc and devastation. One such example is the Czech produced Semtex, used to destroy Pan Am 103; (2) highly sophisticated electronic timing and detonating devices. One such device manufactured by a small electronics firm in Switzerland brought down Pan Am 103, while another triggered a roadside bomb that killed the director of the Deutsche Bank, Alfred Herrhausen near his home in Germany, in November 1989; and (3) readily portable, precision-guided munitions, such as surface-to-air missiles (SAMS) and related antitank weapons.[15]

Third, recent developments in **telecommunications** have unwittingly provided inestimable assistance to terrorist causes. Most terrorists crave publicity. The media, in turn, oblige by televising and broadcasting the high drama of terrorist violence wherever and whenever it occurs throughout the world. Television, in particular, with its communication satellites and minicams has become the handmaiden of modern terrorism. Laqueur speaks of the "close symbiotic relationship between the two, because violence is news, and peace and harmony are not."[16]

The **mass media's role in modern terrorism** cannot be underestimated. They draw the public's attention to terrorist causes. They are instrumental in spreading fear and alarm by publicizing the vivid details of terrorist violence and atrocities. Most important, the media help magnify and exaggerate the power, strength, and importance of individual terrorist groups and movements beyond all reason. Today's terrorists recognize the importance of the media to their causes and measure the success of their movements by the amount of publicity they manage to create. Some literally engineer and choreograph their attacks to guarantee media coverage.

Perhaps the best known example of a choreography of death occurred with the 1972 massacre of Israeli athletes at the Olympic Games in Munich Germany. This barbarous act was engineered by members of the Palestinian Black September Organization, a section of Fatah operating under the auspices of the Palestinian Liberation Organization (PLO). Ingeniously devised, it gave the terrorists instant, worldwide television coverage. It also succeeded in catapulting the PLO from a penny-ante, hit-and-run organization to a globally recognized fearsome household word.

A second illustration of how the mass media can magnify and distort the public's perception of terrorists comes from America's experience with the so-called Symbionese Liberation Army (SLA). Active in California during 1973-74, the SLA appeared almost daily on national television, on radio, and in the newspapers.[17] The group, their logo (a seven-headed cobra), their taped demands, and their outrageous deeds received worldwide publicity thanks to the unmitigated and uncritical media coverage. The SLA was a uniquely American brand of terrorist malefactors, combining sex, violence and racism with revolutionary politics. It also represented an unholy amalgam of criminal know-how, military expertise, and anti-establishment radicalism. But it is important to remember that this "army" never had more than a dozen or so members. Their crimes included the brutal slaying of African-American educator Marcus A. Foster in Oakland, allegedly for oppressing blacks, the kidnapping of heiress Patricia Hearst for the publicity and for extorting her parents, a derailed food distribution program financed by the Hearst family, stolen cars, carjackings, and robberies, including a bank job, in which kidnap victim Patty Hearst appeared to be a willing participant.[18] Each of these activities was an unquestionably serious crime. But the SLA did not constitute a crime wave. That was the impression created by the media.

In sum, the combination of technological developments in travel, weaponry and telecommunications coupled with the unlimited willingness of the media to cover dramatic terrorist incidents, has changed the nature of modern terrorism. Together, these developments not only enhance but also encourage terrorism, whose instigators fully recognize the value of the media in spreading their fearsome propaganda.[19]

Having delineated recent technological developments which have transformed an ancient scourge into a formidable and potent force, the discussion turns to the key characteristics of modern terrorism and working definitions.

DEFINING CHARACTERISTICS OF MODERN TERRORISM

There is currently little appreciation among officials or the public of just how much **modern, industrialized nations are vulnerable to terrorism**. With their surface electric powergrids, nuclear plants, petroleum and natural gas pipelines, public transport systems including airports, commercial and military aircraft and ground transportation, shipping, offshore oil rigs, and countless, centralized computer banks processing and storing vital governmental, private and commercial records, modern societies present unlimited targets to dedicated and ideologically motivated terrorists.[20] The destruction of any of these systems could create far greater losses and disruptions than would have been possible in the past. It is this development that has the most troublesome implications for the future of terrorism in the United States and other highly industrialized countries. Stated succinctly, it means that increasing societal vulnerabilities coupled with increased terrorist capabilities enable ever smaller groups of malcontents, extremists, and even certifiable lunatics to inflict ever greater harm and substantial damage.

WORKING DEFINITIONS OF TERRORISM

The Federal Bureau of Investigation has provided a useful **working definition of terrorism**: "Terrorism is the unlawful use of force or violence against persons or property to intimidate or coerce a government, the civilian population, or any segment thereof, in furtherance of political or social objectives."[21] Beyond this definition it is important to differentiate between **national, international, and transnational terrorism. National** (internal, domestic, or indigenous) **terrorism** is violence principally confined to a single country, or to a specific geographical area within it. As will be seen in a subsequent section of this discussion, America has a continuing problem with domestic terrorism, reflecting a perplexing array of interest groups hell-bent on resolving their grievances through acts of violence.[22]

International terrorism is violence involving two or more countries, with international repercussions. It may involve state-sponsored terrorism directed against foreign countries, or against foreigners and foreign assets located in the terrorist's home state.[23] It may also involve basically autonomous (nonstate sponsored) terrorists striking at foreign nationals or foreign assets in the terrorist's own country or in other nations.[24]

Transnational terrorism first evolved in the late 1970s. Even though this type of terrorism has been responsible for a large portion of terrorist activities in the 1980s, its threat to democratic societies has yet to be fully recognized. Terrorists in this category are not concerned with their own political goals or national identity. Their true interests are nihilistic or anarchistic. Under a thin veil or Maoist/Marxist rhetoric, there is a deep commitment to the destruction of any ruling democratic government. Transnational terrorists have been described as hailing predominantly from affluent societies and who, having rejected their bourgeois background, have committed themselves to support through violence the "struggles of the Third World"[25] Transnational terrorists maintain loose links with one another, function interchangeably, and cooperate on an "as needed" basis. They are literally "for hire" by agents or states bent on using terrorism for their own purposes or as well disguised, surrogate warfare. They come primarily from Europe (Germany, Italy), the Middle East (Palestine, Syria), and the Far East (Japan). Historically, sponsorship, training, and financial, technical and logistical support used to come from the former Soviet Union and other satellite Communist Countries. Today, the support comes from such nations as Algeria, Iran, Iraq, Libya, North Korea, the Sudan, and Syria.

A recent example of a transnational terrorist group active in Europe, Indonesia, the Middle East, and the United States, came to the attention of American authorities with the arrest of Yu Kikumura, a known member of the Japanese Red Army. He was arrested in April of 1988, by the New Jersey State Police while transporting two powerful pipe bombs to be detonated somewhere in New York City. He has been linked by international law enforcement authorities to a shadowy group called Anti-Imperialist International Brigades (AIIB).[26] The AIIB has been linked indirectly (but not tangibly) to Libyan sponsorship and has targeted primarily (although not exclusively) United States interests, ranging from embassies to the United States Information Service Centers and United States Organizations (USO) located in Indonesia, Spain, and Italy.[27]

IS MODERN TERRORISM IRRATIONAL OR ARE THERE UNDERLYING CAUSES?

Terrorism is often viewed as irrational and senseless violence. The fact is that terrorism is anything but that. It is difficult for most Americans to understand how the 1993 bombing of the World Trade Center in New York City and the killing of innocent civilians is supposed to aid the causes of Islamic fundamentalists in Egypt or anywhere else. Nor can one comprehend how the 1975 bombing of LaGuardia Airport and the killing and maiming of police officers by the Armed Forces of National Liberation (FALN) of Puerto Rico are to lever the U.S. government into granting independence to that island Commonwealth. But it is of critical importance to understand that the objectives of terrorism are not those of conventional warfare. To comprehend this kind of terrorist violence, it is necessary to look beyond the seemingly absurd and senseless, to see the theory and the logic behind it.

THE THEORY OF TERRORISM AND THE FUTURE OF POLITICAL VIOLENCE

The upsurge of modern international terrorism during the recent past and the reasons why it will continue into the next century is attributable to certain characteristics of modern societies.

First, **terrorism is effective**. In other words, terrorism works. In an age of super-powers, multinational conglomerates, and military-industrial-complexes, terrorism has become an effective voice of the weak and disenfranchised. Their goals vary and may include: (1) redress for specific grievances; (2) extraction of specific concessions, such as the release of prisoners or payment of ransom; (3) the coercion, destruction or overthrow of a government; or (4) the dissemination by print or electronic media of the group's demands or message.

While scholars debate and even question the effectiveness of terrorism,[28] the record shows that it has been quite effective. Most terrorist incidents such as kidnapping, hijackings, assassinations, and bomb strikes, have at a minimum brought the terrorists publicity or a variety of concessions and money. Examples abound. The previously discussed 1972 invasion of the Olympic Village in Munich rewarded the PLO with worldwide publicity and recognition. In November 1979 a year long process of international trauma and humiliation for the United States began, when fifty-two Americans were held hostage in their own embassy in Tehran, Iran. Captured by Ayatollah Khomeini's Revolutionary Guards, euphemistically described as "students," negotiations dragged on for 444 days. President Carter became a virtual prisoner in the White House, preoccupied with schemes for liberating the captives. The press and the hostage families hounded him to do "something."[29] Eventually, the debacle would cost the president his reelection.[30] To bring the hostages home, the terrorists were rewarded with unlimited publicity, with the release of Iranian assets frozen in the U.S., and by their ability to eclipse the Carter presidency. They were also permitted to meddle in the asylum policies of the United States. This interference occurred when the deposed Shah of Iran, seeking medical treatment for his terminal cancer in New York City, was unceremoniously told by government officials to leave for fear that his prolonged stay might bring about the execution of the hostages.

Still another example of the effectiveness of terrorism involves the October 23, 1983 killing of 241 U.S. marines, when a suicide driver of a truck loaded with high-powered explosives deliberately crashed into their barracks located in close proximity of the Beirut airport. After having told the world many times that America would never be intimidated by terrorism to the point of withdrawing from Lebanon, President Reagan did precisely that in February of 1984. The terrorists scored an undisputed victory.[31]

The second reason why international terrorism will persist in the future is the fact that **terrorism is highly cost effective**. Most nations recognize that conventional warfare is increasingly impractical. Few nations could afford conducting full-fledged war, let alone world wars. Also, nuclear powers must be mindful that any conflict initiated by them has the potential of escalating into a nuclear holocaust, a development most would want to avoid. But more importantly, modern warfare is prohibitively expensive. Recent experiences with modern conventional war have shown that it can severely stress a nation's economy. For example, when Argentina invaded the British owned Falkland Islands in the South Atlantic in 1982, and reclaimed them as their own "Malvinas Islas," Britain launched a counterattack. The naval expedition and the naval and ground warfare proved extraordinarily expensive, leading to tax increases and other financial stress for England.[32] At an earlier date, when Egypt invaded Israel during the Yom Kippur War in the fall of 1973, Israel's defensive and counteroffensive measures proved very costly in men, material, and money.[33]

The third reason why terrorism will continue into the next century is that conventional warfare has become impractical. Accumulating experiences with terrorism have demonstrated its ability of becoming an accepted form of **low-cost, low-intensity or surrogate warfare**. Again, the options and scenarios are almost limitless. For example, for a small investment, governments can hire transnational terrorists or develop their own terrorist cadre. Since the essence of terrorism is stealth and secrecy, governments (or revolutionary movements) can instigate assassinations, bombings, hijackings, or destroy a nation's technological and economic infrastructure. They can also provoke international incidents, while denying any knowledge or involvement in these activities. The former Soviet Union excelled at presenting itself as a "peaceloving" nation, while funding and supporting the formation, training, and fielding of terrorists around the globe.[34] To thwart terrorist campaigns, governments must spend valuable resources and divert them from other critical areas, such as health, education, and welfare.

A fourth reason why terrorism will persist is the fact that globally, **individual state borders have become firmly set** by the victorious allies at the end of World War II. This settlement, coupled with the collapse of colonialism, has left **minority groups few options** to establish their rights while living in the middle of hostile majorities, or to establish their national autonomy.[35]

The Palestinians represent but one of many examples of such minority groups. Most did not accept the creation of the state of Israel by majority vote in the United Nations in 1948, and would not settle for their allotted territory in the West Bank and Gaza Strip. Since those early days, there have been untold bloody clashes and wars between Palestinians, Arab supporters, and the Israelis. Both claim historic ties to the same land. Through the years, world powers and the United Nations have spent much effort and time to mediate the conflict, to no avail.

When Israel decisively defeated Arab military forces in the 1967 war, the Palestinian leadership came to a precedent setting conclusion. Recognizing that they and their usually divided Arab supporters were unlikely to defeat Israel on the battlefield, they decided they would have more to gain by embarking on a systematic campaign of International terrorist violence. The latter would not only be directed against Israel but also against that nation's supporters, the United States and other Western democracies known to support the tiny nation state.[36] This development brought about the growth of the PLO, Fatah, and related terrorist groups, who catapulted their terrorist campaigns onto the world stage.

Given the great publicity accompanying terrorist strikes against the United States citizens or interests, it is unlikely that Palestinian terrorists will give up their deadly games until the fate of the Palestinians is resolved. As such, America has a vested interest in bringing about peace in the Middle East. While peace negotiations between Israel and the PLO are taking place, their outcomes are not guaranteed. More militant Palestinian factions are hard at work not only to derail the peace efforts but also to destroy present Israeli governmental structures in order to establish a state of their own.[37]

Only the foolhardy will assume that the notable success of Palestinian terrorism has not gone unnoticed by other terrorist groups the world over. The elements of contagion and imitation have long been noted in terrorism.[38] Therefore, the possibility is real that other terrorist movements active around the globe will take a page out of the PLO book of horrors and begin to apply the techniques of international terrorism against their enemies.

Nationalist fervor is not an exclusive characteristic of the Palestinians. Examples of other terrorist groups pursuing their dreams of a state of their own include (but are not limited to) the Irish Republican Army (IRA) active in Northern Ireland, the Republic of Ireland, and Britain; ETA (Euzkadi ta Azkazatuna) a Basque terrorist organization active in Spain's Basque provinces; the Tamils active in Sri Lanka; and the Sikhs in the Punjab, India.

At present, it seems as if much of the world is being consumed with the fires of newborn nationalism.[39] For example, the collapse of the former Soviet Union has generated crime, violence, and terrorism in most of the former Republics, most notably in Armenia and Azerbaijan. The disintegration of the former Yugoslavia has brought its own version of nationalist-sectarian hell and terror, the end of which is nowhere in sight. In this instance, a lack of will within the international community in general, and the European Community in particular, has unquestionably contributed to the rise in terror and violence in that region. While inconceivable, it appears that the free world has learned nothing from Fascism, Hitler's holocaust, or Communism's and Stalin's pogroms and mass killings. George Santayana's well known dictum certainly applies here: "Those who cannot remember the past are condemned to repeat it."

TARGET U.S.A. AND THE HOSTAGE PREDICAMENT

Learning from experience, international terrorist groups have long recognized that the taking of hostages substantially improves their bargaining power, especially when dealing with the United States. A hallmark of this nation is the fact that it places great value on individual human lives. It is this characteristic which makes our nation particularly vulnerable to terrorism. For example, the mid-1980s saw a spate of kidnappings of Americans in Beirut, Lebanon.[40] That period also brought a flood of hijackings mainly in Europe, including a fifty-three hour odyssey of TWA Flight 847 on June 14, 1985 on its way from Athens to Greece. In each instance, it was impossible to identify with any precision the kidnappers or their sponsors. Shiite fundamentalists were suspected, possibly members of the Islamic Jihad or the Hezbollah.[41] Given the shadowy nature of terrorism, it is impossible even now to say whether these two groups are distinct entities, or are one and the same.[42] It is one of the more vexing characteristics of terrorism that groups are able to form, strike, disband, and resurface in many permutations, under many noms de guerre, much like the ever shifting sands of the desert.

If there is one lesson in terrorist hostage incidences involving Americans, it is that whenever lives are at stake and the odds clearly favor the hostage takers, deals will be struck for their release, whether or not negotiations are sanctioned or interdicted by government policy.

CHARTING THE PROBABLE FUTURE OF TERRORISM

Predictions of geopolitical developments, including the future of international terrorism are inherently difficult. Analogously, the best political minds in this nation or anywhere else did not envision the collapse of the Soviet Union or that of the regimes of its satellite nations. Nonetheless, it is possible to chart with caution the near future for international terrorism by extrapolating from the developments of the recent past.

Given the uneven but slow rise of international terrorist incidents, we can anticipate a continuation of this progression. We have the ability to predict this because many old grievances fueling past and current terrorist strikes have yet to be resolved, and because new causes and new groups will continue to emerge. The world has certainly no lack of terrorist causes.

The United States and its principal allies, Britain, France, Germany, Israel, and Turkey, will remain key terrorist targets well into the future. These nations have accounted for about half of all the victims of international terrorism.[43] Americans in particular will remain favorite targets for a number of reasons. First, business and personal travel brings Americans into every corner of the world. Their sheer accessibility makes them good targets of opportunity for terrorist strikes. Second, U.S. business interests and military bases span the globe. As such, they represent a virtually unlimited range of targets. Third, as U.S. experience with Middle Eastern terrorism has shown, a number of terrorist groups look upon the United States as the key to the solution of their particular problems and grievances. In this scenario, the U.S. is supposed to exert pressure on its "client states" to yield to terrorist demands, whatever they may be. Fourth, the United States, as virtually the last superpower and self-proclaimed leader of the free world has unwittingly become an almost irresistible symbolic target for a growing number of terrorists movements, who want to strike a blow for the many imagined wrongs committed by America. These wrongs run the gamut of complaints, ranging from imperialism, expansionism, and the economic exploitation of Third World countries, to the degradation of the environment, overconsumption of natural resources, and America's perceived cultural decadence.

FUTURE MODES AND TARGETS OF TERRORISM

According to Jenkins, the "repertoire" of modern terrorism has included six basic tactics: bombings, assassinations, armed assaults, kidnappings, hijackings, and barricade and hostage incidents.[44] He anticipates few changes in this respect. In fact, bombings continue to be the main mode of attack, accounting for almost half of all terrorist attacks worldwide.[45] Bombings bring drama and much publicity. Their production and dissemination require few skills or expertise. Next to bombings, one can anticipate a continuation of terrorist attacks on governmental and business installations, ranging from embassies, military installations, government offices, multinational corporations and other targets with great symbolic value, such as airlines, terminals, trains, railroad stations, to places of worship. While random terrorism has struck at every conceivable human target from airline passengers to babies in carriages, there will be a continuation of targeting persons of "symbolic" value, such as members of the diplomatic corps, military personnel (on and off duty), government officials, businessmen, clergy, as well as journalists.[46]

WILL TERRORISM ESCALATE?

International terrorism has escalated in volume and fatalities during the past few years. While earlier attacks targeted usually vacant buildings, recent developments brought increases in multiple deaths and injuries. Of late, incidents have been of the large-scale, random violence variety, such as car bombs packed with high-powered explosives, detonated on streets, trains, and airliners, and in terminals and railroad stations.[47]

There are many reasons for this change. First, terrorism has become commonplace in the world arena. The public has come to accept terrorist incidents as a modern evil. To the degree that the public has become jaded and desensitized, terrorists feel obliged to "up the ante." By increasing their audacity, violence, and atrocities, they calculate to recapture public attention. Second, there has also been a desensitization of the terrorists. Some movements, such as the Red Army Faction in Germany and some Palestinian terrorist groups, are now in their third generation. As such, they represent a "new breed" of terrorists, brutal, dedicated, and highly proficient. Some of the Middle East terrorists are best described as "Kalashnikov Kids," whose warped sense of violence and merciless actions have been finely honed in Palestinian refugee camps.[48] Third, international terrorists have learned from the experiences of their predecessors. With the aid of ever more sophisticated weaponry discussed earlier in this chapter, they now have the ability to strike with deadly accuracy. They have also learned to evade counterterrorist efforts by governments and Interpol. The final reason for terrorism's increased lethality is attributable to the recent growth of nationalist, separatists, and religious motivated violence.[49] For example, it has been noted that since 1982, Shi'a Islamic groups have been responsible for about 8% of all international terrorist incidents. Yet, they are responsible for 30% of the total number of persons killed.[50]

It is important to note that Islamic terrorists do not have a monopoly on religiously motivated violence. In the United States, white supremacists have bombed and killed with abandon in the name of Christianity. The separatist conflict in Northern Ireland clearly has sectarian attributes, as does the "ethnic cleansing" genocide in the former Yugoslavia. While any terrorism is shocking, religiously motivated terror has especially pernicious qualities to it. As shown in the discussion of the historical roots of terrorism, those motivated by religion look upon violence as a sacred obligation. In this form, terrorist violence assumes a "transcendal dimension," which frees the perpetrators of any "political, moral or practical constraints that would normally affect other terrorists."[51] As a result, religious fanatics, whether they act in the name of God, Allah, or Yahweh, are not only capable of the worst atrocities, but have committed them since the birth of civilization.

PROBABILITIES OF A NUCLEAR OF BIOLOGICAL HOLOCAUST

Given the existence and proliferation of nuclear and biological weapons of mass destruction, there has been much speculation on whether they will be used by terrorists in the near future.[52] Predictions in this respect are most difficult. Some comfort can be taken from remembering the most predominant goals of terrorists: publicity, concessions, and violence tinged symbolism, and theatre of the macabre. Most terrorists want the world to take notice of their existence and to listen to their grievances. Thus far, most incidents have been geared toward having the world watch in horror, and not toward mass murder. Nonetheless, such a turn of events cannot be ruled out. If it happens, it would most likely come from terrorist groups convinced that they have no alternative left, or from groups driven by "intense ethnic enmity or a strong religious imperative."[53]

AMERICAN CRIMINAL JUSTICE AND COUNTERTERRORISM

This chapter has been premised on the assumption that if terrorism is to be countered effectively, it must first be understood. Having looked at the nature, defining characteristics, definitions, motivations, and strategies of terrorism, it is clear that the threat of terrorism to the United States and its citizens is substantial and real. What remains to be discussed is how best to counter the problem.

Responding to terrorist threats against U.S. citizens and American interests abroad, the U.S. Congress has passed the Comprehensive Crime Control Act of 1984 and the Omnibus Diplomatic Security and Antiterrorist Act of 1986. These Acts facilitate counterterrorism efforts by establishing federal jurisdiction over terrorist crimes involving Americans perpetrated outside U.S. territories. Under the provision of the "long arm" statute, terrorists can be pursued around the globe. If apprehended, they can be brought to trial in the United States. Given the shadowy nature of international terrorism, this legislation has had but limited success. In addition, prosecution of terrorists is difficult because U.S. law does not recognize political crimes as such and requires adherence to strict rules of evidence at trial. Additional efforts at the international level include extradition treaties with friendly nations. But even their utility is limited by the fact that a number of countries continue to provide refuge to terrorists. Finally, the U.S. Department of State and the Federal Bureau of Investigation (FBI) have promoted international cooperation among police agencies (including Interpol), and FBI agents are posted in host countries to coordinate vital intelligence and counterterrorism activities.

The leading federal law enforcement agency in fighting terrorism in the United States is the FBI. This agency's counterterrorism efforts are augmented by collaborating with other pertinent federal agencies, such as the Bureau of Alcohol, Tobacco, and Firearms, the U.S. Customs Services, the Secret Service, and the Immigration and Naturalization Service. The FBI has in place a special unit to identify possible targets of terrorist attacks, to develop contingency plans for handling incidents, and to work closely with the Department of Defense, the Department of Energy, and the Nuclear Regulatory Commission, as the occasion may warrant. At the state and local levels, the FBI has formed antiterrorism working groups with law enforcement agencies, and offers specialized counterterrorist training programs for police officers. These multi-faceted efforts to combat terrorism on U.S. soil have brought success on a number of fronts. They range from the early identification and prevention of a large number of planned terrorist attacks, to increased numbers of arrests and successful prosecution of terrorists due to vastly improved information technology, investigatory techniques, and forensic analyses. Finally, the FBI's hostage rescue team deployable throughout the country has succeeded in resolving many high-risk terrorist takeovers and hostage situations.[54]

In spite of these promising developments and notable successes, counterterrorist measures present inherent dangers to civil liberties. The final segment of this chapter briefly discusses this critical issue.

THE EFFECTS OF TERRORISM ON DEMOCRACY, CRIMINAL JUSTICE AND THE RULE OF LAW

The fundamental problem with counterterrorist action lies in the fact that when criminal justice agencies were developed in this country, they were never meant to cope with terrorism. Today, these agencies are straining under severe budget limitations and cutbacks. Should terrorism escalate as predicted, this nation's criminal justice systems will be severely tested in their willingness and ability to adhere to the requirements of the Constitution and the Bill of Rights. The issue is as plain as it is cruel. Terrorists, by definition, do not play by the rules. By contrast, the criminal justice systems must abide by the rules, lest they descend to the same level of lawlessness that characterizes the terrorists.

As noted in the introduction, democracies are particularly vulnerable to terrorism. Bound by the rules of law and due process, a democratic nation cannot resort to the same bloody methods used against it in combating terrorist crime.[55] Looking at the experiences of democratic nations dealing with systematic terrorist assault, one finds not only an expected reduction in the quality of life, but also a disturbing tendency to encroach on the civil liberties of their citizens. Great Britain, for example, is one of the oldest and more stable democracies in the world. Yet, in its struggle with sectarianism and periodic armed insurrection in Northern Ireland, it has instituted at various times such basically undemocratic measures as internment, interrogation-in-depth, as well as search and seizure without warrants, censorship, trials without juries, and the admission of hearsay evidence. There is also a shift in the burden of proof from the government to the defendant. Penalties for activities classified as terrorism are most severe. In the same vein, the governments of Germany and Italy have instituted countermeasures which, although approved by the public, represent clear infringements on the freedoms of their people.

Given the experiences of sister democracies, it is clear that terrorism presents serious challenges to the quality of life, public safety, and the individual rights of affected citizens. The potential loss of individual liberties in the battle to control terrorism is no doubt its greatest threat. This loss is possible because when terrorism seriously threatens public safety, people are more than willing to surrender time-honored civil liberties in exchange for law and order. As a result, the special challenge of terrorism to law enforcement is highly complex. Police must develop response mechanisms that do not endanger existing civil liberties. Since police agencies are most likely to be the primary responders to terrorist acts, they must begin to develop a range of basic services including tactical response, containment, damage control, evidence collection, negotiations, investigations, pursuit, prosecution assistance, as well as intelligence gathering.[56] Since few police departments can provide all of these basic anti-terrorist services, interorganizational coordination and collaboration will become a necessity.

Nationally, an effective apparatus for counterterrorism needs to include:

1. the collection of timely and adequate intelligence nationally and internationally;
2. the formation of alliances with other nations for purposes of sharing intelligence, extradition of terrorists, and denial of refuge or asylum to terrorists;
3. target hardening, including the development of physical and psychological barriers between terrorists and their potential targets;
4. gaining the cooperation of the mass media, a difficult but not insurmountable task;
5. development, deployment, and continued training of a highly specialized cadre of counterterrorist specialists, including experts in intelligence, weaponry, explosives, and behavioral, nuclear, chemical, and biological sciences, computer sciences, medicines, and the military arts; and
6. the development and institutionalization of a national agency for crisis management beyond (or part of) the Federal Emergency Management Agency (FEMA). This agency would develop, control, and deploy regional crisis management teams.

During major terrorist incidents, it is important that government moves quickly to bring aid and assistance to the injured, and to limit the physical damage. Government must also limit the inevitable political and economic fallout. In this regard, it is once again helpful to remember the goals of most terrorist attacks: the creation of widespread fear and alarm. Given that, it is important for government to take all necessary steps to prevent panic and to reassure the public that the situation either is under control, or will be brought under control in short order. In this age of instant television coverage, the appearance of control is almost as important as having it. In the handling of specific incidents, officials must take great care to walk a fine line between two extremes. First, government must not overreact. If it does, there will be more panic, while officials will look incompetent. Second, government must not underreact, lest the public become more alienated and perceive officials as callous and indifferent to pain and suffering.[57]

In summary, it is more than certain that terrorism will continue well into the next century. The reasons include its effectiveness and its shadowy nature, which too often prevent the identification of the perpetrators. The latter is a necessity for nations interested in controlling terrorism and in bringing the perpetrators to justice. Transnational and international terrorists will continue to cooperate with one another and will receive the steady support of rogue nations, including money, material, training, and refuge. Terrorists are also likely to become more proficient and deadly. International terrorism will also be resistant to control by the international community for the reasons discussed in this chapter. These predictions, dire as they are, should not be a reason for despair. While terrorism cannot be defeated, it can certainly be controlled. Even though terrorists take advantage of democracies and deliberately abuse the freedoms guaranteed in such societies, it is essential for governments to uphold the rule of law when taking countermeasures. Adherence to the Constitution and maintaining this nation's highest moral values are essential to America's efforts to control national and international terrorism. State power must be exercised with foresight, caution, and economy, lest

America risk losing its credibility as a true democracy and world leader. Ultimately, it will be the very liberties enjoyed in democracies that will provide the best weapons for limiting the destructive effects of this Twentieth and Twenty-First Century scourge.

STUDY QUESTIONS

1. What is the nature of terrorism? What are its origins and its modern characteristics? What are some of the definitional problems encountered with terrorism? How would you formulate a working definition?

2. What is the role of the mass media in modern terrorism? What are some examples of the interplay between terrorism and the media? What is meant by the symbiotic relationship between terrorists and the media?

3. What are the theory and logic behind politically motivated terrorism?

4. Why is the United States so vulnerable to terrorism?

5. What are the characteristics of modern terrorism? Why does it present such a serious threat to democratic societies? What advice would you give to a democratic government on how best to cope with sustained, serious terrorist assaults?

REFERENCES

1. Aspin, Les. "The Bottom-Up Review: Forces for a New Era." Department of Defense, United States of America. (1993). September 1, p.1.

2. Bush, George. **Public Report of the Vice President's Task Force on Combating Terrorism**. (1986). Washington, DC, Introduction.

3. For an excellent discussion of the problems incurred in defining terrorism see Walter Laqueur, **The Age of Terrorism**. (1987). Little, Brown and Co., Boston, (1987) pp. 142-173.

4. Walter Laqueur, having studied guerrilla warfare notes that the essence of this phenomenon is to establish liberated areas in the countryside and to set up military units that grow in numbers and strength to fight against government troops. Once such areas have been carved out, the guerrillas will set up their own social institutions, ranging from political activities to social control. Op. cit., p. 147.

5. Terrorists (unlike guerrillas) tend to operate in small numbers and in secrecy. They are principally found in urban environments. They also tend to avoid open confrontations with their opponent's military forces. Neither do they take and hold ground, preferring instead to launch surprise attacks, usually, but not always, on civilian targets.

6. History is replete with examples of "legitimate" violence directed, at various times, against unjust governmental oppression: (1) the ancient Greeks recognized tyrannicide as an acceptable outgrowth of the struggle of the rising popular classes against merciless rulers; (2) during World War II and the German occupation of France, the underground French Resistance engaged in sabotage and secret operations against the occupation forces, their civilian supporters and suspected French collaborators; and (3) past and present struggles of the African National Congress (ANC) against the racist South African Government is but the latest of many insurgencies utilizing violence to further their cause. It is important to note, however, that each of the modern insurgencies cited above differ from the terrorist campaigns of small groups such as the **Red Brigades** of Italy in terms of dimensions,

motives, and legitimization. Success for modern insurgencies is always contingent upon wider support among a majority of the people and a vast array of political and military activities geared toward winning the common struggle against oppression.

7. Laqueur, op. cit., p. 11.

8. For a good discussion of this subject, see Stephen Schaefer, **The Political Criminal**. (1974). New York: The Free Press, pp. 5-6.

9. Report of the Task Force on Disorders and Terrorism. **Disorders and Terrorism**. National Advisory Committee on Criminal Justice Standards and Goals. (1976). Washington, DC: U.S. Government Printing Office, pp. 3-6.

10. Schmid, Alex. **Political Terrorism: A Research Guide to Concepts, Theories, Data Bases, and Literature**. (1983). New Brunswick, NJ: Transaction Books.

11. Laqueur, Walter. **Terrorism**. (1977). Little, Brown and Company, Boston.

12. The word assassin comes from the Arabic word "usa sin," signifying a person being under the influence of hashish.

13. The Columbia Encyclopedia. (1963). New York: Columbia University Press, pp. 119-120.

14. Mahmud Abouhalima, the alleged ringleader of the terrorist group that planted a powerful bomb in the parking garage of the World Trade Center in Manhattan, New York, is known to have flown from New York's Kennedy airport to the Middle East within days of the attack to escape apprehension.

15. In September of 1973, Italian police arrested several members of the Popular Front for the Liberation of Palestine (PFLP) near Leonardo da Vinci Airport in Rome, after they had poised a Soviet made, heat-seeking, ground-to-air missile (SA-7) at a jetliner readying for takeoff.

16. Laqueur, op. cit., p. 121.

17. For a good discussion of the Symbionese Liberation Army's criminal exploits, see Albert Parry, **Terrorism From Robespierre to Arafat**. (1976). The Vanguard Press, Inc. New York, N.Y. pp. 342-364.

18. Patricia Hearst was "on the run" for over a year, arrested in the fall of 1975, and put on trial in 1976 for her part in the bank robbery. Found guilty, she served nearly three years in a federal prison. Given today's knowledge grounded in research regarding victim experiences, it is highly probable that she was a victim of thought conversion, better known as brainwashing. For a detailed discussion see Edith E. Flynn. "Victims of Terrorism: Dimensions of the Victim Experience" in **Contemporary Research on Terrorism**. Paul Wilkinson and A.M. Stewart, eds. (1987). Aberdeen University Press, Aberdeen, Scotland, pp. 337-356.

19. In the wake of fast accumulating U.S. experiences with terrorist incidents, such as the Iranian hostage crisis in 1979, and the many kidnappings of Americans and Europeans in Lebanon, there have been several attempts by the public media, most notably the major television networks to impose some measure of self-regulation of their coverage of terrorist incidents. Thus far, these efforts have lost out to the overriding demands of business and "scooping" of the competition.

20. For a good discussion of the physical potential of terrorist disruption, see Robert Kupperman and Darrell Trent. **Terrorism, Threat, Reality, Response**. (1979). Hoover Institution Press, Stanford University, Stanford, CA, pp. 48-74.

21. U.S. Department of Justice. Federal Bureau of Investigation, "Terrorism in the United States 1982-1992." (1993). Washington, DC.

22. See for example the assassination of Alan Berg, a Jewish radio talk-show host in 1984 in Denver, Colorado, by members of "the Order" a covert enforcement and hitman unit of the ultra-rightwing, racist Aryan Nation.

23. The 1988 pre-Christmas downing of Pan American's Flight 103 in which 270 lives were lost over (and in) Lockerbie, Scotland, is but one example of state-sponsored terrorism. The target was clearly the United States. The sponsor of the strike was, in all likelihood, Iran, seeking retaliation for the accidental downing of an Iranian airbus over the Persian Gulf by the USS Vincennes on July 3, 1988. Even though there is no definitive evidence linking Iran to the mid-air explosion, the timing of the incident, the type of target, coupled with Iran's explicit calls for retaliation, point in that direction. (For a good discussion of this and related topics, see Dennis A. Pluchinsky, "Middle Eastern Terrorist Activity in Western Europe in the 1980s: A Decade of Violence," in Yonah Alexander and Dennis A. Pluchinsky, **European Terrorism Today and Tomorrow**. (1992) Brassey's Inc., Washington, DC, pp. 1-29).

24. A good example is the attempted assassination by Germany's Red Army Faction commando "Andreas Baader" of the U.S. Army General Alexander Haig (NATO commander-in-chief at the time), on June 25, 1979, near a small Belgian town.

25. Kupperman, Robert and Darrell Trent. **Terrorism: Threat, Reality, Response**. (1979). Hoover Institution Press, Stanford, CA, p. 25.

26. Pluchinsky, Dennis A. "Middle Eastern Terrorist Activity in Western Europe in the 1980s: A Decade of Violence." in **European Terrorism, Today and Tomorrow**. Yonah Alexander and Dennis A. Pluchinsky eds. (1992), pp. 20-21.

27. Pluchinsky, op. cit., p. 21.

28. Laqueur. (1987). op. cit., p. 75.

29. For the duration, major television networks would begin their evening news with "Day X in the hostage crisis." The latter made Ted Koppel of ABC a media star and his thirty minute program "Nightline" one of the most successful television programs on the late evening program firmament.

30. Kupperman, Robert and Jeff Kamen. **Final Warning**. (1989). Doubleday, New York, p. 156.

31. Turner, op. cit., pp. 161-169.

32. Revel, Jean-Francois. **How Democracies Perish**. (1984). Doubleday and Co., Garden City, NY, pp. 80-90.

33. Ibid., p. 71.

34. For one of the best documented discussions of Soviet involvement in the secret war of international terrorism, see Clair Sterling, **The Terror Network**. (1981). Holt, Rinehart and Winston, New York, NY.

35. Wilkinson, op. cit. p. xv.

36. Wilkinson, op. cit. p. xvi.

37. For an excellent discussion of the Arab-Israeli Conflict, see **The Middle East**. (1986). Congressional Quarterly Inc., Washington, DC, pp. 7-36.

38. Wilkinson, op. cit., p. xv.

39. Gottlieb, Gidon. **Nation Against the State**. (1993). New York: Council on Foreign Relations Press.

40. By 1985, six American hostages were in captivity: Terry Anderson, Associated Press correspondent; David Jacobsen, director of the medical services at the American University; Martin L. Jenco, head of Catholic Relief Services in Lebanon; Peter Kilburn, head librarian at the American University, Beirut; Jeremy Levin, CNN correspondent; and Thomas Sutherland, professor at American University.

41. Turner, op. cit., pp. 161-165.

42. Turner, op. cit., p. 165.

43. Jenkins, Brian M. "The Future Course of International Terrorism." in **Contemporary Research on Terrorism**. Op. cit., p. 583.

44. Jenkins, op. cit. p. 585.

45. Hoffman, Bruce. "Future Trends in Terrorist Targeting and Tactics," in **Special Warfare**. (1993) V. 6, N 3, pp. 30-34.

46. A recent report by Reporters sans Frontieres published in Paris on December 27th 1993, noted that at least fifty-nine journalists had been killed worldwide in 1993. Of these, twenty-three died in Europe, eighteen in Africa, eight in Central and South America, seven in the Middle East and three in Asia. Nations with the highest tolls were Algeria, Bosnia and Russia. (At least nine deaths were attributed to rising Muslim fundamentalism in Algeria and Turkey). **The Boston Globe**, December 28, 1993. p.7.

47. Jenkins, op. cit., p. 583.

48. The Kalashnikov of AK 47 sub-machine-gun was invented by Mikhail Kalashnikov of the Soviet Union. It fires one hundred rounds a minute on automatic and forty rounds a minute in the single shot mode. It is a favorite weapon of terrorists and was amply provided to them by the former Soviet Union. (Dobson, Christopher and Ronald Payne, **The Terrorists: Their Weapons, Leaders and Tactics**. (1979). Facts on File, New York, NY.)

49. Hoffman, op. cit. p. 31.

50. Ibid.

51. Hoffman, op. cit., p. 32.

52. Cetron, Marvin, J. "The Growing Threat of Terrorism," in **The Futurist**. (1989). July-August, pp. 20-24; and Jenkins, op. cit., p. 587.

53. Hoffman, op. cit. p. 35.

54. Sessions, William. "The FBI's Mission in Countering Terrorism." **Terrorism**. (1990). V13:1-6.

55. Flynn, op. cit.

56. Williams, Hubert and James Ginger. "The Threat of International Terrorism in the United States: The Police Response." **Terrorism**. 1987, V 10:219-223.

57. Kupperman, op. cit.

CHAPTER 4

"MURDER AND MAYHEM" IN THE MEDIA

PUBLIC PERCEPTIONS (AND MISPERCEPTIONS) OF CRIME AND CRIMINALITY

Charles B. Fields, Ph.D. and Robert A. Jerin, Ph.D.

ABSTRACT

There are two widely-held assumptions concerning the effects of the media on the public's perception of crime and criminality. The first assumes that the mass media (especially television) are the primary sources of our understanding in these areas. The second assumption is that the media present erroneous and distorted information about crime. Are our views distorted by what we read in the newspaper and what we see on television?

This chapter addresses the various ways in which crime and related issues are reported, their relationship to the actual crime problem and the influences on public perceptions by the media. Both quantitative and qualitative assessments are employed. Future trends in these areas are also addressed.

INTRODUCTION

While the public's reaction to crime is impacted by various sources, it seems that the media have the greatest effect on the perception of crime and criminality. Davis (1952), in one of the first and most important studies examining crime and crime news coverage, presented evidence that there is no relationship between official crime statistics and crime as reported in the print media. In fact, this study indicated that the public perception of crime depends almost entirely on what is read in the newspapers. However, this study was conducted before the proliferation of television.

There are several competing schools of thought in this area that provide interesting study. Ericson (1991) feels that most of the previous research on the mass media and crime is deficient because it has focused too much on the effect of the mass media on our perceptions of crime and criminals. He addresses this "effects" tradition by critiquing several widely-held assumptions, two of which deserve further attention.

The first approach assumes that the mass media (especially television) are the primary sources of our understanding in these areas. It should be noted that some research (Graber, 1979; Graber, 1980), however, points out that our knowledge comes from a variety of sources, the media being but one among several. Nevertheless, most research recognizes the growing influence of the media on public opinion and society's understanding of criminal justice issues (Schlesinger, et al., 1991; Hans and Dee, 1991; Newman, 1990; Page, et al., 1987).

The second assumption is that the media present erroneous and distorted information about crime. The distortion of the extent of crime and its coverage in the news media is well documented. Studies have focused on the extent of crime as reported in local print media (Cohen, 1975, Meyer, 1975, 1976; Antunes and Hurley, 1977; Grabor, 1979; Humphries, 1981; Windhouser, et al., 1990; Marsh, 1991), the amount on television news reports (Graber, 1979; Surette, 1992), and on comparisons with newspaper coverage of crime in other countries (Marsh, 1991). In assessing the literature in the area, Marsh (1991) found that "there is an overrepresentation of violent crimes...and the percentage of violent crimes does not match official crime statistics." Additionally, the "emphasis on relatively infrequent violent crimes may contribute to a heightened concern and fear..." (pp. 67-68). While Ericson (1991) admits that discrepancies can be found between the types and amount of crime reported in the media and official reports of crime, why should we expect the "cultural products of mass media to reflect the social reality of crime" (p. 220)?

These are all important areas of inquiry. This chapter addresses the various ways in which crime and related issues are reported, their relationship to the actual crime problem, the influences on public perceptions by the media, and speculation as to what the future may have in store. Both quantitative and qualitative assessments are employed. This chapter also summarizes data that examine the amount and type of crime news as reported in the only national newspaper, *USA Today*, and attempts to discover if there are any differences in the amount, type, or seriousness of the coverage of statewide news in the national daily as compared to official crime statistics (Uniform Crime Reports), and if state population and crime rates are in any way a determining factor.

CRIME REPORTING AND PUBLIC PERCEPTIONS

Previous research examining the effect of the media's treatment of crime addresses several areas: the study of criminal justice themes in popular culture media (Newman, 1990); the use of public information programming (Sacco and Trotman, 1990); the use of advertising (Eder, 1990); the national print media (Jerin and Fields, 1994); television (Schelsinger, et al., 1991); and combinations of media sources (Sheley and Ashkins, 1981). These studies have all surmised that the true picture of crime, criminals and dangerousness are out of proportion to actual crime statistics.

The accuracy of media reports on crime and criminality can have a direct impact on the public's perception of the extent of the crime problem as well as on the operation of the criminal justice system itself. Hans and Dee (1991) correctly recognize that the public's knowledge and views of the law and legal system are largely dependent on what they read in the newspaper and what they see on television; there is little direct experience by the vast majority of citizens with the entire criminal justice system. Victimization data (Macguire, et al., 1993) establish that over a person's life the likelihood of victimization is very high; however, fewer than half of these cases are even reported to authorities and from the known crimes only a very small percentage are pursued to a conclusion in the justice system.

While the amount of coverage given to crime reporting is significant, it may not be greater than that given to other topics (Graber, 1980); it seems, however, that the crimes covered are largely sensational or extraordinary (Surette, 1984; Marsh, 1991; Roberts and Doob, 1990; Jerin and Fields, 1994) and do not reflect the reality of the type or amount of victimization that is occurring.

This information does not seem to reach the general public. As an example, in a recent *USA Today*/CNN/Gallup Poll (1993), 69% of the one thousand adults polled (plus oversample of 235 Blacks) felt that local television news accurately reflects the amount of crime. It should be noted that only 58% of Blacks in the sample agreed. The poll additionally found that only 25% of those responding believed that TV news exaggerated the amount of crime and nine out of ten believed that crime was worse than it had been a year earlier. These beliefs do not correspond to official data; the actual amount of crime reported to the police actually fell by 5% over the previous year (Macguire, et al., 1993). The link between the public's misconception concerning the amount of crime and the operation of the criminal justice system and whether this trend will continue in the future is an important area for study.

One of the first inquiries into the public's conception of a crime problem and the media's misrepresentation was an examination of how the press fabricated a "crime wave" in 1919 (Schlesinger, et al., 1991). Through the use of increased coverage and a call for governmental action, the public was erroneously led to believe that the crime problem was becoming much worse even though actual change was only minimal.

While misrepresentation of crime information is of serious concern, an additional area is the accuracy in how the media portrays the operations of the criminal justice system. False depictions of "crime waves" and other crime related information (e.g., amount of violent crime) reflect poorly on the police, courts and corrections. The *USA Today*/CNN/Gallup Poll (1993) also found that 86% of those surveyed believed that the courts were not harsh enough in dealing with criminals. Given the public's lack of personal contact with what the courts do, this perception of the quality of justice being dispensed is being driven by other sources.

Research has found that "the content of network television news is shown to account for a high proportion of...U.S. citizens' policy references" (Page, et al., 1987:23). Extending this information to the criminal justice field, the influence of media sources on the public's view of crime and the criminal justice system is apparent. Since most information reported by the different types of media covers similar kinds of stories, inaccuracies in the information presented can lead to inaccuracies in the public's perception of crime and the job the criminal justice is doing.

In a recent study by the authors of this chapter, a content analysis was conducted on articles reported in *USA Today's Across the USA: News From Every State* (Jerin and Fields, 1994). *USA Today* claims to be the foremost daily newspaper in the United States and is the only source that reports news from every state every day. Using Graber's (1979) differentiation of news topics to establish four general headings, the analysis established the central theme of each news *byte* in an effort to reduce duplication of recordings. The topics used in the study were: (1) Crime and Justice, (2) Government and Politics, (3) Economics and Social Issues, and (4) Human Interest and Family.

The initial analysis of the news first examined the different types of news and categorized them according to Graber's model. In *News From Every State*, the crime and justice section received the least amount of coverage. The percentage of stories that fell into the crime category was 16% (n=4236). The percentage of additional news categories was Government/Politics 24.4% (n=6412); Human interest/Family issues 26.7% (n=7015); and Economic/Social issues 32.8% (n=8638). A relatively small number of summaries (n=260) that were difficult or impossible to categorize were excluded from the analysis. This balance of issues is unique when compared to Graber's (1979) earlier study in Chicago (see Table 1). However, further analysis in the crime and justice section confirms previous research.

It is perhaps unusual that crime- and justice-related news summaries make up the smallest category of *News From Every State* in *USA Today* while human interest and family summaries constitute the largest. The three papers examined by Graber (1979) all report more news in the areas of government and politics, while crime and justice, or economic and social issues rank second. Human interest and family news ranks last.

The manner in which crime and justice news is reported in the state section of *USA Today* is similar to what was found in earlier research (e.g. Marsh, 1991). The amount of violent index crimes reported is almost 42% with murder at 28%. Property crimes make up 6% of the crime reported with white collar/corporate crimes totaling about 10%. The level of drug crimes is the third highest recorded category with over 8%. The "other" crime category constitutes 29% of the recordings.

Because of the brevity of the material reported (i.e. two stories per day) the type of crime story that made the news had a uniqueness to it. The material in *USA Today* followed a pattern found in Roshier's work. Roshier (1973) identified four sets of factors which seemed to establish why some crimes are selected in preference to others. These factors are:

TABLE 1

Frequency of News Topics (N) in *USA Today* (1990) and *Chicago Tribune, Sun-times* and *Daily News* (1979)[1]
(Percent)

Topic	USA Today (N=26,301)	Tribune (N=33,200)	Sun-Times (N=581)	Daily News (N=506)
Crime and Justice	16.1	21.8	28.0	26.7
Government and Politics	24.4	41.4	41.5	43.9
Human Interest & Family	32.8	10.6	5.5	7.9
Economic & Social Issues	26.7	26.0	23.5	21.5

---

[1]With the exception of *USA Today* figures, which were collected by the present authors, the primary data included in the table comes from a year-long content analysis of *Chicago Tribune*. The other two Chicago Daily newspapers were analyzed on a more limited basis. For a more detailed discussion of the methodology, see Graber (1979).

1. The seriousness of the offense;

2. "Whimsical" circumstances, i.e. humorous, ironic, unusual;

3. Sentimental or dramatic circumstances; and

4. The involvement of a famous or high status person in any capacity (p. 34-35).

Examples of these factors can be found throughout *USA Today*'s reporting of state events. In many cases a combination of these factors can be observed in the crimes reported.

The differences between the states are somewhat difficult to analyze because of the subjective descriptions of crimes reported in each state. Typically, in a brief sentence or two, routine crime-related summaries list the location of the offense, describe the offense itself (perhaps naming the offender and victim) and little else. It is a little easier, however, to determine a subjective category in which to list the offense.

The total number of crime-related stories by state ranged from thirty-eight in Alaska to 152 in New York. Many crime categories had no reporting in some states; these include drugs, rape, and robbery. The population of the state in many cases seems to establish the frequency of the crime reporting more than anything else. An additional concern is the high percentage of crimes fitting into the other category. There was a need to redefine this category because of the number of crimes and the important social issues that some address (e.g. hate crimes).

CRIME REPORTING AND OFFICIAL CRIME STATISTICS

Many previous studies have dealt with the relationship between the extent of crime reporting and actual crime rates (see, e.g., Antunes and Hurley, 1977; Phillips, 1977; 1979; Fedler and Jordan, 1982). In an attempt to further assess the differences between crime rates and crime reporting, statistics for selected offenses from the Uniform Crime Reports (UCR) were compared with the same offenses reported in *USA Today*.

Using a ranking system, comparisons between states and the UCR offer some interesting information. States were ranked by population, UCR Index crime rate, and number and percent of news summaries relating to crime and justice reported in *USA Today*. In addition, four offense categories (murder, rape, drug violations, and corporate crime) were examined and ranked according to the reporting rate for each state.

The five most populated states—California, New York, Texas, Florida, and Pennsylvania—are among the states with the highest number of reported crimes (Macguire, et al., 1993), but they are not ranked highest in crime and justice related reporting. The inference is that the number of crime and justice summaries is somewhat related to state population.

A comparison of the five areas with the highest UCR Index crime rates— Washington, D.C., Florida, Arizona, Texas, and Georgia—and the reporting of more serious crimes offers additional insight into crime reporting behavior. None of the states with the five highest crime rates are included in the top five rankings of murder and rape. This difference in reporting may be due primarily to the commonality of major crimes in these states so that the newsworthiness of serious crimes in these same states may be minimized and other factors (see Roshier, 1973) may play a larger role.

This comparison is in direct contrast to the five states—West Virginia, South Dakota, North Dakota, Kentucky, and Pennsylvania—with the lowest Index Crime rates. Three of these states (West Virginia, South Dakota, and Kentucky) are ranked in the top five in rape and rape-related news summaries. This discrepancy may be due to the perception in the media that certain sensational crimes are more "newsworthy" in states with low crime rates.

Even the states with the highest rankings in terms of *USA Today's* crime-related reporting—(Arkansas, New Jersey, Wisconsin, Tennessee, and Missouri)—are not states with relatively high crime rates. Only New Jersey is in the top half of the UCR Index offenses (ranked twenty-second). The fact that Arkansas is ranked number one in terms of total crime- and justice-related reporting, number one in murder reporting, and number two in drug reporting, questions the objective reporting of crime related stories in *USA Today.* Further analysis of this phenomenon reveals that certain sensational crimes may be responsible for the extensive coverage of serious crime in Arkansas.

While statistical comparisons between official crime rates and the extent of crime-related reporting in *USA Today* may be problematic, there are at least some preliminary indications of a relationship between the reporting of certain crimes and crime rates (see Table 2).

When correlations between rape as reported in *USA Today* and the UCR Index are examined, it seems that those states with high crime rates were less apt to have rape related summaries during the year. There is, however, a strong positive correlation between drug-related reporting and official crime rates. No relationship was found between reporting of corporate/white collar offenses, murder, and all offenses combined and official crime statistics. Furthermore, *USA Today* had more drug related news summaries and total crime related summaries for small states (in terms of population) than for larger states.

TABLE 2

Simple Correlations Between Uniform Crime Reports (1990) and Crime and Justice Reporting in *USA Today*
(Selected Offenses)

		Crime and Justice Reporting			
	All Offenses	Murder	Rape	Drugs	Corporate
U.C.R.					
Index	.0193	-.0032	-.2346*	.3663**	.1742
Violent	.2313	.1731	-.1166	.3884**	.1830
Murder	.0743	.0259	-.2215	.3699**	.1071
Population	-.6598***	-.1141	-.2557*	-.4250**	-.0935

*   p < .05
**   p < .01
*** p < .001

In the future, the media's representation of crime and criminality will probably follow the same course. With the evolution of 100+ television channel capabilities and the competition which will be generated by these various networks, the use of sensationalism and hyperbole seems unavoidable. The print media could also fall victim to perceived market forces which try to increase the public's interest while at the same time providing the smallest amount of objective information; the use of sensationalized incidents will continue to distort the true picture of crime.

Notwithstanding the possibility of continued misinformation, the increase in news coverage may also tend to educate the public. The use of cameras in the courtroom, which is occurring in over forty-five states (Verhovek, 1991), along with the development of the Courtroom Television Network, will provide the public with coverage of actual court proceedings. While it is likely that initial coverage by these types of media may be limited to only those "sensational" crimes and criminals, watching the actual trial without a media filter will provide the public with a more accurate picture of the criminal justice system.

While sensational crimes have received extensive coverage over the years (e.g., the 1925 Scopes "Monkey" trial and the 1935 Lindbergh kidnapping trial), recent sensational cases have provided the public with a greater interest in watching the actual trial unfold. The William Kennedy Smith and Mike Tyson rape trials captured the attention of the public and every media source (Lacayo, 1991; Corliss, 1992) as has the O.J. Simpson murder trial. Although the coverage of these trials has been characterized as a media "free-for-all" (Pollitt, 1991; Nack, 1992), the ability of the public to watch the actual trials from start to finish allows for an accurate depiction of part of the criminal justice process that most people never experience.

This type of coverage is not only limited to the courts. Law enforcement is also currently the center of attention with television shows such as *COPS* and *Rescue 911*. *COPS* follows actual police officers and allows the officers to narrate the action that the audience is watching. *Rescue 911* reenacts police dramas with the cooperation of the original participants. While what is being covered will focus on appealing law enforcement situations, a more accurate picture of crime and criminals should appear.

The use of these and similar programs is certain to increase due to their low costs of production and the continued prurient interest of the public. The accurate portrayal of the crime problem and the criminal justice system will depend on the media's actions coupled with the public's desire for more information regarding crime and criminality. If the public is only allowed to view a "cut-and-paste" version of these events or has access only to sensational cases, then a distortion of both the crime problem and operation of the system will continue.

CONCLUSION

The reporting of news events across the United States follows previous patterns found in regional newspapers and other media sources. The print media sensationalize certain crimes and ignore many others. Many times lesser crimes are reported not because of the event, but because of the notoriety of the individuals involved or the humor that it evoked. However, the breakdown of crime news in comparison to other areas of interest does not seem out of proportion.

It is suggested that the reporting of major crimes is not based on official crime statistics nor state populations. Furthermore, the media reporting of a few sensational crimes in low crime rate states can distort the true amount of crime in those states. This study has also found that major factors in a crime being reported by the media is not the crime itself, but the circumstances surrounding the crime, the public nature of the offender or victim, and the humorous nature of the incident. This is especially true with minor offenses. It seems that the accuracy of the reporting of criminal acts will always be compromised by the "newsworthiness" of the incident.

The future may hold more promise for accuracy given the possibility of competing news sources and greater variety that may be available to the general public. Live action reporting, gavel-to-gavel coverage of court proceedings, and innovations in information technologies should provide the public with increased and more accurate information.

The conscious decision by the public to use these sources instead of continued reliance on the more traditional "news bits" for information can go a long way in assuring the elimination of the public's misperception of crime and criminality.

STUDY QUESTIONS

1. How are our perceptions about crime and criminality distorted by what we read in the newspaper?
2. ...by what we see on television?
3. What are the primary factors that affect the type of crime related news reporting?
4. How has the reporting of crime related news changed over the past few years?
5. What will influence the ways in which crime related news is reported in the future?

REFERENCES

Antunes, G. E. and Hurley, P. A. (1977). "The Representation of Criminal Events in Houston's Two Daily Newspapers." *Journalism Quarterly* 54:756-760.

Bacon, J. (1992). Personal Communication (2/15).

Cohen, S. (1975). "A Comparison of Crime Coverage in Detroit and Atlanta Newspapers" *Journalism Quarterly* 52:726-30.

Corliss, Richard. (1992). "The Bad and the Beautiful" *Time* 139 (8): 25 (2).

Davis, F. James. (1952). "Crime News in Colorado Newspapers." *American Journal of Sociology* LVII (June): 325:330.

Deaden, J., and J. Duffy. (1983). "Bias in the Newspaper Reporting of Crime News" *British Journal of Criminology* 23: 159-65.

Eder, Peter F. (1990). *The Futurist* (May/June):38-41.

Ericson, Richard V. (1991). "Mass Media, Crime, Law, and Justice." *British Journal of Criminology* 31 (3): 219-249.

Fedler, F. and D. Jordan. (1982). "How Emphasis on People Affects Coverage of Crime." *Journalism Quarterly* 59: 474-78.

Graber, Doris A. (1979). "Is Crime News Excessive?" *Journal of Communication* 29: 81-92.

Graber, Doris A. (1980). *Crime News and the Public.* New York: Praeger.

Hans, Valerie P. and Juliet L. Dee. (1991). "Media Coverage of Law: Its Impact on Juries and the Public." *American Behavioral Scientist* 35 (2): 136-149.

Heath, Linda. (1984). "Impact of Newspaper Crime Reports on Fear of Crime: Multimethodological Investigation." *Journal of Personality and Social Psychology* 47(2): 263-276.

Humphries, Drew. (1981). "Serious Crime, News Coverage, and Ideology: A Content Analysis of Crime Coverage In a Metropolitan Paper." *Crime and Delinquency* 27: 191-205.

Jaehnig, Walter B., David H. Weaver and Frederick Fico. (1981). "Reporting Crime and Fearing Crime in Three Communities." Journal of Communication, Winter: 88-96.

Jerin, Robert and Charles Fields. (1994). "Murder and Mayhem in the *USA Today:* A Quantitative Analysis the Reporting of States' News." in *Media, Process, and the Social Construction of Crime: Studies in Newsmaking Criminology.* G. Barak, Ed., New York: Garland Publishing, Inc.

Jordan, Donald L. (1993). "Newspaper Effects on Policy Preferences." Public Opinion Quarterly 57: 191-204.

Lacayo, Richard. (1991). "Trial By Television." Time 138 (24): 30 (2).

Macguire, Kathleen, et al., eds. (1993). *Sourcebook of Criminal Justice Statistics, 1992.* Washington, DC: USGPO.

Marsh, Harry L. (1991). "A Comparative Analysis of Crime Coverage in Newspapers in the United States and Other Countries from 1960-1989: A Review of the Literature." *Journal of Criminal Justice* 19: 67-79.

Meyer, John C. Jr. (1975). "Newspaper Reporting of Crime and Justice: An Analysis of an Assumed Difference." *Journalism Quarterly* 52: 731-34.

Meyer, John C. Jr. (1976). "Reporting Crime and Justice in the Press: A Comparative Inquiry." Criminology 14: 277-78.

Nack, William. (1992). "A Gruesome Account." *Sports Illustrated* 76 (5): 24-28.

Newman, Graeme R. (1990). "Popular Culture and Criminal Justice: A Preliminary Analysis." *Journal of Criminal Justice* 18: 261-274.

Page, Benjamin I., Robert Y. Shapiro, and Glenn R. Dempsey. (1987). "What Moves Public Opinion?" *American Political Science Review* 81 (1): 23-43.

Phillips, D.P. (1977). "Motor Vehicle Fatalities Increase Just After Publicized Suicide Rates." Science 196: 1464-65.

Phillips, D.F. (1979). "Suicide, Motor Vehicle Fatalities and the Mass Media: Evidence Toward a Theory of Suggestion." *American Journal of Sociology* 84: 1150-74.

Pollitt, Katha. (1991). "Media Goes Wilding in Palm Beach." *The Nation* 252 (24): 833 (5).

Roberts, J.V. and A.N. Doob. (1990). "News Media Influence on Public Views of Sentencing." Law and Human Behavior 14: 451-458.

Robinson, Michael J. and Andrew Kohut. (1988). "Believability and the Press." *Public Opinion Quarterly* 52: 174-189.

Roshier, B. (1973). "The Selection of Crime News by the Press." In S. Cohen, and J. Young (Eds), *The Manufacture of News.* Beverly Hills, CA: Sage, pp. 29-39.

Sacco, Vincent F. and Meena Trotman. (1990). "Public Information Programming and Family Violence: Lessons from the Mass Media Crime Prevention Experience." *Canadian Journal of Criminology* 32 (1): 91-105.

Schlesinger, Philip, Howard Tumber and Graham Murdock. (1991). "The Media Politics of Crime and Criminal Justice." *British Journal of Sociology* 42 (3): 397-420.

Sheley, Joseph F. and Cindy D. Ashkins. (1981). "Crime, Crime News, and Crime Views." *Public Opinion Quarterly* 45: 492-506.

Shoemaker, P.J. and S.D. Reese. (1990). "Exposure to What? Integrating Media Content and Effects Studies." *Journalism Quarterly* 67: 649-652.

Surette, Ray. (1992). Media, Crime and Criminal Justice: Images and Realities. Pacific Grove, California: Brooks/Cole Publishing Co.

USA Today/CNN/Gallup Poll. (1993). "Crime in America," (10/28/93).

Verhovek, S.H. (1991). "News Cameras in Courts? New York's Law Disputed." *New York Times* (May 28); B1, B6.

Windhauser, John W., J. Seiter, and L. Thomas Winfree. (1990). "Crime News in the Louisiana Press, 1980 vs. 1985." Journalism Quarterly *67: 72-78.*

CHAPTER 5

THE SITUATION OF CRIME VICTIMS IN THE YEAR 2020

Andrew Karmen, Ph.D.

FORECASTING FUTURE DEVELOPMENTS

Several different strategies can be pursued to try to anticipate what the situation facing crime victims will be like in the year 2020. One way to make informed guesses about social and political arrangements twenty-five years from now is to look back over the developments of the past twenty-five years in order to see how much can change during this amount of time.

A second way to speculate about what lies just beyond the horizon is to identify the driving forces for change. By projecting emerging social trends, it becomes possible to paint plausible scenarios about developments over the next several decades. Such linear extrapolations basically predict "more of the same" but at higher (or lower) levels or to greater (or lesser) degrees. For example, the trend towards a cashless society might mean there will be fewer victims of muggings but more carjackings in the year 2020. By focusing upon anticipated technological breakthroughs, useful innovations can be predicted. As an illustration, computerized record-keeping could enable victims to monitor from their homes the progress of "their" cases as they are processed by the legal system. However, the extrapolation approach can yield gross inaccuracies, if what are really short-run phenomena are mistaken for long-term trends and are extended too far into the future. For instance, budget cuts and hiring freezes, which currently necessitate reductions in government services provided to victims, may not last long. Vast improvements in victim services may be implemented as soon as economic conditions improve and tax revenues increase again. Furthermore, the extrapolation approach can neglectfully ignore countervailing pressures which might put up enough resistance to hold the driving forces in check.

Still a third way to make predictions is to speculate that completely new and currently unheard of developments will evolve out of familiar situations. Although exercising the imagination is the foundation for good science fiction, it may generate questionable social science. Given the hegemony of punitive approaches, is it not possible that victims soon will be invited to symbolically "lock in" convicts at brief official ceremonies heralding the start of prisoners' sentences? Going further into the realm of revenge fantasies, is it inconceivable that the surviving family members of homicide victims someday will be entitled to "pull the switch" at electrocutions of murderers? Naturally, such conjectures about unprecedented developments run the risk of being way off because they represent an unfettered flight from reality.

Of course, when reviewing the past or describing the present, "what is" must always be distinguished from "what ought to be." The social scientist has to strive for objectivity, and be vigilant that subjective interpretations and personal biases don't find their way into the analysis. Applying this principle of impartiality to forecasting means making a distinction between "what is likely to happen" versus "what would be desirable." Wishful thinking about a better future should not be substituted for a realistic assessment of what is probable.

THE SITUATION FACING VICTIMS TWENTY-FIVE YEARS AGO

When the situation of crime victims in the recent past is reviewed, it becomes clear that sweeping and profound changes can occur in a mere twenty-five-year time span. As recently as 1970, victims were still largely written off as an undifferentiated mass of faceless, pitiful "losers" who were the unfortunate "casualties" of a growing and intractable street crime problem. A number of commentators characterized them as the forgotten people within the criminal justice process, virtually "invisible" (Rieff, 1979), systematically overlooked, totally excluded from meaningful participation, and beset by needs that were routinely ignored (see Carrington, 1975; Barkas, 1978). The plight of crime victims had not yet been rediscovered by the news media, law enforcement officials, political movements, or academic researchers.

Slowly, public consciousness heightened when the women's liberation movement started to expose and critique the way the men at the helm of the justice system callously disregarded the best interests of sexually assaulted girls and women (see Griffin, 1971). There were no rape crisis centers until feminist activists in the San Francisco Bay area challenged police and hospital practices in 1972 (Largen, 1981). In university libraries, students searched in vain for analyses of rape that presented the violated woman's point of view (Schwendinger and Schwendinger, 1983: 10). Similarly, magazine articles rarely addressed the predicament of battered women trapped in romantic relationships that had turned violent. *The Reader's Guide To Periodical Literature* first introduced the subject heading "wife beating" in 1974 (Loseke, 1989). There were no shelters for battered women to flee to, until activists set up a hotline and a refuge in an old house in St. Paul, Minnesota in 1974 (Martin, 1977).

The failure of prosecutors to attend to the needs of their ostensible clients was widespread in criminal courts back in 1970. Many victims never found out if anyone was arrested or convicted in their cases, if their stolen property was ever recovered, or if they were entitled to modest witness fees for missing work when called to testify (Lynch, 1976). Half of the decade would pass before the Law Enforcement Assistance Administration (LEAA) began to channel federal funding to county district attorneys in order to experiment with victim/witness assistance programs. Such programs provide support services to individuals who are needed to testify on behalf of the state (see Schneider and Schneider, 1981; and Roberts, 1990). In 1970, the potential of civil lawsuits as a means of recovering financial losses was not yet realized. It would take a few more years before some legal activists realized that besides suing offenders directly, victims could launch lawsuits against third parties such as businesses, colleges, and psychiatric hospitals whose gross negligence about security matters made it easier for criminals to harm them (Carrington, 1977).

After all the major power struggles of the 1960s, involving African-Americans, students, women, gays, soldiers, and prisoners, were well established, victim activists were inspired to follow their lead, and organize self-help and support groups and advocacy organizations during the 1970s. The loose coalition that constituted the victims' rights movement started the process of redressing grievances by publishing newsletters, demonstrating for reforms, monitoring trials, petitioning criminal justice officials, and lobbying lawmakers (see Friedman, 1985). But the earliest proponents of victims' rights (see Hook, 1972) envisioned these new statutes mostly as weapons to counter or even "trump" the expanding rights of "criminals" (suspects, defendants, and prisoners) granted by landmark decisions handed down by the Warren Court. They did not yet picture victims' rights as a means of empowerment for individuals who deserved input into how "their" cases were resolved by remote and indifferent criminal justice bureaucracies and officials.

Back in 1970, there was no talk about amending the U.S. Constitution to guarantee victims legal standing in criminal justice proceedings. That course of action was not taken seriously until the President's Task Force On Victims of Crime (1982) suggested rewording the Sixth Amendment to include a pledge that "The victim in every criminal prosecution shall have the right to be present and to be heard at all critical stages of judicial proceedings." It took until the mid-1980s before victim advocacy groups realized that they could be much more successful in their drive to secure new rights by organizing campaigns to amend state constitutions, one at a time (NOVA, 1986).

However, one area of legal reform was already well underway by 1970: compensating innocent, physically injured victims for their out-of-pocket monetary losses. A few states set up their own funds during the 1960s, while members of Congress were debating whether it was an appropriate area of responsibility and jurisdiction for federal aid. Before 1970, die-hard believers in rugged individualism denounced the thought of spreading a government-sponsored safety net under wounded victims facing financial ruin as "creeping socialism" (see Meiners, 1978). Congress was unable to muster the majority of members needed to authorize the partial funding of state compensation programs until 1984. But these faltering steps toward helping certain unfortunate victims pay off some of their devastating medical bills had not yet been exposed as largely symbolic political gestures that were grossly underfunded, fiscally inadequate, and personally demeaning (Elias, 1983). Also on the economic front, few judicial systems (except some juvenile courts) had demonstrated a sustained commitment to revive the ancient practice of restitution by offenders to the parties they harmed (Hudson and Galaway, 1975). And it wasn't until 1975 that a religious group in Canada set up an experimental program to enable offenders to repay their victims as part of an effort to resolve their antagonisms and achieve mutual reconciliation (McKnight, 1981).

Victimology—the scientific study of crime victims—had not yet emerged as an area of specialization within criminology. Victimologists from around the world did not hold their first professional conference until 1973 in Jerusalem (Drapkin and Viano, 1974). No journal was devoted to publishing studies about crime victims until 1976 (Viano, 1976). Only one scholarly work that could serve as a textbook (Schafer, 1968) was available for college courses, but it was filled with either historical material about a past "Golden Age" or conjecture about the future because there were very few research findings for the author to cite.

ANTICIPATING THE SITUATION OF VICTIMS TWENTY-FIVE YEARS FROM NOW BY PROJECTING EXISTING TENDENCIES AND TRENDS

To anticipate what the future holds by using the method of extrapolating existing trends, the way to proceed is to identify the most relevant tendencies and then to trace out how they might shape the situation of crime victims. Three tendencies seem to be the most influential: the trend towards greater formal rights, the trend towards privatization, and the trend towards differential case handling.

HOW THE TREND TOWARDS GRANTING VICTIMS GREATER FORMAL RIGHTS WITHIN THE CRIMINAL JUSTICE PROCESS MIGHT LEAD TO THE EMERGENCE OF VICTIM ADVOCATES

One likely development over the next twenty-five years will be the emergence of a new kind of criminal justice professional: the victim advocate (see Karmen, 1995). There will be a growing need for this kind of consultant who can advise victims, one at a time, about their increasingly complicated rights, opportunities, options, and obligations, and look after their best interests in their dealings with detectives, defendants, defense attorneys, prosecutors, judges, probation officers, corrections officials, parole boards, compensation boards, and journalists.

During the past twenty-five years, fourteen state legislatures have amended their state constitutions to guarantee victims certain rights. In other jurisdictions, packages of laws designated as "a Victim's Bill of Rights" have been passed. Now, victims are entitled to know about developments in their cases; to be given timely notification about optional and required appearances at evidentiary hearings, trials, sentencing hearings, and parole board meetings; to pursue a number of strategies for reimbursement of their out-of-pocket expenses (restitution, compensation, civil lawsuits, insurance coverage); and to protect their personal privacy (especially from media exposure in sexual assault cases). In some localities, police chiefs, district attorneys, and judges have granted victims additional privileges above and beyond what procedural law requires as the minimum standard for fair treatment. Special solutions have been devised to address the special problems facing abused children, survivors of childhood incest, abused elders, battered women, rape victims, and targets of bias-motivated hate crimes.

Over the next few decades, the provision of a "crime victim's advocate" will probably become institutionalized on a case-by-case basis. Every complainant, upon filing a report with the police, will be offered the services of this new kind of professional consultant.

To date, scattered individuals—some dedicated volunteers, others overworked and underpaid—are available to assist victims, both outside the criminal justice system (at shelters for battered women and at rape crisis centers, for example) and inside of it (such as guardians *ad litem* in family courts, and counselors working at prosecutors' victim-witness assistance units). But no one looks after the best interests of all kinds of victims (of burglary, robbery, auto theft, and so on) from start to finish in the justice process. By the year 2020, it is likely that victims will be routinely provided with advocates, free of charge, just as attorneys are made available to indigent defendants. Advocates could be furnished by a government agency (comparable to the public defender's office), or supplied by an independent nonprofit organization funded by charitable donations (similar to the Legal Aid Society). Other advocates will have their own private practices, like defense attorneys in law firms, and will be retained for a fee by those who can afford their services.

HOW THE TREND TOWARDS PRIVATIZING CRIMINAL JUSTICE FUNCTIONS MIGHT LEAD TO PRIVATE PROSECUTION

The trend by government to divest, farm out, or share certain responsibilities within the criminal justice process with private enterprises is likely to accelerate in the next few decades. One impact upon victims will be to open up the possibility of private prosecution.

All throughout history, the inherently public and governmental nature of justice and punishment has been symbolized by the badge of the police officer, the robe of the judge, and the uniform of the corrections guard (DiIulio, 1988). However, a number of contemporary developments are undermining the government's monopoly over criminal justice functions. Privatization began by nibbling away at the front and back stages of the criminal justice process. At the front end, privatization took the form of furnishing added protection, above and beyond the minimal degree provided by the state from tax revenues (security firms offering guards for hire) and individually financed tailor-made investigations (carried out for a fee by "private eyes"). At the tail end, privatization took the form of independently operated nonprofit therapeutic communities and profit-oriented residential and outpatient drug treatment programs, plus, since the 1980s, corporate-run detention centers, jails, and prisons. Now, the middle stage of adjudication is undergoing privatization, and a dual court system is emerging: criminal courts handling most cases, and neighborhood justice centers practicing dispute resolution on selected cases diverted from the government's system (see the next section, below, for further implications of this development).

What remains to be privatized is the function of prosecution itself. It is likely that activists and advocacy groups within the victims movement soon will launch campaigns demanding the right to private prosecution (see Cole, 1992: 718). Mounting frustrations with the way that assistant district attorneys handle cases will give this demand broad popular appeal.

Victims and the lawyers assigned by the government to "dispose of" their cases can disagree over the goals of the process. A victim might want to press charges, but the prosecutor's office might want to drop some or all charges (or vice versa). A victim might want the offender to admit guilt and to be held responsible for everything in the indictment, by going to trial if necessary, while the prosecutor's office usually will be satisfied with a conviction on a lesser charge, preferably through a time-saving and cost-effective negotiated plea. A victim might want court ordered restitution from the offender but the government might not consider reimbursement to be an important priority. Likewise, a victim might want the legal system to compel the offender (perhaps a violence-prone husband, or a drug abusing neighbor) to undergo treatment, but the government might be more intent on securing some other disposition, ranging from a suspended sentence to imprisonment.

The seeds of conflict between victims and "their" lawyers are sown by contradictions within each party's roles. One contradiction revolves around the duality of the victim's role: on the one hand, victims are "on the side of the government" in the adversarial system; specifically they are allied with the police and the prosecution in the quest for conviction. On the other hand, victims are independent actors who might want to pursue what they perceive to be their own best interests. Similarly, prosecutors confront a contradiction in their own roles whenever they try to bridge a gap by representing both the interests of the government that hires them and the clients they are assigned to help. The role strain faced by the assistant district attorney was minimal until the last twenty-five years, when victims began to exercise their recently granted rights and started to conceive of their personal interests as being separate from those of the bureaucracy that furnished them with a lawyer for free. Of course, when forced to choose, assistant district attorneys will act in accord with the interests of the agency that employs them rather than on behalf of the injured parties who rely upon them.

The underlying philosophy of jurisprudence (which victims are questioning) is that all criminal acts, including interpersonal violence and theft, should be conceptualized as offenses against the state requiring an official response, and are not simply wrongs inflicted upon innocent parties that could be righted by individually arranged settlements. Because the government gets drawn in, to safeguard the public interest, victims are relegated to the role of mere complainants who set the machinery of justice into motion by reporting incidents to the police. If their cases are solved (most are not; clearance rates are low) and an arrest is made, victims bear the obligation of testifying for the prosecution; but even as star witnesses, they just provide dramatic evidence of criminal conduct on the part of the accused, and otherwise lack legal standing.

A new philosophy is emerging from the ranks of the victims' movement which challenges the government's monopoly on the exercise of prosecutorial discretion. It proceeds from the assumption that person-against-person crimes like rape, robbery, assault, and burglary do more than just violate an abstraction known as the criminal law, or threaten the community's peace, or harm a collectivity like "the People of the State of...," as indictments read. The real flesh-and-blood individual who has suffered emotional damage, physical injuries, and financial losses has a rightful claim to have some input into the way the system handles the case, especially given the great latitude concerning penalties written into the law and the considerable discretion exercised by prosecutors and judges. If the victim is viewed as a "consumer" of prosecutorial "services" made available by the government's "public law firm," shouldn't those attorneys be accountable to their "clients"? If their handling of cases can't be influenced by victims, shouldn't these disgruntled customers be allowed to go elsewhere, and choose a prosecutor of their own, perhaps for a fee?

In anger and frustration, people holding this personalized outlook about justice have sought to gain some leverage over prosecutorial decision-making, in addition to the long-standing negative, self-defeating strategy of discontinuing cooperation with the authorities. In most jurisdictions, victims are now informed about the terms of a negotiated plea, but they cannot exercise the privilege of "veto power" over unacceptable deals. Prosecutors have rejected proposals to permit victims to participate directly in negotiations. Through the vehicles of victim impact statements and allocution (personal appearances), victims have attempted to influence sentencing decisions, but their recommendations are just one of many sources of input influencing judges.

Clearly, the attraction of private prosecution is that it would enable a lawyer hired by the victim to pursue what the victim defines as his or her best interests: some mix of retribution, restitution, rehabilitation (of the offender), and/or reconciliation of the two estranged parties. Victims who did not like the way the government attorney was planning to "dispose of" the case could select their own lawyer to press charges, negotiate a plea, or present the case before a jury.

As recently as 1955, this "do-it-yourself" option was permitted in at least twenty-eight states. But by the 1970s, only a few jurisdictions allowed private lawyers hired by complainants to join forces with government attorneys (Sigler, 1979). Over the years, the Supreme Court has handed down a number of rulings (in 1967, 1973, 1977, 1981, and 1983) establishing that victims cannot compel prosecutors to take action, and that judges cannot intervene in the victim's behalf in their disagreements with prosecutors. Attorneys general and district attorneys retain sole discretion over whether or not to charge defendants with crimes, and over which charges to press or drop (Stark and Goldstein, 1985).

And yet there are two precedents that make the revival of private prosecution seem feasible and reasonable. First of all, victims have long had the opportunity to pursue their private brand of justice in civil court by suing their offenders for monetary damages. Of course, it is at their own expense, and only money, not punishment or compulsory treatment, is at stake. Second, on occasion, victims are already availing themselves of the services of private attorneys. For example, in certain highly publicized cases, rape complainants have retained lawyers; and complainants in high profile bias crimes have consulted with private lawyers who acted as spokespersons and advisors, to protect their clients' interests, and to pressure prosecutors to handle the cases the way the victims wanted them resolved (see Taibbi and Sims-Phillips, 1989).

Private prosecution is relied upon in routine criminal matters in most European countries. The role of government prosecution is limited to major cases raising important principles (for example, in England, the Office of Public Prosecutor; in France, the Procurer Publique; in the Netherlands, the Schout). The victim or the police department (playing the role of complainant) hires a barrister from a pool of lawyers authorized to conduct negotiations and trials. The same barrister may serve as a prosecutor in one case and as a defense attorney in another. The expenses incurred by the prosecuting barrister are paid for either by victims themselves or by government funds set aside for this purpose (Newman, 1986). If European practices are adopted, what will remain to be worked out is whether the victim will be permitted to go forward only if the government prosecutor fails to press charges, and whether private prosecution will be allowed only for certain minor interpersonal offenses like assault and trespass (see Sebba, 1992).

It is likely that federal, state, and country prosecutors will consider private prosecution a threat to their job security and professional stature, and will oppose this trend towards privatization in ways that will retard its acceptance and implementation.

HOW THE TREND TOWARD DEVELOPING MORE ALTERNATIVES TO BOTH ADJUDICATION AND INCARCERATION MIGHT BRING ABOUT A GREATER RELIANCE ON VICTIM-OFFENDER RECONCILIATION PROGRAMS

One trend likely to accelerate is the practice of diverting cases out of the former adversarial system of court adjudication into the informal case processing track of alternative dispute resolution (ADR). Another trend that is sure to persist is the search for effective alternatives to incarceration. The convergence of these two trends is likely to bring about greater reliance upon the use of mediation techniques to arrive at out-of-court settlements, in which offenders make restitution to their victims as the basis for mutual reconciliation, and thereby avoid prison sentences.

For decades, police officers, prosecutors, judges, and court administrators have been taking out what they consider to be the "garbage" from the case flow. What they deem "junk" that doesn't merit much public attention are cases in which people who had prior relationships (as lovers, family members, co-workers, neighbors, and so on) are embroiled in minor disputes and both parties share responsibility for the outbreak of hostilities (Silberman, 1978). But these weeded out cases were not systematically pursued, and were just allowed to fester and sometimes escalate. Finally, in the early 1970s, neighborhood justice centers were set up with LEAA funding to mediate conflicts diverted from the court system. In 1980, Congress passed the Dispute Resolution Act to further the spread of "storefront justice." By the late 1980s, nearly three hundred nonadversarial programs were employing mediators and arbitrators to settle cases in which the labels "innocent victim" and "guilty perpetrator" did not fit the facts.

At the same time that these alternatives to adjudication were developing, a growing chorus of voices were calling for the development of alternatives to incarceration. Jails and prisons have long been indicted for being overcrowded, disease-ridden, explosively violent, and strikingly counterproductive "schools for crime" that churn out hardened convicts prone to recidivate. During the 1960s and early 1970s, a prisoner's rights movement called for a moratorium on new prison construction and for decarceration and deinstitutionalization—symbolically a tendency to "tear down the walls." But the ensuing crackdown on crime demanded by the law and order movement instead generated soaring inmate populations, skyrocketing probation and parole caseloads, and escalating expenditures. During the 1980s, proponents of privatization began to "sell the walls"—giving companies a chance to profit from incarcerating the government's growing number of prisoners (DeIulio, 1988). But the long-standing quest for effective alternatives to locking up lawbreakers was also reinvigorated. Now there is a growing interest in an underutilized option: using mediation to arrange restitution by offenders as a basis for reconciliation.

The first U.S. victim-offender reconciliation program (VORP) was established in Indiana in 1978. The initiators were inspired by biblical teachings: that crime symbolized a rupture or wound that afflicted a whole community and had to be healed through reparation rather than retribution. By taking a restorative rather than punitive approach, these reconciliation programs can help the injured party and the wrongdoer to settle their own differences peacefully. To heal their emotional wounds, both the victim and the offender need to be empowered (authorized to resolve their conflict by themselves). Just as prisons were invented by the Quakers in the early 1800s and then were copied by government, the reconciliation model originated by the Mennonites were replicated by other groups and agencies throughout the 1980s. By 1990, about one hundred reconciliation programs had sprung up across the country, run in most jurisdictions by nonprofit organizations. And the range of cases handled by centers for mediation/restitution/reconciliation was quickly expanding. Originally, only cases embroiling people who previously knew each other, or which involved offenses against property (generally, burglary and other forms of thievery) were considered suitable. But within a few years, cases surrounding acts of violence committed by strangers were being referred for restitution and reconciliation as well (Umbreit, 1990).

In theory, this particular alternative to incarceration offers advantages to victims, offenders, and crime-plagued communities. For victims, these programs provide a safe, secure setting to confront their offenders in the presence of trained and skilled intermediaries. When they meet in person, victims get an opportunity to vent pent-up feelings and ask probing questions. Besides the potential for emotional catharsis, victims ought to be able to leave the negotiations with a satisfactory restitution agreement in hand. For offenders, the encounter offers an occasion to accept responsibility for wrongdoing, express remorse, and ask for the victim's forgiveness. More important to most perpetrators is the chance to substitute restitution obligations (through work at regular jobs) for hard prison time. For the community, the pragmatic benefit is that negotiated settlements relieve court backlogs as well as jail and prison overcrowding and eliminate the need to build more cells to confine greater numbers of convicts at the public's expense. A less tangible but significant spiritual dividend is that "restorative justice" nurtures an atmosphere of forgiveness, redemption, acceptance, and harmony within the community (Umbreit, 1990; Viano, 1990: Galaway and Hudson, 1990; Wright, 1991).

However, if widespread acceptance of the punitive approach to crime persists, the weight of public opinion will act as a countervailing force holding this trend towards "peaceful resolution" of criminal matters in check.

HOW THE TREND TOWARDS DIFFERENTIAL JUSTICE MIGHT INCREASE THE GAP IN THE WAY VICTIMS ARE HANDLED

It is likely that in the near future, obvious "double standards" in the way victims are handled by agencies and officials will become a contentious issue. Whereas in the recent past, just about all victims suffered from neglect, now the potential is developing for some victims to receive "first class, VIP" treatment while others continue to be treated as "second class" citizens.

One obvious and troubling trend within American society does not have an appropriate, evocative, widely accepted name. It is best referred to as "differential access" but is also called "class privilege" and "dual systems." The term "differential" is preferable because it is more accurate; "dual" implies only two distinct systems when actually there usually are several; a top track, a bottom track, and one or more gradations in-between (with people in the middle classes enjoying some privileges but not others). The phrase "class privilege" accentuates the importance of wealth and power, but it overlooks stratification based on gender, race, and age as well. "Differential" or "dual systems" and "class privilege" in other areas of American society have been extensively studied (for example: schooling, health care, transportation, recreation, housing). The persistent pattern in each of these areas is that the affluent benefit from the best goods and services modern technology can deliver and money can buy, while the underclass is grudgingly provided with the minimal, lowest quality services the system can get away with, without fully exposing its false promises of "equality."

Differential access to justice has been the subject of a great deal of interest, research, and debate. Some argue that in America "justice is blind," that the country is run "by laws, not men (sic)," and that there is "equal protection" for all. But others work to expose and put an end to the thinly disguised continuation of the historic trend of differential access to justice, which leads to "double standards," in which a perpetrator's and a victim's characteristics are unfairly taken into account in the handling of cases by the system.

As predicted above, the potential opportunities, rights, and privileges available to victims will proliferate (specifically: providing victim advocates, permitting private prosecution, allowing mediation/restitution/reconciliation). Differential access to justice will become more blatant, in the sense that how the case is resolved will depend primarily upon the victim's status (and secondarily, upon the offender's place in the social order). The victimization of some people will continue to be taken much more seriously than the victimization of others. When "important" members of society are harmed and turn to the legal system for redress, they will receive a more satisfactory and supportive response than they do now. When the meager possessions of "marginal" members of society are stolen, or when they are beaten, robbed, or raped, the same old uncaring, assembly-line disposal of their cases will take place.

Differential handling of cases will show up most clearly when someone from the most affluent and privileged strata is afforded first class, "red carpet" or "VIP" treatment. This class of injured parties will be able to purchase the services of private victim advocates who can devote their undivided attention to their cases, and who are well educated, articulate, dedicated, skillful, knowledgeable, and have all the right networking connections. Victims from privileged backgrounds will receive solid emotional support and effective rehabilitation from experts in the recovery movement, who will endeavor to restore them to the condition they were in before the crimes occurred. Victims who are well off will be able to hire top-notch lawyers to handle their private prosecutions, and get the criminal justice system to resolve their cases in the ways they want (whether severe punishment via lengthy imprisonment, or offender rehabilitation, or diversion/mediation/restitution/reconciliation).

Working class victims will continue to be treated as second class complainants. They will be provided with overworked, underpaid, less trained, and less competent victim advocates, supplied by an underfunded government agency. The cases of these "unimportant" victims will be handled in a brusque, routinized way by government-supplied assistant district attorneys, who will try to dispose of their huge caseloads as quickly and inexpensively as possible.

Pushing these projections still further, a more blatantly unjust situation than exists at present could develop by the year 2020. While more affluent victims might be able to compel the system to delivery satisfactory service, the most underprivileged strata at the bottom of the social class hierarchy might be forced to fend for itself. The rising poor-on-poor crime rate could accelerate the breakdown of over-burdened precincts and courts in high crime neighborhoods. For years, doomsayers have warned about the "collapse" of the criminal justice system; twenty-five years from now what is currently hyperbole might be an accurate description.

The current trend towards a high-tech service economy coupled with de-industrialization (the decline of American manufacturing) is bringing about pervasive long term structural unemployment. Such unemployment will further polarize the population into a prospering upper class, struggling middle classes, and a growing "surplus population" (what some call the "underclass" or "outclass" of marginalized, excluded, demoralized, crushed, defeated, self-destructive, and ineffectively rebellious homeless and hungry people). Contained within urban ghettos and scattered pockets of poverty in suburban and rural districts, these victims of economic dislocations will be viciously preyed upon by their even more desperate neighbors. Their lives will be written off as unimportant, and their life-and-death struggles will be deemed "private matters" not worthy of governmental intervention. As their youngsters engage in endless gang feuds and drive-by shootings, and gunfights to control the neighborhood drug trade, the authorities will turn their backs on these "urban jungles," "free-fire zones" or "no-man's lands." Victims of poor-on-poor crimes will become discouraged about calling the police, who will be widely viewed with hostility as a foreign army of occupation. The profoundly alienated populace in these areas will be forced to defend their lives and possessions as best they can. Given their abandonment by the authorities, law-abiding citizens within the surplus population will be driven to routinely impose their own brands of on-the-spot curbstone justice, vigilante-style. The targets of their wrath will start to mysteriously disappear, as "death squads" carry out nocturnal raids against what they perceive as "predatory members of the criminal element."

In stark contrast to the shantytowns in which street criminals can roam at will, the affluent will reside in isolated, exclusive "gated enclaves," which will rely upon high fences, surveillance cameras, sophisticated alarms, guarded entrances, checkpoints, passes, patrolled perimeters, and high-tech gadgetry to keep intruders at bay. Their "siege mentality" of defending their "turf" against "outsiders who don't belong" will pass for a "sense of community" and "peace of mind" in 2020. Already, by 1994, about 30 thousand gated communities across the country housed an estimated 4 million residents, as personal security became one of the highest priorities of home-buyers ("Circling The Wagons," 1994). In addition to the usual number of police officers, squads of private security forces will watch over members of these privileged strata when they venture from their fortified sanctuaries to shop or pursue leisure activities. Already, by 1994, more than one thousand Business Improvement Districts had been set up nationwide since the early 1970s by real estate interests, merchants' associations, and community organizations to attract and reassure fearful people that they will be safe while in the presence of uniformed guards in these reclaimed sections of town (Lueck, 1994). When they are not backing up the police on occasional raids and forays into high crime hotspots, soldiers and National Guard troops will help patrol heavily used corridors to protect travelers and commuters from highway robbers. The stark contrast between the sheltered lives of the upper classes, (buttressed by a responsive criminal justice system that tends to their needs and wishes should they become victimized), coexisting with the shattered lives of the lower classes (forced to fend for themselves and resort to vigilantism), will serve as an indictment of the gross inequities symbolized by the differential access to justice in 2020, if this nightmare scenario actually materializes.

THE PERILS OF CRYSTAL-BALL GAZING

Will the situation of victims in the year 2020 be marked by institutionalized advocacy, frequent recourse to private prosecution by those who can afford it, widespread reliance on mediation/restitution/reconciliation programs, and more obvious double standards in the handling of cases, as predicted above? Or will countervailing forces arise to keep today's tendencies in check? When gazing into a crystal ball, it is necessary to recognize the possibility that each action can provoke a reaction, and each trend some resistance and opposition.

Will criminal justice officials rally to stop the emergence of dedicated advocates who will force them to live up to their rhetoric about handling victims with dignity and compassion and guaranteeing them notification and participatory rights? Will government attorneys lobby to preserve their virtual monopoly over the exercise of prosecutorial discretion and thereby thwart the revival of private prosecution? Will the punishment-oriented law and order approach stifle the spread of alternatives to adjudication and incarceration that encourage an abandonment of retribution in favor of restorative justice? Will egalitarian-oriented organizations fight against any widening of the gap in the way poor victims are treated in comparison to affluent ones?

Only time will tell.

STUDY QUESTIONS

1. How did the situation of crime victims change from the 1960s to the 1990s?
2. What kinds of services would victim advocates provide to their clients?
3. Why might some victims want a private prosecutor to handle their case, instead of the assistant district attorney provided for free by the government?
4. Why might some victims be interested in restorative justice?
5. What is differential access to justice and why is it a problem?

BIBLIOGRAPHY

Barkas, J. (1978). *Victims*. New York: Scribners.

Carrington, F. (1975). *The Victims*. New Rochelle, NY: Arlington House.

Carrington, F. (1977). "Victims' Rights Litigation: A Wave Of The Future?" U. of Richmond Law Review, 11, 3 (Spring): 447-470.

"Circling The Wagons: More Communities Adopt Gated-Enclave Approach." (1994). *Law Enforcement News*, November 15, p. 6.

Cole, G. (1992). *The American System of Criminal Justice*, 6th Edition. Pacific Grove, CA: Brooks/Cole.

DiIulio, J. Jr. (1988). "What's Wrong With Private Prisons." *The Public Interest*, 92 (Summer): 66-83.

Drapkin, I. and Viano, E. (1974). *Victimology: A New Focus*. Volumes 1-5. Lexington, MA: D.C. Health.

Elias, R. (1983). *Victims of the System: Crime Victims and Compensation in American Politics and Criminal Justice*. New Brunswick, NJ: Transaction Books.

Friedman, L. (1985). "The Crime Victim Movement at its First Decade." *Public Administration Review*, 45 (November): 790-794.

Galaway , B. and Hudson, J. (1990). *Criminal Justice, Restitution and Reconciliation*. Monsey, NY: Criminal Justice Press.

Griffin, S. (1971). "Rape: The All American Crime." *Ramparts* (September): 25-30.

Hook, S. (1972). "The Rights of the Victims. Thoughts on Crime and Compassion." *Encounter* (April): 29-35.

Hudson, J. and Galaway, B. (1975). *Considering the Victim: Readings in Restitution and Victim Compensation.* Springfield, IL: Charles C. Thomas.

Karmen, A. (1995). "Towards the Institutionalization of a New Kind of Criminal Justice Professional: The Victim Advocate." *The Justice Professional.* (Roslyn Muraskin, ed) V9 #1.

Largen, M. (1981). "Grassroots Centers and National Task Forces: A Herstory of the Anti-Rape Movement." *Aegis* 32 (Autumn): 46-52.

Loseke, D. (1989). "'Violence' Is 'Violence'...Or Is It? The Social Construction Of 'Wife Abuse' and Public Policy." Pp. 191-206 in J. Best (ed.), *Images Of Issues: Typifying Contemporary Social Problems.* New York: Aldine de Gruyter.

Lueck, T. (1994). "Business Districts Grow At Price Of Accountability." *The New York Times,* November 20, pp. 1, 46.

Lynch, R. (1976). "Improving The Treatment Of Victims: Some Guides For Action." Pp. 165-176 in W. MacDonald (ed.), *Criminal Justice and the Victim.* Beverly Hills: Sage.

Martin, D. (1977). *Battered Wives.* New York: Pocket Books.

McKnight, D. (1981). "The Victim-Offender Reconciliation Project." Pp. 292-298 in B. Galaway and J. Hudson (eds.), *Perspectives on Crime Victims.* St. Louis: Mosby.

Meiners, R. (1978). *Victim Compensation: Economic, Political, and Legal Aspects.* Lexington, MA: D.C. Health.

National Victim Center. (1990). *Crime Victims and Corrections.* Fort Worth, TX: National Victim Center.

Newman, D. (1986). *Introduction to Criminal Justice,* Third Edition. New York: Random House.

NOVA (National Organization For Victim Assistance). (1986). "NOVA Sponsors Forum On Constitutional Amendment." *NOVA Newsletter,* March, pp. 1-2, 7.

President's Task Force on Victims of Crime. (1982). *Final Report.* Washington, DC: U.S. Government Printing Office.

Rieff, R. (1979). *The Invisible Victim: The Criminal Justice System's Forgotten Responsibility.* New York: Basic Books.

Roberts, A. (1990). *Helping Crime Victims: Research, Policy, and Practice.* Newbury Park, CA: Sage.

Schafer, S. (1968). *The Victim and His Criminal.* New York: Random House.

Schneider, A. and Schneider, P. (1981). "Victim Assistance Programs: An Overview." Pp. 364-373 in B. Galaway and J. Hudson (eds.), *Perspectives on Crime Victims.* St. Louis: Mosby.

Schwendinger, J. and Schwendinger, H. (1983). *Rape and Inequality.* Beverly Hills: Sage.

Sebba, L. (1992). "The Victim's Role in the Penal Process: A Theoretical Orientation." Pp. 195-221 in E. Fattah (ed.), *Toward a Critical Victimology.* New York: St. Martin's Press.

Sigler, J. (1979). "The Prosecutor: A Comparative Functional Analysis." Pp. 53-74 in W. McDonald (ed.), *The Prosecutor.* Beverly Hills: Sage.

Silberman, C. (1978). *Criminal Violence, Criminal Justice.* New York: Random House.

Stark, J. and Goldstein, H. (1985). *The Rights of Crime Victims.* Chicago: Southern Illinois University Press.

Taibbi, M., and Sims-Phillips, A. (1989). *Unholy Alliances: Working the Tawana Brawley Story.* San Diego: Harcourt Brace.

Umbreit, M. (1990). "Victim-Offender Mediation with Violent Offender: Implications for Modifications of the VORP Model." Pp. 337-352 in E. Viano (ed.), *The Victimology Handbook: Research Findings, Treatment, and Public Policy.* New York: Garland.

Viano, E. (1976). "The Study of the Victim." *Victimology*. 1: 1-7.

Viano, E. (1990). "The Recognition and Implementation of Victim's Rights in the United States: Developments and Achievements." Pp. 319-336 in E. Viano (ed.), *The Victimology Handbook: Research Findings, Treatment, and Public Policy*. New York: Garland.

Wright, M. (1990). *Justice for Victims and Offenders*. Philadelphia: Open University Press.

CHAPTER 6

LOOKING FOR A NEW APPROACH TO AN OLD PROBLEM

THE FUTURE OF OBSCENITY AND PORNOGRAPHY

Jay S. Albanese, Ph.D.

ABSTRACT

Explicit songs, movies, cable television, talk radio, and computer services are the latest manifestations of public concern over the proper role of sex and violence in the media and in American life in general. Two national commissions in the last 25 years have investigated these issues and drawn widely different conclusions. A comparison of the method and conclusions of these investigations is used as a backdrop to propose alternative futures in defining and regulating obscenity and pornography. Four major issues are examined: (1) trends in the pornography industry, (2) the effects of pornography on behavior, (3) appropriate action to be taken by private citizens, and (4) legislative and law enforcement remedies. The consequences of a closer examination of the consumers of pornography, and a change in the focus of obscenity from sex to violence, are assessed. Four important questions for the future of obscenity and pornography law and policy are presented.

NEW CONCERN FOR AN OLD PROBLEM

The last twenty-five years have seen two national investigations into obscenity and pornography in the United States. These investigations were paralleled by similar governmental investigations in Canada and England. The interest and concern about the effects of obscene and pornographic material are international in scope, and an examination of the two U.S. Commissions, reporting sixteen years apart, provides some insight into the changing views of pornography in American life and what the future holds.

Indeed, the experiences of the past, informed by current events, help to predict the future of obscenity and pornography. It will be shown that dissatisfaction with past efforts to deal with pornography results in two significant questions for the future: is it more appropriate to shift the legal definition of obscenity from sex to violence in the future, and what are the reasons for the entrenched popularity of pornographic material? A discussion of these issues for the future follow a discussion of the lessons of the past.

All of the past pornography investigation commissions were formed in response to what was seen as a dramatic increase in the availability of explicit materials. In the 1960s and 1970s, this material took the form of books, magazines, television, radio, and films. From the 1980s to the present, concern has focused on new forms of distribution that did not heretofore exist: cable television, video rental and purchases, dial-a-porn, and computer networks. In every instance, the commissions attempted to address the proper balance between free speech, individual privacy, and the public interest.

The mandates of the two U.S. Commissions were remarkably similar. The U.S. Commission on Obscenity and Pornography, reporting in 1970, was established to accomplish four specific tasks. It was to "analyze laws pertaining to the control of obscenity and pornography," to "explore the nature and volume of traffic in such materials," to study its "relationship to crime and other antisocial behavior," and to recommend "appropriate action" to "regulate effectively the flow of such traffic" (1970:1). This four-pronged approach was mirrored by the mandate of the U.S. Attorney General's Commission, reporting in 1986. That Commission was directed to "study the dimensions of the problem of pornography," to examine "the means of production and distribution," to review "available empirical and scientific evidence on the relationship between exposure to pornographic materials and antisocial behavior," and to review "national, state, and local efforts...to curb pornography" (1986:1957).

METHODS AND SOURCES

The two Commissions differed greatly in both the time and money they were allocated to accomplish similar goals. The 1970 Commission was allocated a budget of $2 million and two years to conduct its investigation. The 1986 Commission was granted $500,000 and twelve months to complete its work. These large differences in both time and resources had an effect on both the quality of the investigations of the Commissions and on the nature of their findings.

The 1970 Commission elected not to hold public hearings until late in its investigation because it felt that "public hearings would not be a likely source of accurate data or a wise expenditure of its limited resources" (1970:3). Instead, it chose to conduct basic research due to "the insufficiency of existing factual evidence as a basis for recommendations" (p. 2). The 1986 Meese Commission did "especially regret the inability to commission independent research...," so it relied on public hearings and executive sessions among Commission members to reach its conclusions (p. 218).

As critics of the "public hearing" approach to investigations have recognized, new information is rarely generated in such a forum.

> This tactic [public hearings] was inexpensive, dramatic and promised a few
> good photo opportunities. Unfortunately, hearings were totally ineffective
> for fact-finding purposes. As the 1970 panel noted, views of most witness-
> es were predictable (Nobile and Nadler, 1986:27).

The use of public hearings as an investigative tool is clearly less useful than empirical research, especially when simple baseline data is lacking.

The Meese Commission was criticized as well for its selection of commissioners. Unlike the 1970 Commission, which included a number of behavioral scientists, the Meese Commission was made up of eleven members, six of whom had "well-established public records" against sexually-oriented material. "The Meese Commission lacked the financial resources of its predecessor, but since its conclusions were preordained, it didn't really need them" (Hertzberg, 1986:21).

WHAT IS PORNOGRAPHY?

Every investigation or discussion of pornography gets necessarily bogged down in defining its target. The 1970 Commission correctly noted that the term pornography has no legal significance. Obscenity is material in violation of existing constitutional standards as established by the U.S. Supreme Court in 1973. This material must "taken as a whole, appeal to the prurient interest in sex," portray sexual conduct in a "patently offensive way," and "lack serious literary, artistic, political or scientific value" (*Miller v. California*, 93 S.Ct. 2615, 1973). The 1970 Commission used "erotica," "explicit sexual material," and "sexually oriented material" interchangeably in its report in referring to its subject matter.

The Meese Commission, on the other hand, employed no key term, explaining that either pornography or erotica is often used to connote any "depiction of sex" or "sexually explicit materials" to which the user objects or disapproves (1986:227-231). As a result, the 1986 Meese Commission "tried to minimize" the use of either term, despite the Commission's title.

It is clear that both Commissions, despite vagaries in definition, were referring to explicit depictions of sex in their investigations. Some authors have found the definition of pornography offered by the Williams Committee in England to be the most understandable. The "pornographic representation is one that combines two features: it has a certain function or intention, to arouse its audience sexually, and also a certain content, explicit representations of sexual material" (Committee on Obscenity, 1979:104; Hawkins and Zimring, 1988:27).

THE PORNOGRAPHY INDUSTRY

Both Commissions addressed the size, scope, and operation of the pornography industry. The 1970 Commission conducted basic survey research and found there were approximately 14 thousand movie theaters in the United States, attended by 20 million people each week. General release films were found to be shown in 90% of all theaters, and sexual "exploitation" films were found to be shown in about 6% of all theaters. The Commission noted the rating system implemented by the motion picture industry in 1968 (i.e., G, PG, R, and X) as a step toward industry self-regulation of sexual content, violence, and suitability for children.

An attempt was made to discover the number of "stag" films made each year, but it was found to be "primarily a localized business with no national distribution" that was "extremely disorganized" (p. 22). The Commission found that there was also little money to be made in the stag film industry in the way of large profits.

> There are no great fortunes to be made in stag film production. It is estimated that there are fewer than half a dozen individuals who net more than $10,000 per year in the business (p. 22).

The 1970 Commission also detailed the size and scope of the "adult" book, magazine, bookstore markets. It also found that 85% of men and 70% of women have some exposure to pornographic materials during their lives. It was found that 75% of adult males have some exposure to explicit sexual materials before age twenty-one, although "the experience seems to be more a social than a sexual one" (p. 25). It was found that American patterns of exposure were similar to those in Denmark and Sweden, where pornography has been decriminalized.

The 1986 Commission did not conduct similar research into the nature and volume of traffic in explicit sexual materials. Therefore, it was unable to assess trends in exposure and availability of this material during the intervening sixteen years in any objective way. The Commission drew conclusions anyway, something for which it was the subject of criticism.

The 1986 Meese Commission found that the "men's" magazines, sometimes referred to as "male sophisticate" magazines, were objectionable. The Commission declared that"*all* of the magazines in this category contain at least some material that we would consider 'degrading'" (p.281). Concern was also expressed about the sexual content of material on cable television. The Commission concluded that "approximately 80%" of all American-produced pornographic films and video tapes are made "in and around Los Angeles, California" (p. 285). The source of this information is not noted. Likewise, the Commission found that many video retailers sell or rent pornographic films.

> Based on the evidence provided to us, it appears as if perhaps as many as half of all the general retailers in the country include within their offerings at least some material that, by itself, would commonly be conceded to be pornographic (p. 288).

The Meese Commission also noted that the adult movie theater "is becoming an increasing rarity" (p. 287), and that the growing popularity of videotape also "has hurt the pornographic magazine industry" (p. 289). Unfortunately, no figures were generated to indicate the nature of these apparent changes in the pornography industry.

The other aspect of the pornography industry that was addressed by both Commissions was the influence of organized crime in the manufacture and distribution of pornographic materials. The 1970 Commission found that "there is insufficient data to warrant any conclusion" about the involvement of organized crime in pornography (p. 23). The Commission cited disagreement among both law enforcement officials and researchers in this regard (p. 142).

The 1986 Meese Commission came to a different conclusion. It concluded "we believe that such a connection does exist" (p. 291). This determination was reached despite the fact that the Director of the FBI testified that "about three-quarters of those (fifty-nine FBI field) offices indicated that they have no verifiable information that organized crime was involved either directly or through extortion in the manufacture of pornography" (p. 292). The Commission judged that there exists an organized crime-pornography connection, therefore, "in the face of a negative conclusion by the 1970 Commission, and in the face of the evidence provided by the FBI" (p. 292). Anecdotal evidence was cited to support this position (dealing with alleged organized criminals operating in pornography in certain cities). The Commission's equivocal conclusion reflects the quality of evidence it had on this issue.

> Although we cannot say that every piece of evidence we have received to this effect is true, the possibility that none of this cumulative evidence is true is so remote that we do not take it seriously (p. 296).

This lack of clarity in the Commission's conclusion is matched only by its poor logic in arguing that the lack of reliable evidence reinforces its belief. The first important difference between the two Commissions, therefore, is their conclusions about the link between pornography and organized crime.

THE PORNOGRAPHY-HARM LINK

Perhaps the most significant question to be addressed by these Commissions was the possible effects of pornography in causing antisocial or criminal behavior. The 1970 Commission conducted a great deal of research on the subject due to a lack of existing data. The 1986 Commission conducted no new research of its own, but relied on the results of prior investigations.

In a national poll, the 1970 Commission found that there was no nationwide consensus among the public about the effects of pornography. Empirical studies found that both sexes were equally aroused by explicit sexual material, and that exposure appeared to have no effect on frequency of masturbation or intercourse. Likewise, four separate research studies indicated "little or no effect" of erotic stimuli on attitudes "regarding either sexuality or sexual morality" (p. 29). Finally, it was found that, similar to adults, both delinquents and nondelinquents have similar experiences with explicit sexual material, and that there is no evidence of a pornography-crime link (p. 286).

> In sum, empirical research designed to clarify the question has found no evidence to date that exposure to explicit sexual materials plays a significant role in the causation of delinquent or criminal behavior among youth or adults. The Commission cannot conclude that exposure to erotic materials is a factor in the causation of sex crime or sex delinquency (1970:32).

This conclusion was echoed by subsequent national commissions in both Canada and England reporting in 1985 and 1979, respectively (for a summary of this research, see Malamuth and Donnerstein, 1984).

The 1986 Attorney General's Commission came to a different conclusion on the subject of harm. It admitted that the testimony it received from various offenders and victims of pornography may be suspect, and the report offers an extended discussion of the nature of harm, the standards of proof involved, and the problems of valid and reliable evidence of harm (pp. 302-320).

Nevertheless, the Commission separated sexually-oriented materials into four categories that it admitted may be arbitrary. That is to say, the Commission noted that "some items within a category might produce no effects, or even the opposite effects from those identified" (p. 321). These four categories were: sexually violent material, nonviolent but degrading material, nonviolent and nondegrading material, and nudity. The Commission drew different conclusions for each of these categories.

With regard to sexually violent material, the Commission recognized that there was no consensus about its effects on behavior in the research literature. This difference of opinion led the Commission to make a number of significant assumptions.

> Finding a link between aggressive behavior towards women and sexual violence, whether lawful or unlawful, requires assumptions not found exclusively in the experimental evidence. We see no reason, however, not to make these assumptions (p. 325).

By ignoring a great deal of the empirical evidence, the Commission took an ideological approach to the question of harm and concluded that "substantial exposure to sexually violent materials as described here bears a casual relationship to antisocial acts of sexual violence and, for some subgroups, possibly to unlawful acts of sexual violence" (p. 326). The Commission also found a deleterious effect of this form of pornography on attitudes as well.

The Commission recognized that the empirical evidence is divided concerning the effect of nonviolent but degrading material. Nevertheless, the Commission made "substantially similar" conclusions as it did for the effects of sexually violent material, "although we make them with somewhat less confidence and our making of them requires more in the way of assumption than was the case with respect to violent material" (p. 332).

The conclusions of the 1986 Commission regarding harm were actually based on supposition. "The absence of evidence should by no means be taken to deny the existence of a causal link" (p. 332). In this category, therefore, it was concluded that "substantial exposure to materials of this type bears some casual relationship to the level of sexual violence, sexual coercion, or unwanted sexual aggression in the population so exposed" (pp. 333-4). It was also found that this type of material results in attitudinal changes regarding personal responsibility for actions and attitudes towards victims of sexual aggression. These conclusions have been challenged by several of the researchers relied upon by the Commission. They claim the Commissioners made "serious errors" of "omission" and "commission" in their characterization of the research findings regarding the pornography-harm link (Donnerstein, Linz, and Penrod, 1987).

The Meese Commission found that nonviolent and nondegrading sexual material appear to have no effect on antisocial behavior. It concluded that there "seems to be no evidence in the social science data of a causal relationship with sexual violence, sexual aggression, or sex discrimination" (p. 378). Nonetheless, it found that "the material in this category in some settings and when used for some purposes can be harmful" (p. 346).

With regard to nudity, the 1986 Commission showed little interest. If found that "by and large we do not find that nudity that does not fit within any of the previous categories to be much cause for concern" (p. 349). The differences in the Commissions' conclusions about the harm caused by pornography is perhaps the most significant difference between them.

SEX EDUCATION AND CITIZEN ACTION

The third area of investigation for both Commissions was that of positive approaches to be taken by citizens to effect changes in their local communities. The Commissions addressed sex education and citizen action groups.

The 1970 Commission found that parents are frequently "embarrassed or uninformed" about sex, only about half of all medical schools had even elective courses in human sexuality, and that opportunities for training professional workers "are still not widely available" (p. 34). The Commission also cited a study which found that girls who had a particular sex education course "were less likely to have illegitimate children" than a comparison group. These facts led the Commission to recommend sex education in the schools "because the existing alternatives for communicating about sex with young people are felt by so many people, both adults and young people themselves, to be inadequate or undesirable" (p. 36, 317).

The 1986 Meese Commission also believed that "education is the real solution to the problem of pornography," but it did not recommend sex education in the schools (p. 426). Rather, it limited its attention to the desirability of warnings to children about sexual abuse and exploitation from many sources.

The 1970 Commission noted that an evaluation of two organized citizen action groups found that "their practical effect on the availability of erotica in their respective communities had been quite minimal" (p. 38, 343). On the other hand, the 1986 Commission recommended "protesting near the premises of establishments offering material that some citizens may find dangerous or offensive or immoral" (p. 421-2). Boycotts of an establishment were also seen as desirable.[1]

The 1970 Commission also identified industry self-regulation as an important positive approach to sexual material. It recognized the comic book industry, radio, television, and motion picture industries for their self-imposed standards. Greater than 90% compliance with these voluntary standards was seen as an indication of their success within these industries. The 1986 Commission did not similarly emphasize the role of industry self-regulation as a positive approach to pornography.

LAW AND LAW ENFORCEMENT

The fourth area addressed by both Commissions was the need for laws and changes in law enforcement. Interestingly, both Commissions specifically recognized the inability of law to control behavior effectively. The 1970 Commission found legal regulation "is not the only, or necessarily the most effective, method of dealing with these materials" (p. 32). Similarly, the Meese Commission believed that "to rely entirely or excessively on law is simply a mistake" (p. 428).

The 1970 Commission took its statement to heart and noted that while nearly every state had laws that prohibit the distribution of obscene materials, no federal or state statute defined obscenity at that time. The Commission did not "believe that a sufficient social justification exists for the retention of enactment of broad legislation prohibiting the consensual distribution of sexual materials to adults" (p. 47-8). Therefore, it did not offer a definition of obscenity. In fact, the 1970 Commission made only four legislative recommendations.

First, it recommended that "federal, state, and local legislation prohibiting the sale, exhibition, or distribution of sexual materials to consenting adults be repealed" (p. 57). This proposal was based on the Commission's finding that exposure to explicit sexual material does not play a "significant role" in causing social or individual harm. Public opinion also supported the availability of sexual explicit materials for consenting adults. Furthermore, investigations in other countries have "all concluded that consensual exposure of adults to explicit sexual materials causes no demonstrable damaging individual or social effects" (p. 50).

Second, the 1970 Commission recommended prohibition of the "commercial distribution or display for sale of certain sexual materials to young persons" (p. 62). Although there was no evidence that demonstrated harm to young people, the Commission felt that public opinion, as well as insufficient research on the particular effects on children, made prohibition desirable. The Commission noted problems of definition, but recommended that the prohibited materials be limited to pictures, rather than books, and that the prohibited pictures must depict more than mere nudity.

Third, the Commission recommended legislation prohibiting public displays of sexually explicit pictorial materials in order to protect children and nonconsenting adults from exposure they find offensive.

Fourth, the Commission recommended the establishment of authority for prosecutors to obtain declaratory judgments to determine if material was obscene. This allowance would permit prosecutors to move civilly, rather than criminally, against suspected violators. It would also provide fair notice to the alleged offenders in such actions.

It can be seen that the 1970 Commission made only four legislative recommendations, one of which was to abolish the law as it applies to sexually explicit materials available to consenting adults. The Commission also placed much emphasis on nonlegislative alternatives, noted earlier, such as sex education. As the Commission declared, "much of the 'problem' regarding materials which depict sexual activity stem from the inability or reluctance of people in our society to be open and direct in dealing with sexual matters" (p. 53).

The 1986 Meese Commission took a different approach in its recommendations for change. It made a total of eighty-six recommendations, most of which involved calls for new laws and better enforcement of existing laws. The Commission's conclusion regarding the existence of a pornography-harm link caused it to reject the adult deregulation approach of the 1970 Commission. It also found problems with the city "zoning" approach aimed at grouping or dispersing stores or theaters that offer material containing explicit depictions of sex. The courts have found that "zoning" laws, when used as a guise for "prohibition," are unconstitutional, and "grandfather" clauses in most ordinances do not affect existing establishments, but only future businesses. Likewise, the civil rights approach first attempted in Minneapolis (arguing that pornography violates the civil rights of those portrayed), has been found unconstitutional thus far, because the definitions of obscene material have gone beyond the legal standard set by the U.S. Supreme Court in 1973 (See O'Neill, 1985:177-187).

Similar to the 1970 Commission, the Meese Commission found that there should be preliminary judicial review of material *before* a complaint is filed. This inspection is necessary to protect publishers and distributors from perpetual civil suits.

Of the Meese Commission's eighty-six recommendations, many dealt with the use of forfeiture laws in the prosecution of pornographers to allow for seizure of assets as well as criminal penalties. Fifty of the eighty-six recommendations dealt with child pornography in some manner. This is interesting inasmuch as the Commission made no systematic survey of the extent of the problem. In fact, it concluded that "there now appears to be comparatively little domestic commercial production of child pornography..." and that most is produced as a "cottage industry" rather than through mass production (pp. 409-410).

The emphasis of most of the Commission's recommendations was on *greater priority* to obscenity investigations. It was found that obscenity investigations among law enforcement agencies are not common and that prosecutors rarely take these cases to court. Therefore, many recommendations included suggestions for better training, coordination, and resources for investigations in suspected obscenity cases.

The Commission made a few recommendations for new legislation as well, although the suggestions broke little new ground. Many involved "tightening" of perceived loopholes in existing law. In addition to greater forfeiture provisions, the Commission recommended that *possession* of child pornography be a felony, and that photo labs should be required to report suspected child pornography. Clearly, the 1986 Commission took a regulatory-law enforcement approach to the issue of pornography, whereas the 1970 Commission took a deregulation approach, at least with regard to adults.

EXPLAINING THE DIFFERENCES

Table 1 summaries the major findings of the two national commission investigations of obscenity and pornography during the last twenty-five years. Seven significant issues which the commissions addressed continue to lie at the heart of the pornography debate today.

As Table 1 indicates, the only significant issue on which the two commissions agreed was the prohibition of public displays of explicit material in order to protect children and nonconsenting adults.

The large differences in the findings and recommendations of the two Commissions are not difficult to explain. The 1970 Commission took an empirical approach to the issue. This method was understandable, given the presence of three sociologists and two psychiatrists on the Commission. Absent a finding of a pornog-

---

TABLE 1

Comparisons of Conclusions of Two National Commission Investigations

1970 U.S. Commission on Obscenity and Pornography	1986 Attorney General's Commission on Pornography
1 No demonstrated link between exposure to pornography and sexual activity or crimes.	A pornography-harm link exists, although there may not yet be conclusive evidence.
2 Sex education in school for children and professional workers.	Warn children about sexual abuse and exploitation, rather than sex education in school.
3 Practical effect of citizen protests is minimal.	Protests and boycotts of offending establishments useful.
4 Self-regulation of film, television, and book industry is largely effective.	Greater priority should be given to civil and criminal enforcement.
5 Sale of sexual materials to consenting adults should be permitted.	Greater emphasis on prosecution of producers and distributors of pornographic materials.
6 Prohibit distribution or display of sexual materials depicting more than mere nudity to juveniles.	50 recommendations regarding child pornography, including criminalizing its possession.
7 Public displays of explicit pictorial materials should be prohibited.	Public displays of explicit pictorial materials should be prohibited.

raphy-harm link in its research, legislation to regulate its distribution to consenting adults appeared unnecessary. The 1986 Commission's approach was ideological. Recognizing that the empirical research was imperfect and inconclusive, the Commission chose the route to which the commissioners were predisposed. That is, they *believed* there was some kind of link between pornography and harm, so that is what they concluded (see Albanese, 1987). This bias is evident in that six of the 1986 Commission members had previously established views on the subject, as mentioned earlier. Their efforts to justify their findings based on available research results were feeble, and some of the research the Commission characterized as supportive of its positions was later challenged by the researchers themselves as misinterpretations of their work (see Donnerstein, Linz, and Penrod, 1987).

It is ironic but none of the significant recommendations of either commission has been enacted into law. The same fate met the Williams Committee report in England (Simpson, 1983:57). This inaction is probably due to the fact that there did not exist public support in 1970 for decriminalization of sexually explicit materials for consenting adults. Likewise in 1986, in a more favorable political climate, there did not exist sufficient public interest in the prosecution approach endorsed by the Meese Commission. As the Meese Commission recognized, there were only seventy-one individuals convicted for violation of federal obscenity laws nationwide from 1978 to 1986 (1986:367). There were no federal prosecutions at all from 1984 to 1985 in Manhattan or Los Angeles, the two largest reputed centers of pornography manufacturing and distribution in the United States (1986:504). Finally, from 1977 to 1984 only one person was convicted for production of child pornography under the Protection of Children from Sexual Exploitation Act of 1977 (p. 604). This lack of interest and/or incidence of obscenity cases continues to the present. Convictions obtained by the U.S. Postal Service for mailing pornographic/obscene materials dropped from 250 in 1989 to 206 in 1992 (Flanagan and Maguire, 1990:536; Maguire, Pastore, Flanagan, 1993:550).

ISSUES FOR THE FUTURE

So where does this leave the citizen or policy-maker who perceives an apparent rise in crime and violence in his or her community that appears to correspond with a rise in explicit sex and violence in books, television, and movies? Two significant issues have been either omitted or addressed peripherally in every inquiry into obscenity and pornography: (1) moving from sex to violence in defining obscenity, and (2) reasons for the entrenched popularity of pornographic material. These two issues, perhaps more than any others, will chart the course for the future.

Obscenity: From Sex to Violence

Definitions and prosecutions for obscene materials always have been directed at depictions of sexual conduct. A case can be made, however, that there is nothing inherently obscene about *explicit* depictions of sexual conduct. In fact, explicit depictions of sex have long played a role in psychological counseling, physiological education, and sex therapy. The terms "patently offensive" and "prurient interest" invariably result in subjective line-drawing, attempting to separate the *offensive* from the *indecent* from the *obscene*.

As noted earlier, current legal definitions of obscenity focus on *gratuitous* depictions of sex "lacking serious literary, artistic, political or scientific value" (*Miller v. California*, 1973:2615). An argument can be made, however, that nothing is inherently obscene about gratuitous sex either. The *value* of sex is an elusive concept, difficult to determine in any objective way. When sexual conduct is carried out in a tasteless manner, there is little social interest involved. This apathy makes it difficult to regulate or prohibit, due to its unclear impact on public health, safety, or welfare. Although depictions of sex can be tasteless or offensive, it can be argued that this concern is secondary and not as serious as depictions of gratuitous *violence*.

A significant social concern arises when sex is depicted in a way that involves *force* against an unwilling victim, against children, or even when unjustified *violence without sex* is depicted. Perhaps the future will witness a move from sex to violence in defining obscenity. Obscenity law might prohibit the depiction of gratuitous *violence* rather than sex alone. Depictions of violent assaultive behavior exhibited without legal justification could be held objectionable and punishable under law. The legal justifications for the use of force (e.g., self-defense, defense of others) are well-defined in existing law, as are the definitions of assault. Such a new definition of obscenity might include photographs or broadcasts depicting assaultive behavior committed by persons without legal justification. The inclusion of sex in these depictions of violence could be a sufficient, but not necessary, element of obscenity. The only exception might be factual accounts of real events which have informational or education value.

Unlike the inconclusive link between depictions of sex and sex offenses, there is a growing body of literature that reports on the effects of depictions of violence on aggressive behavior (National Institute of Health, 1982; Donnerstein, Linz, and Penrod, 1987: 108-136). Therefore, it might be argued that descriptions of wanton violence be declared obscene due to their possible effects on behavior. It could also be claimed that violence without justification is something our society sees as more objectionable than sex without social "value."

Before a proposal like this could be considered, changing the focus of obscenity from sex to violence, better answers to at least two important questions are needed:

- How does the effect of depictions of violence on aggressive behavior compare with other possible influences on aggressive attitudes and behavior (such as family and peer groups)?

- If gratuitous violence was determined to be obscene, what deleterious impact would this have on the creative arts, where books, films, and songs portray fictional violence without legal justification?

Why Is Pornography So Popular?

The 1970 Commission conducted studies of the consumers of pornography and found that the vast majority of pornography is directed at the male heterosexual audience. Studies conducted by the Commission in a number of different cities found men also to account for 90% of the consumers of sexually explicit materials (1970: 10ff.; 1971-72, 4:16ff.).

Other studies carried out for the Commission found that "symbolic materials have a noticeably less arousing and erotic effect on women than they do on men." It was found that in both the United States and Sweden (where depictions of sex are more widely available) there is greater "acceptance of pornography" by men than by women and that most pornography is produced by men, rather than by women (1971-71, 9:220; Kinsey et al., 1953). The "traditionally more conservative and restrictive attitudes that women have about virtually all sexual matters" reported by the 1970 Commission might be changing, however. A Gallup Poll reported by the 1986 Commission found that the proportion of young women (eighteen to twenty-four years old) who had rented an X-rated videocassette was two-thirds of the male figure (U.S. Attorney General, 1986:920). Unfortunately, this apparent trend was ignored by the Meese Commission, as was the issue of consumers of pornography in its entirety.

If the availability of sexually explicit materials is identified as a social problem in terms of explicit radio, television, books, films, computer services, and dial-a-porn, it is essential that a better understanding emerge of why those interested in seeing and hearing it are so resilient. It is unlikely that *every* new technology would cater to some degree of those interested in sexually explicit materials, if the market was shrinking. The questions for which better answers are needed are at least two:

- Why are consumers of pornography predominantly male, and are females increasingly consumers of sexually explicit materials?

- Does sex education promote healthier (i.e., less prurient) attitudes toward sex that, in turn, reduces interest in pornography?

These questions underlie the current debate about the effects of pornography on attitudes toward sex and toward men (Assiter, 1989; Downs, 1989; Kendrick, 1987). The answer to these questions through research and experimentation will make future decisions about obscenity and pornography less a matter of taste and more a matter of fact.

STUDY QUESTIONS

1. Argue what you believe is more important in a definition of obscenity: sex or violence. Defend your view, given what is known about the impact of either on human behavior.

2. Why do you believe that men comprise the overwhelming majority of consumers of pornography? Explain why you believe biological, psychological, or social factors may best explain this phenomenon.

3. Most people agree that sex education should occur at home, although it never happens in many homes. What do you believe should be the proper content of sex education whether conducted at home or in the schools?

4. Should there be any restriction on the sale or rental of pornographic material to consenting adults? Defend your position.

5. Explain what you believe to be the best way to inculcate healthy (i.e., nonprurient) attitudes about sex to young people?

FOOTNOTES

[1]It should be noted that early in 1986 the Executive Director of the Meese Commission, Alan Sears, notified several corporations that they had been identified as pornography distribu-

tors and that, unless they proved otherwise within thirty days, they would be described in this way in the Commission's final report. This admonition resulted in several chain-stores dropping such magazines as *Playboy* and *Penthouse*. Following a suit by *Playboy*, *Penthouse*, and the American Booksellers Association, a federal court ordered the Commission to retract its letter, six days before it issued its final report.

REFERENCES

Albanese, Jay S. (1987). "Review Essay: The Accusers, the Accused, and the Victims in the Debate Over Pornography." *American Journal of Criminal Justice*, vol. 11, no. 1.

Assiter, Alison. (1989). *Pornography, Feminism, and the Individual*. Winchester, MA: Pluto Press.

Committee on Obscenity and Film Censorship. (1979). *Report*. London: Her Majesty's Stationery Office.

Donnerstein, Edward I., Linz, Daniel G., and Penrod, Steven. (1987). *The Question of Pornography*. New York: The Free Press.

Downs, Donald Alexander. (1989). *The New Politics of Pornography*. Chicago: University of Chicago Press.

Flanagan, Timothy J. and Kathleen Maguire. (1990). *Sourcebook of Criminal Justice Statistics— 1989*. Washington, DC:U.S. Government Printing Office.

Hawkins, Gordon and Zimring, Franklin E. (1988). *Pornography in a Free Society*. Cambridge: Cambridge University Press.

Hertzberg, Hendrik. (1986). "Big Boobs." *The New Republic*, July 14 and 21, 21-4.

Kendrick, Walter. (1987). *The Secret Museum: Pornography in Modern Culture*. New York: Viking.

Kinsey, Alfred C., Pomeroy, Wardell B., Martin, Clyde E., and Gebhard, Paul H. (1953). *Sexual Behavior in the Human Female*. Philadelphia: Saunders.

Maguire, Kathleen, Ann L. Pastore, and Timothy J. Flanagan. (1993). *Sourcebook of Criminal Justice Statistics—1992*. Washington, DC: U.S. Government Printing Office.

Malamuth, Neil M. and Donnerstein, Edward, eds. (1984). *Pornography and Sexual Aggression*. Orlando: Academic Press.

Miller v. California. (1973). 93 S.Ct. 2607.

National Institute of Mental Health. (1982). *Television and Behavior: Ten Years of Scientific Progress and Implications for the Eighties*. Washington, DC: U.S. Government Printing Office.

Nobile, Philip and Nadler, Eric. (1986). *United States of America v. Sex*. New York: Minotaur Press.

O'Neill, Terry. (1985). *Censorship: Opposing Viewpoints*. St. Paul, MN: Greenhaven Press.

Simpson, A.W.B. (1983). *Pornography and Politics: A Look Back to the Williams Committee*. London: Waterloo.

Special Committee on Pornography and Prostitution in Canada. (1985). *Pornography and Prostitution in Canada*. Ottawa: Minister of Supply and Services.

U.S. Attorney General's Commission on Pornography. (1986). *Final Report*. Washington, DC.: U.S. Government Printing Office.

U.S. Commission on Obscenity and Pornography. (1970). *Report*. Washington, DC: U.S. Government Printing Office.

U.S. Commission on Obscenity and Pornography. (1971-72). *Technical Reports, Vols. 1-9*. Washington, DC: U.S. Government Printing Office.

PART III

INTRODUCTION

POLICING NOW AND INTO THE TWENTY-FIRST CENTURY

The role of the police in contemporary society is one of the most controversial, yet least understood components of the criminal justice process. Police are available twenty-four hours a day. They have the potential as we reach the twenty-first century of maintaining order, improving community unity (Gemeinschaft) and greatly lessening family violence incidents.

Albert Roberts and Vincent Henry in their chapter, "Police Responses to Domestic Violence in the 1990s and Beyond," focus their discussion on the issues of police response to domestic violence and what will occur by the year 2010. They present a case scenario typical of the year 2010 when technology will have greatly increased the efficient response to cases of domestic violence.

The police operate under the democratic rule of law process which means a government of laws not of men. However, it is recognized that the police exercise a great deal of discretion, and at times, this discretion may get out of control. Witness the Rodney King incident. In his chapter, "Policing in the Future: Control and Issues," Robert Meadows indicates that the police officer of the future must be responsive to the community, and accountable for his/her performance. In order for the police to be more responsive, there is a need for greater involvement from the community. Trends in domestic violence legislation suggest that the police will be required to assume a more aggressive posture. Court decisions in search and seizure cases have permitted the police to "bend the rules." A community wide response is needed to address the crime problems of the future.

Taking it a step further, the American economy will become a part of a global economy that becomes feasible with the fall of communism in Eastern Europe in 1989 and the consolidations of Western Europe's economy as of 1992. According to Michael Palmiotto's "The Influence of 'Community' in Community Policing," the perception of crime by the community regardless of worldwide changes will remain stable. Therefore, it is his thesis that community support should increase. The public's demand for extra service will increase at no extra cost. With the police listening to its citizens, it will not be uncommon in the twenty-first century to periodically conduct "customer surveys."

CHAPTER 7

POLICE RESPONSE TO DOMESTIC VIOLENCE COMPLAINTS

BRIDGING THE PRESENT TO THE FUTURE

Albert R. Roberts, D.S.W. and Vincent E. Henry

ABSTRACT

This chapter focuses on police response to domestic violence—past, present, and future. First, the authors present a case scenario typical of the year 2010 when technology has greatly increased the efficiency and speed of police and judicial responsiveness to injured battered women. The next section reviews the literature on police responses to domestic violence, with particular emphasis on the Minneapolis Domestic Violence Experiment and the recent replications in Milwaukee and Omaha. The authors then examine a large data set of domestic violence complaint and arrest rates from a highly populous, ethnically diverse city in the northeastern area of the United States. The study covers six large police precincts during the five-year period 1987-1991.

It was 1400 hours on September 6, 2010. Two police officers were dispatched by headquarters on a report of a domestic violence complaint. Upon arrival at the scene, the officers spoke to the victim, Wilma R. She stated that her boyfriend Louis had been drinking the night before and became involved in an argument with her that ended with his punching her in the face and choking her. The officers observed that Wilma had a cut on her upper lip and swelling in the area between her nose and mouth.

When the police officers questioned Louis, he said he never touched her. He insisted that the bruises on her face resulted from her being clumsy and falling down the steps while carrying the laundry. He said she was making up the story of being beaten because she was angry at him for staying out late with his buddies the previous night.

In order to determine whether or not Louis had choked his girlfriend, the police officer went to the car and brought in the compact portable laser unit. By aiming the laser at Wilma's neck, the officer immediately obtained laser fingerprints which he compared to Louis'. The results showed an identical match. While the first officer was matching the fingerprints, the second officer went to the car and turned on the MDT computer to run a computerized criminal history on Louis. In less than thirty seconds, Louis' history appeared on the screen: two prior convictions for simple assault against a former girlfriend and resisting arrest. The incidents had occurred three years earlier in another state. In addition, Louis' record showed two arrests for driving while intoxicated during the past three years.

The officers' next step was to obtain a temporary restraining order (TRO) to prevent Louis from having any further contact with Wilma. The TRO was obtained by entering a summary of the police officers' findings at the scene on their portable computer and using the cellular phone to call the judge to inform her that the report was being faxed to her courtroom from their car fax.

At the courthouse, the court clerk received the report from the fax machine and brought it to Judge Catherine Sloan for her signature. The court clerk then faxed the TRO back to the police car. The entire approval process took only fifteen minutes.

Next, the police transported Louis to the county jail where the nurse practitioner imprinted a subdural electronic sensor on Louis' wrist. The police gave a sensing receiver to Wilma to wear externally, on a chain around her neck. The computer at police headquarters monitored these sensors as it had done with the three hundred other domestic abuse cases reported to the police department during the past twelve months. The officers informed Louis that if he came within a distance of five hundred meters from Wilma, the sensing device would immediately alert the police officers that he had violated the TRO, and Louis would be sent to prison.

POLICE RESPONSE TO DOMESTIC VIOLENCE IN THE MID 1990s

During the past few years, domestic violence has increasingly been defined by a growing number of state criminal codes and family court statutes as a serious crime (i.e., a felony rather than a misdemeanor). In fact, due to the prevalence and life-threatening nature of woman battering, all fifty states have passed civil and/or criminal statutes to protect battered women (Roberts, 1994). As many as 75% of all police calls in some areas involve domestic conflict and/or violence. In the past, police were often reluctant to respond to family violence calls. When they did respond, they were frequently accused of taking the side of the male batterers and subscribing to the view that "a man's home is his castle." In addition, court staff tended to minimize the dangers that battered women encountered and discouraged the women from filing criminal or civil complaints.

Society-at-large has finally recognized that the beating of women (wives, cohabitants, or companions) is a crime and a major social problem. Societal recognition of woman abuse as a major social problem grew out of four noteworthy activities:

1. the women's movement;
2. two national prevalence studies on the extent of domestic violence in the United States (Straus, Steinmetz and Gelles, 1980; Straus and Gelles, 1990);
3. books and news articles on battered women (Fleming, 1979; Walker, 1979; Roy, 1982; Roberts, 1984; Walker, 1984); and
4. recent litigation and legal reforms (Hunzinger, 1990).

Moreover, many police departments now have a pro-arrest or presumptive arrest policy. The road toward implementing effective mandatory or pro-arrest policies for batterers has, however, been bumpy and uneven. Furthermore, research studies on the short-term deterrent effects of arresting batterers is inconclusive.

Nevertheless, Americans have come a long way from the time when the use of violence by men to control their partners was condoned. Mandatory and warrantless arrest laws are just one part of an improved police response to victims of women battering. In addition, police in highly populated cities and counties throughout the nation now provide immediate protection to battered women.

The complex constellation of social, legal, and political issues surrounding the police response to domestic violence is among the most enduring and contentious problems in the recent history of criminal justice theory and practice. The current salience of domestic violence as an issue of national concern for criminal justice theoreticians and practitioners is well illustrated by the degree of attention this subject has recently received in so many diverse spheres, and by the body of research it has generated. Particularly within the past decade, efforts to define and to institutionalize appropriate roles and responsibilities for police in responding to domestic violence have engendered considerable academic research, generated a significant body of statutory and case law, and been the subject of an uncommon degree of public and political discourse.

Social and political pressures for change, in conjunction with the passage of civil and criminal statutes to protect battered women in all fifty states, have considerably altered the way that police officers and agencies currently respond to domestic violence. Police executives and public policy makers, as well as individual police officers, have become more sensitive to the issues involved as they have faced the burden of making appropriate and effective choices from among a range of competing alternative strategies. Because defining and practicing an appropriate police response to domestic violence necessarily entails consideration of a broad array of practical, legal, political and social variables, supervisors, trainers and street officers confront a difficult task. Despite a host of opinions, policies, agendas, and programs aimed at redressing the social problem and providing relief to victims, there currently appears to be little consensus as to precisely what comprises the most desirable and effective response to domestic violence. It may be that since no single response has proven successful, a multi-level approach should be implemented only after more effective policy research is completed.

Historical Overview

Although the recognition of domestic violence as a pervasive social problem is fairly recent, its cultural bases are deeply embedded in Western history and culture. Even a cursory review of that history reveals the extent to which law and society have traditionally served to implicitly support and perpetuate the subordination of women to their husbands. In South America and Asia, especially in the upper classes, killing a wife for an indiscretion is usually acceptable. The same privilege is not usually extended to women against their husbands. Various cultures and societies have permitted or tacitly encouraged some degree of family violence as a means to maintain that subordination. Demographic analyses of domestic violence offenses reported to the police confirm the observation that domestic violence is most frequently perpetrated by males against their female partners. Males comprise only a small fraction of the total victims in domestic violence cases reported to the police.

As Richard Gelles and Murray Straus (1988) have so aptly noted, domestic violence is intrinsically linked to the maintenance of power and dominance within the family unit. Family violence and spousal assaults are facilitated when a paucity of effective formal and informal social control mechanisms allows the rewards of maintaining power through violence to outweigh the costs of such violence. From this observation, we can infer that cultures which define violence within the family unit as unacceptable behavior and which emphatically communicate an attitude of disapproval by applying potent social sanctions (e.g., ostracizing or publicly humiliating the perpetrator) will exhibit lower rates of domestic violence than societies which ignore the issue or which tacitly approve of intra-family violence will. Similarly, the availability of formal mechanisms of social control (i.e., the legal processes of arrest and punishment) also impacts the incidence of domestic violence. Gelles and Straus (1988) conclude that people use violence against members of their families "because they can (pp. 17-36)."

History reveals that until fairly recently, men were legally empowered to employ relatively unrestrained physical force against their wives and children in order to maintain family discipline. During the 1960s, several discrete trends evolved in policing, in law, and in politics which ultimately converged in the 1970s and 1980s to set the stage for our current concerns and the attention paid to domestic violence issues. The confluence of these trends and pressures created a unique and powerful synergy, forcing American police agencies and law-makers to reexamine their policies and practices, and to adopt the type of strategies which prevail today.

The Impact of Feminism

First, the feminist movement's focus upon the economic, social and legal disparities between men and women in our patriarchal society raised women's issues in general, and domestic violence in particular, to an unprecedented level of public discourse and debate. Because woman abuse is overwhelmingly perpetuated by males against their female partners, and because it serves to degrade women and maintain (through force) their subordinate role within marital or cohabiting relationships, domestic violence quite properly achieved some prominence in the feminist agenda. As the ranks of feminists swelled, and as they achieved increasing political power, they effected legislative changes and influenced public policy. A central premise of the feminist argument for the arrest of batterers was that such arrests have a potent symbolic content in illustrating the equality of women, and that they demonstrate society's refusal to treat women differently than men on the basis of their sex or social condition. Assaulted women, they argued, should expect and should receive the same criminal justice response whether they were assaulted by a stranger or by a spouse, in the home or outside it.

At about the same time, rising national rates of crime focused public attention upon the rights and needs of crime victims, and public policies began to address these needs. Here again, feminist groups took the lead in establishing social service programs for victimized women, and in creating public policies aimed at relieving the traumas experienced by female victims of crime. Prominent among these programs were battered women's shelters (Roberts, 1981). Without the presence of injuries which would raise assault to a felony, police officers frequently remained reluctant to use their discretionary powers of arrest to intrude upon the privacy of the domestic relationship in misdemeanor cases of assault. Partly because of this reluctance, police officers rarely invoked their powers of arrest in domestic violence cases when the offense was a less serious misdemeanor assault. Several other trends and forces also militated against arrest in most misdemeanor domestic assaults.

The Impact of Research

Morton Bard (1970, 1973) was the first researcher to develop training for police officers in family crisis intervention and mediation techniques. Specialized training led to increased officer safety and reduced reported levels of domestic violence. By adopting mediation-based policies, the police and other criminal justice agencies believed they could reduce domestic violence and respond to external pressures for change, at the same time avoiding the expensive and time consuming process of arresting and prosecuting domestic misdemeanor assaults. Bard's research enjoyed great credibility, and consistent with that era's emphasis on enhanced training and police professionalism, many agencies developed mediation-based policies toward policing domestic violence. Since a wealth of federal funds for police training became available through the Law Enforcement Assistance Administration during the late 1960s and early 1970s, many agencies utilized these funds to train officers in family crisis intervention. Sherman and Berk (1984, p. 262), for example, note that by 1977 over 70% of American police departments employing one hundred or more officers had a family crisis intervention training program in place.

In agencies where such mediation-oriented policies existed, the protocol generally called for officers to respond by separating the disputants, interviewing each one to discover the underlying causes for the dispute, and counseling them informally on the spot. In practice, these policies may have helped some families to resolve minor disputes without violence, but in general they rarely proved to be effective deterrents to future disputes or future violence. While the basic theory behind the policies—that mediation and counseling could bring the parties together to work out their difficulties through dialogue rather than through violence—may have had some merit, police were often not trained well enough to deliver effective counseling. Nor did they have the requisite interpersonal skills to identify and deal with the issues leading up to the dispute. Because policing was (and still remains) a male-dominated occupation, it might also be argued that, despite training, male officers were not sensitive enough to the plight of female victims. They may have wittingly or unwittingly been too sympathetic to the male disputant's point of view. In addition, many officers were simply not disposed to practice what they perceived as time-consuming "social work." Officers who saw themselves as "crime fighters," especially those assigned to busy precincts or beats, may have simply been more interested in completing the assignment quickly and getting back to "real" police work.

To understand the failure of mediation-oriented policies to prevent further violence, it is useful to examine the archetypical family dispute from the responding officers' perspective. Indeed, when experienced officers repeatedly encounter similar or apparently identical patterns of family dysfunction and when a cluster of problems or elements appears to contribute to each of these disputes, officers often tend to conceive of family disputes in generic terms. In time, such common features as alcohol abuse, financial problems or accusations of adultery and extra-marital affairs blur the distinctions between disputes. Consequently, officers may lose sight of the unique differences between family disputes. It must also be noted that despite these common features, police officers concurrently view the vast majority of individual family disputes as highly ambiguous and potentially dangerous situations in which the facts and circumstances are not at all clear-cut. The problems and frustrations which give rise to violent disputes are often long-standing and complex, and the disputants themselves may not be fully aware of the causes underlying their present dispute. Instead, the attributed causes they relate to the police may be merely symptomatic of some deep-seated family dysfunction which legitimately lies well beyond the capacity of the police to resolve. Because family crisis intervention is, both by definition and by necessity, short term counseling, even skilled officers who have been trained in counseling techniques may be unable to discover or to address the larger and more complex issues involved. Officers are still overheard to opine that the solutions to most on-going family disputes lie either in divorce court or in long-term intensive psychotherapy. Moreover, these situations are potentially dangerous since the disputants may turn on the officers with violence.

The ever-present demands for expedient resolution of these disputes also impacted the officers' potential for delivering effective counseling during that era. Particularly in busy or high crime districts, where time and resources spent in counseling families means less time and fewer resources available to devote to high priority "real crime" incidents, pressures exist for officers to resolve the disputes as expeditiously as possible so that they are able to return to patrol. Within a context of ambiguity, and in light of the other pressures and constraints placed upon the police officers, it should not be difficult to understand that even the most conscientious officers may quickly become cynical and lose faith in their own ability to resolve complex family problems through short-term counseling. Police cynicism is undoubtedly compounded and reinforced by the ultimate failure of mediation to reduce future assaults or disputes, and by the perception that they have been repeatedly called to the same location to deal with the same individuals and the same problems. Most officers working in a district have intimate knowledge of the family problems they can expect to encounter at a particular chronic call location.

As a consequence of their cynicism, and notwithstanding their training, many frustrated officers have exercised the great discretion afforded them under the mediation model to restore peace temporarily by merely separating the combatants for a period of time. Despite its dubious legality, one strategy frequently employed by police was to order a male aggressor to leave the house for a specified period, threatening arrest if he returned. If the aggressor returned and the dispute continued, the problem would hopefully be passed along to another team of officers.

Several additional factors have possibly contributed to the demise of the mediation model. First, the fact that drug or alcohol abuse, financial difficulties, and other formidable social problems are often correlates of family violence may have impeded the police from dealing with the root causes or the triggers of domestic abuse. The police of that era were (and still remain) largely unable to deal effectively with such profound and deeply embedded problems, which require ongoing therapy and a social support system. In a related vein, and in keeping with the dominant "zeitgeist" of the police professionalism era, the mediation model placed the primary responsibility for crisis intervention and counseling in violent family disputes squarely on the police who were often considered the first social workers or psychologists on the scene.

The rhetoric and dogma of the police professionalism movement argued adamantly that well-trained police officers were capable of performing an entire range of functions and of providing an entire range of services. As a consequence, the police officers and agencies subscribing to this rhetoric were not disposed to cede their authority to external agencies, and were reluctant to utilize services outside the criminal justice sphere. It could well be argued that police reluctance to refer dysfunctional families to community mental health services for ongoing family counseling, as well as an actual paucity of such services within the community, prevented families from accessing the type of long-term counseling which might have reduced further violence. All too often, the police response under the mediation-oriented policies degenerated to a short-term palliative—a "band-aid" approach aimed only at quickly restoring some semblance of order and relieving the critical problem of the moment. Seldom did the police impact the true sources of family dysfunction.

Whatever the reasons, these policies were eventually proven to be ineffective at reducing further incidents of domestic violence: a Police Foundation (1976) study determined that in 85% of spousal homicides, the police had been called at least once in the previous two years, and in over half the cases they had been called five or more times. In time, the practical utility and the underlying philosophical premises of this approach were called into question, and the police began to seek other strategies. Police agencies, though, had at least initiated attempts to address domestic violence issues through policy reform, and had begun to use academic research as a basis for domestic violence policy making.

Research on Deterrent Effects of Arrest

Several studies have been completed on the effect that pro-arrest or mandatory arrest policies have had in reducing repeat calls for domestic violence. The first study, known as the Minneapolis Experiment, found that arrest was more effective than no arrest or mediation in deterring future battering.

The Minneapolis Domestic Violence Experiment (1981-82) (Sherman and Berk 1984; Beck and Newton, 1985) was the first research study to test the short-term deterrent effect of arrest in domestic violence cases with both heterosexual married and cohabitating couples, and same-sex couples. In selected police precincts, domestic violence incidents were randomly assigned to one of three police methods of responding:

1. providing advice and informal mediation;
2. separating the couple by ordering the offender to leave the premises for eight hours to cool off; and
3. arresting the alleged offender and detaining him overnight in the local jail.

Three hundred and thirty eligible cases were tracked for six months. Repeat incidents of domestic violence were measured through official police department record checks to determine if there were additional domestic violence calls to the same address, as well as follow-up interviews with the victim every two weeks. The findings indicated that arrest was more effective than the two other types of police response in deterring subsequent incidents of domestic violence. Repeat violence occurred in only 13% of the arrest cases, compared with a 19% failure rate among the cases assigned to informal mediation, and a 24% failure rate for the cases assigned to "cool off" for eight hours. There were several methodological problems associated with the study: the small sample size; the disproportionate number of cases to which the same officer responded; and inadequate standardization and controls over the treatments actually delivered by the officers. Despite the methodological flaws, the Minneapolis Experiment received widespread national recognition and had a significant impact upon arrest policies nationwide. Between 1984 and 1987, police chiefs in thousands of police departments read the laudatory reports in newspaper articles and the National Institute of Justice (NIJ) report which lauded the study and stated that arrest was the best deterrent for abuse against women.

Between 1984 and 1985, in the aftermath of the Minneapolis study, the percentage of large city police departments with preferred- or pro-arrest "policies increased from 10% to 46%" (Walker, 1992, p. 121). By 1989, thirteen states had enacted mandatory arrest policies for domestic violence perpetrators. In some of these thirteen states arrest is mandatory in misdemeanor and felony level domestic violence charges, as well as for violating a restraining order. However, in two states (Delaware and North Carolina), arrest is mandatory only when the abuser violates a restraining order (Buzawa and Buzawa, 1990, p. 96). In order to determine the validity of the Minneapolis Experiment, the National Institute of Justice funded six replications in Atlanta, Georgia; Omaha, Nebraska; Charlotte, North Carolina; Colorado Springs, Colorado; Dade County, Florida; and Milwaukee, Wisconsin. Similar to the Minneapolis Experiment, the six later studies examined whether arrest is the most effective police response in preventing batterers from committing future acts of abuse.

In sharp contrast to the Minneapolis Experiment, however, none of the six replications found arrest to be a more effective deterrent than other methods of police response. There are three major reasons why arrest was not found to deter future domestic violence at these sites. First, the majority of the batterers in these studies had prior criminal records (50% in Milwaukee; 65% in Omaha; and 69% in Charlotte). Therefore, **arrest in itself does not have the same meaning it would have for first offenders since it is neither innovative nor unexpected by the lawbreaker.** Second, violence is a common and chronic problem among the sample rather than a first time occurrence. Therefore, it is unrealistic to expect a short detention to have much of an impact on changing a long term, chronically violent behavior pattern. Third, there was wide variation in the amount of time arrested batterers were in custody: "short arrests" averaged 2.8 hours; full arrest 11.1 hours. In Charlotte, the average time in custody was 15.75 hours (Sherman, et al., 1991; Dunford, et al., 1990). In contrast, for the Minneapolis study, the time in custody ranged from approximately twenty-four hours to one week (168 hours). Finally, arrest alone does not constitute a strong enough societal stigma among persons with previous arrest histories. In many groups, it is a rite of passage.

Dr. Lawrence Sherman and associates recently found that arrest did not exert a deterrent effect among a particular subgroup of abusers in Milwaukee. The most promising finding of the above cited studies indicates that arrest may well lead to an escalation of violence among unemployed persons, and deterrence of subsequent violence by abusers who are employed, married and white (Sherman, et al., 1992). Because of the large sample size (12 hundred cases were eligible for randomization), the researchers were able to conduct many sub-classification and matched-pair comparisons. The other replications were not able to dichotomize and sub-classify for as many variables as was done in the Milwaukee study.

Pro-arrest Policies

Since 1984 the trend has been for a growing number of police departments in cities with over 100 thousand population to adopt a policy of pro-arrest or probable cause arrests of batterers. Efforts to redefine battering as a crime were boosted significantly by the following four activities and studies:

1. The National Coalition Against Domestic Violence as well as state-wide coalitions and advocacy groups work to protect battered women.

2. The Minneapolis Domestic Violence Experiment on the deterrent effects of arrest (Sherman and Berk, 1984; Beck and Newton, 1985).

3. The final report of the U.S. Attorney General's Task Force on Family Violence (1984) citing the Minneapolis Experiment, documenting the prevalence and intense dangers of battering episodes, and concluding that domestic violence is a major crime problem and that criminal justice agencies should treat it as such.

4. Television network and newspaper accounts of the court decisions which held police liable for failing to protect battered women from severe injuries (e.g. *Thurman v. City of Torrington*, 1984).

A highly publicized Supreme Court case in the mid-1980s led to pro-arrest laws and mandated police training on prevention of domestic violence incidents. Ms. Tracey Thurman of Torrington, Connecticut, who had been beaten repeatedly by her husband, sued the Torrington Police Department. The basis for Thurman's lawsuit was the failure of the police department and its officers to protect Ms. Thurman despite the fact that she had continually and repeatedly requested police protection over an eight month period. Even though Ms. Thurman had obtained a court order barring her violent spouse from assaulting her again, it took the police twenty-five minutes to arrive on the scene of the final and most violent battering. After arrival at Ms. Thurman's residence, the arresting officer delayed arresting Mr. Thurman several minutes, giving the husband, who held a bloody knife in his hand, plenty of time to repeatedly kick his wife in the head, face and neck while she lay helpless on the ground. Ms. Thurman suffered life-threatening injuries as the result of this attack, including multiple stab wounds to the chest, neck and face; fractured cervical vertebrae and damage to her spinal cord; partial paralysis below the neck, lacerations to the cheek and mouth, loss of blood, shock, scarring, severe pain; and mental anguish. Tracey Thurman's award was unprecedented ($2.3 million in compensatory damages against twenty-four police officers). The jury found that the Torrington, Connecticut, police had deprived Ms. Thurman of her constitutional right to equal protection under the law (Fourteenth Amendment of the U.S. Constitution). The jury further concluded that the Torrington police officers were guilty of gross negligence in failing to protect Tracey Thurman and her son, Charles Jr., from the violent acts of Charles Thurman, Sr.

In the wake of the court decision in the Thurman case, police departments throughout the nation began immediately implementing pro-arrest policies and increased police training on domestic violence. As a result, during the last half of the 1980s and the first half of the decade of the 1990s, there was a proliferation of police training courses developed on how best to handle domestic violence calls.

By 1988, ten states had passed laws expanding police arrest powers in cases of domestic assault. Specifically, these new statutes required arrest when there was a positive determination of probable cause (i.e., the existence of visible injury and/or the passage of only a short time between the commission of the act and the arrival of the police on the scene). Police departments are now also legally required to arrest batterers who have violated protective or restraining orders granted to battered women by the courts. As of 1992, protective orders are available to abused women in all fifty states and the District of Columbia. In more and more jurisdictions, women in abusive relationships have been able to obtain protective orders against their abusers from local courts in order to prevent the abuser from coming to their residence. Police are called upon to enforce protective orders and to arrest the abuser if he violates any of the stipulation set forth in the court order.

Several issues limit the effectiveness of pro-arrest policies. First, in many jurisdictions unmarried couples are not included in the policies' definitions of eligibility. This omission certainly limits the effectiveness of the police response, since it is generally recognized that the police receive proportionally more domestic violence calls from cohabiting women than from legally married women. Second, several studies have indicated that 40% to 60% of batterers flee from the residence before the police arrive on the scene. Therefore, the batterer might not be arrested unless the battered victim signed a criminal complaint. The final issue relates to the fact that experienced police officers are accustomed to making their own discretionary decisions regarding whether or not to arrest the abusive person, and they may resent mandated intrusions upon their traditional discretionary authority. As a result, wide-spread police compliance with a presumptive or pro-arrest domestic violence policy is going to be a gradual process, taking several years.

Despite all the inherent limitations of a pro-arrest policy, considerable progress has been made within the past decade. While arrest of all suspects in domestic violence calls is mandated by statute in only a small number of states, thousands of police departments nationwide have implemented their own pro-arrest policies and are now requiring arrests when an officer observes signs of bodily injury on a battered woman.

Secondary Analysis of Police Data from a Large City

We will now examine a large data set of domestic violence complaints and arrest rates from a highly populated city in the northeastern part of the United States. The study covers six large police precincts during the five-year period 1987-1991. The results indicate marked differences in complaint rates for each of the racial groups in the six precincts. The magnitude of these reported differences reveal that domestic violence offenses come to the attention of the police more frequently within predominantly African-American and Hispanic neighborhoods than in predominantly white neighborhoods.

In order to determine the effect of race and ethnicity upon domestic violence reporting and arrest rates in urban areas, the available data from six police precincts in a major East Coast city were obtained and analyzed for a five-year period between

1987 and 1991. Due to the tremendous ethnic and racial diversity in most neighborhoods within that city, the six precincts were selected on the basis of the predominant racial group in each area, and were categorized accordingly (see Table 1).

The authors were able to match three pairs of precincts on the basis of their predominant racial or ethnic population since the percentages and distribution of each racial or ethnic group are approximately equal. The paired samples consisted of two predominantly "white" precincts (designated precincts Ia and Ib), two predominantly African-American precincts (designated precincts IIa and IIb), and two predominantly Hispanic precincts (designated precincts IIIa and IIIb). It should be noted, however, that significant differences existed among these communities and between pairs of communities in terms of per capita income, social mobility, unemployment, overall crime rate, and other factors which might weigh heavily in the domestic violence equation. It was not the authors' intention to measure, quantify, or control for these extraneous variables, nor did the available data set allow them to do so.

It is also important to note that these precincts varied greatly in their respective populations, making whole-number comparisons of the arrest and complaint data impossible. To facilitate comparisons between precincts and between the predominant ethnic and racial groups in each pair of samples, all the data included in this analysis are presented in terms of complaint rates or arrest rates per 100 thousand population.

Unfortunately, the aggregate data examined in this analysis also reflect the police agency's rather broad definition of domestic violence offenses, complicating any attempt to generalize the data to other cities which utilize different definitions. The advantage of this study is that the data collection system utilized by this city's police department is fairly sophisticated, and it accurately reflects the actual number of reports of alleged domestic violence offenses coming to the attention of patrol officers, as well as the actual number of arrests made for these offenses.

TABLE 1

Population Breakdowns in Selected Precincts

	White Nonhispanic	Black Nonhispanic	Hispanic Origin	Other
Predominantly White:				
Precinct Ia	87.2%	3.0%	5.5%	4.3%
Precinct Ib	84.2%	1.2%	7.3%	7.3%
Predominantly Black:				
Precinct IIa	10.7%	78.3%	9.5%	1.5%
Precinct IIb	5.5%	82.9%	10.2%	1.4%
Predominantly Hispanic:				
Precinct IIIa	14.4%	25.2%	58.8%	1.6%
Precinct IIIb	2.1%	38.3%	56.8%	2.8%

To clearly understand the data set upon which this analysis is based, several caveats should be mentioned and a few distinctions drawn. Of primary importance is an understanding of the applicable state law and of the fairly complex set of definitions and policies used to generate complaint and arrest data, as well as the differences between them. For example, this department's rules and regulations require that officers prepare crime complaint reports each and every time they respond to a domestic disturbance in which a felony or a "family offense" is alleged to have occurred. Therefore, the complaint data represents the total number of violent disputes to which the police were summoned, rather than the number of families or households in which such violent disputes have occurred. The resultant data set did not permit the authors to measure the number of households in each community which were affected by domestic violence.

Family offenses consist of simple misdemeanor assaults, aggravated assaults (i.e., those resulting in serious injury or involving use of a weapon), felony assaults, violations of judicial orders of protections, and the lesser offenses of menacing, harassment and reckless endangerment, when they are committed by one household member against another. "Household members" are defined as persons who are or were legally married, who live together or formerly lived together in a family-type relationship, who are related by blood or marriage, or who have a child in common. This broad definition therefore encompasses "common-law" marriages, same sex couples, in-laws, different generations of the same family, and siblings. Officers are allowed no discretion in their mandate to prepare a report when such offenses are alleged between household members. Physical evidence of an offense is not required. Perhaps what is most important is that the mere allegation that a felony or a family offense has been committed between household members is sufficient to generate a crime complaint report.

In contrast, state law requires that probable cause must exist before an officer may legally effect a felony or misdemeanor arrest, whether that crime occurs in his or her presence or not. Arrests for offenses falling within the legal category of "violations" (such as harassment), however, may be legally effected only when the offense is committed in the officer's presence. Although officers are required to arrest suspects for all felony crimes and all violations of judicial protection orders, the law generally allows some discretion in the case of misdemeanors and violations. Department policy removes that discretion in family offense situations. It requires that once probable cause exists, an officer must arrest for any misdemeanor assault between household members (whether in the officer's presence or not), and must arrest for lesser family offenses committed in his or her presence if a complaining witness requests that an arrest be made. Even if the complaining witness does not want an arrest made, the officer may still exercise the discretion to make an arrest for simple misdemeanor assaults committed in or out of his or her presence.

To ensure compliance with these "pro-arrest" policy directives, officers are required to justify the reasons why they have not made an arrest, the complainants who do not wish to press charges must acknowledge their refusal by signing a form. This provision also tends to assure the integrity and the veracity of the statistical data. When the offender is not present at the scene and cannot be readily apprehended, the crime complaint report is forwarded to the local detective squad, whose officers are similarly mandated to apprehend and arrest the offender.

For the purposes of data collection and reporting, this department utilizes the Uniform Crime Reports definitions of "Aggravated" and "Simple" assault. The "Aggravated Assault" category includes all serious and felony assaults, and those misdemeanor assaults involving weapons. The "Simple Assault" category includes less serious assaults in which injuries are not severe and in which no weapons are used.

THE RESULTS

Domestic Violence Complaints

Over the five year period between 1987 and 1991, the number and rate of domestic violence reports coming to the attention of the police within this jurisdiction tended to remain fairly constant within each of the sample precincts, and where variance occurred from year to year, it tended to follow the annual variance in city-wide averages. Table 2 illustrates the aggregate complaint rate per 100 thousand population for all family offenses reported to the police in each precinct. These combined rates, which remained fairly stable over time, reflect the total number of family offenses (i.e., all violations of judicial protection orders, simple assaults, aggravated assaults, and lesser offenses between household members) alleged to have been committed in these precincts. Table 2 also illustrates the degree of concordance in complaint rates among the matched pairs of precincts (Ia and Ib; IIa and IIb; IIIa and IIIb) according to the predominant ethnic or racial groups they represent.

When these matched pairs are compared on the basis of the groups they represent, dramatic differences in the complaint rates for different ethnic and racial groups become evident. The lowest aggregate complaint rates were found in the two predominantly white precincts (Ia and Ib), and the highest in the two predominantly Hispanic precincts (IIIa and IIIb), although the number of alleged family offenses reported in predominantly African-American districts also appears to be quite high. Indeed, over the five year period the complaint rate in one of the predominantly Hispanic precincts (IIIb) was consistently at least ten times greater than in one of the predominantly white precincts (Ia), and about twice the city-wide average. Predominantly black districts (IIa

---

TABLE 2

Domestic Violence Complaint Rate
All Domestic Violence Offenses per 100,000 Population

	1987	1988	1989	1990	1991	5 yr avg.
Ia	131.35	156.01	132.77	117.12	124.71	132.39
Ib	200.68	252.23	308.28	280.26	282.06	264.86
IIa	897.80	929.41	1074.83	738.02	790.02	886.27
IIb	1803.28	1840.66	1468.06	1134.50	1032.46	1459.39
IIIa	1193.05	1368.68	1264.82	1090.04	1328.99	1249.10
IIIb	1378.17	1871.85	1379.64	1284.14	1389.92	1460.74
City-Wide	631.63	761.82	713.82	609.29	640.51	671.41

and IIb) evince a domestic violence report rate at least six times greater than the rate in either of the predominantly white (Ia and Ib) districts.

With several exceptions, the aggregate domestic violence report rate appears to have peaked in 1988, and declined slightly since that year. The highest rate of reported family offenses in any of these districts occurred in 1988 in precinct IIb, when the rate reached 1871.85 complaints per 100 thousand population. The magnitude of these differences in per capita family offense complaint rates strongly suggest that domestic violence offenses come to the attention of the police more frequently within African-American and Hispanic neighborhoods than in white neighborhoods. As noted above, the data set did not permit the authors to discover which, if any, of the uncontrolled variables (unemployment levels, overall crime rate, etc.) may account for this tremendous disparity.

Domestic Violence Arrests

Both the number and the rate of arrests for domestic violence offenses also tended to remain fairly constant within the selected precincts (see Table 3). City-wide, the domestic violence arrest rate rose 8% (from 23.55 to 25.62 arrests per 100 thousand) between 1987 and 1991, but with two exceptions the rate declined in each of the targeted precincts. In predominantly Hispanic district IIIa, the overall rate rose an insignificant 2%, from 18.54 arrests per 100,000 in 1987 to 19.05 arrests in 1991; in predominantly white precinct Ib, the rate increased 34%, from 12.16 in 1987 to 18.59 in 1991. This precinct, however, is somewhat anomalous in that its peak year for arrests occurred in 1988, when arrests there increased a precipitous 36% from the previous year; thereafter, between the peak year of 1988 and 1991, the arrest rate per 100 thousand in precinct Ib declined a modest 5%, from 18.99 to 18.59. Bearing these two exceptions in mind, the relative constancy of these arrest rates and the modest nature of their declines suggest that the statistical decreases found here are not statistically significant.

Further, by comparing the data presented in Table 2 to the data in Table 3, it becomes readily apparent that the tremendous differences in complaint rates found

TABLE 3

Domestic Violence Arrest Rate
All Domestic Violence Offenses per 100 Complaints

	1987	1988	1989	1990	1991	5 yr avg.
Ia	27.43	21.58	24.28	23.07	20.53	23.38
Ib	12.16	18.99	16.71	15.81	18.59	16.45
IIa	32.70	36.54	28.74	30.64	32.68	32.26
IIb	25.37	24.64	24.67	19.77	21.33	23.16
IIIa	18.54	15.98	18.02	18.12	19.05	17.95
IIIb	27.39	23.39	26.83	21.85	25.26	24.94
City-Wide	23.55	23.14	24.34	24.42	25.62	24.21

between precincts and between ethnic or racial groups are not reflected in the annual arrest rates. On the contrary, while these arrest rate data varied, they remained within a fairly consistent and narrow range. As noted above, the family offense report rate in some precincts were as much as ten times higher than in others, but differences of this magnitude cannot be found in the arrest rates. *While we may have observed vast differences in complaint rates on the basis of a precinct's predominant racial or ethnic make-up, the data clearly imply that the police in this city arrest domestic violence offenders at a fairly consistent rate, regardless of the district's racial or ethnic composition.*

Because the complaint rate reflects the total number of domestic violence incidents occurring rather than the number of individuals against whom complaints are made, we might also infer that the pro-arrest policy is a more effective deterrent in some communities than in others. Also, given the depth and the resilience of the social and economic problems within the African-American and Hispanic communities, and perhaps the inability of those communities' members to access social service and counseling programs, arrest alone may not sufficiently deter future violence. It is quite possible that batterers in predominantly white communities have the financial resources to access counseling programs, or that the social stigma attached to arrest within those communities effectively discourages future family violence.

Simple and Aggravated Assaults

The available data set permitted us to isolate aggravated and simple assaults from the aggregate domestic violence complaint and arrest indexes (which encompassed all the

---

TABLE 4

Domestic Violence Complaint Rate
Aggravated and Simple Assaults per 100,000 Population

		1987	1988	1989	1990	1991	5 yr avg.
Ia:	(Aggr.)	45.2	49.3	34.1	33.2	37.9	40.0
	(Simple)	15.6	12.8	14.4	9.9	11.8	12.9
Ib:	(Aggr.)	79.5	77.7	75.9	75.0	86.8	79.0
	(Simple)	22.6	18.1	29.8	32.5	25.3	25.7
IIa:	(Aggr.)	300.8	325.1	313.4	207.7	235.7	276.6
	(Simple)	222.2	194.2	249.3	170.7	139.1	159.1
IIb:	(Aggr.)	377.7	335.4	293.1	229.1	212.6	289.6
	(Simple)	475.8	597.5	466.5	344.7	210.5	419.0
IIIa:	(Aggr.)	253.3	235.6	224.6	184.1	179.0	215.3
	(Simple)	375.7	353.8	320.0	304.0	375.7	345.8
IIIb:	(Aggr.)	246.8	308.5	214.5	179.2	199.8	299.8
	(Simple)	362.9	503.9	355.6	350.5	401.1	400.8
City-wide:	(Aggr.)	115.3	123.9	117.1	97.2	94.9	109.7
	(Simple)	194.7	222.6	204.5	179.7	184.4	197.2

family offenses discussed above), and to differentiate between the two. The complaint rates for these specific crimes are presented in Table 4. The data clearly illustrate a decline in the rate of aggravated assault complaints in each of the subject precincts, as well as in the jurisdiction as a whole. Exceptions were found in the case of predominantly white precinct Ib and predominantly Hispanic precinct IIIa. There, in contrast to moderate declines elsewhere and in the overall city-wide rate, an anomalous and substantial jump in the number of aggravated domestic assault complaints between 1990 and 1991 led to a respective 13% and 19% increase in the aggravated assault report rate. In each of the other districts, however, the aggravated domestic assault report rate declined. The most substantial declines were noted in the predominantly African-American precincts IIb (-44%) and the predominantly Hispanic precinct IIIb (-35%).

Simple assaults also declined overall during the period from 1987 to 1991, with the exception of predominantly white precinct Ib (an 11% increase) and predominantly Hispanic precinct IIIa, where another anomalous increase in simple assault complaints resulted in no substantive change in the complaint rate. The greatest overall decline occurred in the predominantly black IIa and IIb districts, in which reported simple domestic assaults fell 55% and 37%, respectively.

The data presented in Table 5 demonstrate a general decline in the rate of arrest for domestic assaults in most of the precincts. Here it must again be emphasized that these data do not represent the number or percentage of complaints for which arrests are effected, but the overall rate of arrest per 100 thousand population within the subject precincts. With few exceptions, the rate of arrest for domestic assaults tended to

TABLE 5

Domestic Violence Arrest Rate
Misdemeanor and Felony Assaults per 100,000 Population

		1987	1988	1989	1990	1991	5 yr avg.
Ia:	(Aggr.)	12.3	10.4	12.8	11.4	9.9	11.4
	(Simple)	19.9	16.6	12.8	9.9	13.3	14.5
Ib:	(Aggr.)	7.2	14.4	13.6	19.0	19.9	14.8
	(Simple)	8.1	20.8	14.5	12.6	15.4	14.3
IIa:	(Aggr.)	133.7	146.3	142.7	112.9	103.0	127.7
	(Simple)	78.6	90.3	66.8	50.6	77.7	72.3
IIb:	(Aggr.)	228.1	203.3	169.2	116.6	115.6	166.6
	(Simple)	182.7	198.1	142.4	73.3	67.1	132.7
IIIa:	(Aggr.)	127.5	125.8	125.8	96.2	109.8	117.0
	(Simple)	63.3	49.0	54.0	49.8	71.7	57.6
IIIb:	(Aggr.)	148.4	167.5	127.8	102.8	132.2	135.8
	(Simple)	86.7	98.4	76.4	72.0	89.6	84.6
City-wide:	(Aggr.)	67.1	72.6	70.5	59.8	63.0	66.6
	(Simple)	52.8	62.7	57.4	50.8	58.2	56.4

vary in accord with the rate of domestic violence reports received. Thus precinct Ia, which experienced a 16% decline in the per capita rate of aggravated assault complaints received, also experienced a 19% decrease in the per capita rate of arrests made for those crimes; precinct Ib experienced a 15% increase in the complaint rate and a concomitant 28% increase in the per capita arrest rate.

Aggravated Assault Arrest and Complaint Rates

In four of the six precincts studied, the aggravated assault complaint rate declined less substantially between 1987 and 1991 than did the arrest rate during those years; in one precinct (Ib), a net increase in aggravated assault complaints rate (15%) was met with an even more substantial increase in the arrest rate (63%). In only one district, in fact (precinct IIIa), did the decrease in the aggravated assault complaint rate (-29%) exceed the decrease in the arrest rate (-14%). City-wide, aggravated assault complaints fell 18% while arrest rates declined 6%, and a 5% increase in simple assault complaints was offset by a 9% increase in the per capita arrest rate. In almost all cases, then, while the number and rate of aggravated assaults complaints were generally down, the number of arrests for these offenses declined less. We can thus infer that a greater percentage of domestic violence aggravated assaults results in arrests. The data set, unfortunately, did not allow us to measure this phenomenon specifically.

Unlike the aggregated complaint and arrest rates for all the combined family offenses, quite substantial differences were evident in the inter-precinct and inter-group rates of arrest for domestic assaults. Table 4 demonstrates that predominantly white precincts (Ia and Ib) had considerably lower complaint rates for domestic assaults than either the predominantly African-American (IIa and IIb) or Hispanic (IIIa and IIIb) precincts, or than the city as a whole. Moreover, the complaint rates for aggravated assault in predominantly white precincts were proportionally much higher than the rates for simple assault—generally at least three times higher. This pattern was not found city-wide or in the African-American or Hispanic districts, where with the exception of precinct IIa, the rates for simple assaults were consistently higher than for aggravated assaults, and where the difference between the two rates was much less extreme.

By comparing the data in Tables 2 and 4, we see that in both of the predominantly white precincts, approximately 30% of the domestic violence complaints were for aggravated assault, and approximately 10% for simple assault. This finding contrasts sharply with the predominantly Hispanic precincts and with the city as a whole, where aggravated assaults accounted for less than 20% of the total complaints, and simple assaults accounted for nearly 30% of the total complaints. These data suggest that although considerably fewer complaints are received by the police in predominantly White communities, the assaults alleged to have occurred there are more severe.

Simple Assault Complaint and Arrest Rates

The findings obtained from an analysis of the simple assault complaint and arrest rates were similar to those of the aggravated family assaults. In every precinct and city-wide, in fact, the percentage of simple assaults resulting in arrest can be shown to have increased, often substantially (see Table 6). The most dramatic decline in the report rate occurred in the predominantly African-American districts, where the overall report rate plunged almost 44% in precinct IIb between 1987 and 1991, and almost

22% in precinct IIa during this time frame. Somewhat less impressive reductions were found in predominantly white precinct Ia, where a 16% reduction in the complaint rate was realized, and in predominantly white precinct Ib, where the complaint rate actually rose 8.4% during this period. Precinct Ib's aggravated assault complaint rate rose dramatically between 1987 and its peak of 308.28 complaints per 100 thousand in 1989. It has, however, achieved a moderate decline of 8% since that time. The aggravated assault complaint rate also declined dramatically in each of the predominantly Hispanic districts IIa (down 29%) and IIb (down 19%). These decreases tended to accord with the average city-wide decline, where overall aggravated assault complaints fell 17.6%. With the exception of one predominantly white precinct, each of the subject precincts achieved an overall reduction in the number and rate of domestic aggravated assault complaints between 1987 and 1991. These reductions were most pronounced in the predominantly Hispanic districts, which concomitantly experienced the highest per capita rate of complaints.

TABLE 6

Domestic Violence Complaint and Arrest Rates
Percentage Increase or Decrease 1987 to 1991

	1987		1991		% +/-	
	Aggr.	Simple	Aggr.	Simple	Aggr.	Simple
Ia:						
(Compl.)	45.2	15.6	37.9	11.8	-16.1%	-24.3%
(Arrest)	12.3	19.9	9.9	13.3	-19.5%	-33.1%
Ib:						
(Compl.)	79.5	22.6	86.8	25.3	+8.4%	-10.6%
(Arrest)	7.2	8.1	19.9	15.4	+63.8%	+47.4%
IIa:						
(Compl.)	300.8	222.2	235.7	139.1	-21.6%	-37.3%
(Arrest)	133.7	78.6	103.0	77.7	-22.9%	-1.1%
IIb:						
(Compl.)	377.7	475.8	212.6	210.5	-43.8%	-55.7%
(Arrest)	228.1	182.7	115.6	67.1	-49.3%	-63.3%
IIIa:						
(Compl.)	253.3	375.7	179.0	375.7	-29.3%	00.0%
(Arrest)	63.3	49.0	109.8	71.7	+42.3%	+31.6%
IIIb:						
(Compl.)	246.8	362.9	199.8	401.1	-19.0%	+9.7%
(Arrest)	86.7	98.4	132.2	89.6	+34.4%	-8.9%
City-Wide:						
(Compl.)	115.3	194.7	94.9	184.4	-17.6%	-5.3%
(Arrest)	67.1	52.8	63.0	58.2	+9.4%	+9.3%

SUMMARY AND CONCLUSIONS

Based on this data analysis, several important general conclusions can be drawn concerning the effect of race and ethnicity upon domestic violence report and arrest rates. Again, it must be emphasized that the complaint or report data are representative of the total number of family offenses alleged to have been committed between members of the city's households; because the police may have been summoned more than once to these households, the data do not reflect the number of households affected by domestic violence. In contrast, the arrest rate data for aggravated (felony) assaults in a highly accurate depiction of the number of assaults in which police had probable cause to believe that a felony was actually committed; because officers have discretion to arrest in simple (misdemeanor) assault cases where the complaining witness refuses to press charges, that data is a less accurate depiction of the actual rate of bona fide assaults.

The data reveal that the rate of family offenses coming to police attention generally tended to remain fairly constant within precincts between 1987 and 1991, without regard to race or ethnicity. Annual variances in these intra-precinct rates tended to follow the annual city-wide variance.

Nevertheless, dramatic differences in complaint rates are evident for each of the racial or ethnic groups in the subject precincts. The magnitude of these differences in per capita family offense complaint rates strongly suggest that domestic violence offenses come to the attention of the police more frequently within predominantly African-American and Hispanic neighborhoods than in predominantly white neighborhoods. The data set did not permit the authors to discover if this finding was the result of differential police response (an unlikely possibility, given the department's strict regulations) or is attributable to extraneous variables. These extraneous variables might include differences in employment levels, alcohol or drug abuse, or the failure of arrests to deter further assaults in these communities.

Both the number and the rate of arrests for family offenses also tended to remain fairly constant within the selected precincts, and the tremendous differences in complaint rates between ethnically and racially predominant precincts were not reflected in the arrest rates. On the contrary, while these arrest rate data varied, they remained within a fairly consistent and narrow range. Racial and ethnic differences in a neighborhood's composition apparently do not significantly impact the rate of arrest for family offenses.

In contrast to the complaint and arrest rates for the combined family offenses, substantial differences were discovered in both the inter-precinct and inter-group rates of arrest for simple and aggravated assaults. Predominantly white precincts evinced considerably lower complaint rates for domestic assaults than either the predominantly African-American or predominantly Hispanic precincts. The complaint rates for aggravated assault in predominantly white precincts were also proportionally much higher than the rates for simple assault. No similar pattern was found city-wide or in the African-American or Hispanic districts, where the rates for simple assaults were (with one exception) consistently higher than for aggravated assaults. The disparity between simple and aggravated assault arrest rates in minority precincts was also less extreme.

This city's pro-arrest policy in domestic violence cases is inferred to be a more effective deterrent in white communities than in minority communities. This assessment is based on the fact that the complaint rate reflects the total number of complaints received by the police, rather than the number of individuals against whom complaints have been made. Because this department's "pro-arrest" policy is so strictly enforced throughout the agency's jurisdiction, no basis exists to suppose that officers might be enforcing their mandate to arrest more stringently in one neighborhood than in another. Indeed, the compatibility of arrest rates across ethnic and racial lines adds credence to this assertion.

Given the limitations of the data set, an alternative but currently untested explanation for this disparity in complaint rates is that the African-American and Hispanic communities selected for this study are confronted by social problems and conditions which are not as prevalent or as extreme in white communities, and that these problems are contributing factors in the incidence of domestic violence found there. These minority communities may lack many of the resources and continuing social services necessary to achieve a permanent solution to family violence. It is quite possible that batterers in predominantly white communities have the financial resources to access effective counseling programs, or that the social stigma attached to arrest within those communities effectively discourages future family violence.

The aggravated assault arrest rate in predominantly white precincts exceeded the simple assault arrest rate by a substantial margin. In African-American and Hispanic precincts, however, the simple assault arrest rate exceeded the aggravated assault rate. These data suggest that although considerably fewer complaints are received by the police in white communities, the assaults alleged to have occurred there are more severe and result in a greater number of arrests. Two explanations may be posited to account for this finding.

First, police officers in predominantly white neighborhoods may exercise their discretion not to arrest in misdemeanor assaults more frequently than in minority communities. The data did not permit this hypothesis to be tested, and the authors have no empirical reason to assume or question its validity. Another, more intuitively viable explanation may be that assault victims in white neighborhoods are more reluctant to suffer the embarrassment and stigma of calling the police to intervene in family disputes involving less severe injuries. If this hypothesis is valid, it would imply that these victims are more willing to suffer repeated but less severe assaults, until the increasing violence reaches an intolerable threshold. A corollary to this hypothesis is that the actual rate of domestic assaults against white victims is much higher than the complaint data would suggest. Given the acknowledged frailty of the complaint rate data presented here, that possibility should not be ignored.

STUDY QUESTIONS

1. Gelles and Straus (1988) have suggested that domestic violence is often used to maintain power and dominance within families. Historically, how has the law facilitated, or at least failed to punish, domestic violence?

2. How will the social, political and legal trends, which combined in the 1970s and 1980s to initiate change in the police response to domestic violence, continue to impact police policy in the coming decades?

3. The results of the Minneapolis Experiment suggested that police agencies could reduce the level of domestic violence within their jurisdictions by adopting policies

requiring or encouraging officers to arrest batterers. Replications of that study indicate that arrest does not deter domestic violence among all social groups. Should police agencies continue to follow mandatory or pro-arrest policies?

4. Replications of the Minneapolis Domestic Violence Experiment have identified a number of characteristics (e.g., employment status, marital status, race/ethnicity, and criminal record) which appear to influence whether arrest will deter future domestic assaults. Should the police take these factors into account in deciding whether or not to arrest a batterer, or should a uniform policy apply in all domestic violence cases?

5. Domestic violence is a complex social phenomenon, and a variety of social, psychological and economic factors may contribute to the occurrence of violence within a particular family. Should society's primary response to family violence be a legal one? Should police involvement in domestic violence be limited to arrest, or should they also become involved in discovering and solving the family's social, psychological and economic problems? If not the police, what agency should become involved?

6. What reasons, other than the deterrence of future domestic assaults, can be given to justify a mandatory- or pro-arrest policy?

7. Official crime statistics consistently indicate that the vast majority of domestic violence victims are women, and the vast majority of batterers are men. Is this simply because men are generally physically bigger and stronger than women? Are "battered husbands" under-represented in the crime statistics?

8. The data presented here indicate that reported domestic violence offenses are not equally distributed throughout this city's population—domestic violence impacts some ethnic or racial groups disproportionately. What domestic violence policy advice would you give to the police chief of this city?

REFERENCES

Attorney General's Task Force on Family Violence. (September, 1984). *Final Report*. Washington, DC: U.S. Department of Justice.

Bard, M (1970). *Training in Crisis Intervention: From Concept to Implementation*. Washington, DC: U.S. Department of Justice.

Bard, M. (1973). *Family Crisis Intervention*. Washington, DC: U.S. Government Printing Office.

Browne, A. (1984). "Assault and Homicide at Home: When Battered Women Kill." Paper presented at the Second National Conference for Family Violence Researchers, Durham, NH.

Browne, A. (1987). *When Battered Women Kill*. New York: Free Press.

Buzawa, E.S. and C.G. Buzawa. (1990). *Domestic Violence: The Criminal Justice Response*. Newbury Park, CA: Sage Publications.

Dunford, F.W. *et al.* (1990). "The Role of Arrest in Domestic Assault." *Criminology*. Vol. 28, pp. 183-206.

Fleming, J.B. (1979). *Stopping Wife Abuse*. Garden City, NY: Anchor Press/Doubleday.

Gelles, Richard J. and Murray, A. Strauss. (1988). *Intimate Violence*. New York: Simon & Schuster.

Gondolf, E.W. and E.B. Fischer. (1988). *Battered Women As Survivors: An Alternative to Treating Learned Helplessness* Lexington, MA: Lexington Books.

Gondolf, E.W. and E.B. Fisher. (1991). "Wife Beating," in Ammerman, Robert T. and Michael Hersen (eds.), *Case Studies in Family Violence*. New York, NY: Plenum Press. pp. 273-292.

Hart, B. (1992). State Criminal and Civil Codes on Domestic Violence. *Juvenile and Family Court Journal*. pp. 3-68.

Hasselt, V.N., R.L. Morrison, A.S. Bellack & M. Hersen, eds. (1988). *Handbook of Family Violence*. New York, NY: Plenum Press.

Hirschel, J. David., *et al.* (June, 1992). "Review Essay on the Law Enforcement Response to Spouse Abuse: Past, Present and Future." *Justice Quarterly*, Vol. 9, No. 2. pp. 247-283.

Pence, Ellen. (1983). "The Duluth Domestic Abuse Intervention Project." *Hamline Law Review*, Vol. 6, pp. 247-75.

Pleck, E. (1987). *Domestic Tyranny: The Making of American Social Policy against Family Violence from Colonial Times to the Present*. New York, NY: Oxford University Press.

Roberts, A.R. (1981). *Sheltering Battered Women: A National Survey and Service Guide*. New York, NY: Springer Publishing Company.

Roberts, A.R., ed. (1984). *Battered Women and their Families: Intervention Strategies and Treatment Programs*. New York, NY: Springer Publishing Co.

Roberts, A.R. (1988). "Substance Abuse and Battering: The Deadly Mix." *Journal of Substance Abuse Treatment*, Vol. 12, No. 1. pp. 83-87.

Roberts, A.R. and B.J. Roberts. (1990). "A Model for Crisis Intervention With Battered Women and Their Children" in A.R. Roberts, eds. *Crisis Intervention Handbook: Assessment, Treatment and Research*. Belmont, CA: Wadsworth Publishing Co. pp. 105-123.

Roberts, A.R. (1994). "Court Responses to Battered Women and Reform Legislation." in A.R. Roberts, ed. *Critical Issues in Crime and Justice*. Thousand Oaks, CA: Sage Publications. pp. 240-248.

Roy, M., ed. (1982). *The Abusive Partner: An Analysis of Domestic Battering*. New York, NY: Van Nostrand Reinhold Co., Inc.

Sherman, L.W. and R.A. Berk. (1984). "The Specific Deterrent Effects of Arrest for Domestic Assault." *American Sociological Review*, Vol. 49, pp. 267-272.

Sherman, L.W. (1991). "From Initial Deterrence to Longterm Escalation: Short custody arrest for poverty ghetto domestic violence." *Criminology*. Vol. 29, pp. 821-850.

Sherman, L.W., *et al.* (1992). "The Variable Effects of Arrest on Criminal Careers: The Milwaukee Domestic Violence Experiment." *The Journal of Criminal Law and Criminology*. Vol. 83.

Straus, M., R. Gelles, and S. Steinmetz. (1980). *Behind Closed Doors: Violence in the American Family*. Garden City, NY: Anchor Press/Doubleday.

Straus, M. and R. Gelles. (1990). *Physical Violence In American Families*. New Brunswick, NJ: Transaction Publishers.

Sugg, N.K. and T. Inui. (1992). "Primary Care Physicians' Response to Domestic Violence: Opening Pandora's Box." *JAMA*, Vol. 267, No. 23, pp. 3157-3160.

Thurman v. City of Torrington. (1984). 595 F. Supp. 1521 (D. Conn.).

Trafford, A. (February 26, 1991). "Why Battered Women Kill: Self Defense, Not Revenge Is Often The Motive." *Washington Post*.

Walker, L.E. (1979). *The Battered Women*. New York, NY: Harper and Row.

Walker, L.E. (1984). *The Battered Women Syndrome*. New York, NY: Springer Publishing Co.

Walker, L.E. (1987). *Terrifying Love*. New York, NY: Harper and Row.

Walker, L.E. (1993). "Battered Women As Defendants." In N.Z. Hilton (ed.) *Legal Responses To Wife Assault*. Newbury Park, CA: Sage Publications. pp. 233-257.

CHAPTER 8

LEGAL ISSUES IN POLICING

Robert J. Meadows, Ph.D.

ABSTRACT

Policing in the twenty-first century will be a more demanding and delicate process. The police and community will share in the crime control function. Private security services will continue to assist the police in meeting community protection needs. The police will be given more legal freedom mandates, but will continually be held accountable for mistakes. These trends signal a need for the police to be better trained in the total crime prevention process, and functions associated with community service.

INTRODUCTION

The modern police officer is confronted with delicate situations, requiring immediate but appropriate responses. The police are an important link between citizens and their government. However, the police must be not only responsive, but also accountable to those they are sworn to serve. The police operate under the democratic rule of law process which means a government of laws not men. However, it is recognized that the police exercise a great deal of discretion, and at times, this discretion may get out of control. The behavior of the police in the celebrated Rodney King incident demonstrates how the police lost control in a delicate situation. The misuse of discretion in this incident set into motion a series of events where police tactics, policy, and leadership practices were questioned by a number of scholars, public officials, and citizens. The police officers of the future must be responsive to the community and accountable for their performance. This chapter explores the police role in addressing crime and violence in the home and the streets. In order for the police to be more responsive, there is a need for greater involvement from the community. Trends in domestic violence legislation suggest that the police will be required to assume a more aggressive posture. Court decisions in search and seizure cases have permitted the police to "bend the rules." Yet, to assure accountability, legal controls on police behavior and practices will continue to exist.

THE POLICE AND THE COMMUNITY

Given the variety and frequency of police tasks, it is difficult for the police to be totally responsive to the community. A community wide response is needed to address the crime problem. The concept of community policing is based on a working partnership between the police and the community in addressing crime problems (Trojanowicz,

1990; Kelling et al., 1988; Wilson and Kelling, 1982). Generally, the theory of community policing holds that if businesses, community organizations, and residents work together, crime will decrease. In other words, an integrated community effort and a proactive police presence must accompany programs designed to reduce criminal opportunity. In short, the police would go into the community and become not only crime fighters, but community facilitators, working with a law-abiding community. The reactive posture the police have assumed in the past is not enough to address community crime problems. The community must assist in policing itself, and the police must assist in mobilizing the community to accomplish this task. There are three major approaches in meeting future community policing needs. Some of these approaches have already begun.

The first approach is the trend of justice agencies working together in attacking crime problems and targeting serious repeat offenders. In recent years, a number of departments have begun to use proactive, police-initiated procedures in patrolling the community. These programs are referred to as repeat offender programs (ROP). The emphasis on these programs is based on the research findings suggesting that a small number of chronic or repeat offenders commit a disproportionately large number of violent crimes (Blumstein et al., 1983). The juvenile delinquency problem in some communities has forged a working alliance between criminal justice agencies.

A program designed to track serious habitual juvenile offenders, referred to as SHO/DI has been launched in several cities nationwide (Kline, 1993:32-37). The purpose of the program is to develop trust and cooperation between agencies serving juveniles, and to build an inter-agency information process to identify and track serious habitual juvenile offenders. The ultimate goal is to incapacitate the repeat offender, whether through detention, incarceration, probation, or other measures. It is a process to temporarily stop criminal behavior, and institute efforts to modify the behavior. It is a form of crime prevention whereby the police proactively monitor the serious repeat juvenile offender. The SHO/DI program makes rosters of all juveniles meeting the criteria of serious offenders. The police, district attorney's office, and the probation department work together in tracking these offenders. Similar programs are targeting gangs and other at-risk youth. Many of these police sponsored programs not only target the problem offender, but conduct a variety of outreach programs including athletic competition and recreational activities for youth (Weston, 1993:80-84). These approaches are forms of problem oriented policing (POP) strategies practiced by many departments.

As we move into the twenty-first century, the community policing trend is in full swing. Yet, there are concerns as to the required funding to hire more police. Under the proposed 1993 Federal crimes Control Bill, President Clinton's proposal to hire 100 thousand more police nationwide is admirable, but ridiculously low. The nation's capital and crime capital alone could benefit by 100 thousand additional officers, not to mention Miami, New York, and Los Angeles where gang violence has virtually gripped these cities. If community policing is to be effective, there is a need to hire police at a greater pace than current funding allows. And those recruited into the police ranks must view the community as forces of change not adversaries. Community policing requires that the police reorganize their response capabilities. The police must assign beat officers, detectives, and other specialists to certain geographical areas of the city. In other words, the police need to decentralize operations to better serve the community (Donahue, 1993:12-22). This approach includes placing the police in a position where they are more visible to the community. Footbeats and storefronts are two examples where the police are accessible to the public. The use of bicycle patrols has proven successful in a number of cities (Ent,1991).

As pointed out by Goldstein (1990:34-35), "the emphasis on community has two implications. It means looking to the community to define the problems that should be of concern to the police, rather than succumbing to the tendency of the police on their own to define the problems of concern to the community. And it means gaining an understanding of all dimensions of a problem in the total community."

There are a number of examples of community based policing programs. The Los Angeles police have organized citizens to paint out graffiti and have prompted city agencies to tow away abandoned vehicles. This idea is a form of preventive mainte-nance, or the philosophy that if one window is broken and not repaired, then soon all windows will be broken. In other words, when community disorder and decay are not challenged, then the disorder escalates and the decay spreads (Wilson and Kelling, 1989:23).

It is suggested that the community must share in crime control efforts. In 1992, the California Department of Justice published a comprehensive book on community oriented problem solving policing (COPS). According to the Department of Justice publication (1992:4-5), "the community must recognize the conditions that generate crime, and must accept the challenge and responsibility to assume ownership of their community's safety and well being."

There are a number of COPS programs in effect throughout the country. These programs address gangs, drugs, loitering problems, the homeless, residential and business crime prevention, and other proactive attempts to avert crime. However, there are not enough sworn officers available to carry out these programs. Increased budgetary problems confronting many cities are prohibiting the hiring of additional police. If more police are hired, enforcement focus is often directed toward crime repression and other calls for service. In Los Angeles, for example, which has been vic-timized by riots, there are only 2.3 officers for every one thousand residents. This is the lowest officer citizen ratio of the ten largest U.S. cities (*Los Angeles Times*, 1993:26).

In response to the need for increased protection, residents and merchants with the money to spend is hiring private police and security officers to assist in crime con-trol efforts. It is becoming increasingly clear that the police cannot provide the need-ed protection for everyone; thus, the second approach to community policing is through the enlistment of the private security industry. Since the private protection industry outnumbers law enforcement three to one, there is a trend to hire more secu-rity to patrol housing tracts, malls, schools, and a variety of other business establish-ments. Private security is a $64 billion industry, with more than ten thousand firms nationwide. In many respects, real community policing is being done by private secu-rity forces and alarm companies (*Los Angeles Tmes*, 1993:26).

The benefit of private security has been demonstrated in some communities. In Oceanside, California, the downtown area has been plagued with prostitution and drug activity. The police department has lost thirty officers in three years to budget cuts. In 1992, the city hired a private patrol company on a three-month trial program.

The funding was provided by redevelopment funds. The program was so successful that when the funds ran out, downtown merchants each contributed $50.00 a month to keep the security force. The police, as a result, are able to devote more time and respond more quickly to serious calls.

The increased use of private guards in shopping malls is another trend. Shopping malls are becoming new cities, with some of the same problems as outdoor areas. Increased problems in loitering, gang activity, thefts, and other crimes are finding their way indoors, including the parking lots. Local governments are passing ordinances allowing security officers to write parking citations and enforce reckless driving. Security officers provide valuable public relations for tenants and patrons (*USA Today*, Dec. 3, 1993:1).

In 1993, a bill came under review before the Texas legislature requiring shopping centers to employ security officers. In Minnesota, there is a senate bill under review that would authorize private security officers to request identification of persons who are on the premises. These legislative trends signal an increased recognition of the value of security. In Philadelphia, the police have embraced the support of the private security sector to assist in crime control efforts. The program, entitled "security watch," utilizes security officers in the downtown area to perform building checks and patrol areas frequented by shoppers, theater goers, and residents. Security officers are trained by the police and their respective agencies. A true partnership has been formed between the police and the private security sector. There has been tangible gain from this partnership, both in the reduction of crime, and in the police ability to respond to calls for service (Zappile, 1991:22-23).

Private security officers have replaced police officers in one jurisdiction. In Sussex, New Jersey, a four member police department was replaced by a private security company. The security company was given a six-month contract to provide police services to the small town. The use of security saved the town over $93,000. More important, the security officers did a good job, and were well received by the citizens (*Crime Control Digest*, 1993). However, a court order forced the town to discontinue the security services because of potential liability in the training of the officers, a problem that could be resolved by legislation.

There are a number of other positive examples of working relationships between public policing and private security. The University of New Haven and Yale University security staffs have developed relationships with the local police. The agencies have carried out a community based policing philosophy. The police and security staffs meet monthly to discuss mutual crime problems, and are involved in joint patrols. The Connecticut Police Chiefs Association has formed a private security committee. The committee is composed of security managers from a number of companies, including Fortune 500 companies (Cain, et al., p. 25, 1993). The call for increased use of private security to assist the police has come from scholarly sources as well. The police and community would benefit from the assistance of security and thereby allow the police more control over the security industry. In other words, instead of harassing and resisting the security industry, the police need to coordinate efforts in order to meet the community crime challenges (Sherman, 1983).

The growth of private protection is attributed to the rising incidents of workplace crime, funding problems in the public sector, fear of lawsuits for inadequate protection, and the growing realization by the public of the availability of protection measures. In five states, the leading cause of death is murder in the workplace. The tragic slayings by disgruntled employees and others in post offices and other public buildings suggest a need to increase security measures. Particularly at high risk are people working with valuables or money in the retail setting (*Los Angeles Times*, Nov. 29, 1993).

In order for community policing to be effective, there must be increased use of private security; however, it is recognized that private security officers are not trained as well as the police. There is a fear that many security officers are simply thugs in uniform. This perception has some validity. There are trends to upgrade security professionalism, specifically in the training domain. In New York, the legislature in 1992 studied a bill that would establish new mandatory training, licensing, and registration requirements for private security officers employed as contract or proprietary officers. In the same year, there was a bill before the Virginia legislature providing campus security officers the same powers as the police.

Although a number of states mandate security training, the protection industry lacks serious regulation. There are federal legislative efforts to improve the security industry. These efforts are referred to as the Gore-Martinez training proposals. The bills would not only standardize the training of private security officers in every state but also mandate examination, certification, classroom instruction, and on the job training for security officers. The 1992 Martinez bill, referred to as House Bill 5931, is more specific than the 1991 Gore Bill, in that it provides for specialized training in such areas as law and patrol procedures.

The third approach to meeting the community policing need is the utilization of police reserves and cadet programs stressing higher education. Many law enforcement agencies utilize the services of citizen-reserve officers. In Los Angeles, for example, candidates for the reserve corps must undergo the same pre-service training as regular police officers. Reserves are required to volunteer their services every month, without pay. Communities need to recruit qualified citizens to serve as reserves. As in the teaching and nursing profession, funds must be set aside to pay citizens on a per diem basis to assist the police in meeting the community crime challenges.

Reserve programs provide a quality pool of officers. There is a need to pass legislation where these officers are paid for their part-time services. In many cities, high school youths begin their police careers in cadet or explorer programs. However, New York City allows youth as young as sixteen to take the written exam for a police officer. Those students who pass the exam, and stay out of trouble, are guaranteed a job when they reach the appropriate age (Osborn, 1992:23).

There is a movement to recruit qualified candidates by offering grants for educational expenses. The New York City Cadet Corps program pays $3,000 toward a cadet's last two years of college. After graduation, the student must serve two years with the police department in order to pay the loan in full. There is a need to hire more college educated officers. While there is no conclusive evidence that college educated officers make better officers, there is some evidence that they are more efficient and are less likely to use force than noncollege educated officers (Carter, 1989). The success of community policing depends upon the use of citizens, security officers, and quasi-professionals to perform certain law enforcement tasks freeing the police for more serious problems.

DOMESTIC VIOLENCE AND THE POLICE

Domestic violence accounts for a significant proportion of calls for police service. It is a problem that pervades every community. Domestic violence includes injuries to married, separated, divorced, and cohabiting couples. While males can be victims of domestic violence, this aggression is usually directed against females. Verbal threats are also considered abusive, but are less likely to result in police intervention (Hirschel et al., 1992:250). There has been an inconsistent response by law enforcement to domestic violence complaints. Reasons for this ambivalence are grounded in policing attitudes about the seriousness of these cases, and the reluctance of the police to intervene into private matters. Thus, there is a form of unofficial approval of violence (Gelles and Straus, 1988:25).

However, since the 1970s, increased attention in domestic violence cases has surfaced. The police are undergoing training in crisis intervention and other types of violence reduction programs. These training programs are necessary given that between 25 and 30% of couples will experience a violent incident in their lifetime. Although domestic violence incidents cut across all socioeconomic classes, the poor and undereducated are most often represented in these cases (Hamberger and Hastings, 1988). It is clear that one of the major problems in domestic violence matters is under reporting. Fearing social disapproval or embarrassment, the middle-class and upper-class are less likely to report these offenses than are nonwhite and lower income women (Schulman, 1979).

In the past, domestic violence calls received low police priority (U.S. Commission on Civil Rights, 1982). Police usually viewed these calls as a nuisance and typically left after advising the parties to keep the peace. In recent years, the police have undergone training in crisis intervention and mediation, but there is little evidence that such training has reduced the police handling of these complaints (Oppenzander, 1982).

A further problem concerns the attitudes of the police. Generally, the police did not welcome these changes often viewing domestic violence training as social work. A number of women's groups filed suits demanding that the police take a more responsive and proactive role in enforcing domestic violence laws. These suits filed on behalf of women victims were based on the denial of due process and equal protection of the law. In other words, in some situations, the police have a duty to the victim to respond in a timely manner to domestic violence complaints. This duty is based on a special relationship to the victim, when there is evidence that violence is directed at another, and the police have been notified but fail to respond (*Thurman v. City of Torrington* 1984; *Balistreri v. Pacifica Police Department* 1990).

The current law enforcement movement in addressing domestic violence is termed preferred arrest. In other words, a number of state statutes have been revised providing the police with broader arrest powers. In 1983, twenty-seven states expanded police arrest powers in domestic violence cases. (Lerman et al., 1983:44). In 1986, six states passed laws requiring arrest with probable cause and the presence of the offender (Ferraro, 1989:61). However, the victim must have signs of physical injury. The police are also asked to arrest abusers who have violated protection orders. Currently, forty-eight states have such orders (Finn and Colson, 1990). In ten states, violation of these orders must result in an arrest. Thus, statutory law is limiting police discretion in domestic abuse matters.

The police arrest policy as a means of addressing domestic violence gained support from the Minneapolis domestic violence study (Sherman and Berk, 1984). The study conducted in 1981-82 was the first to test the deterrent effect of arrest in spousal abuse cases. In this experiment, police arriving to the scene of a domestic violence complaint were assigned one of three responses: (1) advising the couple; (2) separating the couple by ordering the offender to leave the scene for a few hours; and (3) arresting the offender. After a six-month follow-up, it was revealed that arresting the offender resulted in fewer repeat offenses than the other responses.

The study concluded that arrest was more effective in deterring repeat violence. Although there were problems with the study methodology, the finding received national attention and is credited with the movement toward police arrests as the preferred response in domestic violence cases. The validity of arrest as a preferred response was further tested by additional research funded by the National Institute of Justice. The studies conducted in six cities (Omaha; Atlanta; Colorado Springs; Dade County, Florida; Milwaukee; and Charlotte) tested the arrest hypothesis.

Although there was a difference in research designs, the results generally indicated that arrest was not found to be a deterrent to domestic violence. There were a number of reasons for these conclusions, including the fact that some offenders had criminal histories and that arrests are not a new or unusual experience (Dunford et al., 1990:194; Hirschel et al., 1991:37; Sherman et al., 1991:827). More recent research in Dade County, Florida, however, suggests that mandatory arrest practice does have a deterrent effect on employed suspects. Thus, those offenders who are employed or part of the workforce have more to lose than their unemployed counterparts, and are less likely to repeat their abusive patterns (Pate and Hamilton, 1992:691-697).

The future of police responses to domestic violence is not limited to stricter laws and more arrests. As in the community policing concept, a coordinated community response approach to the problem is needed. Spousal abusers, like a number of other violent offenders, suffer from social and/or psychological disorders which rehabilitation or prison confinement is unable to cure. Unless legislation is passed requiring mandatory long term sentencing for abusers, many abusers will leave jail and repeat their crimes. As part of the tough crime control legislation efforts, there is a bill before congress requiring mandatory life sentencing for those convicted of three violent crimes; however, there are doubts that this bill will pass (*Congressional Quarterly*, 1993:3200).

Congress is currently considering other punitive approaches. The House Judiciary Committee proposed several crime bills in 1993. The committee approved a measure to establish new legislation aimed at reducing domestic violence. Under the proposed 1993 bill, referred to as HR 1133, the measure would require the police to arrest in cases of domestic violence. The bill would also create a new federal crime for stalkers and provide education programs for judges dealing with domestic violence cases.

As with many other offenses, the punitive response of arrest and imprisonment is often the preferred approach. For many offenders, these approaches are necessary. If for no other reason, these social outcasts will be temporarily out of "the business of abusing." The trends in most states suggest that arrest be the preferred police response, regardless of research findings questioning the value of this approach. However, arrest is only one part of the justice response. Community efforts after the arrest may dictate the success of programs designed to deter domestic violence. An example of a community response program is the Duluth, Minnesota Domestic Abuse Intervention Project. This project coordinates the efforts of nine law enforcement, criminal justice, and human service agencies. In other words, after an arrest, other agencies intervene providing victim/offender counseling and so forth (Pence, 1983:258-59).

In California, legislation requires the police to arrest anyone inflicting injury to a spouse or to persons of the opposite sex who are cohabitating. The infliction of injury is a felony punishable of up to four years in prison. However, there must be visible injury, not verbal injury (Penal Code Section 273.5). Upon conviction, where probation is granted, the law in California requires the abuser to participate in a batterer's treatment program. This treatment is designed to address the abuser's propensity for violence; in other words, to address the cause of violence rather than treat the symptoms. The role of counseling is introduced to both the victim and the abuser.

The legislative intent in California, as in a number of other states, is to identify domestic violence as a community problem. Spousal abusers are recognized as a "clear and present danger to the citizens." The legislature further finds that the concept of vertical prosecution in which a trained deputy district attorney or prosecution unit is assigned to a case from its filing to its completion is an effective way to assure that abusers are convicted and sentenced (California Penal Code: 273.8). There is a welcome trend to protect the victims. It is a misdemeanor in California to disclose the location of domestic violence shelters or safe houses without the authorization of that shelter (California Penal Code: 273.7). The protection of the victim after an arrest is a high priority.

Another legal approach to enhance the law enforcement role are restraining orders. Most states allow victims to obtain these protection orders if there is evidence of harassment, threats, and so forth. Violation of a protection order is a misdemeanor; however, if the victim suffers injury, the law requires that the abuser serve forty-eight hours in jail whether or not a fine, jail term, or other punishment is imposed (California Penal Code: 273.6(b)). The problem and treatment of domestic violence are clearly becoming an integrated justice problem solving approach. In 1994, California has several new laws addressing domestic violence. State marriage fees have increased from $19 to $23 to help finance domestic violence prevention programs. Another new law prohibits any person from owning a firearm for ten years, upon conviction of spousal abuse or violating a court protection order. In addition, husbands who rape their wives are subject to the same prison penalties as other rapists, and conviction can result in imprisonment for a period of three, six, or eight years (California Penal Code Section 264).

The role of technology is entering the domestic violence arena. In Delaware, there is an experiment with seven county police departments where women who are potential victims of physical abuse have installed silent alarms in their homes. The alarms are installed by a security alarm company and are activated by pressing a button in the home or are triggered by pressing a button on a necklace. As can be seen from the discussion, the police are becoming more proactive in terms of training and arrest practices. The responsibility of the police will be to respond quickly to spousal abuse incidents. Upon arrival, the police are accountable for controlling the situation.

However, the response doesn't stop with arrest. Legislation has been enacted in some states to assure that both the offender and victim receive the appropriate assistance. While it can be criticized that arrest practices are not effective in deterring domestic violence, arrests are valuable in bringing to the attention the problem of violence. In other words, arrest is just the first step in the justice process. The arrest is not always viewed as a punitive response, but could serve as the catalyst for offender/victim treatment. In any event, the laws in some states are getting tougher on those who physically abuse their spouses.

CONTROLLING THE POLICE

While there are increasing trends to promote and expand community policing, and address problems such as domestic violence, the police will continually be scrutinized by the community and the courts. It is understandable that the police will make mistakes; but they may not always be at fault for their actions. If the public expects more proactive community oriented policing, then there is a risk of the police abusing their authority in carrying out their crime control mandates. Most police departments have some form of administrative control of their officers. Some agencies have civilian review boards that review allegations of police misconduct and other policy matters. However, only about 17% of the 132 largest cities have a citizen board (Walker, 1991). Most departments have internal review boards consisting of officers who investigate misconduct of other officers. Regardless of the method of review, the police can expect increased public scrutiny especially when the police are accused of corruption or serious misconduct.

The Rodney King incident in Los Angeles resulted in the formation of the 1991 Christopher Commission investigation, which recommended a number of policy changes within the department. This type of investigation illustrates how civilians can influence the policy making of a police agency. Following on the heels of the Christopher report was the Kolt's report (1992) of the L.A. County Sheriff's Department. This report, like the Christopher report, was critical of the sheriff's office on matters concerning use of force, hiring, and supervision and other procedural concerns. Other than internal administrative controls and civilian reviews, two legal methods of controlling police conduct are civil litigation and the exclusionary rule. These methods are expected to continue in the future, but with varying results. Unless the police are totally irresponsible, or act without just cause or good faith, their actions, however inappropriate to some, are usually defensible. The courts generally favor police practices, as long as the police do not "break the rules."

CIVIL LIABILITY IN POLICING

The police are confronted with enormous pressures daily. The impact of the Rodney King incident left many citizens wondering if the behavior of the four L.A. Police Officers was a planned response, or a demonstration of atypical police behavior. The police can be held liable for inappropriate or wrongful behavior, regardless of their intention. Law suits brought against the police can be filed in either state or federal courts.

One of the most common approaches of suing the police for misconduct is under federal law. There are several statutes that allow citizens to file actions against the police. However, the most common is referred to as Title 42 of the United States Codes, Section 1983. This law has its roots in the early civil rights act of 1871, which is also referred to as the Ku Klux Klan Act. The law was written to protect citizens against the violence of the Klan. The law has been expanded to allow citizens to bring suit against law enforcement officers, police agencies, and municipalities. Title 42 of the United States Codes, Section 1983, reads:

> Every person who, under color of any statute, ordinance, regulation, cus-tom, or usage, of any State or Territory, subjects, or causes to be subjected, any citizens of the United States or other person within the jurisdiction thereof to the deprivation of any rights, privileges, or immunities secured by the Constitution and laws, shall be liable to the party injured in an action at law, suited in equity, or other proper proceeding for redress.

The application of Section 1983 became entrenched in *Monroe v. Pape*, 365 U.S. 167 (1961). The Monroe case held that a Section 1983 case can be brought against the police any time a constitutional right is violated, whether or not the officer was acting within authorized limits. The Monroe case opened the door to a flurry of lawsuits against the police, and is currently a popular remedy for a number of reasons. It is expected that this type of action will be used extensively in the future. The popularity of this type of suit as opposed to state actions, is based on the following reasons: first, civil lawsuits are filed in federal court, where discovery is often more liberal than in state courts. This process makes it easier for the plaintiff, or the injured party, to obtain the necessary records and documents from the defendant. Secondly, suits filed in federal courts do not have to exhaust state remedies, thus reducing delays in the justice process. Another reason for filing in federal court is that the prevailing plain-tiff may recover attorney's fees under the Attorney's Fee Act of 1976. In other words, if the case has merit, attorneys are more inclined to accept cases where their fees can be paid by the defendant police officer or agency.

Civil rights lawsuits are used by plaintiffs even though there are also criminal sanctions available. In other words, 1983 suits can be filed whether or not a criminal action is initiated. Civil lawsuits normally follow criminal actions. However, prosecu-tors may be reluctant to file cases against police officers, or grand juries may not be inclined to indict officers, unless there has been some gross or blatant conduct. Therefore, 1983 actions are filed since only a preponderance of evidence is required to prove wrongdoing, rather than beyond a reasonableness as in criminal cases.

There are two basic requirements for a Section 1983 lawsuit. First, the defen-dant must be acting under color of the law; second, there must be a constitutional violation or violation of some federally protected right. The first requirement requires that the defendant officer be performing an act of public authority. This means that the on-duty officer is performing an act lawfully or unlawfully. Police officers who arrest without probable cause, or administer excessive force, are misus-ing their authority under the color of law. Committing unlawful acts while on duty (e.g. sexual assaults) can fall under this principle. The second requirement refers to violations of protected rights. Some examples are fourth and fifth amendment viola-tions or police actions violating a person's due process rights. Thus, an officer who maliciously beats a prisoner or denies an arrestee needed medical treatment would fall under this principle.

Civil liability under state law is divided into intentional tort and negligent tort. An intentional tort is a commission of an act of which an officer intended. An officer who falsely detains another, or uses unreasonable force resulting in injury is committing an intentional tort. Intentional torts result from a wanton disregard for a person's rights. In contrast, negligence is the failure to act or to do something that ought to be done.

Negligence generally occurs when an officer fails to protect the public from harm or injury such as in the case of failure to respond to 911 calls. For negligence under state law to prevail, four elements must be met:

1. There must be a duty on the part of the defendant police officer.
2. There was a failure to perform that duty.
3. There is a proximate cause or relationship between the duty and failure to perform.
4. There is actual damage or injury to the person.

There are a number of court cases that illustrate negligence. In *Sorichetti v. City of New York*, 484 N.E., 2d 70 (1985), for example, a judgment for two million dollars against the New York Police Department was upheld for failing to protect a child who was under an order of protection issued by the court. In this case, the police, knowing that a father was in custody of his child in violation of a court order, failed to intervene at the request of the mother. The child was later attacked by the father and severely injured.

In *Irwin v. Town of Ware*, 467 N.E. 2d 1292 (1984), the court found that the police had a duty to arrest a drunk driver as required by state statute. The police stopped a drunk driver but failed to make an arrest, resulting in the driver subsequently injuring the plaintiff. In both of these cases, negligence was established because of a special relationship between the police and the plaintiff. The special relationship was established by statute.

In general, the police are not legally obligated to protect an individual from harm. The public duty doctrine holds that the police owe a duty to the public, and not specific individuals. This doctrine was established by the U.S. Supreme Court in *South v. Maryland*, 59 U.S. 396 (1896). The public duty doctrine prevails in most states, but is not without controversy. In *Simack v. Risely*, 804 F. 2d 143 (1986), a seventh circuit decision ruled that the police were not liable for failing to assist a woman who was robbed during an undercover police surveillance. The police owed no duty to protect the woman since there was no special relationship established, or expectation by her for police assistance. The police waited until the attack occurred before they intervened. The court reasoned that being in a position to observe did not make the police liable for the attack.

If a plaintiff feels that there is a constitutional right to protect, then a 1983 action can be filed in federal court. However, it is difficult to establish liability under federal law. The landmark case in this regard is *DeShaney v. Winnebago County Department of Social Services*, 57 U.S.L.W. 4218 (1989). In this case, a four-year old was beaten and seriously injured by his father who had custody of the child after a divorce. Despite a number of complaints by the boy's mother that the child was being abused, the social service agency took various steps to protect the boy, but did not remove him from the father's custody. The agency knew that the boy was being abused. The father was later convicted of the crime. A law suit was filed alleging that the boy's due process right was violated under the constitution. The Supreme Court ruled that the due process clause does not impose a duty to protect an individual not in state custody. The boy was in the custody of his father.

The use of force is one of the most common suits brought against the police. The police are entitled to use nondeadly or deadly force if the situation allows it. The use of force must be reasonable and appropriate. Otherwise, as seen in the Rodney King incident, the police can be tried criminally under state or federal law. After being acquitted for state charges, two Los Angeles police officers were later convicted in federal court. However, as of this writing, the civil portion of the King case is still pending.

The landmark case on police use of deadly force is *Tennessee v. Garner*, 471 U.S. 1, (1985). The case limited the broad shooting discretion used by the police in some jurisdictions. In other words, police officers may not shoot any fleeing felon. The use of deadly force may only be used when a fleeing felon poses a serious physical threat or risk to others. Despite this limitation, the courts recognize the need for the police to use force in split second decisions (*Graham v. Conner* (1989)).

In *Smith v. Freland* (1992), the courts balanced the behavior of the police with the need of the situation. In this case, the police shot and killed a suspect in a high speed chase. The police were sued for excessive force, but prevailed. The court opined that the police must make instantaneous decisions under very threatening circumstance.

The number of lawsuits filed against the police continues to grow. A survey of police chiefs from the twenty largest cities with populations over 100 thousand revealed that most officers and supervisors have been sued in the past and expect to be defendants in the future (McCoy, 1987). The survey revealed that the litigations most often brought against the police are:

1. use of force
2. auto pursuits
3. arrests/searches
4. employee drug tests
5. hiring and promotion
6. discrimination based on race, sex, or age
7. record keeping and privacy
8. jail management

In Houston, Texas, the number of complaints filed against the police increased by 245% from 1980 to 1985 (*The Houston Chronicle*, August 8, 1986). However, while the number of the lawsuits filed against the police continues to increase, the number of cases imposing liability against the police is low (de Carmen, 1991:3). The number of complaints filed against the police will rise in the future. This increase will be due in part to public awareness of their rights, and the stress of policing, where officers may employ force unnecessarily. A survey of police officers indicates that there is fear of being sued by the public. Some officers experienced stress when another officer was sued (Scogin and Brodsky, 1991).

Recent research has indicated that the number of cases brought against the police for civil rights (1983) actions is continuing. In a study by Kappeler, et al. (1993), there were 1,359 section 1983 actions brought against the police between 1978 and

1990. Most claims were for false arrest, excessive force, and search and seizure violations. While the police prevail in over 50% of the cases, there are expenses in defending these cases, as well as negative publicity and morale problems.

In response to the threat of civil liability, police departments are making changes
in policies and practices. These changes reflect current movements to increase professionalism and accountability. The crime picture for the future looks bleak. The
police will be expected to be more proactive and aggressive.

As discussed, some laws are being revised requiring the police to arrest in some
situations (e.g. domestic violence). The movement toward community policing may
also create more civil liability problems. In other words, as the police assume a more
proactive role in community crime control, there may be situations where the police
exceed their role. Mandatory arrest policies, for example, may increase the likelihood
of violence or abuse initiated against or by the police. In response to these threats, the
police need to recruit persons representative of the community, and to prepare these
officers to respond to community problems. Police managers must plan now for
future recruitment and training. It is expected that there will be rapid changes in the
demographics of our population. According to Trojanowicz and Carter (1991), "by the
year 2010, more than one third of all American children will be Black, Hispanic, or
Asian." Thus, Caucasians will become a minority within America in less than one hundred years. There is a need to recruit more women into the police ranks. During the
next ten years, it is anticipated that women will dominate the workforce. The need to
hire additional women may reduce the problem of civil litigation. One study suggests
that women are less likely to use force, are less likely to seriously injure a citizen, are
no more likely to suffer injuries, and are more emotionally stable (Grennan, 1988).

In the future, recruitment will focus on multilevel assessments for recruiting
police officers. In other words, the emphasis will be on screening out undesirable candidates through a variety of measurements. The assessment center approach utilizes
intelligence tests, paper-pencil tests, and role playing exercises to evaluate a person's
capabilities and decision making abilities. The assessment center approach provides
evaluators with an understanding on how the candidate will react under stressful situations. Persons successfully completing the assessment phase will be eligible for
employment. Reports on the effectiveness of the assessment approach in selecting
police officers have been documented (Pynes and Bernardin, 1992). The assessment
approach focuses on measuring the candidate's perception, decision making decisive-
ness, ability to direct others, adaptability to policing, oral communications, interpersonal skills, and written communications. This recruitment approach is becoming
more popular and is expected to gain in popularity in the future.

In addition to comprehensive recruitment programs, quality police training is
necessary to assure the effectiveness and performance of police officers. Not only must
the police receive training in traditional topics such as firearms and patrol procedures,
but training must focus on communication skills, cultural relations, and an understanding of ethnic diversity. Police departments are undergoing training in verbal judo,
which is training on the proper use of language as opposed to forcing a physical confrontation. Many police agencies are requiring officers to undergo this training.

The New York and Los Angeles police departments have instituted training on
gay and lesbian issues. The Los Angeles Police Department requires officers to com-

plete training in conversational Spanish. In some cities recruit officers are assigned to work in prosecutors' offices, public defenders' offices, and placed with judges to learn about the complexities of sentencing (McCampbell, 1986). Police training in the future will become more holistic and humanistic, incorporating decision making exercises, not just rudimentary "how to" training that stresses only tactics and procedures.

THE EXCLUSIONARY RULE AND POLICING

The U.S. Constitution prohibits unreasonable searches and seizures of people, houses, and personal property. The Fourth Amendment provides:

> The right of the people to be secure in their persons, houses, papers, and effects, against unreasonable searches and seizures, shall not be violated, and no warrant shall issue, but upon probable cause, supported by oath or affirmation, and particularly describing the place to be searched, and the persons or things to be seized.

Although violation of the rule is not a major problem in policing, it comes into play when a court determines that a search or seizure was unreasonable. Under the rule, which was created to encourage proper police conduct, evidence that results from an illegal (unreasonable) search or seizure is excluded at trial. It is suppressed (inadmissible), and cannot be brought to the jury's attention.

A major case involving the exclusionary rule is *Mapp v. Ohio* (1961). The Mapp case specifically required the states to exclude from trials evidence that had been seized illegally by the police. In other words, the police need a warrant based upon probable cause to search a premises, vehicle, or individual. However, it is not always possible to get a warrant every time the police encounter a situation in which there may be contraband. Consequently, there are judicially interpreted exceptions to the warrant requirement. These exceptions or attacks on the exclusionary rule began about 1970. Since that time, there have been a number of cases limiting the scope of the exclusionary rule. There are a number of cases that have limited the intent of the exclusionary rule; however, only a few significant cases are discussed.

Following the "rights for the offenders trend" of the 1960s, the Supreme Court has been gradually chipping away at an offender's Fourth Amendment. The conservative Burger and Rehnquist courts have granted the police additional search and seizure exceptions to the warrant requirement. In 1961, the court in *Mapp v. Ohio* allowed the police to "pat down suspicious persons." In this case, the court ruled that if the police have cause to believe that a person may be armed, and for officer safety, the police can perform a limited search for weapons. In the 1966 case of *Schmerber v. California*, the court allowed the police to use blood samples taken from a drunk driver who was involved in an accident, despite the fact that the driver did not give consent.

The 1970s introduced further erosion to the exclusionary rule. In *Cupp v. Murphy* (1973), the court allowed evidence to be used against a defendant arrested for strangling his wife. Despite his refusal, the police scraped the defendant's fingernails for blood residue before being placed under arrest. One of the exceptions of the search warrant requirement is consent of the citizen. In other words, unless the police have other causes for conducting a search, a citizen has a right to refuse a police search.

In *Schneckloth v. Bustamonte* (1973), the police stopped a car for a traffic violation. After the stop, the police asked the occupants if they could search the vehicle. The occupants consented, and the officers recovered evidence of a theft. The occupants were convicted but appealed their conviction on the grounds that the police did not tell them that they had a right to refuse. The Supreme Court upheld the conviction.

Once a person is arrested and placed into police custody, the police may perform a full scale search of his person. Any evidence discovered by the police, even though unrelated to the initial crime, may be used against the defendant. This was the decision in *United States v. Robinson* (1973). In *Rakas v. Illinois* (1978), the Supreme Court permitted evidence against an occupant of a car. In this case, the passenger Rakas was arrested for robbery. Even though the police conducted an illegal search resulting in the conviction of Rakas, he had no standing to object to the search because he was only a passenger.

In the 1980s, the assault on the exclusionary rule continued. In *Illinois v. Gates* (1983), the Supreme Court ruled that the search and subsequent conviction of two drug dealers based entirely upon an anonymous letter sent to the police (accompanied with police surveillance) was permissible. The court departed from earlier precedent that required corroboration from informants to justify the issuance of a search warrant.

One of the most serious assaults on the Mapp case and the exclusionary rule is *United States v. Leon* (1984). In Leon, the Supreme Court established the so called "good faith" exception to the exclusionary rule. In other words, if the police conduct a search with a defective warrant, the evidence obtained is still admissible if the police honestly believed that the warrant was valid.

The court has ruled that there is no privacy protection in open fields. In *Oliver v. United States* (1984), narcotics agents relying on a tip, and without a warrant, observed marijuana growing in an open field. The county ruled that there was no expectation to privacy even though there was posted a no trespassing sign on the property. In *California v. Greenwood* (1988), a warrantless police search of garbage placed on the curb for collection was admissible, despite defendant objections that the garbage was subject to privacy protection.

The conservative trend of the Supreme Court is continuing its march into the 1990s. In *Illinois v. Rodriguez* (1990), the police entered a home without a warrant. The police were granted entry by a person who was victimized by the defendant (the victim did not reside at the home). Upon entry, the police observed drugs that led to the arrest of the defendant. The trial court excluded the evidence based upon the warrantless entry; however, the Supreme Court ruled that the police had a good basis for entering because the woman said she lived there. In other words, the police were acting under good faith.

In *Maryland v. Buie* (1990), the Supreme Court extended the right of the police to conduct protective sweep searches of closets and other rooms near the area where a defendant is arrested. This ruling extends the right of the police to protect themselves from harm while making an arrest in a home. Within these protective sweeps, any evidence observed can be used against the defendant.

The problem of drunk driving has created a serious safety problem to the public. In response, the police have instituted checkpoints to detect drunk drivers. Drivers stopped and detained at these checkpoints have raised fourth amendment claims. In

Michigan v. Sitz (1990), the Supreme Court ruled that the fourth amendment does not apply to drivers stopped and detained at these checkpoints.

In a recent Supreme Court decision, the court again tackled the issue of pedestrian searches. In *Minnesota v. Dickenson* (1993), the court ruled that the police pat-down of a suspect revealing drugs was admissible. In this case, the police patted down a suspect for weapons. During the pat-down, the officer felt a soft object in the suspect's pocket. The officer seized the item that turned out to be illegal narcotics. The court agreed that the officer's "sense of touch" justified seizing the contraband, even though there was no other reason to suspect that the suspect had narcotics. In short, the case further expanded the Terry decision allowing the police to retrieve items suspected of being weapons or contraband.

The courts do have limits on how far they will go in allowing the police to search. In *Winston v. Lee* (1985), the Supreme Court ruled that the police seizure of a bullet taken from a robbery suspect violated the defendant's Fourth Amendment rights. In this case, a robbery suspect was shot by the victim, arrested by the police, and taken to a hospital where the bullet was extracted to be used as evidence against the accused. The court ruled that the surgery violated the defendant's right to privacy.

The famed Miranda warning is another area that has seen some erosion. As in search and seizure cases, the courts have allowed the police to exceed certain limits as long as their tactics were reasonable and/or in good faith. Under the Miranda rule, the police must advise a suspect of his/her rights before asking incriminating questions or seeking confessions. Suspects must make reasonable waivers before discussing their involvement in a crime. Yet, the courts have allowed the police to use trickery and deceit to obtain incriminating evidence. In *Holland v. McGinnis* (1992), the police told a suspect that his vehicle was seen at the scene of a crime (a lie). The suspect confessed and the court ruled that the confession was admissible. In a related case, a suspect was told that his fingerprints were found at a crime scene (another lie), tricking the suspect into confessing. The court ruled in this case that the police tactic was permissible (*State v. Haywood*, 1989).

In *Ahmad A. v. Supreme Court* (1989), a juvenile suspect in police custody for murder asked to have a private visit with his mother in the police interrogation room. The youth confessed to his mother his involvement in a killing. The conversation was recorded and the statements used against the youth. The court ruled that there is no expectation to privacy in police custody, and the statements are admissible. In other words, the court adopted the concept that the "walls have ears," and that there is no expectation to privacy in police custody. There are limits as to how far the court will go in permitting police to obtain a confession. When the police threaten a suspect with physical violence, a subsequent confession will not be admitted (*Cooper v. Scroggy* 1985). However, threatening a suspect to add additional charges unless the defendant confesses is not always inadmissible. Thus, a little threat is permissible as long as it is not physical (*Lindsey v. Smith*, 1987).

There are also trends by legislatures, and proposals by governors in several states, to weaken exclusionary rule laws (Glick, 1993:436). In California, for example, the voters passed proposition eight in 1982 that allows the use of evidence even though it violated the California Constitution (but not the Federal Constitution). It is unlikely that the exclusionary rule or Miranda warnings will be abolished. However, there will continue to be cases where defendants will find it difficult to challenge police practices as long as the police continue to act reasonably. As long as violent crime continues, and society continues to be threatened by ill-intentioned individuals, the courts will follow the path of law and order allowing the justice system greater leeway in using evidence to convict criminals.

CONCLUSIONS

There are indeed challenges for the police in the years ahead. As society experiences more violence from within the household or from the streets, more pressure will be placed upon the police to respond. Generally, there is a cry for more punitive approaches to counter violence. These approaches may not solve the underlying social ills resulting from rampant drug use, gangs, unemployment and so forth. But punitive legislation, aggressive policing, and an integrated community/justice response can reduce the threat of victimization. The police will need help from the community in order to meet the crime problem. There is a welcome trend from the courts and legislatures to warn criminals that enough is enough and violence will not be tolerated in the community. The rights of citizens must take precedence over the rights of the criminals, even if the police need to bend the rules. In other words, a utilitarian enforcement philosophy is needed which may require curbing legal escapes for factually guilty offenders.

STUDY QUESTIONS

1. Discuss the strengths and weaknesses of community policing, and the requirement for an effective community policing program.
2. Evaluate the preferred arrest policy in domestic violence cases utilized by a number of jurisdictions.
3. Discuss how the police can be sued under the federal civil rights law.
4. Identify how the police in the future will be held more accountable and responsible for procedure and policy.
5. Discuss the advantages and disadvantages of retaining the exclusionary rule.

SOURCES

Blumstein, Alfred, Jacqueline Cohen, Susan E. Martin, and Michael H. Tonry, eds. (1983). *Research on Sentencing: The Search for Reform*, Vol. 1. Washington, DC: National Academy Press.

Cain, Candy M., et al. (1993). "No Agency Is an Island," *Security Management*, December: 25-28.

Carter, D.L. (1984). "Theoretical Dimensions in the Abuse of Authority by Police Officers" *Police Studies.*

Carter, D.L. (1991). "Your Education and Minority Recruitment: The Impact of a College Requirement," Washington, D.C. Police Executive Research Forum.

Carter, D.L. (1993). "Tough Minded Senate Adopts Crime Crackdown Package" *Congressional Quarterly*, November 20.

Corwin, Miles, "Guns For Hire." *Los Angeles Times Magazine*, 28 November 1993.

Crime Control Digest. 1993, Vol 27:1

Crime Control Digest. *1993, Vol 27:32.*

delCarmen, Roland V. (1991). *Civil Liabilities in American Policing,* Prentice Hall: NJ.

Donahue, Michael E. (1993). "A Comprehensive Program to Combat Violent Crime: The Savannah Experience," *Police Chief,* September: 9.

Dunford, Franklyn W. (1990). "System Initiated Warrants for Suspects of Misdemeanor Domestic Violence: A Pilot Study" *Justice Quarterly* 7:631-53 Foundation.

Ent, Carl Lt. and James E. Hendricks (1991). "Bicycle Patrol: A Community Policing Alternative," *The Police Chief,* November: 58-60.

Ferraro, Kathleen J. (1989). "Policing Women Battering," *Social Problems* 36:61-74.

Finn, Peter and Sarah Colson. (1990). "Civil Protection Orders: Legislation Current Court Practice, and Enforcement," Washington DC: U.S. Dept. of Justice.

Gelles, Richard J. and Murray A Straus. (1988). *Intimate Violence* (New York: Simon and Schuster).

Glick, Henry R. (1993). Courts, Politics and Justice (New York: McGraw Hill).

Goldstein, Herman. (1990). *Problem Oriented Policing* USA: McGraw-Hill Inc.

Goulds, California Penal Code Handbook. (1993). Gould Publishing Co.: Longwood, FL.

Grennan S. (1988). Findings on the Role of Officer Gender in Violent Encounters With Citizens," *Journal of Police Science and Administration,* 15: 78-85.

Hamberger, L. Kevin and James Hastings. (1988). "Characteristics of Male Spouse Abusers Consistent With Personality Disorder," *Hospital and Community Psychiatry* 39: 763-70.

Hirschel, David et al. (1992). "Review Essay on the Law Enforcement Response to Spousal Abuse: Past, Present, and Future", *Justice Quarterly* 9:2.

Hirschel, David J., Ira W. Hutchison, Charles W. Dean, Joseph J. Kelley and Carolyn E. Pesackis. (1991). *Charlotte Spouse Assault Replication Project: Final Report,* Washington DC: National Institute of Justice.

Kappeler, Victor E., Stephan F. Kappeler and Roland V. del Carmen. (1993). "Police civil liberty cases: Decisions of the Federal District courts 1978-1990." *Journal of Criminal Justice,* 21:4.

Kelling, George L., et al. (1988). *Perspectives on Policing: Police Accountability and Community Policing,* Washington DC: National Institute of Justice.

Kline, E.M. (1993). "Colorado Springs SHO/DI: Working Smarter With Juvenile Offenders," *Police Chief,* April.

Kolts, James G. and Staff. (1992). *A Report on The Los Angeles Country Sheriff's Department* (Los Angeles, CA).

Lerman, Lisa G, Leslie Landis and Sharin Goldweig. (1983). "State Legislation on Domestic Violence": In J.J. Costa, ed. *Abuse of Women: Legislation, Reporting, and Prevention,* Lexington, MA: Heath.

The Los Angeles Times, "Laws 1994," December 31, 1993.

McCampbell, Michael S. (1986). "Field Training for Police Officers: State Of The Art," (Washington DC: National Institute of Justice.

McCoy, C. (1987). "Police Legal Liability is Not a Crisis," *Crime Control Digest,* January: 1.

"Murder Leads Workplace Deaths in Five States," *Los Angeles Times,* 29 Nov. 1993.

Oppenlander, Nan. (1981). "The Evaluation of Law and Wife Abuse" *Law and Police Quarterly* 3:382-405.

Osborn, Ralph. (1992). "Police Recruitments Today's Standard—Tomorrow's Challenge," *FBI Law Enforcement Bulletin,* June: 21.

Pate, Anthony M., and Edwin E. Hamilton. (1992). "Formal and informal deterrence to domestic violence: The Dade County spouse assault experiment," *American Sociological Review,* Vol 57:5

Pence, Ellen. (1983). "The Duluth Domestic Abuse Investigation Project," *Hamline Law Review*, 6: 247-75.

Pynes, Joan and H. John Bernardin. (1992). "Entry level police selection: the assessment center as an alternative," *Journal of Criminal Justice*, 20:1.

Schulman, Mark. (1979). "A Survey of Spousal Violence Against Women in Kentucky," Washington DC: U.S. Department of Justice.

Scogin, F. and S.L. Brodsky. (1994). "Fear of Litigation Among Law Enforcement Officers." *American Journal of Police* 10:41-45.

Sherman, Lawrence W., et. al. (1991). "From Initial Deterrence to Long Term Escalation: Short Custody Arrest for Poverty Ghetto Domestic Violence," *Criminology* 29: 821-50.

Sherman, Lawrence W. and Richard A. Berk. (1984). *The Minneapolis Domestic Violence Experiment* Washington DC: Police Foundation.

Sherman, Lawrence W. (1983). "Patrol Strategies for the Police," In: *Crime Control and Public Policy*, Ed: James Q. Wilson, (ICS Press: San Francisco, CA).

"Tough Minded Senate Adopts Crime Crackdown Package." (1993). *Congressional Quarterly*, November: 20.

Trojanowicz, Robert and Bonnie Bucqueroux. (1990). *Community Policing—A Contemporary Perspective*, OH: Anderson Publishing.

U.S. Commission on Civil Rights. (1982). "Under the Rule of Thumb Battered Women and the Administration of Justice," Washington DC: U.S. Government Printing Office.

Walker, S. and V.W. Bumpus. (1991). *Civilian Review of the Police: A National Survey of the 50 Largest Cities*, University of Nebraska, Omaha.

Weston, Jim. (1993). "Community Policing: An Approach to Youth Gangs in a Medium-Sized City," *Police Chief*, August: 8.

Wilson, J.Q. and G. Delling. (1982). "Broken Windows...," *Atlantic Magazine* 249 (March): 29-38.

Zappile, Richard A. (1991). "Philadelphia Implements Security Watch," *Police Chief*, August.

CASES

Ahmad A. v. Superior Court, 263 Cal. Rptr. 747, (1989)

Balisteri v. Pacifica Police Department, 901 F.2d, 696, 9th Cir. (1990)

California v. Greenwood, 486 U.S. 35 (1988)

Cooper v. Scroggy, 848 F.2d 1385, (1985)

Cupp v. Murphy, 412 U.S. 291 (1973)

Deshaney v. Winnebago County Department of Social Services, 489 U.S. 189 (1989)

Graham v. Conner, 490 U.S. 386 (1989)

Holland v. McGinnis, 763 F.2d 1044 (1992)

Illinois v. Gates (1983)

Illinois v. Rodriguez, 110 S.Ct. 2793 (1990)

Irwin v. Town of Ware, 467 N.E. 2d. 1292, (Ma. 1984)

Lindsey v. Smith, 820 F.2d 1137 (1987)

Mapp v. Ohio, 367 U.S. 643 (1961)

Michigan Department of State Police v. Sitz, 110 S.Ct. 2481 (1990)

Minnesota v. Dickenson, 113 S.Ct. 2130 (1993)
Monroe v. Pape, 365 U.S., 167 (1961)
Rakas v. Illinois, 439 U.S. 128 (1978)
Schmerber v. California, 384 U.S. 757 (1966)
Schneckloth v. Bustamonte, 412 U.S. 218 (1973)
Simack v. Risely, 804 F. 2d 143 (7th Cir. 1986)
Smith v. Freland, 984 F.2d 343 (1992)
South v. Maryland, 59 U.S. (18 How.) 396 (1986)
State v. Haywood, 439 N.W. 2d 511, (1989)
Tennessee v. Garner, 471 U.S. 1 (1985)
Thurman v. City of Torrington, 595 F. Supp. 1521, D. Conn. (1984)
United States v. Leon, 82 U.S. 667 (1984)
United States v. Robinson, 414 U.S. 218 (1973)

CHAPTER 9

THE INFLUENCE OF "COMMUNITY" IN COMMUNITY POLICING IN THE TWENTY-FIRST CENTURY

Michael J. Palmiotto, Ph.D.

ABSTRACT

What influence will the "Community" have in community policing in the twenty-first century? The difficulty of projecting the influence of the "Community" on community policing lies with the fact that there exists limited concrete data that community policing is successful. Although community policing is in its infancy and will be evolving within the next decade it appears logical that some influences of community policing will be around in the twenty-first century.

Although gazing into the crystal ball of the future is nebulous, certain facets of the community policing concept will survive and have an impact on policing and crime control. The impact and influence of the "Community" on policing should grow and be greater than it was in the last decades of the twentieth century. This chapter reviews the influence of the "Community" on policing in the twenty-first century.

INTRODUCTION

In the last quarter of the twentieth century police practitioners have come to the realization that the traditional reactive approach to crimes already committed was not working and the development of a new police strategy was imperative. This new concept was to become known as "community policing." The philosophy of community-oriented policing grew out of police strategies known as team policing and mini-stations which were established in many of our cities during the 1960s and 1970s.

A driving force behind "community policing" was the desire to maintain the quality of neighborhoods on the part of citizens who lived in these neighborhoods and the police who had the legal authority to maintain social order in the neighborhoods. Former California Governor Pat Brown had this to say: "As I see it, the single greatest problem over the next twenty years will be keeping the quality of life in the state from deteriorating any further than it already has" (Brown, 1990, p. 8). Citizens' concern about the "quality of life" has influenced the police to examine the service orientation philosophy of community policing at the expense of the traditional law enforcement model. The average citizen has indicated his or her concern about incivilities that can often devastate a neighborhood.

Herman Goldstein, a noted police scholar of the late twentieth century, developed the concept of "problem-oriented policing," which compelled police officers to solve nuisance or crime problems. The problem-oriented philosophy became the foundation for the community-oriented approach to policing.

Under the community-oriented policing concept, the police are recognizing that they need the support of the community in order to solve crime. With crime on the rise, especially crimes of violence, the fear of crime has also increased. The big hope that community-oriented policing offered was that crime could be prevented and reduced. If the police were successful in these areas, the fear of crime would decline. The major question that has not been answered is whether community-oriented policing will be successful in keeping crime under control. Initially, there existed a wide approach to community-oriented policing, but eventually evaluation of community-oriented programs made it possible to select its most successful aspects. Both police administrators and line officers came to realize that community-oriented policing had to work if they were to obtain community support and cooperation. The police of the twentieth century became aware that they were only successful in solving crimes when the public cooperated by providing information that could lead to the arrest and conviction of law violators.

During the 1970s research on policing increased substantially. These findings indicated that the police must make a serious effort to work with people whom they were to serve and protect. The police could not deal with the crime problem alone. The citizen also had a role in preventing and controlling crime. The research of the latter twentieth century was an eye-opener for the police. The major research findings came to the following conclusions.

1. Increasing the numbers of police does not necessarily reduce crime rates, nor raise the proportion of crime solved.... Such social conditions as income, unemployment, population, and social heterogeneity are far more important predictors of variation in crime and clearance rate....

2. Randomized motorized patrolling neither reduces crime nor improves the chances of catching criminals....

3. Two-person cars neither reduce crime nor catch criminals more effectively than one-person cars. And police are no more likely to be injured in one-person cars....

4. Although saturation patrolling does reduce crime, it does so at the cost of displacing it to other areas....

5. The legendary "good collar" is a rare event. Even more rarely do police patrol confront a crime in progress....

6. Response time doesn't matter....

7. Criminal investigations are not very effective in solving crime.... (Manning, 1988, pp. 41-44).

CRIME PROBLEM

The last decades of the twentieth century saw a substantial increase in the crime rate in America. The final decade of the century saw violent crimes—which include murder, rape, robbery and aggravated assault—reach two million. The clearance rate for violent crimes hovered around 45%. In the 1990s the number of murders approached 25 thousand compared to eight thousand murders during the 1960s (a two-thirds increase in murders in a very short time span). With the increase in the number of murders, the police were less successful in solving them. The solvability rate was over 90% when there were eight thousand murders in our country. The solvability rate dropped to less than 70% when the number of murders approached 25 thousand. During this period the concept of serial murders evolved. A serial murderer is an individual who kills a number of people over a period of time. An accurate account of serial murderers on the loose in American society was unknown. This era also saw the evolution of the mass murderer, an individual who kills a number of people at the same time. Individuals have gone into fast food restaurants, shopping malls, and work places and killed whoever was in the area. The 1990s observed the initiation of the recreational murderer as an individual who kills for the sheer pleasure. Most of the murders committed were senseless, done for the sake of cruelty and without any feeling for the victim as a human being. Many of our murderers were juveniles who appeared to have no sense of the value of a human life.

The last decades of the twentieth century saw an increase in the use of drugs and their acceptance by large segments of our society. With the increase in the use and availability of drugs there was also an increase in the availability and use of firearms. Firearms were used in over 60% of the killings. Social scientists enumerate several factors that may contribute to the violence:

- Increase in drug use has spurred deadly competition among rival drug suppliers.

- The growth of juvenile gang activity has further promoted the subculture of violence, particularly within the inner cities.

- The general disintegration of the family and the community as value-stamping mechanisms may be leaving young people with a limited sense of traditional moral direction; consequently, they may be more likely to engage in instinctual violence.

- Though we decry its use in our own homes and neighborhoods, Americans' cultural values glorify violence in a number of areas (i.e. sporting events, television, cartoons, movies). As a result of this mixed message, there seems to be some spillover into communities.

- Decades of high unemployment in our inner cities have resulted in strong feelings of relative deprivation among many inner-city residents....

- The number of children growing up in violent-prone families who, as they leave their homes and families, are more prone to inflict violence on their own spouses, children, and others is rising.

- An increasing sense of frustration and futility harbored by residents of the inner cities seems to have resulted in a measure of violent vigilantism, intensifying the circle of violence.

- Increases in media violence may be contributing to a sense of callousness toward real-world violence (Eskridge, 1992, pp. 5-6).

Whatever the cause of the violence, it has been accepted that America is a violent country. Crime scholars recognize that the police can only attempt to prevent crime or solve a crime after it occurs. Cooperation from informed citizens who are actively involved in crime prevention is required if the police hope to curb the rising crime rate. Using traditional police strategies, the police have been unable to control crime. The police would not have initiated community-oriented policing if the professional model of policing had been successful in curbing the crime rate. Not only was the violent crime rate high, property crime rates were also high, reaching thirteen million crimes in the last decade of the twentieth century. Property offenses include burglary, theft, and arson. With the increase in crime, the public's fear of crime, and the news media's onslaughter of crime news, the police had their backs to the wall. Therefore, they adopted a policing philosophy with the argument that it offered a better strategy for preventing crime and reducing the public's fear of crime than did the professional police model.

COMMUNITY DEFINED

What does the term "community" mean? The term community is loosely used and often has a variety of meanings and perceptions. Peter Wilmot expounds that we may want to distinguish between "**territorial community**, defined by geography and meaning the people living in a specific area; the **interest community**, a set of people with something in common other than just territory (the black community, the Jewish community, the gay community); and the **attachment community**, where there is a kind of attachment to people or place which gives rise to a 'sense of community'" (Wilmot, 1987, p. 2). Wilmot believes the three types of community can overlap. For example, interest communities can be geographically dispersed. Also, an attachment and sense of community can join people into territorial or interest communities.

The community has functioned as a means of social control and its importance to the community-oriented policing concept seems evident. The term community is often used interchangeably with neighborhood. The majority of Americans live in urban and suburban neighborhoods in contrast to rural communities. In an industrialized civilization, communities or neighborhoods are drawn along socio-economical lines described as underclass or lower class, working class, middle class, and upper class. One's status in this socio-economical structure is based on wealth, material possession and the importance of one's position in society's structure.

The lower socio-economic classes commit the predatory crimes which the rest of society considers intolerable. The police have always functioned in controlling the lower socio-economic classes with the political and economic support of the middle and upper classes. With traditional policing strategies not succeeding in controlling predatory crimes, another strategy was needed. Community-oriented policing became the panacea for preventing and controlling crime. It was also offered as a means to diffuse the fear of crime.

COMMUNITY-ORIENTED POLICING PHILOSOPHY

Mollie Weatheritt writes that "community policing is a conveniently elastic term which is often loosely used to accommodate virtually any policing activity of which its proponents approve" (1987, 7). Weatheritt claims that there exists no agreed definition of community policing nor should there be one. Contrary to Weatheritt, Robert Trojanowicz and Bonnie Bucqueroux have a basic definition for community policing:

> Community policing is a new philosophy of policing, based on the concept that police officers and private citizens working together in creative ways can help solve contemporary community problems related to crime, fear of crime, social and physical disorder, and neighborhood decay. The philosophy is predicated on the belief that achieving these goals requires that police departments develop a new relationship with the law-abiding people in the community, allowing them a greater voice in setting local police priorities and involving them in efforts to improve the overall quality of life in their neighborhoods. It shifts the focus of police work from handling random calls to solving community problems... (1990, p. 5)

Community-oriented policing means a shift away from centralization and control of the line officer. The philosophy of community-oriented policing allows the line officer to be a decision maker and problem solver. The structure of police departments requires them to be more flexible and democratic. Under the concept of community-oriented policing, police work is not incident-driven any longer but instead emphasizes community problem solving. The goal will be to solve the problem in order to eliminate incidents of disturbances or annoyances to the community or neighborhood. L. Brown distinguishes community policing from traditional policing:

1. Community policing is oriented to problem-solving and focuses on results. It encourages techniques such as problem identification, problem analysis, and problem resolution.

2. Community policing demands that police departments organize to incorporate citizen input in matters that affect the safety and quality of neighborhood life. Police citizen partnerships and power sharing in crime control efforts are encouraged. Police are expected to be accountable to the community for their actions and results.

3. Decentralization is encouraged. Beats are drawn to coincide with natural neighborhood boundaries to encourage responsibilities for shared "turf." Beat officers are given permanent beat assignments and are encouraged to become actively involved in the affairs of the community and to initiate creative solutions to neighborhood problems. The patrol officer becomes the "manager" of their assigned beat.

4. Performance evaluations are based on problem-solving ability and success in involving citizens in crime fighting efforts. The criterion for success becomes an absence of incidents such as criminal offenses, traffic accidents, and repeat calls for service (Brown, 1988).

Herman Goldstein claims that if policing is to be improved, the public's expectation of the police must change. Goldstein advocates realistic expectations of what the police can accomplish. By taking a realistic approach, the impossible job the police are asked to perform becomes possible. The police should concentrate on analyzing and responding to specific citizen problems that are brought to their attention. For community policing to be successful, the relationship between the community and the police has to improve. A partnership must develop (1993, pp. 4-6).

EARLY TWENTY-FIRST CENTURY

American society exists in a changing world. The society in which we will live in the early twenty-first century will be different from what it is in the late twentieth century. The age of information will have taken hold. We will be able to communicate visually and orally with anyone in the world instantaneously. Information about scientific, business, and political issues will be obtained in seconds. The cities of rust, making steel and automobiles, will be replaced by communities concerned about pollution products produced by automation. The American economy will become a part of a global economy that became feasible with the fall of communism in Eastern Europe in 1989 and the consolidation of Western Europe's economy in 1992. Educational institutions will be a key component to the success of individuals and business. The work force will be trained in high tech equipment and people will be constantly retrained to keep up to date in new technological developments. More individuals will be working from their homes than in an office or factory. A substantial portion of the population will be over 65 years of age. The baby boomers of post World War II will have reached senior status. White males will be a minority in the work force. They will be replaced by females and other minorities. The Hispanic population should be approaching 30% while the Asian and Black population will each have about 12% of the population. America will have become a culturally diverse society.

Futurist Gene Stephens believes that the justice process will be participatory, a mediation process where victim and defendant come to a satisfactory agreement. Stephens claims police will possess tools that could invade individual privacy (1992, 22). A California study found six trends that can affect policing of California cities going into the twenty-first century:

1. There will be decreased resources.
2. The population will be wealthier, older, and more culturally diverse.
3. There will be a steady increase in the crime rate and the diversity of crime will increase.
4. The perception of crime by the community will remain stable.
5. Community support should increase.
6. The public's demand for extra service will increase at no extra cost (Schwab, 1992, pp. 16-19).

COMMUNITY INFLUENCE

With approximately three hundred police departments claiming to utilize the community-oriented policing philosophy in the mid 1990s and most police departments being influenced by its policing strategy, the community policing concept will have an influence on policing in the early decades of the twenty-first century. Community-oriented policing emphasizes listening rather than just talking to people. It takes seriously the concerns and input of citizens who live and work in the community or neighborhood. The police listen because they realize that:

1. Citizens may legitimately have ideas about what they want and need from the police that may be different from what police believe they need;

2. Citizens have the information about the problems and people in their areas that police need in order to operate effectively; and

3. Police and citizens each hold stereotypes about the other that, unless broken down by nonthreatening contacts, prevent either group from making effective use of the other (Wycott, 1988, pp. 105-106).

With the police listening to its citizens it will not be uncommon for the police in the twenty-first century to periodically conduct "customer surveys." The police need regular feedback on how they are doing. This feedback can only be obtained for the citizen-client whom the police serve. The police will survey victims, witnesses, and complainants on how the police are performing their job. Customer surveys will ask the citizen to rate the police on such areas as concern, helpfulness, knowledge, quality of service, solving the problem, putting the citizen at ease, and professional conduct (Couper and Lodbitz, 1991, p. 74). Based on customer service feedback the police will make adjustments and improvements in their actions.

CITIZEN POLICE ACADEMIES

With limited resources in the initial decades of the twenty-first century, the police will need the assistance of citizen volunteers if they are to keep crime under control. There should be an increase in direct citizen participation to keep crime and neighborhood disturbances under control. One commonly used avenue will be Citizen Police Academies which advance police interaction with citizens and can extend police accountability to the community. These training academies, which are usually offered once a week and taught by police officers, can provide the citizen with realistic expectations of what the police can achieve in controlling and preventing crime. Citizens can learn how to prevent crime and how to control the fear of crime and disorders, and they can bring back this information to their communities where they can put it to practical use. This concept may allow the citizens in the neighborhood to police themselves.

COMMUNITY ADVISORY COUNCILS

A common practice in the initial decades in the twenty-first century will be the development of Community Advisory Councils. These Advisory Councils will meet on a regular basis and work with operational commanders and police department policy makers to decrease the crime rate, disorder, and the fear of crime. A partnership between the Community Advisory Council and the police will be linked to improving the "quality of life" for community citizens. The Community Advisory Council will identify and prioritize problems within the community that a majority of residents want rectified. Once problems are identified, strategies will be devised to solve the problems. There will be an evaluation by the Advisory Council to determine if the problems identified have been corrected or at least kept under control.

The Council will have a variety of activities at its disposal. Under its bailiwick is the Neighborhood Information Network which provides information about crime in the area. The Information Network will be a direct source of crime information providing accurate information in place of rumors, gossip, and accounts from the news media. The Advisory Council would print a newsletter to inform residents of recent crime trends and provide crime prevention techniques to help citizens avoid becoming victims. The Council will also have the responsibility to organize citizen patrols and to oversee the selection for this activity with the approval of the police department. Considering the "broken window" concept which advocates that graffiti and rundown neighborhoods leave an impression of lack of concern and a crime-infested community, the Council working with the police will have graffiti and abandoned cars removed and will strive to clear the neighborhood of any appearance of disorganization. The goal is to establish a sense of community. The Council will function as an advisory board to the police and work to provide solutions to community problems.

CIVILIAN OVERSIGHT

In the last half of the twentieth century there existed an on-again off-again movement to have civilian review boards or, as it became known in the 1980s and 1990s, civilian oversight of police behavior. In the late twentieth century because of police violence and police corruption, community residents demanded the opportunity to review police conduct. In the 1990s it became apparent that the police were unable to clean their own house. The Mollen Commission in New York City discovered that police officers were robbing drug dealers of their money and drugs and going into business for themselves. Police officers would not only sell drugs but use illicit drugs such as cocaine while on duty. Officers intentionally abused citizens without any legal reason other than that an individual had annoyed the officer. High ranking administrators and supervisors looked the other way. They did not want a scandal or negative publicity. Police violence and corruption were not unique to New York; they existed in urban, suburban, and rural communities. In Detroit, two police officers beat a suspect to death. Atlanta police officers were arrested for burglarizing adult entertainment clubs. Savannah, Georgia had a drug ring operated by a police officer.

Because of police scandals in the last decade of the twentieth century, community leaders have been given the authority to oversee police conduct, directed by the community-oriented police concept which can only operate successfully if a partnership exists between the community and the police. Under a closed system a partnership does not exist. When police organizations opened their operations to the public then a legitimate partnership came into existence. No longer did the wall of silence exist among police officers. Police administrators and supervisors came to realize that it was in the best interest of the police department to open up their organization to the community. If they did not allow or cooperate with the community in civilian oversight of police behavior, then the philosophy of community policing that they advocated would be a fraud.

Civilian oversight would consist of only civilians who will have the power to investigate and to review allegations of police misconduct by members of the police department. The civilian oversight committee will review any police activity involving unnecessary or excessive use of force, discourtesy, abuse of authority, and conduct or behavior. All accusations will be promptly and thoroughly investigated, and upon completion of the investigation, the Civilian Oversight Committee will turn over its findings to either the prosecutor for criminal prosecution or the department for appropriate actions, or if the allegation is unfounded or uncorroborated, the officer, the department and the accuser will be notified.

The Civilian Oversight Committee will also have input on police promotions, hirings, and reassignments. This committee will provide insight to department policies directly affecting police interaction with citizens. The committee will have the authority to recommend specific training that may be lacking in a police department. For example, some officers may need sensitivity training if they are abrasive and rude when dealing with the community. The committee would be a partner with the police and not function as an adversary. Members of the committee would be recommended by the police department, community organizations, such as the Chamber of Commerce, and elected political officials.

If the police are to be recognized as professionals, then their activities have to be an open book. Their conduct and behavior should be above approach. For community-oriented policing to be successful, the community and its citizens must trust and respect the police. How can the community be coproducers in crime prevention, eliminating neighborhood disorganization and controlling the fear of crime, if their only intention is to manipulate the community? There must be a sincere police-community partnership if community-oriented policing will be successful. This means that in the twenty-first century the community will have a voice in policing.

PRIVATIZING THE POLICE

Because of an anemic economy in the early 1990s and slow economic growth in this decade, some communities have looked at alternative means for public safety. The police, because of financial cutbacks and stagnant budgets, have forced the affluent, businesses and those elements of the community who were concerned about their personal safety to play a larger role.

The community-oriented philosophy of policing has been forced to include private security organizations. The conclusions drawn by the Hallcrest Report provides the justification for the partnership of private policing agencies with public policing agencies. The Hallcrest report states: "Law enforcement resources have stagnated and in some cases are declining. This mandates greater cooperation with the private sector and its private security resources to jointly forge a partnership on an equal basis for crime prevention and reduction. Law enforcement can ill afford to continue isolation and, in some cases, ignoring these important resources" (Cunningham and Taylor, 1985, p. 275).

Private police agencies can be involved in a variety of ways. They can function as alarm monitors and respond to intrusions when burglary and robbery alarms go off. The private police will respond in lieu of the public police. There can be a volunteer police organization under the supervision of the county sheriff or local police chief. The volunteer police organization can operate under a nonprofit, tax exempt private organization under state law. The organization would have a board of directors with limited police powers. The volunteer police organization can free the police to perform proactive police work. They can check vacant homes while residents are on vacation or direct traffic.

Privatizing of the police includes establishing guard forces for public housing, directing traffic, and providing security and crowd control for civil centers and public owned buildings. The guard force will be used for the management of parking enforcement. Regional shopping centers can use guard forces for public safety. Private police can perform patrol service. For example, San Francisco has had licensed private individuals provide patrol services to those neighborhoods who wanted additional police protection. They go to the city's Police Academy to qualify as peace officers; they are armed, uniformed, and are given full police powers. The private patrol officers are expected to respond to calls in their neighborhood just as public police officers do. The key difference is that the private police officers are entrepreneurs.

More private police will man switchboards in the twenty-first century than in the twentieth century. Public police will contract for this service as well as for records and property management, data processing and so forth. It will be more cost effective to contract with private police than for the public police to perform these functions.

The list of activities performed by private police involving the privatization of public policing services will be substantial during the twenty-first century. In the twenty-first century the citizens of American communities will decide that private policing agencies have an important role to play in crime prevention and control. The private police and the public police will be partners. The community-oriented policing philosophy will be extended to private police. Since the private police are citizens from the community, their role in private policing will increase the influence of the "community" in community policing.

SUMMARY

In the last quarter of the twentieth century police practitioners have come to the realization that the traditional reactive approach to crimes already committed has not worked and the development of a new police strategy is imperative. This new philosophy has become known as "community policing." A driving force behind "community policing" has been the desire to maintain the quality of life in neighborhoods for citizens who lived in these neighborhoods.

The last decades of the twentieth century have witnessed a substantial increase in the crime rate in America. In the final decade of the century, violent crimes will reach two million. Not only are violent crime rates high, property crime rates are also high. With the increase in crime, the public's fear of crime, and the news media's onslaught of crime news, the police have their backs to the wall. Therefore, they have adopted a policing philosophy with the argument that it offers a better strategy for preventing crime and reducing the public's fear of crime than the professional police model does.

Community-oriented policing means a shift away from centralized and control of the line officer. The philosophy of community-oriented policing allows the line officer to be a decision maker and problem solver. The structure of the police department requires it to be more flexible and democratic. Under the concept of community-oriented policing, police work is not incident-driven any longer but instead emphasizes community problem solving.

American society exists in a changing world. The society of the early twenty-first century will be different from that of the late twentieth century. The age of information will have taken hold. We will be able to communicate visually and orally with anyone in the world instantaneously. The American economy will become a part of a global economy, made feasible with the fall of communism in Eastern Europe in 1989 and the consolidation of Western's Europe's economy in 1992. A substantial portion of the population will be over sixty-five years of age. White males will become a minority of the work force, replaced by women and minorities.

In the twenty-first century the community-oriented policing concept will be come imbedded in the strategies of policing. It will be uncommon for the police to periodically conduct "customer surveys." The police will survey victims, witnesses, and complaints on how the police are performing their job. Citizen Police Academies will become common with citizens being directly involved in crime prevention and control strategies.

A common practice in the twenty-first century will be the formation of Community Advisory Councils. These advisory councils will meet on a regular basis and work with operational commanders and police policy makers to decrease the crime rate, disorder, and the fear of crime. The council will have a variety of activities at its disposal. Because of police scandals in the last decade of twentieth century, community leaders have been given authority to oversee police conduct. They have been directed by the community-oriented policing concept which can only operate successfully if a partnership exists between the community and the police.

Because of the anemic economy in the early 1990s and slow economic growth in this decade some communities have looked at alternative means for public safety. The police, because of financial cutbacks and stagnant budgets, have forced the affluent, businesses and those elements who were concerned about their personal safety to play a larger role. The community-oriented philosophy of policing has been forced to include private security organizations. Private police have functioned as alarm monitors, volunteer police, guard force, and switch board operators.

STUDY QUESTIONS

1. What influence will the community have in community policing in the twenty-first century?

2. How can the public help the police in solving/preventing crimes?

3. Describe what is known as a participatory system as it impacts on policing and the criminal justice system.

4. How will technology impact on the solving of crimes and therefore the role of the police?

5. Will privatizing the police force be an answer in the twenty-first century?

REFERENCES

Brown, E.G. (1990, January). "To Preserve the Quality of Life," *California Journal.*

Brown, L. (1988). "Community Policing: A Practical Guide for Police Officials." *Perspectives on Policing*, No. 12, Washington, DC: National Institute of Justice.

Cunningham, W.C. and Taylor, Todd H. (1985). *Private Security and Police in America: The Hallcrest Report*, Portland, OR: Chancellor Press.

Couper, D.C. and Lodbitz, S.H. (1991). *Quality Policing: The Madison Experience*, Washington, DC: Police Executive Research Forum.

Eskridge, C.W. (1992). *Criminal Justice: Concepts and Issues*, Los Angeles, CA: Roxbury Publishing Company.

Goldstein, H. (1993, August). "The New Policing: Confronting Complexity," paper presented at the Conference on Community Policing, National Institute of Justice, U.S. Department of Justice, Washington, DC.

Manning, P.K. (1988). "Community Policing as a Drama of Control," In J.R. Greene and S.D. Mastrofski (Eds.) *Community Policing: Rhetoric or Reality*, New York: Praeger (pp. 27-45).

Schwab, S. (1992, February). *Restructuring Small Police Agencies: A Transition Toward Customer Service*, Sacramento, CA: Peace Officer Standards and Training (POST).

Stephens, G. (1992, May-June). "Drugs and Crime in the Twenty-First Century," *The Futurist*.

Trojanowicz, R. and Bucqueroux, B. (1990). *Community Policing: A Contemporary Perspective*, Cincinnati, OH: Anderson.

Weatheritt, M. (1987). "Community Policing Now," In Peter Wilmot, *Policing and the Community*, London, England: Policy Studies Institute, (pp. 7-20).

Wilmot, P., ed. (1987). *Policing and the Community*, London, England: Policy Studies Institute, 1987.

Wycott, M.A. (1988). "The Benefits of Community Policing: Evidence and Conjecture," In J.R. Greene and S.D. Mastrofski, *Community Policing: Rhetoric or Reality*, New York, NY: Praeger Publishers, (pp. 103-120).

PART IV

INTRODUCTION

THE COURTS AND FUTURE LAW

The operation of the criminal courts is surrounded by conflicting pressures and controversies. As we reach the twenty-first century, constitutional violations have worsened, the constitutional rights of the crime victim are often ignored, while aggressive defense attorneys play legal games like delaying court dates and attempting to suppress DNA evidence.

Kenneth Haas reviews court decisions regarding capital punishment in his chapter, "The United States Supreme Court and the Future of Capital Punishment." The United States is the only western democracy that still executes its citizens. Haas ultimately tries to convince the reader of the need for the Supreme Court to declare the death penalty to be unconstitutional by the year 2050 at best.

Alexander Smith and Harriet Pollack talk about "The Bill of Rights in the Twenty-First Century." The U.S. Supreme Court for the past thirty years has interpreted the Fourth, Fifth, Sixth and Eighth Amendments of the Bill of Rights in a manner protective of the rights of suspects, defendants, and prosecutors. In recent years, the focus of the Court has shifted from restrictions on the police and the conduct of trials, to concerns about sentencing and punishment. What the future holds depends largely on government policy in relation to drug use and trafficking, and gun control, the chief elements of our crime problem.

CHAPTER 10

THE UNITED STATES SUPREME COURT AND THE FUTURE OF CAPITAL PUNISHMENT

Kenneth C. Haas, Ph.D.

ABSTRACT

This chapter analyzes the United States Supreme Court's past, present, and future role in monitoring the American system of capital punishment. In *Gregg v. Georgia* (1976), the Court upheld the constitutionality of death-penalty laws that permit a judge or a jury to impose a death sentence only after weighing all of the relevant "aggravating" and "mitigating" factors concerning the defendant's crime and character. In the years following *Gregg*, the Court proceeded cautiously, setting strict limits on the applicability of the death penalty by refusing to allow the executions of those who did not actually take another human life and by insisting that judges and juries give due consideration to all mitigating factors in the defendant's conduct and background. Since 1983, however, the Court has taken a much more aggressive and activist approach toward death-penalty cases, rejecting every major constitutional challenge to the fairness of death-penalty laws and sanctioning the execution of sixteen year old offenders, mentally retarded defendants, and those who neither killed nor intended to kill. These kinds of decisions make it very likely that by the year 2010, both the rate and geographical reach of executions will have expanded significantly. Ironically, however, it is predicted that this increase in executions will ultimately convince the American people that the death penalty simply cannot be administered without error, caprice, and discrimination. Abolitionist movements will gain momentum in an increasing number of states, and the Supreme Court will declare the death penalty to be unconstitutional by the year 2050 if not sooner.

INTRODUCTION

In 1972, the U.S. Supreme Court, ruling in *Furman v. Georgia*, put a halt to all executions, thereby removing 558 condemned prisoners from the nation's death rows (Marquart and Sorensen, 1989: 5). *Furman* held only that all *then existing* state and federal death-penalty laws violated the Eighth Amendment's cruel and unusual punishment clause because of the arbitrary and discriminatory way in which they were applied (*Furman* at 239-374).[1] The decision, nevertheless, was greeted with a sense of euphoria by opponents of capital punishment. Many were convinced that the United

States had joined the worldwide trend towards abolition, and that the gallows, gas chambers, and electric chairs would soon be relegated to museums and history books (Meltsner, 1973: 289-291).

In 1976, however, the Supreme Court refused to take the next step—declaring the death penalty in and of itself to be unconstitutional. In *Gregg v. Georgia* and its companion cases,[2] the Court upheld new death-penalty laws that require the jury (or in a few states, the judge) to conduct a separate penalty hearing in order to consider "aggravating" and "mitigating" factors concerning the capital offender's crime and character. Under most of these laws, the jury is instructed to weigh all of the relevant factors and circumstances, and to return with either a sentence of death or life imprisonment. On the same day *Gregg* was decided, the Court also struck down another type of death-penalty law that several states had enacted in the aftermath of *Furman*. In *Woodson v. North Carolina* (1976) and *Roberts v. Louisiana* (1976), a 5 to 4 majority found mandatory death-penalty laws to be violative of the Eighth Amendment because such laws would undermine the Court's new requirement that sentencing authorities must consider *all* relevant information concerning the nature of the offense and the character of the defendant as an indispensable part of the process of determining which defendants shall live and which shall die (*Woodson* at 302-304).[3]

Today, not even a quarter century after *Furman*, the turnabout can only be described as stunning. Since the *Gregg* decision, the Supreme Court has rejected every major constitutional challenge to the death penalty. The result is that while every other western industrial nation in the world has abolished capital punishment, the United States has a death-row population that will soon exceed three thousand men and women (NAACP, 1994-95).

This chapter examines the Supreme Court's past, present, and future role in breathing life back into the death penalty. In particular, the chapter analyzes some of the Court's most important post-*Gregg* decisions on the legal status of capital punishment. It is argued that the predominant trend is typified by decisions that limit capital defendants' rights of appeal while expanding the reach of the death penalty to include children, the mentally retarded, and those who have not taken another human life. These decisions make it very likely that by the year 2010, both the rate and geographical reach of executions will have increased significantly. It is also predicted that the growth in executions will ultimately convince the American people—and the Supreme Court—that the time has come to abolish the death penalty. An increasing number of states will abolish capital punishment in the second, third, and fourth decades of the twenty-first century. Citing this movement away from capital punishment, the Court will conclude that the American people of the middle decades of the twenty-first century have reached a sufficient consensus against capital punishment to justify a Supreme Court holding that the death penalty must be abandoned altogether.

THE POST-*GREGG* ERA

Gregg and *Woodson* established the framework for evaluating the constitutionality of all American death-penalty laws. *Gregg* made it clear that the death penalty *per se* is not forbidden by the Eighth Amendment. But many important questions concerning the constitutional status of capital punishment remained unanswered. Indeed, the 1976 decisions arguably added to the confusion by articulating two major goals that seemed to be quite contradictory. On the one hand, the sentencing authority is commanded by the *Gregg* majority to apply the death penalty even-handedly and without arbitrariness, thus suggesting that it is paramount to provide judges and juries with clear and objective standards that can be applied the same way in all cases. On the other hand, both *Woodson* and *Gregg* arguably stand for the proposition that the sentencing authority is obligated to place great emphasis upon the individual characteristics of each offender and the particular circumstances surrounding his or her crime. These two goals will strike nearly everyone as incompatible; how can the sentencing authority be expected to give full consideration to the uniqueness of each individual defendant when its discretion has been sharply limited in order to promote fairness and consistency?[4]

This question has still not been resolved by the Supreme Court and as a result, it is particularly difficult to predict the future of capital punishment in the United States. The best way to proceed, however, is to examine how the Court has dealt with other important death-penalty issues since 1976. As we will see, the clear trend has been to expand the reach of the death penalty. As of today, there is little reason to believe that the Court is likely to alter its course in the near future. It therefore seems likely that there will be fewer procedural safeguards for capital defendants and an increasing rate of executions by the year 2010.

The Post-*Gregg* Years: 1976-1983

In his book, *The Death Penalty in the Nineties*, Professor Welsh White (1991) suggests a useful framework for studying the post-*Gregg* era. As White sees it, from 1976-1983, the Supreme Court attempted to clarify the constitutional boundaries of capital punishment by identifying the specific protections that must be afforded capital defendants (White, 1991: 5-8). From 1983 to the present, however, the Court has increasingly sought to promote "expeditious executions" (White, 1991: 8-24). Professor White's two-phase analysis strikes me as substantially correct, although I would argue in even stronger terms that the Court has increasingly become an activist, pro-death-penalty tribunal. For the most part, the justices, particularly Chief Justice Rehnquist and Justices O'Connor, Kennedy, Scalia, and Thomas, have made little or no effort to camouflage their intentions. These justices exercise their judicial power zestfully while pursuing an activist jurisprudence that emphasizes great deference to legislative bodies and values states' rights far more than individual rights. As a result, the Eighth Amendment has been pushed far into the woodwork and out of the way of the legislative power, thereby expanding the category of death-eligible offenders and curtailing the appellate rights of death-row inmates.

From 1976 and 1983, however, the High Court proceeded carefully. *Gregg* and *Woodson* had invalidated mandatory death-penalty laws, but had given states the green light to enact capital statutes that provide for a bifurcated trial and clear guidelines—aggravating and mitigating factors—for judges and juries to consider in deciding whether to sentence the offender to death. This suggested that guided-discretion statutes such as the one upheld in *Gregg* were generally constitutionally acceptable. But no two states had identical death-penalty laws, and many important questions remained to be addressed.

In the years immediately following *Gregg*, the Court seemed inclined to resolve the aforementioned conflict between consistent sentencing and individualized sentencing in favor of the latter alternative. In 1977, for example, the Court reaffirmed its *Woodson* stance against mandatory death-penalty laws. In *Roberts v. Louisiana*, a sharply divided Court struck down a Louisiana statute that made death the mandatory punishment for anyone convicted of the first-degree murder of a police officer engaged in the performance of his or her lawful duties. A five-justice majority made it clear that the fact that a murder victim was a police officer could be regarded as an aggravating circumstance (*Roberts* at 636). However, the majority held that the sentencing authority must always be permitted to consider such mitigating facts as the youth of the offender, the absence of any prior convictions, or the influence of extreme emotional disturbance (*Roberts* at 637). Because the Louisiana law did not allow the jury to consider these kinds of mitigating factors when the victim was a law-enforcement officer, it violated the Eighth Amendment (*Roberts* at 637-638).

A year later, the Court again indicated that promoting individualized sentencing was its foremost priority. In *Lockett v. Ohio*, (1978), with Justices Rehnquist and White as the only dissenters, the Court invalidated the sentence of Sandra Lockett, a young black woman who had been condemned to die on the basis of her participation in a pawnshop robbery in which one of her confederates shot and killed the pawnshop owner while Lockett waited in the getaway car. The trial judge had found two statutory aggravating circumstances to exist but could not consider the full range of possible mitigating factors under Ohio's law. This restraint was a result of the law's stipulation that the judge *must* impose a death sentence unless he found by a preponderance of the evidence that (1) the victim had induced or facilitated the murder; (2) the offender was under duress, coercion, or strong provocation; or (3) the murder was primarily attributable to the offender's psychosis or mental deficiency. By so sharply limiting the number of mitigating circumstances that could be considered, the Ohio statute deprived Lockett of the opportunity to offer into evidence such mitigating factors as her youth and her relatively minor role in the crime (*Lockett* at 589-594).

Reaffirming its commitment to promoting individualized sentencing in capital cases, the Court held that "in all but the rarest kind of capital case," the sentences must not be precluded from considering any mitigating factors bearing on the defendant's character, prior record, or the circumstances of the offense (*Lockett* at 604). The Constitution may not require individualized sentencing in noncapital cases, wrote Chief Justice Burger, but preventing a judge or a jury from giving "independent mitigating weight" to all aspects of the defendant's character, record, and offense is incompatible with the Eighth Amendment (*Lockett* at 604-605). "The need for treating each defendant in a capital case with that degree of respect due the uniqueness of the individual is far more important in capital cases" (*Lockett* at 605). With these words, the Chief Justice established the primacy of individualized decision making in capital cases. Although *Lockett* did not explicitly renounce the objective of reducing arbitrariness and bias in capital sentencing, it certainly signaled that this objective was now subordinate to the goal of promoting individualized capital sentencing. But as will be explained later, the tension between these two conflicting goals still exists and may yet work to the advantage of those who oppose the death penalty.[5]

In the first few years after *Gregg*, the Court also refused to extend death-penalty eligibility to crimes other than murder. Thus in *Coker v. Georgia*, decided in 1977, six justices agreed that death is an impermissible punishment for the rape of an adult woman. Writing on behalf of a plurality and joined by Justices Brennan and Marshall, both of whom concurred in the judgment on the basis of their belief that capital punishment is in all circumstances unconstitutional, Justice White took the position that rape, though a reprehensible crime deserving of severe punishment, simply does not compare to murder in terms of the harm done to the victim and to society (*Coker* at 597-598).

> The murderer kills; the rapist, if no more than that, does not. Life is over for the victim of the murderer; for the rape victim, life may not be nearly so happy as it was, but it is not over and normally is not beyond repair (*Coker* at 598).

Stressing that the Court must look to objective indicators as to whether contemporary society's "evolving standards of decency" (*Trop v. Dulles* at 101) are incompatible with executing rapists, Justice White found it particularly significant that only three of the thirty-five states that had enacted post-*Furman* death penalty laws had authorized the death penalty for the rape of an adult woman (*Coker* at 591-594). Thus, the judgments of state legislatures, though not unanimous, weighed very heavily against death as an acceptable punishment for rape (Coker at 596). Moreover, the sentencing decisions actually made by juries in cases in which the prosecutor seeks the death penalty for rape also pointed to a growing consensus that death is a disproportionate punishment for rape (*Coker* at 596-597). In Georgia, for example, juries had sentenced to death only six of sixty-three convicted rapists since 1973 (*Coker* at 596-597). The jury's rejection of capital punishment for rape in the vast majority of cases, like the legislative response to *Furman*, provided significant and reliable evidence that the American people were now in agreement with the Court's "own judgment, which is that death is indeed a disproportionate penalty for the crime of raping an adult woman" (*Coker* at 597).

Five years later, in *Enmund v. Florida* (1982), the Court stood by the principle arguably established by *Coker*—that the death penalty is unique in its severity and irrevocability, and therefore must be reserved only for those who take another human life or at least intend or attempt to take another human life. Indeed, Earl Enmund, the getaway driver for two robbers who shot and killed an elderly farm couple who resisted their hold-up attempt, was parked approximately two hundred yards from the scene of the murders (*Enmund* at 784). He did not shoot the victims and there was no evidence that he had planned or even anticipated that lethal force would or might be used in the course of the robbery (*Enmund* at 788). A Florida judge nevertheless sentenced him to die, a decision upheld by the Florida Supreme Court (*Enmund* at 784-787).

With Justice White again writing on behalf of the majority, the Court, by the narrowest of margins, struck down Enmund's death sentence. Justice White began by stressing that "to the maximum possible extent," the Court's decisions as to whether a particular punishment is grossly disproportionate to a particular crime must be informed by objective criteria (*Enmund* at 788-789). Accordingly, he turned first to an analysis of legislative judgments on the appropriateness of executing a nontriggerman such as Earl Enmund (*Enmund* at 788-793). Pointing out that only eight of the thirty-six states with capital-punishment statutes allowed the death penalty to be imposed solely because the defendant somehow participated in a robbery in the course of which an accomplice committed a murder, Justice White found that the legislative consensus "weighs on the side of rejecting capital punishment for the crime at issue." (*Enmund* at 792-793). The sentencing behavior of juries provided even stronger evidence that contemporary American society rejects the death penalty for accomplice liability in felony murders (*Enmund* at 794). Of the 362 executions that had been carried out since 1954, only six were for merely participating in a felony in which a confederate had committed a murder (*Enmund* at 794-795). Moreover, only three of the 739 people who were under sentence of death as of late 1981 had been condemned to die without a finding that they did more than merely participate in an underlying felony that had led to an unplanned murder (*Enmund* at 795).

The final decision, however, must always be made by the Court, and the majority of the justices were in agreement with the judgments of legislators and jurors (*Enmund* at 797). The executions of offenders such as Earl Enmund would serve neither the goal of deterrence (since the threat of death is unlikely to deter when murder is not premeditated) nor the purpose of retribution (since retribution requires penalties that are tailored to fit the offender's *personal* responsibility and moral guilt) (*Enmund* at 798-801). Such executions, therefore, accomplish "nothing more than the purposeless and needless imposition of pain and suffering" and thus are prohibited by the Eighth Amendment (*Enmund* at 798). Accordingly, death is an impermissible punishment for "one who neither took life, attempted to take life, nor intended to take life" *(Enmund* at 787).

Decisions such as *Lockett*, *Coker*, and *Enmund* typify the Court's cautious approach to death-penalty issues in the 1976-1983 period. With very few exceptions,[6] the Court insisted that the states follow strict procedural guidelines and make reasonable efforts to ensure fairness, reliability, and individualized consideration in the capital-sentencing process. Thus, the Court repeatedly reaffirmed the *Lockett* holding that the sentencer must consider all relevant mitigating circumstances proffered by the defense (*Bell v. Ohio* (1978); *Green v. Georgia* (1979); *Eddings v. Oklahoma* (1982)). Similarly, in *Gardner v. Florida (1977)*, the justices held that capital defendants must always be permitted to confront and cross-examine witnesses who present aggravating-circumstances evidence at the penalty phase. *Godfrey v. Georgia* (1980) established that the aggravating circumstances considered by capital juries must be defined clearly enough to avoid the arbitrary imposition of the death penalty. Also in 1980, the Court invalidated an Alabama law that prohibited the trial judge from instructing the jury as to its option to find a capital defendant guilty of a lesser included noncapital offense *(Beck v. Alabama)*. And in 1981, the Court held that a jury's initial vote for life over death was an implied acquittal of death-penalty eligibility, thus precluding reimposition of the death penalty after the defendant's reconviction for the same crime *(Bullington v. Missouri)*. In these and in other cases that invalidated death sentences, the High Court seemed to be acutely aware that "death is a different kind of punishment from any other" *(Beck at 637)* and must always be accompanied by stringent safeguards designed to ensure fairness and consistency in capital sentencing.

The Post-*Gregg* Years (1983-Present)

Toward the end of the 1982-83 term, the Court began to retreat from its cautious, "go-slow" approach to capital punishment. The insistence on strict procedural safeguards was replaced by an attitude that it was time to "get on with it" and stop interfering with the will of the people as reflected by the laws passed by state legislatures.[7] Such deference to the political branches of government would broaden the class of death-eligible defendants and weaken the special safeguards against unfairness and caprice. But as the majority commented in a 1983 case, the states had a legitimate interest in finding a speedier way of handling death-penalty appeals and "not every imperfection in the deliberative process is sufficient...to set aside a state court judgment" (*Zant v. Stephens*: 884-885).

Space limitations preclude a discussion of all or even most of the dozens of death-penalty decisions handed down by the Supreme Court since 1983. But we will look at some of the decisions that most accurately reflect the Court's evolving view of capital punishment, with special emphasis on the holdings that demonstrate the Court's head-long retreat from the positions it had taken in the 1976-1983 period. It should be noted, however, that the Court has not dismantled all of its earlier holdings. For example, the justices have continued to demand that the sentencing authority must be permitted to consider any relevant mitigating circumstances when deciding whether or not to sentence a defendant to death (*Skipper v. South Carolina*, 1986; *Hitchcock v. Dugger*, 1987).

Neither has the Court fully retreated from its *Woodson-Roberts* stance against laws that mandate the death penalty for particular categories of offenders. Most notably, in *Sumner v. Shuman* (1987), the Court struck down a Nevada law that required the jury to impose the death penalty in all cases in which a prisoner is convicted of murder while serving a life sentence without the possibility of parole. Interestingly, Justice Blackmun, who had voted to uphold the mandatory death-penalty laws at issue in *Woodson* and *Roberts*, wrote the majority opinion in *Shuman*. He reasoned that even when an inmate serving a life-without-parole sentence commits a murder, there might be mitigating factors such as the defendant's age or mental condition, which weigh against a death sentence (*Shuman* at 81-82). To the argument that a mandatory death sentence is necessary in order to deter and provide retribution against life-termers, the majority responded that under a nonmandatory guided-discretion sentencing law, those who deserve to die are likely to receive the death penalty in most cases and those not condemned to die can still be punished in other ways, "such as through a transfer to a more restrictive...correctional facility or deprivation of privileges." (*Shuman* at 83-84). Since the state's legitimate interests in deterrence and retribution can be satisfied through the use of a guided-discretion statute, the Court would not depart from the position that mandatory death-penalty laws violate the Eighth Amendment (*Shuman* at 85).

Although *Shuman* remains in effect, the Court in 1990 embraced an element of mandatoriness in capital sentencing. In *Blystone v. Pennsylvania*, a five-justice majority held that the existence of a mandatory component in a guided-discretion death-penalty statute does not always violate constitutional strictures. Specifically, the *Blystone* Court upheld the constitutionality of a Pennsylvania law that requires the jury to impose the death penalty if it finds that the aggravating circumstances in the case outweigh any mitigating circumstances. Writing for the majority, Chief Justice Rehnquist distinguished *Woodson*, stressing that under the Pennsylvania statute:

> Death is not automatically imposed upon conviction for certain types of murder. It is imposed only after a determination that the aggravating cir-

cumstances outweigh the mitigating circumstances present in the particular crime committed by the particular defendant, or that there are no such mitigating circumstances (*Blystone* at 305).[8]

In *Blystone*, the Supreme Court merely "chipped away" at past precedents requiring strict scrutiny of death-penalty laws. For opponents of the death penalty, this was ominous enough in itself. But in other important cases, the Court has gone much further, jettisoning prior holdings and retreating from the pursuit of fairness and consistency in death-penalty cases. To be sure, the Court has continued to invalidate egregiously unconstitutional capital-sentencing provisions.[9] However, the predominant trend has clearly been in the direction of expanding the reach of the death penalty and promoting expeditious executions.

Several 1983 decisions marked the High Court's movement away from the strict regulation of capital sentencing procedures. For example, in *California v. Ramos*, the Court found nothing constitutionally deficient in a law that seemingly gives the jury the mistaken impression that the *only* way to keep the defendant off the street is to execute him. The law in question required judges to instruct the jury that the governor had the authority to reduce a life-without-parole sentence to a sentence that includes the possibility of parole. But it did not require the judge to call the jury's attention to the governor's power to commute a death sentence (*Ramos* at 994-998).

In two 1983 cases (*Barclay v. Florida*; *Zant v. Stephens*), the Court refused to invalidate death sentences even though the sentencer had considered an illegitimate aggravating circumstance along with two or more legitimate aggravating circumstances. The majority's determination that a sentence of death could rest upon both valid and invalid aggravating circumstances provoked a strong dissent from Justice Blackmun, who wrote, "[t]he end does not justify the means even in what may be deemed to be a 'deserving capital punishment situation'" (*Barclay* at 991).

In a particularly controversial 1983 case dealing with Texas' death-penalty statute, the Court upheld the admissibility of testimony by state-hired psychiatrists who routinely predicted that capital defendants would commit future crimes. Writing for the majority in *Barefoot v. Estelle*, Justice White acknowledged research studies showing that "expert" predictions about future dangerousness turn out to be incorrect 66% of the time (*Barefoot* at 898-903). He dismissed the importance of such studies, however, noting that psychiatrists are not wrong all of the time, only "most of the time" (*Barefoot* at 901). Since the defense will have the opportunity to cross-examine the state's witnesses and can always call its own witnesses, the jurors will hear both sides of the debate over the defendant's dangerousness and can sort out the differences themselves (*Barefoot* at 898-899). Thus, the scientifically dubious expert testimony does not in and of itself render the sentencing hearing to unfair as to violate the Constitution (*Barefoot* at 905-906). The Barefoot majority also bestowed its approval on "expedited review procedures" to be followed by federal courts in order to speed death-penalty appeals toward a final resolution (*Barefoot* at 887-896). Ironically, as several legal commentators have pointed out, the procedures approved in Barefoot give capital defendants *less time* to prepare their appeals than prisoners who do not face the death penalty (Mello, 1988: 547-548; Amsterdam, 1987: 889-890).

In 1984, the Court signaled unmistakably that it would no longer uphold all of the strict procedural safeguards that the *Gregg* Court thought would protect capital defendants from the arbitrary, aberrant, or excessive infliction of the death penalty. Both the plurality and concurring opinions in *Gregg* had emphasized the importance of the Georgia statutory provision requiring the state supreme court to "compare each death sentence with the sentences imposed on similarly situated defendants to ensure that the sentence of death in a particular case is not disproportionate" (*Gregg* at 198, 211-212). Indeed, a fair reading of *Gregg* would indicate that the Court viewed such a comparative proportionality review as an *indispensable* aspect of any constitutionally sound capital-sentencing system. Justice Stewart, after all, had written that "[i]n particular the proportionality review substantially eliminates the possibility that a person will be sentenced to die by the action of an aberrant jury" (*Gregg* at 206). And Justice White had added that he was confident that the Georgia Supreme Court would see to it that "death sentences imposed for discriminatory reasons or wantonly or freakishly for any given category of crime will be set aside" (*Gregg* at 224).

In 1984, however, Justice White, writing for a six-justice majority, repudiated the argument that the outcome of *Gregg* had hinged on mandatory proportionality review. In *Pulley v. Harris*, the Court considered the case of Robert Harris, a convicted murderer who was sentenced to death under a California law that provided for an automatic appeal of the factual validity of each death sentence, but did not require the state's highest court to conduct a comparative proportionality review in all cases. Although Justice White conceded that *Gregg* had "made much of the statutorily required comparative proportionality review," neither he nor the other justices who constituted the *Gregg* majority meant to declare that such a review "was so critical that without it the Georgia statute would not have passed constitutional muster" (*Harris* at 45). What the *Gregg* justices really meant to say, according to Justice White, was that whether such a proportionality review would be constitutionally mandated in any given state would depend upon what other checks against arbitrariness were included in that state's statutory death-sentencing scheme (*Pulley* at 51-53).

Since the California statute requires the jury to find that at least one aggravating circumstance exists before imposing the death penalty, the statute operates to limit the death sentence to a small subclass of cases, thus minimizing the risk of capricious and standardless sentencing (*Pulley* at 53). The occasional "aberrational outcomes," reasoned Justice White, "are a far cry from the major systematic defects identified in *Furman*" (*Pulley* at 54). Such inconsistencies, he concluded, are inevitable, since there can be no perfect procedure for deciding when to extinguish life (*Pulley* at 54). The California procedures provided Robert Harris with enough protection against the evils identified in *Furman* to satisfy constitutional requirements (*Pulley* at 54).

Justice Brennan, joined by Justice Marshall, rebuked the majority for departing from the promises seemingly made in *Furman* and *Gregg* (*Pulley* at 61-64). Arguing that *Gregg* stands for the principle that the irrational imposition of the death penalty can *never* be constitutionally defended (*Pulley* at 63-64), Justice Brennan described comparative proportionality review as an imperfect but necessary method for eliminating some of the racial discrimination and arbitrariness that all too often surrounds the imposition of death sentences (*Pulley* at 71). A growing body of scholarly evidence, he contended, demonstrated that racial discrimination and other irrationalities continued to infect the post-*Gregg* imposition of the death penalty (*Pulley* at 64-67). He predicted that the majority's refusal to mandate comparative proportionality review would only increase the arbitrariness and racial bias already inherent under the various state capital-sentencing schemes (*Pulley* at 70-73).

With only a few exceptions, the High Court continued to demonstrate its new attitude toward capital punishment in the 1984-85 and 1985-86 terms. For example, in *Wainwright v. Witt* (1985), the Court by a 7 to 2 vote relaxed the longstanding standard that required judges to remove a prospective juror from both phases of a capital trial only when the juror made it "unmistakably clear" that he or she could never vote to impose death in the penalty phase of the trial. This standard, derived from a 1968 decision, *Witherspoon v. Illinois*, helped to make capital juries at least somewhat representative of the community at large—a community that typically includes some people who are potentially receptive to the defense attorney's arguments for life as well as the prosecutor's arguments for death. But the *Witt* holding replaced *Witherspoon* with the rule stating that a prospective juror could be eliminated merely on the ground that the judge believed that the juror's doubts about capital punishment would "substantially impair" his or her ability to impose a death sentence (*Witt* at 424-425).

One year later, Justice Rehnquist, the author of the *Witt* majority opinion, again wrote for the Court in *Lockhart v. McCree* (1986). Here the holding was that "death qualification"—the practice of removing from capital juries those who were reluctant to impose death in the penalty phase—does not violate the defendant's Sixth Amendment right to a fair trial in the guilt phase of the trial. The *McCree* decision contradicted the findings of numerous social-science studies showing that death-qualified juries were significantly more likely to impose the death penalty than were juries in noncapital cases (Ellsworth, 1988). To opponents of capital punishment, the *Witt* and *McCree* holdings were seen as heralding a new era in which the scales of justice would be weighted against life and in favor of death.

In 1987, many of the worst fears of death-penalty abolitionists were realized. In a trilogy of 5 to 4 decisions, the Court rejected two important challenges to death-penalty laws and extended death-penalty eligibility to an entire new group of defendants—those who did not actually take another human life. First, in *California v. Brown*, Chief Justice Rehnquist authored a majority opinion upholding a death sentence imposed by a jury that had been instructed by the trial judge that it "must not be swayed by mere sentiment, conjecture, sympathy, passion, prejudice, public opinion or public feeling" (*Brown* at 540). The California Supreme Court had found that an instruction to disregard any sympathy factors raised by the defense violated the *Lockett* mandate that juries must be permitted to consider all relevant mitigating evidence before reaching a decision (*Brown* at 539-540). Chief Justice Rehnquist, however, asserted that a reasonable juror would read the instruction as a whole rather than focus only on the admonition against being swayed by sympathy (*Brown* at 542-543). Therefore, he reasoned, the instruction did nothing more than advise jurors to ignore emotional responses that are not rooted in the aggravating and mitigating evidence, thereby minimizing the risk of arbitrary and capricious decisions (*Brown* at 543).

In dissent, Justice Brennan contended that the state supreme court was right in the first place: the anti-sympathy instruction would almost certainly lead jurors to believe that they could not consider the very kind of mitigating factors that the *Lockett* majority "[had] decreed must be considered by the sentencer" (*Brown* at 555). The result will be that juries will be confronted with confusing and contradictory instructions, a state of affairs that should not be tolerated when life itself is at stake (*Brown* at 560-561).

Several months after *Brown*, the Court rejected a major systemic challenge to the constitutionality of capital punishment. In *McCleskey v. Kemp* (1987), the Court was confronted with strong statistical evidence that post-*Gregg* capital-sentencing procedures were still saturated with arbitrariness and racial discrimination, and thus violated both the Eighth Amendment and the Fourteenth Amendment guarantee of equal protection under the law. A comprehensive study (known as the Baldus study)[10] of two thousand murder cases that occurred in Georgia during the 1970s revealed that defendants charged with killing white victims were 4.3 times as likely to receive a death sentence as those whose victims were black (*McCleskey* at 287). Moreover, the death penalty had been imposed in 22% of the cases involving black defendants and white victims; 8% of the cases involving white defendants and white victims; 3% of the cases involving white defendants and black victims; and 1% of the cases involving black defendants and black victims (*McCleskey* at 286).

Did such overwhelming evidence of racial discrimination in capital sentencing establish a constitutional violation? Writing for the majority, Justice Powell answered this question in the negative. The majority assumed that the Baldus study was reliable, but held that to prevail under the equal protection clause, a capital defendant would have to meet the difficult burden of proving "that the decisionmakers in *his* case acted with discriminatory purpose" (*McCleskey* at 292). To the argument that the statistical evidence demonstrated that the death penalty in Georgia was arbitrarily applied in violation of the Eighth Amendment, Justice Powell responded:

> At most, the Baldus study indicates a discrepancy that appears to correlate with race. Apparent disparities in sentencing are an inevitable part of our criminal justice system...Where the discretion that is fundamental to our criminal process is involved, we decline to assume that what is unexplained is invidious. In light of the safeguards [Georgia has] designed to minimize racial bias in the process...we hold that the Baldus study does not demonstrate a constitutionally significant risk of racial bias affecting the Georgia capital sentencing process (*McCleskey* at 312-313).

In a dissenting opinion, Justice Brennan, joined by Justices Marshall, Stevens, and Blackmun, accused the majority of ignoring "precisely the type of risk of irrationality in sentencing that we have consistently condemned in our Eighth Amendment jurisprudence" (*McCleskey* at 320-321). He vehemently objected to Justice Powell's assertion that the risk of racial bias in Georgia's capital-sentencing system was not "constitutionally significant" (*McCleskey* at 325-328). Pointing out that the Baldus study showed that "blacks who kill whites are sentenced to death at nearly *twenty-two times* the rate of blacks who kill blacks and more than *seven times* the rate of whites who kill blacks," Justice Brennan contended that "we should not be willing to take a person's life if the chance that his death sentence was irrationally imposed is *more* likely than not" (*McCleskey* at 327-328).[11]

The *McClesky* decision dealt a major blow to opponents of the death penalty, but many abolitionists were even more dismayed by the Court's 1987 holding in *Tison v. Arizona*. The *Tison* decision significantly modified the Court's aforementioned 1982 ruling in *Enmund v. Florida*, forbidding the execution of those who participate in a felony that leads to murder but who do not actually kill or intend to kill the victim. In *Tison*, the justices considered the fate of Ricky and Raymond Tison, two young brothers who helped their father, Gary Tison, and his cellmate, Randy Greenawalt, escape from the Arizona State Prison in 1978. Several days later, the escape car lost a tire on a desert road, and the group decided to flag down a passing motorist and steal his car. After a Mazda occupied by John Lyons, his wife, his two-year-old son, and his fifteen-year-old niece pulled over to offer help, Gary Tison and Randy Greenawalt took the family back to the escape car, held them there at gunpoint, and told the brothers to go back to the Mazda to get some water. When they did so, their father and his friend brutally shotgunned their four captives to death. Although Ricky and Raymond subsequently testified that they were surprised by the shooting, they nonetheless stayed with their father until they were captured several days later after a shootout with the police in which Randy Greenawalt was also captured and their father was killed (*Tison* at 139-141).

The Tison brothers and Randy Greenawalt were all convicted for the murder of the Lyons family and sentenced to death. Randy Greenawalt, one of the actual murderers, certainly was eligible for the death penalty. But could the Tison brothers be executed for murders that the state could not prove that they committed or even intended to commit? The *Enmund* holding would seem to answer this question in the negative, but the Supreme Court disagreed. Writing for the majority, Justice O'Connor reasoned that there was nothing cruel and unusual about executing defendants who neither committed nor intended to commit murder (1) if they participated in a "major" way in the underlying felony that led to murder and (2) if they demonstrated a "reckless indifference to human life" while doing so (*Tison* at 158). As Justice O'Connor explained it, the defendant's role in the armed robbery and murders in *Enmund* was "minor"; the Tison brothers, on the other hand, participated fully in the escape, kidnapping and robbery "and watched the killing after which [they] chose to aid those whom [they] had placed in the position to kill rather than their victims" (*Tison* at 152). Focusing only on the question of whether or not the defendant intended to kill, she continued, did not take into account that "reckless disregard for human life may be every bit as shocking to the moral sense as an 'intent to kill'" (*Tison* at 157). She added that "in these midrange felony murder cases...the majority of American jurisdictions clearly authorize capital punishment" (*Tison* at 155).

In a lengthy dissenting opinion joined by Justices Marshall, Stevens, and Blackmun, Justice Brennan challenged both Justice O'Connor's mathematics and her logic (*Tison* at 159-185). Pointing out that Justice O'Connor had excluded from her survey the fourteen states that do not authorize capital punishment, Justice Brennan declared that when these states are included along with those that require proof of intent to kill in order to impose a death sentence, "one discovers that approximately three-fifths of American jurisdictions do not authorize the death penalty for a non-triggerman absent a finding that he intended to kill" (*Tison* at 175). He accused the majority of creating "a new category of culpability" and blithely discarding a fundamental principle found in virtually all European and Commonwealth countries, that the death penalty—if it is ever to be used—must be reserved for those who either killed or intended to kill another human being (*Tison* at 170-171). The Court's holding, he concluded, was inconsistent with *Enmund*, violated basic standards of fairness and proportionality, and went well beyond the retributive principle of "an eye for an eye..." (*Tison* at 174-185).[12]

To those who oppose capital punishment, the *Tison* ruling was a chilling indication that the Supreme Court's future decisions would continue to expand the category of death-eligible defendants. This is what the Court in fact has done and is likely to continue to do. Two important 1989 decisions, both announced on June 26 of that year, illustrate the current trend in the Court's death-penalty jurisprudence. First, in *Penry v. Lynaugh*, the Court held that executing a person who is mentally retarded does not constitute cruel and unusual punishment. Johnny Paul Penry, who was twenty-two at the time he committed murder, was diagnosed as "moderately" mentally retarded with an IQ ranging between 50 and 63. This meant that he had the mental capacity of an average 6 1/2 year-old child (*Penry* at 308). But according to Justice O'Connor's majority opinion, this circumstance was outweighed in importance by the fact that the State of Texas had found Penry to be competent to stand trial and to have "a reasonable degree of rational understanding...as well as factual understanding of the case against him" (*Penry* at 333). Justice O'Connor suggested that it might be cruel and unusual to execute "profoundly" or "severely" retarded people, but that the mental limitations of someone who was merely "moderately" retarded did not automatically preclude imposition of the death penalty (*Penry* at 333-340). Four dissenting justices failed to convince the majority that "[t]he impairment of a mentally retarded offender's reasoning abilities [and] control over impulsive behavior limit his or her culpability so that, whatever other punishment might be appropriate, the ultimate penalty of death is always...disproportionate to his or her blameworthiness and hence is unconstitutional" (*Penry* at 346).[13]

On the same day the holding in *Penry* was decided, the Court announced its decision in a case that raised the issue of whether the prohibition against cruel and unusual punishments precluded the execution of defendants who were under the age of eighteen at the time of their offense. One year earlier, a closely divided Court had held that fifteen-year-old offenders could not be executed unless and until more states enacted laws authorizing such executions (*Thompson v. Oklahoma*, 1988). But in *Stanford v. Kentucky*, the Court found that it was already sufficiently clear that there was no national consensus against imposing capital punishment on sixteen-year-old and seventeen-year-old offenders. Writing for the majority, Justice Scalia noted that of the states that permit capital punishment, fifteen declined to impose it on sixteen-year-olds and twelve declined to impose it on seventeen-year-olds (*Stanford* at 372). These numbers, according to Justice Scalia, did not establish enough of a national consensus to show that executing such young offenders was contrary to America's evolving standards of decency and thus violative of the Eighth Amendment (*Stanford* at 372-373). As Justice Brennan pointed out in dissent, the majority's holding would ensure that the United States would remain in the embarrassing company of Rwanda, Barbadus, Pakistan, and Bangladesh as the only nations in the world that still execute children (*Stanford* at 389).[14]

Justice Scalia, however, rejected such international comparisons as irrelevant, emphasizing that "only *American* conceptions of decency are dispositive" (*Stanford* at 369 n. 1). He also repudiated another of Justice Brennan's arguments: that executing those who are too young, immature, and impulsive to take full responsibility for their actions fails to serve the only two penological goals the Court has recognized as legitimate in capital cases—retribution and deterrence (*Stanford* at 377).[15] Indeed, it is this part of Justice Scalia's opinion that is most troubling for those who do not want the United States to become the world leader in executions.

Writing for a plurality (since Justice O'Connor did not join this part of the Court's opinion), Justice Scalia asserted that arguments grounded in the claim that juveniles are less mature, more impulsive, and less likely to possess fully developed cognitive skills than adults must fail because they rest on social-science studies rather than the judgment of the American people (*Stanford* at 377-378). Social-science studies, according to Justice Scalia, are irrelevant because the Court has no business evaluating such studies in order to determine whether a particular punishment violates the Eighth Amendment (*Stanford* at 378). It is the citizenry of the United States, not judges, who must be persuaded that children are less blameworthy and are therefore ineligible for the death penalty (*Stanford* at 378). Accordingly, the Court in future death-penalty cases would ignore "ethioscientific" evidence and consider only "objective indicia"—the most important of which are the laws passed by Congress and the state legislatures (*Stanford* at 377-378). In the future, Justice Scalia warned, the Eighth Amendment would be taken literally. A challenged punishment would have to be *both* cruel *and* unusual, as determined by objective factors, to fail the Court's Eighth Amendment tests (*Stanford* at 369). In other words, a cruel punishment will withstand constitutional scrutiny if enough states still authorize it. Just how many states are enough will be determined by the Court on a case-by-case basis.[16]

In the years since *Stanford*, Justice Scalia's brand of jurisprudence—extraordinary deference to laws and procedures that broaden the application of the death penalty—has clearly been in the ascendancy. In the majority of the most important death-penalty cases, the conservative majority, led by Chief Justice Rehnquist and Justice Scalia, has prevailed. For example, in *Payne v. Tennessee*, Chief Justice Rehnquist ended the 1990-91 term by authoring a majority opinion that reversed the Court's previous holdings (*Booth v. Maryland* (1987); *South Carolina v. Gathers* (1989)) prohibiting the use of so-called "victim-impact" statements in the penalty phase of capital trials. In *Payne*, a six-justice majority rejected Justice Stevens' dissenting argument that permitting juries to base death-penalty decisions on such idiosyncratic factors as the victim's reputation and the persuasiveness of the victim's family in describing their loss would distract jurors from examining the character of the defendant and the nature of the crime. This consideration, in turn, would pose a "constitutionally unacceptable risk" that juries would impose the death penalty in an arbitrary and discriminatory manner (*Payne* at 2628-2631).[17]

One other area of the Supreme Court's recent death-penalty jurisprudence deserves to be mentioned before we turn to the risky enterprise of predicting the Court's future role in capital punishment. In a series of cases beginning in the 1988-89 term, the Court has erected exceptionally strict substantive and procedural roadblocks to the use of the federal habeas corpus statute by state death-row inmates who wish to appeal their state criminal convictions.[18] Indeed, the Court has managed to eviscerate nearly all of its prior holdings in this area, thereby crippling the power of federal courts to overturn even the most questionable state-court convictions and/or sentences of capital defendants.

Federal habeas corpus law is extraordinarily complex, and space limitations preclude an examination of all of the Supreme Court's recent rulings. However, in the next section we will see that the Court's most recent habeas holdings have so strictly limited death-row inmates' rights of appeal that in 1994 Justice Harry Blackmun, citing the growing likelihood of erroneous convictions and unfair death sentences, renounced his former position in support of the constitutionality of capital punishment. Ironically, this reversal indicates that the best hope for the abolitionist dream of eliminating capital punishment may lie in the very trends so far discussed. It is possible that the contemporary Supreme Court's growing willingness to expand the death-penalty's reach and tolerate arbitrariness and discrimination in its application will eventually lead a future Court to outlaw capital punishment as a cruel and unusual punishment forbidden by the Eighth Amendment.

THE SUPREME COURT AND THE PROSPECTS FOR ABOLISHING CAPITAL PUNISHMENT

The recent trends in the Supreme Court's death-penalty jurisprudence suggest that the pattern of American executions is about to change dramatically. Until quite recently, actual execution had been the *least* common cause of death for those condemned to die under post-*Furman* capital-punishment statutes. Death-row inmates more commonly died from old age, suicide, or murder at the hands of their fellow prisoners (Streib, 1984: 443). Indeed, from 1976 to 1983, only eleven death-row inmates were executed. In 1984, twenty-one inmates were executed, followed by eighteen in 1985, eighteen in 1986, twenty-five in 1987, eleven in 1988, sixteen in 1989, twenty-three in 1990, and fourteen in 1991 (NAACP, 1994-95: 3). But while executions were carried out from 1984 to 1991 an average of less than nineteen times per year, the number of defendants sentenced to death each year averaged approximately 250 (Haas and Inciardi, 1988: 12). This sharp numerical discrepancy may reflect deep ambivalence toward the death penalty on the part of the American people, indicating that peoples' willingness to endorse capital punishment in the abstract is not necessarily an accurate measure of their willingness to put it into practice. Indeed, recent research shows that even though public opinion polls continue to measure public support for capital punishment at approximately 70%, most of these death-penalty supporters acknowledge that they would favor abolishing capital punishment if offenders were given a sentence of life imprisonment without parole combined with a restitution requirement (Bowers, 1993). The result of this ambivalence toward the penalty of death has been obvious—a relatively small number of executions and a burgeoning death-row population that reached 2,976 as of January 31, 1995 (NAACP, 1994-95).

To some extent, the gap between the death-row population and the number of people executed could be attributed to the length of the appeals process. It generally takes anywhere from six to ten years, and sometimes longer, for condemned inmates to exhaust all of their appeals and postconviction remedies (Haas and Inciardi, 1988:13). And these appeals have often been successful in reversing death sentences. Since 1976, 1,439 death-penalty convictions or sentences have been reversed and seventy-two death-row inmates have had their sentences commuted (NAACP, 1994-95:1). But as we have seen, over the past decade, the U.S. Supreme Court has expanded the category of death-eligible defendants, weakened safeguards against unfair death sentences, and streamlined the death-penalty appeals process. Will this, in fact, result in the execution of more people in the years to come?

Almost certainly, the answer is "yes." Indeed, the general trend toward a greater number of executions appears to have already begun. In 1992, there were thirty-one executions followed by thirty-eight in 1993, and thirty-one in 1994 (NAACP, 1994-95). It stands to reason that as the final appeals are exhausted for those now on death row, many of whom have been there for more than six years, the annual execution total will rise.

Equally important, over the next ten to fifteen years, we will undoubtedly see an expansion of the geographical reach of the death penalty. As of January 31, 1995, 239 of the 267 post-*Gregg* executions (91%) had been carried out by fourteen states—Texas (89), Florida (33), Virginia (25), Louisiana (21), Georgia (18), Missouri (11), Alabama (10), Arkansas (9), North Carolina (7), South Carolina (4), Mississippi (4), Delaware (4), Oklahoma (3), and Maryland (1). Thus, capital punishment remains largely a southern phenomenon; only twenty-four (9%) post-*Gregg* executions had been carried out in non-southern states—Nevada (5), Utah (4), Arizona (3), Indiana (3), California (2), Illinois (2), Washington (2), Idaho (1), Wyoming (1), and Nebraska (1) (NAACP, 1994-95). But even this represents a noteworthy increase in less than six years. As of March 22, 1988, only six persons had been put to death in nonsouthern states—Nevada (2), Indiana (2), and Utah (2) (Haas and Inciardi, 1988: 12). Among the states that have only recently begun to execute offenders are Missouri (11 since January 1989), Arkansas (9 since June 1990), Delaware (4 since March 1992), Oklahoma (3 since September 1990), California (2 since April 1992), Illinois (2 since September 1990), Washington (2 since January 1993), Wyoming (1 in January 1992), Idaho (1 in January 1994), Maryland (1 in May 1994), and Nebraska (1 in September 1994) (NAACP, 1994-95).

Even so, thirteen out of the thirty-eight states that currently have capital-punishment statutes have not yet executed anyone in the post-*Gregg* era—Colorado, Connecticut, Kentucky, Montana, New Hampshire, New Jersey, New Mexico, New York, Ohio, Oregon, Pennsylvania, South Dakota, and Tennessee (NAACP, 1994-95). But many of these states, most of which are nonsouthern, are moving toward the first of what could turn out to be a significant number of executions. For example, fifty of the 171 inmates currently sentenced to death in Pennsylvania have exhausted all of their state appeals, and a state court recently ordered the governor to speed up the process of issuing warrants (Eshelman, 1994). Once all fifty warrants are signed, most of the affected inmates will pursue federal appellate remedies, a process that—because of the U.S. Supreme Court's approval of expedited procedures in habeas corpus cases—may not take nearly as long as it has in the past. Other states with growing death-row populations that are moving steadily towards a resumption of executions are Ohio (137), Tennessee (102), and Kentucky (28), (NAACP, 1994-95). Even in New Jersey, with a relatively small death-row population (9), the state's highest court began to uphold death sentences in 1991, ending a nine-year period in which the court had consistently reversed such sentences (Bienen et al., 1990: 713-714).

Abolitionists also cannot ignore the possibility that one or more of the twelve states without a capital-punishment law may resurrect the death penalty. On March 7, 1995, New York became the thirty-eighth state with capital punishment when Governor George Pataki signed into law a thirty-one page death penalty law that takes effect September 1, 1995 (Dao, 1995). Similarly, in Massachusetts, Governor William

Weld is attempting to reinstate the death penalty (Death Penalty Information Center, 1992: 8). Moreover, it is quite possible that the U.S. Government and the U.S. Military will resume executions before the end of the twentieth century. There currently are thirteen people under a federal sentence of death, and as this book was going to press, the U.S. Congress was on the verge of passing a new crime bill that would add nearly seventy new federal death-penalty offenses (Wines, 1994).

All things considered, it seems quite likely that by the year 2010 we will see a significant increase in executions and in the number of jurisdictions that execute offenders. The death penalty almost surely will become more of a national phenomenon, no longer isolated in the South (although southern states can be expected to execute significantly more offenders than nonsouthern states). But how high will the number of executions go? Will the number rise to levels approaching the average of 152 per year who were executed in the 1930s? Or even to the annual average of 118 in the 1940s or sixty-eight in the 1950s? (Bowers, 1984: 50.)

My prediction is that the United States will not return to the levels of the 1930s or 1940s, but it may very well return to levels comparable to the 1950s. It is not unreasonable to expect that the average annual number of executions in the first decade of the twenty-first century will be somewhere between fifty to eighty. The reason that it is not expected to go higher is that, as explained earlier, support for the death penalty is not nearly as deep as it is broad. The public's ambivalence toward capital punishment may very well turn to discontentment once the number of executed offenders reaches higher levels. Even now, American juries, showing that their "bark is worse than their bite," return death-penalty verdicts in less than 25% of first-degree murder cases (Haas and Inciardi, 1988:11).

Moreover, a growing number of public officials in such death-penalty states as Texas and Florida have complained about the crushing financial costs of the death penalty. In Florida, for example, it costs six times more to execute a person than to incarcerate a prisoner for life with no parole. As a result of the heightened due process required in the pretrial, trial, and post-trial stages of capital cases, Florida by 1988 had spent $57.2 million to execute eighteen people. Yet a mid-year budget cut of $45 million for the Florida Department of Corrections forced the early release of three thousand inmates (Death Penalty Information Center, 1992: 4). As the number of execution rises (and in all probability without a corresponding decline in murder rates),[19] a growing number of Americans may become increasingly reluctant to allow the death penalty to siphon off scarce resources that could be used to strengthen the police, courts, and correctional agencies.

The best hope for an abolitionist future almost certainly lies in greater public knowledge concerning the death penalty. In *Furman v. Georgia*, Justice Marshall asserted that if the American people were given accurate information about capital punishment—its failure to deter crime any more effectively than life imprisonment, its high costs relative to life imprisonment, and the many cases of wrongfully executed defendants—they would renounce the death penalty and replace it with lengthy prison sentences (*Furman* at 360-363). Studies lend support to what has become known as the "Marshall hypothesis." Interview and questionnaire studies have shown that support for the death penalty is indeed founded on misinformation about the effects of capital punishment and how it is used in our society (Ellsworth and Ross,

1983). Moreover, when representative samples of the American adult population are presented with pamphlets that provide factual, unbiased material on the realities of capital punishment, enough people change their minds to turn what had been minority opposition to the death penalty into a majority (Sarat and Vidmar, 1976).

If anything will turn the current minority position on capital punishment into a majority position, it is the cumulative impact of the Supreme Court death-penalty decisions discussed earlier. For example, how will Americans react when the evidence mounts that *McCleskey v. Kemp* (1987) was wrongly decided? One indication came when the U.S. House of Representatives recently voted to add a racial justice provision to a prospective crime control law. Citing the studies put forth in *McCleskey*, this provision would effectively reverse *McCleskey* by permitting condemned defendants to challenge their state or federal death sentences by using statistical evidence to show a pattern of racial bias in the past capital sentences meted out in their jurisdictions (Wines, 1984). Noting that opponents of the provision, led by Representative Bill McCullom of Florida, vehemently argued that it would "abolish the death penalty in America," a *New York Times* editorial raised an obvious question: "What more damning statement could be made of capital punishment than that it could not survive if applied with racial justice?" (*N.Y. Times* Editorial, 1994). If the evidence becomes irrefutable—and well-known—that human beings simply are incapable of administering the death penalty without racial discrimination, the pendulum of public opinion may very well begin to swing back toward the prevailing attitude in 1966 when a Harris survey found 47% of the public opposed to capital punishment, 38% in favor of it, and 15% unsure (Haas and Inciardi, 1988: 11).

A similar shift in public opinion might become evident when the long-term effects of the Supreme Court's 1989 decisions in *Stanford v. Kentucky* and *Penry v. Lynaugh* become clear. Public support for the death penalty may very well erode noticeably as children increasingly are selected to receive the ultimate penalty. So far only nine of the 227 post-*Gregg* execution victims have been juvenile offenders (NAACP, 1993-94), but this figure can be expected to rise in the aftermath of *Stanford*. The impact of *Penry* could also contribute to public doubts about the morality of capital punishment. The Court held that Johnny Paul Penry was eligible for the death penalty even though he had a mental age of 6 1/2. One can only wonder where—if anywhere—the Court will draw the line here. The *Penry* Court suggested but did not clearly hold that the execution of "severely" or "profoundly" retarded offenders would constitute cruel and unusual punishment (*Penry* at 333). Will the Court countenance the execution of those with a mental age of two, three, or four? And if it does, will the majority of Americans defend such executions as having deterrent or retributive value? What will happen, as seems inevitable, when a greater number of women are executed? Although there are now forty-eight women on death rows around the country, only one of the 263 post-*Gregg* executions was of a female offender (NAACP, 1994-95). This statistic suggests a certain squeamishness on the part of the public when it comes to executing women—a chord that may not evoke approval when, as is now possible under current Supreme Court rulings, a sixteen-year-old girl with a mental age of 6 1/2 is put to death.

Tison v. Arizona (1987) also could eventually lead people to rethink their assumption about the fairness of capital punishment. It is not at all certain that the killing of those offenders who themselves never killed, intended to kill, or attempted to kill will ultimately square with basic American notions of fairness and justice.[20] Are Americans so fearful and angry about crime that they will reject the longstanding principle of "an eye for an eye" and replace it with a principle calling for "an eye for an eye and then some?" (Haas, 1994.) This may be a hotly debated issue by the year 2010. And possibly by the year 2025, if not sooner, the answer may turn out to be "no." There is still another eventuality—made all the more likely by the Supreme Court's recent decisions curtailing habeas corpus appeals by death-row inmates—that may prove pivotal in convincing the public that the death penalty can no longer be tolerated. Indeed, it was the chilling impact of this particular eventuality that helped lead to the abolition of capital punishment in England—the execution of defendants who are later discovered to be innocent (Christoph, 1962). Legal scholars have already convincingly demonstrated that the erroneous conviction of people charged with capital crimes has long been—and continues to be—a major problem in the United States. In the most thorough study to date, Michael Radelet, Hugo Bedau, and Constance Putnam (1992) carefully documented the cases of 416 innocent Americans convicted of capital crimes between 1900 and 1991. Although some two dozen of these people were executed—and although the problem of wrongful capital convictions appears to be growing—the magnitude of the problem has so far eluded the American public.

But as a result of inherent human fallibility, the process of determining guilt in capital cases will always be plagued by such problems as mistaken eyewitness identification, perjured testimony, coerced confessions, laboratory errors, overzealous officials who conceal exculpatory evidence, and inattentive or confused jurors. And these kinds of errors can only become more difficult to discover and correct than they have been in the past. The Supreme Court's recent efforts to expedite the capital-appeals process may help to reduce somewhat the crushing financial costs of the death penalty, but they will also deprive those who have been wrongfully convicted of a full and fair opportunity to prove their innocence. As more such cases occur and become highly publicized in the print and broadcast media, it stands to reason that a growing number of Americans will have second thoughts about the wisdom of imposing an irreversible punishment on criminal defendants.

My prediction, therefore, is that the Supreme Court's recent death-penalty decisions will increase both the number of executions and the geographical reach of executions by the year 2010. The number of executions will also most likely reach levels comparable to the 1950s—fifty to eighty per year—but will never return to the levels of the 1930s of approximately 150 per year. While it is unlikely that more than a few states will statutorily abolish capital punishment by 2010, we should see a growing pattern of reluctance to perform executions in many states.

Although there will not be a "deluge" or "avalanche" of executions, there will be enough executions to force Americans to rethink the death penalty in the first decade of the twenty-first century. As a result of the Supreme Court's expansion of the categories of death-eligible defendants, there will be more executions of juvenile offenders and mentally retarded offenders, and it will be more clear than ever that racial bias is the key factor in determining who dies. There will also be more cases in which the death penalty is imposed on nonmurderers and, most disturbingly, on defendants who will be conclusively—but too late—shown to be innocent.[21] As a result, perhaps as early as 2010, a majority of Americans will begin to turn against capital punishment.

Abolitionist movements will gain momentum in an increasing number of state capitols and in the U.S. Congress, and a growing number of jurisdictions will abolish capital punishment. Sometime in the mid-twenty-first century, with no more than eight states retaining death-penalty statutes, the U.S. Supreme Court, citing the dwindling number of death-penalty laws, and executions, as convincing evidence of a new societal consensus against the death penalty, will declare capital punishment in all cases to be a violation of the cruel and unusual punishment clause of the Eighth Amendment.

If this scenario proves correct the American public will have gone through the same transition as Justice Harry Blackmun. Justice Blackmun had joined not only in the *Gregg* majority, but had supported the *mandatory* death-penalty laws under review in *Woodson v. North Carolina* (1976) and *Roberts v. Louisiana* (1977). But on February 23, 1994, after twenty-four years on the Supreme Court, Justice Blackmun repudiated capital punishment. In *Callins v. Collins*, he pointed to the central dilemma underlying all of the Supreme Court's post-*Gregg* jurisprudence. How can an appropriate balance be struck between the promise of consistency and equality in capital sentencing and the seemingly contradictory requirement of individualized sentencing in capital cases? Justice Blackmun's answer was that these two goals simply cannot be reconciled. "It seems that the decision whether a human being should live or die is so inherently subjective—rife with all of life's understandings, experiences, prejudices and passions—that it inevitably defies the rationality and consistency required by the Constitution" (*Callins* at 1134-1135). A quarter of a century of handling the hundreds of death-penalty cases that came to the nation's highest court, he wrote, had convinced him that human beings are not capable of devising procedural or substantive rules that can prevent the inevitable intrusion of arbitrariness and racial discrimination into the capital-sentencing process (*Callins* at 1135-1136).

Justice Blackmun also made it clear that his decision to renounce capital punishment was heavily influenced by what he called the Court's "obvious eagerness to do away with any restrictions on the states' power to execute whomever and however they please" (*Callins* at 1137). He singled out the Court's 1993 decision in *Herrera v. Collins* for especially strong criticism (*Callins* at 1137-1138). The *Herrera* majority, he asserted, had not only refused to afford Leonel Torres Herrera an evidentiary hearing "despite his colorable showing of actual innocence," but it had erected "nearly insurmountable barriers" to any capital defendant's ability to get a federal habeas corpus hearing on a claim of actual innocence (*Callins* at 1138). The result of *Herrera*, he predicted, will be an increasing number of innocent people who will never have a full and fair opportunity to challenge their conviction and death sentence (*Callins* at 1138). Under these circumstances, he concluded, he would no longer "tinker with the machinery of death" (*Callins* at 1130) and he was optimistic that "this Court will eventually conclude that...the death penalty must be abandoned altogether" (*Callins* at 1138).

To be sure, Justice Blackmun's hope will not become a reality in the very near future. On April 6, 1994, he announced that he would resign from the Court at the end of the 1993-94 term. President Clinton, a death-penalty supporter, is not likely to go out of his way to select a death-penalty opponent to replace Justice Blackmun. Moreover, Senate conservatives have stated that they would view any lack of support for capital punishment as a fatal flaw for a potential nominee and do what they could to block his or her confirmation (Reske, 1994: 14). Although Justice Ruth Bader

Ginsburg, President Clinton's 1993 choice to replace retiring Justice Byron White, has not yet stated her views on capital punishment (Cohen, 1993: A19), it seems safe to say that no current justice supports the position taken by Justices Brennan and Marshall in *Furman*—that the death penalty in all cases violates the Eighth Amendment (*Furman* at 257-306, 314-374). But there will undoubtedly be some changes in the composition of the Supreme Court by the year 2010 and, of course, *many* more by the year 2050. If by then, the American people, like Justice Blackmun, become convinced by the weight of the evidence that the death penalty is useless, dangerous, and self-defeating, the Supreme Court will surely reach the same conclusion.

CONCLUSION

In their thought-provoking book, *Capital Punishment and the American Agenda*, Franklin Zimring and Gordon Hawkins (1986: 148) argue that "America has outgrown the death penalty but is reluctant to acknowledge [it]." But what will it take to convince the American people to "acknowledge it"? Ironically, the answer may lie in the U.S. Supreme Court's recent death-penalty jurisprudence. Since 1983, the Court has weakened the procedural protections available to convicted defendants, created formidable procedural obstacles to federal appellate review of capital appeals, ensured the continuing pervasiveness of racial discrimination in capital sentencing, and extended the reach of the death penalty to juvenile offenders, mentally retarded offenders, and those who never killed nor intended to kill. By the year 2010, the short-term effects of these decisions will be evident—more executions in more states. But with more executions will come more erroneous executions, more evidence of arbitrariness and racial bias in capital sentencing, and more questions about the morality of executing children, the mentally retarded, nonmurderers, or anyone else in a world where human error, caprice, and prejudice are inevitable. By the middle part of the twenty-first century, the American people will repudiate capital punishment and the Supreme Court will declare it in all cases to be a cruel and unusual punishment forbidden by the Eighth Amendment.

STUDY QUESTIONS

1. Is there any way to resolve the conflict between the goals of *consistent sentencing and individualized sentencing* in capital cases? Does the tension between these two seemingly contradictory goals expose a fatal flaw in the Supreme Court's death-penalty jurisprudence—one that will ultimately lead to the demise of capital punishment in America?

2. The author is highly critical of the Supreme Court's decision in *Tison v. Arizona* (1987) and suggests that the death penalty, if used at all, should be reserved only for those who intentionally take another person's life. But are there crimes that do not result in murder that are nevertheless heinous enough to warrant the death penalty? How about a kidnapper who mutilates his victims but does not kill them? How about a serial rapist who tortures his victims unmercifully?

3. The author cites *Sumner v. Shuman* (1987) as demonstrating the Supreme Court's refusal to sanction any kind of *mandatory* death-penalty law. What is wrong with a law that mandates the death penalty for a convicted murderer serving a life-without-parole sentence who kills again?

4. The author commented that even though scholars have carefully documented over four hundred twentieth-century cases of erroneous capital convictions in the United States, the scope of this problem seems to elude the American public. Newspapers and other media regularly cover numerous cases of wrongful criminal convictions and yet this issue seems to have had little effect on the death penalty debate. In the face of overwhelming evidence of inevitable, and all too frequent, human fallibility, why do so many Americans assume that erroneous convictions are extremely rare and aberrational rather than a regular part of the death-penalty process?

NOTES

1. For detailed discussions of *Furman*, see Polsby (1973) and McFadden (1972).

2. See *Proffitt v. Florida* (1976) and *Jurek v. Texas* (1976).

3. Among the many good analyses of *Gregg, Woodson,* and the other 1976 death-penalty cases are Barry (1979) and Rhoads (1977).

4. This issue is discussed at length by Sundby (1991).

5. This possibility and other implications of the *Lockett* decision are examined by Radin (1980).

6. See, for example, *Dobbert v. Florida* (1977) (holding that changes in Florida's capital punishment law between the time of the murder and the defendant's sentencing did not amount to an *ex post facto* violation) and *Estelle v. Smith* (excluding psychiatric testimony on *Miranda* grounds, but pointedly noting that psychiatric evidence as to a defendant's "future dangerousness" is generally admissible).

7. Arguably, the Court's emerging new attitude first became apparent in Justice Rehnquist's dissent from a denial of certiorari in *Coleman v. Balkcom* (1981). Urging his colleagues to take all necessary steps to expedite the administration of the death penalty, Justice Rehnquist referred to the slow pace of executions as a "mockery" of our criminal justice system" (*Balkcom* at 958). Pointing to the lengthy appeals process in capital cases, Justice Rehnquist lamented that "[g]iven so many bites at the apple, the odds favor petitioner finding some court willing to vacate his death sentence because in its view his trial or sentence was not free from constitutional error" (*Balkcom* at 957).

8. See also *Boyde v. California* (1990) (applying the reasoning of *Blystone* and thus upholding a sentencing scheme that requires the imposition of a death sentence when aggravating circumstances outweigh mitigating circumstances).

9. See, for example, *Ake v. Oklahoma* (1985) overturning a death sentence on the ground that an indigent capital defendant was defied access to a psychiatric examination that was necessary to prepare an effective defense based on his mental condition); *Francis v. Franklin* (1985) (invalidating a conviction and death sentence on the ground that the instructions to the jury violated the Fourteenth Amendment requirement that the state must prove every element of a criminal offense beyond a reasonable doubt); *Caldwell v. Mississippi* (1985) (vacating a death sentence because the prosecutor, citing the inevitability of appellate review, urged the jury not to view itself as actually determining whether the defendant dies); *Maynard v. Cartwright* (1988) (reversing a death sentence because one of the statutory aggravating circumstances was unconstitutionally vague); *Mills v. Maryland* (1988) (vacating a death sentence imposed under a state law that led jurors to believe that they could not consider all relevant mitigating factors); *Lankford v. Idaho* (1991) (invalidating a death sentence in a case in which the prosecution announced that it would not seek the

death penalty and the trial judge failed to provide adequate notice that death could still be imposed as the punishment); *Dawson v. Delaware* (1992) (reversing a death sentence imposed by a jury that had been told to consider the defendant's racist political views as an aggravating circumstance); and *Morgan v. Illinois* (1992) (invalidating a death sentence because the defense was not permitted to challenge the eligibility of jurors who would *automatically* impose the death penalty after a conviction).

10. For a detailed analysis of the study, its implications, and its treatment by the courts, see Baldus, D.C., Woodworth, G., and Pulaski, Jr., C.A. (1990).

11. See Holland, M.E. (1988) for a good critique of *McCleskey v. Kemp*.

12. The *Tison* holding is critically analyzed by Bass (1988).

13. The *Penry* decision ha been greeted with an outpouring of criticism. See especially Reed (1993), Cohen (1991), and Dick-Hurwitz (1990). It will strike many as paradoxical that in *Ford v. Wainwright* (1986), the Court held that the Eighth Amendment prohibits the execution of insane death-row inmates. The *Ford* case and its implications are examined by Miller and Radelet (1993).

14. For a penetrating critique of *Stanford* and *Penry*, see Miller (1990). The most comprehensive overview of the historical and contemporary practice of subjecting minors to capital punishment is by Streib (1987).

15. In *Gregg v. Georgia* (1976: 184-187), the Court cited retribution and deterrence as two legitimate penological rationales for the death penalty. Surprisingly, the Court has never officially recognized a third justification—incapacitation. Many avowed opponents of capital punishment will acknowledge that this rationale is not totally without merit. Studies consistently show that convicted murderers are less likely to commit murders in prison or after release than are inmates convicted of such lesser crimes as robbery, burglary, and aggravated assault (Sellin, 1980: 103-120). Nevertheless, there are some death-row inmates who appear to be incorrigible, willing to kill guards or fellow inmates, and capable of escape. It thus can be argued that the death penalty is the only way to be 100% certain that a sociopath or a serial killer will never kill again. On the other hand, the noted attorney and abolitionist Anthony Amsterdam has responded to this argument by declaring that "[y]ou cannot tell me...that a society which is capable of putting a man on the moon is incapable of putting a man in prison, keeping him there, and keeping him from killing while he is there." (Amsterdam, 1982: 354).

16. See Gey (1992) for an insightful analysis of Justice Scalia's death-penalty jurisprudence.

17. The *Payne* decision continues to provoke highly critical commentaries in law reviews. See, for example, Levy (1993), Casimir (1993), and Oberlander (1992).

18. See especially *Teague v. Lane* (1989) (determining that new constitutional rulings benefiting defendants cannot be applied retroactively in habeas corpus proceedings), *Murray v. Giarratano* (1989) (holding that indigent death-row inmates have no right to counsel in habeas corpus petitions), *Butler v. McKellar* (1990) (holding that the *Teague* retroactivity doctrine bars state death-row inmates from invoking a new rule—one that was "susceptible to debate among reasonable minds" and was not clearly dictated by precedent—in a federal habeas corpus proceeding), *McCleskey v. Zant* (1991) (finding that a death-row inmate's failure to raise a Sixth Amendment claim—a claim based on facts that he and his attorney did not become aware of until later—in his first habeas corpus petition constituted "an abuse of the writ" that precluded a second habeas corpus hearing); *Coleman v. Thompson* (1991) (deciding that an attorney's error in filing a notice of appeal from the denial of state postconviction relief one day late did not constitute a "cause" for death-row inmate's procedural default and that the inmate thus was procedurally barred from

seeking federal habeas corpus relief), *Keeney v. Tamayo-Reyes* (1992) (holding that the "cause-and-prejudice standard" governs question of whether a death-row inmate forfeited his right to federal habeas corpus review by failing to fully develop his claim in state court proceedings), *Gomez v. District Court* (1992) (ruling that the claim that execution by cyanide gas violates the Eighth Amendment was waived when not presented in an earlier federal habeas corpus petition), *Sawyer v. Whitley* (1992) (requiring a federal habeas petitioner bringing a successive claim to prove by clear and convincing evidence that but for a constitutional error, no reasonable juror would have found him eligible for the death penalty), and *Herrera v. Collins* (1993) (finding that a death-row inmate's claim of actual innocence based on newly discovered evidence did not entitle him to federal habeas corpus relief). These and other noteworthy decisions are explained by Robbins (1994).

19. After over fifty years of research and dozens of published studies, the evidence is overwhelming that the death penalty is no more effective than life imprisonment in deterring murder. Moreover, a growing body of research indicates that executions may have a "brutalizing effect" that causes a small but discernible short-term *increase* in the murder rate. See generally Cochran et al. (1994) and Bowers (1988).

20. In fact, recent studies indicate that the majority of Americans soundly support the principle of proportional justice and reject the death penalty as a fair punishment for felony-murder accessories. See Finkel and Smith (1993) and Finkel and Duff (1991).

21. It is also inevitable that there will continue to be executions in which the condemned inmate suffers an especially prolonged, painful, or horrifying death, such as occurred in (1) a 1983 gassing in Mississippi during which the inmate had convulsions for eight minutes; (2) a 1983 electrocution in Alabama during which the inmate took fourteen minutes to die, but not before smoke and flame erupted from his head; and (3) a 1985 lethal injection in Texas in which technicians took forty-five minutes to search the inmate for a suitable vein in which to insert the needle (Amnesty International, 1987: 117-119). As more Americans become aware of such cases, their instinctive sense of mercy may prevail over their desire for lethal revenge.

REFERENCES

Amnesty International U.S.A. (1987). *The Death Penalty*. New York: Amnesty International.

Amsterdam, A. (1987). In Favorem Mortis. *Human Rights*, 14: 889-890.

Amsterdam, A.G. (1982). Capital Punishment. In H.A. Bedau (Ed.), *The Death Penalty in America, 3rd ed.* (pp. 346-358). New York: Oxford University Press.

Baldus, David C., Woodworth, C., and Pulaski, Jr., C.A. (1990). *Equal Justice and the Death Penalty: A Legal and Empirical Analysis*. Boston, MA: Northeastern University Press.

Barry, R.V. (1979). *Furman* to *Gregg*: The Judicial and Legislative History. *Howard Law Journal*, 22: 53-117.

Bass, W.K. (1988). *Tison v. Arizona*: A General Intent for Imposing Capital Punishment upon an Accomplice Felony Murderer. *University of Toledo Law Review*, 20: 255-292.

Bienen, L.B., Weiner, N.A., Allison, P.D., and Mills, D.L. (1990). The Reimposition of Capital Punishment in New Jersey: Felony Murder Cases. *Albany Law Review*, 54: 709-817.

Bowers, W.J. (1993). Capital Punishment and Contemporary Values: People's Misgivings and the Court's Misperceptions. *Law and Society Review*, 27, 157-175.

Bowers, W.J. (1984). *Legal Homicide: Death as Punishment in America, 1864-1982*. Boston, MA: Northeastern University Press.

Bowers, W.J. (1988). The Effect of Execution is Brutalization, Not Deterrence. In K.C. Haas and J.A. Inciardi (Eds.), *Challenging Capital Punishment: Legal and Social Science Approaches* (pp. 49-89). Newbury Park, CA: Sage Publications.

Casimir, G. (1993). *Payne v. Tennessee*: Overlooking Capital Sentencing Jurisprudence and Sate Decisis. *New England Journal on Criminal and Civil Confinement*, 19: 427-458.

Christoph, J.B. (1962). *Capital Punishment and British Politics: The British Movement to Abolish the Death Penalty* 1945-57. Chicago: University of Chicago Press.

Cochran, J.K., Chamlin, M.B., and Seth, M. (1994). Deterrence or Brutalization? An Impact Assessment of Oklahoma's Return to Capital Punishment. *Criminology*, 32: 107-134.

Cohen, R. (1993, June 22). Where Does Ginsburg Stand on the Death Penalty? *Washington Post*, p. A19.

Cohen, U.S. (1991). Exempting the Mentally Retarded from the Death Penalty: A Comment on Florida's Proposed Legislation. *Florida State University Law Review*, 19: 457-474.

Dao, J. (1995, March 8). "Death Penalty in New York is Restored after Eighteen Years; Pataki Sees Justice Served." *New York Times*, p. A1.

Death Penalty Information Center. (1992). *Millions Misspent: What Politicians Don't Say About the High Cost of the Death Penalty*. Washington, DC: The Center.

Dick-Hurwitz, R. (1990). *Penry v. Lynaugh*: The Supreme Court Deals a Fatal Blow to Mentally Retarded Capital Defendants. *University of Pittsburgh Law Review*, 51: 699-725.

Ellsworth, P.C. and Ross, L. (1983). Public Opinion and Capital Punishment: A Close Examination of the Views of Abolitionists and Retentionists. *Crime and Delinquency*, 29, 116-169.

Ellsworth, P.C. (1988). Unpleasant Facts: The Supreme Court's Response to Empirical Research on Capital Punishment. In K.C. Haas and J.A. Inciardi (Eds.), *Challenging Capital Punishment: Legal and Social Science Approaches* (pp. 177-211). Newbury Park, CA: Sage Publications.

Eshelman, R.E. (1994, April 22). State Court Orders Casey to Sign 2 Death Warrants. *Philadelphia Inquirer*, p. A1.

Finkel, N.J. and Duff, K.B. (1991). Felony-Murder and Community Sentiment: Testing the Supreme Court's Assertions. *Law and Human Behavior*, 15: 405-429.

Finkel, N.J. and Smith, S.F. (1993). Principals and Accessories in Capital Felony-Murder: The Proportionality Principle Reigns Supreme. *Law and Society Review*, 27: 129-156.

Gey, S.G. (1992). Justice Scalia's Death Penalty. *Florida State University Law Review*, 20: 67-132.

Haas, K.C. (1994). The Triumph of Vengeance Over Retribution: The United States Supreme Court and the Death Penalty. *Crime, Law and Social Change*, 21:127-154.

Haas, K.C. and Inciardi, J.A. (1988). Lingering Doubts About a Popular Punishment. In K.C. Haas and J.A. Inciardi (Eds.), *Challenging Capital Punishment: Legal and Social Science Approaches* (pp. 11-28). Newbury Park, CA: Sage Publications.

Levy, J.H. (1993). Limiting Victim Impact Evidence and Argument After *Payne v. Tennessee*. Stanford Law Review, 45: 1027-1060.

Marquart, J.W. and Sorenson, J.R. (1989). A National Study of the Furman-Commuted Inmates: Assessing the Threat to Society from Capital Offenders. *Loyola of Los Angeles Law Review*, 23: 5-28.

McFadden, G.T. (1972). Capital Sentencing—Effect of *McGautha and Furman*. *Temple Law Quarterly*, 45: 619-648.

Mello, M. (1988). Facing Death Alone: The Post-Conviction Attorney Crisis on Death Row. *American University Law Review*, 37: 513-607.

Meltsner, M. (1973). *Cruel and Unusual: The Supreme Court and Capital Punishment*. New York: Random House.

Miller, E. (1990). Executing Minors and the Mentally Retarded: The Retribution and Deterrence Rationales. *Rutgers Law Review*, 43: 15-52.

Miller, K.S. and Radelet, M.L. (1993). *Executing the Mentally Ill: The Criminal Justice System and the Case of Alvin* Newbury Park, CA: Sage Publications.

NAACP Legal and Educational Defense Fund. (1993-94). *Death Row U.S.A. Reporter*. New York: NAACP Legal and Educational Defense Fund.

New York Times Editorial. (1994, April 22). For Racial Justice in Executions. *New York Times*, p. A26.

Oberlander, M.I. (1992). The Payne of Allowing Victim Impact Statements at Capital Sentencing Hearings. *Vanderbilt Law Review*, 45: 1621-1662.

Polsby, D.D. (1973). The Death of Capital Punishment? *Furman v. Georgia*. In P. Kurland (Ed.), *The Supreme Court Review: 1972* (pp. 1-40). Chicago, IL: University of Chicago Press.

Radelet, M.L., Bedau, H.A., and Putnam, C.E. (1992). *In Spite of Innocence: Erroneous Convictions in Capital Cases*. Boston, MA: Northeastern University Press.

Radin, M.J. (1980). Cruel Punishment and Respect for Persons: Super Due Process for Death. *Southern California Law Review*, 53: 1143-1185.

Reed, E.F. (1993). *The Penry Penalty: Capital Punishment and Offenders with Mental Retardation*. Lanham, MA: University Press of America.

Reske, H.J. (1994). Liberal Detectors: Judicial Nominees Sized Up Based on Death Penalty Stance. *ABA Journal* 80, 14.

Rhoads, M.D. (1977). Resurrection of Capital Punishment—The 1976 Death Penalty Cases. *Dickinson Law Review*, 81: 543-573.

Robbins, I.P. (1994). *Habeas Corpus Checklists: 1994 Edition*. New York: Clark Boardman Callaghan.

Sarat, A. and Vidmar, N. (1976). Public Opinion, the Death Penalty, and the Eighth Amendment: Testing the Marshall Hypothesis. *Wisconsin Law Review*, 1976, 171-206.

Sellin, T. (1980). *The Penalty of Death*. Beverly Hills CA: Sage Publications.

Streib, V.L. (1984). Executions Under the Post-Furman Capital Punishment Statutes: The Halting Progression from "Let's Do It" to "Hey, There Ain't No Point in Pulling So Tight." *Rutgers Law Journal*, 15: 443-487.

Streib, V.L. (1987). *Death Penalty for Juveniles*. Bloomington, IN: Indiana University Press.

Sundby, S.E. (1991). The Lockett Paradox: Reconciling Guided Discretion and Unguided Mitigation in Capital Sentencing. *UCLA Law Review*, 38: 1147-1208.

White, W.S. (1991). *The Death Penalty in the Nineties: An Examination of the Modern System of Capital Punishment*. Ann Arbor, MI: University of Michigan Press.

Wines, M. (1994, April 22). House Adopts Crime Legislation to Build Jails and Hire Officers. *New York Times*, p. A1.

Zimring, F.E. and Hawkins, G. (1986). *Capital Punishment and the American Agenda*. Cambridge: Cambridge University Press.

CASES

Ake v. Oklahoma, 470 U.S. 68 (1985).

Barclay v. Florida, 463 U.S. 939 (1983).

Barefoot v. Estelle, 463 U.S. 880 (1983).

Beck v. Alabama, 447 U.S. 625 (1980).

Bell v. Ohio, 438 U.S. 637 (1978).

Blystone v. Pennsylvania, 110 S. Ct. 1078 (1990).

Booth v. Maryland, 482 U.S. 496 (1987).

Boyde v. California, 494 U.S. 370 (1990).

Bullington v. Missouri, 451 U.S. 430 (1981).

Butler v. McKellar, 494 U.S. 407 (1990).

Cage v. Louisiana, 111 S. Ct. 328 (1990).

Caldwell v. Mississippi, 472 U.S. 320 (1985).

California v. Brown, 479 U.S. 538 (1987).

California v. Ramos, 463 U.S. 992 (1983).

Callins v. Collins, 114 S. Ct. 1127 (1994).

Coker v. Georgia, 433 U.S. 584 (1977).

Coleman v. Balkcom, 451 U.S. 949 (1981).

Coleman v. Thompson, 111 S. Ct. 2546 (1991).

Dawson v. Delaware, 112 S. Ct. 1093 (1992).

Dobbert v. Florida, 432 U.S. 325 (1977)

Eddings v. Oklahoma, 455 U.S. 104 (1982)

Enmund v. Florida, 458 U.S. 782 (1982).

Estelle v. Smith, 451 U.S. 454 (1981).

Ford v. Wainwright, 477 U.S. 399 (1986).

Francis v. Franklin, 471 U.S. 307 (1985).

Furman v. Georgia, 408 U.S. 238 (1972).

Gardner v. Florida, 430 U.S. 349 (1977).

Godfrey v. Georgia, 446 U.S. 420 (1980).

Gomez v. District Court, 112 S. Ct. 1652 (1992).

Green v. Georgia, 442 U.S. 95 (1979).

Gregg v. Georgia, 428 U.S. 153 (1976).

Herrera v. Collins, 113 S. Ct. 853 (1993).

Hitchcock v. Dugger, 481 U.S. 393 (1987).

Jurek v. Texas, 428 U.S. 262 (1976).

Keeney v. Tamayo-Reyes, 111 S. Ct. 1715 (1992).

Lankford v. Idaho, 111 S. Ct. 1723 (1991).

Lockett v. Ohio, 438 U.S. 586 (1978).

Lockhart v. McCree, 476 U.S. 162 (1986).

Maynard v. Cartwright, 486 U.S. 356 (1988).

McCleskey v. Kemp, 481 U.S. 279 (1987).

McCleskey v. Zant, 111 S. Ct. 1454 (1991).

Mills v. Maryland, 486 U.S. 367 (1988).

Morgan v. Illinois, 112 S. Ct. 2222 (1992).

Murray v. Giarrantano, 492 U.S. 1 (1989).

Payne v. Tennessee, 111 S. Ct. 2597 (1991).

Penry v. Lynaugh, 492 U.S. 302 (1989).

Proffitt v. Florida, 428 U.S. 242 (1976).

Pulley v. Harris, 465 U.S. 37 (1984).

Roberts v. Louisiana, 428 U.S. 325 (1976).

Roberts v. Louisiana, 431 U.S. 633 (1977).

Sawyer v. Whitley, 112 S. Ct. 2514 (1992).

Skipper v. South Carolina, 476 U.S. 1 (1986).

South Carolina v. Gathers, 490 U.S. 805 (1989).

Stanford v. Kentucky, 492 U.S. 361 (1989).

Sumner v. Shuman, 483 U.S. 66 (1987).

Teague v. Lane, 489 U.S. 288 (1989).

Thompson v. Oklahoma, 487 U.S. 815 (1988).

Tison v. Arizona, 481 U.S. 137 (1987).

Trop v. Dulles, 356 U.S. 86 (1958).

Wainwright v. Witt, 469 U.S. 412 (1985).

Whitmore v. Arkansas, 495 U.S. 149 (1990).

Witherspoon v. Illinois, 391 U.S. 510 (1968).

Woodson v. North Carolina, 428 U.S. 280 (1976).

Zant v. Stephens, 462 U.S. 862 (1983).

CHAPTER 11

THE BILL OF RIGHTS IN THE TWENTY-FIRST CENTURY

Alexander B. Smith, Ph.D. and Harriet Pollack, Ph.D.

❖

ABSTRACT

The U.S. Supreme Court for the past thirty years has interpreted the Fourth, Fifth, Sixth, and Eighth Amendments of the Bill of Rights in a manner protective of the rights of suspects, defendants and prisoners. In recent years, the focus of the Court has shifted from restrictions on the police and the conduct of trials, to concerns about sentencing and punishment. What the future holds depends largely on government policy in relation to drug use and trafficking, and gun control, the chief elements of our crime problem.

When the text of the Constitution emerged from the Constitutional Convention in 1787 and was presented to the states for ratification, it was by no means greeted with universal acclaim. The compromises struck by the Founding Fathers in relation to representation of large states versus small, the slave trade, and other controversial issues left many people unhappy. The biggest complaint, however, was that the proposed Constitution provided insufficient protection for individual rights, and indeed, that the new government-to-be might be as tyrannical as the old British monarchy. In many states, it was the only promise that a bill of rights protecting individual liberties would be enacted immediately that enabled the Constitution to be ratified.

It is, in fact, true, that while the Constitution itself set up the framework for a majoritarian representative government, it is the Bill of Rights, that is, the first ten amendments to the Constitution, that protects individuals from the unwarranted intrusion of government into their daily lives. It is the Bill of Rights that guards personal integrity, that gives us the right to be let alone.

The government is the only institution in society that has a legitimate right to exert physical force over us. Therefore, the right to be let alone means, above all, the right not to be arrested and punished for what we have said or done except under certain clearly specified conditions. It is not surprising, thus, that five of the first ten amendments concern the workings of the criminal justice system. It is our purpose in this chapter to discuss first, how U. S. Supreme Court interpretations of those five amendments, the First, Fourth, Fifth, Sixth, and Eighth, have shaped the substance of the criminal law as well as the rules of criminal procedure, and secondly, those questions currently unresolved, which have the potential for further changes in the system.

PART I—THE STATE OF THE LAW

Amendment I

> Congress shall make no law respecting an establishment of religion, or pro-
> hibiting the free exercise thereof; or abridging the freedom of speech, or of
> the press; or the right of people peaceably to assemble, and to petition the
> Government for a redress of grievances.

The First Amendment is not usually discussed in terms of its impact on the criminal
justice system, yet in the context of the right not to be arrested or punished for speech
related activities, it is very important. Actually, with the exception of the short-lived
Alien and Sedition Act of 1798, there was no federal regulation of speech until the
World War I Sedition and Espionage Acts. While the states may have punished certain
types of speech, the federal government did not, and though the road from the post
World War I period to the present traversed serious bumps in the form of Red scares
and McCarthyism, at the present time we are living in an era of great freedom for both
speech and religion. The U.S. Supreme Court has held virtually all speech to be constitutionally protected, except for speech which is pornographic or creates a danger of
imminently inciting riot or rebellion. Speech, moreover, has been broadly defined as
communication: art, music, sculpture, drama, picketing, and street demonstrations.
Some of these forms of communication obviously involve action as well as speech,
and can be restricted more than speech unmixed with action. Nevertheless, the
Supreme Court generally has sided with the speaker, going so far as to indicate that
in the case of a speaker with a hostile audience, the police, wherever possible, must
restrain the audience and protect the speaker.

Religion has been almost entirely free from regulation by the criminal law except
for two recent cases, one involving the use of peyote, a hallucinogenic drug, in religious rituals, and the other a form of animal sacrifice. In both cases the U.S. Supreme
Court upheld the state law and outlawed the forbidden practice.

Fourth Amendment

> The right of the people to be secure in their persons, houses, papers and
> effects, against unreasonable searches and seizures shall not be violated,
> and no Warrant shall issue but upon probable cause supported by Oath or
> affirmation, and particularly describing the place to be searched or the per-
> son or things to be seized.

The Fourth Amendment is the amendment which quintessentially restrains the police.
It tells the police that they must have probable cause to arrest, that they must have a
warrant to search, and that the warrant must specify where and what is to be seized.
Given the complexity of the interactions between the public and the police, there is an
enormous body of law dealing with the details of these restrictions on police action.
The Court has said that probable cause is something more than mere suspicion and
that the permissible thoroughness of the search must vary with the degree of certainty that the police officer has regarding the guilt of the suspect. *Terry v. Ohio* (1968)
held that where a police officer merely suspects that someone is about to commit a
felony, he may stop and frisk the individual in a public place, but he may not conduct
a full-scale search or arrest such a person without additional information.

A police officer may also conduct a search *without* a warrant if given consent by a person authorized to give such consent, e.g., the owner of the premises the police wish to search. In the case of a valid arrest, the officer may also, without a warrant, search the premises immediately adjacent to the suspect. These procedural rules regarding arrests and searches are, for the most part, not new, but within the last thirty-five years the Court has greatly expanded their impact on the police by ruling that evidence illegally seized, i.e., in violation of these rules, cannot be used in court to obtain a conviction. Evidence gained through leads obtained by illegal means, moreover, is to be considered fruit of the poisonous tree and cannot be used either.

This exclusionary rule led to a revolutionary change in police training and attitudes. It is generally agreed that, historically, American law enforcement, especially on the local level, was conducted without regard for constitutional niceties, until the decision in *Mapp v. Ohio* (1961), which removed most of the incentive and imposed penalties for illegal police activity. Gradually since then, the police have become both better trained and more professional. The exclusionary rule, of course, was criticized severely by those who felt that the hands of law enforcement officials were being tied and criminals were being coddled. Crime *has* increased since *Mapp*, but the exclusionary rule seems to have had little to do with the increase, and most police departments live quite comfortably with the rule, especially since it was been modified by the Supreme Court to provide for good faith exceptions where the totality of the circumstances were such that the officer had reason to believe that he was acting legally. (See *Illinois v. Gates*, 1983; *United States v. Leon*, 1984; *Nix v. Williams*, 1984; and *New York v. Quarles*, 1984).

The Court has also dealt with other intrusions on personal privacy, such as wiretapping, and after a long period of denying that wiretapping fell under the aegis of the Fourth Amendment, finally admitted that wiretapping was indeed a search which should be regulated by Fourth Amendment standards (*Berger v. New York*, 1967). Subsequent to the *Berger* decision, Congress enacted legislation regulating wiretapping and while wiretapping still remains the dirty business that Justice Holmes called it, the situation is much better controlled.

In more recent times, the Court has dealt with more esoteric issues such as the question of whether a person has a right to privacy in the garbage he has discarded. In *California v. Greenwood* (1988), a warrantless search of garbage revealed drug paraphernalia which the court admitted into evidence, holding that Greenwood had no right to privacy in the garbage once it has been placed on the curb. Similarly, in *Oliver v. United States*, (1984), marijuana growing in a secluded, fenced, open field marked "No Trespassing," was permitted into evidence on the ground that there was no right to privacy in an open field.

The Court also addressed the problem of warrantless *arrests*. Such arrests are permitted when in hot pursuit of the suspect, but traditionally, had also been permitted when the suspect was thought to be hiding in private premises. The Court held that not only did the police require an *arrest* warrant to enter such premises, but a *search* warrant as well, if there was no prior consent to their entry. (See *Payton v. New York*, 1980, and *Steagald v. United States*, 1981.)

One of the most difficult areas for the Court has been deciding the constitutionality of various types of automobile searches and seizures, particularly in illegal drug cases. The multitudinous decisions of this area are truly bewildering and require a chapter of their own, but the clear tendency has been to allow the police more latitude in making such searches, both of the vehicle itself and of containers within the vehicle.

Fifth Amendment

> No person shall be held to answer for a capital, or otherwise infamous crime, unless on a presentment or indictment of a Grand Jury, except in cases arising in the land or naval forces, or in the Militia, when in actual service in time of War or public danger; nor shall any person be subject for the same offense to be twice put in jeopardy of life or limb; nor shall be compelled in any criminal case to be witness against himself, nor be deprived of life, liberty, without due process of law; nor shall private property be taken for public use, without just compensation.

Of all the guarantees mentioned in the Fifth Amendment, probably the most important in terms of impact on the criminal justice system is the protection against forced self-incrimination. In British law, from which we derive many of our legal traditions, suspects are warned that incriminatory statements that they make can be used against them, and that they have a right to remain silent under police questioning. In the United States, the Fifth Amendment was thought to provide the same protection. However, until *Miranda v. Arizona* (1966), there was no specific penalty imposed on the police for ignoring this protection. *Miranda* for the first time required that the police give a specific set of warnings to suspects under arrest, informing them of their right to remain silent and their right to have a lawyer present during questioning by the police. Any statements obtained without regard for these protections would be inadmissible for the purpose of obtaining a conviction at a trial.

Like *Mapp*, *Miranda* was extremely unpopular not only with the police but with the public as well, who felt that voluntary admissions of guilt were being excluded on the basis of technicalities. Despite the furor, *Miranda* has never been overruled, although it has been modified in many respects. *Miranda* applies only to suspects who are in custody at the time of questioning, and custody has been defined very narrowly by the Court. Thus, people brought in by the police for questioning, unless they have been formally arrested, are not covered by *Miranda*, even though they may think that they are under arrest.

The Court, however, refused to overturn *Miranda* even in a case which presented an excellent opportunity. In *Brewer v. Williams* (1977), the suspect, accused of kidnapping, raping and killing a child, was being transported on Christmas eve from one city to another. In the course of the ride, the sheriff who had promised the suspect's counsel not to question him, made remarks designed to elicit a confession from Brewer, a known religious zealot. The Court refused to admit Brewer's confession holding that the sheriff's statement, although not direct questioning, was designed to improperly pressure the suspect to confess.

Another modification of *Miranda* was the *Quarles* decision where Quarles, while attempting to hold up a supermarket, was captured and handcuffed. While thus confined, the police, without giving him *Miranda* warnings, asked him where he had thrown his gun. Quarles told them, and the gun was admitted into evidence at the trial. The Court held the admission proper, holding that because of the imminent danger to public safety, the police had not had time to give *Miranda* warnings.

Another protection of the Fifth Amendment is the protection against double jeopardy. Double jeopardy basically means that a person cannot be tried and punished for the same crime twice. However, since the United States is a federation of states rather than a unitary system, there is dual sovereignty exercised over every individual. It is settled law that while a state may not try an accused person twice for the same crime, the federal government may institute a second prosecution for that crime regardless of the outcome of the first prosecution, and *vice versa*. Thus, when the local sheriff was acquitted of murder charges in the case of three civil rights workers in Mississippi, he was tried and convicted in Federal court of violating the civil rights of the three men by murdering them.

Sixth Amendment

> In all criminal prosecutions, the accused shall enjoy the right to a speedy and public trial, by an impartial jury in the State and district wherein the crime shall have been committed, which district shall have been previously ascertained by law, and to be informed of the nature and cause of the accusation; to be confronted with the witnesses against him; to have compulsory process for obtaining witnesses in his favor, and to have the Assistance of Counsel for his defense.

Closely related to the privilege against self-incrimination is the right to counsel at all times after arrest. At the pretrial stage, the purpose of the attorney is to see that the defendant's rights are not violated by torture, or improper questioning. The purpose of the attorney at trials is to see that the defendant receives a fair trial with the opportunity to confront and cross examine witnesses against him, present evidence in his own behalf, and have a judge untainted by pretrial prejudicial publicity. *Escobedo v. Illinois* (1964), a forerunner to *Miranda*, involved a defendant who asked for, but was denied, the presence of his lawyer during police questioning. The Court held his confession inadmissible.

Similarly, in *Massiah v. U.S.* (1964), Massiah, an indicted defendant in a drug case, was induced by his indicted codefendant who had turned informer, into making incriminating statements. The Court refused to admit Massiah's confession on the ground that after indictment, questioning of a defendant may not take place outside the presence of his lawyer, and that the use of an undercover informer constituted improper questioning.

Eighth Amendment

> Excessive bail shall not be required, nor excessive fines imposed, nor cruel and unusual punishment inflicted.

The purpose of bail is to insure the presence of the defendant at trial. If the crime, however, is egregious enough, there is a strong possibility that the defendant may run away and never come back. Therefore, very large amounts of bail, or indeed, the total denial of bail, have been imposed on certain kinds of cases.

The courts have always been conflicted over whether it is proper to use a money device to insure the presence of the defendant at trial. On the one hand, the effect of money bail may be to keep poor people who pose little risk to the community in jail because they cannot make bail. On the other hand, releasing a defendant who *can* make bail may mean releasing a dangerous criminal. The riddle has not yet been resolved.

To alleviate the hardship of money bail on the poor, there have been many pilot projects which enable suspects with roots in the community and stable life styles to be released without bail. These projects have had a mixed record or success, depending on how well they have been administered, but well-run programs have managed to allow poor defendants their freedom pending trial, and to insure their return for adjudication.

To address the second part of the bail riddle, some communities have enacted preventive detention laws which deny bail altogether to suspects thought to be too dangerous to be released. Such laws must be narrowly drawn and contain safeguards against long term, unreasonable pretrial detention if they are to pass constitutional muster. In short, not much has changed since 1835 when a Judge Krantz was asked to set bail for a suspect who had attempted to assassinate President Jackson. He set bail at $1,500, but complained that "If the ability of the prisoner alone were to be considered, $1,500 is too much, but if the atrocity of the offense alone were to be considered, it was too small" (see Caleb Foote as quoted by Ronald Goldfarb in *Ransom*, New York: Harper and Row, 1965, pp. 13-14).

The cruel and unusual punishment clause of the Eighth Amendment was probably meant to prevent the infliction of barbarous methods of punishment, such as boiling in oil, or drawing and quartering. However, in more recent years, the cruel and unusual punishment clause has been used to challenge the conditions under which prisoners have been incarcerated. In the earlier cases, the conditions brought to light were truly horrifying as in *Holt v. Sarver* (1972), where the Arkansas prison system used inmate trustees to perform the duties of prison guards. Trustees flogged inmates, used electric shock devices attached to their genitals, and applied burning cigarettes to their bodies. Many inmates were murdered and their bodies buried. In the more recent cases, however, the abuses charged have been much less flagrant and relate to overcrowding, lack of medical care, poor food, etc.

There have also been challenges to restrictions of prisoners' First Amendment rights, including the right to receive uncensored mail, to be interviewed by journalists, and the right to practice their religion and observe special holy days. At the present time, as a result of suits brought by inmates under the Eighth Amendment, a large proportion of the state prisons systems of the United States are under Federal Court orders to improve the conditions under which inmates are held.

The cruel and unusual punishment clause has also been used to attack inequities in sentencing. Imbedded in our legal traditions, is the notion that there must be proportionality between a crime and its punishment. As far back as 1910, the U.S. Supreme Court held that a fifteen-year sentence at hard labor, chained at the ankle and wrist, was a disproportionate sentence for a wrongful entry in a cash book by a government employee (*Weems v. U.S.*). In more recent times, disproportionality in sentencing has been challenged in relation to mandatory sentencing laws for drug offenders, which have resulted in very harsh sentences for what are frequently low level offenders.

The main challenges in sentencing, however, have come in relation to the death penalty. The death penalty was at first challenged on a *per se* basis, that is, that execution in and of itself was unconstitutional. The Court, in *Furman v. Ga.* (1972) denied that argument. Since then, however, the Court has attempted, by imposing rigorous procedural requirements, to eliminate the randomness of the death penalty and its possible racial bias, and to limit the kinds of offenses for which the death penalty may be imposed. In capital cases, two trials are now required, one for the determination of guilt, and one to decide whether the death penalty should be imposed.

From 1967 to the 1977 the federal courts declared a moratorium on executions pending resolution of legal challenges to their constitutionality. Since the moratorium ended, executions have taken place at an increasing pace, although fewer than before the moratorium, and mainly in the southern states.

NEW ISSUES FOR THE TWENTY-FIRST CENTURY

Despite a change in the political climate of the country and of the membership on the Court, it is unlikely that the major decisions made by the U.S. Supreme Court which have had substantial impact on the criminal justice system will be overturned. Instead, a series of modifications of earlier decisions is most likely. The *Mapp* and *Miranda* decisions with the imposition of the exclusionary rule on illegally obtained evidence and confessions were, in many ways, the high water marks of constitutional change in our criminal justice system. The tide of protection for defendants has been ebbing since, but slowly and not very substantially. Most of the issues that we will discuss now are, relatively speaking, details in an overall grand design, and indeed, many of them will be resolved and others will take their places in the remaining few years of the century. Nevertheless, they are of interest as a reflection of changes in our society.

One *caveat* needs to be addressed, however. While it is true that the substance of Fourth, Fifth, Sixth and Eighth Amendment jurisprudence has not changed substantially, the *procedural* rules for getting such cases to the U.S. Supreme Court have changed substantially, especially in relation to *habeas corpus* petitions. A *habeas corpus* petition is a device for bringing the custodian of an accused person or prisoner into court for the purpose of challenging the legality of the confinement. It is used, for example, to challenge the admissibility of evidence that might have been seized illegally, and most importantly, in death penalty cases, the constitutionality of an impending execution. The most significant use of *habeas corpus* has been to obtain federal oversight of state criminal procedure, since a writ of *habeas corpus* obtained in a federal court commands state officials to justify their actions. In legal cases, this is called collateral relief, and is of great importance because, in effect, it creates federal supervision of state practices. Understandably, state officials resent such suits and the collateral relief process results in very long, complex, and expensive litigation, which congests both state and federal courts.

The U.S. Supreme Court has responded to this situation by limiting the granting of *habeas corpus* in certain kinds of situations. In 1976 in *Stone v. Powell*, the Court ruled that federal courts could not hear *habeas corpus* petitions from state prisoners arguing that illegally seized evidence should have been excluded from their trials, as long as each inmate had received a full and fair chance to make the argument in state court appeals. More recent restrictions on *habeas corpus* will be discussed below.

Fourth Amendment

Outside of *habeas corpus* restrictions, there have been very few changes in Fourth Amendment jurisprudence. In *Florida v. Bostick* (1991), a police officer who had no legal basis for suspecting a particular passenger, boarded a bus and at random, asked for and received a passenger's consent to search his luggage, after telling the passenger that he could refuse permission to search. The resulting search revealed contraband. The U.S. Supreme Court held that as long as the officer's request was not so coercive that the passenger was not free to refuse, the search was a legal consent search, even though the passenger, being on a bus, was not free to leave. *Bostick* expanded the meaning of "consent" in consensual searches, which are free from the requirements of probable cause or a warrant. In *Minnesota v. Dickerson* (1993), a police officer conducted a "frisk" search under the guidelines set down by *Terry v. Ohio*, (1968). The permissible pat down search in a public place, for weapons, revealed a lump which the officer proceeded to investigate. The object being soft was obviously not a weapon, but the officer investigated it and found it to be crack cocaine. The question presented was whether the officer had a right to seize a non-weapon, since the purpose of allowing the frisk is the officer's protection. The Court upheld the legality of the search on the ground that the drug seizure had been in "plain view," that is, that while legitimately searching for a weapon the officer found the drugs. Under the search and seizure law of conventional searches, anything found while legitimately searching for the object specified in a warrant is seizable. By analogy, the drugs found in the frisk were also seizable.

Fifth Amendment

The most notable development in Fifth Amendment jurisprudence was the refusal of the Court to extend *habeas corpus* restrictions which it had applied to cases relating to illegally seized physical evidence to cases involving allegedly illegally obtained confessions.

In *Withrow v. Williams*, (1993), in a 5 to 4 decision, the Court refused to extend the limitation on *habeas corpus* that it had imposed on search and seizure cases in *Stone v. Powell*. *Withrow* involved a defendant who claimed a violation of the *Miranda* rule and as such, challenged admission of his incriminating statements. To the surprise of most Court watchers who expected the ban on *habeas corpus* in cases involving searches and seizures to be extended to cases involving confessions, the Court granted his petition. The issue may not be entirely closed, however, because of the closeness of the vote and the fact that in another case, *Brecht v. Abrahamson* (1993), in another 5 to 4 decision, the Court refused to permit *habeas corpus* petitions challenging constitutional errors committed by the state at trial, unless the defendant could show that the error had a "substantial and injurious effect on the jury's verdict," and that he suffered from "actual prejudice from the error."

The position of the court in relation to double jeopardy is unchanged. In *United States v. Dixon* (1993), the Court upheld a second prosecution for a man who had beaten his wife, after he had already been tried for violation of a court order of protection. The decision was 5 to 4, and some recent events have reopened public discussion of the fairness of the dual sovereignty dual jeopardy rules.

In Los Angeles, CA, the acquittal in a *state* trial of four white policemen shown on television tape severely beating a black man in the course of an arrest, aroused such public outrage that the federal government instituted a new trial. Although the *acts* were the same, the charge in federal court was a violation of the victim's civil rights, and some of the previously acquitted defendants were convicted. The original state verdict, however, had led to severe rioting in Los Angeles, in the course of which, a white truck driver was badly beaten by black rioters. The beating was filmed by a reporter. At the ensuing trial, only one defendant was convicted of a felony which carried punishment far less than the original highest count in the indictment. There were some calls for a federal trial of the defendants, on the ground that the jury had been terrorized by the fear of a replay of the riots. There was no retrial of the black defendants, but the two cases provoked much discussion of when and whether a second trial by a different sovereign (i.e. the state or federal government) was appropriate.

Eighth Amendment

In the two hundred plus years of its existence, the U.S. Supreme Court paid almost no attention to the criminal justice system until the 1960s. The post World War II years have been a period when increasingly the Court has been concerned with individual rights rather than property rights, and part of that concern reflected itself in new interpretations of the Fourth, Fifth, Sixth and Eighth Amendments. The Fourth Amendment dealing with police procedure was the first to receive attention, followed over the years by the Fifth Amendment dealing with confessions and double jeopardy and the Sixth Amendment dealing with the right to counsel and fair trial. At the present time, however, it is unquestionably the Eighth Amendment dealing with sentencing that is at the top of the Court's agenda and which is now receiving, and in the future probably will receive, the lion's share of the Court's attention in the area of criminal justice.

The Eighth Amendment speaks of cruel and unusual punishment. The cases coming before the Court divide themselves roughly into three categories: cases dealing with the death penalty; those with unsatisfactory prison conditions; and those with disproportionate sentencing in nondeath penalty cases. Most of the appeals from the death penalty come via a writ of habeas corpus asking the federal court to review certain procedural questions which the prisoner alleges violated his constitutional rights.

In *Herrera v. Collins* (1993), Herrera alleged that newly discovered evidence of his innocence had been discovered that entitled him to a new trial. The evidence consisted, in part, of affidavits tending to show that his now dead brother had committed the murders, evidence which was not available to him at the time of his original trial. Herrera's claim, however, was made ten years after his original conviction, while under Texas law a new trial motion based on newly discovered evidence must be made within thirty days of the imposition of sentence. The U.S. Supreme Court denied Herrera's motion holding that the Texas limitation on the introduction of new evidence, even evidence purporting to show the defendant's innocence, was not a denial of fundamental fairness and did not violate Herrera's due process rights.

In another case, *McCleskey v. Zant*, 1993, McCleskey claimed in his petition for habeas corpus that the evidence used to convict him had been obtained improperly from a prisoner in an adjoining cell and should have been excluded on the basis of the decision in *Massiah v. U.S.* (1964). In *Massiah* the police had wired Massiah's codefendant who had agreed to turn informer, and had him elicit damaging admissions after Massiah had been indicted and was outside the presence of his attorney. McCleskey's problem, however, was that although he might have prevailed on the merits of his *Massiah* claim, he had previously made several petitions for habeas corpus at both the state and federal levels, some of which did not include the *Massiah* claim although eighteen other claims had been made. The U.S. Supreme Court rejected his application for habeas corpus on the ground that he had abused the writ by filing multiple claims some of which did not raise the *Massiah* issue. In both *Herrera* and *McCleskey* three justices dissented, holding that in the case of the death sentence and its ultimate finality, technical procedural rules should not bar meritorious claims.

Another death penalty case not involving the propriety of a request for a writ of habeas corpus was *Payne v. Tennessee* (1991). Payne was convicted of first degree murder of a mother and her two-year-old daughter and assault on her three-year-old son. At the penalty phase of Payne's trial, the state called as a witness the victim's mother, who described the devastating effect on the family, and especially on the remaining child, of the crime. The constitutional question presented was whether a capital sentencing jury could, under the Eighth Amendment, consider victim impact evidence. Two previous precedents, *Booth v. Maryland* (1987), and *South Carolina v. Gathers* (1989), barred the admission of victim impact statements during the penalty phase of a capital trial, on the ground that the jury should consider only the evidence relevant to the character of the offense and the character of the defendant. Impact statements which tend to differentiate victims on the basis of their different roles or value to society served no purpose but to inflame the jury. In *Payne* the Court overruled the two previous precedents and held that the impact might properly be considered as an aggravating circumstance, related to the crime itself.

Another group of cases decided recently by the U.S. Supreme Court deals with prison conditions. In *Wilson v. Seiter* (1991), Wilson claimed that the overall prison conditions under which she was confined constituted cruel and unusual punishment. The Court rejected her claim, holding that it is incumbent on the petitioner to specify both the particulars of the allegedly unconstitutional conditions of confinement and to relate them to a policy of deliberate indifference on the part of prison officials.

On the other hand, in *Hudson v. McMillian* (1992), Hudson alleged that his Eighth Amendment rights were violated by the beating he received by state correctional officers. He was beaten while handcuffed and shackled following an argument with Officer McMillian, one of the prison guards. Hudson received minor bruises, facial swelling, loosened teeth, and a cracked dental plate. The supervisor on duty watched the beating and simply told the guards "not to have too much fun." At the Federal Court of Appeals level, Hudson's claim was disallowed on the ground that inmates alleging excessive force in violation of the Eighth Amendment must prove significant injury, and since Hudson required no medical attention, his claim was dismissed. The U.S. Supreme Court, in a 7 to 2 decision disagreed, holding that unnecessary and wanton infliction of pain violated the Constitution regardless of the extent of the injury.

In 1993, in *Helling v. McKinney*, McKinney brought suit against Nevada prison officials, claiming that his health was jeopardized by his cellmate who was a heavy smoker, forcing him to breathe second-hand smoke whenever he was in his cell. The U.S. Supreme Court agreed that it was not necessary for McKinney to show that his confinement represented deliberate indifference on the part of the prison administration to his health needs, but that he was not entitled to a directed verdict, only to a hearing in which he could prove that the cigarette smoke was injurious to his health. McKinney's case may be mooted since he has been moved to a new prison with a cellmate who does not smoke and a prison policy which restricts smoking to certain areas.

The remainder of the Eighth Amendment cases relate to disproportionate sentences—determining whether, as Gilbert and Sullivan said, "the punishment fits the crime." Many of these cases were triggered by the relatively recent implementation of Federal Sentencing Guidelines which punish drug possession, even in small quantities, very harshly, and also allow for forfeiture of property thought to have been obtained through illegal drug activities. RICO (Racketeer Influenced Corrupt Organizations), a federal law which provides for property seizure *before* conviction is also giving rise to increasing litigation in this area.

In *Harmelin v. Michigan*, 1991, the Court permitted imposition, under Michigan law, of a mandatory sentence of life imprisonment without parole for a nonviolent first offense: possession of more than 650 grams of cocaine. Harmelin contended that the mandatory nature of the sentence did not permit consideration of mitigating factors in his case. In a 5 to 4 decision, the Court held that while such a severe penalty might be unconstitutional for some crimes, Harmelin's sentence under Michigan law for having two pounds of cocaine in his possession was constitutional, even though under federal law he would have been sentenced to about ten years. Two justices, Scalia and Rehnquist, went so far as to say that short of the death sentence, proportionality in sentencing was irrelevant in terms of the Eighth Amendment—that any prison sentence was constitutional. Justices Kennedy, O'Connor, and Souter, however, said that while Harmelin's sentence was acceptable, the Eighth Amendment could invalidate grossly disproportionate sentences. White, Blackmun, Stevens, and Marshall dissented, holding that the sentence was disproportionate and unconstitutional. White noted that only one other state, Alabama, imposed a mandatory life sentence without parole for a first time drug offender. Under Alabama law, Harmelin would have received a five-year sentence.

Several 1993 cases related to seizure of property from criminals and suspects, particularly in drug cases. In *United States v. Parcel of Land* (1993), the Court, by a 6 to 3 vote, interpreted a federal drug forfeiture law to provide an exception for innocent owners. A woman was permitted to defend her house against forfeiture on the ground that she did not know that the money used to buy the house came from her boyfriend's drug dealing. In a second case, *Austin v. United States* (1993), the Court unanimously left to the lower courts the decision as to when a forfeiture violated the Eighth Amendment. Austin was the owner of a small body shop in South Dakota and lost his business and his mobile home worth a total of $38,000, in addition to $4,000 in cash, when he sold two grams of cocaine to an undercover agent.

In a third case, *Alexander v. United States* (1993), the owner of a chain of adult bookstores and movie houses forfeited his businesses and almost $9 million in profits after he was convicted of racketeering by selling obscene material. Alexander had raised both an Eighth Amendment claim against excessive fines and a First Amendment claim relating to the destruction of books and other materials that were not obscene. His Eighth Amendment claim was unanimously upheld, but his First Amendment claim was narrowly rejected by a 5 to 4 vote. A remaining issue that the Court has undertaken to decide is the right to advance notice and hearing in forfeiture cases.

Another sentencing issue addressed by the Court recently, concerned the issue of whether a state may enhance criminal penalties because of the political motives of the offender. In *Wisconsin v. Mitchell*, No. 92-515, 1993, Mitchell, a black man, was convicted of leading a racially motivated assault on a white teen-ager. The maximum sentence for such an assault would have been two years in prison, but under the terms of Wisconsin's hate crime law, because Mitchell had selected his victim on the basis of race, the sentence was increased to four years. Mitchell charged that the statute abridged his First Amendment rights, in that his political beliefs were used to enhance his sentence. The state contended that it was the additional potential for violence that led to the increased sentence, not Mitchell's political beliefs. The U.S. Supreme Court agreed that in this case, the state's interest in controlling violence outweighed Mitchell's First Amendment claims.

The function of the Bill of Rights in the twenty-first century, even as in the eighteenth century, will be to protect minorities, even minorities of one, against majorities. Criminal defendants are minorities and the last thirty years have seen a generous interpretation of the Bill of Rights in their favor. But the body of the Constitution exists to create and maintain a government for the benefit of the *majority*. The question then becomes: whose rights shall prevail?

The post World War II era has been a time of concern for minority rights, probably in reaction to the horrors resulting from the wholesale overriding of those rights in such countries as Germany and the Soviet Union. At the present time there seems to be no likelihood that there will be a sweeping denial of basic human right in the foreseeable future in the United States, but increasing crime and violence are straining the social fabric. The degree of success in dealing with those strains will determine the shape of the criminal justice system in the twenty-first century.

STUDY QUESTIONS

1. What kind of future policies are needed to see changes in the way the Fourth, Fifth, Sixth and Eighth Amendments will be interpreted come the twenty-first century?

2. Compare the way the Founding Fathers envisioned the Bill of Rights with the way the criminal justice system uses these rights.

3. Is there such a thing as "cruel and unusual punishment"?

4. How far should the criminal justice system go in solving a case?

REFERENCES

Goldfarb, Ronald. (1965). *Ransom* New York: Harper and Row.

CASES

Alexander v. United States, 113 S.Ct. 2766 (1993).

Austin v. United States, 113 S.Ct. 2801 (1993).

Berger v. New York, 388 U.S. 41 (1967).

Booth v. Maryland, 482 U.S. 496 (1987).

Brecht v. Abrahamson, 113 S.Ct. 1710 (1993).

Brewer v. Williams, 430 U.S. 387 (1977).

California V. Greenwood, 486 U.S. 35 (1988).

Escobedo v. Illinois, 378 U.S. 478 (1964).

Florida v. Bostick, 111 S.Ct. 2382 (1991).

Furman v. Georgia, 408 U.S. 238 (1972).

Harmelin v. Michigan, 111 S.Ct. 2680.

Helling v. McKinney, 113 S.Ct. 2475 (1993).

Herrera v. Collins, 113 S.Ct. 853 (1993).

Hold v. Sarver, 309 Fed. Supp. 881 (1972); affirmed 501 F.2d 1291 (5th Cir. 1974).

Hudson v. McMillian, 112 S.Ct. 995 (1992).

Illinois v. Gates, 462 U.S. 2113 (1983).

Mapp v. Ohio, 367 U.S. 642 (1961).

Massiah v. United States, 377 U.S. 201 (1964).

McCleskey v. Zant, 111 S.Ct. 2841 (1991).

Minnesota v. Dickerson, 113 S.Ct. 2130 (1993).

Miranda v. Arizona, 384 U.S. 436 (1966).

New York v. Quarles, 467 U.S. 649 (1984).

Nix v. Williams, 467 U.S. 431 (1984).

Oliver v. United States, 466 U.S. 170 (1984).

Payne v. Tennessee, 111 S.Ct. 2597 (1991).

Payton v. New York, 445 U.S. 573 (1980).

Steagald v. United States, 451 U.S. 204 (1981).

South Carolina v. Gathers, 109 S.Ct. 2207 (1989).

Stone v. Powell, 428 U.S. 465 (1976).

Terry v. Ohio, 3992 U.S. 1 (1968).

United States v. A Parcel of Land, 61 U.S.L.W. 4189 (1993).

United States v. Dixon, 113 S.Ct. 2849 (1993).

United States v. Leon, 468 U.S. 897 (1984).

Weems v. United States, 217 U.S. 349 (1910).

Wilson v. Seiter, 111 S.Ct. 2321 (1991).

Wisconsin v. Mitchell, 113 S.Ct. 2194 (1993).

Withrow v. Williams, 113 S.Ct. 1745 (1993).

PART V

INTRODUCTION

CORRECTIONAL ISSUES OF THE FUTURE

The central task of administering large jails and state correctional institutions is an extremely challenging problem for criminologists. The prison is supposed to incapacitate the offenders, control and restrict their movements, change the offenders' value orientations and vocation skills, and deter future offenders from committing crimes. The chapters in this section examine major problems inherent in today's correctional institutions and predict major riots and skyrocketing crime rates, if prisons do not change in the twenty-first century.

In the lead chapter, Lori Scott discusses "Probation: Heading in New Directions." She assumes that, as more offenders are diverted from the criminal justice system, probation will be addressed more and more by the issues expected to be handled within the correctional facilities. She predicts that there will be more cooperation between the public and private sectors with cost effective systems in place.

"Prison Violence," by Michael Welch, tells us that a major dilemma of criminal justice in a democratic society is how to process suspects and punish law violators in a humane and rational manner. His chapter states that since violence clearly takes place when existing controls are strained or break down, institutional violence continues to remain a problem throughout the history of American corrections, and is likely to remain a critical issue in the near and distant future. As the populations of prisons and jails continue to grow, institutional programs, services and security will fail to keep pace with the demand ensuring that institutions will remain dangerous for inmates and staff alike.

In the chapter, "Jail Overcrowding and Court-Ordered Reform: Critical Issues," Wayne N. Welsh points out that the widespread prevalence of court orders to reform unconstitutional conditions of confinement in American jails and prisons, including unprecedented overcrowding, indicates a significant gap in the current ability of courts to do so with an opportunity to change. A coordinated approach to problem analysis and policy design is needed as we deal with the scope of jail overcrowding and court-ordered reform. We have yet to learn how to punish in a humane and rational manner. Long-neglected economic and social realities suggest a pressing need to reexamine our willingness and capability to punish. There needs to be acknowledgment that jail overcrowding and court orders result from a dynamic confluence of social, political and legal forces, and that solutions to complex problems are unlikely to be quick or easy.

In the area of correctional health issues we turn to James M. Tesoriero's and Malcolm McCullough's work on "Substance Abuse, HIV/AIDS, and Tuberculosis in

American Prisons: Key Factors in Today's Correctional Health Care Crisis." These authors examine the delivery of medical services within the correctional system of the United States. Their emphasis is on correctional policies of education, testing and treatment of these diseases as well as the known efficacy of existing education treatment interventions with particular focus on the impact these issues are likely to have on correctional health care in the twenty-first century.

Edna Morgan-Sharp and Robert Sigler argue, in "Sentencing Into the Twenty-First Century: Sentence Enhancement and Life Without Parole," that punishment and treatment represent two extremes on a continuum of approaches for the disposition of offenders who have been found or pled guilty to the offenses for which they have been committed. They indicate that punishment stresses the protection of society through the use of incarceration and tends to have elements of retribution, incapacitation and deterrence. Treatment stresses the protection of society by changing the offender so that he or she stops committing crimes. Orientation toward the punishment or treatment of convicted offenders has vacillated from treating the offender as if he or she had no rights or reason to expect help to treating the offender as a person who retains his or her rights and who should receive education, training, and psychological services. The authors point out that society is moving toward dependence upon punishment to deter criminals from criminal activity. They indicate that as a result of a situation in which public sentiment for treatment will develop, there will be produced a new wave of treatment-oriented reform.

CHAPTER 12

PROBATION

HEADING IN NEW DIRECTIONS

Lori Scott, M.C.

ABSTRACT

Probation's role in the future of corrections should be one of expanding community-based intervention programs, based upon an increasingly sophisticated ability to assess risk, and the technological capacity to supervise even high-risk offenders. The emerging use of technology will allow for more flexibility and efficient use of resources, in both space and personnel.

As more offenders are diverted into the system with higher needs, probation will be expected to address issues such as literacy, drug treatment, job counseling, mental illness, and parenting skills in the struggle to help probationers succeed. More professionalism and specialization, more cooperation with other agencies and the private sector, and more creativity in the development of intermediate sanctions are improvements already working in progressive probation departments throughout the country. The real challenge will continue to be to convince legislators and others to fund those programs and procedures which are effective, both in outcome and in cost savings.

INTRODUCTION

It was 5 p.m., June 25, 2010. Probation Officer Dave Smith of Phoenix drove his car around the corner and pulled to a stop as he answered his mobile phone. At the same time he glanced at the computer screen beside him and noted two items: his surveillance officer, Debra Watson, had just checked in for the evening shift, and Joe, one of their forty-five sex offenders, had just returned home and activated the electronic voice monitor. This information would be recorded a part of Dave's case file on Joe, who rated high on the risk scale, and was therefore assigned a tight curfew, electronic checking, and two officers instead of one. And even though the sensors installed in Joe's apartment were sensitive enough to pick up any voice other than his, his manipulative history required in-person checks to verify that he was never in contact with children.

The department was in the process of awarding contracts for a new sensing device placed just under the defendant's skin, which identified him by his DNA, and would record a touch by any other human. Joe knew that he would be required to account for any such contacts. If and when he lived with a permanent partner, she would be able to stay with him only if she were to allow a comparable sensing device. Even though the equipment was costly, it would eventually allow gradual shifting of intense in-person monitoring to more electronic control. A cost analysis had proven to the legislature that even the most intensive community supervision was less than half that of an expensive prison bed, and offenders such as Joe could be safely monitored while working to further pay some of the cost of supervision.

When Dave answered the phone, it was his surveillance officer, who wanted to go over the details of her scheduled search of Joe's apartment for drugs. Ordinarily, one of the drug specialists would perform this type of search, but Debra or Dave always went along on sex offender cases. They both were well aware that drug use was a significant factor in sex offender recidivism. Dave again hoped that the DNA sensor contact would be approved, as it would automatically record any use of drugs or alcohol, eliminating the random and time-consuming process of collecting urine samples for urinalysis. Since Joe had been a high user of methamphetamines, his terms of probation required random periodic searches of his residence, as well as testing. These searches were programmed by the computer, and neither Dave nor his partner knew when they would be done. Of course, they always had the option of scheduling searches on their own judgment.

On the surface, Joe was doing well. Nineteen years old and unskilled and unemployed at the time of his offense, he had been ordered to the department's Literacy Center every Sunday, where his presence was entered into Dave Smith's case file. He was now reading at a sixth grade level and was working at one of the companies which contracted with the probation department. They needed reliable employees for assembly line work; they liked the intensive supervision given some probationers, who were likely to be drugfree and dependable. Again a computer at his employer's recorded his work hours for Dave Smith's file.

> Dave knew, however, that Joe was struggling in his therapy group, and would need months, maybe years of additional treatment before supervision could be significantly reduced. Dave had a master's degree in Psychology; to be a specialized officer in his area required an advanced degree in human behavior. His job required him to work closely with therapists in implementing the "team" approach which worked so well with sex offenders. Outcome studies of the last twenty years had shown that treatment was most effective when combined with surveillance. With a sophisticated risk instrument, the use of computer technology, teamwork with fellow officers and therapists, and Dave's talent and experience, the department could move offenders like Joe up and down the continuum of less to more intensive supervision without having to go back to court every time, allowing for the most effective use of people and time.

Can this be the future for probation in the community? Is it fantasy or reality, wishful thinking, or somewhere in between? Criminal justice experts here and abroad predict that technology and specialization will be trends that can make community corrections safer, increasingly innovative, and cost-effective alternatives to expensive prisons. Before we begin such a discussion, however, we should consider the words of H.L. Mencken, who observed decades ago that our increasing knowledge of human behavior would soon make prisons obsolete. Looking back seventy years, we have indeed increased our knowledge, but we have been paralyzed and handicapped by political and extremist pressures to use that knowledge effectively.

We will examine in detail a large probation department which is heading progressively toward the twenty-first century, often at a gallop, and sometimes at a crawl. Other innovations around the country will illustrate the efforts of modern day community corrections leaders to manage the increasing numbers placed under their care. Driven by the numbers, by liability cases, by growing community violence, hampered by bureaucracy, concerned about officer safety, they are struggling to fulfill their mandate to lower risk and change behavior, all at the lowest cost possible.

TECHNOLOGY

Ask any probation officer what he or she hates most about the job, and chances are the answer would be "paperwork." But ask most heads of departments if their budget allows for notebook computers for their staff, and they would probably laugh. Then again, if the average taxpayer knew that a $1200 device might allow field officers to safely increase their caseloads and work more efficiently, they might not think it's such a bad investment. The technology is here; private industry doesn't hesitate to use every means available for efficiency; why not government?

With this in mind, the Maricopa County (Phoenix, Arizona metropolitan area) Probation Department is engaged in an ambitious move to automate its entire system. Information is originally entered in the computer when the defendant is interviewed for the presentence report. Soon presentence writers can check out computer notebooks to interview defendants in jail. Terms will be entered by the judge's clerk at sentencing. If probation is granted, all data can be electronically transferred to the field officer's computer and to any other officer who may need it, such as a jail work furlough program. There will be no lost files, no delays in transferring the basics of a case. Most duplication of effort in entering information will ultimately be avoided.

Field officers will begin adding and building onto this basic information. With notebook computers, they can input data from the field, and access any collateral data for inquiries in the case. With the use of a cellular phone and less paperwork, officers can spend more time in the field, carrying their mobile offices with them. Clerical staff can be reduced, or trained and promoted to track paper caseloads, such as restitution or fine-only cases. Office space will shrink, allowing officers to telecommute and share workstations which they will need only one or two days a week.

As telecommunication advances are made, it is the hope of progressive chief probation officers such as Norman Helber of Maricopa County that private industry can be convinced to work with government in determining the fastest, easiest, and most efficient ways to utilize that technology. He predicts that in government areas in which technology has been advanced, agencies such as NASA will be sharing space-age innovations which can help with the job of monitoring people and maintaining safety. Bullet-proof yet lightweight clothing, advanced techniques in biomedical monitoring, and improvement in electronic surveillance technology are realistic possibilities.

All that data will automatically produce the numbers and information needed by the department's planning and programs division. In a system which manages 20 thousand probationers a year in a geographic area roughly the size of Israel, planning for the future means analyzing past and present trends and accommodating the needs of probationers, always mindful of budgetary restraints. The division has been aggressively pursuing grant monies where available, and utilizes staff creativity and flexibility to design and implement programs in which probationers can be monitored in a variety of ways.

THE AGE OF SPECIALIZATION

Literacy Centers. A program which makes a dramatic and personal impact on the lives of probationers and illustrates the use of technology and cooperation among county agencies is the Literacy Center. Its impetus came from a former judge who was disturbed at the number of defendants who could not read or write and asked the state's two largest probation departments in Maricopa and Pima (Tucson) Counties to join with local school districts and the State Department of Education to develop a literacy and learning center which would be state of the art, and a resource to the whole community as well as probationers. It demonstrates that technology should not only be used to monitor and regulate probationers, but can be helpful in improving their lives:

> Janelle is twenty-four. She is a mother of three who followed her ex-husband into several years of drug use and eventual sales. Sitting in front of a computer, she inserts a laser disc and finds her place at Lesson 10. As she watches intently, the brightly colored screen flashes pictures and letters that she is finally learning to decode as words. Janelle wants to be able to read to her children, help them with school, and go back to school herself to be able to support them without state aid. Erin, the instructor, recalls the difference between the Janelle who reluctantly walked in five weeks ago and the woman who is now talking about going to college.

The Literacy Center is an example of the increasing use of specialized programming as Maricopa County's aggressive response to the need for "intermediate sanctions." Many of the intermediate sanctions have been adopted in response to the needs of probationers, and while they cannot always be considered diversions from incarceration, they can reduce revocation rates in their attempt to improve a probationers' ability to live crime-free in the community. The need for remedial education is acute: 65% of U.S. prison inmates are functionally illiterate, as compared to 13% of the total population; 90% of Arizona's prisoners are high school dropouts; 75% of Arizona's prison inmates have not even reached high school; 60% are recidivists (Siegel, 1994). To focus resources and personnel on this preventive obstacle to healthy citizenship makes fiscal and social sense.

A followup study of the recidivism of Pima County's GED graduates showed a significant difference in new conviction rates when compared to a group of GED dropouts and a control group (Siegel, 1994). In a 1991 study in Harris County, Texas, it was found that participants in their Adult Education/Literacy Project were revoked at a significantly lower rate than the general population (Harris County Annual Report, 1992). Considering the increasing correlation evident between learning disabilities and the prison population, probation departments of the future may have to compensate for the failure of schools and parents to focus attention on these problems at an early age. Could the future also include teams of senior citizen volunteers recruited from their increasing numbers to aid in this important work? Only if the growing concepts of "intermediate sanctions" receives wider acceptance by the community, and a reduction of the "us vs. them" mentality.

Drug Court. The "war on drugs" campaign has resulted in a huge increase in the number of drug offenders in our jails and prisons. Since 1980, the population of drug offenders in U.S. prisons has increased by 650%, more than five times the rate of increase for other offenders (Clear and Cole, 1994). If the defendant remains in the community, much of the probation officer's time is spent trying to help the probationer stay clean; he or she may be in or out of various treatment programs, on a continuum from less to more intensive. Since drug addiction is rarely dealt with in prisons, probation is often the best chance for effective treatment. Maricopa County is experimenting with two programs: Drug Court, and the Community Punishment Program.

> At 10:30 every Friday morning in Judge Susan Bolton's courtroom in downtown Phoenix, twenty to thirty probationers gather for "Drug Court." Modeled after a Florida program, it's part of a unique experiment in impacting first-time drug offenders with a carrot-and-stick approach; they must participate in intensive treatment, frequent urinalyses, and return to the courtroom as often as every week to report on their progress. On this Friday, Judge Bolton alternates encouragement for those who are fulfilling their contracts with disappointment and sanctions for those who are not. She listens to Kenneth try to explain why he didn't have the required urine sample last Wednesday...a lack of transportation, a missed bus, a misunderstanding about time. The others in the courtroom look at each other, grinning and shaking their heads; they've been through it; they know his excuses won't hold up. As a consequence, and because this is not his first infraction, Kenneth is handcuffed and led off to serve a week in jail, where he will be given a chance to think and try again.
>
> But more often, there is praise for the others who are drug-free; who have fulfilled the terms of Phase I, II, or III, who in return will incrementally earn days off a sixty-day deferred jail term, and months off their three-year probation. Twenty-three-year-old Craig triumphantly hands Judge Bolton the last of his paperwork, having completed every stage and every contract and earned a release from probation after eight months.

The two specialized probation officers staff every case with the judge, attend many of the counseling sessions, and all work together to support their probationers' small successes in the struggle to overcome their dependency on drugs. Begun with a small federal grant, the Drug Court program is now self-sufficient. Probationers pay the cost of their counseling; both prosecution and defense support it; and preliminary studies show that it is definitely having an impact on jail overcrowding, as many of the participants manage to earn their way out of the jail sentence which would have been imposed. It is a small attempt to attack one of the leading reasons for failure on probation. According to criminologists Norval Morris and Michael Tonry, "it is well established that drug users account for a grossly disproportionate amount of street crime: it is also well established that it is possible without excessive expense greatly to reduce the ingestion of drugs by addicts and consequentially greatly to reduce their criminal depredations. It is astonishing to us that this path is not well trodden" (p. 196).

While a program like Drug Court can work well for some offenders, unfortunately, in Maricopa County as in most jurisdictions nationwide, there is a severe shortage of in-patient beds for the more severely addicted offender. In periodic surveys of the county's probation officers, this shortage always ranks as the number one need. As prison beds continue to rise in cost, it is hoped that the future will bring enlightened and increased public and legislative support for the investment of criminal justice monies into more community-based programs, which are certainly cheaper and can transition the nonviolent offenders into halfway houses while still under various levels of probation supervision. As police and prosecutors waged the war on drugs, jail and prison beds were added, but in the ten years from 1983 to 1993, not a single additional in-patient treatment bed became available for Maricopa County probation officers to utilize for their own indigent offenders who needed a safe and drug-free living space, away from their drug-using friends and families.

For the state of Texas, the impetus was a federal court order in 1989 on both prison and jail overcrowding, forcing the release of such monies into the community. In Harris County (Houston metropolitan area), the situation was compounded by a local lawsuit resulting in the need to lower the population of the jail (*Alberti vs. the Sheriff of Harris County*). As a result, Harris County now has a huge probation department second to none in its selection of "intermediate sanctions." For example, they now have almost two thousand residential beds which provide not only substance abuse treatment, but educational services, training in life skills, job search assistance, and other needs of probationers. The goal has been to directly reduce the number of probation revocations for technical violations, and it seems to be working. Services and programs to deal with all the issues facing offenders are offered county-wide to its 60 thousand probationers. Some of the options available include: "Project Action," which services the mentally ill; "Super-intensive" probation, which focuses on the higher-needs, high security population; and a Diagnostic Center which will soon be the central referral source of all new probationers.

Sex Offenders. A fast-growing development in probation supervision in many larger jurisdictions is the specialization in populations such as sex offenders and the mentally ill. As an example, Maricopa County has had specialized sex offender officers for many years; a detailed protocol has been developed for supervising sex offenders which combines treatment with intensive surveillance. Together with states such as Washington, Oregon, Colorado, Vermont, and Texas, they have pioneered innovative supervision strategies for sex offenders utilizing the polygraph, penile plethysmograph, and up-to-date assessments addressing known risk factors. The addition of seventeen specialized terms to most sex offenders' probation gives officers better control over their behavior in the community, and with the ability to use electronic monitoring and periodic polygraphs, it is expected that many of these offenders can continue to be safely monitored in the community. Arizona judges now have the option of imposing lifetime probation for almost all sexual crimes, using the rationale that "such offenders can never be cured, but can learn to control their behavior" (Scott, 1994). It is expected that more states will add lifetime probation to the sentencing possibilities for certain high-risk sex offenders.

By strictly controlling the offender's environment, Maricopa County's nine specialized officers supervise five hundred of the thirteen hundred sex offenders in the current probation population, utilizing the services of four surveillance officers who work evenings and weekends. They all have undergone intensive training on the psychology and treatment of sexual deviancy. Because some sex offenders are now being sentenced to several years in prison on one count and lifetime probation on another, there will be an increasing demand for personnel willing to specialize in the treatment and supervision of this very difficult caseload. As future research and outcome studies on treatment and supervision become more reliable, risk assessments should become more sophisticated, allowing for continued community supervision at various levels.

Future technology and national data networks will definitely aid in the overall surveillance of sexual abusers. There is also the possibility that much more can be accomplished with drug therapy to help these offenders focus on making the necessary behavioral changes, at least in the initial stages of treatment (Bradford, 1993). Perhaps the future may bring further acceptance of pharmacological treatment for certain offenders, especially as drugs are being developed which are less expensive and do not have the adverse side effects present in the anti-androgens used by some offenders today.

Mentally Ill. Specialized officers already supervise a population in which medication is generally accepted as a term of probation: the seriously mentally ill. In another effort to attend to probationer's needs while vacating jail space, Maricopa County in 1990 opened the Transitional Living Center (TLC) for this problem probationer. With twenty-five beds, it allows for the offender who might have committed a petty crime or series of technical violations to participate in a humane living environment while undergoing a diagnosis and evaluation. After he or she is stabilized, caseworkers help the transition back to appropriate lodging in the community. The program has received widespread support from other agencies, including the Maricopa County Jail, which presently can be considered the second largest mental hospital in the state as a result of inadequate funding for Arizona's mentally ill.

Houston's Community Supervision and Corrections Department lists specialized caseloads for the following: developmentally disabled, domestic violence, mental health, female offenders, special needs for Spanish speaking, and intensive sex offender caseload. They offer Restitution Centers, among other residential facilities, to ensure that crime victims are compensated financially for their losses, providing special counseling for probationers so that employment is maintained.

Day Reporting Center. Another concept taken from successful programs tried elsewhere is the Phoenix Day Reporting Center. Patterned after a Massachusetts experiment, probationers in jail are screened, and if found eligible, are allowed to leave the jail early to serve their time under house arrest, reporting to the Probation Office every day to participate in a wide variety of activities. These may include literacy skills, drug treatment, employment search and counseling, and life skills training. They are assigned both a regular probation officer and an intensive surveillance officer, and can be sent back to jail without a hearing if they break the rules. As in the Houston area's recent expansion of programs, the focus is to release people from jail if enough controls and requirements can be administered.

ADDITIONAL INTERMEDIATE SANCTIONS

Day Fines. In their discussion of intermediate sanctions, Morris and Tonry make an excellent case for the imposition and collection of fines, a "financial disincentive" as a punishment for crime. A grant from the Vera Institute allowed for the experimental establishment of a Maricopa County day-fine program (F.A.R.E.), taking into account the various economic circumstances of offenders who have committed similar crimes.

An assessment of the probationer's financial situation and income might merit wide differences in the amount of money assessed by "unit" or percentage, rather than the same flat amount. Day fines are widely used in Europe; in fact, they are the punishment of choice for many crimes. In West Germany in 1979, for example, 82.4% of all sentenced criminals were ordered to pay a fine as the primary sanction (Morris and Tonry, 1990). In the United States we place incarceration first and work our way back from that point.

As of January, 1994, after thirty-three months of operation, Maricopa County's day fine program had collected over a half million dollars from 505 defendants. The collection rate has consistently been above 97%. Only two have been revoked to prison, and eighteen had to be moved up to regular probation. This finding suggests that the program is definitely working, and that it is meeting the guidelines set up for it. One of the problems with many intermediate sanctions is that often they are not focused on the right defendants, or there is not enough enforcement and followup. With ordinary fines or community service tacked on as an adjunct to regular probation, the requirements can become excessively burdensome and unrealistic for both offender and probation officer, especially if the main focus of probation should be substance abuse treatment. If, on the other hand, the day fine is the primary and meaningful sanction and enforced as such, many experts think it can be much more effective than it is now.

Presently the typical defendant profile of F.A.R.E. probation is a young offender guilty of a nonviolent offense of the lowest class felony. Maricopa County would like to expand this program to more serious felons, again, if they can continue to control the candidates. With a caseload of three hundred, one probation officer and a clerk can easily manage such a population, leaving the more dangerous offenders to more intensive supervision. Does the future hold more use of the day-fine concept? Only if the prosecutors, judges, and the public can be convinced that it is viable and as punitive as incarceration. If a fine, for example, caused enough economic hardship that the offender might have to sell his house or car and live in greatly diminished circumstances, then it might be considered as punitive as two or three years in prison. He would also be turning over money to the state, instead of the state paying his room and board and ultimately causing the same economic hardship on his family.

Collecting Money. In 1993, Maricopa County's probation officers collected a record $7 million in a combination of restitution, probation service fees, court reimbursement assessments, and fines. And there is a growing trend in government to impose or increase "user" fees, probation departments nationwide have assessed probation fees, but often have poor collection rates. Maricopa County has experimented recently with a "collections team" of professional money managers in one regional field office. All new probation cases (655 to date) are assigned to the collection team in addition to their regular probation officer. Preliminary results show a collection rate of 83% versus a departmental rate of 60%. The team reports that because they spend the initial two or three months with clients helping them with budgeting and making their probation payments a priority, it becomes a habit. "Most research on the payment and nonpayment of fines reveals that the single most important step in ensuring the payment of fines is the prompt notification to the debtor if his payment or payments fall even briefly into arrears" (Morris and Tonry, 1990, p. 140).

Again, it must be emphasized that while the use of the fine as punishment should be enforced, adding a fine to a long list of other punishments meted out to a probationer makes it difficult to collect. For example, several years ago the Arizona Legislature mandated a minimum fine of $1050 (with surcharges) for the possession of even a small amount of marijuana. This fine was combined with three years' probation (monthly fee $30) and 360 hours of community service. Low-income probationers who manage to successfully complete treatment programs and pay their probation fees often struggle on for extra months or years to pay off their fines when they could easily receive an early termination.

Community Service. As in the example above, community service often becomes an additional add-on to probation terms, and can be so excessive that it loses its impact. It can leave officers and offenders both scrambling to find ways to fill out the required hours, instead of being a meaningful way of "giving back" to the community for harm done. In San Diego County, California, an enlarged community service component is a visible and meaningful sign to the public that probationers are working hard. With a fleet of several vans and buses, they have contracted with San Diego and surrounding cities to perform jobs that would otherwise use city employees. In their bright orange vests, probationers can be seen maintaining the areas along the extensive trolley system, cleaning up the beaches, picking up trash after city or nonprofit events, painting over graffiti, and working in city, county, or state parks. In addition, as in most cities, probationers are individually assigned work for a large number of nonprofit agencies. The future could find many departments focusing on community restitution as a viable intermediate sanction which can stand on its own.

Intensive Probation. Much has been written about the use of intensive probation for high-risk offenders, and many states now utilize some form of intensive probation as a sentencing option. This probation may or may not be combined with attendance at a "boot camp" or perhaps electronic monitoring. "Intensive" can mean, as it does in Phoenix, two officers for every twenty-five probationers and mandated contacts of at least four per week plus forty hours a month of community service. In Houston, there are many levels of intensive probation, such as a secure residential facility for offenders age seventeen to twenty-five, or "super-intensive" probation, mandating daily contacts and numerous other requirements. In Arizona, at a cost of $10.81 a day, IPS lines up as an affordable alternative to a $44.00 a day prison bed. It is expected that the future will see the expansion of intensive-type programs which are more politically popular then other less restrictive programs.

Risk Assessments. As increased specialization of officers and programs evolves, there will be more emphasis on effective risk assessments to place offenders appropriately. The field officer's discretion and independence may be reduced; in many ways, such discretion relies rather haphazardly on each officer's individuality. At the same time, well-trained specialized officers can be the key to the probationer's long-term success. There will be more and more a "team" approach, as programs are developed to meet probationer's needs.

In Marion County, Oregon, the principle of "limited risk management" is being developed to balance the need for punishment with the individual's risk of reoffending. Corrections Department Director Billy Wasson believes that "the model is explicitly seen as reducing rather than widening the net of social control while containing costs and limiting the risk of new crime" (Clear and Cole, 1994, p. 215). Limited risk management requires a continuum of intermediate sanctions; it means imposing only those conditions which are enforceable; it presumes that decision making at both individual and organizational levels will be visible and regularly reviewed, and that the system will routinely be assessed and modified in order to attain "measurable objectives and clearly stated goals." Most importantly, Mr. Wasson states that it requires a "widely shared vision of what the organization is and ought to be."

That "widely shared vision" will have to be shared by the numerous other components of the system, by legislators, prosecutors, judges, and the public, who need to hear more facts and numbers regarding the cost of our present system of punishment and less political rhetoric which plays on the public's fear of crime and criminals. The "measurable objectives" do not necessarily have to mean the rate of recidivism." Nationally, the Bureau of Justice Statistics has formed a study group which is presently challenging criminal justice professionals to formulate new performance measures that expand and complement the conventional measures such as rates of crime and recidivism (Dilulio, 1992).

Interagency Cooperation. Teamwork with other agencies will be crucial in managing future offenders as there is more demand for a limited amount of funding. In Maricopa County, for example, an agreement was reached with the Sheriff to utilize funds earmarked for work furlough beds to help open the Day Reporting Center. At a cost of $15.94 a day, versus $37 for a jail bed, it has so far diverted a total of 34,337 jail days, for a net cost saving of $723 thousand. Work is underway on a small experiment to combine supervision and treatment resources in families with both juvenile and adult offenders; traditionally the juvenile system has more treatment dollars, while the adult system might focus more on supervision. Many states are looking at the issue of prosecuting and sentencing the increasingly violent juvenile offender, and examining ways in which the traditional separation of adult and juvenile corrections might allow for more serious punishment while still placing an emphasis on rehabilitation.

In sex offender cases involving incest and reunification, much more could be accomplished in many jurisdictions to systematically coordinate the treatment and supervision of offender, family, and victim. The state of Washington's SSOSA (Special Sex Offender Sentencing Act) allows for effective teamwork and management of such cases from investigation to sentencing to supervision. Protocols have been written in Phoenix and Tucson to coordinate the reporting, investigation, prosecution, court proceedings, sentencing, supervision, and treatment of child sexual abuse cases, with the goal of reducing the trauma to the child, and maintaining consistency. Such protocols are easier to write than to put into practice, but at least they can be a beginning.

What part private industry will play in future community corrections is unknown, but it is expected that as corrections administrators expand their supervision options, the demand for services will grow. In cities with high-tech industries, there could be agreements, for example, to utilize field officers to test new and experimental equipment. Why couldn't probation officers try out new types of phones, surveillance equipment and even electric cars? Private vendors and monitors will no doubt play an increasing role in supervision and surveillance as the efficiency and capabilities of technology increase. Various types of treatment, residential facilities, life skills management, urine screening, and numerous other services can often be provided more cheaply by outside contractors, and defendants frequently can pay all or part of the cost. Probation department may be able to utilize a portion of RICO funds and vehicles, provided they aided in some way in the apprehension of certain absconded offenders.

CONCLUSION

In spite of the logical and cost-effective benefits of intermediate sanctions to both offender and taxpayer, a 1990 report revealed that only 5% of the 2,670,234 persons on probation in this country were involved in some type of correctional option other than jail. The hard work of many agencies in the past three years has undoubtedly increased that percentage. We know that many nonviolent offenders can change their behavior while in the community with programs specifically designed to meet their needs. As society's other institutions increasingly fail to turn out productive citizens, the traditional lessons of family, school, church, and workplace will have to be learned in the expensive "classrooms" of the criminal justice system.

The reality of corrections, however, is that there has always been little planning; the pendulum swings whichever way the political wind blows; in the present "get tough" attitude on crime there is little discussion of costs involved as we continue to imprison people in record numbers. Yet the worst case scenario for probation departments would be the sentencing or the release of huge numbers of offenders into the community system with no funding for increased and intensive supervision, and no attempt at distinguishing risk levels or planning for appropriate management. Probation departments know that they can do the job with many offenders who might easily be sentenced to prison, but they need the right tools to be effective and safe. If we are fortunate, the future might allow their vision to become reality.

STUDY QUESTIONS

1. What are some of the barriers that keep probation and other corrections entities from adapting as quickly to high technology as private industry?

2. Discuss some of the ways technology can help probation departments become more efficient in the future.

3. Discuss the impact of illiteracy rates on the prison/probation population.

4. Give some examples of the cost-effectiveness of the imposition of community sanctions as compared to incarceration, and why you think such programs have not been used more extensively.

5. What do you think probation departments of the future will have to do to "sell" their programs to the appropriate decision-makers?

REFERENCES

Bradford, J. and Kafka, M. (1993, November). "Sexual Impulsivity, Mood Disorders, and Psychopharmacology." Paper presented at the Twelfth Annual Research Conference of the Association for the Treatment of Sexual Abusers, Boston, MA.

Clear, T.R. and Cole, G.F. (1994). *American Corrections*. Belmont, CA: Wadsworth.

Dilulio, Jr., J.J. (1992). *Rethinking the criminal justice system: Toward a new paradigm*. Washington, DC: U.S. Department of Justice, Bureau of Justice Statistics.

Harris County Community Supervision and Corrections Department. (1992). *Annual Report*. Houston, TX.

Morris, N., & Tonry, M. (1990). *Between prison and probation*. New York: Oxford University Press.

Scott, Lori. (1994). "Sex Offenders: Prevalence, Trends, Model Programs, and Costs." In A. Roberts (Ed.), *Critical Issues in Crime and Justice*. Thousand Oaks, CA: Sage.

Siegel, Gayle. (1994). The effect of literacy and general education development programs on adult offenders on probation. *Perspectives*, 18, 1, 38-43.

Taxman, Faye S. (1994). Correctional Options and Implementation issues: results from a Survey of Correctional Professionals. *Perspectives*, 18, 1, 32-37.

CHAPTER 13

PRISON VIOLENCE IN AMERICA

PAST, PRESENT, AND FUTURE

Michael Welch, Ph.D.

ABSTRACT

The history of American prison violence is as old as the nation itself, dating back to 1774 when a major uprising occurred in the Simsbury prison in Connecticut. Since then few American prisons have been immune to violence. This chapter explores various levels (collective versus individual) and forms (inmates versus inmates, inmates versus staff, staff versus staff) of institutional violence. In addition to introducing an historical and futuristic view of prison violence, several theoretical considerations are presented: the motives and goals of prison violence, the sources of prison violence, as well as strategies to reduce violence.

ESCAPE INTO THE FUTURE

The scene is 1997, where the once great city of New York becomes the one maximum-security prison for the entire country. (The plan to convert the island of Manhattan into penitentiary emerged in 1988, when the crime rate nationwide increased 400%. This crime wave forced government officials to rethink the traditional penitentiary. As a result, the New York Maximum-Security Penitentiary, Manhattan Island, became the ultimate futuristic prison.) A fifty foot containment wall has been constructed around Manhattan Island along the Jersey shore, around the Harlem River, and down the Brooklyn shore. All bridges and waterways are mined with explosives. The United States Police Force—like an army—is encamped outside the containment wall. Liberty Island and the Statue of Liberty function as the control station from which surveillance helicopters patrol the harbor. Officers manning these helicopters have orders to shoot escaping inmates. There are no guards inside the penitentiary, only prisoners and the world they create. The rules are simple: "Once you go in, you don't go out." Prisoners sentenced to Manhattan Island, however, are given a choice: to enter the penitentiary for life or be terminated and cremated at the control center. The name of this film was "Escape from New York."

Kurt Russell plays the role of Snake Plissken who sports an unshaven face, eye-patch, and leather jacket—looking much like a futuristic buccaneer. Plissken, a war hero, is sentenced to life for robbing the federal reserve depository. As Plissken enters the underworld of Manhattan Island Penitentiary, he learns of the harsh reality of survival. Prisoners live in subway tunnels and sewers. Moreover, inmates rely on heightened vigilance to fend off predatory attacks from street gangs, punk rockers, and crazies who continuously battle over turf.

Though the movie "Escape from New York" is an engaging science fiction exercise, it does address some real notions and trends in incarceration. At the societal level, the film illuminates the classic "lock 'em up and throw away the key" sentiment which remains popular today. The movie also reflects a current trend in correctional policy which places more emphasis on constructing super-maximum security penitentiaries.

At the institutional level, the movie introduces a new style of prisoner surveillance; that is, placing guards on the outside of the prison, leaving inmates to their own devices for survival. Today, corrections officials certainly have not turned prisons over to the inmates. However, due to overcrowding and staff shortages, prisoners cannot rely on guards for protection against physical and sexual assault. Instead, prisoners must resort to carrying concealed homemade knives, known as "shanks," to defend themselves. Similar to those on the futuristic Manhattan Island, inmates in today's prisons must live in the world that they create, and typically the convict world is a violent one.

INTRODUCTION

The first major prison riot recorded in American history was in 1774 at the Simsbury prison—a primitive institution which was constructed over an abandoned copper mine in Connecticut (Dillingham and Montgomery, 1985). Hence, the history of prison violence is as old as the nation itself. Between 1990 and 1985, more than three hundred riots have been documented in American corrections (Dillingham and Montgomery, 1985). Although not all of these disturbances resulted in deaths and major destruction, some riots are remembered as devastating events: in particular, the uprisings at Attica and the Penitentiary at New Mexico.

Since incarceration involves the practice of warehousing criminals (many of whom are violent) in overcrowded and understaffed institutions, it stands to reason that prisons continue to be among the most dangerous places in society. Indeed, danger is intimately associated with life in prison, where both inmates and staff struggle to avert victimization.

In this chapter, various levels (collective versus individual) and forms (inmates versus inmates, inmates versus staff, staff versus inmates) of institutional violence will be discussed. In addition to describing theories of violence, this chapter discusses the riots at Attica and the Penitentiary at New Mexico. In doing so, we shall explore institutional violence in the past and present, especially as they relate to future trends.

MOTIVES AND GOALS OF PRISON VIOLENCE

Recognizing and identifying the types of prison violence is crucial to our understanding of why and how violence emerges. Just as there are different levels and forms of violence, there also exist various motives or goals. At the most fundamental level of analysis, the motives and goals of prison violence are characterized as either *instrumental* or *expressive* (Bowker, 1985).

Instrumental Violence

Instrumental violence is rational or calculative because it sets out to achieve a particular goal. This aspect of reasoning is especially true of inmate-inmate violence in which an inmate physically or sexually assaults a fellow prisoner for the purpose of garnering power and status within the prison society. In pursuit of dominance, an inmate may employ violence (or the threat of violence) to get what he wants: a more desirable living situation, sexual satisfaction, commodities (sneakers, junk-food), contraband (drugs, weapons), and/or various services (laundry tasks, paper work for legal matters). Through instrumental violence, the aggressor may enhance his self-image (Bowker, 1985). Instrumental violence is not restricted to individual violence; it also emerges within collective disturbances, especially when goals, usually in the form of demands, are pronounced (Welch, 1996, 1995).

Expressive Violence

Expressive violence is not rational, insofar as goals are not consciously pursued. Rather, such violence is expressive in the emotional sense, such as spontaneous release of tension. Expressive violence is apparent in individual outbursts of violence as well as in collective disturbances, as depicted by a "mob mentality." In either case, expressive violence requires a psychological state of readiness coupled with a conducive situation, or precipitating event.

It needs to be emphasized that instrumental and expressive violence are not mutually exclusive; many violent incidents involve a combination of the two. For instance, in the hostile world of prison, inmates have consciously engaged in assaults so that others would perceive them as being savagely violent. Such displays of expressive violence are instrumental because it bolsters the inmate's reputation, thereby enhancing his or her power and status. For example, in the years leading up to the riot at the Penitentiary at New Mexico, inmates felt vulnerable to snitches and other violent cliques of prisoners. Consequently, some inmates reinforced their own "macho" reputations by unleashing emotional outbursts of violence. Bolstering a violent reputation among one's peers serves a form of self-protection (Welch, 1996, 1995; Colvin, 1982; also see Abbott, 1981).

SOURCES OF PRISON VIOLENCE

Although there are literally dozens of factors attributed to prison violence, we are served best by concentrating on three of the most instrumental sources of institutional disturbances: the violent inmate, the social climate of violence, and overcrowding. We should stress that these factors are regarded as *sources* and not *causes*, since they are not solely responsible for violence.

The Violent Inmate

It stands to reason that prisons are violent places because they house violent offenders. Indeed, that is one of the purposes of prisons in society—to protect nonviolent citizens from those who are violent. This line of reasoning is especially true of maximum security penitentiaries which hold the most violent criminals. Therefore, violence in prison is, in part, explained by the fact that inmates attempt to settle their disputes in a manner to which they are accustomed—through violence.

However, prison violence is not the domain of maximum security penitentiaries housing violent offenders. Prison violence also takes place in medium (and some minimum) security facilities. Moreover, violence also arises among prisoners who do not have violent histories. Therefore, we must look to other sources of violence, such as the social climate of violence and overcrowding.

The Social Climate of Violence

A major axiom of sociology is that some actions are *motivated*, whereas others are *situated*. Applying this notion to prisons, it is proposed that inmates (even those who are generally nonviolent) may resort to violence because of the contextual features of their environment. Toch (1985) examined the social climate of violence in prisons and concluded that the situational context is not the sole producer of violence, but it may enhance or reduce the likelihood of occurrence. Toch identifies a number of contextual features which contribute to prison violence:

- *By Providing "Pay-offs."* Acting violently in prison has rewards, such as peer admiration or the creation of fear (which may be instrumental by serving as a form of protection).

- *By Providing Immunity or Protection.* Violence in prison is perpetuated because victims generally adhere to a code of silence by not "ratting" on the aggressor(s).

- *By Providing Opportunities.* Due to the institutional routine and internal architecture, there are numerous opportunities for assaults. Violence often takes place when the risk of being seen by staff is minimal and in places which conceal the attack.

- *By Providing Temptations, Challenges, and Provocations.* The climate of violence is replete with temptations, challenges, and provocations to engage in violence against inmates who are regarded as deserving an assault.

- *By Providing Justifactory Premise.* Since prisons are viewed as violent places, especially by inmates themselves, violence is justified because the norms permit it.

As we shall see in the section on intervention, the prevalence of violence can be reduced by attending to each of these contextual features of the prison climate.

Does Overcrowding Contribute to Violence?

At a glance, it makes sense that overcrowding contributes to prison violence. However, we must remain mindful that almost all correctional facilities are overcrowded, and violence varies from institution to institution. Therefore, it is important to determine more precisely what effect overcrowding (in addition to other factors) has on institutional violence. A report by the Bureau of Justice Statistics (1988) finds little evidence that prison population density is *directly* associated with inmate-inmate assaults and other disturbances. Nevertheless, most forms of aggression are *indirectly* fueled and exacerbated by overcrowding. The Bureau of Justice Statistics emphasizes that violence occurs more frequently in maximum security facilities, irrespective of their population densities. However, other studies have found that overcrowding *is* an important factor affecting institutional violence (Gaes and McGuire, 1985; Farrington and Nutall, 1985). Clearly, additional research is needed to assess more precisely the impact that overcrowding has on prison violence; moreover, this knowledge should be taken into account to formulate preventative measures.

THE RIOT AT ATTICA

Perhaps no other prison riot has received as much notoriety as the uprising at Attica, in upstate New York. From the onset, Attica became a metaphor for numerous social problems, including racism, oppression, and injustice. Yet, metaphors aside, indepth investigations of Attica have concluded that racism, oppression, and injustice were salient features before, during, and after the riot (*Attica: The Official Report*, 1972; Useem and Kimball, 1987, 1985; Useem, 1985; Mahan, 1985; Wicker, 1975; also see Oswald, 1972 and the 1991 Commemorative Issue of *Social Justice* devoted to Attica).

Between September 9 and 13, 1971, forty-three persons died at the upstate New York maximum security prison. Most alarmingly, thirty-nine were killed, and more than eighty others were wounded by gunfire during the fifteen minutes it took the State Police to retake the institution. "With the exception of Indian massacres in the late nineteenth century, the State Police assault which ended the four-day prison uprising was the bloodiest one-day encounter between Americans since the Civil War" (*Attica: The Official Report*, 1972: 130).

The storming of the prison did not end the violence; for many inmates, it was the beginning. Hundreds of inmates were subsequently stripped naked and beaten by correction officers, troopers, the sheriffs' deputies. The agony was prolonged because prison officials withheld immediate medical care for those suffering from gunshot wounds and injuries stemming from the widespread reprisals. In fact, when the shooting stopped, there were only ten medical personnel available to treat more than 120 seriously wounded inmates and hostages, and only two of them were physicians. Doctors at local hospitals who could have assisted the wounded were not dispatched by prison officials until four hours later.

Reprisals by officers against inmates were characterized as brutal displays of humiliation:

> Injured prisoners, some on stretchers, were struck, prodded or beaten with sticks, belts, bats, or other weapons. Others were forced to strip and run naked through gauntlets of guards armed with clubs which they used to strike inmates as they passed. Some were dragged on the ground, some marked with an "X" on their backs, some spat upon or burned with matches, others poked in the genitals or arms with sticks (from *Inmates of Attica v. Rockefeller*, 1971, quoted in Deutsch, Cunningham, and Fink, 1991: 22).

The Prisoners' Class Action Suit

On February 27, 1991, the United States Court of Appeals for the Second Circuit removed the final obstacle which permitted a class action civil rights suit to proceed. The suit (*Al-Jundi v. Mancusi*, 1991) was filed on behalf of the 1,200 prisoners who were killed, wounded, denied medical care (following the storming of the prison), and beaten by officers. Following years of legal resistance, the case went to trial on September 30, 1991 in Buffalo, New York. The suit sought to hold liable four top supervisory officials: Russell Oswald (Commissioner of Corrections), Major John

Monahan (commander of the assault force), Vincent Mancusi (Attica's Prison Warden), and Karl Pfeil (Deputy Warden).

The jury found Deputy Warden Pfeil liable for violent reprisals following the riot for permitting police and guards to beat and torture inmates. The jury deadlocked on the liability of the three other state officials (Oswald and Monahan are deceased). Additional litigation has also stemmed in the aftermath of the uprising. For example, in 1989, seven former Attica inmates and their families were awarded nearly $1.3 million for injuries suffered during the storming of the prison. Such legal action demonstrates that state prison officials are not above the law, even during such horrific situations as large-scale riots.

It should be noted, that due to litigation and the prisoners' rights movement, a new breed of prison administrators have emerged. Today, increasingly more corrections commissioners, directors, superintendents, and wardens are now expected to be proficient in law. In fact, many newly-recruited administrators are themselves attorneys. It is understood that a good administrator can spot legally problematic issues quickly and resolve them before they surface as lawsuits (Welch, 1996).

THE NEW MEXICO STATE PRISON RIOT

Whereas Attica symbolizes the political struggles which often occur between inmates and staff (and administration), the uprising at the New Mexico State Prison (February 2, 1980) stands as an example of sheer brutality among inmates. In a most accurate characterization, Mahan (1985) refers to the New Mexico riot as a "killing ground."

Similar to the riot at Attica, the officials at New Mexico were not prepared to deal with a large scale riot. In fact, the institution was inexcusably understaffed: at the time of the riot there were only twenty-two guards supervising 1157 inmates in a prison built to hold eight hundred. Moreover, the riot might have been prevented from spreading, but other officers were unable to produce a complete set of prison keys. Perhaps the worst institutional flaw of all, though, was the failure of a "shatter-proof" glass installed at the control center, the prison's life line. When the inmates broke the protective glass and seized the control center, they had full access to the facility. Here they pushed buttons which electronically opened all interior gates. The violence quickly spread, but the degree of brutality that awaited other inmates was simply horrible (Saenz, 1986).

Small cliques of inmates sought revenge against snitches and other prison outcasts, including convicted child molesters known as "diddlers" or "short-eyes." The string of violent encounters that erupted was preceded by several preparatory events. First, prisoners stormed the institution's pharmacy where they consumed massive doses of drugs such as amphetamines, or "speed." Such a "high" generated thirty-six hours of frantic and savage destruction. Others preferred alternative sources of mood alteration; for example, some inmates broke into the shoe shop where they sniffed the intoxicating fumes of glue (*Newsweek*, 1980).

To further prepare themselves for the impending acts of revenge, inmates confiscated prison records identifying informers and those convicted of sex offenses, the two most despised criminal types in the prison society. Finally, inmates added to their arsenal of shanks by equipping themselves with tools and blowtorches stolen from the prison maintenance supply room. Now they were ready to create a nightmare that would shock even the most jaded prison expert. The impending rampage would exceed the typical forms of beatings characteristic of prisons. For the next several hours, inmates unleashed their rage by raping, burning, decapitating, castrating, and eviscerating fellow prisoners (Stone, 1982).

Unlike Attica, the riot had no identified course of action; it simply constituted a series of independent acts of revenge. "There was no carnival atmosphere, no leadership, no lists of grievances, no organization, nothing. Only unspeakable brutality" (Dinitz, 1981: 4). In large part, the violence was the direct work of small cliques of prisoners, mostly Chicano (58% of the inmate population), who took full advantage of the uprising to settle their differences with rival Chicano inmates (Colvin, 1982: 1992). Additional acts of brutality consisted of the following: a snitch had a steel rod driven through one ear and out the other; another was stomped to death and a perpetrator carved "rat" into his abdomen; seven inmates were found slashed to death in their cells; a rope was tied to the neck of an inmate who was nearly decapitated when his body was thrown off the tier; and a prisoner whose eyes were nearly gouged out was beheaded with a shovel (*Newsweek*, 1980). In thirty-six hours, $36 million of damage was incurred; all the more tragic, though, thirty-three inmates were killed at the hands of other prisoners (Office of the Attorney General of the State of New Mexico, 1980).

When we examine the Attica and New Mexico riots, numerous lessons present themselves; for example, institutional conditions (i.e. crowding, inadequate services and programs), inmate-staff/administration relations and violence. Though uprisings are relatively rare events, conditions which contribute to riots are often ignored in most prisons. Other large scale riots have since erupted in prisons and jails across the nation over the past twenty-five years. For example, when George Jackson was shot in San Quentin in 1971, three inmates and three guards were killed during a riot. In 1978, three officers were murdered during an uprising in Pontiac Correctional Center (Illinois) and two prisoners and a guard were killed at Georgia State Prison (Reidsville). Other violent disruptions have occurred in the State Prison at Southern Michigan, Joliet Correctional Center (Illinois), Marion Federal Penitentiary (Illinois), Rikers Island (New York), Atlanta Federal Penitentiary, and Oakdale Detention Center, just to name a few. In each of the institutions, the conditions for a riot had existed for a considerable length of time, but few meaningful attempts had been made to alter them.

INMATE-INMATE VIOLENCE

A careful examination of riots helps us understand collective violence, whether that aggression transpires among inmates or staff. Whereas riots are relatively uncommon events, physical assaults between inmates constitute a daily problem in most prisons and jails. Several institutional features contribute to such violence. First and foremost, violence is attributed to lack of adequate supervision by officers. That is, as overcrowding outpaces the hiring of guards, violence becomes increasingly imminent. For example, leaders of the corrections officers' union at Rikers Island (New York) report that more than three thousand assaults on inmates and staff occur each year (Welch, 1991). Assaults are more likely to take place in facilities that do not have adequate supervision, especially if the interior architecture limits supervision. The proliferation of weapons in an institution is also the result of security lapses, and when officers feel that they do not have the ability to control inmates, they often permit prisoners to protect themselves by any means necessary (Welch, 1996, 1995; Colvin, 1982).

SEXUAL ASSAULT IN PRISON

A particularly alarming form of violence among inmates is sexual assault. However, the issue of sexual assault in prison is complicated because while brutal attacks do take place, we must *not* be led to believe that rape in correctional institutions is a common occurrence. In fact, research demonstrates that the frequency of sexual assault in prisons (and jails) is exaggerated (Lockwood, 1980; 1982; 1985; Nacci, 1982; Nacci and Kane, 1984).

Lockwood (1980; 1982) systematically examined sexual assault in correctional institutions and found that sexual violence falls into two groups. In the first category, sexual violence is a form of domination that is used to coerce one's victim. "The primary causes of violence are subcultural values upholding men's rights to use force to gain sexual access" (Lockwood, 1982: 257). The other category includes cases in which the target reacts violently to propositions perceived as threatening; therefore, sexual assault emerges as a form of self-protection.

What is far more common than homosexual rape in correctional institutions is *sexual harassment* in which the *threat* of sexual assault by one inmate over another is used as a form of dominance. Moreover, it is the frequency of sexual harassment (insults and offensive propositions) that may lead some observers to believe that rape is rampant in prisons, largely attributable to the level of fear generated. Accordingly, Nacci's (1982) study of sexual assault in the Federal Prison System found that only two out of 330 inmates surveyed had been compelled to perform undesired sex acts, but 29% had been propositioned by other inmates. Similarly, Lockwood's (1980) examination of sexual assault in the New York State Prison System found 28% of the inmate surveyed had been aggressively approached by inmates seeking sexual favors. Lockwood (1985: 90) concludes: "the problems caused by sexual propositions in prison affect far more men than those suffering the devastating consequences of sexual assault." Problems stemming from sexual assault include fights, social isolation, racism, fear, and crisis (also see Lockwood, 1991).

Although some recent research endeavors to explore sexual assault in prisons (Chonco, 1989; Jones and Schmid, 1989; Tewksbury, 1989), future studies are necessary to further establish the prevalence and dynamics of sexual victimization, especially in light of the emergence of AIDS.

INMATE-STAFF VIOLENCE

Because work as a correctional officer is characterized as hazardous duty, most officers are routinely reminded of the dangers of working in a tense atmosphere. Officers must supervise inmates who have the potential to direct and vent their anger at the staff. For safety purposes, most guards prefer to work alongside a fellow officer. Due to overcrowding and budgetary constraints, however, such arrangements are difficult to maintain. Today, officers are guarding increasingly more inmates; consequently, the potential for violence has increased proportionately as well.

Whereas systematic examinations of prison riots are plentiful, few researchers have explored patterns of individual assaults on correctional officers by inmates.

Bowker (1980) offered two categories which help us to distinguish between fundamentally different types of assaults on officers. First, assaults are sometimes spontaneous attacks which occur during volatile situations: for example, an officer being assaulted when intervening between fighting inmates. Second, some assaults may be categorized as planned attacks. Unlike the former, these assaults do not take place "in the heat of the moment"; they are premeditated. Consequently, officers have difficulty anticipating such violence.

More recently, Light (1991, 1990a, 1990b) investigated patterns of assaults on officers and found numerous interactional themes which help explain the motives of violence. One interactional theme encompasses assaults ensuing from an officer's command that the inmate objects to. The following case illustrates this type of assault: "Inmate was standing on stairs leading to the gym and correctional officer told him to move. Inmate refused and correctional officer repeated his order. Inmate punched correctional officer on side of face" (Light, 1991: 251).

Inmates may also lash out against staff to express their protest of being unjustly treated. Similarly, prisoners may react violently to an officer's attempt to search the inmate's person, cell, or property. Light (1991: 253) recorded the following incident from staff records: "CO was pursuing inmate who had fled from [the] area to avoid being frisked before entering the mess hall, when inmate turned around and punched CO in the mouth." Officers also run the risk of assault when approaching emotionally unstable inmates. For example: "As inmate was entering mess hall, he broke from line and struck correction officer with his fists. As he was being subdued by CO, inmate slashed him with a razor blade on left arm and side of face (Report cites 'apparent psychotic episode' as cause, and refers to inmate's 'catatonic state')" (Light, 1991: 256-257). Other assaults are categorized according to the following interactional themes: inmates fighting; movement; restraint; contraband; sexual and remaining categories. Light's study found that most assaults on officers are reported as having unexplained motives, or taking place for no apparent reason. For instance: "While checking that inmate's cell door was locked on rounds, correctional officer received urine thrown in his face by inmate. Inmate then attempted to hit CO with broom and glass jar" (1990: 249).

While officers cannot expect to work in prisons which are complete free of violence, they can exercise caution in dealing with inmates. Training helps officers to deal effectively with violent inmates and to identify volatile situations (or "hot spots"), thereby reducing the risk of assaults. Just as important, prison administration also has the responsibility to improve those institutional conditions which engender violence (see Fleisher, 1989).

STRATEGIES TO REDUCE VIOLENCE

It is unreasonable to presume that all incidents of prison and jail violence can be prevented. However, policy makers and administrators can employ measures to make correctional institutions safer places for officers to work and for inmates to live. We must acknowledge that all levels and forms of prison and jail violence are associated with institutional conditions. While overcrowding has been cited as one factor, there are multiple sources of stress and frustration (poor food services, inadequate health care, lack of meaningful programs, etc.) that, when left unchecked, may lead to violence (Welch, 1996, 1995).

Administrators need to focus on staff training that addresses both levels of violence. At the individual level, officers must learn skills (i.e., conflict resolution) that permit them to deal effectively with frustrated and angry inmates. At the collective level, officers must be prepared to prevent and control large scale disturbances. Explicit policies and procedures, ranging from strategies for containing the disturbance to the appropriate use of force, are necessary components of institutional control (American Correctional Association, 1991).

Other preventative measures focus on the following: better screening of inmates to determine who is more likely to resort to aggression; the introduction of ombudsmen, formal procedures of filing grievances, and dispute resolutions which are taken seriously by inmates, staff, and administration; and neutralizing the impact of gangs by denying them the recognition they need to generate power.

Architecture and the New Generation Philosophy

Since the future of corrections entails the construction of additional institutions, it is imperative that more attention be given to architectural designs. Zupan (1991) emphasizes the importance of architecture in corrections by pointing out that better designed correctional facilities can lead to safer and more humane environments. The traditional architecture of correctional institutions features the linear/intermittent surveillance design which has serious limitations. For example, the linear/intermittent design limits supervision, thereby contributing to violence and misconduct because it provides more opportunities for these acts with less fear of detection (Welch, 1991b). Zupan proposes greater use of New Generation jails to reduce violence. "Underlying the New Generation philosophy is the assumption that inmates engage in violent and destructive behavior in order to control and manipulate a physical environment and organizational operations which fail to provide for their critical human needs" (Zupan, 1991: 5).

The New Generation philosophy is driven by widely accepted assertions regarding human (not necessarily criminal) behavior. Individuals tend to engage in violence and misconduct when their critical needs (such as safety, privacy, personal space, activity, familial contact, social relations, and dignity) are not met. In attempting to meet these critical needs in the New Generation jail, inmates are divided into manageable groups (between sixteen and forty-six) and housed in modules in which the correctional staff has maximum observation, supervision, and interaction with inmates (Zupan, 1991; Welch, 1991b).

Critics, however, argue that New Generation jails are limited because they can only control "softer prisoners," and not hard-core violent offenders. Yet, the New Generation approach has never been systematically tested with a high security inmate population. Instead, current and future trends suggest that more attention is being given to technological advances to improve supervision (e.g., monitors, video taping, etc.) as well as traditional "nuts and bolts" and "bricks and mortar."

Super-Maximum Security Penitentiaries and Allegations of Human Rights Violations

In terms of "nuts and bolts" and "bricks and mortar," one of the most significant trends that promises to impact the future of corrections is the construction of super-maximum security penitentiaries. For example, the Federal Penitentiary at Marion (Illinois), a super-maximum security unit has taken the role of a modern-day Alcatraz.

Marion holds four hundred of the federal system's most incorrigible and high risk inmates. For years, Marion has been operating under a "lock-down," meaning that all inmates are confined to their cells for twenty-three hours per day and allowed one hour of exercise outside their cell. As repressive as it is, "locking-down" the institution is the ultimate method of preventing riots and various forms of violence.

Human rights advocates, however, criticize the repressive practices at Marion, particularly the long-term chaining of prisoners to their beds. Though prison officers are permitted to restrain inmates only as long as necessary, Amnesty International criticizes Marion officials for violating the United Nation's Minimum Rules for the Treatment of Prisoners. Allegedly, numerous inmates have been routinely chained to their beds (merely concrete slabs) for periods lasting several days (see Dickey, 1990; Whitman, 1988; Welch, 1996).

Similarly, Human Rights Watch investigated human rights violations to other super-maximum security units across the nation and concluded that units in thirty-six states featured some type of human rights violations. Many super-maximum security prisons confine inmates to poorly ventilated cells where they are denied access to educational classes and outdoor exercise. Moreover, Human Rights Watch also criticized these institutions for the procedures utilized in determining which inmates are remanded to the super-maximum security units; they charge that it is an administrative decision which few inmates are allowed to appeal. In their report, Human Rights Watch also cited human rights violations in the super-maximum security unit for women at Broward Correctional Institution in Miami, where inmates were routinely handcuffed while outside their cell as a means of punishment, regardless of the infraction. At the super-maximum security wing of Oregon's maximum security prison, the administration was ordered to stop the practice of stripping inmates and having them earn back their clothing through good behavior (*The New York Times*, 1991).

Analogous to the Federal Bureau of Prisons' use of the penitentiary at Marion, the California correctional system has designated the Pelican Bay State Prison to serve as their "Alcatraz"—housing the system's most incorrigible and dangerous prisoners. Approximately twelve hundred inmates, the system's worst, are incarcerated in this super-maximum security unit which was recently characterized by a former guard as the "toilet of the corrections system" (Hentoff, 1993a: 21). Also, like Marion, corrections watchdog groups (ACLU Prison Project and the Pelican Bay Information Project) have repeatedly criticized the institution for its inhumane conditions. For example, inmates are routinely confined to their cells (eight-by-ten-foot cells) 22 1/2 hours per day, where heat causes headaches, nausea, dehydration, and drains the inmates of their energy. According to one inmate: "The inside of your body always feels as though you have a fever and your skin is always moist with sweat, whether you move or not" (Hentoff, 1993a: 20; also see Haney, 1993). Inmates are not permitted to work or study; hence, they are deprived of educational and vocational programs, as well as counseling and religious services. Ironically, inmates often do not visit the exercise yard for their ninety minutes of recreation because it serves as just another form of isolation. "When they go up to the bare, concrete space—where there is no exercise equipment, not even a ball—they are still under the blinking eye of Big Brother...They cannot see any of the surrounding landscape because of the solid concrete walls that extend up some twenty feet around them..." (Hentoff, 1993a: 20).

Another point of controversy at Pelican Bay concerns its practice of cell extraction. When an inmate confined in his cell refuses an order from an officer, the prisoner is subject to cell extraction insofar as a team of specially-trained guards (sporting helmets and riot gear, and equipped with a shield, a baton, and guns which fire gas pellets, rubber and wooden bullets) forcibly remove the inmate from his cell. The tactic of cell extraction is regarded as excessively coercive and brutal. The team hog-ties the inmate into a fetal position, inflicting injuries by way of kicks and punches. A class-action suit has been filed, containing more than 2500 individual grievances focuses on excessive force, inadequate medical treatment, and deliberate, pervasive sensory deprivation—isolation in many forms (Hentoff, 1993b, 1993c; Welch, 1996).

To prevent riots and other forms of violence, a current trend that will reach well into the future is the reliance on more repressive measures of controlling inmates (i.e., solitary confinement and super-maximum penitentiaries). Such measures are directed primarily at those prisoners deemed violent or incorrigible. However, this approach is extremely limited because it reflects a correctional philosophy which emphasizes *control* without necessarily addressing the root causes of violence: whether those causes are institutional, individual, or a combination of the two.

Correctional philosophies, which dictate the course of daily operations, are important in preventing violence. Colvin (1992) argues that rehabilitative ideologies coupled with meaningful programs are more effective and efficient in maintaining order and safety than the repressive and rigid custodial philosophy. Since maintaining stability in prison requires the cooperation of inmates, administrators can encourage inmate participation to help create a less violent environment. It is important to note that strict coercive and punitive controls, which resort merely to warehousing prisoners, often undermine long-term institutional stability.

Clearly, violence takes place when existing controls are strained or break down. DiIulio (1987) contends that despite overcrowding, budget limitations, and racial polarization, disruption can be reduced by establishing what he calls "good government." He proposes that a prison can operate as a constitutional government which holds inmates, staff, and administrators to the same standards of the law. Through the introduction and maintenance of constitutional government, prisons can promote civility and justice (see also Martin and Ekland-Olson, 1987; Useem and Kimball, 1989; Colvin, 1981).

CONCLUSION

Institutional violence has remained a problem throughout the history of American corrections, and is likely to remain a critical issue in the near and distant future. Yet, even though prison officials are aware that the necessary conditions for riots exist within their institutional walls, they continue to play the game of chance. And more often than not, they win, because riots and major disturbance are rare events (Martin and Zimmerman, 1990). Because of the relative infrequency of large-scale disturbances, it is likely that during the 1990s only a few *major* riots will occur nationwide.

However, in terms of other forms of violence, it is expected that assaults among inmates (and between inmates and staff) will continue to proliferate throughout the next decade. As prison and jail populations continue to grow, institutional programs, services, and security will fail to keep pace with demand, thereby ensuring that institutions will remain dangerous for inmates and staff alike.

Reiman (1990) raises several key questions about the role of corrections in society, and in the context of prison violence, he helps us identify and confront the institutional conditions and effects of incarceration. Reiman proposes that prisons should be both *civilized* and *civilizing*. One can hardly conclude that violent prisons are civilized, a point which should concern us because most inmates eventually return to society. If prisoners do not become more civilized during their incarceration, then how can citizens feel safe when inmates are released?

Insofar as single incidents of victimization rarely transform a nonviolent person into a dangerous marauder, we should be concerned about the impact that persistent assaults have on individuals. Even for those who have not been assaulted in prison, the experience of incarceration is profound. Yet, for those who have endured violence, the effects of prison are all the more dramatic. It is no exaggeration to say that these inmates suffer a level of punishment exceeding the sentence imposed by the courts (Welch, 1996, 1995).

STUDY QUESTIONS

1. Based on this chapter, what are prisons really like? What are the myths and what are the realities?
2. Distinguish between collective and individual levels of prison violence.
3. What are the various forms of prison violence? Give examples.
4. What are the key features of the riots at Attica and New Mexico?
5. Explain the nature of super-maximum security penitentiaries and what are the allegations of human rights violations?

REFERENCES

Abbott, Jack Henry. (1981). *In the Belly of the Beast: Letters from Prison*. New York: Vintage Books.

American Correctional Association. (1991). *Riots and Disturbances in Correctional Institutions*. College Park, MD: American Correctional Association.

Attica: The Official Report of the New York State Commission. (1972). New York: Bantam Books

Bowker, Lee. (1985). "An Essay on Prison Violence." In M. Braswell, S. Dillingham, and R. Montgomery, eds. *Prison Violence in America*. Cincinnati: Anderson.

Bowker, Lee. (1982). "Victimizers and Victims in American Correctional Institutions." In R. Johnson and H. Toch, eds. *Pains of Imprisonment*. Beverly Hills, CA: Sage Publications.

Bowker, Lee. (1980). *Prison Victimization*. New York: Elsevier.

Chonco, N. (1989). "Sexual Assaults Among Male Inmates: A Descriptive Study." *The Prison Journal*, Volume LXVIX, 1: 72-82.

Colvin, Mark. (1992). *The Penitentiary in Crisis: From Accommodation to Riot in New Mexico*. Albany, NY: State University of New York Press.

Colvin, Mark. (1982). "The New Mexico Prison Riot." *Social Problems*, 29, 5: 449-463.

Colvin, Mark. (1981). "The Contradictions of Control: Prisons in Class Society." *The Insurgent Sociologist*, Vol. X, No. 1—Vol. X, No. 1: 33-45.

Deutsch, Michael, Dennis Cunningham and Elizabeth Fink. (1991). "Twenty Years Later—Attica Civil Rights Case Finally." *Social Justice*, 18, 3: 13-25.

Dickey, Christopher. (1990). "A New Home for Noriega." *Newsweek*, January 15: 66-69.

Dillingham, S. and R. Montgomery. (1985). "Prison Riots: A Corrections Nightmare Since 1774." In M. Braswell, S. Dillingham, and R. Montgomery, eds. *Prison Violence in America*. Cincinnati: Anderson.

DiIulio, John J., Jr. (1987). *Governing Prisons*. New York: Free Press.

Farrington, David and C. Nutall. (1985). "Prison Size, Overcrowding, Prison Violence, and Recidivism." In M. Braswell, S. Dillingham, and R. Montgomery, eds. *Prison Violence in America*. Cincinnati: Anderson Publishing Company.

Fleisher, Mark. (1989). *Warehousing Violence*. Newbury Park, CA: Sage.

Gaes, G. and W. McGuire. (1985). "Prison Violence: The Contribution of Crowding and Other Determinants of Prison Assault Rates." *Journal of Research in Crime and Delinquency*, 22, 1: 41-65.

Hentoff, Nat. (1993a). "Buried Alive in Pelican Bay." *The Village Voice*, June 22: 20-21.

Hentoff, Nat. (1993b). "The Bloody Art of Prison Cell Extraction." *The Village Voice*, July 6: 20-21.

Hentoff, Nat. (1993c). "Charles Dickens's Report to Janet Reno." *The Village Voice*, June 15: 22-23.

Jones, R. and T. Schmid. (1989). "Inmates' Conceptions of Prison Sexual Assault." *The Prison Journal*, Volume LXVIV, 1: 53-61.

Light, Kevin C. (1991). "Assaults on Prison Officers: Interactional Themes." *Justice Quarterly*, 8, 2: 243-262.

Light, Kevin C. (1990a). "Measurement Error in Official Statistics: Prison Infraction Data" *Federal Probation*, 52: 63-68.

Light, Kevin C. (1990b). "The Severity of Assaults on Prison Officers: A Contextual Study." *Social Science Quarterly*, 71: 267-284.

Lockwood, Daniel. (1991). "Target Violence." In K.C. Haas and G.P. Alpert (eds.) *The Dilemmas of Corrections*. Prospect Heights, IL: Waveland Press.

Lockwood, Daniel. (1985). "Issues in Prison Sexual Violence." In M. Braswell, S. Dillingham, and R. Montgomery, eds. *Prison Violence in America*. Cincinnati: Anderson.

Lockwood, Daniel. (1982). "Contribution of Sexual Harassment to Stress and Coping in Confinement." In. N. Parisi, ed. *Coping With Imprisonment*. Beverly Hills, CA: Sage Publications.

Lockwood, Daniel. (1980). *Prison Sexual Violence*. New York: Elsevier Books.

Mahan, Sue. (1985). "'An Orgy of Brutality' at Attica and the 'Killing Ground' at Santa Fe." In M. Braswell, S. Dillingham, and R. Montgomery, eds. *Prison Violence in America*. Cincinnati: Anderson.

Martin, Randy and Sherwood Zimmerman. (1990). "A Typology of the Causes of Prison Riots and an Analytical Extension to the 1986 West Virginia Riot." *Justice Quarterly*, 7, 4: 711-737.

Nacci, Peter L. (1982). "Sex and Sexual Aggression in Federal Prisons." Unpublished Manuscript. U.S. Federal Prison System: Office of Research.

Nacci, Peter L. and Thomas R. Kane. (1982). *Sexual Aggression in Federal Prisons*. Washington, DC: U.S. Department of Justice Federal Prison System.

Nacci, Peter L. and Thomas R. Kane. (1984). "Sex and Sexual Aggression in Federal Prisons: Inmate Involvement and Employee Impact." *Federal Probation*, 8, March: 46-53.

Newsweek, "The Killing Ground." February 18, 66-76.

Office of the Attorney General of the State of New Mexico. (1980). *Report of the Attorney General on the February 2 and 3, 1980 Riot at the Penitentiary of New Mexico*. Santa Fe: Office of the Attorney General of the State of New Mexico.

Oswald, Russell B. (1972). *Attica: My Story*. New York: Doubleday and Company.

Reiman, Jeffrey. (1990). *The Rich Get Richer and the Poor Get Prison*, (3rd Ed.). New York: MacMillan Publishing Company.

Saenz, Adolph. (1986). *Politics of a Riot*. Washington, DC: American Correctional Association.

Social Justice. (1991). Attica: 1971-1991, A Commemorative Issue, 18: 3.

Stone, W.G. (1982). *The Hate Factory: The Story of the New Mexico Penitentiary Riot*. Agoura, CA: A Dell Book.

The New York Times. (1991). "Study Finds Abuse in High Security Prisons." November 15: A-15.

Toch, Hans. (1985). "Social Climate and Prison Violence." In M. Braswell, S. Dillingham, and R. Montgomery, eds. *Prison Violence in America*. Cincinnati: Anderson Publishing Company.

Useem, Bert and Peter A. Kimball. (1989). *States of Siege: U.S. Prison Riots 1971-1986*. New York: Oxford University Press.

Useem, Bert and Peter A. Kimball. (1987). "A Theory of Prison Riots." *Theory and Society*, 16, 87-122.

Useem, Bert. (1985). "Disorganization and the New Mexico Prison Riot." *American Sociological Review*, 50, 5: 677-688.

Welch, Michael. (1996). *Corrections: A Critical Approach*. New York: McGraw-Hill.

Welch, Michael. (1995). "A Sociopolitical Approach to the Reproduction of Violence in Canadian Prisons." *Violence in Canada: Sociopolitical Perspectives*, Jeffrey Ian Ross, ed. Toronto: Oxford University Press.

Welch, Michael. (1991a). "Institutional Conflict in Jail: The Crisis at Rikers Island During the Summer of 1990." A Paper Presented at the Annual meeting of the Academy of Criminal Justice Sciences, Nashville, TN.

Welch, Michael. (1991b). "A Review of *Jails: Reform and the New Generation Philosophy*." *American Jails: The Magazine of the American Jail Association*, March/April: 132-135.

Whitman, Steve. (1988). "The Marion Penitentiary: It Should Be Opened Up, Not Locked Down." *The Southern Illinoisean*, August 7: 25.

Wicker, Tom. (1975). *A Time to Die*. New York: Quadrangle.

Zupan, Linda L. (1991). *Jails: Reform and the New Generation Philosophy*. Cincinnati, OH: Anderson Publishing Company.

CHAPTER 14

JAIL OVERCROWDING AND COURT-ORDERED REFORM

CRITICAL ISSUES FOR THE FUTURE

Wayne N. Welsh, Ph.D.

ABSTRACT

A major dilemma of criminal justice in a democratic society is how to process suspects and punish law violators in a humane and rational manner. The widespread prevalence of court orders to reform unconstitutional conditions of confinement in American jails and prisons, including unprecedented overcrowding, indicates a significant gap in our current ability to do so and an important opportunity for change. In this chapter, the scope of jail overcrowding and court-ordered reform is discussed, and critical issues for the future are presented. A coordinated approach to problem analysis and policy design is emphasized.

INTRODUCTION

If the public, through its judicial and penal system, finds it necessary to incarcerate a person, basic concepts of decency, as well as reasonable respect for constitutional rights, require that he be provided a bed.[1]

Not the least of the Sheriff's problems is the abysmal design of the jail. Architecturally, the jail is a gross case of malpractice in design.[2]

Replacement [of the jail] must occur regardless of the source of funds...The Court's power in this regard is a negative one: it cannot order respondent board of supervisors to appropriate funds. But it can, and will, order the facility closed, if necessary, to eliminate unlawful conditions.[3]

This court will not tolerate the miserable overcrowding in the jail which was existent in March when these hearings began. The responsible executives in the Sheriff's Office, Board of Supervisors, and the County Executive have offered nothing whatever in response to this most pressing problem.[4]

Such judicial pronouncements have become a common feature of American corrections in recent years. Over the past twenty years, courts have found conditions of confinement in numerous American jails to be in violation of constitutional guarantees such as the Eighth Amendment (banning cruel and unusual punishment) and the Fourteenth Amendment (guaranteeing due process rights). In 1992, 27% of the nation's large jails (i.e., one hundred inmates or more) were under court order to reduce overcrowding or improve general conditions of confinement (U.S. Department of Justice, 1993). At midyear 1992, American jails held a record 444,584 persons. Overcrowding, the problem most frequently cited in court orders, severely limits an institution's capacity to provide adequate safety, medical care, food service, recreation, and sanitation. Correctional and government officials have been ordered to make sweeping changes to comply with court directives: to reduce chronic overcrowding, to improve medical care and recreation services, to increase staffing levels and improve training, to make use of early release mechanisms, even to build new facilities—all under the watchful eye of the court.

Change will be neither immediate nor wholesale. Current trends will not be easily reversed. Problems shaped by powerful forces over time are likely to persist into the twenty-first century:

- Overcrowding will persist in spite of the continued proliferation of intermediate sanctions and community corrections.

- Crime rates will continue to fluctuate up and down, but punishments will remain driven more by political forces than by any documented "crime problem." Criminal justice as a policy priority will diminish, however, as economic conditions command greater attention.

- We will observe an increasingly rule-oriented correctional environment, but fewer lawsuits challenging jail conditions. Basic inmate rights will be upheld, but courts will be increasingly hesitant to institute large-scale reforms.

- The major advocates of jail reform will be a select group of highly specialized, experienced attorneys ("repeat players").

However, there is also reason to expect more effective and coordinated policy responses based on lessons from the past:

- Interagency problem-solving and initiatives involving criminal justice, government, and community agencies will increase.

- As resources dwindle, public officials will be held more accountable for their policies: there is greater need to match resources to policy. There will be greater need for cost-effective, alternative punishments.

- Standards for correctional confinement will become increasingly clarified and mandatory; there will be fewer "deviant jails."

The outcomes of countervailing trends cannot be easily predicted. Any prediction of future events, of course, must be based on observations from the past.

OVERVIEW

Despite its priority as a policy issue, the causes of court-ordered jail reform and its impacts remain poorly understood. Jails, in contrast to prisons, are operated at the municipal or county, rather than state or federal level; they house convicted offenders generally serving one year or less of time; and they also house pre-trial detainees, typically about half of the jail's daily population (Advisory Commission on Intergovernmental Relations, 1984). Jails are also characterized by a high rate of turnover. There is a constant flow of inmates into and out of the jail, with the average inmate staying less than one week. The politics and demographics of jails, therefore, are quite different from those of state or federal prisons, and separate analyses of court intervention and its causes are required.

Examinations of impact have rarely extended beyond the walls of the institution (e.g., changes in rules and procedures, effects on correctional staff and institutional control). By overemphasizing institutional responses, we have largely ignored the interactive responses of criminal justice agencies to court orders. Jail problems and court-ordered reform can be understood only by tracing the jail's interdependence with local agencies of criminal justice and county government. Court orders against county jails put pressure on entire criminal justice systems to alter the processing of accused and convicted offenders. Police book suspects into the jail, the courts try them, jails house them, and probation provides programming for both pretrial and sentenced offenders. Pressures are also felt by city or county government officials, who are responsible for financial and personnel allocations to the jail.

CAUSES OF OVERCROWDING

Overcrowding has consistently been identified by criminal justice practitioners as one of the most serious problems facing criminal justice systems (Gettinger, 1984; Grieser, 1988; U.S. Department of Justice, 1988). However, potential driving forces of problems such as overcrowding often remain undiagnosed. Judges who order change and government officials who formulate policies often make decisions on the basis of very limited causal theories. Like most social problems, jail overcrowding is multiply determined, and informed policy choices require careful analysis of the causes and scope of the problem.

Crime Rates

To what degree, if any, do increases in crime over the last twenty years explain jail overcrowding? Did crime rates explode without warning, leading to drastic shortfalls in correctional capacities? Although problems with official crime statistics are well known (e.g., Skogan, 1975), there is little support for the crime-causes-overcrowding hypothesis. In fact, the National Crime Surveys (NCS) show relatively *stable* crime victimization rates in the 1970s (U.S. Department of Justice, 1991a), and *declines* in personal theft (-15%), household crimes (-18%), and violent crimes (-10%) between 1981 and 1988 (U.S. Department of Justice, 1991a). Stabilization or declines in most crime rates continued up to 1991. The Uniform Crime Reports (UCR), based upon crimes reported to police, show increases in reported crime for most categories between 1964 and 1980. From 1980 to 1989, total UCR index crimes *decreased* by 3.5%, although violent crimes increased by 11.1% for this period (U.S. Department of Justice, 1992a). Although the two measures of crime yield somewhat different results, dramatic increases in crime are not substantiated.

Over the same period, correctional populations have soared. The number of prisoners under the jurisdiction of state or federal correctional authorities reached a record high of 823,414 in 1991, an increase of 150% since 1980 (U.S. Department of Justice, 1992b). The number of jail inmates incarcerated by local authorities rose from 158,394 in 1978 to 426,479 in 1991, an increase of 169% (U.S. Department of

Justice, 1992a). Clearly, these dramatic increases in incarceration rates were *not* driven by comparable increases in crime.

Legal and Political Environments

Variations in local punishment practices influence overcrowding and the probability of judicial intervention. Incarceration rates seem to reflect differences in the laws and legal cultures of different areas, and differences in the harshness of local policies regarding punishment (Kizziah, 1984; Klofas, 1987; 1990; Welsh, Pontell, Leone, and Kinkade, 1990). For example, to the degree that particular jurisdictions use incarceration as a preferred sanction, there are increased demands for correctional space and services. Where high incarceration rates are accompanied by low rates of prisoner expenditures, it becomes less likely that constitutionally acceptable standards of conditions (e.g., adequate medical care, food services, clothing, sanitation, inmate safety) will be met, and prisoner lawsuits become more likely (Welsh, 1992a; 1992b). Inadequate correctional spending may reflect a punitive political climate, a fiscally strapped county, or both, but the net effect is that jail conditions deteriorate and judicial intervention becomes more likely.

Demographic, Economic, and Social Conditions

To what degree do social conditions contribute to jail overcrowding? Conflict theorists have suggested that incarceration rates are influenced by the fluctuating needs of dominant elites to maintain social control. High unemployment, for example, may lead to an unproductive and frustrated "surplus population." Dominant interests may feel threatened and increase their use of incarceration as a means of controlling the underclass (Carroll and Doubet, 1983; McCarthy, 1990; Rusche and Kirchheimer, 1939). Others have suggested that economic inequality fuels incarceration. Areas characterized by higher minority compositions and higher poverty also display more aggressive criminal justice responses and expenditures, including higher rates of imprisonment (Myers and Talarico, 1987).

Another approach examines how demographic shifts contributed to overcrowding (Blumstein, 1988). The mid-teens are the peak risk years for criminality, but the mid-twenties are the peak risk years for imprisonment, due to the greater seriousness of offenses committed by older offenders. According to Blumstein, crime rates began to rise in 1964 (when a large 1947 birth cohort reached age seventeen), but imprisonment rates didn't begin to rise until 1972 (when the 1947 cohort reached age twenty-five). Crime rates began to increase again in 1980, when a large 1961 birth cohort ("echo" boomers) reached age nineteen. Because the 1961 cohort will have passed the peak age for imprisonment by 1990, Blumstein predicted prison populations would begin to decline once again. Unfortunately, record increases in jail and prison populations have continued each year into 1992. Two other factors provide additional explanations for jail overcrowding and court orders.

Resources and Expenditures

Criminal justice expenditures have traditionally been the primary responsibility of local (county and city) governments, but an increased burden on cities and counties over the past few years has further constrained options to reduce jail overcrowding. From 1985 to 1988, justice spending increased more than government spending for any other activity, including education, health, and welfare (U.S. Dept. of Justice, 1990a). Increases in correctional expenditures have been by far the most pronounced. These trends reflect the increased priorities of jail and justice issues on the policy agenda and increased strain on local government budgets.

According to government and correctional officials, resource shortages contributed to court orders by limiting new jail construction, and by limiting the implementation of improvements (e.g., increased staff levels, improved medical care) needed to comply with court decrees (Welsh et. al., 1990). However, policymakers must share responsibility for historically placing jail needs low on the list of policy priorities. Inadequate resources can never be an adequate justification for the state's depriving people of their constitutional rights (see *Gates v. Collier*, 1974; *Miller v. Carson*, 1975).

Public Attitudes and the "Get-Tough" Movement

To what degree has the public thirst for punishment contributed to jail overcrowding and court orders? Recent reforms have included restrictions or abolition of parole, mandatory minimum sentences, determinate sentencing, sentencing enhancements (e.g., for weapons, use of violence), and longer sentences. Cullen, Clark, and Wozniak (1985) trace much of this development to a growing crisis in authority which confronted the nation in the 1960s. Diminished confidence by voters in the nation's leaders created a threat to some politicians (electoral vulnerability) and an opportunity for others who could convince voters that they were capable of re-establishing the moral order.

While conservative values have dominated recent political responses to crime, public opinion is less retributive and more complex than is commonly thought. For example, Cullen et al. (1985) found that a majority of Texas residents polled felt that the courts were too easy on criminals (77%), and felt that prison inmates should serve their full sentence (58%). However, many of these same respondents said that rehabilitation was an important function of prison (79%), and 72% favored some type of community-based corrections instead of simply "building as many prisons as needed." In surveys of two Ohio cities, Skovron et al. (1988) found that a majority of respondents (80% and 70% for the two cities) favored allowing prisoners to earn early release credits through good behavior and to participate in education or work programs while in prison. A large majority (90% and 87%) also favored the development of local programs to keep nonviolent and first-time offenders active and working in the community. There is little doubt that the "get-tough" movement has strongly influenced criminal justice policy, but the public's many voices, and many perceive a need for rational change in correctional planning and operations.

COURT INTERVENTION

The Role of the Courts

Until recently, the courts followed a "hands-off" policy regarding corrections. Courts refused to hear prisoner rights cases, essentially viewing the inmate as a "slave of the state" who had forfeited his/her rights as a consequence of his/her crime (Bronstein, 1980). This trend was reversed by the Supreme Court decision in *Cooper v. Pate* (1964).

Reviews of court decisions can be found elsewhere, (e.g., Bronstein, 1980; Call, 1986; Cooper, 1988; Jacobs, 1980). The most important of these was *Rhodes v. Chapman* (1981), which represented the first time that the Eighth Amendment had been interpreted by the Supreme Court in the context of jail or prison overcrowding. The Court indicated that: "...conditions must not involve the wanton and unnecessary infliction of pain, nor may they be grossly disproportionate to the severity of the crime warranting punishment" (Call, 1986:245). In a more recent ruling (*Wilson v. Seiter*, 1991), the Supreme Court ruled that conditions of confinement were not unconstitutional unless deliberate indifference to basic human needs could be demonstrated. It is not yet clear to what degree this ruling has exerted a chilling effect on prisoner litigation, but it certainly has increased the burden of proof upon prisoners.

The Legal Process: Judges, Lawyers, and Defendants

Different judges adopt different roles in crafting remedies and monitoring compliance, and they may do so at different stages of a case. Early in the remedy-crafting stage, judges often adopt a "facilitator" role, encouraging litigants to negotiate and develop plans to address jail problems (Cooper, 1988). Over time, though, judges often find it necessary to set limits as negotiations stall. Judges then shift toward a more active "ratifier/developer" role whereby they approve some plans presented by litigants but begin adding their own modifications and remedies. Judicial options are limited when resistance to change by county officials is pronounced, leading to a more autocratic and tough-minded judicial role.

The type of legal representation that prisoners obtain critically influences the outcome of lawsuits. Prisoner advocacy groups such as the ACLU have an ideological commitment toward jail reform, and tend to seek extensive relief for plaintiffs. Repeat players, (frequent litigants such as the ACLU) also enjoy competitive advantages (Galanter, 1974): greater ability to structure the transaction; expertise; lower start-up costs; informal relations with court and government officials; ability to adopt optimal litigation strategies and issues; and bargaining credibility. Indeed, "ideologically committed" attorneys tend to target jail jurisdictions with histories of underfunding and overcrowding; they tend to file more allegations of constitutional violations; and they tend to receive greater relief than either private attorneys or public counsel who represent inmates in jail cases (Welsh, 1992a).

When the leaders of county government (e.g., county supervisors or commissioners) are named by inmate attorneys as defendants, lawsuits are often bitterly contested. Because these officials are responsible for allocating funds and personnel to jails, it seems a wise strategy to include them as defendants. However, they also command considerable resources, including a well-staffed legal department which handles the county's legal business. Not surprisingly, lawsuits involving county officials tend to last a long time, and often involve bitter disputes not only with plaintiffs but with different county agencies, as government officials attempt to deflect blame for jail problems (Welsh and Pontell, 1991; Welsh, Leone, Kinkade, and Pontell, 1990).

Court-Ordered Change and Compliance

Court-ordered remedies have shaped dramatic policy changes. For example, court-imposed jail population caps have resulted in the early release of sentenced inmates, citation release of arrestees, expanded pretrial release programs, and the construction of new jails. Orders to protect inmate safety and provide adequate supervision often require substantial increases in staffing levels. Orders to provide inmates with adequate recreational time outside cells require both equipment and staff manpower. Orders to improve medical care may require that doctors and nurses be hired, that medical equipment and supplies be purchased, and that medical records be kept. If prison officials are ordered to ensure inmates' access to lawyers and legal material, visitation rights may need to be extended, and prison libraries may need to be created or expanded to provide access to law books.

Just because a court issues *orders* to improve jail conditions, however, does not necessarily mean that action by county officials is immediate or automatic. One study found that jail lawsuits lasted four to five years on average (Welsh, 1992a), with some extending as long as thirteen years.

One of the judge's most flexible means of monitoring compliance is the appointment of a special master to act as the "eyes and ears" of the court. Special masters have increasingly been used by judges to gather information on jail conditions and procedures, to monitor compliance with court directives, and in some cases, even to informally mediate disputes between litigants (Brakel, 1979; Montgomery, 1980; Nathan, 1979; Yale Law Journal, 1979). Special masters may be most needed in lengthy, contested cases where compliance is most difficult. Cases involving special masters tend to last much longer than other cases; they are characterized by more orders over the history of the case; and they are more likely to include orders to reduce overcrowding, raise staffing levels, improve pre-trial release procedures, and release sentenced inmates early (Welsh, 1992a). The intrusive nature of such remedies calls for a labor-intensive compliance monitoring effort which can best be provided by a skilled special master.

The threat of a contempt order may be used as a method of last resort when all other attempts to enforce compliance with the court's orders fail. A finding of civil contempt may lead to fines or even jail sentences for recalcitrant defendants. For example, on March 16, 1987, Judge Spurgeon Avakian found Santa Clara, California county supervisors in contempt of court for failing to build ninety-six new jail cells on time. He fined the supervisors $1,000 each and sentenced them to serve five days in their own jail. In response, the county launched an aggressive media campaign criticizing the judge, and successfully lobbied the state legislature to reduce the liability of government officials. The point became moot when the contempt order was annulled by the California Court of Appeals on September 17, 1987 (*Wilson v. Superior Court*, 1987), and Judge Avakian resigned from the case. Potential benefits of contempt orders, therefore, must be carefully weighed against the possibility of further retrenchment.

IMPACTS OF COURT-ORDERED REFORM

Changes in Institutional Conditions

While the impact of court orders is limited by legal and pragmatic constraints (e.g., limited judicial authority; defendants' willingness and ability to comply), significant changes have certainly occurred. Evidence from cases in Alabama (Yackle, 1989), Georgia (Chilton, 1991), Texas (Crouch and Marquart, 1989; Martin and Ekland-Olson, 1987), Louisiana (Harris and Spiller, 1977), and New York (Harland, 1991;

Storey, 1990) suggests that court orders have contributed to improvements in staffing levels, disciplinary procedures, inmate safety, medical care, recreation, visitation, food services, sanitation, inmate classification procedures, and access to courts.

Certain issues, such as jail capacity, the physical condition of jail facilities, and staffing are generally perceived by the courts as necessary components of reform. In thirty-four of forty-three California jail lawsuits examined by Welsh (1992a), courts ordered jail officials to reduce overcrowding. In thirteen cases, direct orders to improve staffing levels were issued. In sixteen cases, judges handed down orders to build new jails or expand existing capacity.

Several examples illustrate the centrality of these issues and the ability of the courts to motivate change. In Alameda County (*Smith et al. v. Dyer*, 1983), Judge Richard A. Bancroft proclaimed that "the time for footdragging is over," and "replacement must occur regardless of the source of funds." In Placer county (*Offield v. Scott*, 1977), Superior court Judge William A. Newsome stated: "the county jail is an antiquated facility designed to meet the needs of a different era" (May 12, 1977, p. 1). In Fresno (*In re Morgan, In re Ransbury, and Consolidated Cases*, 1983), Superior Court Judge Frank J. Creede stated: "Full compliance with recognized constitutional standards and with the 1980 California Minimum Jail Standards can be achieved only with the construction of a new detention facility" (March 27, 1985, p. 12). In San Diego (*Hudler et al. v. Duffy*, 1980), Superior Court Judge James L. Facht diagnosed the major jail problems as overcrowding and inadequate staffing, calling the jail an "architectural nightmare" which mitigated against proper supervision and observation of inmates.

Organizational Impacts

Jail administration has changed substantially as a result of court orders. Modern information systems and scientific classification procedures have replaced archaic methods in many jails. The courts have also helped define clearer professional standards and guidelines for institutional living conditions (Feeley and Hanson, 1986, 1990), and have created a need for better-educated, modern correctional "managers" who can anticipate and prevent problems (DiIulio, 1987, 1990; Jacobs, 1980). There is little doubt that court orders have increased the bureaucratization of the jail and required more accountability from public officials.

Unintended Impacts

There has been much speculation about the negative or unintended impact of court orders. Critics have attributed diverse effects to court orders: reduced inmate respect for staff; increased rule violation by inmates; reduced staff morale; uncertainty in decision-making by guards, and increased assaults by inmates on guards and on each other (Alpert et al., 1986; Crouch and Marquart, 1989; Ekland-Olson and Martin, 1988; Glazer, 1975, 1978; Martin and Ekland-Olson, 1987; UCLA Law Review, 1973). It is likely, however, that disruptions attributable to court orders are temporary aberrations brought about by rapid shifts in the power structures and regulatory mechanisms of institutions (Crouch and Marquart, 1989). Management and administration practices play a large role in shaping the new order that emerges in the post-decree phases of lawsuits.

Systemwide Impacts

Although the criminal justice system is often viewed as a "nonsystem" due to its decentralized and fragmented nature, dramatic changes in political environments, such as the imposition of court orders, create demands to tighten the "loose coupling" that normally characterizes criminal justice organizations (Hagan, 1989). Responses may include the formalization of exchange relations between different agencies (e.g., creation of jail task forces and committees) and the development of cooperative, inter-agency innovations (e.g., new criminal justice programs). Less positive responses include struggles for resources and disagreements over appropriate agency responses to jail problems.

In jurisdictions from California (Welsh and Pontell, 1991) to New York (Harland, 1991; Storey, 1990), city and county jails have implemented or increased the use of various pre-trial release mechanisms to reduce jail populations to court-imposed limits. For example, "citation release" in California and "Desk Appearance Tickets" in New York require that misdemeanor suspects sign a written promise to appear in court, and suspects are then released at the jail prior to arraignment. In a recent study (Welsh, 1993), police officials reported adjustments in arrest policies in response to jail release procedures. Police officials perceived that jail citations had hurt police credibility and morale, and some suggested that officers wouldn't "waste their time" booking misdemeanors any more. They also suggested that officers were less likely to enforce outstanding warrants as a result of liberal jail release policies. However, neither large-scale nor long-term changes were detected by statistical analyses. Police organizational culture (i.e., a "crime-fighting" orientation) and a motivation by public officials to avoid blame for unpopular policies may partially explain pronouncements by police officials that court orders to reduce jail overcrowding have impaired police capacity to protect public safety.

Numerous case processing and sentencing alternatives have been adopted by local criminal courts as a result of court orders against jails in Baltimore (Dunbaugh, 1990); California (Welsh, 1990; Welsh and Pontell, 1991), New Orleans (Baiamonte, 1990), New York (Harland, 1991; Storey, 1990), and Philadelphia (Babcock, 1990). For example, early screening programs have been implemented in attempts to remove weak cases that are likely to be discharged later, and to speed processing of those that are being held awaiting decisions on bail or some other form of pre-trial release. Pre-trial release programs such as ROR (release on own recognizance), more liberal forms of bail (e.g., 10%), and supervised release are now widely used in many jurisdictions.

Post-conviction sentencing alternative such as work programs, community service, boot camps, and electronic surveillance have also proliferated (U.S. Department of Justice, 1990b) as a result of court orders. The utility of these "intermediate sanctions" (Morris and Tonry, 1990) in reducing jail populations may be limited, however, as perceived liability by public officials often results in stringent eligibility criteria (e.g., no history of violence or drug abuse).

Without the specter of court orders, it is unlikely that we would have witnessed this bandwagon return to what was known as "alternatives to incarceration" a few years ago (Austin and Krisberg, 1982). The popularity of such programs lies largely in their "band-aid" utility for reducing soaring incarceration costs and complying with court-imposed jail population caps rather than a liberal shift in correctional philosophy.

Finally, there is little doubt that correctional systems have been forced to increase their expenditures as a result of court orders, at least temporarily. Increases in institutional capacity, staffing, and service delivery surely require expenditures, and courts have occasionally been quite explicit in directing such expenditures (Welsh, 1992b). What is not so clear is whether court orders have merely brought offending counties and states up to levels previously demonstrated by facilities not under judicial scrutiny, or whether changes in conditions and procedures mandated by court order have actually necessitated "excessive" expenditures (Glazer, 1978). The degree and persistence of such effects awaits further empirical study.

IMPLICATIONS FOR CRIMINAL JUSTICE POLICY

Jail overcrowding is the result of a complex interaction of social and political forces. Competing problem definitions and casual explanations have been accompanied by uncertainty and a sense of urgency. Under such conditions, a "garbage-can" model of decision-making prevails: policy makers seize upon readily available solutions rather than weighing options and formulating an optimal plan (Cohen, March, and Olson, 1972). As a result, policies adopted may be ineffective, inefficient, or inconsistent. For example, early release policies may be implemented by local officials to reduce jail overcrowding at the same time as mandatory sentences adopted by the state send more people to jail. To counteract such tendencies, more attention needs to be paid to structuring and defining the jail overcrowding problem. If problem analysis is incomplete or inaccurate, then policies may fail because they either find the wrong solution to the right problem, or they are aimed at the wrong problem. A policy design approach focuses attention on the match between problem definition and proposed solutions. Seven aspects of policy design (adapted from Ingraham, 1987) are relevant to local jails:

1. Degree of goal consensus vs. level of conflict: At present, jail policies are rarely tied to explicitly stated goals, purposes of fiscal limitations. More consideration needs to be devoted to the unique purposes of jails, tempered by practical and fiscal constraints. If consensus is not possible, reasonable compromises must be realized.

2. Placement on policy agenda: Time and resources must be devoted to arriving at a solution. Conflict resolution and group-building techniques have proven effective in gaining consensus in a wide variety of policy settings (e.g., Susskind and Cruikshank, 1987). Kaufman (1985) describes team-building techniques used by the National Institute of Corrections to facilitate the formulation of solutions to prison overcrowding by state policymakers; Harland (1991) describes similar strategies with New York jail policymakers.

3. Availability of alternative choices: A complete list of policy alternatives and consequences should be articulated. For example, neither building nor using intermediate sanctions will be effective in all settings. Comprehensive needs assessments in each locality should be undertaken so as to define the need for future jail space, the feasibility of intermediate sanctions, and the costs (both financial and social) of pursuing different policy alternatives.

4. The diversity of stakeholders: The more heterogeneous are participants in the policy process, the more likely is conflict over policy options. Jail overcrowding

is the policy arena for diverse actors: county supervisors, district attorneys, sheriffs, probation departments, judges, and state legislators. Absent interagency cooperation or communication, many policies meet unexpected resistance and noncompliance. The diverse views of key actors must be identified and considered if effective responses are to develop.

5. Level of required expertise to formulate policy: Expertise includes technical and political competence, level of direct contact with the problem, and level of understanding of the problem. Policymakers must carefully locate and integrate expertise in a variety of areas: jail population forecasting; jail policy advocacy; design and administration of programs in jails, courts, probation, and other agencies; and planning. It must not be assumed that policymakers themselves possess the necessary range of required expertise.

6. Resources demanded by the policy versus those available: Assuming that agreement can be reached on problem definition and policy goals, it is essential to match resources on policy (Mullen, 1985). Either resources must rise to the level required by policy, or policy must be tailored to meet resource constraints. "Get-tough" sentencing policies, for example, should not be contemplated unless necessary jail and prison space can be ensured. Minnesota's sentencing guidelines are explicitly tied to resource considerations (Blumstein, 1987; Miethe and Moore, 1989).

7. Implementation responsibility and determination of performance criteria: Assuming that other policy requirements can be met (e.g., resources, agreement on problem and goals, commitment to achieving a solution), any new policy must contain a plan for monitoring its progress and evaluating its effectiveness over a specified period of time. A dearth of valid evaluations of new policies has seriously hindered progress in solving the jail crowding problem.

CONCLUSION

This chapter has attempted to advance our understanding of jail problems and reforms by integrating diverse perspectives on the causes, evolution, and impacts of court orders against jails. Substantial shortcomings in both policy design and research on jail problems have hindered solutions to overcrowding and other problems. We may not yet have learned how to punish in a humane and rational manner, but the courts have contributed enormously to an important window of opportunity to do so.

Over the past ten years or so, court orders have forced social systems to become more selective about the use of incarceration. Court orders have raised awareness of jail problems, and have created a more receptive climate for sentencing alternatives, public education, and other innovations. Building new jails has proven to be a simplistic, expensive, and ineffective response to litigation (Busher, 1983; Hall, 1985), while increased law enforcement and incarceration have proven to be simplistic responses to crime (Clear and Harris, 1987; Walker, 1990). Even in jurisdictions that have undergone extensive building programs, overcrowding persists and little change in crime has resulted. Fiscal crisis and court-imposed population caps have contributed to the widespread adoption of intermediate sanctions. It is not yet clear, however, that intermediate sanctions signal the emergence of a more rational system of sentencing and punishment (Morris and Tonry, 1990). Such policies may merely provide temporary "band-aid" solutions for over-burdened correctional systems.

Long-neglected economic and social realities suggest a pressing need to re-examine our willingness and capability to punish. The "get-tough" anti-crime policies of the 1970s and 1980s contributed to jail overcrowding, court orders, and resource crisis in local government. Such policies have also contributed to an increasingly criminalized urban underclass (Wilson, 1987). The United States now has the highest rate of incarceration in the world, and incarcerates black males at a rate four times that of South Africa (Mauer, 1990). We must acknowledge that jail overcrowding and court orders result from a dynamic confluence of social, political, and legal forces, and that solutions to complex problems are unlikely to be quick or easy:

> If jail reform is to be effective, it must transcend the individual jail and must be conceived in a broader, more systematic manner, which sees the jail problem as an integral part of the entire criminal justice system (Mattick, 1974:822).

At the same time, the current state of affairs should be viewed as a considerable opportunity. Our need for efficient and just policy choices requires a more careful process of problem analysis, policy design and evaluation than ever before. Well-planned research can open the door for coordinated policy innovation rather than a "piecemeal political patchwork of minor ameliorations" (Mattick, 1974: 822). The major obstacle to a more rational system of punishment is the tendency to seize upon unrelated, simplistic solutions at the expense of more coordinated but complex plans informed by police-relevant research. The dangers of faulty problem analysis, "knee-jerk" change, and poor evaluations of new criminal justice policies should by now be clear. While the future should be informed by the past, it need not be doomed by it.

STUDY QUESTIONS

1. Public officials often disagree over appropriate solutions to jail problems. Some argue that the rights of inmates to sue over jail conditions should be severely limited; others argue that more money must be raised to build newer, larger jails. What are some problems with each of these strategies? Are other strategies possible?

2. To what degree did increased crime contribute to jail overcrowding? Provide evidence for your answer.

3. How did public opinion contribute to jail overcrowding? What role might public opinion play in developing solutions?

4. Discuss the different roles that judges play and their effects on solutions to jail overcrowding.

5. "The popularity of intermediate sanctions lies largely in their band-aid utility for reducing soaring incarceration costs, rather than a liberal shift in correctional philosophy." Do you agree or disagree with this statement? Why?

6. What is meant by a "garbage-can" model of decision-making? How can public officials who formulate jail policy avoid this problem?

FOOTNOTES

1. Judge William P. Gray, *Stewart et al. v. Gates et al.*, 450 F. Supp. 583 (C.D. Cal. 1978), 450 F. Supp. at 588.
2. Judge James L. Facht, *Hudler et al. v. Duffy et al.*, No. 404148 (Cal. Super. Ct., County of San Diego, May 12, 1980, p. 21).
3. Judge Richard A. Bancroft, *Smith et al. v. Dyer et al.* Nos. 74184, 63779, 76086, 750121 (Cal. Super. Ct., County of Alameda, August 15, 1983).
4. Judge Bruce Allen, *Branson et al. v. Winter et al.*, No. 78807 (Cal. Super. Ct., County of Santa Clara, Order of November 22, 1982: 4).

REFERENCES

Advisory Commission on Intergovernmental Relations. (1984). Jails: Intergovernmental Dimensions of a Local Problem. Washington, DC: Advisory Commission on Intergovernmental Relations.

Alpert, Geoffrey P., Ben Crouch and C. Ronald Huff. (1986). "Prison reform by judicial decree: The unintended consequences of Ruiz v. Estelle." In Kenneth C. Haas and Geoffrey P. Alpert, eds. *The Dilemmas of Punishment* (pp. 258-271). Prospect Heights, IL: Waveland.

Austin, James, and Barry Krisberg. (1982). The unmet promise of alternatives to incarceration. *Crime and Delinquency* 28:374-409.

Babcock, William G. (1990). "Litigating Prison Conditions in Philadelphia: Part II." *The Prison Journal* 70(2):38-49.

Baiamonte, John V. Jr. (1990). "Holland v. Donelon Revisited: Jail Litigation in Jefferson Parish, Louisiana, 1971-1991." *The Prison Journal* 70(2):38-49.

Blumstein, Alfred. (1987). "Sentencing and the Prison Crowding Problem." In Stephen D. Gottfredson and Sean McConville, eds. *America's Correctional Crisis: Prison Populations and Public Policy*. Westport, CT: Greenwood.

Blumstein, Alfred. (1988): "Prison Populations: A System out of Control?" In Michael Tonry and Norval Morris, eds. *Crime and Justice: A Review of Research*. Vol. 10. Chicago: University of Chicago Press.

Brakel, Samuel J. (1979). "Special masters in institutional litigation." *American Bar Foundation Research Journal* 3:543-569.

Bronstein, Alvin J. (1980). "Offender rights litigation: historical and future developments." In Ira P. Robbins, ed. *Prisoners' Rights Sourcebook* (Vol. 2) (pp. 5-28). New York: Clark Boardman.

Busher, Walter. (1983). *Jail Overcrowding: Identifying Causes and Planning for Solutions*. Washington, DC: Office of Justice Assistance, Research and Statistics.

Call, Jack E. (1986). "Recent case law on overcrowded conditions of confinement: An assessment of its impact on facility decisionmaking." In Kenneth C. Haas and Geoffrey P. Alpert, eds. *The Dilemmas of Punishment. Readings in Contemporary Corrections*. Prospect Heights, IL: Waveland.

Carroll, Leo and Mary Beth Doubet. (1983). "U.S. Social Structure and Imprisonment: A Comment." *Criminology* 21:449-456.

Chilton, Bradley S. (1991). *Prisons Under the Gavel: The Federal Court Takeover of Georgia Prisons*. Columbus: Ohio State University Press.

Clear, Todd R., & Harris, Patricia M. (1987). "The costs of incarceration." In Stephen D. Gottfredson & Sean McConville, eds. *America's Correctional Crisis*. Westport, CT: Greenwood.

Cohen, Michael D., James G. March, and Johan P. Olsen. (1972). "A Garbage Can Model of Organizational Choice," 17 *Administrative Science Quarterly* 1.

Cooper, Phillip J. (1988). *Hard Judicial Choices*. New York: Oxford University Press.

Crouch, Ben M., and James W. Marquart. (1989). *An Appeal to Justice*. Austin, TX: University of Texas Press.

Cullen, Francis T., Gregory A. Clark, and John F. Wozniak. (1985). "Explaining the get tough movement: Can the public be blamed?" *Federal Probation*, 49:16-24.

DiIulio, John J., Jr. (1987). *Governing Prisons: A Comparative Study of Correctional Management*. New York: The Free Press.

DiIulio, John J., Jr., ed. (1990). *Courts, Corrections, and the Constitution*. New York: Oxford University Press.

Dunbaugh, Frank M. (1990). "Prospecting for Prospective Relief: The Story of Seeking Compliance with a Federal Court Decree Mandating Humane Conditions of Confinement in the Baltimore City Jail." *The Prison Journal* 70:57-73.

Ekland-Olson, Sheldon, and Steven J. Martin. (1988). "Organizational compliance with court-ordered reform." *Law and Society Review*, 22:359-383.

Feeley, Malcolm M., and Roger P. Hanson. (1986). "What we know, think we know and would like to know about the impact of court orders on prison conditions and jail crowding." Presented at the meeting of the Working Group on Jail and Prison Crowding, Committee on Research on Law Enforcement and the Administration of Justice, National Academy of Sciences, Chicago, IL.

Feeley, Malcolm M., and Roger P. Hanson. (1990). "The Impact of Judicial Intervention on Prisons and Jails: A Framework for Analysis and a Review of the Literature." In John J. DiIulio, Jr., (ed.) *Courts, Corrections, and the Constitution*. New York: Oxford University Press.

Galanter, Marc. (1975). "Afterword: Explaining Litigation." *Law and Society Review*, 9:347-368.

Gettinger, Stephen H. (1984). *Assessing Criminal Justice Needs*. Washington, DC: U.S. Department of Justice, National Institute of Justice.

Glazer, Nathan. (1975). "Towards an Imperial Judiciary?" *The Public Interest* 41:104.

Glazer, Nathan. (1978). "Should judges administer social services?" *The Public Interest* 50:64-80.

Grieser, Robert C. (1988). *Wardens and State Corrections Commissioners Offer Their Views in National Assessment*. Washington, DC: U.S. Department of Justice, Research in Action, NCJ-113584.

Hagan, John. (1989). "Why is there so little criminal justice theory? Neglected macro- and micro-level links between organization and power." *Journal of Research in Crime and Delinquency* 26:116-135.

Hall, Andy. (1985). *Alleviating Jail Overcrowding: A System Perspective*. Washington, DC: U.S. Department of Justice, National Institute of Justice, Office of Development, Testing and Dissemination.

Harland, Alan T. (1991). "Jail Crowding and the Process of Criminal Justice Policymaking." *The Prison Journal* 71(1):77-92.

Harris, M. Kay, and Dudley F. Spiller, Jr. (1977). *After Decision: Implements of Judicial Decrees in Correctional Settings*. National Institute of Law Enforcement and Criminal Justice, Law Enforcement Assistance Administration. Washington, DC: GPO.

Ingraham, Patricia. (1987). "Toward More Systematic Considerations of Policy Design." *Policy Studies Journal* 15:611-628.

Jacobs, James B. (1980). "The prisoners' rights movement and its impacts, 1960-80." In N. Morris & M. Tonry, eds. *Crime and Justice*. Vol. 2. Chicago, IL: University of Chicago Press.

Kaufman, Gerald. (1985). "The National Prison Overcrowding Project: Policy Analysis and Politics, a New Approach." *Annals of the American Academy of Political and Social Sciences* 478:161-172.

Kizziah, Carol A. (1984). *The State of the Jails in California.Report #1: Overcrowding in the Jails*. Sacramento, CA: Board of Corrections, State of California.

Klofas, John. (1987). "Patterns of jail use." *Journal of Criminal Justice* 15:403-412.

Klofas, John. (1990). "The Jail and the Community" *Justice Quarterly* 7:69-102.

Martin, Steve J., and Sheldon Ekland-Olson. (1987). *Texas Prisons: The Walls Came Tumbling Down*. Austin, TX: Texas Monthly Press.

Mattick, Hans W. (1974). "The contemporary jails of the United States: An unknown and neglected area of justice." In Daniel Glaser, ed. *Handbook of Criminology* (pp. 777-848). Chicago: Rand McNally.

Mauer, Marc. (1990). *Americans Behind Bars: A Comparison of International Rates of Incarceration*. Washington, DC: The Sentencing Project.

McCarthy, Belinda R. (1990). "A Micro-Level Analysis of Social Structure and Social Control: Intrastate Use of Jail and Prison Confinement," *Justice Quarterly* 7:325-340.

Miethe, Terance D., and Charles A. Moore. (1989). "Sentencing Guidelines: Their Effect in Minnesota" Research in Brief, NCJ-111381. Washington, DC: U.S. Department of Justice, Office of Justice Programs, National Institute of Justice.

Montgomery, Elizabeth. (1980). "Force and Will: An Exploration of the Use of Special Masters to Implement Judicial Decrees." *University of Toledo Law Review* 52:105-123.

Morris, Norval, and Michael Tonry. (1990). *Between Prison and Probation: Intermediate Punishments in a Rational Sentencing System*. New York: Oxford University Press.

Mullen, Joan. (1985). "Prison crowding and the evolution of public policy." *The Annals of the American Academy of Political and Social Science* 478:31-46.

Myers, Martha and Susette Talarico. (1987). *The Social Contexts of Criminal Sentencing*. New York: Springer-Verlag.

Nathan, Vincent M. (1979). "The use of masters in institutional reform litigation." *University of Toledo Law Review* 10:419-464.

Rusche, Georg and Otto Kirchheimer. (1939). *Punishment and Social Structure*. New York: Russell and Russell.

Skogan, Wesley G. (1975). "Measurement Problems in Official and Survey Crime Rates." *Journal of Criminal Justice* 3:17-32.

Skovron, Sandra E., Joseph E. Scott, and Francis T. Cullen. (1988). "Prison Crowding: Public Attitudes Toward Strategies of Population Control." *Journal of Research in Crime and Delinquency* 25:150-169.

Storey, Ted S. (1990). "When Intervention Works: Judge Morris E. Lasker and New York City Jails." In John J. DiIulio, Jr., (ed.), *Courts, Corrections, and the Constitution*. New York: Oxford University Press.

Susskind, Lawrence and Jeffrey Cruikshank. (1987). *Breaking the Impasse: Consensual Approaches to Resolving Public Disputes*. New York: Basic Books.

U.C.L.A. Law Review, Note. (1973). "Judicial intervention in corrections: The California experience—An empirical study." *UCLA Law Review*, 20:452-580.

U.S. Department of Justice. (1988). *Police chiefs and sheriffs rank their criminal justice needs* NCJ-113061. Washington, DC:GPO.

U.S. Department of Justice. (1990a). *Justice Expenditures and Employment, 1988*. Bulletin NCJ-124132. Washington, DC:GPO.

U.S. Department of Justice. (1990b). *A Survey of Intermediate Sanctions*. Bulletin NCJ-124132. Washington, DC:GPO.

U.S. Department of Justice. (1991a). *Criminal Victimization in the U.S.: 1989*. NCJ-129391 Washington, DC: GPO

U.S. Department of Justice. (1991b). *Criminal Victimization in the U.S.: 1973-88 Trends*. NCJ-129392. Washington, DC:GPO

U.S. Department of Justice. (1992a). *National Update*. (Vol. II, No. 1) NCJ-137059. Washington, DC:GPO.

U.S. Department of Justice. (1992b). *Prisoners in 1991*. NCJ-134729. Washington, DC:GPO.

U.S. Department of Justice. (1993). *Jail Inmates 1992*. NCJ-143284. Washington, DC: GPO.

Walker, Samuel. (1990). *Sense and Nonsense about Crime*. Belmont, CA: Brooks/Cole.

Welsh, Wayne N. (1990). *A Comparative Analysis of Court Orders Against California County Jails: Intervention and Impact*. Ph.D. Dissertation, University of California, Irvine.

Welsh, Wayne N. (1992a). "The Dynamics of Jail Reform Litigation: A Comparative Analysis of Litigation in California Counties." *Law and Society Review* 26(3): 591-625.

Welsh, Wayne N. (1992b). "Court Orders and County Correctional Expenditures: Power of the Purse?" *Law and Policy* 14:277-311.

Welsh, Wayne N. (1993). "Changes in Arrest Policies as a Result of Court Orders Against County Jails." *Justice Quarterly* 10:89-120.

Welsh, Wayne N., and Henry N. Pontell. (1991). "Counties in court: Interorganizational adaptations to jail litigation in California." *Law and Society Review* 25:73-101.

Welsh, Wayne N., Henry N. Pontell, Matthew C. Leone, and Patrick Kinkade. (1990). "Jail Overcrowding: An Analysis of Policymaker Perceptions." *Justice Quarterly* 7:341-370.

Welsh, Wayne N., Matthew C. Leone, Patrick T. Kinkade, and Henry N. Pontell. (1991). "The politics of jail overcrowding: Public Attitudes and official policies." In: Joel A. Thompson and G. Larry Mays, (eds.), *American Jails: Public Policy Issues* (pp. 131-147). Chicago, IL: Nelson-Hall.

Wilson, William Julius. (1987). *The Truly Disadvantaged*. Chicago: University of Chicago Press.

Yackle, Larry W. (1989). *Reform and Regret*. New York: Oxford University Press.

Yale Law Journal. (1979). Note, "'Mastering' intervention in prisons." *Yale Law Journal* 88:1062-1091.

CASES CITED

Cooper v. Pate, 378 U.S. 546 (1964).

Gates v. Collier, 501 F.2d 1291 (5th Cir. 1974).

Hudler et al. v. Duffy et al., No. 404148 (Cal. Super. Ct., County of San Diego, May 12, 1980).

Miller v. Carson, 401 F. Supp. 835 (M.D. Fla. 1975).

In re Morgan, In re Ransbury, and consolidated cases, Nos. 281302-0, 281438-2, 284164-1, 308318-5, 316580-0, 286040-1, 285427-1, 289487-1, 289488-9, 287160-6 (Cal. Super. Ct., County of Fresno, January 12, 1983).

Offield et al. v. Scott, No. 46871 (Cal. Super. Ct., County of Placer, May 12, 1977).

Rhodes v. Chapman, 452 U.S. 337 (1981).

Smith et al. v. Dyer et al., Nos. 74184, 63779, 76086, 750121 (Cal. Super. Ct., County of Alameda, August 15, 1983).

Wilson v. Seiter, 49 U.S.L.W. 2264 (1991).

Wilson v. Superior Court (Branson), 240 Cal. Rptr. 131 (Cal. App. 6 Dist. 1987).

CHAPTER 15

CORRECTIONAL HEALTH CARE NOW AND INTO THE TWENTY-FIRST CENTURY

James M. Tesoriero and Malcolm L. McCullough

❖

ABSTRACT

The neighborhoods from which prisoners reside often lack adequate health care. Coupled with their tendency to engage in unhealthy lifestyles, prisoners in the United States usually enter prisons with more medical needs than average U.S. citizens. Prison officials are often slow or unable to respond adequately to these needs. Lack of proactive planning by correctional administrators nationwide has resulted in severe prison overcrowding, increased prevalence of communicable diseases, and a prison population which has large concentrations of injecting drug users. Current funding for correctional health care in this country is vastly inadequate.

This chapter reviews the current state of correctional health care in the United States, focusing on the areas most likely to impact prison health care into the twenty-first century. Areas covered include the communicable diseases of tuberculosis and AIDS, and the perennial issue of substance abuse and drug treatment.

SUBSTANCE ABUSE, HIV/AIDS, AND TUBERCULOSIS IN AMERICAN PRISONS: KEY FACTORS IN TODAY'S CORRECTIONAL HEALTH CARE CRISIS

Hearings conducted by the National Institute of Corrections (NIC) Advisory Board in April of 1993 included correctional officials and administrators representing every region of the nation. **Prison Health Care** was identified as the most critical current and future issue within the prison profession (NIC, 1993). Included among the most important correctional health care issues were the inter-related areas of substance abuse, HIV/AIDS, and tuberculosis[1].

This chapter examines the condition of medical service delivery in U.S. correctional systems, focusing on substance abuse, HIV/AIDS, and tuberculosis. Particular

---

[1]Other important factors identified were mental illness, the aging of the inmate population, and the special needs of female inmates (e.g., prenatal care and pregnancy issues). These topics are beyond the scope of this chapter, however.

importance is paid to the prevalence of these conditions in American prisons; correctional policies concerning education, testing, and treatment of these diseases; the known efficacy of existing education/treatment interventions; and the probable impact these issues are likely to have on correctional health care into the twenty-first century.

SUBSTANCE ABUSE

Prevalence of Substance Abuse Among U.S. Prison Inmates

U.S. jails and prisons house one of the highest concentration of substance abusers in the world, and current sentencing practices assure that this situation will only worsen.

The U.S. prison population has increased over 50% since 1981, due in large part to a national crackdown on drug-related crimes (Lipton, et al., 1992). Forecasted trends in sentencing predict a worsening of this already troubling situation. Murry (1992) reported that almost 50% of Federal Bureau of Prison Inmates were incarcerated for drug-related crimes, and this percentage is projected to rise to 70% by 1996.

The National Institute of Justice's Drug Use Forecasting (DUF) data reveal that 60% of arrestees in twenty-two of America's largest cities tested positive for at least one drug (excluding alcohol) at the time of arrest (Leukefeld and Tims, 1993). Likewise, Wish et al. (1984) found that 80% of those arrested and charged in New York with serious *nondrug* crimes, tested positive for drugs, primarily cocaine and heroin.

When one progresses from arrestee to those actually incarcerated, the concentration of drug users becomes even higher. In fact, the majority of our nation's prison and jail inmates are thought to be regular users of drugs. Lipton (1994) reports that "Of the 800,000 inmates that Bureau of Justice Statistics (BJS) indicate are now in federal and state prisons, and of the 9.7 million that are admitted to the Nation's 3,500 jails each year, probably 50% to 66% are regular users of controlled substances." Similarly, Innes (1988) reported that 62% of all U.S. prisoners used drugs on a regular basis prior to their imprisonment.

Overcrowding and Opportunity for Positive Impact

Prisons in the United States have become vastly overcrowded. All but ten states are currently under court order or consent decree to reduce overcrowding (Lipton, 1994). As mentioned, tougher sentencing during the 1980s, aimed disproportionately at drug users and dealers (e.g., mandatory sentencing for drug-related offenses), resulted in a high concentration of drug-abusing offenders in our prisons. The most serious of these offenders, the heroin and crack addicts, are responsible for a disproportionate amount of crime. Chaiken (1986) reports that heroin using offenders were responsible for ten times as many thefts, fifteen times as many robberies, and twenty times as many burglaries, when compared to their nondrug using counterparts. Research by Ball, et al., (1986) and Johnson, et al., (1986) demonstrates that predatory crime increases during periods of active heroin use by a factor of between four and six. Recent research has found that similar effects are produced from cocaine/crack usage (Fagan, et al., 1990). The National institute on Drug Abuse estimates that drug-related crime costs the country sixty to seventy billion dollars every year.

Evidence also suggests that the "revolving door" analogy is more applicable to drug users. Wexler, et al., (1988) report that up to three-quarters of parolees with a history of cocaine or heroin use (who were not treated for their substance abuse problem), return to drug use and criminal activity within three months of release from prison.

Some have pointed out that the high concentration of drug users in our nation's prisons represents a tremendous opportunity for both correctional and public health officials. From a public health perspective, most drug abusers spend at least some time in prison, making the prison a sensible place to establish treatment programs. The ability to treat large numbers of highly addicted substance abusers is a welcomed opportunity, since these individuals are unlikely to seek substance abuse services on their own (Lipton, 1994). The vast majority of inmates have never received treatment in the community. Moreover, evidence suggests that they have little or no interest in obtaining such treatment (Lipton, 1994). From a criminal justice perspective, any measurable reduction in an inmate's dependency on drugs can be expected to result in a decrease in disruptive behavior while in prison, and a reduction in criminal behavior upon release.

History of Drug Abuse Treatment in the Prison Setting

Leukefeld and Tims, (1993) point to the opening of two U.S. Public Health Services Hospitals in 1935 (Lexington, Kentucky) and in 1938 (Fort Worth, Texas) as the beginning of prison-based drug treatment. These "Narcotics Farms" eventually evolved into clinical research centers, and are now part of the Federal Bureau of Prisons. Others point to the passage of Title II of the Narcotic Addict Rehabilitations ACT (NARA II), allowing federal judges to mandate offender examinations to determine if rehabilitation through drug treatment was possible, as the start of drug treatment in correctional settings (Rouse, 1991). NARA II allowed judges to sentence inmates to one of three federal drug treatment institutions for a period of not more than ten years or the maximum allowable sentence for the crime committed (whichever was shorter).

Just as prison-based drug treatment was becoming part of many correctional settings, a paradigmatic switch away from a rehabilitative correctional model towards a "Just Deserts" philosophy was emerging. This movement was fueled by studies such as the Martinson Report, which reviewed research findings from prison rehabilitation studies and concluded that rehabilitative efforts did not work (Martinson, 1974). Notwithstanding a reversal of his position after additional investigation, the momentum away from a rehabilitative model was inevitable. Existing treatment programs were terminated, as were plans for the creations of new ones (Leukefeld and Tims, 1993). The number of NARA inmates also declined during the 1970s, and NARA II was eventually repealed by the Crime Control Act of 1984 (Rouse, 1991).

America's get-tough attitude on crime and criminals resulted in a drastically overcrowded prison system by the late 1980s, with an enormous concentration of offenders with substance abuse problems. The need to do something, coupled with encouraging new findings from several evaluations of prison-based drug treatment programs, has resulted in a revitalization of drug treatment in correctional settings. The Anti-Drug Abuse Act of 1986 included substantial funding for the support of prison-based drug treatment programs. In fact, the federal government is allocating money for drug abuse treatment, prevention, and research (as well as drug interdiction and drug-related crime control) at unprecedented levels (Wexler, 1994).

Types of Substance Abuse Treatment Offered in Prison

Current drug treatment programs being utilized vary in the amount of time and energy they demand from both prison staff and inmates. They also vary in appropriateness, with the more intensive (and expensive) programs being reserved for the most seriously addicted. Brown (1992) points out that the most common "treatment" model available to inmates, experienced by at least 65% of all those in need of such treatment, is incarceration without any specialized drug treatment services.

For those facilities with specialized drug treatment components, drug education and counseling, either at the individual or group level, are the most common services available to inmates. A variety of techniques are utilized by institution-funded caseworkers or psychologists, aimed at making the inmate aware of the dangerous consequences of his drug using behavior. The emergence of intravenous drug use as the number one transmission vector for HIV/AIDS, gives particular credence to their arguments (Brown, 1992).

Client-initiated and maintained self-help groups comprise a third treatment model used in the prison setting. Alcoholics Anonymous (AA), Narcotics Anonymous (NA), and Cocaine Anonymous (CA) are examples of such programs. Lipton, et al. (1992) characterizes these programs as follows:

> Using the AA 12-step model, [these programs] insist on sobriety, encourage sharing experiences and programs related to drug dependence, teach constructive tools to deal with the triggers to relapse, urge positive alternatives to a drug-dependent lifestyle, and perhaps most importantly, provide an important aftercare link—a network of supportive human resources to help offenders returning to the community avoid relapse provoking pitfalls.

Such programs are available at little if any cost. This is perhaps their greatest attribute.

Residential treatment settings, isolated from the general prison population, represent a more intensive level of drug treatment service. They require more commitment on the part of both correctional staff and inmate participants. Most often, prison-based residential drug treatment programs are modeled after the therapeutic community (TC) approach[2]. The TC approach stresses paced individual growth, where residents are given increasing levels of responsibility for the upkeep of the environment, the monitoring of fellow residents, and their own behavior change. In addition to the use of peer pressure as a stimulus for change, a variety of other techniques, including individual and group counseling, community sessions, and traditional rehabilitative programs (e.g., vocational education), are employed. Community status is achieved as one progresses through the program, demonstrates positive behavior change, and is given responsibility for encouraging change in others (Brown, 1992).

TCs do not follow the traditional medical model of treatment, in that there is not a clear line drawn between the staff and the inmates. TC staff are usually not reflective of the typical corrections officer. In fact, some TC-based residential programs employ recovering addicts and even convicted felons on their staff. Evidence suggests that TC

---

[2]See Jones (1980) for a discussion of successful features of prison-based therapeutic community models.

staff view themselves as "special" and are more committed to the inmates than other corrections staff (Brown, 1992).

Not surprisingly, residential drug treatment programs are more expensive to operate than the aforementioned modalities. Costs can often be reduced, however, through federal grant money, and through funding from drug abuse, mental health, and other state agencies.

The Scope of State Prison Based Drug Treatment

What is the current state of drug treatment services available to inmates? Lipton, et al. (1992) reviewed the literature and reported that:

> ...recent incomplete surveys of treatment for incarcerated drug abusers show that thirty-nine states use preliminary assessment procedures with newly sentenced inmates; forty-four states allow Narcotics Anonymous (NA), Cocaine Anonymous (CA), or Alcoholics Anonymous (AA) self-help group meetings once or twice a week; forty-four states have some form of short term (thirty-five to fifty hours) drug education programming; thirty-one states have some form of individual counseling available for drug users...; thirty-six states have group counseling in which small groups of inmates meet once or twice weekly with a therapist; and thirty states have some type of intensive residential program, often based on the TC model...

Thus, the vast majority of states have some type of drug treatment services available. Many states offer more than one treatment program, to accommodate the varying degrees of addiction experienced by their inmates. But how pervasive are these services? Are they available to all those inmates in need?

The NIDA conducted a survey of all fifty states and the District of Columbia in 1979, in order to assess the state of drug abuse treatment programs in our Nation's prison system. Results indicated that only 4% of the prison population (about 10 thousand inmates) were being served by a drug treatment program (National Institute on Drug Abuse, 1981). Chaiken (1989) estimated that in 1987, the number of inmates in drug treatment had increased to over 50 thousand, representing around 11% of the prison population. Thus, notwithstanding an increase in services available to inmates, the overwhelming majority of inmates with drug abuse problems are still receiving no treatment while in prison (recall that at least 50% of all inmates have substance abuse problems).

Evaluation of Prison-Based Substance Abuse Treatment Programs

Unfortunately, there is little if any research to support the effectiveness of the treatment modalities discussed above, with the exception of the TC approach. Anecdotal evidence notwithstanding, there is a lack of scientific research supporting the effectiveness of AA, NA, or CA type programs. Likewise, "most research studies of the effectiveness of individual counseling have shown little evidence of success in reducing recidivism (and other negative behaviors), although positive psychological changes have been demonstrated" (Lipton, et al., 1992). As for substance abuse education, aimed at increasing user's knowledge about the personal and social ramifications of their addiction, Lipton, et al., (1992) remark that "most drug-using inmates do not lack information about the drug or their consequences; in fact, most drug users are fairly sophisticated street pharmacologists, and it is naive to think that improving [drug education] will deter future use."

The TC approach, however, has recently received substantial evaluative focus, and contrary to Martinson's statement that "nothing works," there is a vast amount of research to indicate that residential drug treatment in a prison setting does produce favorable outcomes: "In every case where statistics are available the recidivism rates of program participants are at least 10% lower than a control group" (Rouse, 1991). Rouse also points to the potential for reducing prison overcrowding and the cost effectiveness as benefits of prison-based drug treatment.

One example of a prison-based residential TC approach that has undergone rigorous evaluation is the Stay'n Out program operated by New York Therapeutic Communities, and currently funded by the New York State Department of Correctional Services. There are two sites, a male program located at the Arthur Kill Correctional Facility, and a female program at the Bayview Correctional Facility. The female program has a single forty bed unit, while the males have three treatment units and a total capacity of 146 beds (see Wexler and Williams, 1986 for a detailed discussion of the admissions criteria and program features of the Stay'n Out program).

Narcotic and Drug Research, Inc. (NDRI) received a federal grant in 1984 to evaluate the Stay'n Out program. Using a quasiexperimental design, NDRI compared male and female participants to no-treatment and alternative treatment control groups, along several recidivism measures (percent rearrested, mean number of months until rearrest, percent successfully completing parole, and percent not re-incarcerated). NDRI found, among many other things, that: 1) Stay'n Out participants had significantly lower re-arrest rates compared to control groups; and that 2) For Stay'n Out clients, those remaining in treatment for nine to twelve months had significantly lower recidivism rates (however measured) than those spending time in the program. Oddly, as time in the program increased beyond twelve months, there was some reduction in program effectiveness (Lipton, et al., 1992).

A comprehensive discussion of prison-based TC evaluations is beyond the scope of this chapter. The reader is referred to Rouse (1991), Leukefeld and Tims (1993), and Lipton (1994) for excellent discussions of several specific evaluation studies. General features of successful programs have been identified, however. Wexler (1994) describes the features as follows:

- Treatment services should be based on a clear and consistent treatment philosophy.
- An atmosphere of empathy and safety.
- Recruitment and maintenance of committed, qualified staff.
- Clear and unambiguous rules of conduct.
- Use of ex-offender and ex-addicts as role models, staff, and volunteers.
- Use of poor role models and peer pressure.
- Provision of relapse prevention programs.
- Establishment of continuity of care throughout custody and community aftercare.
- Integration of treatment evaluations into the design of the program.

Research also suggests that isolating drug treatment inmates from the general population is an important ingredient for program success (Wexler and Williams, 1986), and that it is important to gauge the intensity of the program to the level of need/addiction in the population to be served (McLellan, et al., 1986). Also, requiring inmates to participate may not produce undesirable results. Research has demonstrated that individuals mandated by legal sanction to participate in *community based* drug treatment programs do as well as those who participate voluntarily (Hubbard, et al., 1989).

Evaluations of prison-based drug treatment efforts must consider that these programs exist in an atmosphere of suspicion and mistrust, often requiring program participants to engage in activities directly against the inmate code of conduct (e.g., "snitching" on fellow inmates who break program regulations is required). Coupled with the overcrowded conditions and the constant need for security, prison-based treatment has several obstacles not encountered by community-based programs.

In concluding this section, it is appropriate to point out that many evaluations of residential drug treatment programs have been seriously flawed in several respects. Perhaps the most threatening to the validity of prison-based drug treatment evaluations is self-selection bias. This bias can occur when program clients possess higher levels of motivation to succeed than control group members, thus leading to the spurious attribution of favorable experimental group outcomes to the drug treatment program. Even if experimental and control groups are fairly equivalent on motivation at the start, the high attrition rates in these programs often leave only a core of highly motivated individuals by the end of the study. The reader is referred to Fletcher and Tims (1992) for a detailed discussion of threats to internal and external validity in prison-based drug abuse treatment research.

Substance Abuse: A Look Toward the Twenty-First Century

There has been a recent trend on the part of correctional administrators towards the adoption of comprehensive correctional models with strong rehabilitation and drug treatment components. It is not important whether this trend is being fueled by the need to relieve prison overcrowding, to maintain prison security, the realization that prison-based drug treatment may actually be working and that crime and drugs are inherently linked. The fact is, there is more help available to the drug addicted inmate today than ever before, and evidence suggests that this trend will continue into the twenty-first century. The importance of this cannot be overstated, because there are currently insufficient treatment options available to the vast majority of substance abusers in American prisons. The current lack of adequate service options, together with the projected rise in the concentration of drug users in prison, poses a great challenge for correctional administrators, researchers, and health providers. The challenge remains that of finding the most effective ways to reach the majority of inmates still in need of substance abuse services.

HIV/AIDS IN AMERICAN PRISONS

Although there are many important issues contributing to today's correctional health care crisis, the key factor in this crisis has been AIDS and the correlation between preincarceration injecting drug use (IDU) and HIV infection (National Institute of Corrections, 1993). Acquired Immune Deficiency Syndrome (AIDS): **represents the final stage** in a spectrum of disease caused by infection with Human Immunodeficiency Virus (HIV). HIV assaults and impairs the immune system, exposing the individual to a broad variety of unusual illnesses that rarely occur in people with healthy immune systems. Evidence continues to validate that there are three primary modes of HIV transmission: sexual contact with the exchange of genital secretions (i.e., semen, vaginal and cervical secretions); intravenous drug use through the use of contaminated needles or syringes; and perinatally through the passage of HIV from infected mother to child, either across the placenta, during delivery, or by breast feeding. (National Academy of Sciences, 1988)[3].

PREVALENCE OF HIV/AIDS IN AMERICAN PRISONS

In November 1981, the first confirmed case of AIDS among United States prison inmates appeared in New York State, just six months after CDC announced the existence of the disease (Coughlin, 1988). By the end of March 1993, only the states of West Virginia and South Dakota had not reported an AIDS case within its correctional system. The total number of AIDS cases reported by the other forty-eight states and the Federal Bureau of Prisons was 8,525. Of these, there have been 2,858 inmate deaths from AIDS, 39% of which occurred after 1990 (Hammett, et al., 1994).

A 1992/1993 National Institute of Justice survey reflected an *AIDS incidence rate* in prison that was twenty times higher than the 1992 U.S. general population (Hammett, et al. 1994). Seroepidemiological surveys have established that *HIV infection rates* in prisons exceeded the general population by as much as five or six to one (Lurigio et al. 1991).

The best indicator of an overall HIV seroprevalence rate in American prisons is 2.2%, as reported by the U.S. Department of Justice (Harlow, 1993). There is great state-by-state variance in this figure, however. A nationwide study conducted in ten correctional systems with moderate to high rates of HIV infection, assessed 10,944 prisoners and found seroprevalence rates ranging from 2.1% to 7.6% for males and 2.5% to 14.7% for females. Nine of the ten correctional facilities reported higher rates of HIV infection for women (Vlahov, et al., 1991).

The high rates of seroprevalence among inmates is directly due to the increasing significance of intravenous drug use (IDU) as a transmission vector for HIV/AIDS. By the start of the decade, 24% of new AIDS cases in the United States were attributed to IDUs (Centers for Disease Control, 1990). Among inmates, intravenous drug use is responsible for the vast majority of HID/AIDS cases (Greenspan, 1988).

An extreme example of the relationship between intravenous drug use and HIV infection exists in New York State. The increase in court commitments for drug offenses during the 1980s increased the percentage of IDUs in New York state prisons (estimated to be as high as 85%). This led to an increase in the percentage of HIV infected inmates. By the end of 1989, approximately one inmate per day was dying of AIDS-related illnesses (Greifinger, 1989). In 1992, it was estimated that one out of every eight inmates in NYS was HIV infected (Glaser and Greifinger, 1993).

---

[3]Prior to 1985, the receipt of blood and blood products (blood transfusions) was a major route of transmission, but, due to stricter safeguards regarding blood donation, is now considered a secondary means of transmission. Although rare, HIV transmission can also occur through occupational exposure. The health care profession is the only place where occupational transmission of HIV has been documented to date.

The dramatic impact of policies targeting drug-related crimes is reflected by changes in the AIDS incidence rate in state and federal prisons, which have risen from 181/100,000 in 1990, to 362/100,000 in 1992/1993 (Hammett, et al., 1994). This ongoing "get tough" national stance on drugs should impact on American prisons into the twenty-first century, with a continued increase in inmate AIDS cases/mortality.

Like crime, AIDS disproportionately plagues minorities. In the general population, minorities accounted for roughly one-half of the total AIDS cases through 1992, yet they represent only about 20% of the total population. When discrepancies in socio-economic status are reduced by looking exclusively at the prison population, minorities continue to exhibit higher infection rates than whites (Hammett et al., 1994). Perhaps minority inmates are more likely to live in and frequent neighborhoods with higher background seroprevalence rates and prevalence of intravenous drug use. Due to residential patterns, therefore, the probability of contracting HIV per given sexual contact or needle sharing episode would be greater for Blacks and Hispanics than it would be for whites.

HIV Testing in American Prisons

The advent of a blood test for HIV antibodies in 1985 ignited intense national debates concerning the nature of HIV testing. This debate centered around the moral and legal issues of mandatory testing. In the nation's general population, voluntary HIV counseling and testing is the norm, with the exception of mandatory testing for U.S. military personnel and for foreign nationals applying for permanent resident status.

However, because prison inmates tend to demonstrate higher HIV infection rates and because inmates have diminished privacy rights under the constitution, many lawmakers and correctional administrators advocated mandatory testing among prison populations. Indeed, for the Federal Bureau of Prisons, the order for mandatory testing came from President Reagan in 1987 (Belbot and del Carmen, 1991). The NIJ/CDC survey indicated that, for approximately 80% of the prison systems in 1992, the primary type of HIV testing was voluntary. However, sixteen state correctional systems had policies which required all inmates to be screened for HIV (Hammett, et al., 1994). Other testing methods utilized by prisons include targeting risk groups, routine testing where all the inmates are tested unless declination occurs, testing of inmates if clinical manifestations of HIV/AIDS surface, and "incident testing" of inmates involved in the possible exposure of blood, mucous or other body fluids (Hammett, et al., 1994). HIV testing can also originate in the judicial system, and court-ordered HIV testing has occurred with inmates in the state correctional departments of Arizona, California, Kansas and Washington (Lillis, 1993).

Regardless of the testing policy adopted by individual prison systems, public health officials deem the following elements crucial to any HIV screening program:

- Pretest counseling focusing on the significance of the test.
- HIV/AIDS education stressing risk reduction behaviors.
- Referrals for any health or medical needs.
- Adoption of confidentiality measures, especially with test results.
- Support for HIV seropositive inmates including medical, mental, and social services.

- Post-test HIV counseling and education for inmates to facilitate behavior change (Freudenberg, 1989).

Housing and Security

As the number of inmates with HIV/AIDS grows, correctional administrators in the nation are increasingly faced with the issue of where to place them. In the beginning of the AIDS epidemic, segregation policies in prisons were favored in order to protect the inmate population from HIV infected inmates, who were considered contagious. There has been a shift in housing policy over time, however, and HIV seropositive prisons now tend to be mainstreamed into the general prison population. The NIJ/CDC survey found that 42% of State/Federal systems had some sort of segregation policy for HIV infected inmates in 1985, but this percentage had decreased to just 8% by 1993 (Hammett, et al., 1994). This shift towards allowing HIV infected inmates into the general population was due, in part, to the spacing constraints faced by prison officials. It has also been due to litigation by HIV infected inmates, challenging the right of correctional administrators to segregate them from the general prison population (see, for example, *Cordero v. Coughlin, Dunn v. White, Harris v. Thigpen, Judd v. Packard, Powell v. Dept. of Corrections*). Today, the decision to place an inmate in special HIV/AIDS housing is most typically dealt with on a case-by-case basis, contingent on the inmate's medical stage of the disease.

Certainly, the great majority of HIV asymptomatic prisons do not require special housing. Special housing needs primarily occur when full blown AIDS is manifested. The shift in policy towards a case-by-case approach has assured that the limited correctional resources available for HIV/AIDS-related activities can be targeted for effective HIV prevention programs, the purchase of needed life-sustaining prophylaxis, and the development of special AIDS wards/infirmaries or longterm medical care facilities.

Consideration of AIDS-afflicted inmates' individual circumstances has also resulted in the emergence of early release policies by prisons, allowing terminally ill inmates to be at home upon their deaths. However, given that many inmates come from disadvantaged backgrounds and may not be eligible for medical care or treatment outside prison walls, it is imperative that prison officials verify that they are not releasing dying inmates into precarious medical situations.

Medical Treatment for HIV- and AIDS-Afflicted Inmates

Once a correctional system has identified an inmate as HIV infected, it has a duty, guaranteed by the constitution, to protect the prisoner and provide adequate medical care and treatment (see, for example, *Estelle v. Gamble*, 1976). While the interpretation of "adequate medical care" is a subjective one, courts have generally held that the care must meet community standards, but need not employ "cutting edge" technology. Ideally, penal institutions should provide this health care in the least restrictive environment given existing security needs.

The level of care provided to HIV positive inmates varies greatly from state to state, with at least one state (Texas) providing inmates with the same level of medical services and therapeutic drugs that are available to the general population (Hammett, et al., 1994). Inmate access to experimental trials of new drugs has been extremely limited. In part, this restriction has been due to federal regulations limiting the use of inmates in clinical trials (originally adopted to protect inmates from exploitation). Currently, fewer than 20% of state correctional systems offer experimental HIV therapies to their inmates (Hammett et al., 1994).

Early diagnosis of HIV by correctional medical staff is crucial in developing the most comprehensive treatment plan for the inmate. Treatment for HIV infection involves trying to manage the disease with prophylactic and therapeutic drugs, theoretically increasing the life expectancy of the inmate. The efficacy of early treatment with zidovudine (AZT), thought to prevent the onset of AIDS to asymptomatic HIV seropositive individuals, has recently been questioned with the release of the "Concorde Study" (Aboulker and Swart, 1993). Drug-related treatment is very expensive, and most inmates are not given AZT until they meet Federal Drug Administration (FDA) eligibility criteria [CD4 (T4) cell count below five hundred] (Hammett and Moini, 1990). The NIJ/CDC survey found that AZT is available to HIV infected inmates within 98% of the nation's correctional systems (Hammett, et al., 1994). Approximately 80% percent of the prisons in the survey also offer the antiretroviral drug of ddI and Bactrim/Septra or aerosolized pentamidine to treat Pneumocystis carinii pneumonia (PCP) (Hammett, et al. 1994).

Treatment needs differ by sex. For example, women with AIDS are more likely to develop PCP but rarely develop Kaposi's Sarcoma (KS), which is much more frequent among men. Pregnant inmates with HIV infection should be monitored closely, since they are more susceptible to opportunistic infections during their pregnancies (Lawson and Fawkes, 1993). Findings from a new study, yet to be corroborated, indicate that the risk of perinatal transmission may be cut drastically by administering AZT to HIV-infected women in the weeks immediately preceding delivery (National Institute of Health, 1994).

Prevention and treatment of HIV/AIDS have been financially draining on state prison budgets. In 1992, the Centers for Disease Control began partial funding of State HIV Prevention Projects (Centers for Disease Control, 1992). This type of assistance came as a welcome relief to the nation's correctional system, where the costs for testing and treatment of inmates with HIV/AIDS continue to rise. A report issued in mid-1993 found that 76% of the state correctional systems in this nation reported their health care budgets had increased in the past year and that, on average, 10% of their total correctional budgets were now allotted for health care (Lillis, 1993).

Psychological and Social Services for HIV/AIDS Afflicted Inmates

Psychological and social support services needs are extensive for those suffering with AIDS. Such needs are further compounded by the prison environment. At the very least, individual therapy should exist to help inmates deal with the anger, denial, and fear that often occur after the notification of a positive test result. If group therapy is available, it can be used to help address the stigmatization that many HIV-infected inmates experience in the penal setting.

The NIC/CDC survey found that 95% of state/federal correctional systems offer support services for inmates with HIV, which are usually provided by correctional services staff (Hammett et al., 1994). However, very few systems employ full-time HIV counselors. There is also a tremendous need for Spanish-speaking HIV counselors. Hispanics are over-represented in American prisons (especially in the Southwest), and have among the highest inmate seropositivity rates, underscoring the need to reach this population.

Often, psychosocial support for HIV positive inmates is derived from inmate-run HIV peer counseling and support programs. The NIJ/CDC survey found that 52% of state/federal systems had such programs in 1992-1993 (Hammett et al., 1994). The AIDS Counseling and Education (ACE) program at the Bedford Hills female facility in New York State has been identified as an exemplary peer education and support program for women. In addition to educating women about HIV/AIDS, ACE offers a variety of support services: "Various bilingual programs are offered by ACE, including medical advocacy, individual counseling, peer support and counseling, support groups for people with AIDS, and video discussion groups" (Hammett et al., 1994). ACE also works with various community organizations to establish appropriate HIV/AIDS linkages for inmates upon release.

Prevention of HIV Transmission through Education

Without a cure or vaccine for AIDS, behavior change through HIV education is the only method to combat the spread of HIV infection. Given the fact that the prison population is at high risk for HIV/AIDS, and that many inmates receive little or no access to health care outside prison, the prison offers an excellent venue for HIV education, counseling and testing, and medical intervention. A recent survey of state correctional departments, funded by the National Institute of Justice and the Centers for Disease Control (hereafter referred to as the NIJ/CDC survey) found that forty-eight states have some type of AIDS education for inmates. Ninety-four percent of state correctional agencies have AIDS educational programs on intake, with half of those states also conducting AIDS education upon release. Moreover, HIV education was mandatory in 63% of state/federal prison systems (Hammett et al., 1994).

The majority of states have implemented their programs for the following reasons (in rank order):

1. enhancing of institutional safety for both inmates and staff,
2. commitment to public health,
3. a desire to improve the prison environment,
4. and the need to protect the institution from inmate litigation. (Martin, et al., 1993).

Litigation against the correctional departments of Alabama and Connecticut has recently been levied by inmates to ensure that those states provide adequate AIDS education (Freudenberg, 1989).

Most typically, HIV/AIDS education is delivered to inmates in group settings by correctional health staff or outside contractors. Most state correctional systems (nearly 90%) offer "live" sessions, in addition to or instead of audiovisual presentations, where inmates have the opportunity to interact with the instructor (Hammett et al., 1994). The content of the educational material typically includes the modes of HIV transmission, signs of HIV infection and disease progression, implications concerning the HIV antibody test, symptoms and signs of AIDS, HIV infection control procedures and confidentiality requirements, and information on assistance for those inmates testing positive for HIV. In addition, the NIJ/CDC survey found that nearly all states

(96%) discuss HIV prevention through safer sexual practices and that most states (71%) discuss prevention through the cleaning of drug injection paraphernalia (Hammett, et al., 1994). HIV/AIDS education is often utilized as an important lead-in component to counseling inmates both before and after HIV antibody testing.

Virtually all states offer HIV/AIDS education to their correctional staff. Education is mandatory for correctional staff in thirty-eight states, and for the most part includes the same information presented to inmates (Hammett, et al., 1994). In addition, staff are trained on topics relating to the care and security of HIV inmates. This is a major area of concern for correctional staff. Notwithstanding urging on the part of staff and their unions to adopt policies of universal testing and disclosure of inmate serostatus, very few systems currently have such policies. In their absence, correctional staff are instructed to adopt "universal precautions," treating all inmates as if they are HIV positive. There have been no documented inmate-to-staff HIV transmissions to date (Hammett, et al., 1994).

Peer education programs are also becoming an important part of many state HIV prevention efforts. Up from 22% in 1990, roughly 33% of states offered peer education programs in 1992-1993 (Hammett, et al., 1994). These programs are desirable for a number of reasons. They are much less expensive to administer than programs utilizing outside professionals. More importantly, they are probably less likely to engender feelings of mistrust on the part of inmates, who will identify more closely with fellow inmates. Peer educators are also more accessible to inmates, whose questions and concerns may arise outside the educational sessions.

A clear distinction has been drawn between provision of *information* about HIV risk-reduction techniques (given by almost all states) and the provision of the *means* to achieve these reductions. Due to the proscription of sex and drug use in prison, most correctional authorities have been reluctant to provide condoms to inmates, and no system currently provides bleach explicitly for the purpose of cleaning drug-injecting equipment. There have been no major security-related or other reported problems in the six states that do make condoms available to inmates (Hammett, et al., 1994).

Evaluations of HIV Education Programs

The presence of even an extensive HIV/AIDS education program does not guarantee reductions in risk-related activities by inmates. In fact, it may not even guarantee an increase in knowledge about HIV/AIDS. A recent study of Pennsylvania prisons revealed that, despite comprehensive HIV/AIDS educational programs for inmates, large percentages of inmates still possessed misconceptions regarding the modes of HIV transmissions:

> Forty-six percent of inmates surveyed believed that they could be infected by eating food prepared by an HIV-infected person, 44% said that transmission could occur through coughing or sneezing, and more than two-thirds stated that mosquitoes and other insects transmit the virus. (Zimmerman and Martin, 1994).

In fact, there is virtually no research on the paramount goal of prison-based HIV education programs: the reduction of HIV risk-related behaviors once released from prison. The tracking of inmate risk behavior after release is a difficult if not an impossible task. Martin et al. (1993), found that only 20% of states had made any attempt to evaluate their HIV education programs. Moreover, previous evaluation attempts have been methodologically flawed to the point that their results are of little utility. Research outside the prison setting does suggest that education alone will not produce positive behavior change (Kelly and Murphy, 1992). More intensive treatment of high-risk inmates, including behavior modification techniques, may be necessary for desired changes to occur.

HIV/AIDS: A Look Toward the Twenty-First Century

Given the projected rise in HIV seropositive inmates in the next decade, and the continuing threat of inmate litigation, it appears that the correctional health care crisis will continue for some time. The medical and custodial needs of HIV/AIDS inmates will be one of the most, if not the single most, important considerations for correctional administrators well into the twenty-first century.

There is a dire need for evaluations of HIV/AIDS service delivery in correctional settings. Particularly, methodologically sound research into the efficacy of prison based HIV education programs at stimulating risk reduction of inmates upon release is needed. Correctional administrators should also work together with community leaders to develop more extensive linkage to community-based HIV services for inmates being released. Such linkages are severely lacking in most states today.

TUBERCULOSIS

Tuberculosis Defined

Tuberculosis (TB) is a disease caused by the microorganism called "Mycobacterium tuberculosis." Although it sometimes infects extrapulmonary sites of the body (usually in those co-infected with HIV or other immune-suppressing illnesses), it most often infects the lungs (AIDS Institute, 1993). The vast majority of those infected with TB (90%-95%) never develop symptoms of the disease, because their bodies can fight it off. This symptomless TB is referred to as TB *infection*. Individuals with TB infection can *not* infect others.

For some individuals, however, TB infection progresses to *Active TB disease*. This progression occurs when the body is unable to ward off the disease, due to conditions such as old age, malnutrition, HIV/AIDS, and/or substance abuse. Young children are also at heightened risk, due to the fact that their immune systems are not fully developed. Symptoms of active TB include persistent coughing, weight loss, fatigue, and night sweats (AIDS Institute, 1993). Active TB can be passed on to others, and, if not treated properly, can result in death.

Transmission of Tuberculosis

TB is an airborne virus, and can be spread when an individual with active TB coughs, sneezes, or talks to others. The most effective mode of transmission is through tiny airborne droplets (sputum). Individuals exposed to air infected with these droplets can become infected themselves. TB is usually not transmitted as the result of a single exposure to an individual with active TB, even if that exposure occurs in a closed environment. It has been estimated that a *healthy* individual exposed to a person with active TB for eight hours a day over a six-month period has only a 50-50 chance of becoming infected (Burroughs Wellcome, 1993).

Most prison environments today are extremely conducive to TB transmission. They are vastly overcrowded (e.g. double bunking), have poor ventilation systems, and are comprised of individuals most likely to be TB infected (e.g. minorities and low SES individuals). How much TB transmission is actually occurring in prison is not known, since many inmates are TB infected upon admission. There are many documented transmissions of TB to both inmates and staff within prison settings, however (Braun, et al., 1989). A recent study comparing female inmates hospitalized with HIV infection to a group of hospitalized noninmate HIV infected controls, found that rates of TB were significantly higher in the prison group (Ross, 1991). Notwithstanding the use of small, nonrepresentative samples (e.g. only those with HIV infection) and lack of adequate statistical controls, this study suggests that TB can be transmitted in prison settings at rates far exceeding the general population.

Testing for TB

A Corrections Compendium survey published in 1993 found that only the state of Nebraska did not test for the presence of TB in its inmate population. The most common (and least expensive) method to test for TB is called the "Mantoux" or "PPD" skin test, in which small quantities of fluid protein are injected under the skin. A positive result is indicated by a bump at least ten millimeters in size, occurring within forty-eight to seventy-two hours of the test (AIDS Institute, 1993). A positive test is usually followed by a chest x-ray and microscopic examination of sputum to determine if the TB is active/contagious.

TB is harder to diagnose in individuals with HIV/AIDS. Some individuals with HIV infection or full blown AIDS, due to their compromised immune systems, may test negative for the PPD test, despite being TB infected or even having active TB. The more immunosuppressed an individual is, the greater the likelihood that he will provide a false negative PPD test. As many as 70% of TB-infected patients with CD4 (T-Cell) counts less than two hundred will test negative for TB using the PPD skin test (AIDS Institute, 1993). As a result, HIV-infected individuals are often tested with two PPD skin tests, as well as chest x-rays and sputum analysis. All these tests are less reliable (in the direction of finding more false negatives) when dealing with HIV/AIDS infected individuals (AIDS Institute, 1993). Because of this unreliability, different standards have emerged in dealing with tuberculosis testing and treatment of HIV-infected individuals.

Prevalence of TB Infection and Active TB in Prison

Once a leading cause of death, TB was thought to be well under control by the 1950s (AIDS Institute, 1993). Due to a variety of factors, including a shift of attention away from TB prevention and treatment, a rise in homelessness, substance abuse, poverty, and the emergence of HIV/AIDS, TB has resurfaced and is on the rise again. New York State has the highest incidence of TB in the nation. Over 80% of New York's TB cases originate in New York City. In fact, New York City accounts for only 3% of the nation's population, but over 14% of its TB cases (AIDS Institute, 1993).

Given what has already been said about the demographic and structural conditions necessary for the spread of TB, it should not be surprising to learn that TB infection rates are very high among some prisons in the United States. According to CDC statistics, the incidence of TB in prison populations overshadows that in the general population by a ratio of at least four to one (Burroughs Wellcome, 1993).

In New York State, which does mandatory TB testing upon admittance to the prison system, active TB has increased seven-fold, from 15.4 per 100 thousand in 1976 to 105.5 per 100 thousand in 1986 (Braun, et al., 1989). Moreover, this rate is projected to continue rising for the foreseeable future (Machon, 1992). Minorities are disproportionately affected by TB, as well as by HIV and substance abuse. Incidence rates (per 100 thousand) for active TB among inmates in New York between 1984 and 1986 were as follows: whites, 35.3%; blacks, 76.0; and Hispanics, 98.7 (Braun, et al., 1989). As foreboding as these statistics are, the potential situation is much worse. Twenty-eight percent of New York State's more than sixty thousand inmates have tested PPD positive, with an additional 5% estimated to have received false negative test results due to immunosuppression (Machon, 1992).

Co-Infection with HIV and TB

HIV and substance abuse are two important risk factors for the development of active TB. CDC reported that studies of AIDS patients in Florida, New York City, Connecticut, and New Jersey, found that anywhere between 5% and 21% had histories of TB. Minorities accounted for between 80% and 100% of these co-infections. In San Francisco, nearly 30% of TB patients aged eighteen to sixty-five were co-infected with HIV (Centers for Disease Control, 1989).

The likelihood of TB infection progressing to active TB is much greater for those HIV infected (estimated to be 8% *per year*) than it is for those without weakened immune systems (estimated to be 10% in a *lifetime*) (Selwyn, et al., 1989).

Given their poor history of medical care and their high prevalence of substance abuse and HIV, prisoners in some states are often co-infected with HIV and TB. In New York State, where the situation is among the worst, it is estimated that 65% of inmates with TB also have HIV infection, and 80% are substance abusers (AIDS Institute, 1993). In other states, such as Nebraska and Oklahoma, there is much less evidence of co-infection in or out of the prison setting (Burroughs Wellcome, 1993).

Treatment and Prevention of TB in Prisons

TB is a very curable disease, even among those HIV-infected. Perhaps the single largest barrier to cure is the duration of treatment needed to eradicate the disease: anywhere from six to twelve months of antibiotics is necessary (AIDS Institute, 1993). In the general population, this duration is especially problematic, given the highly transient nature of the typical TB patient. Patients begin to feel good again in just a few weeks and the incentive to continue treatment diminishes. One study reported that of 178 patients admitted to, and subsequently released from, Harlem Hospital with TB in 1988, nearly 30% were readmitted within one year with active TB (AIDS Institute, 1993).

One might assume that a prison environment would be more conducive to treatment, since the inmate's whereabouts are known at all times. However, short prison terms, numerous transfers, and exorbitant amounts of time between entry to prison and diagnosis and isolation of active TB, make treatment and control in the prison environment equally challenging.

Inmates found to have active TB should be held in isolation for at least two weeks or until their symptoms show improvement. This isolation should include closed doors and a ventilation system with negative air flow (e.g., from the room directly to the outside) (AIDS Institute, 1993). TB-killing ultraviolet lamps and sophisticated air filtration systems can also be used to prevent transmission to other inmates. The New York State correctional system currently has 150 isolation rooms for inmates with active TB. A separate facility for active TB inmates is being considered (AIDS Institute, 1993).

What about inmates who are diagnosed TB infected, but who don't have active TB? It is highly recommended that such individuals be given six to twelve months of preventative medication (e.g., isoniazid) so as not to develop active TB. Preventative therapy decreases the likelihood that active TB will materialize, including Multiple Drug Resistant TB (discussed below) (Burroughs Wellcome, 1993). This therapy is especially important for immunosuppressed individuals, who are much more likely to develop active TB and who are much more likely to die from it.

Multiple Drug Resistant TB

Multiple Drug Resistant TB (MDRTB) is not a new phenomenon. It dates back to 1945 when streptomycin was used to treat TB patients (Burroughs Wellcome, 1993). The major cause for concern today is the threat MDRTB poses to HIV-infected individuals, where it is occurring in its highest concentrations. Studies of MDRTB outbreaks have shown that over 90% of these cases involve HIV positive individuals, and over 70% have been fatal. In New York State in 1991, twelve inmates died of MDRTB, all of whom were HIV seropositive (AIDS Institute, 1993).

MDRTB is often caused by inadequate treatment, or premature termination of treatment by patients. When the treatment does not completely eviscerate the TB, drug-resistant organisms can emerge and grow to the point where the person becomes sick again, this time with a more formidable form of TB. Once MDRTB has manifested, it can be transmitted to others the same way nonresistant TB is transmitted (AIDS Institute, 1993).

A Look Toward the Twenty-First Century: Improving the TB Situation in Prisons

For the reasons outlined above, many correctional systems in the United States are (or will be in the near future) experiencing major outbreaks of TB. There are several policy recommendations on what correctional departments can do to eradicate active cases of TB, and to prevent the development of future cases. The following recommendations have been gleaned from various sources, including extant literature, conversations with public health professionals, and from personal observations and experiences:

- Perform chest x-rays on all incoming inmates, in an effort to identify active pulmonary TB, the most common form of infectious TB.

- The above point is especially important in states that do not have mandatory HIV testing of inmates. HIV-infected inmates are more likely to falsely test negative for PPD skin tests (compared to chest x-rays). Moreover, PPD skin tests only identify TB infection, not active TB.

- It is imperative that the length of time it takes to diagnosis active TB (whatever method is used) be shortened, thereby reducing the likelihood of further transmission. A definitive TB diagnosis can often take up to a month to occur (due primarily to multiple shipments of the cultures to multiple laboratories performing various portions of the test). Those individuals with a positive PPD test, as well as those suspected of being HIV positive could be isolated and observed, either until a negative test result is returned or until suspicions are otherwise allayed.

- There should be further coordination of HIV, substance abuse, and TB education and testing services in prisons. Certainly, any patient diagnosed with one of these three illnesses, should be educated and tested (when appropriate) for the presence of co-infection.

- It is absolutely crucial that TB-infected inmates be linked with community-based TB services upon release. For most states, the creation of such links first needs to be developed before utilization can occur. Given what is known about the difficulties of self-administered TB therapy, it would be preferable to link such therapy to conditions of parole or to place the inmate in residential treatment facilities.

- Ensure that federal requirements for proper ventilation of correctional facilities are met. Also, provide correctional staff with proper barrier masks and respirators during times of active TB outbreaks.

- Take measures to alleviate the overcrowded conditions contributing to the resurgence of TB in prison.

CONCLUSION

This chapter has examined three areas identified as crucial to the future of correctional health care: substance abuse, HIV/AIDS, and tuberculosis. Although each was discussed in its own section of this chapter, it should be apparent how inevitably intertwined they are. Substance abuse can be viewed as a direct cause of both HIV/AIDS (through intravenous drug use) and TB (through weakened immune systems). HIV/AIDS and TB clearly have reciprocal effects on one another. The presence of HIV/AIDS weakens the immune system and makes TB more likely to occur, while TB can hasten the progression of AIDS patients towards death.

Absent independent interventions (e.g., a vaccine for AIDS), as the concentration of substance abusers in prison increases, so will the concentration of HIV- and TB-infected inmates. This will pose a tremendous challenge to correctional policy makers, researchers, and health providers, to find innovative ways to deal with these trends. The coordination of substance abuse, TB, and HIV/AIDS-related services to inmates (e.g., all-encompassing educational sessions and treatment opportunities) will be an important ingredient for coping with correctional health-related challenges into the twenty-first century. Correctional health care will also need to advocate/lobby for the establishment of adequate community-based linkages, capable of finishing vital treatment or rehabilitation efforts begun in the correctional facility.

STUDY QUESTIONS

1. What is the major cause in the rise of HIV infection and AIDS in the American penal system?

2. What U.S. Supreme Court case guaranteed the right to adequate medical care and treatment for prisoners?

3. Absent a cure or vaccine for AIDS, what is the best method to combat the spread of HIV infection?

4. What is the major cause of multiple drug-resistant TB?

5. Which type of substance abuse treatment programs have received the most research attention?

REFERENCES

Aboulker, J.P. and A.M. Swart. (1993). "Preliminary Analysis of the Concorde Trial." *Lancet*, 341: 889-890.

AIDS Institute. (1993). *AIDS in New York State: A Newsletter from the New York State Department of Health AIDS Institute*, Albany: New York State Department of Health.

Ball, J.C., Shaffer, J.W., and D.N. Nurco. (1986). "The Hyper-Criminal Opiate Addict." In B.D. Johnson and E.D. Wish, (Eds.), *Crime Rates Among Drug Using Offenders: Final Report to the National Institute of Justice* (pp. 81-104). New York: Narcotic and Drug Research, Inc.

Belbot, B.A. and R.V. del Carmen. (1991). "AIDS in Prison: Legal Issues." *Crime and Delinquency*, 37 (1): 135-153.

Braun, M.M., Truman, B.L., Maguire, B., DiFerdinando, G.T., Wormser, G., Broaddus, R., and D.L. Morse. (1989). "Increasing Incidence of Tuberculosis in a Prison Inmate Population." *Journal of the American Medical Association*, 261 (3): 393-397.

Brown, B.S. (1992). "Program Models." In C.G. Leukefeld and F.M. Tims (Eds.), *Drug Abuse Treatment In Prisons and Jails* (pp. 31-37). Washington, DC: Government Printing Office.

Burroughs Wellcome. (1993). *HIV Infection and Tuberculosis in the Correctional System*. USA: Burroughs Wellcome Co. (RTY0496920M).

Centers for Disease Control. (1989). "Tuberculosis and Human Immunodeficiency Virus Infection: Recommendation of the Advisory Committee for the Elimination of Tuberculosis." *Morbidity and Mortality Weekly Report*, 38, no. 14:236-250.

Centers for Disease Control. (1990). *HIV/AIDS Surveillance Report*. Rockville, MD: National AIDS Clearinghouse.

Centers for Disease Control. (1992). "Guidelines for the Performance of CD4+ T-cell Determinations in Persons with Human Immunodeficiency Virus Infection." *Morbidity and Mortality Weekly Report*, 41, no. RR-8:1-17.

Chaiken, M.R. (1986). "Crime Rates and Substance Abuse Among Types of Offenders." In B.D. Johnson and E.D. Wish, (Eds.), *Crime Rates Among Drug Using Offenders: Final Report to the National Institute of Justice*. New York: Narcotic and Drug Research, Inc.

Chaiken, M.R. (1989). *In-Prison Programs for Drug Involved Offenders*. Washington, DC: National Institute of Justice.

Cordero v. Coughlin, 607 F.Supp. 9 (S.D.N.Y. 1984).

Corrections Compendium. (1993). "Dealing with HIV/AIDS-Positive Inmates." *Corrections Compendium*, June 1993.

Coughlin, T.A. (1988). "AIDS in Prison: One Correctional Administrator's Recommended Policies and Procedures." *Judicature*, 72 (1): 63-66, 70.

Dunn v. White, 880 F.2d 1118 (10th Cir. 1989).

Estelle v. Gamble, 429 U.S. 97 (1976).

Fagan, J.S., Belenko, B., Chin, K.L., and E. Dunlap. (1990). *Changing Patterns of Drug Abuse and Criminality Among Crack Cocaine Users. Summary Final Report*. New York: New York Criminal Justice Agency, January.

Fletcher, B.W. and F.M. Tims. (1992). "Methodological Issues: Drug Abuse Treatment Research in Prisons and Jails." In C.G. Leukefeld and F.M. Tims (Eds.), *Drug Abuse Treatment in Prisons and Jails* (pp. 246-259). Washington, DC: Government Printing Office.

Freudenberg, N. (1989). "Prisoners" In *Preventing AIDS: A Guide to Effective Education for the Prevention of HIV Infection* (Chapter 11). Washington, DC: American Public Health Association, 1989.

Glaser, J.B. and R.A. Greifinger. (1993). "Correctional Health Care: A Public Health Opportunity." *Annals of Internal Medicine*, 118(2): 139.

Greenspan, J. (1988). "National Prison Project Gathers Statistics on AIDS in Prison." *National Prison Project Journal*, Summer 1988.

Greifinger, R.B. (1989). Oral Presentation as the Deputy Commissioner for Health Services and Chief Medical Officer for the New York State Department of Correctional Services, before the New York State AIDS Institute Ad Hoc Committee on AIDS in Correctional Facilities, September 19, 1989.

Hammett, T.M. Harrold, L., Gross, M. and J. Epstein. (1994). *1992 Update: HIV/AIDS in Correctional Facilities Issues and Options*. Washington, DC: National Institute of Justice.

Hammett, T.M. and S. Moini. (1990). *1989 Update: AIDS in Correctional Facilities: Issues and Options*. Washington, DC: National Institute of Justice.

Harlow, C.W. (1993). *HIV in U.S. Prisons and Jails*. Washington, DC: U.S. Department of Justice, Bureau of Justice Statistics Special Report.

Harris v. Thigpen, 727 F.Supp. 1564 (M.D.Ala. 1990).

Hubbard, R.L., Marsden, M.E., Rachal, M.E., Harwood, H.J., Cavanaugh, E.R., and H.M. Ginzburg. (1989). *Drug Abuse Treatment: A National Study of Effectiveness*. Chapel Hill: University of North Carolina Press.

Innes, C.C. (1988). *Profile of State Prison Inmates, 1986*. Special Report. Washington, DC: Bureau of Justice Statistics.

Johnson, B.D., Lipton, D.S., and E.D. Wish. (1986). *Facts about the Criminality of Heroin and Cocaine Abusers and Some New Alternatives to Incarceration*. New York: Narcotic and Drug Research, Inc.

Jones, M. (1980). "Desirable Features of a Therapeutic Community In a Prison." In H. Toch (ed.), *Therapeutic Communities in Corrections* (pp. 34-40). New York: Praeger.

Judd v. Packard, 669 F.Supp. 741, 742 (D.Md. 1987).

Kelly, J.A. and D.A. Murphy. (1992). "Psychological Interventions with AIDS and HIV: Prevention and Treatment." *Journal of Consulting and Clinical Psychology*, 60:576-585.

Lawson, W.T. and L.S. Fawkes. (1993). "HIV, AIDS, and the Female Offender." In American Correctional Association (ed.) *Female Offenders: Meeting Needs of a Neglected Population*. Baltimore, MD: United Book Press, Inc.

Leukefeld, C.G. and F.M. Tims. (1993). "Drug Abuse Treatment in Prisons and Jails." *Journal of Substance Abuse Treatment*, 10:77-84.

Lillis, J. (1993). "Dealing with HIV/AIDS-Positive Inmates." *Corrections Compendium*, 18(6): 1-3.

Lipton, D.S. (1994). "The Correctional Opportunity: Pathways to Drug Treatment for Offenders." *The Journal of Drug Issues*, 24(2):331-348.

Lipton, D.S., Falkin, G.P. and H.K. Wexler. (1992). "Correctional Drug Abuse Treatment in the United States: An Overview." In C.G. Leukefeld and F.M. Tims (Eds.), *Drug Abuse Treatment In Prisons and Jails* (pp. 8-30). Washington, DC: Government Printing Office.

Lurigio, A.J., Petraitis, J. and B. Johnson. (1991). "HIV Education for Probation Officers: An Implementation and Evaluative Program." *Crime and Delinquency*, 37(1): 125-134.

Machon, S.C. (1992). "Prisoners with HIV/AIDS and TB/MDR-TB: The Epidemic within the Epidemic." Paper presented at the VIII International Conference on AIDS, Amsterdam: MoD-0036.

Martin, R., Zimmerman, S. and B. Long. (1993). "AIDS Education in U.S. Prisons: A Survey of Inmate Programs." *The Prison Journal*, 73 (1): 103-129.

Martinson, R. (1974). "What Works? Questions and Answers about Prison Reform." *Public Interest*. 35:22-54.

McLellan, A.T., Luborsky, L., Obrien, C.P., Barr, H.L., and F. Evans. (1986). "Alcohol and Drug Abuse in Three Different Populations: Is It Predictable?" *American Journal of Drug and Alcohol Abuse*, 12:101-120.

Murry, D.W. (1992). "Drug Abuse Treatment Programs in the Federal Bureau of Prisons: Initiatives for the 90's." In C.G. Leukefeld and F.M. Tims (Eds.), *Drug Abuse Treatment In Prisons and Jails* (pp. 62-83). Washington, DC: Government Printing Office.

National Academy of Sciences, Institute of Medicine. (1988). *Confronting AIDS: Update 1988* (App. A at 72-73, and APP. B 74). Washington, DC: National Academy Press.

National Institute of Corrections. (1993). *Advisory Board Hearings Report*. Washington, DC: U.S. Department of Justice, Prisons Division.

National Institutes of Health. (1994). "Important Therapeutic Information on the Prevention of the Transmission of HIV From Mother to Infant." Preliminary information presented to health departments. Publication of formal study currently under journal review.

Powell v. Dept. of Corrections, 647 F.Supp. 968 (N.D.Okla. 1986).

Ross, T. (1991). "Imprisonment and Tuberculosis in HIV-Infected Women." *JANAC*, 2(3):9-15.

Rouse, J.J. (1991). "Evaluation Research on Prison-Based Drug Treatment Programs and Some Policy Implications." *The International Journal of the Addictions*, 26(1): 29-44.

Selwyn, P.A. Harte, I.D., Lewis, V.A., Schoenbaum, E., Vermund, S., Klein, R., Walker, A. and G. Friedland. (1989). "A Prospective Study of the Risk of Tuberculosis among Intravenous Drug Users with Human Immunodeficiency Virus Infection." *New England Journal of Medicine*, 320:545-550.

Vlahov, D., Brewer, T.F., and K.G. Castro, et al. (1991). "Prevalence to Antibody to HIV-1 among Entrants to U.S. Correctional Facilities." *Journal of the American Medical Association*, 265(9): 1129-1132.

Wexler, H.K. and R. Williams. (1986). "The Stay'n Out Therapeutic Community: Prison Treatment for Substance Abusers." *Journal of Psychoactive Drugs*, 18(3): 221-230.

Wexler, H.K., Lipton, D.S., and B.D. Johnson. (1988). *A Criminal Justice System Strategy for Treating Cocaine-Heroin Abusing Offenders in Custody. Issues and Practices in Criminal Justice*. DOJ Pub. No. NCJ-108560. Washington, DC: Supt. of Docs., Govt. Print. Off.

Wexler, H.K. (1994). "Progress in Prison Substance Abuse Treatment: A Five Year Report." *The Journal of Drug Issues*, 24(2): 349-360.

Wish, E.D., Brady, E., and M. Cuadrado. (1984). "Drug Use and Crime Arrests in Manhattan." Paper presented at the 47th meeting of the Committee on Problems of Drug Dependency, New York: Narcotic and Drug Research, Inc.

Zimmerman, S.E. and R. Martin. (1991). "AIDS Knowledge and Risk Perceptions Among Pennsylvania Prisoners." *Journal of Criminal Justice*, 19:239-256.

CHAPTER 16

SENTENCING INTO THE TWENTY-FIRST CENTURY

SENTENCE ENHANCEMENT AND LIFE WITHOUT PAROLE

Etta Morgan-Sharp and Robert T. Sigler, Ph.D.

ABSTRACT

Throughout recorded history the approach to disposition of convicted offenders has tended to cycle from periods in which the dominant paradigm can be characterized as punishment or retribution to periods in which the dominant paradigm is rehabilitation or treatment. At present, the dominant paradigm in the United States appears to be punishment or retribution. Punishment-oriented periods are characterized by the enactment of statutes which focus on the offense rather than the offender, increase penalties, and reduce variability. In the coming years, this approach will fall out of favor with the public and will be replaced by the treatment or rehabilitation paradigm. New statutes will reduce or eliminate punitive statutes such as habitual offender statutes. The medium which is likely to be adopted in this next cycle is the expanded use of community based alternatives. Statutes expanding and establishing the development of community corrections as sentencing alternatives will continue to emerge as the twenty-first century approaches.

CYCLES IN ORIENTATION TOWARD THE SENTENCING OF CRIMINAL OFFENDERS

Punishment and treatment represents two extremes on a continuum of approaches for the disposition of guilty offenders. Punishment stresses the protection of society through the use of incarceration and tends to have elements of retribution, incapacitation, and deterrence. Treatment stresses the protection of society by changing the offender so that he or she stops committing crimes, and it tends to have elements of rehabilitation and reintegration. It is rare in practice to have one extreme to the exclusion of the other, with most systems changing emphasis rather than eliminating programs when public sentiment changes. Orientation toward the punishment or treatment of convicted offenders has vacillated from treating the offender as if he or she had no rights or reason to expect help to treating the offender as a person who retains his or her rights and who should receive education, training, and psychological services (Smith and Berlin, 1988).

In the United States, orientation toward the offender in the latter part of the twentieth century can be characterized as dominated by the punishment orientation. As the twenty-first century emerges, it is likely that the wheel will turn and public sentiment toward the offender will shift toward treatment as a preferred alternative. If present trends continue, the next wave of treatment options will emerge and become dominant in the context of community corrections. Support for this method can be found in an historical review of the cyclic patterns in the treatment/punishment orientation of the public and in an assessment of the potential power of the emerging field of community corrections.

Bartollas (1980) identifies four waves of treatment reform. During the colonial period in the United States, punishment dominated as the philosophy for disposition of convicted offenders with severe penalties, such as the stocks, whipping post, and gallows seen as appropriate dispositions. Treatment-oriented reform emerged after the war for independence, producing the prison. A second wave of reform in the latter part of the nineteenth century produced the reformatory. A third wave of reform in the early twentieth century produced individual treatment, and the medical model emerged during the mid 1900s in a fourth wave of reform. He notes that punishment became dominant in the 1970s but suggests that support for rehabilitation will reemerge in the coming years.

Jails and prisons are overcrowded; restrictive statutes prevent effective and efficient operation of the justice system; and, as a result, citizen unrest is growing. The pressure caused by this unrest will become intense as the media focuses on the misfunctioning of the justice system. As the twenty-first century approaches this pressure can be anticipated to produce impetus for change. It is likely that the change, a shift toward treatment, will be reflected in the development of expanded community corrections. Legislation and funds will be directed toward establishing and promoting the adoption of community corrections as the appropriate approach to the disposition of the convicted offender.

While shifts in orientation are not necessarily distinct or universal, clear trends can be observed. When punishment dominates, laws are passed making incarceration easier to apply with provisions for longer sentences; the use of prison as a disposition increases, putting pressure on correctional systems. The response of correctional systems combined with factors such as increasing costs, overcrowding, the incarceration of relatively mild offenders for long periods of time, and deterioration of the quality of life in prisons produces a reaction against the use of prisons. Crime rates do not decline and punishment is projected in the media as an ineffective strategy. Public sentiment changes and treatment-oriented reformers press for a treatment-oriented response to the criminal offender to reduce crime. Laws, policies, and practices are adopted to change the orientation of the correctional system. At the extreme point in the swing to treatment, the system "treats" and releases all offenders. Offenders spend very little time incarcerated, and some of the released/nondetained offenders commit spectacular new crimes. Crime is not reduced. Treatment is projected as a failure in the public media. Public sentiment changes and treatment falls into disfavor. Punishment-oriented reformers press for a more restrictive system to provide protection from criminal offenders and to reduce crime. As we move into the twenty-first century, treatment will re-emerge as the preferred approach to the disposition of convicted criminal offenders.

HISTORICAL ANTECEDENTS

When looking to the future it is informative to look to the past. The examination of past cycles in the orientation toward punishment and treatment provides a basis for projecting present trends into the next century.

The rehabilitation ideal is believed to have dominated corrections throughout the nineteenth and twentieth centuries (Allen, 1981). Although the treatment/punishment cycle is relatively pervasive, there appears to be a continuous shift toward more humane, if not more treatment-oriented, use of incarceration. That is, with each cycle some treatment-oriented programs tend to remain in place (education, vocational training, work release) and, with the exception of the death penalty, punishments have tended to become less severe than has historically been the case (corporal punishment, severity of the prison environment).

The alternating preference for punishment or treatment predates the use of the prison as a sentence. Shifts in the cycle from treatment to punishment can be seen in the development of the work houses or the development of the English Poor Laws. The development of the prison as a disposition in the late 1600s was the product of a reform movement which sought to reduce crime through the treatment of criminal offenders and was to replace less humane dispositions, such as corporal punishment and capital punishment. By the early 1700s, sentiment had changed and while the prison was maintained, the colonial assembly reimposed the English criminal code, including capital punishment and whipping (McKelvey, 1977).

In the early 1800s, treatment preference produced the use of indeterminate sentences, prison societies, probation and parole, and the reformatory movement with firm discipline and education defined as part of the treatment process (McKelvey, 1977). Houses of refuge emerged for the treatment of children with an emphasis on training and inculcation of proper moral standards (Bernard, 1992). By the end of the 1800s, the cycle was shifting, as reflected in statutes providing for longer sentences for minor offenders, the use of mandatory sentences, habitual offender statutes, restrictions on the use of parole, and statutes criminalizing vagrancy.

At the turn of the century, reform emerged in the form of the separation of children from adult offenders, the development of the juvenile court (Bernard, 1992), and the reemergence and expansion of the reformatory movement (McKelvey, 1977). Growing interest in mental health and its application to criminal offenders led to expanded indeterminate sentencing and defective delinquent statutes. In practice, treatment-oriented reformers sought to replace mark and ratings systems (an earlier treatment innovation) with clinical prognosis as a basis for determining release of imprisoned offenders. The medical model for treating offenders began to emerge.

In the late 1920s the focus shifted to the failure of the system to correct offenders, with studies indicating high failure rates on parole and among released offenders. The use of prison as a disposition increased, overcrowding became an issue, and most states undertook construction of expanded prison systems.

In the 1930s and 1940s the medical model emerged and an emphasis on classifying inmates for treatment and on an upgrading of the status of parole emerged, beginning with the federal system and moving to the states (McKelvey, 1977). Studies of the impact of prisonization (Clemmer, 1958) appearing in the 1940s added to the shift toward treatment as did rapidly emerging therapies such as psychodrama and guided group interaction. Legislation and practice permitted the implementation and expansion of the medical model of treatment, including enabling statutes, modified death penalty statutes, and the expanded good time provisions (McKelvey, 1977).

By the 1970s sentiment had shifted away from treatment. Rehabilitation was perceived as a failure with the severity of crime perceived as increasing and the safety of the public decreasing because of the emphasis on treatment in the correctional system (Allen, 1981; Fogel, 1978). The juvenile court became more legalistic (Bernard, 1992). Reformers who advocated punishment as the correct function of sentencing prevailed, and incarceration became prominent. Legislative initiatives resorted determinate sentences, abolished parole, reestablished or strengthened habitual offender provisions, increased the use of sentencing enhancement, and developed sentencing guidelines. As a result, the incarceration rate more than doubled between 1973 and 1983 (Currie, 1985). This trend has continued, and presently correctional systems are unable to house all of those sentenced to state incarceration, in spite of aggressive construction programs.

MEDIATING INFLUENCES

As the trend toward treatment of the convicted offender moves to dominance in the twenty-first century, a number of factors will not only mediate the impact of the shift, but also frequently serve as markers of the move to a new paradigm. First, the shift is not complete. There is an identifiable group of treatment-oriented reformers which is relatively stable over time. When punishment is dominant, such reformers continue to argue for treatment.

There is a similar group of punishment-oriented reformers who continue to argue for punishment when treatment dominates orientation toward the disposition of criminal offenders. While the size of these groups is undetermined, it appears probable that most people are relatively uninformed and uncommitted to punishment or to treatment; thus, the shift from one extreme to the other is likely to reflect a relatively small part of the uninvolved majority, permitting justice agencies to resist full implementation of reform measures.

Diffusion of concepts, particularly as reflected in legislation and policy development, is slow. Reform will begin in one state and spread to other states over many years. As a result, at any one time there are likely to be states in which punishment is still dominant, while in others treatment orientation prevails. In addition, later adaptations may be less extreme than the original models, whether it be legislation or policy. System resistance to change also moderates the impact of extreme legislation. Judges may choose to avoid judicial notice of sentence enhancement conditions, particularly in plea bargained cases when punishment is dominant, or give longer sentences from a range of sentences when treatment dominates. Correctional institutions may maintain treatment programs with decreased emphasis during punishment peaks and find ways to retain "dangerous" offenders during treatment peaks.

CONTEMPORARY PRACTICES

The factors which will propel the change in treatment/punishment orientation into the next century are in place today. Punishment presently dominates policy, legislation, and practice regarding convicted offenders. Society is moving toward dependence upon punishment to deter criminals from criminal activity. The inclination to punish is an emotional reaction which becomes salient with the violation of social sentiments (Garland, 1990). The social sentiments which Garland addresses are referred to as the conscience collective by Durkheim (1965).

If punishment is merely an expressive institution which serve to release psychic energy, then it has no objective or intended goal. If punishment simply occurs without an objective to be achieved, then it is not particularly useful other than in the context of retribution. If there is no action against the collective sentiment, then there is no need for a reaction to protect the collective sentiment. If punishment functions to create a community that is harmonious and unified, then the effects of punishment are positive. Punishment should be perceived as part of the cultural matrix which supports a complex pattern of rules and sentiments (Garland, 1990). Punishment can be perceived as a symbolic issue in society which directly affects the psychological and overall development of individuals in a society. Politically, the extent of punishments in a society represents the definitive authority that is maintained by the political order of that society.

Because all of the facets of a society are interrelated in the social order, punishments and all other dispositions available to the justice system, like other social factors, are determined by means of inclusion or exclusion in the social group (Garland, 1990). It is the preferences of the conscience collective that are implemented by a select few who are elected to office. In most cases, legislators attempt to codify in law what they believe to be the wishes of the public, or at least that portion of the public who elected them to office. Other agencies such as the police and the courts are also sensitive to what is perceived to be the wishes of the public. It should be noted that these wishes generally are not empirically determined but reflect the beliefs of the elected or appointed officials. It has been suggested that to some extent, legislation and its implementation tend to reflect the sentiments of those persons with political and personal power (Headley, 1989).

Three types of legislative initiatives reflect a shift in orientation toward punishment: habitual offender statutes, other sentence enhancement alternatives, and determinate sentencing (with a reduction/elimination of the use of parole). These statutes are enacted to control dangerous or serious criminal offenders. The desire for an increase in public safety through the use of incarceration to control severe offenders is characteristic of periods in which punishment dominates disposition philosophy.

These initiatives developed in the federal system. Sentencing disparity, particularly insufficiently punishing sentences for some offenders, became an important issue for Congress during the 1970s. Congress charged the U.S. Parole Commission with the task of developing a plan to address the problems involved in sentencing offenders. The plan was short-lived because of lack of judicial acceptance. The second plan involved rewriting the federal criminal code, but it, too, was not implemented successfully. The third plan focused on sentencing reform and proposed a comprehensive criminal law package, the Comprehensive Crime Control Act of 1984, and included the Sentencing Reform Act (Wilkins, Newton, and Steer, 1993).

The purpose of the Sentencing Reform Act was to enhance the ability of the criminal justice system to combat crime through an effective, fair sentencing system. In order to achieve this goal, Congress identified three objectives:

- the sentence imposed would be the actual sentence served, except for "good-time" credits, and the possibility of parole would not be a factor;

- there would be uniformity in sentencing practices; and

- the sentence would be proportional to the defendant and the offense (Wilkins, Newton, and Steer, 1993).

Several states have followed the federal model by enactment of similar sentencing procedures that provide for sentence enhancements for the career criminal. Common characteristics of sentence enhancement statutes are:

- imposition of a greater sentence for persons convicted under another statutory provision;

- procedures for sentence hearings; and

- titles that classify them as sentence enhancing statutes (Rafaloff, 1988, p. 1090).

HABITUAL OFFENDER STATUTES

Habitual offender statutes and other sentence enhancement statutes are central to the complex of factors which will influence the shift to treatment in the twenty-first century. In an attempt to reduce recidivism, many states have enacted habitual offender acts. This enactment is a direct response to evaluations that question the effectiveness of correctional programs in reducing criminality (Maltz, 1984). Maltz concluded that nothing works or is an effective deterrent to reducing recidivism, and that getting tough works if the intervention is tough enough. States that have enacted habitual offender acts hold the belief that getting tough works.

Much of the research in this area has focused on the career patterns of dangerous and repeat offenders who are the targets of habitual offender legislation. One group of studies, which focuses on the operation of special programs at the law enforcement and prosecution level, reports mixed results (Weimer, 1980; Blumstein and Moitra, 1980; Phillips and Cartwright, 1980). A number of studies focus on the outcomes of special programs for the treatment of dangerous and career criminals and also tend to report mixed results (Tennent and Way, 1984; van der Werff, 1981; Hoffman and Beck, 1982).

Habitual offender statutes tend to reflect most clearly the preference for incarceration as a disposition. By 1983 forty-three states had adopted legislation providing for mandatory sentencing for offenders who demonstrated repeated violations of felony statutes (U.S. Department of Justice, 1983). This approach to controlling the crime problem was adopted without the benefit of supporting research and with, at best, limited consideration of the potential consequences. Reservations have been expressed by both correctional professionals and academic researchers who suggest that habitual offender acts may prove to be costly and ineffective, while others suggest that the use of imprisonment would be cost effective.

Attempts to understand the "criminal," the individual who earns his or her livelihood by committing criminal acts, have dominated criminology since its inception. Research indicates that as much as 80% (Shinnar and Shinnar, 1975) or 85% (Wolfgang, Figlio, and Sellin, 1972) of serious crimes committed are committed by habitual offenders. Habitual offender acts attempt to control this population by assigning longer sentences to repeat felony offenders.

Concern about repeat offenders is not new. Proposed solutions are varied and have been present since the beginning of the use of prisons. Judges have taken prior criminal history into account when sentencing an offender, and they have used and continue to use longer sentences to control habitual or career criminals. The indiscriminate use of longer sentences for repeat offenders is not effective because plea bargaining, lack of information, and other factors can and do reduce the judge's freedom in assigning a sentence. The use of automatic sentencing has been present since as early as 1926 (Inciardi, 1986) when legislation very similar to current habitual offender legislation was introduced in the New York legislature, with a mandatory life sentence following a fourth felony conviction. Contemporary proposals for selective incapacitation (Blackmore and Welsh, 1983; Janus, 1985) which are the product of both a desire to control career offenders and pressure to contain the growth of prison populations, are an updated version of an old response to an enduring problem.

Attempts to develop an effective operational definition for habitual offenders have led to the reduction of this concept to a specific number of felonies, thus creating a condition in which the offenders captured by the statute may not be the career criminals sought. Relatively nondangerous offenders could commit three mild felonies (a popular threshold for many legislatures), plead guilty to all three, and receive a harsh sentence for a fourth mild felony offense. The career criminal or the individual with a criminal orientation would avoid the statute by bargaining for a plea to a reduced charge (a misdemeanor), by leaving the jurisdiction after posting bond and avoiding a conviction, or by moving from jurisdiction to jurisdiction during his or her criminal career.

Habitual offender acts have sentence enhancement provisions (add one or more years to the sentence when two or more prior convictions exist) which mandate the use of a life without parole sentence for some (usually on the fourth felony conviction), regardless of the dangerousness or level of commitment to criminal behavior. Other statutes provide for life without parole sentences because of the severity or offensiveness of the act. These statutes permit the assignment of a life without parole sentence when an offender's behavior is so dangerous that society has an interest in incarceration for public safety and/or for punishment. If the statutes are effective, there should be two life without parole populations. One is composed of offenders (who may not be career criminals) who have committed extremely offensive and dangerous acts, usually involving an element of physical assault; the other is a group of career criminals who frequently have no personal violence in their offense history. Habitual offenders tend to be the younger, more violent, and more assertive offenders (Flanagan, 1982; Irwin, 1981). If the habitual offender acts are ineffective, a third group of life without parole inmates is created. This group of offenders exhibits relatively mild levels of criminal activity and is not dangerous.

The growth in prison populations has been attributed to changes in the orientation of the justice system (MacKenzie, Tracy, and Williams, 1988). Prior to 1980, growth in Louisiana prisons was related to demographic changes in the general population, but the rapid growth of Louisiana's prison population in the early 1980s has been attributed to a number of changes in the law which increased the severity of sentences (MacKenzie, Tracy, and Williams, 1988). Similar statutes have been adopted in many states.

The cost of maintaining the life without parole population is high. If the use of these recent, more severe statutes is heavy, a department of corrections might be required to build a new prison every two or three years to accommodate new life without parole offenders. These prisons would be expensive, secure facilities requiring more and better qualified staff. Thus, in addition to adding the cost of staffing and maintaining new institutions to the operating budget of the department of corrections, the cost per inmate would increase as well.

SENTENCE ENHANCEMENT

Common characteristics of sentence enhancement statutes are: imposition of a greater sentence for persons convicted under another statutory provision; procedures for sentence hearings; and titles that classify them as sentence enhancing statutes (Rafaloff, 1988, p. 1090). Legislators failed to realize the impact that sentence enhancements would have on prison populations and prison management. Sentence enhancements have contributed greatly to the problem of prison overcrowding in many states. For this reason, many prison officials have reconstructed their programs to accommodate the increase in population. The overall effects of punitive sentence reforms extend beyond the inmate population increase and prison management to include the management of human and material sources (Luttrell, 1990, p. 54).

Many sentence enhancement acts focus on the use of firearms. The federal model is the Armed Career Criminal Act. Criminal Justice administrators trying to comply with the requirements of the Armed Career Criminal Act found that its application as a sentence enhancement depended on judicial interpretation. The Armed Career Criminal Act's original objective was to punish habitual and/or repeat offenders, who are sometimes referred to as career criminals. However, the statute failed to define the career criminal, thereby leaving the definition of such a person to the sentencing authority.

On the state level, firearm laws have been changed to shift discretionary powers in some states from the judges and parole boards to the prosecutors and police. In some states, there tends to be an overuse of sentence enhancements with those identified as serious repeat offenders, while in others there is a tendency to avoid using these enhancements as the law mandates.

California's gun crime sentence enhancements include a one-year additional sentence if the offender or the accomplice is in possession of a gun during the commission or attempted commission of a felony. Actual use of a gun during a felony mandates an additional two-year sentence. An additional two years is added to the sentence if the perpetrator is armed during a sexual offense; in all cases using a firearm adds a third year to the sentence (Lizotte and Zatz, 1986).

In a study conducted by Lizotte and Zatz (1986) which covered a three-year period, data revealed that use of a firearm does not significantly affect the length of sentence to prison. The sentence enhancer is not used for first convictions of any type, and sentences were influenced more by the length of time required to process the case than by mandatory sentences. The use of firearms did begin to influence the sentence length, with the fourth or later arrest increasing the sentence length by fourteen months. For the fifth and subsequent arrests, the sentence length increased by twenty-nine months whether or not the prior arrests involved firearms (Lizotte and Zatz,

1986). The firearm sentence enhancer is not used until the fifth and later offenses for rape, although California Penal Code mandates a three-year add-on sentence to the sentence for rape when a firearm is used. Courts in California, like those in many other states, only use the sentence enhancer for the most serious repeat offenders (Lizotte and Zatz, 1986).

Massachusetts statutes mandate a sentence of one year for persons illegally carrying a firearm. This enhancer does not establish an add-on sentence in relation to another felony; it is directly associated with possession of a firearm. With this enhancer in place, police officers have been granted unlimited discretion in terms of selective policing. As a means of "protecting" a particular group of citizens, the police decide who will be frisked and whether or not to report when a gun is found (Lizotte and Zatz, 1986).

In Michigan, if a person is convicted of possessing a firearm during the commission of a felony, the law mandates a two-year add-on sentence. Michigan officials have responded in two different ways to this law. In some instances, they have chosen to "throw the book" at the defendant if the defendant is considered a serious repeat offender. Michigan officials have also found ways to avoid using or lessening the effect of the Felony Firearm Law, such as adjusting the sentence for the mandatory two-year add-on sentence; adjudicating the defendant as innocent of all charges; adjudicating the defendant as guilty of all charges except the Felony Firearm Law; or adjudicating the defendant guilty of a misdemeanor, at which point the Felony Firearm Law cannot be applied (Lizotte and Zatz, 1986).

In addition to firearm sentence enhancers, there are also drug enhancement sentences. In response to citizen outcry for more stringent drug laws, Congress passed the Anti-Drug Abuse Act in 1986. Under this Act, mandatory provisions concerning the quantity of drugs involved were established. Mandatory sentences range from a minimum of ten years without parole for one kilogram or more of heroin or five kilograms or more of cocaine to a minimum of five years for lesser amounts of either drug (Wilkins, Newton, and Steer, 1993). If an offender has prior convictions, the mandatory sentence is doubled. In instances in which death or serious bodily injury occurred due to the use of a controlled substance, the mandatory minimum sentence is twenty years. The 1986 Act also provided sentence enhancements for the location of the distribution, the age of purchaser, and pregnancy of the purchaser (Wilkins, Newton, and Steer, 1993).

Habitual offender acts are also sentence enhancement acts. In addition to the use of life without parole, habitual offender statutes use sentence enhancements for lower levels of repeat offenses. Thus, a second conviction might call for two to four additional years, while a third conviction might call for five to ten additional years.

RESTRICTED HOUSING

Statutes have been enacted that limit the ability of the departments of corrections to house some offenders in specific types of housing which also contribute to the conditions which will produce change in the twenty-first century. Some of these restrictions are explicit; others are implicit or related to classification restrictions. Explicit statutes identify classes of offenders who cannot be housed in specific types of facilities. For example, Alabama statutes prevent murderers, drug dealers, and offenders convicted of a sexual offense from receiving community status. Thus, they cannot be placed in facilities such as halfway houses or work release centers. As a result, these offenders are returned to the community from at least a minimum security correctional facility.

Habitual offender statutes, particularly those with life without parole provisions, produce a similar effect. Because a life without parole offender has no reason to avoid escape, he or she must be kept in at least medium security correctional facilities. Sentencing enhancing provisions have a lesser impact, but delay the time the offender will spend in secure facilities (most classification schemes consider length of sentence remaining to be served as well as severity in determining classification).

DETERMINATE SENTENCES/PAROLE

The final set of factors to be considered in terms of pressures for system change in the coming decades are changes in sentencing structures. In the middle 1970s, justice-model-based determinate sentencing began to emerge as an alternative to rehabilitation-based indeterminate sentencing (Cullen & Gilbert, 1982). Determinate sentencing was used until the latter part of the nineteenth century. Indeterminate sentencing developed as a product of treatment-oriented reform and was well established by the beginning of the twentieth century. In the 1970s, punishment-oriented reformers pressed for sentences to be suited to the crime. The provisions for shorter sentences were acceptable to many rehabilitation-oriented reformers who perceived the justice system as victimizing the offender, with set sentences reducing the degree of victimization. Programs to help offenders could remain in place, but would not be related to release. By the beginning of the 1980s, twelve states and the federal system had adopted some form of determinate sentencing, but the justice model was not fully adopted in any jurisdiction. In many cases, the differences in legislation reflected the outcome of a debate between conservatives and liberals about the severity of the sentencing provisions and the range of offenses which should be addressed with incarceration. Other differences include the amount of discretion permitted, the abolishment or modification of parole, and the use of good time to reduce prison sentences (Cullen & Gilbert, 1982).

INTO THE TWENTY-FIRST CENTURY

Punishment as the appropriate disposition of convicted offenders is dominant at the present. The preference for punishment developed in the 1970s and has influenced legislation, policy, and practice. Legislation enhancing habitual offender statutes, providing for determinate sentencing, restricting the ability of departments of corrections from housing some offenders in some types of housing, and providing longer sentences when specific conditions are present have increased the number of offenders sentenced to prison, provided for longer sentences, and made prisons more difficult to administer. The practical consequences of these actions has been to produce overcrowded prisons and to reduce ability to use punishment to control offenders.

Punishment tends to become dominant when treatment is perceived as ineffective in curing offenders, crime is perceived as increasing, and the risk of the public to criminal victimization is seen as increasing. Punishment is perceived to have a deterrent effect, and long incarceration is perceived to have an incapacitation effect. It is anticipated that the combination of deterrence effect and incapacitation effect will reduce victimization by reducing crime. In particular, the identification of severe and persistent offenders and their subsequent incarceration is expected to greatly reduce crime by incarcerating a relatively small number of offenders. It was noted earlier that this strategy as reflected in the application of habitual offender statutes has not effectively removed serious offenders from society.

The ability to sentence severe offenders to prison and to maintain them for long periods of time is effectively prevented by overcrowding caused by implementation of the various sentencing reform statutes. Prisons were overcrowded when the shift from treatment to punishment began. A series of judicial decisions in the 1960s established minimal standards for humane living conditions which continued to be reinforced into the seventies. A central position in many of these decisions addressed population density, forcing many prison systems to reduce the number of inmates housed in existing facilities thus defining many operating prisons as overcrowded. In many cases, court orders prevented, and in some cases still prevent, exceeding specific population limits for specific jails, correctional facilities, and correctional systems. While more recent decisions have modified the earlier rulings, higher population limits are in place for many correctional institutions. The mandatory provisions of many statutes force the placement of specific offenders in prison for minimum periods of time. In order to accept these prisoners, other offenders must be released. When mandatory provisions apply to relatively mild offenders such as shoplifters, more serious offenders are released through a number of compensatory provisions enacted by legislatures at the request of system components. While most correctional systems have responded with rapid expansion, new construction cannot keep up with the flow of new inmates into the system.

When overcrowding occurs and is capped at the state level, prisoners sentenced to the department of corrections remain in the county jail until a bed becomes available. In most states, the county jails are full. In many instances, they are under a court order capping jail population and pressure is brought to bear on the court system to reduce the flow of offenders sentenced to incarceration. As a result, more serious offenders with fewer convictions (e.g., those who commit assault) are given probation, and less serious offenders with longer records (e.g., shoplifters) are incarcerated.

As the problems develop, secondary adaptations that avoid some of the statutory provisions emerge. For example, the court might not take judicial notice of the presence of three prior felony convictions when sentencing a specific offender thus avoiding the mandatory prison sentence or the need to enhance the sentence appropriate for the offense. Pressure to use incarceration remains, producing an uneasy balance in the sentencing process which causes some less severe offenders to be incarcerated while more severe offenders are released. When added to the process which causes some of the more severe offenders to be released, the degree of risk to which society is exposed increases rather than decreases.

Statutes with mandatory sentence enhancement and mandatory life without parole provisions are vulnerable to court challenge. The mandatory provision in many of these statutes has been included to answer criticism that such acts are discriminatory. If the imposition of a sentence is automatically applied to a set of circumstances related to the offense, it is not discriminatory. The decision to avoid taking judicial notice of conditions requiring the application of a mandatory sanction effectively removes the direct link between the conditions relative to the crime and the sentence. At some point, it is probable that the application of these statutes will be challenged as discriminatory.

As we enter the twenty-first century, it is probable that there will be a shift in philosophy from a preference for punishment to one of treatment as a disposition for criminal offenders. It will be held that punishment is expensive and does not work. The construction costs of new prisons are high; however, the more substantial costs lie in operating budgets. As more prisons are brought on line, the operating budgets of correctional systems increase. This growth mandates either increased taxes or reduction in the budgets of other state government activities. News articles will begin to focus on the cost issue and ask the questions "What are we receiving for this investment?" and "Is what we receive worth higher taxes or poorer highways?" The belief that offenders who are incarcerated become worse and that all offenders cannot be locked up for life will grow along with examples of mild offenders who are serving life without parole sentences. The argument will emerge that it is not enough to lock people up—something must be done to reduce the likelihood that they will continue to commit crimes. As a result, public sentiment for treatment will develop, producing a new wave of treatment-oriented reform.

While the exact nature of these reforms cannot be determined, a number of reactions are probable. Community corrections is presently advanced as the next stage in the development of an effective treatment agenda for offenders. Community corrections continues to refer to a variety of programs which are located in the community with little attention given to conventional definitions of community corrections or to purpose and function. As a result, community corrections is a relatively vague entity encompassing such a variety of programs that most people can identify a community corrections program that they find acceptable. In essence, many programs defined as community corrections are not treatment-oriented in the pro-offender sense. Home detention, halfway houses, shock probation, and similar programs all have punishment elements. Although statutory revision would not be required to implement community corrections as a disposition, it is probable that statutes defining or expanding the scope of various community corrections sentencing alternatives will be enacted. It is also likely that additional enabling legislation and legislation supporting development and dissemination of community corrections will be enacted.

Contemporary concern with the perceived increase in the amount and severity of violence may moderate the response to pressure to modify sentencing provisions. If the focus on sentence enhancement and life without parole sentences focuses on the number of relatively mild offenders captured by these statutes, these statutes may be revised such that they apply only to those who commit the most serious assault/weapons linked felonies. It is likely that mandatory sentence enhancements will be softened. Drug-related enhanced sentencing provisions may prevail unless the tendency to identify drug use as a cause of crime moderates. The expansion of the adoption of determinate sentencing will moderate; however, statutes in place are likely to remain in place. While determinate sentences reflect the positivist perspective and are keyed to the crime rather than to the characteristics and needs of the offenders, determinate sentences do not prevent the application of treatment programs, particularly if the next shift to a treatment perspective focuses on community corrections as treatment.

STUDY QUESTIONS

1. Discuss the validity of the argument that cycles in the preference for punishment over treatment are caused by the continuous failure of the justice system to control crime regardless of the approach to sentencing offenders in use.

2. Is it possible to define community corrections as treatment? What elements of community corrections are punishment rather than treatment? What aspects of community corrections are clearly treatment?

3. How likely is it that habitual offender statutes will be narrowly focused (only severe offenders or removal of life without parole provisions) rather than eliminated?

4. What types of articles, news stories, and features will appear prominently in the news media as the shift to treatment begins?

5. Will the shift to the use of community based alternatives in sentencing solve the underlying problem—the need to reduce crime?

BIBLIOGRAPHY

Allen, F.A. (1981). *The decline of the rehabilitative ideal: Penal policy and social purpose.* New Haven, CT: Yale University Press.

Bartollas, J.S. (1980). Practitioner's attitudes toward the career criminal program. *Journal of Criminal Law and Criminology, 71*, 113-117.

Bates, R.L. (1981). Search and seizure—the effect of unrecorded misdemeanor corrections on enhancement statutes. *American Journal of Trial Advocacy, 4*, 739-760.

Bennett, R. (1983). A favorable decision for recidivists facing life sentences without parole. *St. Louis U.L.J., 27*, 883-894.

Bernard, T.J. (1992), *The cycle of juvenile justice.* New York: Oxford University Press.

Blackmore, J., and Welsh, J. (1983). Selective incapacitation: Sentencing according to risk. *Crime and Delinquency, 29*(4), 505-527.

Blumstein, A., and Kadane, J. (1983). An approach to the allocation of scarce imprisonment resources. *Crime and Delinquency, 29*(4), 546-559.

Blumstein, A., and Moitra, S. (1980). The identification of career criminals from chronic offenders in a cohort. *Law and Policy Quarterly, 2*, 321-334.

Bonticy, M.K. (1983). Proportionality review of recidivist sentencing. *DU Paul Law Review, 33*, 149-182.

Brauchi, R. (1983). From the wool sack: Inconsistencies in supreme court decisions on recidivists. *Colorado Law, 12*, 1658-1659.

Carney, L. (1980). *Corrections: Treatment and philosophy.* Englewood Cliffs, NJ: Prentice Hall.

Clemmer, D. (1958). *The prison community.* New York: Holt Rinehart, and Winston.

Connour, W.F. (1982). Habitual offender issues. *Res Gestae, 26*, 86.

Cullen, F.T., and Gilbert, K.E. (1982). *Reaffirming rehabilitation.* Cincinnati, OH: Anderson Publishing Co.

Currie, E. (1985). *Confronting crime.* New York: Pantheon Books.

Davis, W.L. (1982). Recent developments in persistent felony offender cases. *Kentucky Bench & Bar, 46,* 100.

Dunford and Elliott. (1984). Identifying career offenders using self-reported data. *Journal of Research in Crime and Delinquency, 21,* 57-86.

Durkheim, E. (1965). *The rules of the sociological method.* New York: Free Press.

Feldman, S.W. (1984). The habitual offender laws of Tennessee. *Memphis State U.L. Rev., 14,* 293-335.

Flanagan, T. (1982). Correctional policy and the long-term prisoner. *Crime and Delinquency,* 28(1), 82-95.

Flanagan, T. (1985). Sentence planning for long-term inmates. *Federal Probation,* 49(3), 23-28.

Fogel, D. (1978). *We are the living proof,* 2nd ed. Cincinnati, OH: Anderson Press.

Forst, B. (1984). Selective incapacitation. *Judicature, 68,* 153-160.

Garland, D. (1990). Frameworks of inquiry in the sociology of punishment. *British Journal of Sociology, 41,* 1-15.

Gottfredson, M., and Hirschi, T. (1986). The true value of lambda would appear to be zero: An essay on career criminals, criminal careers, selective incapacitation, cohort studies, and related topics. *Criminology,* 24(2), 213-233.

Grant, I. (1985). Dangerous offenders. *Dalhousie Law Journal, 9,* 347-382.

Greenwood, P., Chaiken, J., Petersilia, J., & Peterson, M. (1978). *The Rand habitual offender project: A summary.* Santa Monica, CA: Rand Corporation.

Greenwood, W. (1980). Career criminals presentation: Potential objectives. *Journal of Criminal Law and Criminology, 71,* 85-8.

Headley, Bernard. (1989). Introduction: Crime, justice, and powerless racial groups. *Social Justice,* 16(4), 1-9.

Hochberger, R. (1980). Justice bar recidivist sentence. *N.Y.L.J., 83,* 1.

Hoffman, P.B., and Beck, J.L. (1984). Burmont—age at release from prison and recidivism. *Journal of Criminal Justice, 12,* 617-623.

Inciardi, J. (1986). *Criminal justice.* New York: Harcourt Brace, Jovanovich.

Irwin, D. (1981). Sociological studies of the impact of long-term confinement. In D. Ward & K.F. Schoen (Eds.) *Confinement in Maximum Custody.* Lexington, MA: Lexington Books.

Jackson, F. (1984). Second-degree burglary held a serious felony. *LA Daily J, 97,* 2.

Janus, M. (1985). Selective incapacitation: Have we tried it? Does it work? *Journal of Criminal Justice, 3,* 117-129.

Kindell, L.R. (1983). Ohio adopts a mandatory sentencing measure. *U. Dayton L. Rev., 8,* 425-441.

Kramer, R.C. (1982). From habitual offenders to career offenders: The historical construction and development of criminal categories. *Law and Human Behavior, 6,* 273-293.

Langan, P., and Greenfeld, L. (1983). *Career patterns in crime.* Washington, DC: U.S. Department of Justice, Bureau of Statistics.

Lizotte, A., and Zatz, M. (1986). The use and abuse of sentence enhancement for firearms offenses in California. *Law and Contemporary Problems,* 49(1), 199-221.

Luttrell, M. (1990). The impact of the sentencing reform act on prison management. *Federal Probation,* 55 (4), 54-57.

MacKenzie, D.L., Tracy, G.S., and Williams G. (1988). Incarceration rates and demographic change hypothesis. *Journal of Criminal Justice,* 16(3), 212-253.

Maltz, M. (1984). *Recidivism.* Orlando: Academic Press, Inc.

Marshall, L. (1980). The constitutional informities of Indiana's habitual offender statute. *Indiana Law Review*, *13*, 597-626.

McKelvey, B. (1977). *American prisons: A history of good intentions*. Montclair, NJ: Patterson Smith.

Monohan, J. (1981). Identifying chronic criminals. In D. Ward & K.F. Schoen (Eds.), *Confinement in Maximum Custody* (NCJ-77087). Lexington, MA: D.C. Heath and Company.

Moran, T.J. (1982). Separation of powers and the Illinois habitual offender act: Who sentences the habitual criminals? *Loyola University of Chicago Law Journal*, *13*, 1033-1053.

Morris, N. (1951). *The habitual criminal*. Cambridge: Harvard University Press.

Morris, W. (1983). Colorado's habitual criminal act: An overview. *Colorado Lawyer*, *12*, 215.

Mueller, N.R. (1982). Attacking prior convictions in habitual criminal cases: Avoiding the third strike. *Col. Law.*, *11*, 1225-1230.

Peck, D., and Jones, R. (1981). The high cost of Alabama's habitual felony offender act: A preliminary assessment. *International Journal of Offender Therapy and Comparative Criminology*, *29*(3): 251-264.

Petersilia, J., Honig, P., and Huboy, C. (1980). *Prison experience of career criminals*. Washington, DC: U.S. Department of Justice.

Phillips, J., and Cartwright, C. (1980). The California career criminal prosecution program zone one year later. *Journal of Criminal Law & Criminology*, *71*, 107-112.

Pindur, W., and Lipec, S.P. (1981). Prosecution of the habitual offender: An evaluation of the Portsmouth commonwealth's attorney major offender program. *University of Detroit Journal of Urban Law*, *58*, 433-457.

Radzinowicz, L., and Hood, R. (1980). Incapacitating the habitual criminal: The English experience. *Michigan Law Review*, *78*(3), 1305.

Rafaloff, J. (1988). The armed career criminal act: Sentence enhancement or new offense? *Fordham Law Review*, *56*, 1085-1099.

Shinnar, E., and Shinnar, K. (1975). The effects of the criminal justice system on the control of crime: A qualitative approach. *Law and Society Review*, *23*(4), 547.

Shore, J.M. (1984). An evaluation of Canada's dangerous offender legislation. *Les Cahiers Droit*, 411-426.

Smith, A.B., and Berlin, L. (1988). *Treating the criminal offender*. New York: Plenum Press.

Sorenson, C.W. (1980). The habitual criminal act. *Nebraska Law Review*, *59*, 507-537.

Supreme Court. (1980). Cruel and unusual punishment: Life sentences for repeated nonviolent felonies. *Harvard Law Review*, *94*, 87-96.

Tennent, G., and Way, C. (1984). The English special hospital—A 12-17 year followup study. *Medical Science and Law*, *24*, 81-91.

U.S. Department of Justice. (1983). *Setting prison terms*. Washington, DC: Bureau of Justice Statistics.

van der Werff, C. (1981). Recidivism and special deterrence. *British Journal of Criminology*, *21*, 136-147.

Weimer, D.L. (1980). Vertical prosecution and career criminal bureaus: How many and who? *Journal of Criminal Justice*, *8*, 369-378.

West, D.J., and Wright, R.S. (1981). A note on long-term criminal careers. *British Journal of Criminology*, *21*, 375-376.

Wilheim, M.G. (1982). Recidivist statutes. *Washington Law Review*, *57*, 573-598.

Wilkins, L.T. (1980). Problems with existing prediction studies and future research needs. *Journal of Criminal Law & Criminology*, *71*, 98-101.

Wilkins, Jr., W., Newton, P., & Steer, J. (1993). Competing sentencing policies in a "war on drugs" era. *Wake Forest Law Review, 28,* 305-327.

Williams, K.M. (1980). Selection criteria for career criminal programs. *Journal of Criminology Law & Criminology, 71,* 89-93.

Wolfgang, M., Figlio, M., & Sellin, T. (1972). *Delinquency in a birth cohort.* Chicago: University of Chicago Press.

Young, J. (1980). Constitutional Law—Texas habitual offender statute. *American Journal of Criminal Law, 8,* 209-216.

PART VI

INTRODUCTION

TECHNOLOGY AND THE TWENTY-FIRST CENTURY

Joseph Grau in his chapter, "The Use of Technology in the Twenty-First Century," demonstrates how an understanding of the crime problem, the nature, and the role of the crime and criminal justice systems will require elaborate ways that technological innovation will bring, transforming the social context in which the crime of tomorrow will occur. Quantum leaps in technology have grown out of basic science research and are and will continue to impact the way crime is being viewed and handled.

Workforce investment has become a major development theme in the 1990s. Complex demographic, economic, and educational conditions force the emerging workforce problems to center around a shortage of skilled workers—a trend that will affect the quality and quantity of the workforce into the twenty-first century. Rosemary Gido's chapter, "Organizational Change and Workforce Planning—Dilemmas for Criminal Justice Organizations and the Year 2000," discusses the criminal justice workplace of the future and the dilemmas that it will face, dilemmas similar to those of the private sectors, i.e., managing an increasingly diverse workforce; affording opportunities to women; retraining and training seasoned and new employees; and embracing new organizational models which permit flexibility, employee participation and proactive human resource strategies. She looks at an emerging model of criminal justice organizational change that will promote flexibility, employee participation and proactive human resource strategies—essential elements to a strategic criminal justice resource plan for the year 2000.

The process of criminalization of human behavior judged to be harmful to the public is typically one that builds slowly in common law jurisdictions. Momentum gained through problem identification and pressures exerted by special interest groups can easily span decades before undesirable actions are classified as "crime" through legislative enactment. Donald Rebovich, in "Prosecuting Environmental Crime in the Twenty-First Century," describes how a rare exception to the problem of identification is the relatively speedy transformation of acts of pollution into official crimes against the environment. Currently, community leaders and the public they represent, are turning to their elected crime control leader—local prosecutors—for the type of protection they have come to expect from these officials on more traditional predatory crimes. Local prosecutors are gearing themselves up to prosecute crimes against the environment with the same or similar vigor used in prosecuting crimes on the street.

In "Impact of Computer Based Technologies on Criminal Justice: Transition to the Twenty-First Century," William Archambeault describes for us the nature of the information society and its impact on American criminal justice. How computers and computer based technology apply to the system is the topic of his discussion. What the future holds for society in its use of this information has far reaching implications for us.

CHAPTER 17

TECHNOLOGY AND CRIMINAL JUSTICE

Joseph J. Grau, Ph.D.

ABSTRACT

Quantum leaps in technology, growing out of basic science research, are transforming societies around the world, and consequently the crime scene, criminals, and the criminal justice system. The crime scene is worldwide and crime is being democratized. As technology knits societies together through rapid, easier communication, the world shrinks to a "global village."[1] One's "neighbor" may be on another continent, reached in seconds, and capable of responding immediately.

Although technology is changing the social context within which wrongdoing occurs, it does not cause crime; rather, by adding a new dimension to the social situation, it opens new opportunities for expanded freedom and more effective social control. Human beings can use it for good or evil, for legal or illegal purposes. Personal and corporate assets take new forms, such as plastic and electronic money; greater availability and expanded use of intangible property, e.g., information, raise intriguing legal questions concerning human rights of freedom and privacy. In technological society, tangible and intangible property can be exchanged legitimately or fraudulently; personal space can be subtly invaded or expanded.

TECHNOLOGICAL SOCIETY

Criminal justice is an integral concern of all human beings and societies around the world. Understanding the crime problem, the nature and role of the criminal, and criminal justice systems requires elaboration of the ways technological innovations have transformed the social context within which crime occurs. "Data highways" supplement transportation systems. Cyberspace is the new milieu overlaying physical space; it does not replace, but adds a new dimension, to the crime scene. *Time* magazine defines cyberspace and its social consequences:

> Cyberspace is the globe-circling, interconnected telephone network that is the conduit for billions of voice, fax and computer-to-computer communications.... Every night on Prodigy, CompuServe, GEnie and thousands of smaller computer bulletin boards, people by the hundreds of thousands are logging on to a great computer-mediated gabfest, an interactive debate that allows them to leap over barriers of time, space, sex and social status. Computer networks make it easy to reach and touch strangers who share particular obsessions or concerns.[2]

Within cyberspace love notes, explicit sexual messages, graphics, coded plans for terrorist attacks, and invasions of personal space may be communicated. In this environment, for example, "two anonymous people (or maybe more) may sit at their computer terminals in different parts of the world, exchanging written descriptions of erotic acts performed with each other in an imaginary boudoir."[3] John Schwartz, a reporter for the *Washington Post*, brings "net sex" or "virtual sex" closer to home with the story of "an eight-year-old girl attempting computer conversations with a group of transvestites. Seemingly safe at home, the child was playing with her favorite $2,000 toy, using her computer and modem to make new friends online."[4] Internet can be used to "wire digitized child pornography to those who want it."[5] One can enter a computer discussion group where questions can be raised, such as: "Has anyone ever experimented with flogging or caning on the soles of the feet? Is there any reason this should be avoided? If not, is there a preferred way to go about it? Anyone with knowledge please advise."[6] In the flow of data and information through computer networks, such as Internet, ethical and law enforcement controls are lacking. No one is in charge, not even the government. Legislation and regulations are urgently needed to assure decency, justice, and fairness.

This chapter focuses on cyberspace and information technologies which have a significant impact on: 1) the crime scene, 2) forms, rates and qualities of crime, and 3) the criminal justice system. Reference will be made to technological developments in other fields, such as molecular biology and social science research, but no extensive treatment of these aspects of the technological revolution will be developed. To begin, we point to a few technological resources available and used in crime control: remotely controlled surveillance, chemical and genetic testing, DNA typing, and a wide array of computer and telecommunications exchange systems; computer models, psychological profiles, composite sketches and maps that facilitate tracking offenders and assessing potential recidivists; electronic events scheduling, task coordination and monitoring to replace paper-based manual procedures; computer caseload management for moving criminal cases through the criminal justice system for report-investigation-arrest to judicial proceedings and various correction applications.

Before discussing the relationship between technology and the criminal justice system, the "global village" concept requires further elaboration because it sets the parameters for the discussion that follows. Teleputing—the convergence of television, telephone and computer—has intensified the cybernetic revolution. Whereas mechanical inventions, one by one, increased our physical powers, electricity has expanded mental functions; electronics created a new dimension—cyberspace. As industrialization gave birth to urban and suburban areas, electrification internationalized and, to some extent, democratized human societies. Now, billions of people around the world can reach out to the minds, hearts and emotions of each other. In the 1970s during the Vietnam War, we experienced televised military conflict in our living room; more recently we shared in the suffering of people in Somalia, the Middle East, and the former Yugoslavia through televised newscasts, while at the same time and in the same way experiencing the tragedies, disasters, violence, and crimes of our "local" neighbors. Russian newscasts for the Russian people are simultaneously received by us and many other people around the world through satellite transmission. Wilson P. Dizard, Jr., former consultant on telecommunications and information policy for the U.S.

Department of State said that "for the first time in human history, there is a realistic prospect of communication networks that will link everyone on earth." He was optimistic that the "United Nation's goal of a telephone within an hour's walk of every village" would "be realized in the next century," despite the fact that presently there are some gaps in the "basic connection for most people" and in the "array of computers and other information resources," especially in Third World countries.[7]

Already, telecommunication linkage among the powerful, volatile financial, commercial, and industrial centers of the world, such as New York, London, and Tokyo is operating around the clock. Simultaneously, each receives the same, updated information, such as stock quotes, interest rate...and currency changes. All these markets are sensitive to the slightest change in the financial fortunes, productivity, and political developments in European, Asian, and Pacific Rim countries, to mention only a few. This "new global financial market" was poignantly described by Walter Wriston, former chairman of Citicorp:

> The new global financial market is not a place on the map; it is more than 200 thousand monitors in trading rooms all over the world that are linked together. With this technology no one is really in control. Rather, everyone is in control through a kind of global plebiscite on monetary and fiscal policies of the governments issuing currency...news will march across the tube, traders will make judgments and a value will be placed on a currency that will be known instantly all over the globe.[8]

At the present time, the world socio-economic fabric is knit together into a "global village." For example, by the use of only one computer network, Internet, an estimated fifteen million people in fifty countries are connected; nearly 40% of personal computers have modems facilitating the transmission of messages—often by fax.[9]

Telecommunication is pulsating through the academic community, not only in research endeavors, but also in the social life of students. *The Wall Street Journal*, in a special report on technology, described one of the "hottest night spots" on the campus of the University of Michigan, namely, the courtyard at Angell Hall:

> Students flock here to write love notes, send letters to their parents, turn in homework to their professors, post classified ads, catch up on campus news, talk about Rousseau and Locke on a special bulletin board for members of a political science class (more than 25% of all classes have their own discussion boards), and look one another up in an electronic phone directory (complete in some cases, with such personal details as "male, blond, nice guy").[10]

They engage in, what *Newsday* called, "Riding the Information Highway." In this electronic social center, that from the outside "looks like a giant funky cafe," it is chic to have a computer address with "the funny @ in the middle."[11]

Although this chapter focuses on this global electronic information world, we shall also refer to genetic and chemical research contributions insofar as they significantly impact criminal justice. Through biologically based techniques, human birth and death are engineered; individuals are genetically tested and evaluated. The fifteen-year, $3 billion federally funded Genome Study, begun in 1988 by the National Research Council of the National Academy of Science, is currently identifying and mapping the estimated 100 thousand human genes. Further research will demonstrate genetic relationships to specific human physical, behavioral, and psychological conditions. An in-depth treatment of genetic engineering would require detailed discussion well beyond the limits of this chapter. However, biologically based techniques, such as DNA fingerprinting and other biometric identification measurements, deserve a special note. Genetic research, at this time, does not impact all aspects of the criminal justice system as does information technology. In the future, molecular biology may have more extensive applications as suggested by the fact that gene technology research is being applied today for identification of war crimes perpetrators in Yugoslavia, Korea, and Argentina.[12]

THE HIGH TECH CRIME SCENE

The high tech crime scene is set on a technosocial stage, being integrally woven into the global social fabric. Advanced electronics provides an easily accessed, user-friendly environment for wrongdoing. In a button-pushing society, young and old, weak and strong, brilliant and the less intelligent, male and female, high and low social status people have equal opportunities for instantaneously transferring assets or obtaining money and information. It is not unusual for us to draw or transfer money through an automatic teller machine (ATM) or to engage in computerized credit or debit card purchases at local stores, by telephone or computer. Modem data bank access to valuable information is so easy that even a grade school child can do it. The purchase and "know-how" for using advanced electronic equipment are available everywhere—in magazines, catalogues, and newspapers at local stores, by merchants, and on electronic bulletin boards. For example, *Virtual Reality World*, a magazine devoted to the "hottest" advanced technology, appears regularly on newsstands; academic institutions and entertainment centers, such as Disney World...offer virtual reality experiences.[13]

Note that this electronic world of teleputing, telecommunicating, computing, and, in fact, any electrical device operate rain or shine, day or night, in any place (home, bedroom, office, car, airplane, satellite or outer space), as well as within and across national and international jurisdictional lines.

In this technological, user-friendly, easily accessed, electronically-wired social setting, the crucial issue is access control. This access raises many questions concerning personal identification. Which person (or persons) has been authorized? For what specific purpose? To use which electronic equipment? These questions surfaced when a highly publicized crime, the case of the Hannover Hacker, occurred in 1980.[14] Young West German hackers, operating from a small cramped room in Hamburg, Germany, logged onto computers without authorization at the University of California's Lawrence Berkeley Laboratory and at NASA headquarters in Washington, D.C. They found access to Internet through University College, London, and then to a computer bank of Mitre Corporation modems which saved the last number dialed. By easily redialing these numbers, they happened to enter a computer at the Anniston Army Depot and Optimis, a U.S. Defense Department computer base, with information about military studies.[15] The unsophisticated computer security of that time allowed the hackers to type "anonymous," as a log-in and "guest" as a password. In another case (1988), Robert T. Morris, a twenty-two-year-old Cornell University graduate student gained notoriety by placing a flawed computer program, a worm, into a network system. He experienced how quickly and easily it moved through the telecommunications system. After putting final touches on his program around 7:30 p.m., he typed in a few commands, hit the return button and went out to eat. "In the time it took Robert to put on his jacket after pressing Return the program began to spread. Within a few minutes it was already fanning out over the network. Computers started infecting one another like toddlers in a day care center."[16] The released worm quickly jammed about six thousand computers linked to Internet because of the speed with which the command was executed.[17] Today, this spread would be considered slow time because electronic impulses are often measured in as little as a nanosecond, or billionth of a second.

Not only can hackers disrupt computer systems and enter cybernetic space unauthorized, but thieves easily and quickly tap phone systems, running up exorbitant toll charges on other people's bills. For example, Ron Hanley, an executive at Dataproducts in New England in Wallingford, Connecticut, was notified by ATT that his company had been hacked. Within two days he had a bill confirming that "in one twenty-four-hour period, street corner phone users in New York had made some two thousand calls to the Caribbean on the company's line, ringing up about $50,000 in tolls."[18]. Don Delaney, New York State Police Senior Investigator and computer consultant, explains how the complex network allows phone freaks almost impenetrable cover of anonymity:

> Tens of thousands of computers are interconnected nationwide and internationally over telephone lines. These interconnections are networks with such names as Internet, Milnet, Arpernet, Telenet, and Tymnet. Many of these linked computers enable the individual dialing in to out-dial to another computer. If a criminal initiates the first call using a stolen telco credit card or a PBX on an 800 number, and then loops through several network computers, he or she virtually ensures anonymity.[19]

Note that the convergence of telecommunication systems involves transmission through both fiber optic wires and airwaves. Furthermore, hundreds of thousands of mobile cellular phones, using both types of transmission, have been cloned, i.e., reprogrammed with illegally copied numbers. A user can make roughly a month's worth of free international calls before being caught.[20] Clone phone cheats park their large, expensive cars along city streets where people, migrant aliens and nonaliens who cannot afford telephone service, enter and make calls to their relatives and friends in far away places in the Middle East and South America.

A group of hackers, Masters of Deception (MOD), led by Mark Abene alias Phiber Optic, got access to computers that controlled all the regional telephone companies and ATT. They made unbillable calls and freely used other services that cost hundreds of thousands of dollars. They traveled the Tymnet highway frequented by banks and the government. Just before being arrested at his parents' house, Phiber Optic had been using his laptop computer in his bedroom, but he did not know that he was being hacked back by two New York Telephone employees.[21]

The high tech crime scene, characterized by wire and wireless communication that links commercial and government computers locally, nationally, and internationally, creates opportunities for savvy criminals. Only a few of their many fraudulent scams have been illustrated, and they were basically at the individual and lower level of the financial system. In addition, more costly crimes at the upper institutional level occur, where on an average day trillions of dollars are moved by electronic funds transfer (EFT). National and international money exchange involves wire transfers, automated clearing house (ACH) procedures, cash management, online teller, and computerized check processing which are vulnerable to high tech fraudulent manipulations.

To prevent such fraud, personal identification numbers (PINS) and passwords are standard safeguards. Computer security experts have implemented sophisticated protection programs to keep one step ahead of hackers and criminals who also use computers to transfer and launder money, steal commercial inventories, and communicate with each other.[22] In this teleputing environment, the thief's traditional tools— mask, gun, and getaway car—are crude instruments. Theft and misuse of passwords and access codes, manipulation of computer programming and system glitches present opportunities for wrongdoing that never existed before, furthermore, plastic and electronic money are new forms of assets waiting to be misused. The criminal has adapted quite well to the high tech crime scene by implementing a variety of effective electronic modi operandi that fit with the electronic world.

HIGH TECH CRIME SCENE INFOBANKS

The high tech crime scene provides not only opportunities for costly telecommunications disruptions, fraudulent use of services, and financial scams, but also easy button-pushing access to a new type of bank, the infobank which holds computer-generated information. The introduction of the microchip in the 1970s and the inundation of our homes and offices with personal computers made it possible for anyone with a modem to obtain invaluable personal information from thousands of data bases or mainframe infobanks in the United States and around the world. Again, global source access has shrunken this plant so that "global villagers" can know just about everything about anyone.

The basis for this statement is the fact that for several decades computers have been collecting, filing, and storing private details gathered from personal applications. Few people realize that whenever they apply for a mortgage, license, or even telephone service, their personal life history enters the infobank system. We all know that a driver's license contains much more information than one's driving history. Among the computerized items on that little card are: date of birth, place of residence, color of eyes, height, weight, color of hair and even a photograph of the driver. Because of all this information, it is the most readily accepted and frequently used form of identification. Furthermore, credit bureaus, such as TRW in Orange (Calif.), Equifax in Atlanta, and Trans Union Credit Information in Chicago, collect and store financial status information on about 170 million people on a half million computer files. To this must be added all the financial information held by Internal Revenue Service from income tax returns which reveal more about one's life style than is apparent. Credit bureaus, in preparing credit profiles, look into a subject's payment history, public records that may contain liens, judgments or bankruptcies, personal debt load, banking relations or affiliations, employment, credit performance, and verification of social security number.

Although access restrictions apply to credit bureau reports and income tax returns, many other data banks in the public domain, are computer accessible without many restrictions. They contain information on property ownership, professional licenses, bankruptcy searches, professional reputation, criminal convictions, address verification, bank affiliations, lien/judgments, civil litigations, motor vehicle ownership, business affiliations, education verification, employment history, secondary residence, and telephone verification. Incidentally, public domain refers to information available to everyone. In addition, there is an almost inexhaustible supply of infobanks related to other areas of life, such as health, entertainment, sports, etc. For our purposes, we shall focus on those most relevant to law enforcement and the high tech crime scene.

The National Crime Information Center (NCIC), monitored and controlled by the Federal Bureau of Investigation (the FBI), contains computerized files on criminal histories, missing persons, warrants, stolen property and securities, registered property, such as guns and vehicles, and even persons considered dangerous to the President of the United States. NCIC holds criminalistic lab information and Canadian arrest warrants. It is consulted approximately a half million times a day by local authorities.

The Treasury Enforcement Communications System (TECS) was instituted for the U.S. Treasury Department and operated by the U.S. Customs Service in the fight against crime, especially in the areas of money laundering and drug smuggling. Scrambled messages are transmitted through more than sixteen hundred terminals throughout the country. To log on, users must identify themselves to the operation systems and enter the day's secret access code. An agency uses the TECS hardware and generic software, but sets up its own data base. An agency may shield its information from other agencies on the system. Upon written request, other federal agencies and even Interpol may seek the input data from a TECS subsystem.

Organized Crime Information System (OCIS) is a computerized data base, maintained and controlled by the FBI to provide specific information about known and suspected organized crime figures and their activities.

Some computer systems, e.g. "Big Floyd" and "Scorecard," were designed to access data banks on known and potential criminals for the purpose of "thinking through" their activities. When operative, they can identify the contacts and associates of wanted individuals and make suggestions on where a fugitive might be or which other parties might be able to lead to that individual. This type of relational data base file retrieves and searches out clues and relationships between clues.

All states have computerized law enforcement networks with subsystems that include criminal history, firearms control, stolen vehicles identification, wanted individuals, missing persons, stolen property identification, and many others. Information can be accessed by local, state, and federal law enforcement agencies, even from mobile units in the field.

The Automatic Fingerprint Identification System (AFIS) scans fingerprints submitted by law enforcement agencies, thereby creating a unique pattern and library index of individual prints, even latent prints. The American Standard for Information Exchange allows the matching of fingerprints taken from crime scenes with known prints from other jurisdictions. In addition to traditional finger and palm prints, research in molecular biology provides support for DNA fingerprinting tests that involve comparing the DNA of blood, semen or hair roots found at the scene with the DNA of a suspect. This technological enhancement is virtually foolproof because no two people, other than identical twins, have the same genetic characteristics.

The National Center for the Analysis of Violent Crime (NCAVC), located in the FBI's National Academy, Quantico, Virginia, is comprised of two units: the Behavioral Science Instruction and Research Unit and the Behavioral Science Investigative Support Unit. The overall Behavioral Science Unit, formerly known as a psychological profiling unit, identifies characteristics of offenders based on their behavior before, during, and after committing the crime to requesting law enforcement agencies in the United States and free world.[23] Violent crime is reported to NCAVC for pattern analysis and classification which can reveal multidimensional trends and profiles in the crime data.

The FBI Violent Crime Apprehension Program (VICAP) computer system stores information on unresolved homicides reported to the NCAVC. Crime reports are entered online from NCAVC at Quantico using a secure telecommunication network. The VICAP compares over one hundred selected categories of each new case with all other cases stored in the data base, producing a hardcopy report listing in rank order the top ten matches in the violent crime data bank, i.e., a template pattern match.

The profiling and consultation program uses a series of crime pattern recognition computer programs to detect and predict the behavior of violent criminals. The Arson Information Management System, applying the same approach, facilitates law enforcement's ability to predict the time, date, and location of future incidents and the most probable residence of the suspect. In general, artificial intelligence procedures are being used to manipulate data and compute the probable hierarchies and interactions of complex organizations to interdict organized crime, terrorist, and gang activity. Computer-assisted linguistic analysis techniques facilitate content evaluation of written and oral communication in extortions, bombings, and terrorist incidents to assess authorship and threat viability.

As we have seen, not only the criminal justice system, but countless other services and agencies collect and record data about people living in the United States and around the world. Thirty or forty years ago, this information was paper-recorded and filed in large cabinets; today a pinhead microchip can electronically classify, store, and retrieve the same data. What was costly, time-consuming and limited by space, has become inexpensive, lightning fast, and almost boundless. As a result, public and private institutions collect, maintain, and exchange huge quantities of data, much of it personal. Instantaneously, one's personal life may become an open book, flashed to the mass media and across the city, to a mobile police cruiser or credit office, or even the whole world.

The computer transforms raw data into meaningful, usable information. Infobanks organize, cross-index, and create composite files from which conclusions are drawn and decisions made. Police, license and credit bureaus, housing and welfare agencies, insurance and mortgage companies, educational institutions and innumerable government agencies routinely exchange this information about people without their knowledge or consent. Exchanges between the Central Intelligence Agency, Internal Revenue Service, and the Federal Bureau of Investigation are sometimes performed without adequate audit trail procedures. As a result, the original source of the data and the circumstances under which it was gathered cannot be traced. Data accumulates in public and private administrative institutions that may limit a person's benefits or preclude employment.

The standards for maintaining confidentiality in information transferral from one agency to another vary, not only between the public and private sectors, but also among federal, state, and local governments. This sharing can lead to privacy invasion, especially when public officials are not sensitive to privacy concerns. However, even in private business transactions confidentiality may be violated, information divulged, misused, or at least not handled in a way that indicates personal consideration. The following incident reported in *Business Week* some time ago, illustrates the point.

> Last spring, the long arm of American Express Co. reached out and grabbed Ray Parrish. After getting his credit card in January, the twenty-two-year old New Yorker promptly paid bills of $331 and $204.39 in February and March. Then he got a surprising call. His credit privileges were being suspended, an American Express clerk informed him, because his checking account showed too small a balance to pay his April charge of $596. A contrite American Express now says that it should have asked before peeking, and it reinstated Parrish after he paid his bill from his savings and cash on hand. But that was besides the point. "I felt violated," says Parrish who has kept his card because he needs it. "When I gave them my bank account number, I never thought they would use it to routinely look over my shoulder."[24]

That was his introduction to the information age. In the beginning he did not realize that by signing the credit card application, he allowed American Express the right to snoop.

The establishment of data banks at all levels of government, business, and military service and subsequent information exchanges subtly whittle away rights to privacy. *Business Week* succinctly summarized the privacy protection legislation that has been passed and the many loopholes that in practice make it quite ineffective. For example, The Fair Credit Reporting Act restricts the sharing of information, but allows it for "legitimate business needs." The Privacy Act "bars federal agencies from letting out information they collect for one purpose to be used for a different purpose," but "exceptions let agencies share data anyway," and the law only applies to federal agencies. The Right to Financial Privacy Act sets procedural rules when federal agencies go through a customer's bank records, but does not cover state and local governments. Furthermore, the FBI and U.S. government agencies are exempt in an increasing number of instances. The computer Matching & Privacy Protection Act "regulates computer matching of federal data for verifying eligibility for federal benefits programs or for recouping delinquent debts" and gives the individual an opportunity to respond before the federal government takes adverse action, but because of the law's narrow scope, matches for "law enforcement and tax purposes" are now exempt. New privacy protection legislation is forthcoming as we move into the twenty-first century. For example, when the video rentals of Robert Bork, a nominee for the U.S. Supreme Court, were identified through a computer search and published in *The City Paper*, lawmakers were outraged. As a result they passed the (1988) Video Privacy Protection Act.[25]

Not only the large number of infobanks, but also their vulnerability to searches creates enormous problems. It is relatively easy, or at least an exciting challenge, for someone who understands computer technology to search an infobank with or without authorization. Even the computer illiterate through social engineering can gain access to computerized information. Many low level computer operators, unconcerned about keeping their records private, provide medical and financial data to anyone who gives a good reason for wanting to know. Private investigators are particularly adept at obtaining confidential information.

Difficulties involved in controlling the quality of input data and the individual's limited opportunities to expunge or delete errors in a file open a Pandora's box of personal problems and legal questions. Even if a person knows or suspects that certain files are being kept, the specific information and its accuracy often cannot be verified. Information in government or private files may be misleading or blatantly false because it was not checked thoroughly. For example, an insurance company investigator may ask a neighbor a question. The response received is local gossip, hence false, or at least, of questionable reliability and validity. If the investigator has no way of knowing this, it may enter the infobank as fact. To delete false or irrelevant information, assuming that the individual has had an opportunity to identify it, can be a long, tedious, costly struggle.

HIGH TECH CRIME SURVEILLANCE TECHNOLOGY

In addition to computer-driven searches, relatively inexpensive and widely available sophisticated surveillance technology has expanded the power of our five senses, especially the eye and ear. Parabolic listening devices, night vision cameras and scopes, cellular and laser devices, motion detectors, and microwave developments enhance our ability to see and hear. A former New York City detective and presently a corporate business investigator, in summarizing available technological equipment, identifies more than two pages of eavesdropping devices (bugs) used by law enforcement personnel as well as by ordinary citizens. "In today's business climate, the availability of over-the-counter products and inventions have fashioned a growing recourse to industrial espionage, armchair private investigators, do-it-yourselfers and the professional eavesdroppers."[26] Other electronic equipment described includes: the 360 Tracking System, the LoJack system activated through computerized microprocesssing and coding, video and infrared surveillance, voice scramblers, digital voice changers, mail screening, x-ray spray, fiber optic video transmission, wireless alarm systems, teleconferencing, and satellite communications. As noted, technological equipment is neither good nor bad, but rather more effective or efficient. It can be and, in fact, is used by criminals, law enforcement personnel, and also the average person. For example, a mother may buy an eavesdropping device (bug) to monitor the crying of her baby in another room, or a husband and wife may find surveillance instruments useful during their breakup.

In addition to the availability of surveillance and teleputing equipment in local stores and through catalogues, extremely deadly, rapid-fire weapons and explosives can also be obtained legally or illegally with little difficulty. Even the material and know-how for constructing and detonating a nuclear bomb are not beyond the reach of some people and nations. As a general safeguard against misuse of telecommunications by criminals, especially in plotting criminal activities, the United States Government introduced an encrypting device, the Clipper Chip, in 1994.

THE CLIPPER CHIP

The Clipper Chip, a tiny computer ship attached to telephones, scrambles sounds and information for privacy protection. As with all technology, it is a double-edged sword, raising a storm of controversy among law enforcement officials, the computer industry, and civil libertarians. "Vice President Al Gore dubbed encryption a 'law and order issue' because criminals use it to bypass wiretaps."[27] The Clinton Administration wants it adopted by the United States as the one and only legitimate coding system for protecting telephone and computer communications. Controversy is currently raging over who should hold the decoding or unscrambling key. In response to the computer industry and civil libertarians' fear that it would violate privacy rights, the Administration proposed the following measures to protect the public against misuse or abuse by the government:

> One of the two components of the key embedded in the chip would be kept with the Treasury Department and the other component with the Commerce Department's National Institute of Standards and Technology. Any law enforcement official wanting to wiretap would need to obtain not only a warrant but the separate components from two agencies. This, plus the super strong code and key system, would make it virtually impossible for anyone, even corrupt government officials, to spy illegally.[28]

Presently, law enforcement engages in eavesdropping, i.e., interception of telecommunication through electronic surveillance, by obtaining court authorization that includes stringent requirements for execution. In somewhat the same way, the FBI wants universal application and control of the Clipper Chip by the U.S. Government so that it will be able to intercept teleputing communications by organized crime. If criminal elements are allowed to have their own coding and decoding system, the agency contends that it would not be able to function effectively. Dorothy E. Denning, chair of computer science at Georgetown University and author of *Cryptography and Data Security*, said that "the constitution does not give us absolute privacy from court-ordered searches and seizures, and for good reason. Lawlessness would prevail."[29] The computer industry and civil libertarians believe that people should be free to use their own scrambling codes and that the Government's exclusive control of the Clipper Chip would be an invasion of privacy.

Such controversies will continue into the twenty-first century because of the basic dilemma involved, namely freedom vs. control. The key issues are crucial to the maintenance of our way of life and security. How can we balance the individual's rights to privacy with the government's need to know? When "technology as a productive force rolls on, while its contribution to social stability grows weaker" it may be worthwhile to consider the following paradoxes catalogued by the French sociologist, Jacques Ellul:

- All technical progress exacts a price; that is, while it adds something on the one hand, it subtracts something on the other.

- All technical progress raises more problems than it solves, tempts us to seek the consequent problems as technical in nature, and prods us to seek technical solutions to them.

- The negative effects of technological innovations are inseparable from the positive. It is naive to say that technology is neutral, that it may be used for good or bad ends; good and bad effects are, in fact, simultaneous and inseparable.
- All technological innovations have unforeseeable effects.[30]

THE HIGH TECH CRIMINAL

Who can be a high tech criminal? Anyone who participates in, or has access to an advanced technological society that, as we have seen, shapes the crime scene. Teleputing and surveillance equipment is user-friendly and available to anyone at a relatively modest cost. Therefore, assuming a high tech scene, anyone can be a criminal. Indeed, technology has democratized crime. August Bequai, attorney and author of several books on technological society, entitled a chapter, "Democratizing Crime: The Myth of the Supercriminal." He said that "even the amateur with access to a keyboard can do it." For example:

> Michele Cubbage, twenty-seven, was a housewife in Oxon Hill, Maryland. There was nothing unusual about her; she had no computer training. She learned from watching the television program "60 Minutes" how easy it was to steal by computer. And she did, taking People's Security Bank for more than $36,000.
>
> Until May 1983, Stanley Slyngstad worked for the Washington State Division of Vocational Rehabilitation. An unemployed friend of his needed money to buy a truck, and Stanley decided to help. He took more than $17,000 from his employer by programming the department's computer to issue twenty-five bogus checks to "people who were down on their luck." Stanley had never stolen a nickel before this; neither did he know what "computer crime was all about."
>
> Eryie Ann Edgerly, thirty-seven, and Jennie L. Barger, thirty-eight, were two inconspicuous Maryland housewives. Their neighbors were startled to learn that the two had been implicated in a $500,000 fraud involving a Washington, D.C., pension fund. They did it by filling out phony computer sheets, which listed Eryie as a beneficiary; the computer issued a total of 608 checks to her.
>
> In England a salesman for a chemical company defrauded his employer out of more than $100,000 by programming the computer to double his sales commissions. This was his first brush with the law.[31]

Despite the fact that, theoretically, all have an equal chance to engage in telecommunication and computer fraud, persons directly involved with computer functions on a daily basis, such as data entry operators, computer operators who control and monitor, programmers who test and maintain programs, system analysts who design and implement systems, and data base administrators who design and provide guidelines for use have greater and more frequent opportunities.

They are in a position to engage in internal computer crimes, employing covert instructions that alter the computer program, e.g. a Trojan Horse, Logic Bomb, Trap Door, or virus infection; they are able to access teleputing systems through phreaking, hacking, misuse of telephones, and use of illegal bulletin boards. They can undertake manipulative fraudulent acts, electronically without manual, paper pushing and a paper trail. Law enforcement needs more than a fingerprint on a keyboard to get a conviction. Indeed, computer button-pushing facilitates the creation of fictitious loans, insurance policies, membership lists, or addresses as well as the deletion or change of grades, inventory, or merchandise shipments.

Computers can assist criminals by providing data bases to support criminal enterprises, such as drug distribution, prostitution, pornography, and illegal gambling. Finally, theft of high tech equipment is a lucrative business, especially microchips, which are tiny and much more difficult to trace than paper money, coins, and drugs.

Applying a modus operandi based on advanced technology has given rise to a new vintage of criminals, such as techno-terrorists, software pirates, infobank blackmailers, and extortionists, and even those ingenious murderers by computer. Techno-terrorists' strategic global plans can be implemented through remotely controlled or time-delayed, high explosive detonations. Within our advanced technological age, their methods are beginning to shift from seizing radio and television stations to invading and attacking computer network systems and infobanks to bring about a serious social disruption.[32] Software piracy has become commonplace, and opportunities for blackmail and extortion, personal and international, multiply with the infobank explosions. Computer monitored life-saving hospital equipment is vulnerable to deadly reprogramming or deletions.

Hackers can be utilized in spy operations. In the following incident, hacking, but not espionage, was involved. The Belgian newspaper *De Standaard* reported that a man using a personal computer spent three months rummaging through the electronic mail and files on the Belgian Prime Minister and other Cabinet members. Apprehended, he showed reporters exactly how he broke into and "read the personal files of about ten government ministers" and gained access to the government's agenda.[33] While demonstrating his skills, he met up with and talked to another "burglar" via his computer. Although this crime did not become a serious international or even a national problem, deceptive access and illegal use of government information did become a crucial matter in the Aldrich Ames CIA spy case. Hackers can play a key role in spy operations as revealed in the Hannover Hacker case when unauthorized computer accessed information was sold to the former Soviet Union. The hacker may be the only distinctly new type of criminal. Be that as it may, the fact remains that this form of criminal behavior will only increase and play an ever more significant role in the crime scene as the technological developments advance.

TECHNOLOGY AND CRIMINAL JUSTICE MANAGEMENT

Advanced technology has transformed the crime scene, facilitating both crime commission and control. At the same time, criminal justice management has changed from reliance on manual, paper-based procedures to electronics. High tech teleputing assists by providing a fast, effective way of communicating through the bureaucratic quagmire and coordinating activities so that steps in the justice process occur in a more orderly manner.

Teleputing helps by saving wasted resources and by building public confidence in the administration of justice through more efficient case handling. Engulfed by its sheer number of cases, persons involved, and the complexity of the system, this bureaucracy can employ teleputing for working out solutions to some of its problems. Consider how it could be applied in the following situations:

1. A police officer appears in court on his day off, drawing overtime pay. The hearing is rescheduled, but he/she never received a notice.

2. A laboratory technician works long hours on a piece of evidence, but the case was dismissed and that person does not know about it.

3. A prosecuting attorney informs appropriate personnel that he/she will be out of town at a law seminar, but a case is scheduled for the prosecuting attorney on that day.

4. One municipal courtroom is jammed to capacity, while another down the hall is empty and not used because its caseload was disposed early due to many no-shows.

5. A justice professional tries to find a case folder, but it is not where it should be, and no one knows where it might be.

6. A probation officer spends an hour investigating a new probationer, only to discover later that all the information he or she gathered had been acquired previously by another agency.

7. A detainee whiles away many hours in a detention center because that unit did not receive notification that bail was paid. Furthermore, the detainee was not even guilty.

Teleputing, by electronically controlling events scheduling, task coordination, and task monitoring, can facilitate the resolution of such situations. In general, each event in the criminal justice system, e.g., an arraignment, has a number of tasks associated with it, such as a formal complaint. The arraignment cannot occur and the case moved on to the next event until the task of filing the complaint is accomplished. Computerized management makes it easier to complete these functions and their associated tasks. Teleputing has extensive applicability because the criminal justice system is complexified by innumerable other tasks requiring coordination, such as preparing investigation reports, serving subpoenas, and preparing for the hearing. Computerization of bureaucratic operations assists in the smooth running of any system.

Furthermore, telecommunication infobanks, discussed previously, employ computer crime mapping analysis to handle the huge volume of information generated in the investigative process. Electronically, clusters of criminal activity are located and graphically mapped in terms of such variables as time of occurrence, place, and type of crime. Moreover, through computer analysis trends are extrapolated and probable future events predicted. As a result, law enforcement's ability to properly identify and apprehend criminals improves, internal operations become more efficient, and, in general, the public benefits.

The following teleputing pilot program, New York City's I-Net (international network) project, illustrates high-tech application of video, voice, and data transmission in criminal justice management at the precinct level. Ross Daly, reporting for the *Newsday* Series, "Riding the Information Highway" describes an application of teleputing at the police precinct level.

Officer Tom Buckley sat down in front of the assistant district attorney, calmly reviewing the facts of a domestic assault the night before. The husband, Buckley told Phil O'Hene, had battered his wife with a baseball bat. The attorney and the cop reviewed the facts, O'Hene typed up a criminal complaint, and Buckley signed it.

Their meeting finished, Buckley stood up from the table in the 122nd Precinct station house in Staten Island. O'Hene stood, too—at the Targee Street Criminal Court, a 45-minute drive away. But Buckley didn't have to make that drive because he was using a video link-up between the precinct station house and the court.[34]

The dedicated, fiber optic, coaxial cable lines carry interactive pictures that allow participants to share each other's personal expressions and to make eye contact. As one officer said: "It's just like being there." Forty cities have brought forth suggestions for other applications and the city Department of Telecommunications and Energy will be outlining future uses of the network.

CONCLUSION

Technological society introduced the high tech crime scene and electronic criminal justice management. Teleputing—the convergence of telephone, television and computer—added a new dimension, cyberspace. Sophisticated surveillance technology surfaced an almost inexhaustible supply of public and private information. Stored like money in the bank, this intangible asset assists law enforcement in identifying, apprehending, processing, convicting, and punishing offenders. At the same time, computers house invaluable information assets that can become targets for criminal activities.

The critical issue in this cybernetic world is how to work out a fair, equitable balance between freedom and social control. Knowledge is a powerful tool in the hands of social controllers. The government as a social control agent needs to know. Therefore, it conducts a census. Payment for services provided requires taxation, which to be equitably applied, necessitates information gathering. The criminal justice system functions to ensure lawful exercise of power. Technology has enhanced the government's capacity to know and, as a result, its power lays at the expense of personal and collective freedoms and privacy. Adjusting to this dilemma is the challenge of the future.

Being a double-edged sword, technology provides the means for our becoming a more fully informed society in which individual members can exercise self-control and informally regulate their behavior in the interest of social harmony, thus offering the possibility of a "Computopian" society. On the other hand, advanced electronics also presents the potentiality for implementing an Orwellian Big Brother "global village." Jacques Ellul suggested a third most likely possibility, namely, that good and bad effects are inseparable. Hence, we may continue to experience both positive and negative effects simultaneously.

In general, the high-tech stage is set: 1) Cyberspace overlays a more powerfully explosive physical environment. 2) Teleputing provides abundant opportunities for mental wrongdoings as well as crime control. 3) Remotely controlled operations provide the cover of anonymity for the criminal as well as a means for more effective and efficient criminal justice management.

As actors on the stage we write the script, create social space, and design the beliefs, values, and standards by which we live. Fortunately, in this creative role we have the power to rearrange society to better meet our needs and express our values, always remembering that every action has intended and unintended consequences which may not always occur at the same time.

STUDY QUESTIONS

1. How can we achieve an equitable solution to the dilemma of the government's right to know and individual rights to privacy? How much does the government need to know about us?

2. Should individuals be free to use their own scrambling codes to protect their computer communications or should the government have exclusive control of encrypting devices?

3. A federal jury in San Jose, California is examining whether Mr. Zimmerman, the creator of an unbreakable encrypting code, Pretty Good Privacy, broke U.S. laws against exporting encryption codes. How can the fact be established that he put the codes on Internet, thereby making it available to terrorists around the world? If it is established that he did, should he face criminal charges?

4. In what specific ways has teleputing—the convergence of telephone, television, and computers—democratized crime?

5. How do you put a price tag on a fact or an idea obtained through unauthorized access of infobanks?

END NOTES

1. "Technology-Global Villager," *The Wall Street Journal Reports*, November 15, 1993, p. R12.

2. "Cyberpunk: Cover Story," *Time Magazine*, February 8, 1993, 59-65, p.60.

3. "The Love Connection," *Newsday*, November 7, 1993. p.3.

4. Ibid.

5. "Technology," *The Wall Street Journal Reports*, November 15, 1993, 1-27, p.R16.

6. Ibid.

7. Wilson P. Dizard, Jr., *The Coming Information Age*, 3rd ed. New York: Longman, 1989, p.1.

8. "The Decline of the Central Bankers," *The New York Times*, Forum, September 20, 1889.

9. Opus. Cit. "Technology," *The Wall Street Journal Reports*, p.R4.

10. Ibid.

11. Ibid.; also see "Riding the Information Highway," *Sunday Newsday, Special Reprint*, July 1993.

12. "Scientist As Detective," *Newsday*, February 21, 1994, p.14.

13. *Virtual Reality World*, Mecklermedia, 11 Ferry Lane West, Westport, CT. 06880.

14. Katie Hafner and John Markoff, *Cyberpunk: Outlaws and Hackers on the Computer Frontier* New York: Simon & Schuster, 1991, p. 141-249; also see: Cliff Stoll, *The Cuckoo's Egg* New York: Pocket Books, 1990.

15. Ibid. *Cyberpunk*, p. 186-187.

16. Ibid. p. 301-302.

17. "Computer Terrorism," *The National Times*, February 1993, 56-59, p.58.

18. "Hanging up on Hackers," *Crain's New York Business*, October 12, 1992, p. 21.

19. Donald P. Delaney, "Investigating Telecommunications Fraud" in *Criminal and Civil Investigation Handbook*. 2nd edition, Editor Joseph J. Grau, New York: McGraw-Hill, 1994, p. 35-5; also see: "Investigating Computer Crime" 34: 1-16.

20. "2 Charged in Big 'Clone' Scam," *Newsday*, February 17, 1993.

21. "Hacker Gets Logged into U.S. Prison," *Newsday*, November 4, 1993. p.6.

22. John F. Markey, "Money Laundering: An Investigative Perspective" in *Criminal and Civil Investigation*, 2nd edition, Editor Joseph J. Grau, New York: McGraw-Hill, 1994, 36: 1-16.

23. Raymond M. Pierce, "Criminal Investigative Analysis" in *Criminal and Civil Investigative Handbook*, 2nd Edition, Editor Joseph J. Grau, New York: McGraw-Hill, 1994, 28: 1-14.

24. "Is Nothing Private?" *Business Week*, September 4, 1989, 74-77. p. 74.

25. Ibid. p. 77.

26. Ben Jacobson, "Technological Advances and Investigations" in *Criminal and Civil Investigation Handbook*, 2nd edition, Editor Joseph J. Grau, New York: McGraw-Hill, p. 47: 1-12.

27. "White House Faces Backlash on Policy to Protect Private Telecommunications," *The Wall Street Journal*, February 7, 1994, p. B4.

28. Dorothy E. Denning, "The Clipper Chip will Block Crime," Viewpoints in *Newsday*, February 22, 1994, p. 35.

29. Ibid.

30. Jacques Ellul, "The Technological Order," *Technology and Culture* 3 (Fall 1962):394 as referenced and quoted by Wilson P. Dizard, Jr. in *The Coming Information Age*, p. 13.

31. August Bequai, Techno-Crimes Lexington, MA: Lexington Books, 1987, p. 49-50.

32. opus. cit. *The Coming Information Age*, p. 209.

33. "A Byte Back at Crime," *Newsday*, October 22, 1988, p. 8.

34. Ross Daly, "Taking a Byte Out of Crime," Newsday, Special Reprint July 1993, p. 16.

CHAPTER 18

ORGANIZATIONAL CHANGE AND WORKFORCE PLANNING

DILEMMAS FOR CRIMINAL JUSTICE ORGANIZATIONS FOR THE YEAR 2000

Rosemary L. Gido, Ph.D.

ABSTRACT

Workforce investment has become a major economic development theme in the 1990s. Fueled by complex demographic, economic and educational forces, the emerging workforce problem centers around a shortage of skilled workers—a trend that will affect the quality and quantity of the workforce into the twenty-first century. The criminal justice workplace of the future will face similar dilemmas to that of the private sector: managing an increasingly diverse workforce, affording opportunities to women; retaining and retraining seasoned and new employees; and embracing new organizational models which permit flexibility, employee participation, and proactive human resource strategies. This chapter addresses some of the existing organizational barriers and management and human resource practices that will inhibit criminal justice agencies from recruiting and retaining qualified personnel. It highlights emerging models of criminal justice organizational change that promote flexibility, employee participation and proactive human resource strategies—essential elements to a strategic criminal justice human resource plan for the year 2000.

INTRODUCTION

Workforce investment has become a major economic development theme in the 1990s. One reason for this emphasis is that the 1980s produced the greatest increase in income inequality since World War II. Economists report that U.S. men in the bottom fifth of the income distribution experienced nearly a 1% annual decline in hourly wages between 1979 and 1989. In contrast, men in the top fifth saw their hourly wages rise about 0.6% a year. While 35.5% of the poor moved into the middle class between 1967 and 1980, only 30.4% advanced to the middle class in the 1980s (Morin, 1991).

Such wage gap statistics are cited as evidence of the decline in the average American worker's standard of living. Fueled by complex demographic, economic, and educational forces, the emerging workforce problem centers around a shortage of skilled workers—a trend that will affect the quality and quantity of the workforce into the twenty-first century.

On the supply side, the annual rate of growth of the population and labor force is slowing. The pool of younger workers is more likely to come from minority or immigrant groups with lower levels of education and entry level work skills (Johnston, 1987). On the demand side, global economic competition and the shift to a predominantly service economy are pushing private and public sector employers to seek productivity gains in technology, work reorganization, and worker training/retraining (Task Force on the New York State Public Workforce in the 21st Century, 1989; Drucker, 1991).

The stagnation of earnings among the young and less educated raises even more critical long-term issues. High level jobs resulting from technological change in the workplace are not likely to go to those most disadvantaged by lack of education, discrimination, or language barrier. To what degree will such patterns of uneven economic growth and opportunity and change in the structure of jobs erode communities and increase the risks of crime and violence (Currie, 1987)? Will national policy priorities for the year 2000 emphasize job creation and training/retraining for disadvantaged and displaced workers? Will our nation continue to rely on expansion of the criminal justice system as a response to those displaced from the labor market who turn to crime?

The answer to these questions lies in the development and implementation of long-term, proactive national employment and worker training policies. The degree to which there is public commitment to these labor market strategies will directly affect the role of the criminal justice system in the twenty-first century. At the same time, the criminal justice workplace will face similar dilemmas to that of the private sector: managing an increasingly diverse workforce; affording opportunities to women; retaining and retraining seasoned and new employees; and embracing new organizational models which permit flexibility, employee participation, and proactive human resource strategies.

This chapter reviews the current "state of the art" on work force issues for the year 2000. First, it reviews several major work force studies on the changing composition of the workforce and the impact of these workforce changes on the criminal justice workplace. Second, it delineates some of the existing organizational barriers/management and personnel practices that will inhibit criminal justice agencies from recruiting and retaining qualified personnel. And finally, it highlights emerging models of criminal justice organizational change that support flexibility, employee participation, and proactive human resource strategies—essential elements to a strategic criminal justice human resource plan for the year 2000.

WORKFORCE ISSUES FOR THE YEAR 2000

Changes in America's Workforce Composition

Over the last ten years, an increasing number of studies has emerged regarding the skills gap in the American workforce and the growing concern of private and public employers to fill this gap. The first labor force analysis to gain national attention was *Workforce 2000*, published in 1987 (Johnston, 1987). *Workforce 2000* focused on the

changing composition of the workforce and the demographic, economic, and educational trends that will exacerbate the skills deficit of U.S. workers into the next century.
Among the major trends the report identified include:

> The rate of growth of the U.S. workforce is declining.
>
> The U.S. population and the workforce is aging while the numbers of
> "replacement youth" in the labor pool is declining. The twenty-five to fifty-
> four-year-old age group will represent an increasing percentage of the labor
> force, growing from 61% in 1975 to 73% in 1995. Between 1984 and 1996,
> 21.6 million workers aged twenty-five to fifty-four will come into the labor
> market, while employees aged sixteen to twenty-four will decline by 2.7
> million. Workers fifty-five and over will decline by .8 million.
>
> The jobs that are being created for the year 2000 will require a higher
> caliber of worker.
>
> The shift from a manufacturing to service-based economy will change
> the type of job skills in demand. New job creation will be concentrated in
> occupations emphasizing literacy, problem-solving, communication, and
> analysis skills. New technology will further restructure the nature of work
> and job skill requirements.
>
> New workforce entrants will not match the requirements of emerging
> high level professional and technological occupations.
>
> Women will comprise about three-fifths of new entrants into the labor
> force between 1990 and 2000. Blacks, Hispanics, and other minorities will
> comprise about 57% of labor force expansion for this decade. Two-thirds
> or more of immigrants of working age will also join the job force.
> However, the economy's emphasis on higher-skill occupations will disad-
> vantage women and minorities who will be overrepresented in shrinking
> "low tech" and entry-level job categories and underrepresented in "high
> tech" positions.

These dramatic predictions signaled the end of an era of "workforce homogeneity,
high skill levels, and big labor pools" (Schuler, 1989:258). And as the "economic
boom" of the Reagan-era 1980s declined, there was growing recognition of deep
"structural" problems in the American economy. These problems include lagging productivity, a rising budget deficit, and strong foreign market competition (Congress of
the United States, 1990).

With the continuing effects of the recession came a flood of studies which
were more policy focused than *Workforce 2000* (U.S. Departments of Labor,
Education, and Commerce, 1988; U.S. Department of Labor, 1989; Jasinowski,
1990). Two major themes for attacking America's skills gap predominated: the
restructuring of the U.S. education system and long-term investment in worker
development.

America's Choice, High Skills or Low Wages, published in 1990 by the National
Center on Education and the Economy, called for reorganizing the workplace through
worker training and retraining. It was highly critical of current U.S. employers and
their failure to invest in employee development. For example, it found that 95% of
U.S. employers continue to rely on outmoded, low performance, low productivity
forms of work organization which require no upgrading of worker skills. *America's
Choice* prescribed a national program to improve our schools, reorganize work, and
invest in "frontline" worker training.

Echoing similar themes of work reorganization and training investment, *The Myth of the Coming Labor Shortage*, released by the Economic Policy Institute in 1991 (Mishel and Teixeira, 1991) summed up what U.S. labor market priorities must be for the year 2000:

> The key lies in improving the skills of the workforce as a whole, both workforce entrants (including minority entrants) and those already in the workforce.... In this sense, broad upgrading of worker skills, coupled with policies that encourage employers to utilize a more highly skilled, more empowered workforce, can become a constituent part of a policy mix favoring a "high skill path" for the U.S. economy as a whole (Mishel and Teixeira, p. 41)

Workforce Retrenchment and Re-engineering

The economic recession of the last five years has largely precluded a comprehensive national program for worker development as envisioned in these studies. Without the "big engines" of manufacturing companies to create new jobs and ensure long-term economic growth, the U.S. private sector has responded to the economic slowdown with widespread employee layoffs. White collar workers from Fortune 500 companies like IBM and General Motors have joined the ranks of unemployed blue collar workers as consumer product demand has declined. National, state, and local government budget deficits have also caused government workforce reduction and retrenchment (Levine, 1984).

Beyond the use of such short-term "downsizing," public and private sector employers have begun to realize productivity gains through organizational restructuring and work re-engineering (Osborne and Gaebler, 1992; Martin, 1993). Such organizational innovation calls for a radical departure from traditional bureaucratic, hierarchical forms of authority structure (Tull and Bukiewicz, 1991). Instead, the workplace is "re-engineered" to include work teams, the "cross training" of employees in multiple skills, and the empowerment of workers to make decisions and take responsibility for quality and productivity (Kochan, et al., 1989; Ban and Riccucci, 1991).

Recent studies indicate that re-engineering, particularly through the application of technology, is producing productivity gains and improved services in both the public and private workplace (Ehrbar, 1993; Martin, 1993). While this improvement is a proactive response to the skills gap, the downside is that re-engineering is eliminating jobs, as more output can be gained with fewer workers. It is estimated that as many as 2.5 million jobs could be done away with each year, primarily among service industry clerical, supervisory, and middle management staff and manufacturing support workers (Ehrbar, 1993).

Twenty-First Century Workforce Trends: Personnel Dilemmas for Criminal Justice Organizations

The workforce trends outlined above will present significant personnel-related dilemmas for criminal justice administrators in the future. Specifically:

- The creation of higher paying, higher skill jobs in the private sector will make it more difficult to attract such talent to the traditional criminal justice work environment. The smaller size of the labor pool will increase competition for such qualified workers, driving up salaries that will be impossible to match by police and corrections agencies.

- The remaining worker pool will be largely semi-skilled and unskilled. Even more qualified workers displaced by re-engineering may not be available to the criminal justice workplace, as they are likely to be quickly absorbed by the private sector, given the smaller labor pool. As entry level jobs decline and re-engineering or slow economic growth stall new job creation, will the criminal justice system have to recruit from a less qualified labor pool?

- The "aging" of the current workforce will result in the retirement of the most experienced criminal justice staff and administrators. Given increased public concerns about police use of force, public safety, and prison overcrowding, will younger, inexperienced police and corrections officers be up to the task (Wilson, 1992)? Will continued government budget deficits preclude adequate training of these new recruits? To what degree will such trends increase liability actions against criminal justice organizations?

- Women, minorities, and immigrants represent a potential resource for recruitment to the criminal justice workplace. Women are now more likely than men to graduate from high school and complete college (Mishel and Teixeira, 1991). Will criminal justice administrators attract these groups through gender-, racial-, and ethnic-sensitive human resource policies? Will the entrance of greater numbers of diverse workers eradicate remaining vestiges of race and gender discrimination (Maghan, 1992; Hale and Wyland, 1993)?

- The implementation of organizational innovations which flatten the organization and encourage employee participation is "catching on" in today's workplace. To what degree will such criminal justice innovations as community policing and unit management go forward if more qualified employees cannot be attracted and retained? Similar to the private sector, will re-engineering and technology be introduced into the criminal justice workplace to enhance productivity with fewer workers?

- The Clinton administration is currently recommending to Congress a long-term proactive national education and worker training improvement program (Celis, 1993). Will such "school-to-work" programs for students not headed to college include training for criminal justice occupations?

The effects these trends will have on the criminal justice work environment of the future are directly related to present criminal justice management and personnel practices. It is clear that criminal justice agencies need to currently address both organizational structures and human resource policies that are resistant to internal and external change. These structural and cultural barriers are obstacles to the development of proactive human resource policies, flexible organizational models, and employee decision-making—all essential elements to survival in the workplace of the future.

BARRIERS TO CRIMINAL JUSTICE ORGANIZATIONAL CHANGE

Retrenchment and Declining Resources

Foremost among the impediments to change across criminal justice agencies is the reactive nature of the "criminal justice business." Unlike private sector employers, the public sector serves the public, and public safety dictates often preclude long-term fiscal and personnel training. In recent years, the unabated growth in criminal violence stemming from illicit drugs and the increasing reliance on incarceration as a criminal justice response have created a shortage of resources directed to public safety and the support of correctional institutions at all levels (Currie, 1987). Funding has been directed at building more prisons but little has been allocated for employee development. Local criminal justice networks, in particular, have experienced problems as city and county budgets spiral downward with eroding local tax bases and declining federal government support.

A 1987 national survey asked 2,500 police chiefs, sheriffs, jail administrators, prosecutors, chief judges, and probation/parole agency chiefs to rank the most serious problems in the criminal justice system (Guynes, 1988). It is not surprising that resource shortages and personnel issues were at the top of the list—jail crowding, staff shortages, and prison crowding. Low salaries and the low image of jail work were cited as the most serious recruitment and retention problems at the local level. Sixty to 75% of the respondents cited a range of training needs, from managing stress, handling special need inmates, crisis intervention, civil liability, and interpersonal communication.

Given that in government settings, there is more reliance on "decrementalism," uncoordinated, short-term, incremental and piecemeal problem solving methods (Levine, 1984), it is difficult to move "overnight" from public sector retrenchment to work force planning (New York State Department of Civil Service, 1990).

Organization Inertia

Organizational inertia is often cited as the enemy of change and innovation. Recent analyses of criminal justice organizational culture underscore the intractability of its hierarchical, paramilitary structures and conservative values and practices (Menke et al., 1990).

The extent to which policing has changed in America has been the topic of recent assessments, given the increased visibility of problem-oriented and community policing. Mastrofski (1990) has done a comprehensive review of change in police patrol practices over the last ten years. While he acknowledges that American police are "becoming more susceptible to broader forces of purposive change" (Mastrofski, 1990:2), he believes "patrol officers of today can be expected to do their work by and large as they did a decade ago and as they will do a decade hence" (Mastrofski, 1990:62). This reinforces the notion that the police "command and control" bureaucracy survives because it protects the organization from outside forces which threaten established police "routines." (Mastrofski, 1990:2). In light of the riots following the Rodney King incident in Los Angeles, there is renewed public attention on the failure of police "to respond creatively to changing social problems, changing race relations, and changing public expectations" (Walker, p. 359, 1992).

The transformation of the rank and file reactive style of policing and corrections to a proactive professional model will require revolutionary changes to the structures which support the hierarchical system. This transformation would include revising the basic rank system, substituting nonmilitary titles for selected personnel grades and decreasing the number of authority levels (Meese, 1993:2). As innovative unit management and strategic policing models have primarily been introduced and supported by "enlightened administrators," the inability to recruit a "different type" of officer is a significant impediment to long-term institutional change.

Gender and Racial Barriers

Current assessments of the status of women and minorities in police work indicate that most of the "blatant" discrimination practices have been eliminated (Martin, 1989; Sullivan, 1989). There are, however, still major obstacles in the formal and informal structures of police work organizations related to gender and race (Martin, 1992:302; Sullivan, 1989).

Hale and Wyland (1993), for example, find that in spite of evaluation studies which indicate that women are successful as patrol officers, the organizational culture of policing has resisted women's integration into this role over the last twenty years. They cite three types of organizational resistance as blocking the recruitment and retention of female patrol officers. Technical resistance includes both the failure to adequately adapt police uniforms and equipment for women, as well as the continued emphasis on physical testing and firearms during training. Political and cultural resistance is evidenced in the failure to develop child care programs, flexible and gender neutral shifts, and maternity/paternity policies (Hale and Wyland, 1993:5).

Zupan (1992) has also documented cultural and structural roadblocks to women correctional officers in all-male prisons. Tokenism, differential treatment and discrimination by first-line officers in the assignment of women officers, and the continued opposition to women by male co-workers still exist.

While some researchers have noted the dramatic effects on police agencies of the assimilation of African-Americans and other minorities into the police (Maghan, 1992), the recruitment and promotion of minority police officers is still at issue. Continued reliance on written examinations and the negative image of policing as an occupation for people of color hinder recruitment efforts. The underrepresentation of minority officers above the patrol level as well as lack of access to informal "white power networks" within and outside police departments represent obstacles to promotion (Sullivan, 1989:342-43).

In spite of these major obstacles to organizational change and overcoming the very dilemmas that will challenge the work organization of the year 2000, there are some positive "models of change" that have been developed and implemented in criminal justice agencies of today. These innovations represent the basic change agents that will enable criminal justice organizations to become more flexible, respond to employee needs and attract and retain qualified personnel.

EMERGING MODELS OF CRIMINAL JUSTICE ORGANIZATION CHANGE

Police Models

Despite the intransigence of policing resistance to change, problem-oriented and community policing hold out the best hope for institutional change. While there is not sufficient data to assess the degree of dissemination of the proactive policing model, police departments in large and small cities are experimenting with the model. Some experts locate the chances of long-term success for strategic policing in the qualitative changes which are taking place in police recruitment and training.

Bittner (1990) acknowledges that a college degree is a key factor in police officer candidates who will be successful in proactive policing. As there may be significant competition for college graduates for other occupational fields, the essential element for change must take place within training academies. These graduates are a cadre of young officers who have the potential to change existing departments, particularly as senior officers who have maintained the "old ways" are leaving in record numbers (Wilson, 1992).

There is evidence of significant curriculum revamping at the training academy level. Dr. Elsie Scott has become the first black female deputy commissioner for training of the New York City Police Department. She is overhauling the police academy curriculum to "reschool" 29,000 rank and file officers in community policing. The goal is to integrate community policing training into every course and to support more in-service training (Wolff, 1992).

On the national level, the Executive Session on Policing has been formed to support and disseminate knowledge on community policing. Sponsored by the National Institute of Justice and the John F. Kennedy School of Government at Harvard University, the Session brings together scholars, police chiefs and mayors to discuss community policing and new state-of-the-art management tools to support innovative policing. Clearly, more research is needed to document the implementation of participative management structures into police agencies.

For example, Gray et al. (1990) studied the Washington State Highway Patrol TEAMS Program, a participatory management program that evolved out of efforts to implement productivity enhancements in police patrols in the early 1980s. This case study illustrates the importance of a number of factors in introducing change into police organizational structure:

1. The role of leadership—the commitment of the police chief to a participatory management philosophy and implementation.

2. The need for continuous, long-term training in participatory management and team-building with application of training to actual problems for all levels of the organization.

3. The evolution of "verteams" (vertical teams) to facilitate information exchange and monitor the process, as well as make policy recommendations.

Such evaluation studies are essential for assessing the "transferability" of models across police organizational settings and tracking such issues as the degree to which such models become "permanent" or whether they survive retrenchment.

Correctional Models

The New Generation Direct Supervision model of correctional facility operation represents the most promising criminal justice model of organizational effectiveness as outlined in this chapter.

First introduced in 1974 by the Federal Prison System and since replicated at the local jail level, modular, direct supervision facilities are designed to maximize direct staff supervision of inmates. Each unit is typically staffed by one officer who controls forty to fifty inmates. Compared to indirect models where reactive "guarding" is the norm, the direct supervision model is built on a proactive management philosophy that seeks to shape and reinforce positive inmate behavior (National Institute of Corrections, 1991).

As the work of Zupan (1991) and Menke et al. (1990) illustrate, the success of direct supervision jails depends on the explicit linkage of this proactive management style to both architectural design and personnel practices. In direct supervision facilities, personnel, not technology, is the critical investment. Recruitment and training emphasize staff communication skills; the management style is one of team work and facilitation.

Similar to problem-oriented policing, direct supervision organizational models and human resources strategies point the way to the future of criminal justice agencies. If criminal justice organizations are to move forward into the twenty-first century, transformational leaders must move boldly to change inflexible cultures and practices. Critical to moving from a reactive societal institution to a catalyst for change, criminal justice must begin now to recruit and retain the men and women who will ensure a quality and human workplace for the year 2000.

STUDY QUESTIONS

1. What are the major demographic, economic, and educational trends that will result in a "skills gap" in the American workforce of the future?

2. How will social workforce trends affect the quantity and quality of the workforce available to criminal justice organizations?

3. Give specific examples of "inertia" in policing organizations. What are the "roots" of this tendency to resist change?

4. Give examples of current workplace barrier that still exist for minorities and women.

5. Discuss emerging changes in police organization and training which are challenging the barriers to workforce quality and organizational flexibility.

REFERENCES

Ban, C. and N.M. Riccucci. (1990). *Personnel Systems, Labor Relations, and Government Performance*. Prepared for the National Commission on the State and Local Public Service. Albany, NY: State University of New York Graduate School of Public Affairs.

Bittner, Egon. (1990). "Some Reflections on Staffing Problem-Oriented Policing." *American Journal of Police* 9, 3:189-196.

Bureau of Justice Statistics. (1992). *National Update* 1, 3 (January): 1-11. Washington, DC.

Celis, W. (April 22, 1993). "Administration Offers Plan for Better Schools." *The New York Times*: A20.

Congress of the United States, Office of Technology Assessment. (1990). *Worker Training: Competing in the New International Economy (Summary)*. Washington, DC.

Currie, Elliott. (1987). "What Kind of Future? Violence and Public Safety in the Year 2000." San Francisco, CA: National Council on Crime and Delinquency.

Currie, Elliott. (1989). "Confronting Crime: Looking Toward the Twenty-first Century." *Justice Quarterly* 6, 1 (March): 5-25.

Director, S.M. (1985). *Strategic Planning for Human Resources*. New York: Work in America Institute Studies in Productivity.

Drucker, P.F. (1991). "The New Productivity Challenge." *Harvard Business Review* 69, 6 (November-December): 69-79.

Ehrbar, A. (March 16, 1993). "Re-Engineering Gives Firms New Efficiency, Workers the Pink Slip,: *The Wall Street Journal*: A1, A11.

Goldstein, H. (1979). "Improving Policing: A Problem Oriented Approach." *Crime and Delinquency* 25, 2:236-258.

Gray, K., Stohr-Gillmore, M.K. and N.P. Lovrich. (1990). "Adapting Participatory Management for a Paramilitary Organization: The Implementation of TEAMS in the Washington State Patrol (manuscript).

Guynes, R. (1988). "National Jail Managers Assess Their Problems." *Research in Action*. Washington, DC: National Institute of Justice.

Hale, D.C. and S. M. Wyland. (1993). "Dragons and Dinosaurs: The Plight of Patrol Women." *Police Forum* 3(2):1-6.

Jasinowski, J.J. (1990). *America's Work Force in the 1990's: Trends Affecting Manufacturers*. Washington, DC: National Association of Manufacturers.

Johnston, W. (1987). *Workforce 2000*. Prepared for the U.S. Department of Labor. Indianapolis, IN: Hudson Institute.

Johnston, W. and A. Packer. (1988). *Civil Service 2000*. Prepared for the U.S. Office of Personnel Management. Indianapolis, IN: Hudson Institute.

Kantor, R.M. (1989). *When Giants Learn to Dance*. New York: Simon and Schuster.

Kennedy, D. (1993). "The Strategic Management of Police Resources." *NIJ Perspectives on Policing*. Washington, DC: U.S. Department of Justice.

Kochan, T., Cutcher-Gershenfeld, J. and J.P. MacDuffie. (1989). *Employee Participation, Work Redesign and New Technology: Implications for Public Policy in the 1990s*. Prepared for the Commission on Workforce Quality and Labor Market Efficiency. Washington, DC: U.S. Department of Labor.

Levine, C.H. (1984). "Retrenchment, Human Resource Erosion, and the Role of the Personnel Manager." *Public Personnel Management Journal* 13,3:249-263.

Maghan, J. (1992). "Black Police Officer Recruits: Aspects of Becoming Blue." *Police Forum* 2,1 (January): 8-11.

Martin, J. (March, 1993). "Re-Engineering Government." *Governing*: 27-30.

Martin, S. (1989). "Female Officers on the Move? A Status Report on Women in Policing." in R.G. Dunham and G.P. Alpert (eds.) *Critical Issues in Policing*. Prospect Heights, IL: Waveland Press.

Martin, S. (1992). "The Changing Status of Women Officers, Gender and Power in Police Work." in I. Moyer (ed.) *The Changing Roles of Women in the Criminal Justice System*. 2nd Edition. Prospect Heights, IL: Waveland Press.

Mastrofski, S.D. (1990). "The Prospects of Change in Police Patrol: A Decade in Review." *American Journal of Police* 9,3:1-79.

Mease, E. (1993). "Community Policing and the Police Officer." *NIJ Perspectives on Policing*. Washington, DC: U.S. Department of Justice.

Menke, B.A., Zupan, L., Stohr-Gilmore, M.K., and N.P. Lovrich. (1990). "Human Resource Development: An Agenda for Jail Research." Paper presented at the National Institute of Corrections Conference: "Setting the Jail Research Agenda for the 1990s," Denver, CO, September 1990.

Miller, R., Sexton, G.E. and V.J. Jacobsen. (1991). "Making Jails Productive." *Research in Brief*. Washington, DC: National Institute of Justice.

Mishel, L. and R.A. Teixeira. (1991). *The Myth of the Coming Labor Shortage: Jobs, Skills and Incomes of America's Workforce 2000*. Washington, DC: Economic Policy Institute.

Morin, R. (1991). "America's Middle-Class Meltdown." *The Washington Post* (December 1, 1991), C2+.

National Center on Education and the Economy. (1990). *America's Choice: High Skills or Low Wages: The Report of the Commission on the Skills of the American Workforce*. Rochester, NY.

National Institute of Corrections. (1991). *Popular, Direct Supervision Jails*. Boulder, CO.

New York State Department of Civil Service. (1990). *New York State Work Force Plan 1990: Building the State Work Force in the 1990s*. Albany, NY.

Osborne, D. and Gaebler, T. (1992). *Reinventing Government: How the Entrepreneurial Spirit is Transforming Government*. New York: Addison-Wesley Publishing Co.

Peters, T. (1987). *Thriving on Chaos: A Handbook for a Management Revolution*. New York: Jossey-Bass.

Schuler, R. (1989). "Scanning the Environment: Planning for Human Resource Management and Organizational Change." *Human Resource Planning* 12,4:157-276.

Sparrow, M.K. (1993). "Information Systems and the Development of Policing." *NIJ Perspectives on Policing*. Washington, DC: U.S. Department of Justice.

Task Force on the New York State Public Workforce in the 21st Century. (1989). *Public Service Through the State Government Workforce: Meeting the Challenge of Change*. Albany, NY.

Tull, M.R. and J. Bukiewicz. (1991). "Manager/Staff Partnerships: A Strategy for Leading Organizations in the 90s." *HR Horizons*, Summer: 7-12.

U.S. Department of Labor. Commission on Workforce Quality and Labor Market Efficiency. (1989). *Investing in People: A Strategy to Address America's Workforce Crisis*. Washington, D.C.

U.S. Departments of Labor, Education and Commerce. (1988). *Building a Quality Workforce*. Washington, DC.

Walker, S. (1992). *The Police in America*, 2nd Edition, New York:McGraw-Hill, Inc.

Wilson, J. (March 15, 1992). "D.C.'s Other Crime Crisis: Our Vanishing Veteran Cops." *The Washington Post*: C1, C4.

Wolff, C. (October 8, 1992). "To Teach New Policing, A New Kind of Teacher." *The New York Times*: B5.

Zupan, L. (1992). "The Progress of Women Correctional Officers in All-Male Prisons." in I. Moyer (Ed.) *The Changing Roles of Women in the Criminal Justice System*. Prospect Heights, IL: Waveland Press.

Zupan, L. (1991). *Jails: Reform and the New Generation Philosophy*. Cincinnati: Anderson Publishing.

CHAPTER 19

PROSECUTING ENVIRONMENTAL CRIME IN THE TWENTY-FIRST CENTURY

Donald J. Rebovich, Ph.D.

ABSTRACT

This chapter on environmental crime prosecuting in the twenty-first century traces environmental crime prosecution from its early days in the 1970s at the federal level, through the 1980s when state attorneys general office proceeded to initiate environmental crime prosecutions at growing levels, to the present where many of the prosecution responsibilities have shifted into the hands of district attorneys and county prosecutors. Based upon these trends—and recent empirical research—projections are furnished that characterize environmental prosecutions of the future.

Part of the discussion on environmental prosecution in the future centers on the building pressure of the public to demand criminal punishment of offenders and protection from the results of their criminal activities and the manner in which prosecutors will likely respond to such pressure. Recent role expansions of local district attorneys are emphasized as the wave of the future for environmental prosecution. The chapter concludes with discussion of a future research agenda in this area.

INTRODUCTION

The process of criminalization of human behavior judged to be harmful to the public is typically one that builds slowly in common law jurisdictions. Momentum gained through problem identification and pressures exerted by special interest groups can easily span decades before undesirable actions are classified as "crime" through legislative enactment. A rare exception to this phenomenon is the relatively speedy transformation of acts of pollution into official *crimes against the environment*. National media coverage of toxic tragedies like those occurring at Love Canal, New York in the late 1970s and at Times Beach, Missouri in the early 1980s altered forever the American public's perception of the improper disposal of hazardous waste and sparked the quick passing of criminal laws on both federal and state legislative levels prohibiting offenses against the environment.

Entrusted with implementing these new laws is a growing army of prosecutors specializing in environmental crime prosecution that will assume broad responsibilities for the control of environmental crime as we enter the twenty-first century. Once found exclusively within the U.S. Department of Justice, environmental crime prosecutors now populate many state attorney general offices, as well as the offices of local district attorneys in urban/metropolitan jurisdictions. This chapter examines the problems that these prosecutors will face, the future implications of recent environmental studies of local, state, and federal environmental crime prosecutions, and how certain key factors can be expected to affect the prosecution of environmental crime in the future. These factors include recent changes in standards for the admissibility of scientific evidence into the courtroom, an enhanced public awareness of the dangers of environmental crime, the growing acceptance of the crime problem as an equity issue, and criminal displacement caused by tougher enforcement. The article also projects improvements in the effectiveness of environmental crime prosecution brought about by the widened availability of specialized training and greater experimentation with new technology and prosecution strategies. Concluding the piece is an agenda for prospective research that can serve to complement the work of criminal prosecutors in the forefront of this rapidly evolving crime area.

A NEW CRIMINAL ROLE: THE LOCAL ENVIRONMENTAL PROSECUTOR

Gradually, and without abatement, "grass roots" movements have helped elevate the issue of environmental protection to a serious matter of community safety that, increasingly, is being seen by *local* police officials as an important obligation (Bullard, 1991). Community leaders, and the public they represent, are turning to their elected crime control leaders—local prosecutors—for the type of protection they have come to expect from these officials on more traditional predatory crimes. In response to this groundswell, district attorneys, particularly in densely populated jurisdictions, are preparing their personnel to confront the mammoth task of solving and prosecuting these crimes locally, rather than passing them up to federal or state agencies, a common practice in the past (Metz, 1985). Through this direct involvement, local prosecutors are seizing the opportunity to demonstrate their level of concern for constituents' well being, rather than deferring enforcement responsibilities to other government agencies through claims of lack of ability or expertise (Meehan, 1991).

State and federal agencies traditionally responsible for the enforcement of environmental laws have been characterized by some in the early 1990s as isolated, specialized, and only mildly empathetic to local issues (Murphy, 1991). Lack of involvement of state/federal environmental enforcement agencies in local issues has tended to further their isolation from other public safety functions of local government. As we move toward the twenty-first century, local prosecutors are filling this vacuum by bringing to this area an integration of environmental prosecutions into the routine function of law enforcement at the local level. Counteracting what some have called the Federal "boutique" approach to environmental crime enforcement, this response by local prosecutors symbolizes their sensitivity to a crime problem too long overlooked (Jensen, 1991).

As seen by the Environmental Protection Agency (EPA) in its *Enforcement in the 1990s Project Report*, greater district attorney involvement in criminal prosecutions would provide a faster response to environmental crimes, reducing environmental risk or damage. Prosecution by district attorneys is also expected to deter criminal behavior within a class of violators too numerous for EPA and the states to reach. In addition, operations can be tailored to indigenous community conditions to meet community needs and cooperative relationships can be built among local, state, and federal agents to form task forces necessary to investigate and prosecute environmental crimes efficiently and effectively (Herrod, et al., 1991).

BARRIERS TO EFFECTIVE ENVIRONMENTAL PROSECUTION: WHAT IS CURRENTLY KNOWN

In spite of recent gains made in the investigation of environmental offenses (Hawke, 1987; Metz, 1985), hurdles to achieving consistency in environmental prosecution success remain. The most frequently expressed prosecution-related problems, as reported through a 1988 prosecutors' survey, dealt with difficulties in juror and judicial interpretation of complex criminal laws and regulations (Rebovich, 1992). Ohio, Pennsylvania, Vermont, and Virginia were states that found this complexity to be particularly troublesome. In these states, juror and judicial uncertainty of interpretation of relevant laws and regulations was thought to jeopardize the attainment of guilty verdicts. Even cases resulting in convictions, prosecutors in Virginia claimed that time spent on the courtroom clarification of the statutes resulted in substantial processing time delays. There have been some indications that local prosecutors have avoided the prosecution of clearly criminal environmental violations out of fear of losing the cases because of such cases' highly technical nature.

Since 1992, three separate publications were produced that furnish valuable, new insight into characteristics of environmental crime and its prosecution. A fourth work, unpublished at the time of this printing, presents results of a national survey that can help us in taking a peek at what is in store for all with regard to environmental crime/crime control.

Dangerous Ground: The World of Hazardous Waste Crime (Rebovich, 1992) laid out the results of a study of hazardous waste crime in the northeastern U.S. between 1977 and 1985, and efforts to stem its growth on the state enforcement/prosecution level. While state criminal enforcement/prosecution agencies studied were found to be dedicated and responsible for major inroads into environmental crime, they were also found to be routinely undercut by failures of state regulatory agencies and by a paucity of resources to adequately address all environmental crime reported. The book warns of the potential of amendments to the Resource Conservation and Recovery Act (Pub. L. No. 98-616, 1984, U.S.C., 6901-6987, 1982) in widening the defining parameters of environmental crime and, in turn, widening the population of those subject to criminal prosecution.[1]

M. Cohen, in *Environmental Crime and Punishment: Legal/Economic Theory and Empirical Evidence on Enforcement of Federal Environmental Statutes* (1992), presented empirical information on 703 environmental crime prosecutions on the *federal* level by the Department of Justice's Environmental Crimes Section between 1983-1990.

---

[1] A host of heretofore unregulated industry procedures related to hazardous waste generation are now regulated under the 1984 amendments. Most significant is the amendment regarding small waste generators. Section 221 lowers the cut-off volume level of those previously exempt because of low levels of waste generation.

Cohen's analysis found that the average firm changed with environmental crime on the federal level is larger than the average firm charged with nonenvironmental federal crimes. Cohen further projects the growth of the proportion of large companies charged with federal environmental crimes based on his assertion of a trend toward criminalizing and prosecuting regulatory noncompliance and street liability offenses on the federal level.

Hammett and Epstein's NIJ-supported *Local Prosecution of Environmental Crime* (1993) shifts the focus of environmental crime control to the local government level in the presentation of its results of case studies of five local prosecutors' offices. The report portrays some progressive local prosecutors' offices as vigorously taking on the challenge of controlling environmental crime and dispelling the myth that these cases are inherently too complex and expensive for district attorneys to handle. Environmental crime is presented as varying in its makeup from locality to locality with local prosecutors and police departments representing agencies appropriately attuned to local community needs, but heretofore underused in the fight against environmental crime.

The most recent empirical study of environmental prosecution was a NIJ-supported national assessment of the abilities and needs of environmental prosecutors on the local government level: district attorneys (American Prosecutors Research Institute, 1994). The study found that over 75% of one hundred urban prosecutors' offices surveyed have prosecutors assigned specifically to environmental crime cases with half of the offices operating special environmental prosecution units. According to the study, between January of 1990 and June of 1992 the volume of environmental cases prosecuted by the prosecutors more than doubled (i.e., 667 to 1352). Community pressure to criminally prosecute environmental offenses was perceived by the majority of respondents as far outweighing pressures applied by the business community to withhold prosecutions. The access to and use of technical experts in environmental crime cases were considered to be of extraordinary value to prosecutors' decision-making in charging, and to their effectiveness at trial[2]. To improve their effectiveness, respondents were almost unanimous in their expression of need for increased technical assistance and specialized training.

Synthesized along with qualitative case study data, the study results illustrate how district attorneys have been compelled to assume greater responsibility for controlling environmental crime and have gravitated toward specializing professional personnel in this crime area. But the data also show that local prosecutors have struggled to keep pace with the demand for technical assistance and education to achieve and sustain a competitive edge over their defense adversaries. Further, results appear to reveal that local prosecutors have yet to observe convincing evidence of acceptable levels of sensitivity to the criminal nature of environmental offenses by their system counterparts: police and judges.

---

[2]More than 75% of those environmental prosecutors responding to the survey believed these utilities of technical experts (e.g., expert witnesses on properties of wastes disposed) to be important. Supplemental qualitative data indicated that defense knowledge of the technical capacity of prosecutors strengthened the environmental prosecutor's position during plea negotiations and during trial, and the use of technical expert testimony strengthened evidence credibility in the eyes of jurors.

FACTORS AFFECTING ENVIRONMENTAL PROSECUTION IN THE FUTURE

Based upon our knowledge of environmental crime, its prosecution and the needs of environmental prosecutors, it is apparent that the future offers many new challenges for those prosecuting environmental crime. There are several key areas, however, that warrant special attention. They are areas in which patterns of change should have noticeable impact on the manner in which environmental crime is prosecuted in the future and the level of its effectiveness. These areas include changes in public and system sentiment toward environmental crime, particularly with regard to punishment, growing dissent in low income areas about environmental crime control, and the spillover of environmental crime to suburban and rural districts. Of a more technical nature, changes in evidence admissibility standards, in education for improvement of prosecutorial skills, and in the testing of new technologies/strategies will likely influence the state of environmental crime prosecution in the twenty-first century. The following is a projection of what we can come to expect in each of these areas.

Wider Acceptance of Strict Penalties for Environmental Offenses

After years of setbacks in their plight to raise environmental violations to the level of "criminal behavior," prosecutors of environmental crime are now on the verge of witnessing a change in the winds of sentiment on this issue. In the 1991 second national environmental opinion study conducted by Environmental Opinion Study Inc., American citizens were found, overwhelmingly, to favor terms of incarceration for corporate or government officials convicted of deliberately violating pollution laws (Environmental Opinion Study, 1991). The U.S. Sentencing Commission's proposal on how to sentence corporations for environmental crimes seemed to further reflect a toughening on acts of environmental crime. Determination of fines under the proposed guidelines requires sentencing judges to calculate factors such as economic gain derived from the criminal act and costs attributed to the pollution (e.g., clean-up costs, actual environmental harm), and to merge their calculations with an ordinal grading of offense severity set out by the Commission. Judges are also encouraged, through the proposed guidelines, to put defendants on probation for one to five years. Altogether, the guidelines have drawn much protest from certain business community groups and conservative legal foundations as being "draconian" in nature (DeBenedictis, 1993).

The public's disgust with environmental crime and the government's new proclivity to react was typified by the "Rocky Flats Affair," a case that should prove to be a lasting catalyst to intensified criminal prosecution of environmental offenses and sentence impositions for some time to come. In 1992, Rockwell Corp., a nuclear weapons facility in Rocky Flats, Colorado pled guilty to federal criminal violations involving the illegal disposal and storage of hazardous wastes. While the plea bargain did result in a $18.5 million penalty for Rockwell, federal prosecutors sought no individual indictments against Rockwell employees. The most noteworthy aspect of the case is that federal grand jury members chose to disregard the prosecutor's decision not to pursue individual indictments and attempted, instead, to indict Rockwell employees on their own.

This incident, plus questions regarding the handling of other environmental pollution cases by federal prosecutors, eventually became the target of a House oversight committee chaired by Rep. John Dingell (D-Mich.). The Dingell panel was assembled to review Justice Department policy on environmental crime and to investigate changes of leniency toward polluting corporations. While the panel ostensibly represented a viable avenue for unearthing information on patterns of a "soft" approach under the Bush Administration toward violations of federal environmental laws, it also received sharp criticism for what was charged as an assault against the concept of prosecutorial discretion. These allegations became more pronounced when Dingell's staff was allowed by Attorney General Janet Reno to interview career attorneys at the Department of Justice about their cases (LaFraniere, September 18, 1992; *The Wall Street Journal* July 8, 1993).

The genesis of environmental offense criminalization has taken us from a point in the past where the average American equated hazardous waste dumping to "throwing out the garbage," to a point where after years of rising numbers of incidents of these offenses—and media attention to them—the public outcry to punish severely has reached a pitch heard plainly by those in political power. Environmental crime control officials have worked diligently to change the normative climate on pollution and are finally seeing some genuine results.

Federal sentencing patterns for environmental crimes analyzed by Cohen highlight a sentencing toughness unparalleled in the past. Federal sentencing guidelines propose to put more teeth into punitive options. And leniency toward corporate polluters is questioned at the highest levels of government. But while environmental prosecutors, overall, should be satisfied with such results, the possibility exists that their voracity aimed at tendering more punitive sanctions may become their own unique conundrum—*How "tough" is "tough" when it comes to environmental crime?* By raising the level of consciousness of the public and government officials on the "criminality" of acts of pollution, prosecutors may have also raised expectations that even they cannot meet. A more aware public will, in the coming years, be more demanding of prosecutors on all government levels to treat polluters harshly. This means an expectation of a reduction in "leniency" in plea negotiations in cases that will now place prosecutors under a magnifying glass much like their experiences with more traditional high profile crime cases. As state and local prosecutors intensify their efforts to prosecute environmental crimes, they will also undergo greater public/media scrutiny, held to a higher standard than they themselves will have created, a standard that may indirectly limit prosecutorial discretion.

Environmental Equity

As environmental prosecutors enter the twenty-first century, it is likely that they will, more than ever, be required to carefully consider the ramifications of the issue of *environmental equity*. As defined by the EPA, environmental equity refers to the distribution of environmental risks across population groups and policy responses to them. In 1990, EPA's thirty-member task force on environmental equity concluded that minority communities experience greater than average exposure to environmental hazards including lead, air pollutants, and toxic wastes (EPA, 1990). Activists representing the lower class lay claims that industry consciously locates its most polluting plants in low income, minority areas with the tacit approval of government (Weisskopf, 1992). The close proximity of these plants, landfills, and incineration facilities add up to a disproportionate amount of pollution in these areas along with the creation of a local culture tolerant of the illegal abandonment of hazardous waste. This has taken its most insidious form in areas like the Altgeld district of Chicago where "fly dumping"—hit-and-run waste dumping—has become a common practice (Ervin, 1992).

In *Environmental Equity: Reducing Risk for All Communities* (EPA, 1992), the EPA pledges to address the inequity of low-income population proximity to chemical dangers by making a number of recommendations for improvement. These include the selective review and revision of EPA's permit, grant, monitoring, and enforcement procedures in low-income communities, and the improvement of the manner in which EPA communicates with racial minorities. Criminal enforcement, however, has yet to effect a plan to address the environmental crime violations occurring as byproducts of the disproportionate presence of plants, landfills, and incinerators in these areas. As pressure grows from activist groups to arrest this problem, the crime control burden will likely fall on the shoulders of state and local prosecutors. It is foreseen that those prosecutors progressive enough to realize the gravity of environmental equity, will open avenues of communication with minority group community leaders to identify environmental patterns in low-income areas, and begin to direct their task force resources toward those locations at greatest risk.

Displacement of Environmental Crime

As prosecutors become more proficient at controlling environmental crime in those urban, highly populated areas most likely to be victimized, it is anticipated that rising incidents of environmental crime will "spill over" into adjoining suburban and rural districts. In the previously mentioned APRI study (1994), interviews with local prosecutors warn that this infiltration is occurring now in some areas. Less populated counties with less experienced enforcement units are becoming the unsuspecting recipients of environmental offenders migrating from those areas where environmental enforcement task forces have perfected their crafts, and where prosecutors are aggressive in their prosecution. In addition, in many cases poorer, rural counties make some of the best targets for midnight dumpers because of their isolated geography.

One recent examination of district attorneys prosecuting environmental crime in the South noted that prosecutors there were observing an influx of companies and individuals possessing records of environmental offenses. Some speculation by the Bureau of National Affairs in 1991 offered to explain this trend was that environmental offenders from the North were keenly aware of the relatively lower level of sophistication of environmental crime control in the South and were capitalizing on this knowledge. A more recent assessment of charging trends among rural prosecutors by the Bureau of Justice revealed that environmental crime was considered to be one of a select number of emerging areas in rural jurisdictions that posed special complications for those uninitiated to cases of this type.

The solution to this problem may well lie in the wisdom of prosecutors in suburban and rural America to accept the spread of environmental crime into their districts as inevitable and to consider the dire consequences of *not* preparing their work forces with adequate training in environmental investigation and prosecution. If they ignore the problem, they risk becoming an unintentional casualty of the earnest control efforts of their urban neighbors. Absent organized education programs for prosecutor offices in nonurban regions, these regions could conceivably become "legal havens" for the future's environmental criminals.

Standards for the Admissibility of Specific Evidence: The Daubert Test

A looming problem for prosecutors of environmental crime cases is the degree to which recent Supreme Court decisions affect their capacity to prove physical harm or the extent of physical harm caused by wastes improperly disposed. At the heart of this problem is the change in the standards of admissibility of scientific evidence in the courtroom, evidence that could be pivotal in determining the dimensions of harm posed that can have a significant bearing in penalty severity at conviction.

The traditional standard emerging in *Frye v. U.S.* (293) F. 1013 [D.C. Cir. 1923]) was that the validity of scientific evidence considered for admission must be ensured through general acceptance within the relevant scientific community. The standard was developed as a fairly strict test of acceptance through evaluation of those most qualified to determine the worth of the scientific technique in question. This long-standing test has recently been replaced by one born out of a 1993 Supreme Court decision in *Daubert v. Merrell Dow Pharmaceutical, Inc.* (113 S. Ct. 2786, 53 CrL 2313, 1993) in which Merrell Dow was sued by the guardians of infants to recover from birth defects allegedly caused by the mothers' ingestion of an oral drug. The decision dramatically liberalizes the standard for admissibility of scientific evidence in that the trial judge largely becomes the determinate of evidential validity. As described by Busloff in her analysis of the landmark decision's effect on the horizontal gaze mystagmus test for sobriety,

> The trial judge must determine whether the subject of an expert's testimony is "scientific knowledge" and whether the testimony can be supported by appropriate validation. Moreover, there must be a valid scientific connection between the testimony and the pertinent inquiry. In other words, *Daubert* asks judges to make decisions on a case by case basis (Busloff, 1993, p. 221).

The *Daubert* decision may prove to be a double-edged sword for prosecutors of environmental crime. The relaxing of standards of scientific evidence admissibility may open the door for the use of expert testimony on scientific techniques demonstrating connections between chemical exposure and physical harm that may have been considered inadmissible under the prior standard due to the relative newness of the particular methods. Thus, prosecutors may find themselves in a better position to rely on such emerging technology to verify resultant harm and buttress arguments for the imposition of tougher penalties. On the other hand, presenting the trier of fact with expanded authority in concluding scientific method validity can also have a damaging impact for environmental prosecutors. The shift in standards conceivably can have the effect of turning the courtroom into a raging battleground pairing expert witnesses for the prosecution against those for the defense, arguing over the finer points, levels of toxicity and degrees of harm of wastes disposed, with the judge wielding wide discretion in deciding which information meets the test of acceptability at trial. Prosecutors can find themselves at a distinct disadvantage in light of the deep pockets corporate defendants may have to call upon for persuasive technical testimony.

Furthermore, the *Daubert* decision may act to unintentionally elevate the credibility of certain "coincidence" defenses. These defenses allow the proliferation of hazardous chemicals by widening the latitude of acceptability for waste sample analysis results matching disposed wastes to their sources.[3]

Training

The national survey of local environmental prosecutors stressed the growing need for specialized training in environmental prosecution skills. It wasn't until 1981 that any organized training in environmental crime prosecution was generated for state government prosecutors. At that time, the Northeast Hazardous Waste Coordination Committee—a regional consortium of state attorney general offices and state regulatory agencies—began developing and administering specialized training to state prosecutors. Since then, the EPA has provided funding for the creation of three similar regional consortiums covering most of the United States. Environmental crime prosecution training on a national level directed exclusively at local prosecutors was established in 1993 by the National Environmental Crime Prosecution Center. Training of federal prosecutors in environmental crime prosecution is ongoing and predates those of state and local prosecutors. It is furnished by the EPA and the FBI.

Although the past has seen a paucity of channels for environmental crime prosecution training, it is clear that we are now embarking upon a period in which government is more willing to fund formal education for those responsible for prosecuting offenses against the environment. Some training programs like that of the National Environmental Crime Prosecution Center, are supported primarily through forfeiture funds contributed by local district attorneys. In the early 1990s a degree of fractionalism arose between the four regional consortiums and the National Center. In some respects local prosecutors became the beneficiaries of this dispute with competition spurring the establishment of more training programs for local prosecutors than were ever before available. However, the hope is that the training providers will collaborate to complement programs to ensure that training *quality* is not sacrificed for training *quantity* in the quest to equip prosecutors with necessary skills. One recent attempt to coordinate such training efforts on local, state, and federal government levels has been the development of EPA's National Environmental Training Institute, the results of which remain to be seen.

For now, we can say that environmental prosecutors of the future should at least have greater access to organized education programs. Those who avail themselves of these programs should be better able to lead effective environmental crime investigations taking advantage of knowledge gained from investigative strategies from other crime-

---

[3]One of the most well-known incidents where this position was used recently involved the Monsanto Co. plant in Sauget, IL, the nation's largest producer of PCBs before PCBs were banned in 1979. EPA officials found themselves deadlocked by Monsanto claims that their generation of PCBs and the clusters of PCB dumps along nearby Dead Creek were mere coincidence. Monsanto's position that their proximity to Dead Creek and likelihood of disposal there was irrelevant and that the disposal could have been committed by others, was found to present early obstacles to the strategy of matching chemical composition of wastes to their source.

specific areas (e.g., drug enforcement) and from veterans of successful environmental crime investigations.[4] In addition, those trained should be prepared to understand the nuances of directing multi-agency responses, to make decisions to initiate civil or criminal proceedings, to use technical experts at trial, and to present at trial general and defense strategies common to environmental crime cases.

Experimentation with New Technologies/Strategies

Findings of the American Prosecutors Research Institute's national survey of local prosecutors exposed this group's wish for a marked upgrading of their technical abilities to match those of environmental case defense attorneys. In the courtroom, this desire translates, to a great degree, into a need for the capacity to simplify complicated descriptions of the harmful chemical properties of wastes that are illegally disposed, transported or stored. Also needed are skills to reduce the complexities entailed in depicting chemical procedures used during investigations to link illegally disposed wastes to their source to verify criminal culpability of the defendant(s).[5]

As prosecutors continue to pursue environmental crime cases and begin to take advantage of the wider array of training opportunities offered by regional/national environmental control education organizations, it is expected that they will display a greater tendency to rely on technological advances in the submission of complex evidence. This presentation can include experimentation in areas such as the use of three dimensional computer simulations to recreate the commission of environmental crimes, the tracing of disposed wastes to their source, and the events leading up to accidents resulting in hazardous disasters like oil spills.[6] Experience with refined methods of presenting simple demonstrative evidence in these cases is also anticipated as being enhanced in the future.

With regard to special strategies that environmental crime prosecutors will be more likely to use in the future, the use of Racketeer Influenced and Corrupt Organizations laws (RICO) on local, state, and federal levels holds much promise.

---

[4]An example of this type of investigative strategy training is environmental "reverse sting" operations, presented at the National Environmental Crime Prosecution Center's National Conference on the Prosecution of Environmental Crime in Phoenix, AZ in April 1993. A traditional part of the drug investigators' repertoire, it involves the use of undercover agents posing as business officials paying the suspected offenders to dispose of hazardous wastes. Although heretofore used rarely by environmental prosecutors, instances where it has been used have led to fruitful results. One of the most notable was orchestrated by the Suffolk County, NY District Attorney's Office in 1992. The "toxic avenger" sting took four months for investigators to set up the transaction with representatives of plating industry/silicon transistor manufacturing companies to transport and dispose of hazardous wastes illegally (National Environmental Crime Prosecution Center, 1992). Information from successful operations such as this, are increasingly forming the foundation of new training programs for environmental prosecutors.

[5]These methods can include the injection of chemical dyes into the waste stream and the tracing of the journey of the dyed wastes, or the physical tracing of special painted markings, or qualities of drums containing wastes.

[6]Such technology has already been employed in criminal trials involving vehicular homicide and in manslaughter cases against police in which trajectory angles are critical to the determination of the physical positions of victims and defendants.

Enacted in 1970 on the federal level (RICO, 18 U.S.C. 1961-1965), the law makes it a crime to acquire, receive income from, or operate an enterprise through a pattern of racketeering and permits prosecutors to abandon a reliance on discrete statutes. Instead, RICO allows prosecutors to prosecute *patterns* of criminal acts committed by direct and indirect participants in criminal enterprises. Twenty-nine states have enacted their own versions of this law. So far, there have only been a handful of situations where prosecutors have turned to RICO in environmental crime cases.[7]

A 1993 national survey on the use of state RICO statutes by local prosecutors provided information that while RICO statutes were found to be used infrequently by local prosecutors overall, metropolitan prosecutors were showing signs of greater willingness to employ these statutes in organized/white collar crime cases. With adequate training and the development of effective screening criteria for its use, local prosecutors claimed a higher likelihood that their confidence in using this progressive prosecutorial tool would be enhanced (Rebovich, Coyle and Schaaf, 1993).[8] These statutes, in many states, carry criminal penalties stricter than those associated with more traditional laws typically used in environmental crime cases. They also provide prosecutors with other powers, like those relating to the forfeiture of assets, that can prove to be potent weapons in the battle against environmental crime.

DISCUSSION AND IMPLICATIONS FOR FUTURE RESEARCH

Since the emergence of environmental pollution offenses as bona fide environmental crime, there has been increasing concern regarding the refinement of prosecution capabilities to effectively catch up to the maturing crime commission patterns of environmental offenders. In terms of sheer numbers of environmental prosecutors, we are light-years ahead of where we were only two decades ago. Tracing the history of environmental prosecution in the U.S. is analogous to picturing an inverted funnel with

---

[7]On the state government level, one of the most well-known RICO prosecutions associated with environmental crime occurred in 1983 in Pennsylvania State Attorney General's case against *Lavalle & Son Co.*. Lavalle, the head of a trucking company that transported hazardous wastes, was charged with illegally disposing hazardous wastes and using more than $580,000 in illegal profits to create a "legitimate" transport business. Through the use of its state RICO law, Pennsylvania was able to prove that there was an organized and consistent pattern of criminal activities which surrounded Lavalle's operations. Lavalle was found guilty of violating the RICO statute on two separate counts: theft by deception and use of stolen funds (Rebovich, Coyle and Schaaf, 1993).

The most noteworthy federal RICO prosecution in an environmental crime case is U.S. v. A&A Land Developmental, et al., a 1990 case in which three individuals and seven waste disposal and real estate development agencies were convicted of RICO and mail fraud violations. The violations involved the illegal transfer and disposal of hazardous wastes on Staten Island. Penalties resulted in the seizure of the companies and assets for liquidation and recovery and sentences of incarceration for all three individuals.

[8]Sixty percent of the respondents reporting the prosecution of organized crime were from jurisdictions representing over 250,000 in population. Prosecutors who used RICO statutes contended that they offered versatile sanctions to a wide variety of offenses and that these sanctions were not available under other laws. Some advantages specified included the obtaining of injunctions to prevent RICO violators from continuing to operate businesses in which criminal activity was focused. RICO laws were also asserted to be valued as prosecution "hammers" during plea negotiations because of the strict penalties that could result from conviction.

the top represented by the small number of federal environmental prosecutors beginning their campaigns in the 1970s, the middle represented by the somewhat greater number of state attorneys general expanding the prosecution coverage in the 1980s, and the widest area symbolizing the much larger number of local prosecutor's offices prosecuting environmental crime in the 1990s. While we can feel fairly secure that even more will be prosecuting environmental offenders in the future, there is less certainty on how effective environmental prosecutors will be and by what measure they will be judged.

This chapter has offered some projections on what environmental prosecution will be like in the future given certain events and patterns forming at the present. The important factors presented can be categorized as those that are sociopolitical in nature (e.g., public/system sentiment on environmental crime, equity in the distribution of environmental risk, the burden of increased environmental crime in suburban/rural regions caused by effective control programs in urban areas) and those that are profession-specific technical issues (e.g., changes in evidentiary standards, progress in training, advances in methods and technologies). Though some of these may not materialize as *leading* change elements, clearly, the role diversification of this profession should be emphasized as the wave of the future for environmental prosecutors.

Undoubtedly, tomorrow's environmental prosecutor will be required to wear several hats: those of law enforcer, protector of public health, environmental technician, and community leader. This diversity will mean that certain inevitable compromises will be forced upon the environmental prosecutor in order to satisfy new community expectations. The increasing public/media pressures to vigorously prosecute polluters *and* to simultaneously safeguard the welfare of the general public will prompt prosecutors to carefully weigh issues that, given fallout from the Rocky Flats affair, may not be easy to balance. To guarantee the expedient elimination of health threats emanating from criminal disposals, prosecutors may sometimes be obliged to structure plea negotiation decisions to revolve around promises of defendant remediation of the disposal sites (i.e., environmental cleanup) and grudgingly forsake desired degrees of punitiveness. Prosecutors may also find they will have to reconcile public insistence on the imposition of tough penalties with some residual judicial hesitancy to mete out such penalties. Consequently, we may see more environmental prosecutors exploring the possibilities of subtly graduated penalties for situational offenders that could include community service and more creative alternatives like the disqualification of professional certifications and the newspaper publication of criminal act admissions by offenders.

Though some of these predictions may be arguable, it is generally agreed that whatever course the environmental prosecutor of the future takes, changes in role definition will necessitate a new agenda for future research that will supply the environmental prosecutor with information facilitating a proactive position and permitting him/her to meet the challenges of the new role. Though not exhaustive, the following list provides a glimpse at some of the possible research endeavors that could help usher the environmental prosecutor into a new era of professional growth.

- *The Study of Offender Behavior* so that appropriate proactive enforcement mechanisms can be identified and targeted for specific crime commission types.

Prosecutors could establish the relationships, if any, between the financial status of offenders at the time of the offense and the offense committed. Prosecutors could also isolate characteristics common to offending corporations. This information is vital to EPA ideas of "pollution prevention" to target only "good citizen" corporations for voluntary compliance.

- *The identification of the types of business most likely to commit environmental offenses and their location* in rural or urban areas of county/jurisdiction, etc. to predict the kinds of individuals and companies likely to commit environmental crimes (e.g., profile study of criminal corporations with comparison control group of noncriminal corporations).

- *Significant Outsiders to Criminal Core Acts* (e.g., unregulated "treatment brokers," "private labs"). A comparison study of prosecutors' offices in states with regulation in these areas and those without such regulation. This study would be an examination of the extent to which significant outside groups/individuals can pave the way for the unencumbered commission of environmental offenses at the local level and the avoidance of meaningful punishment.

- *Decision to Charge.* Content analysis study of a comparison of environmental crime cases dismissed vs. cases charged. What factors are most important in charging/not charging? Are they the best reasons for all? What formal and informal procedures are used by prosecutors to reduce felonies to misdemeanors, to relegate criminal cases to civil proceedings or to dismiss altogether?

- *Success/Failure of Environmental Crime Cases Prosecuted.* Discriminate analysis of environmental crime conviction rates by characteristics of cases (level of evidence, complexity of cases, source of discovery, degree of harm, type/volume of chemical, proximity to popular areas). The independent variable would be success/failure of the cases. With this study we could establish predictability standards as is done in other crime areas so that planning can be done efficiently. In essence, this type of analysis would be the foundation of a system to statistically predict the chances of conviction for use in helping to decide which environmental cases to criminally prosecute.

- *The Study of Penalties.* Studies on sentencing at local level—quality, types of penalties by types of offenses. Data could lead to study of environmental offense recidivism and collection of supplemental data on impact of sanctions on company profits in later years as well as on attitudes of shareholders.

- *The Study of Intermediate Environmental Sanctions and Prevention Strategies.* The equations of "risk" and "harm" with levels of punitive sanctioning (e.g., occupational disqualification of corporate executives, community service, tax incentive programs for waste reduction).

STUDY QUESTIONS

1. Public pressures to control pollution in the U.S. helped lead to the criminalization of offenses against the environment. In what other crime areas has such public pressures similarly led to the criminalization of social behavior that may have been considered improper but legal? What role did the media play in this

criminalization process? How are these crime areas similar to environmental crime? How are they different?

2. Consider and discuss how society tends to categorize environmental crime (e.g., white collar crime, predatory crime, violent crime). How might these categorizations of environmental crime differ by political orientation (i.e., political liberal, political conservative)? By special interest groups (i.e, business groups, groups representing minorities)? How might these orientations affect the decisions of elected criminal justice officials like district attorneys? How might they affect the decision of jurors?

3. Discuss the issue of environmental equity. Are there any parallels with other crime areas affecting impoverished groups? What direction do you see this issue talking? What special concerns does it present to prosecutors of environmental crime?

REFERENCES

Abt Associates Inc. (1985). *National small quantity hazardous waste generator survey.* Washington, DC: Environmental Protection Agency, Office of Solid Waste.

Adler, F. (1991). *Offender specific versus offense specific approaches to the study of environmental crime.* American Society of Criminology, Annual Conference, November 21, San Francisco, CA.

American Prosecutors Research Institute. (1994). "Environmental Crime Prosecution." Unpublished report.

American Prosecutors Research Institute. (1992, August 14). "The Local Prosecution of Eenvironmental Crimes: A Literature Review." Alexandria, VA.

Benson, M.L., W. Maakestad, F. Cullen and G. Geis. (1988). "District Attorneys and Corporate Crime: Surveying the Prosecutorial Gatekeepers." *Criminology*, 24(3): 505-519.

Blumenthal, R. (1983, June 5). "Illegal Dumping of Toxins Laid to Organized Crime." *The New York Times*, pp. 1 and 44.

Bullard, D. (1991, June). "Environmental Racism in America?" *Environmental Protection*, 25.

Bureau of Justice Assistance. (1993). *Violent Crime and Drug Abuse in Rural Areas: Issues, Concerns, and Programs.* Washington, DC: Justice Research and Statistics Association.

Busloff, S. (1993). "Can Your Eyes Be Used Against You? The Use of Horizontal Gaze Mystagmus Test in the Courtroom." *The Journal of Criminal Law and Criminology*, 84(1), 203-238.

California Bureau of Criminal Statistics and Special Services. (1988). "Racial, Ethnic and Religious Crimes Project." *Criminal Justice Analysis in the States: The Role of Measurement in Public Policy Development.* Washington, DC: Criminal Justice Statistics Association.

Catterson, J. (1992). *Criminal Prosecution of Environmental Violators.* pp. 7-8.

Cohen, M. (1992). "Environmental Crime and Punishment: Legal/Economic Theory and Empirical Evidence on Enforcement of Federal Environmental Statutes." *The Journal of Criminal Law and Criminology.* 82(4), 1055-1107.

Criminal Justice Statistics Association. (1988). "Measuring Bias Motivated Crime." *Criminal Justice Analysis in the States: The Role of Measurement in Public Policy Development.* Washington, DC.

Daubert v. Merrill Dow Pharmaceutical, Inc. (113 S. Ct 2786, 53 CRL 2313, 1993).

De Benedictis, D. (1993, June). "Few Like Pollution Guidelines." *ABA Journal*, 25-26.

Environmental Opinion Study, Inc. (1991). "Environmental Issues Ranked." Washington, DC: Environmental Opinion Study, Inc.

Environmental Protection Agency. (1992). "Environmental Equity: Reducing Risk for All Communities." Washington, DC.

Environmental Protection Agency. (1990). "Reducing Risk: Setting Priorities and Strategies for Environmental Protection." Washington, DC.

Epstein, S., L. Brown and C. Pope. (1982). *Hazardous Waste in America*. San Francisco: Sierra Club Books.

Ervin, M. (1992, January). "The Toxic Doughnut." *The Progressive*, 15.

Frye v. U.S. (293) F1013 [D.C. Cir. 1923]

Gold, A. (1991, February 15). "Increasingly, Prison Term is the Price for Polluters." *The New York Times*.

Hammett, T. and J. Epstein. (1993). "Local Prosecution of Environmental Crime." *Issues and Practices*. Washington, DC: The National Institute of Justice.

Hammett, T. and J. Epstein. (1993). "Prosecuting Environmental Crime: Los Angeles County." *Program Focus*. Washington, DC: The National Institute of Justice.

Hammitt, J.K. and P. Reuter. (1988). *Measuring and Deterring Illegal Disposal of Hazardous Waste*. Santa Monica: Rand Corporation.

Hawke, N. (1987). "Crimes Against the Environment." *Anglo-American Law Review*. 16(1): 90-96.

Herrod, S., L. Paddock, S. Patti, H. Holden, G. Lie, and J. Baylson. (1991). "Utilizing Local Government." *Enforcement in the 1990's: Recommendations of the Analytical Workgroup*. Washington, DC: U.S. Environmental Protection Agency.

Hollinger, G. and M. Atkinson. (1988). "The Process of Criminalization: The Case of Computer Crime Laws." *Criminology*. 26(1).

Jensen, G. (1991). "America's New Environmental Populism." *Prosecutor's Brief*. 2nd Quarter, 4-5.

Krajick, K. (1981, May). "When Will Police Discover the Toxic Time Bomb?" and "Toxic Waste is Big Business for the Mob." *Police Magazine*, pp. 6-20.

LaFraniere, S. (1992, September 18). "Pollution Leniency Alleged: Dingell Panel to Review Justice Department Policy." *The Washington Post*, 1.

Meehan, J. (1992). *Policy issues in environmental crimes for America's metropolitan prosecutors*. NDAA Annual Conference for Metropolitan Prosecutors, Washington, DC.

Metz, B. (1985). *No more Mr. Nice Guy: Hazardous waste enforcement management in the USA*. Groningen, The Netherlands: Ministry of Housing, Physical Planning and Environment, Regional Inspectorate for the Environment.

Mugdan, W.E. and B.R. Adler. (1985). "The 1984 RCRA Amendments: Congress as a Regulatory Agent." *Columbia Journal of Environmental Law*, 10(2), 215-254.

Murphy, W. (1991). Presentation at the National Environmental Enforcement Council, Washington, DC.

Mustokoff, M. (1981). *Hazardous waste violations: A guide to their detection, investigation and prosecution*. Washington, DC: The National Center on White Collar Crime, Department of Justice, Law Enforcement Assistance Administration.

Rebovich, D., K. Coyle and J. Schaaf. (1993). *Local Prosecutor of Organized Crime: The Use of State RICO Statutes*. Washington, DC: Bureau of Justice Statistics.

Rebovich, D. (1992). *Dangerous ground: The world of hazardous waste crime*. New Brunswick, NJ: Transaction Publishers.

Rebovich, D. (1987). "Exploring Hazardous Waste Crime Characteristics." *Law Enforcement Intelligence Digest*, 2(1).

Rebovich, D. (1987). "Policing Hazardous Waste Crime: Issues in Offense Identification and Prosecution." *Criminal Justice Quarterly*, 9(3).

Reuter, P. (1983). *Disorganized crime: The economics of the visible hand*. Cambridge, MA: MIT Press.

Sherman, R. (1987, August 6). "Pillars or Polluters: Prosecutors Play Hardball with Corporate Managers." *The New Jersey Law Journal*, p. 1.

Szacz, A. (1986). "Corporations, Organized Crime, and the Disposal of Hazardous Waste: An Examination of the Making of a Criminogenic Regulatory Structure." *Criminology*. 24(1), 1-28.

U.S. Department of Justice. (1991, January). *Environmental crimes manual*. Washington, DC.

Wald, M. (1992, September 30). "Jury Battled Prosecutor on Nike Plant." *The New York Times*.

The Wall Street Journal. (1993, July 8). General Dingell, *Review and Outlook*, A12.

Weisskopf, M. (1992, January 16). "Minorities Pollution Risk is Debated." *The Washington Post*.

Wolf, S. (1983, Winter). "Hazardous Waste Trials and Tribulations." *Environmental Law*, 13(2).

CHAPTER 20

IMPACT OF COMPUTER BASED TECHNOLOGIES ON CRIMINAL JUSTICE

TRANSITION TO THE TWENTY-FIRST CENTURY

William G. Archambeault, Ph.D.

ABSTRACT

This chapter explains the nature and impact of the information society on American criminal justice. It logically links information dependency to computer dependency. It traces the evolution of computers and computer based technologies, then discusses the applications of computers in American criminal justice of the 1990s. Computer applications are discussed under the headings of Data Based Management, Organizational Communications, Computer Assisted Diagnosis/Education/Training, Computer Assisted Monitoring of Offenders, and Computer Related Crime. Evolving technologies, including artificial intelligence and virtual reality, are discussed in terms of their future applications. The chapter concludes by noting that the future applications of computers in criminal justice will be limited only by human imagination, ethics and law.

INTRODUCTION

As twentieth century yields to the twenty-first, computers and computer based technologies (CBTS) play critically important roles in American criminal justice. Computers, as defined today, are electronic devices that have at least four basic definable functions: input[1], storage[2], processing[3] and output[4]. There are at least three common groupings of computers: PCs or microcomputers[5], minicomputers[6] and mainframe computers. Computer based technologies (CBTS)[7] refer to a wide range of integrated technologies that employ computers (PC, mini or mainframe) or computer microchip integrated logic circuitry into their design as critical or essential components.

Computers and CBTS are the heart of organizational information systems. In a recent National Institute of Justice Report discussing the importance of computers to law enforcement, Sparrow (1993, 1) notes:

> At one time, information technology was thought to be best left to technicians so managers could concentrate on the serious business of management. However, that might have been an effective division of labor only when computers were used solely to automate well-defined administrative functions, such as batch processing of payroll...Now, information systems are the essential circuitry of modern organizations, often determining how problems are defined and how progress is evaluated. They frequently determine how work gets done, often who does it, and sometimes what the work is...Organizational strategy no longer can be separated from informational technology strategy, for the organizational effects of information systems no longer are limited to efficiency gains.

Sparrow's comments are indicative of a fundamental reality in the external environment of all criminal justice organizations, namely, that the U.S., like most other industrialized countries of the world, has evolved into a society which is totally dependent on information: its content, its flow and its speed of delivery.

This dependency manifests itself in two fundamental ways in all criminal justice organizations. *First, information and its flow within organizations are critical to efficient operations, the delivery of services, and the safety of criminal justice workers*. The most obvious example of this need is seen in the dispatching and delivery of police emergency services. Accurate information and its rapid flow can literally have life or death consequences. Similar levels of criticality and information dependency can also be seen in the operation of courts, jails and correctional facilities.

Second, the criticality of information and its flow in American criminal justice has led to the widespread use of computer based technologies and recurring cycles of ever increasing dependency on the technology. Most criminal justice organizations are totally dependent on information and the technology for managing it. Within these organizations there is great pressure to acquire, store, manage, retrieve and analyze raw data, and to convert it to usable information[8]. This continuing pressure propels these organizations to apply more powerful computers to handle the information load. The irony of this process is that more powerful computers produce more data and information than the humans in the organizations can utilize or even comprehend. In turn, this multiplication increases the pressure to obtain ever more powerful computers that lead to even greater dependency and produce even more information. Paradoxically, computer dependency is a relatively recent phenomenon as the following sketch of history indicates.

RISE OF THE INFORMATION SOCIETY AND COMPUTER DEPENDENCY

For centuries the term *computer* referred to human beings who performed mathematical computations in accounting, budgeting, engineering, astronomy, and navigation-related computations. When President John F. Kennedy announced the goal of landing men on the moon, NASA was still using human computers. However, by July 20, 1969, when American astronauts first walked on the moon, the word *computer* had evolved into its present meaning, but only a few programmers and systems analysts had any contact with computers. A small number of large police departments or government agencies used computers or computer services. The vast majority of criminal justice organizations maintained manual (paper and file folder) records and information storage. The ideas of using computers in police cars or courtrooms or officers carrying video-telephone devices were *Dick Tracy-* or *Flash Gordon*-quality comic book fiction.

By 1979, a decade later, much had changed. Most criminal justice organizations were automating or at least experimenting with the use of computers in a desperate effort to keep up with the demand for information. However, it was still science fiction:

1. that humans could interact verbally with computers,

2. that computers could "learn" anything on their own,

3. that CBTS retinal scans could be used for the identification of persons entering or leaving correctional confinement,

4. that CBTS crime labs could conduct DNA analysis and identify rapists,

5. that police could use computers in routine police cars,

6. that CBTS CADS could interact with satellites, dispatch emergency vehicles to specific locations, or provide electronic maps of the shortest way to travel to the scene of the emergency, or

7. that computers could be effectively used in employee training or offender education.

By 1989, however, the computer revolution and the information society were realities. Most of what had been "science fiction" in 1969 or even 1979 had become operational realities of American criminal justice. In society, computers were as normal as pencils. Computer literacy became second in importance only to reading literacy. The use of computer based education and training became common in criminal justice organizations.

COMPUTER BASED TECHNOLOGIES AND CRIMINAL JUSTICE OF THE 1990s

Ongoing research into computer technology and CBTS applications continue to redefine human definition of computers and of their potentials. Changes as radical as the cumulative changes experienced since the 1970s may occur by the year 2000 or shortly thereafter. Anticipation and understanding of these projected changes begin with a comprehension of today's computers. With few exceptions, most contemporary computers and CBTS devices exploit defendant fourth generation computer technologies which are human dependent: humans enter data, input processing instructions, instruct computers on how to analyze data and how to output the results. There are, however, some exceptions. These are computers with some attributes of evolving fifth generation technology.

Emerging fifth generation computers add a fifth function to the basic definition of a computer: *the capacity to learn without human assistance*. This ability is loosely called *artificial intelligence* or *AI*. At the present time, true artificial intelligence does not exist. What does exist are incremental technological steps leading to AI and rudimentary forms of artificial intelligence which are often labeled "smart," "expert," "brilliant," or even "genius." These have some, but not all the characteristics of AI.

True artificial intelligence has two sets of functional "learning" characteristics. Without human intervention, the computer has the ability to acquire new data or information and to alter its basic programming. Learning, in the first context, refers to a computer's capability to acquire new data, analyze them, and make decisions based on them without human direction or control. Today's most advanced computers are programmed to acquire new data or information on their own, but in a very narrow frame of reference. These computers are labeled "smart," "expert," or "brilliant." These are illustrated by the performance of the computer-directed guidance system of the Patriot Missile during the 1991 Gulf War. Hundreds of times a second the missile was able to receive data on its location and that of its target, analyze it, and alter its course. These functions are also found in the most sophisticated computers in American criminal justice such as the computers used by the FBI's National Center for the Analysis of Violent Crime (NCAVC) (Reboussin, 1990), the Automated Fingerprint Identification Systems (AFIS) in wide use today, in genetic research and DNA matching, in telecommunication, and in emergency dispatching systems.

Current "smart" or "expert" systems are incremental developments which will eventually lead to true artificial intelligence, but are not true AI. Although such machines can "learn" or acquire new data, they can do so only within narrow parameters controlled by the computers' basic programming. For true AI to exist, a computer must be able to "learn" on its own from a wide range of inputs in its environment, just as humans can learn from a wide variety of different life experiences and integrate them into some new conceptual model of reality. More importantly, the true AI computer must be able to modify its own programming through a process that parallels that of a human child who is developing a sense of personal morality about the world. By way of analogy, a Patriot missile guidance system in flight cannot suddenly decide that it no longer wants to be a missile, conclude that all killing is wrong and resolve not to destroy what it hits. An "expert" AFIS system cannot suddenly decide that it wants to become a communications system instead. A "brilliant" genetics research computer cannot suddenly reach a dilemma and philosophize about the ethics and morality of genetic engineering. Only true artificial intelligence could do any of these things. In the near future, AI research may totally redefine current ideas of what computers are and what they can do. Before exploring future potentials of AI, it is necessary to understand how computers and CBTS are applied in American criminal justice.

In the operational environment of the 1990s, computers and computer based technologies are extensively used in at least four areas of American criminal justice: (1) data base management, (2) computer assisted communication, (3) computer assisted instruction and training, (4) computer assisted monitoring of offenders. In addition to being tools of criminal justice, computers are also creating new crime forms. Space limitations permit only a superficial description of each of these areas.

Data Base Management

Data base management or *DBM* is the application of computer based technology to the systematic input, storage, retrieval and analysis of data (encoded facts) or information (encoded facts with meaning). Computers make it possible to store and access huge volumes of data and information that could not be done manually with any acceptable degree of efficiency.

Data base management is the core of most computer utilization in criminal justice that depends on rapid access to accurate information which may have life and death consequences. Most other application areas interface with DBM. Consequently, it is not surprising to find that there are many different kinds of DBM applications in criminal justice. Some involve the simple storage of files or records. Others, called management information systems (MIS), are designed to provide managers with information on organizational activities, budgets, personnel actions, historic and projected future demands for services needed for planning. They may track employee work and vacation schedules; personnel records dealing with payroll, promotions, retirement; vehicle mileage, replacement and maintenance schedules; and other related information that managers and administrators need to make decisions about the organization.

Other types of DBM systems provide information needed for criminal justice operations. Jails and courts use DBM to ensure that offenders are properly charged, booked, scheduled for hearings or trials, as well as to make sure that the right offender shows up in the right courtroom with the right assigned judge (Weinberg, 1989; Block, 1990; Manchester, 1991). Court DBM systems manage case dockets, maintain files on offenders, enter official court decisions when rendered. Many courts can directly access current laws and case precedents (Gruner, 1989; Churbuck, 1991) as well as offender records at time of sentencing. DBMs interface with telephone and tele-video CBTs to produce closed circuit television systems that make it possible for courts to conduct remote bookings, initial hearings and preliminary arraignments from miles away. DBMs make it possible to track offender cases through the maze of legal and judicial steps that comprise the American criminal justice system.

In jails, prisons and other custody settings, retinal scan identification, as well as hand-palm and fingerprint matching, are used to control access to restrictive areas of institutions. A DBM system contains identification files that contain previously recorded retinal, hand-palm and fingerprint data. Voice print recognition is also used and information stored in a similar manner.

Still other DBMs store all known information on characteristics, behavioral patterns, actions and victims of known serial killers (Larson, 1989; Bardege, 1990; Clede, 1990). The Federal Bureau of Investigation (FBI) employs "expert systems" to analyze criminal behavior stored in the DBM at the National Center for the Analysis of Violent Crime (NCAVC) (Reboussin and Rafoya, 1990). Other DBMs may contain information on known terrorists such as the ones who placed a car bomb in the New York Trade Center parking garage or may contain general information on offenders in a prison system (Saylor, 1990; Jameson and Megerman, 1990). Many DBMs record information and evidence as it is collected and evaluated, while others allow police officers to run a records check in seconds, such as searching the files of the National Criminal Information Center (NCIC) in Washington, D.C.

Portable crime lab computers operate in the field at crime scenes to collect data and analyze some evidence. Other collected field data is transmitted to powerful forensic computers in crime labs for detailed analysis. Analysis possibilities include a broad array of evidence, including DNA typing, blood matching, microscopic fiber analysis, computer enhanced imaging of the facial features of persons long dead, behavioral profiling of serial killers, among others.

Police and other 911 emergency dispatchers can receive a call for service, verify caller's address and phone number, prioritize the call, determine which available units are closest to dispatch and notify these units of the call and the best route to follow in getting to the emergency—all in a matter of seconds. Some systems require human dispatchers to access data bases that store addresses, phone numbers, and street maps (Dertouzos, 1991; Sikes, 1991); others perform this function automatically. Some "smart" systems are capable of interfacing with communications satellites which can pinpoint objects and terrain features of only a few inches from thousands of miles out in space, determine the exact location of any vehicle on a computerized street map, and dispatch units without human intervention. Computers in police cruisers and computer aided dispatch (CAD) of emergency services are common in many large metropolitan areas today.

Sheriff's deputies in New York City carry hand held computers that allow satellite interface with mainframe computers which contain hundreds of thousands of unpaid parking tickets and public ordinance fines (Parks, 1990), allowing the City of New York to collect millions of dollars in unpaid fines. Other DBM systems may contain plans to buildings, including banks, high rises, apartment buildings and others. Crime pattern analysis allows police agencies to deploy limited patrol resources most efficiently in any geographical area by time of day.

Computer Assisted Organizational Communications

There are three areas of organizational communications which employ CBTS extensively: written, electronic, and verbal. *Written communications* refers to operational manuals, memos, letters, or any other form of information communications that requires a reader to see and interpret meaning from printed words or symbols. *Electronic communications* refers to the transmission and reception of written communications via a video screen or CRT, fax machines or the transmission of voice messages through "voice mail." With the advent of in-car computers, electronic communications is rapidly replacing many forms of both verbal and written communications. *Verbal communications* refers to the transmittal of human voice communications through interpersonal exchanges, over the air waves or through some other medium.

Computer assisted writing or *CAW* is the application of CBTS to the preparation, editing and dissemination of printed documents in an organization. Word processing and desk publishing are two of the most common uses of CBTS in any organization. CAW allows writers to assemble their written statements or documents, then edit them for readability and reading comprehension before they are distributed. CAW can also be used to distribute the completed information as well. Many criminal justice organizations have tried, with varying degrees of success, to become "paperless" so far as the distribution of internal documents are concerned. The CAW signals the intended recipient that a message is waiting. The recipient can read the message (document) on the computer screen, then print it out if a hard or paper copy is needed (Dean, 1989). Other CAW systems allow the message to be sent to all intended recipients through a facsimile or FAX system. The document is prepared in the word processor, then sent to the FAX system to be distributed to from one of several hundred different locations ranging from a few feet away to thousands of miles. Still other CAW systems make it possible to send documents directly to a central distribution center where it is printed on paper and sent to intended recipients. Often, these communications are prepared through the use of desktop publishing programs that give a professional print quality to the final publication.

In addition, most justice organizations also depend on CBTS radio, microwave or cellular technologies to send human voice communications as well (Parks, 1990; Harman, 1991; Dertouzos, 1991). However, perhaps the most important of the recent CBTS developments is in the area of computer assisted dispatch systems or CADS. Sparrow notes:

> The development of police technology during the 1980s focused principally on the acquisition by police departments of two major types of systems: CAD (computer-aided dispatch, sometimes called "enhanced") and AFIS (automated fingerprint identification systems). CAD systems have been augmented by the use of mobile display terminals (MDTs) in patrol cars, by automatic vehicle locator systems, and by integrations of geographic information (GIS) capabilities into CAD control systems. AFIS frequently has been tied to existing criminal history data bases (Sparrow, 1993: 6).

In many metropolitan areas an emergency call for assistance might be received either by a human dispatcher or by a computerized voice recognizer. Under optimal operating conditions, within one to three seconds after a call is received, the information is entered into a data base, the priority determined, and an order to respond is sent to the closest available unit. The CAD systems can then route the emergency unit to the scene of the emergency by the quickest route. Additional information on the call is transmitted while police cruisers are heading toward their destination. Unfortunately, in many areas the high volume of high priority calls (e.g., shootings, robbery in progress, major traffic accidents with life threatening consequences) utilize all available units. Consequently, CADs often do not result in improved response time to less serious emergency calls (e.g., minor traffic accident, home burglary not-in-progress). Also, field computers and portable crime lab computers are used to collect and measure crime scene field data which is often transferred electronically via CBTS microwave radio technology back to base stations and powerful forensic crime computers for detailed analysis.

Federal agencies such as the FBI and DEA employ video-telephones that allow agents in the field to see and talk to superiors in Washington D.C. They also allow interaction with agency data bases as well as giving supervisors data on the location of agents.

CBTS high tech monitoring devices make it possible to aim a microwave dish at a building or automobile hundreds of feet away, listen in on conversations, obtain video images and other information. CBTS observation and intelligence gathering equipment employ technologies that do not fit traditional definitions of "wire tapping" about which right to privacy laws have been written in many states. There are issues of concern and debate.

Computer Assisted Diagnosis, Instruction and Training

CBTS are being employed in all forms of diagnoses techniques from assessing the operation of a modern automobile to medical diagnosis of illnesses to psychological testing of human beings (Anthes, 1991; Cash and Brown, 1989; Waldron et al., 1987: 41-58). Computer assisted diagnosis of personality disorders, or reading and educational deficiencies are commonplace in many clinics and school settings today. Some probation departments are generating pre-hearing and pre-sentence evaluations, social history reports and risk analysis ratings using computers. While there are many different forms of this technology in use today, most involve sitting a person down in front of a computer that asks the subject to respond to questions. Sometimes the person is aided by another person who may read the questions to the test subject and record the subject's responses. In all forms, the computer scores and analyzes the test results, producing a report. Some research suggests that computers are much more accurate than human testers in administering psychological tests. The FBI and other law enforcement agencies employ programs that allow the analysis and profiling of criminal personality types. Psychological and psychiatric diagnoses of human pathologies are also possible using current technology.

Computer assisted diagnosis is also used with two other CBTS applications: Computer assisted instruction (CAI) and computer based training (CBTS). CAI is a term that is used for a variety of applications which involve using computers to augment or substitute for human classroom teaching. The vast majority of CAI applications involve augmentation, rather than substitution. CAI places the learner in direct inter-action with a computer and a computer program that presents information to the learner and then tests learning levels. CAI was generally unheard of two decades ago. Today, it is used in hundreds of thousands of classrooms throughout the United States. CAI often combines video and CD-ROM technologies to place the learner in a two-dimensional video learning environment.

CAI is used in correctional institutions in teaching subjects ranging from GED (General Education Development) preparation to teaching academic subjects such as math, reading and history. CAI is also useful in alternative school settings. Some students who have trouble relating to human authority figures or who find traditional classrooms to be too difficult can find great success in learning through CAI. Consequently, CAI has great utility for various kinds of alternatives to traditional schools.

Computer based training refers to the application of the same technology to the training of people and employees for specific jobs or positions (Orlin, 1991; Booker, 1990; Fritz, 1991). It is extensively used in police training simulations and to a lesser extent in the training of correctional personnel. It is used in the skill training of offenders both inside and outside correctional institutions. Much more sophisticated computer based training has been borrowed from military simulation trainers. Simulators present pilots and tank drivers with video scenery that interacts with the actions of the trainee. Simulation training has led to the development of *virtual reality* (VR) technologies that allow humans to become part of the computer generated "reality." Through virtual reality, human body movement is part of the computer program allowing the human to move about the three-dimensional surrealistic world of the computer in much the same manner as did the fictional characters in the movie *TRON*.

VR allows architects, as well as aircraft designers, to "see" and "walk" through computer-generated simulations based on the plans. Changes and errors can be detected in construction before the plans are ever built. Current discussions and debates revolve around how VR technology could be used in teaching and training people, as well as how it might be used in the treatment of the mentally ill. VR may also have great potentials for the treatment and rehabilitation of offenders in the future.

Computer Assisted Monitoring of Offenders

Computer Assisted Monitoring of Offenders or *CAMO* is defined (Archambeault and Archambeault, 1989, pp. 170-171) as having two unique properties:

> First is the notion that a computer, through some form of sensory input and with minimum human intervention, can systematically assimilate, store, analyze and retrieve information about individual offenders.
> Second is the notion that the computer assisted monitoring system has the ability to directly or indirectly influence or control the behavior of the offender.

CAMO is commonly discussed under the heading of "electronic monitoring" or "home arrest." CAMO is in its infancy and may become the single most significant sentencing and correctional alternative of the twenty-first century. Currently, there may be as many as seventy thousand offenders under some form of CAMO control and this number may well triple by the year 2000.

However, current legal, ethical and economic issues, combined with a lack of creative thinking, have retarded the development of CAMO technologies thus far this century. Legal controversies involving CAMO often revolve around issues of privacy—that of the offender and those who live in the same location with him or her. Current "rule of thumb" legal standards generally hold that it is legal to monitor an offender's time related activities and location. However, unless there is a substance abuse issue involved, it may not be legal to monitor offender physiology or biology. It may also not be legal to invade the privacy of other people (e.g., family, friends) who may live with the offender. These standards restrict the type of CBTS that can be incorporated into legal CAMO devices.

Ethical issues are many and varied. Some revolve around questions such as "How much external State control over an offender's life, outside a prison or jail, is justified?" Does the State, through its law enforcement and correctional control social institutions, have the right to monitor every aspect of an offender's life? To what degree must the offender be free to choose whether or not to commit crime again? If the State is allowed to restrict to the maximum degree that CBTS allows the rights and movement of offenders in the community, then what is to stop it from using the same "Big Brother" technology to restrict the rights of other classes of citizens?

Economic issues are directly linked to legal and ethical issues. Although manufacturers have the capability of producing significantly more sophisticated CAMO systems, they would be much more expensive than current products. Legal and ethical considerations have influenced manufacturers to concentrate on marketing less controversial and less effective CBTS devices.

The problems associated with current market driven CAMO technologies prompt some critics to argue that electronic monitoring and criminal justice related CBTS are merely passing fads (Corbett and Marx, 1991). Others disagree (Lilly, 1992). Moreover, such conclusions often do not reflect an accurate understanding of the range of CBTS applications that could be employed in a CAMO context. To aid in the understanding of the real potential of CAMO, this writer developed and presented a seven category continuum typology (Archambeault and Archambeault, 1989: 170-187) and later elaborated upon it (Archambeault and Gould, 1990). This continuum typology includes:

1. computer assisted diagnosis and instructional systems;
2. computerized offender transaction data bases;
3. fixed location detector devices;
4. mobile location detectors;
5. mobile location and biophysical data transmission devices;
6. external behavior altering and monitoring systems; and
7. intracranial stimulation and subcutaneous control devices. Space limitations will not allow a detailed discussion of each. However, the following seven summary comments are appropriate.

First, moving from CAMO Type 1 to 7, the extent of external control or influence over offender behavior and activities increase in addition to the amount of information on subjects which is collected and analyzed by computer.

Second, computer assisted diagnosis and instructional systems[9] (CAMO Type 1) and computerized offender transaction data bases (CAMO Type 2) are the most common and widely accepted forms of CAMO.

Third, although there is a wide variety of CBTS integrated technologies used in "offender monitoring" devices today, most are CAMO Type 3 which transmit only three basic pieces of information: (1) time, (2) fixed location and (3) subject identification using early 1980s technology[10]. Currently, there are many problems with CAMO Type 3 devices. For example, to track an offender's movement from point A (home) to B (work), fixed monitors must be installed in both locations. There is no continuous monitoring during movement. Perhaps the worst feature of current monitoring practices is the great number of paper reports that must be read by human probation, or parole or community control officers to detect patterns of violating behavior. Often, stacks of daily reports are placed in files, lost, thrown away, but not read. Reports are sometimes generated on a twenty-four hour basis, while monitoring agencies themselves are only open eight to twelve hours a day. When a violation occurs during an agency's "closed hours," it may be twelve to eighteen hours before anyone knows it. This is obviously time enough for the offender to disappear or return to his/her assigned location. Consequently, the effectiveness of the "control" aspect is sometimes questioned.

Fourth, the technologies for CAMO Type 4, mobile location detectors, and Type 5, mobile location and biological data transmitters currently exist, but few products are currently marketed in the United States. For example, CAMO Type 4 devices could be constructed out of the same technologies which create CAD (computer aided dispatch), AVL (automatic vehicle locator) and other emergency CBTS systems. Mobile emergency medical technologies monitoring systems could be added to create CAMO Type 5 devices. These systems would allow continuous point to point monitoring of offender behavior and actions. However, this technology is much more expensive than Type 3 devices. Additionally, legal and ethical issues concerning their use are still unresolved in some jurisdictions.

However, during the 1980s, the emphasis on DWI or DUI enforcement led to the acceptance of the use of some of this technology in detecting substance abuse violations. Consequently, there are several devices that are capable of detecting substance abuse violations and reporting them in the process of offender monitoring. Most of these either use the breath from the subject or measure toxins on the surface of the skin to detect violations. Although the products currently on the market are fairly primitive, much more sophisticated technology already exists in the medical, bio-medical and space research programs. These "state of the art" biomedical sensors and transponders are able to monitor a wide range of biological and biophysical functions of the human body, in addition to the detection of a wide spectrum of gasses and toxin exposures to human skin surface. For example, in Japan, a system is being developed that will allow drivers, as well as monitoring authorities, to detect when a driver is too tired to drive safely by reading the buildup of certain chemical compounds on the skin surface. Similar systems already exist in other countries that alert drivers and authorities when too much alcohol has been consumed.

Fifth, external behavior altering and monitoring systems (CAMO Type 6) and inter-cranial stimulation and subcutaneous control devices (CAMO Type 7) offer the most potential for correctional control of offenders, but are also the most controversial. Currently, these CBTS applications are not legal correctional control methods and exist only as theoretical CAMO types. They extend the concept of monitoring from that of simply collecting information on offenders to that of directly intervening in offender behavior and actions. Arguably, crude forms of CAMO Type 6 can be seen in the devices that will not permit a driver who has consumed alcoholic beverages from being able to start his vehicle. Slightly more advanced prototype devices contain prom chips and voice synthesizers; when alcohol or drug toxins are detected and devices can make instant records and generate verbal warnings. In theory, these could warn a pro-bationer or parolee that he or she is around illegal substances and might, as a conse-quence, have his/her probation or parole revoked. Others might produce minor shocks and be used in combination with a behavioral modification reinforcement regime. Still other devices might allow the release of drug agents onto the surface of the skin that counter the effects of the drug or produce an adverse physical reaction.

However, much more sophisticated mechanisms are currently in use in medical treatment and biotechnical research. Computers are now able to communicate directly with brain cells; future potentials may allow computers to abstract information from human brains that may be lost to the conscious mind. Many forms of medical patches or external devices are used to monitor patient electrochemical balances in the body. These patches might also offer potential application in the control, monitoring, and treatment of selected offenders with biological or physical based mental problems or with substance abuse addictions.

CAMO Type 7 devices extend this technology of control into the human body itself through implants. Although no devices are currently marketed for use in moni-toring offenders, much of the technology needed to implant miniaturized computer devices in the body, especially the brain, already exists. For decades there has been continuous medical and physiological research into human brain-body connections. Research, for example, has shown that the artificial stimulation of selected parts of any organism's brain can give that organism the greatest pleasure or pain that the organism is capable of experiencing. Other research has extended the use of minia-turized computers that are surgically implanted in the brain, central nervous system, or other parts of the body. These devices can monitor body motor activities or functions, or stimulate brain or sensory feelings and sensations. Other devices can regulate the body's own chemistry and electrophysiology. When combined together, these technologies make it theoretically possible to both monitor and control the organism. The implications of this technology for the future are awesome.

Sixth, the range of CBTS biomedical technologies that could potentially be used for the monitoring and control of offenders is developing much more rapidly than the legal and ethical issues which they create can be resolved. More sophisticated CBTS human control technologies currently exist than were ever conceptualized by George Orwell in his book *1984.*

Finally, a lack of creative thinking and void of adequate theory also hinder the efficient use of CAMO. The phenomena of CAMO has not been adequately conceptualized in terms of theory development. Terms such as "electronic monitoring" or "house arrest" obscure the nature of CAMO and hinder understanding. Combined with a lack of creativity in thinking about how current CBTS could be used, CAMO has not advanced much beyond the early 1980s capabilities.

Computer Related Crime

Computers have also altered the nature and characteristics of crime and criminals. The 1990s continue to experience an increase in computer related crime, including: electronic fraud, viruses, terrorism, and security system violations (Alexander, 1991; Rotenberg, 1991; McCullock, 1990; Rosenblatt, 1990). This technological crime has engendered much debate about privacy issues (Weinberg, 1991) and the potential threats posed by the emerging "electronic information highway." It has also increased the demand and utilization of more powerful and "smarter" computer systems for the protection of data systems as well as the detection and investigation of computer related crimes (Clede, 1990). The nature of computer crime will change in the future as will the investigative tools of law enforcement as a function of the development of artificial intelligence and virtual reality.

CRIMINAL JUSTICE 2000: IMPLICATIONS AND CONCLUSIONS

If the past two decades are indicators of the future, then the line between science fiction and scientific fact will continue to blur as the twenty-first century approaches. On any given day, computer research may dramatically redefine "state of the art" technology as it has so many times over the past few years. Computer technology which only existed in "sci-fi" movies and literature of the 1960s and 1970s became operational realities of the 1980s and early 1990s. In part, this progress occurs because computer technology evolves as an end in itself and is propelled by theoretical, futuristic thinking. It is left up to others to determine how to apply the technology to different functions.

If the past is an indicator of the future, then it is logical to take current evolving technologies and project their usage into the future. Three emerging computer technologies have significant implications for criminal justice of the twenty-first centuries: artificial intelligence, virtual reality and biomedical research into direct brain-computer linkage.

Research in artificial intelligence may totally revolutionize current concepts of computers. In the near future, for example, it may be possible for users to verbally interact (talk) with computers, inputting data and instructions without having to touch a keyboard. Computers will clarify what they are supposed to do by asking the user questions. Computers will be able to provide users with verbal output information, in addition to printing reports or graphics. Emerging AI technology will also make it possible to develop network linkages among currently incompatible data bases.

These advances will be incorporated into criminal justice communication and crime analysis capabilities. Increasingly, crime scene evidence will be collected and analyzed in the field or at crime scenes. New verbal interactions between officers on the street and centralized computers may change the meaning of "partner." These advances may result in improved accuracy of evidence. Courts—judges, prosecutors, defense attorneys—may be able to directly interface with legal data bases during trials, allowing the introduction of higher court decisions to be applied instantly after they are made. Computers may guide all the court actors as to procedures, leading to fewer errors.

Corrections will use AI to manage its huge offender data systems. However, AI advancements will also lead to more secure correctional facilities and more effective treatment programs. CAMO effectiveness will be strengthened by allowing AI to screen offender "monitoring" reports and making more efficient use of probation officer or community control officer time.

AI, in combination with Virtual Reality technology, may have tremendous implications for criminal justice. For example, today computer generated graphical arrays and displays are already being used to illustrate events surrounding crime scene investigations and traffic accidents in American courts. Future developments in AI-VR CBT may enable computer simulations to be generated as witnesses testify as to what they observed. Drawing from current research on direct brain-computer interface, VR-AI may allow witnesses to recall subconscious or suppressed memories. Conceivably, it may even be possible to question a subject and obtain accurate perceptions of facts and events without consent; such usage would have obvious constitutional implications.

The integration of artificial intelligence, virtual reality, and computer assisted instruction may have great potential for offender therapy and rehabilitation. For example, in the future it may be possible for people to read sensory or action words (e.g., hot, ice, wind, run) and experience the physiological sensations associated with them. In this context, it may enhance the learning process and enable students who have difficulty learning through conventional methods to learn better. It may also speed up the process of learning for normal learners, allowing the acquisition of knowledge more rapidly than through conventional methods. Under therapeutic counseling conditions, offenders may be able to relive their crimes and experience the reactions and feelings of their victims. Similar technology may allow the probing of deep psychological, emotional and social learning problems.

The VR-AI technology may have some negative effects as well. The same technology may also create new forms of addiction that could be more powerful than biology-based drug addiction. It could also be used to "brainwash" or alter human learned value systems. The future applications of computers in criminal justice will be limited only by human imagination, ethics and law.

STUDY QUESTIONS

1. Discuss the implications of Computer Based Technologies (CBTS) on the management of criminal justice organizations in an information dependent society. How is this dependency manifested in all criminal justice organizations today? How might it be manifested in the twenty-first century?

2. What are the requirements of true Artificial Intelligence (AI)? Does AI actually exist today? What are "smart," "expert," and "brilliant" computers? What bearing will artificial intelligence have on the operations of criminal justice agencies and institutions of the future?

3. What is CAMO? What are the seven categories of CAMO? What are some of the ethical, moral, and legal questions that surround the use of CAMO today?

4. Discuss the potential combined effects and uses of AI and Virtual Reality (VR) on criminal justice of the twenty-first century.

5. Discuss and debate the statement: "If the past two decades are indicators of the future, then the line between science fiction and scientific fact will continue to blur as the twenty-first century approaches." What significance might this statement have on the fundamental concept of American criminal justice?

END NOTES

1. *Input* refers to the fact that the device is capable of receiving electronic coded data or information. Input can come from a *user* or person who operates the computer through keyboard commands, or from already stored data, or from the output of some other program. Input can also come from sensor readings; from data transmitted over wire, radio waves or microwaves; or from hundreds of other sources.

2. *Storage* refers to the fact that the electronic device is capable of storing or saving the input data or information for some future use. Storage can either be for a short period of time or for permanent or long-term. For example, data saved by a computer only until it is turned off is said to be *held in memory*. On the other hand, data is said to be "stored" when it is saved to electronic media, such as disks, tapes, CD Roms or other devices, and if it is present even after a computer is turned "off" and "on" again. The distinction between "memory" and "storage" in many computers is whether the user input data remains and is retrievable after the computer is turned off.

3. *Processing* refers to the capability of the device to do something with the input data or information. Normally, processing involves the manipulation, use or analysis of the stored data or information. It is the reason for the computer in the first place. The user controls the computer either through direct instructions to it, which is another form of input, or through programs. *Programs* are sets of pre-written instructions or applications. A few of the most common application programs today are: word processing, spreadsheets or accounting ledgers, statistical analysis, games, telecommunications processing to mention only a few.

Through all of these, the input data is transformed into a more usable format by the computer for the human user. Word processing or telecommunications facilitate human communications. Statistical analysis and spreadsheets allow the user to summarize and analyze numerical data. Games allow the user to play according to the rules of the program. Processing may also involve the monitoring or controlling of production machines, robots, the flight of aircraft, or thousands of different functions.

4. *Output* refers to the ability to get the processed data or information out of the computer. Frequently, output takes the form of alpha-numeric or graphic print formats such as those that are produced through word processing, statistical analysis or graphics. Other times, the output function is to cause another device to be manipulated or controlled, such as the use of computers to regulate heating and cooling in a building or regulate the flow of fuel in a modern car's injector's system. Other times, the output function of one program may be the input functions of another. Where these functions occur, they are said to be looped or linked together. For example, the output function of a word processing program may be the simultaneous printing of a document, the saving of the document file, and the creation of a backup of the file. Many other types of output functions are also possible.

5. Personal computers (PCs) are stand alone systems which include CPU, disk drive(s), CRTs or monitors and keyboards. These may be connected to peripheral devices including: modems, faxes, printers, tape drivers among others. PCs are generally intended for one user, although PC networks can interconnect many PCs and users.

6. Mini-computers and mainframe computers are central memories that are accessed through remote terminals. Both mini and mainframe computers are designed by multiple users to run multiple programs. "Mini" computers are small main frame computers which are generally much more powerful than PCs. Mini-computers are sometimes used in PC networks as file servers or central computers. Mainframe computers are the most powerful computers in existence. They are often able to service thousands of users who are running hundreds of different programs.

7. In the environment of the 1990s, there are literally tens of thousands of different CBT applications in use and hundreds more being created daily. These include programmable TVs, radios, VCRs, satellite dishes, coffee pots, alarm clocks, digital wrist watches or video games, microwave ovens, memory typewriters, motion detectors or lights, voice activated security systems, voice activated dictation equipment, cellular telephones, printers, modems, fax machines, copying machines, memory telephones, electronic fuel injection and emissions systems in most newer vehicles. Whole areas of operations depend on integrated computer technologies, including: robotics, telephone, cable, microwave and radio wave communications devices, biomedical treatment and research monitors, laser surgery, CAT Scans, radiation therapy, among others.

8. Data are raw facts or computer encoded numeric symbols. Information refers to facts that communicate meaning to the human being.

9. For discussions on why these are included in the CAMO typology refer to citations given above.

10. Refer to Archambeault and Archambeault, 1989, 172-180 for discussion of different specific characteristics of different types of equipment used.

BIBLIOGRAPHY

Alexander, M. (1991). "Justice Unit Spurred on by Cross-border Hackers." *Computerworld*. (October 21, Vol XXV, No. 42):5.

Alexander, M. (1989). "Hacker Stereotypes Changing." *Computerworld*. (April):101.

Alleman, T. (1990). "The Computerized Prison: Automation in a Penal Setting." in Schmalleger, F. (ed.) *Computers in Criminal Justice: Issues and Applications*. Wyndham Hall Press.

Anthes, G.H. (1991). "Computers Play Part in Addicts' Recovery." *Computerworld*. (September):45.

Archambeault, W. and L. Gould. (1990). "The Computer Assisted Monitoring of Offenders (CAMO): an Emerging Alternative to Incarceration." in Schmalleger, F. (ed.) *Computers in Criminal Justice: Issues and Applications*. Wyndham Hall Press: Bristol, TN.

Archambeault, W.G. and B.J. Archambeault. (1989). *Computers in Criminal Justice Administration and Management*. 2nd Edition. Anderson: Cincinnati, OH.

Bardege, S. (1990). "Technology Boosts Law Enforcement." *American City & County*. (February):14.

Block, M.H. (1990). "Computer-integrated Courtroom: Moving the Judicial System into the Twenty-first Century." *Trial*. Vol. 26 (September):30-52.

Booker, E. (1990). "Grading High-tech Teaching." *Computerworld*. (February 19):114.

Branscomb, A.W. (1991). "Common Law for the Electronic Frontier." *Scientific American*. (September):154-158.

Branwyn, G. (1990). "Computers, Crimes and the Law." *The Futurist*. (Vol. XXIV, 5):48.

Cash, T.F. and T. Brown. (1989). "Validity of Millon's Computerized Interpretation System for the MCMI: Comment on Moreland and Onstad." *Journal of Consulting and Clinical Psychology*. (Vol. 57, No. 2):311-312.

Churbuck, D. (1991). "The Computer as Detective." *Forbes*. (December):150-155.

Clede, B. (1990). "Computer-Aided Investigation." *Police Chief*. (April):45.

Corbett, R. and G.T. Marx. (1991). "Critique: No Soul in the New Machine: Technofallacies in the Electronic Monitoring Movement." *Justice Quarterly*. Vol. 8 (3):399-414.

Dean, J.M. (1989). "Computers are like Cars..." *Federal Probation*. (June):61-64.

Dertouzos, M.L. (1991). "Communications, Computers, and Networks." *Scientific American*. (September):63-69.

Dworetzky, T. (1991). "Mechanimals." *Omni*. (March):50-56.

Fritz, M. (1991). "Future Looks at Little Brighter for CBT." *Computerworld*. (April):16.

Geake, E. (1991). "Transputers Speed up Medical Diagnosis." *New Scientist*. (24, August):24.

Gruner, R.S. (1989). "Sentencing Advisor: An Expert Computer System for Federal Sentencing Analysis." *Santa Clara Computer and High Technology Law Journal*. (February):51-73.

Harman, A. (1991). "Photophone." *Law and Order*. (February):28-30.

Hitt, J. and P. Tough. (1990). "Terminal Delinquents." *Computerworld*. (December):174-178; 182-183; 211-219.

Jameson, R. and C. Megerman. (1990). "Automation in Medium-Sized Jail." *Corrections Today*. (July):180-182.

Johnson, W. (1989). "Information Espionage: An old problem with a New Face." *Computerworld*. (October):85.

Kapor, M. (1991). "Civil Liberties in Cyberpsace." *Scientific American*. (September):158-164.

Larson, R. (1989). "The New Crime Stoppers." *Tecknology Review*. (Nov/Dec):28-31.

Lilly, J.R. (1992). "Review Essay: Selling Justice: Electronic Monitoring and the Security Industry." *Justice Quarterly*. Vol. 9 (3, September):493-503.

Manchester, R.E. (1991). "Office Organization in the Computer Era." *Trial*. Vol. 27 (January):29-31.

McCullock, D.J. (1990). "Computer Based Security Systems Save Money Boost Safety." *Corrections Today*. (July):86, 88, 90-91.

Meyer, G. and J. Thomas. (1990). "The 'Baudy' World of the Byte Bandit: A Postmodernist Interpretation of the Computer Underground." in Schmalleger, F. (ed.) *Computers in Criminal Justice: Issues and Applications*. Wyndham Hall Press: Bristol, TN.

Moreley, H. (1990). "Computer Viruses: High Technology Automated Crime." in Schmalleger, F. (ed.) *Computers in Criminal Justice: Issues and Applications*. Wyndham Hall Press: Bristol, TN.

Nagelhaut, M. (1992). "Caller ID: Privacy and Blocking Issues." *Public Utilities Fortnightly*. (March 1):31-33.

Orlin, J.M. (1991). "Alien Technology Made Familiar." *Training and Development*. (November):55-58.

Parks, C.M. (1990). "Handheld Police Computers: the Ticket of the Future." *Police Chief*. (April):36-40.

Reboussin, R. (1990). "An Expert System Designed to Profile Murderers." in Schmalleger, F. (ed.) *Computers in Criminal Justice: Issues and Applications*. Wyndham Hall Press: Bristol, TN.

Reboussin, R. and W. Rafoya. (1990). "The Development of Artificial Intelligence Expert Systems in Law Enforcement." in Schmalleger, F. (ed.) *Computers in Criminal Justice: Issues and Applications*. Wyndham Hall Press: Bristol, TN.

Roberts, L. (1991). "GRAIL Seeks out Genes Buried in DNA Sequence." *Research News*. (8, November):805.

Rosenblatt, K. (1990). "Deterring Computer Crime." *Technology Review*. (February/March):35-40.

Rotenberg, M. (1991). "Lets Look Before we Legislate: Laws are adequate to Handle Computer Crime; 'Net Police' Not Needed." *Computerworld*. (October 21, Vol. XXV, No. 42):40.

Saylor, W. (1990). "Federal Bureau of Prison Systems Tracks Inmate Populations." *Corrections Today*. (July):24, 26, 28.

Schmalleger, F. (ed.) (1990). *Computers in Criminal Justice: Issues and Applications*. Wyndham Hall Press: Bristol, TN.

Sikes, A. (1991). "Brink of Revolution." *Newsweek*. (January 14):8.

Sparrow, W. (1993). "Information Systems and the Development of Policing." *Perspectives on the Police*. United States Department of Justice. United States Printing Office, Washington, DC. (March):1-11.

Stephens, G. (1990). "Impact of Emerging Police and Corrections Technology on Constitutional Rights." in Schmalleger, F. (ed.) *Computers in Criminal Justice: Issues and Applications*. Wyndham Hall Press: Bristol, TN.

Waldron, J., B. Archambeault, W. Archambeault, L. Carsone, J. Conser and C. Sutton. (1987). *Microcomputers in Criminal Justice*. Cincinnati, OH:Anderson.

Weinberg D. (1989). "Computers are Talking in America's Courts." *The Judges' Journal*. Vol. 28 (Spring):4-7.

Weinberg D. (1990). "Prison a la Carte." *The Economist*. (September 8):57.

Weinberg D. (1992). "Police Computer fuels fears of 'European Connection'" *New Scientist*. (4, January):14.

Weinberg D. (1991). "Computers and Privacy: The Eye of the Beholder." *The Economist*. (May 4, Vol. 319, 7705):21-23.

PART VII

INTRODUCTION

GENDER ISSUES NOW AND IN THE NEXT CENTURY

Roslyn Muraskin reviews the subject of "Women and the Law: Future Issues" and discusses how historically women have always been discriminated against by the criminal justice system. Women were not considered "citizens" and did not enjoy the same rights and privileges that men did. As we approach the twenty-first century, what conditions will prevail and what differences will be seen in the handling of women and their continuing cry for equal justice?

As we look to the twenty-first century, we note that the HIV virus and AIDS are posed to create unprecedented administrative, custodial, economic and health care changes within the correctional facilities. Most research has been concentrated on the male inmates, but what about the female inmates? Mark Lanier's chapter, "Justice for Incarcerated Women with HIV in the Twenty-First Century," discusses such issues. This population is the fastest growing population in the correctional facilities, and is fast growing in numbers having the AIDS virus. New policies need to be developed regarding female correctional health policies. This circumstance will not go away and action is needed desperately.

In another area that focuses on women and minorities, Sean Grennan deals with "Women as Police Supervisors in the Twenty-First Century: A Decade of Promotional Practices by Gender in Three Major Police Agencies." As police departments enter the twenty-first century, they must realize that the growing female population is just as competent as anyone in the ever present male contingent. The time is long overdue for female police supervisors to be promoted above the highest rank of civil service testing, usually captain, into the politically appointed positions from Deputy Inspector to Assistant Chief. It is anticipated, according to Grennan, that as women continue to enter law enforcement that their total percentage in policing will reach the 30-35% bracket by the year 2010. Women are a viable asset to the police departments and must be recognized as such.

CHAPTER 21

WOMEN AND THE LAW

WHAT THE FUTURE HOLDS

Roslyn Muraskin, Ph.D.

ABSTRACT

Females are not catching up with males in the commission of violent, masculine or serious crimes. What is happening to females is they are becoming victims of more violent crimes. There are arguments that females have more equality than ever before, and in some cases this might be true, but unfortunately females are also being victimized in more areas than ever before. As women have gained more equality, they have become harassed by employers in a manner akin to rape and cases of domestic violence. There needs to be developed for the twenty-first century a strategy that will provide law enforcement personnel with a better understanding of the kinds of crime that are being committed against women. The argument is made that while the public is slowly starting to realize the dynamics of rape, domestic violence, and sexual harassment and its aftermath, there are many experts in the field of criminal justice who feel more has to be done.

INTRODUCTION

Historically, women have been discriminated by law. Women, in fact, have been victimized by policies designed to protect them. Women, during the last decades, have taken their cases to court to argue for equality. The history of women's struggles teaches us that litigation is but a catalyst for change. A change in attitude is still needed. Discrimination still exists. Women still continue to struggle. Controversy still abounds.

Women's issues infuse every aspect of social and political thought. Women's basic human rights are inextricably linked to our treatment by and with their participation in today's political world. Due to the fact that the lives of women are reflections of what they do, what they say, and how they treat each other, women as participating members of the human race are ultimately responsible for human affairs.

What then is the agenda for change in the criminal law as we approach the twenty-first century? There is no way to automatically allow both sexes to enjoy the equal protection of the laws unless we are committed to the elimination of all sexual discrimination. The criminal justice system over the years has slowly come to grips with the needed understanding of women and justice. As we approach the twenty-first century more and more cases will be heard in the courts where legal procedures and precedent have been established to insure that complainants will receive a fairer hearing than before. Courts will need to allow time for discovery of evidence and the opportunity to hear expert testimony in cases of sexual violence.

Crimes such as rape, domestic violence, and sexual harassment are all part of the continuum of violence against women. Rape is not a crime of sex, it is a crime of power. It is "an act of violence, an assault like any other, not an expression of socially organized sexuality" (MacKinnon, 1979:218). The fact that rape is acted out of sex does not mean that it is an act of male sexuality. Rape is simply an act of violence. As of late the act of sexual harassment has drawn parallels to the crime of rape. If sex or sexual advances are unwanted, if they are imposed on a woman who is in no position to refuse, why is this act any different from rape? It may be a lesser crime, but yet it is an act of violence against women. Perhaps by the twenty-first century, acts such as sexual harassment will be illegal under the criminal law. Sexual harassment **is** sexual discrimination and laws are needed to remedy such disparities.

According to MacKinnon, "a crime of sex is a crime of power" (220). Taken together, both rape and sexual harassment eroticize women's subordination. This eroticization continues the powerlessness of women as a gender by the criminal law. "If sexuality is set apart from gender, it will be a law unto itself" (MacKinnon:221).

History

The fact of the matter is that when this country was founded, it was founded on the two principles that (1) "all men are created equal" and that (2) "Governments derive their powers from the consent of the governed." Women were not included in either concept. The Constitution of the United States did not include women as citizens or as individuals with legal rights. Women were not considered persons under the Fourteenth Amendment to the constitution which guaranteed that no state shall deny to "any person within its jurisdiction the equal protection of the laws." Therefore, in the face of the law women had no rights, as they did not exist.

The women's movement has been the most integrated and populist force in this country. Seven years after women won the right to vote—a right granted to women **after** slaves were freed—women still wait for the promise of the Declaration of Independence, that of equality before and under the law.

There existed under the English common law the "rule of thumb," which allowed a husband to beat his wife with a whip or stick no bigger than his thumb. The husband's prerogative was incorporated into American law. The sad fact is that several states had laws on the book that essentially allowed a man to beat his wife with no interference from the courts. Blackstone referred to this action as the "power of correction." For too many decades women have been victims of sexual assault. Each act of "sexual assault is recognized as one of the most traumatic and debilitating crimes for adults...." (Roberts, 1993:362). The victimization of women has been most prevalent and problematic for the criminal justice system.

As pointed out by Susan Faludi

> women's advances and retreats are generally described in military terms: battles won, battles lost, points and territory gained and surrendered. In times when feminism is at a low ebb, women assume the reactive role— privately and most often covertly struggling to assert themselves against

the dominant cultural tide. But when feminism becomes the tide, the opposition doesn't simply go along with the reversal, it digs in its heels, brandishes its fists, builds walls and dams (1991).

In the past decade, we have seen sexual assault reform legislation resulting "in several long-overdue improvements in the criminal justice processing of sexual assault cases, for example, passage of rape shield laws, confidentiality laws to protect communications between the victims and their counselors, and laws designed to preserve medical evidence" (Roberts: 370). Additionally, victim assistance programs have been developed.

Sexual Harassment

The female represents half of the national population. She is deserving of the same rights and opportunities afforded all men. There exists the rhetoric of gender equality but it has yet to match the reality of women's experiences. The case of Anita Hill and Judge Clarence Thomas brought to light the words, **sexual harassment**, words that have gained new meaning.

In 1980 the Equal Employment Opportunity Commission defined sexual harassment as occurring when unwelcome sexual advances, requests for sexual favors, and other verbal or physical conduct of a sexual nature are made a condition of employment, are used in employment decisions, affect an employee's work performance or create an intimidating, hostile or offensive working environment. The Supreme Court upheld these guidelines in 1986 in the case of *Meritor Savings Bank v. Vinson*, where it ruled sexual harassment is sexual discrimination and illegal under Title VII of the Civil Rights Act of 1964. Throughout this country, Task Force Committees have been established to combat the charges of sexual harassment. It was almost as if the Thomas-Hill hearings brought people "out of the closet."

Cases have come to light such as the *Wagenseller v. Scottsdale* (1990) in Arizona where the Arizona Supreme Court overruled earlier law and recognized a public policy exception to discharge at will in the case of an emergency room nurse, who allegedly was terminated because she refused to "moon" on a rafting trip.

A worker who continuously harasses female co-workers and is discharged does not have a right to reinstatement for failure of the employer to follow the notice provisions of the contract (*Newsday v. Long Island Typographical Union* (1990)).

In the case of *Ellison v. Brady* (9th Cir. 1991) the trial court had dismissed "love" letters, which the plaintiff had received from a co-worker along with persistent requests for dates, as trivial. However, the Ninth Circuit disagreed. The court stated that the perspectives of men and women differ. Women, the court indicated, have a strong reason to be concerned about sexual behavior, due to the fact that they are the victims of rape and sexual assault.

A court in Florida ruled in the case of *Robinson v. Jacksonville Shipyards* (M.D. Fla. 1991) that the display of nude women can lead to the creation of a hostile environment, and therefore is deemed an act of discrimination.

In Minnesota the State Supreme Court in the case of *Continental Can Co. v. Minnesota* upheld an action against the employer because of the failure to take timely and appropriate action to stop harassment by fellow employees. In still another case, *EEOC v. Sage Realty Corp.*, the court held that an employer may impose reasonable dress codes for its employees, but the employer cannot require its employees to wear "revealing and sexually provocative uniforms" that would subject the employee to a form of sexual harassment. This constitutes sex discrimination.

What has increased is the notice that sexual harassment is more than mere physical touching. It exists if the employer/supervisor or co-worker subjects an individual (usually a woman) to the following:

- obscene pictures in the workplace or at a work sponsored activity
- leering at your body
- sexually explicit or derogatory remarks
- unnecessary touching, patting or pinching your body
- subtle pressure for sexual activities
- demanding sexual favors for a good work assignment, performance rating and/or promotion.

In the case of *Bundy v. Jackson* (1981) the plaintiff had been subjected to sexual propositions by five of her supervisors during a period of two and one-half years. Because the plaintiff was unable to demonstrate that her rejection of the supervisor's advances had resulted in loss of job benefits or promotions, she lost in the lower courts; but, in reversing the decision of the lower courts, the judge held that an employer violates Title VII merely by subjecting female employees to sexual harassment in the absence of the deprivation of tangible job benefits.

In *Vinson* Judge Rehnquist indicated that the proper questions to be asked was whether the plaintiff indicated that the alleged sexual advances were "unwelcome." It is not surprising that women would not complain of experiences for which there has been no name. Until 1976, lacking a term to express it, sexual harassment was literally unspeakable, which made generalized social definitions of it inaccessible (MacKinnon, 1979).

Originally thought to be limited to those relatively rare situations where women are compelled to trade sexual favors for professional survival, sexual harassment is now recognized more broadly as "the inappropriate sexualization of an otherwise nonsexual relationship, an assertion by men of the primacy of a woman's sexuality over her role as worker or student."

Legal scholars like Catherine MacKinnon, a law professor at the University of Michigan and activists like Susan Brownmiller are accredited with initiating the view of sexual harassment that has radically changed the way sexual harassment complaints are treated under the legal system. Shifting the focus of sexual harassment from the belief that males' sexual pursuit of a woman in the workplace or the classroom is essentially biological and that sexual harassment is therefore a "normal" consequence of attraction between the sexes, MacKinnnon, Brownmiller and others advocate a "dominance" approach. *Sexual harassment* is *sexual discrimination*. It occurs in the workplace because women occupy largely inferior job positions and roles. At the same time it also works to keep women "in their place."

Litigation

The law sees and treats women the way men see and treat women. The first litigation of sexual harassment claims did not occur until the mid-seventies. Title VII of the

Civil Rights Act prohibiting sex discrimination in the workplace was followed eight years later by Title IX of the 1972 Higher Education Amendments prohibiting sex discrimination in educational institutions receiving federal assistance. But in much of the early adjudication of sex discrimination, the phenomenon of sexual harassment was typically seen "as isolated and idiosyncratic, or as natural and universal, and in either case, as inappropriate for legal intervention." It was not until 1980 that the Equal Employment Opportunity Commission's "Guidelines on Discrimination" explicitly defined sexual harassment under Title VII as a form of unlawful, sex-based discrimination.

Victims' rights to collect damages continue to be limited under federal law. While the 1991 Civil Rights Act does not limit awards for back pay and past out of pocket damages like medical bills, the compromise forged to ensure passage of the bill in Congress and gain White House approval to limit other damages according to the size of the employer's work force. Unlike the potential damages available to victims of racial discrimination, damages for sex discrimination are capped at $50,000 for small companies and $300,000 for larger ones.

As the law has been interpreted, prohibition against sexual harassment in the workplace technically covers any remark or behavior that is sufficiently severe and perversive that not only the victim's but also a "reasonable person's" psychological well-being would be affected. A 1991 landmark ruling by the Court of Appeals for the Ninth Circuit in California held that "the appropriate perspective for judging a hostile environment claim is that of the 'reasonable woman' and recognized that a woman's perspective may differ substantially from a man's. There may be a difference between intent and impact. Many men may not intend it, but some things they do may be experienced by women as sexual harassment. A touch or comment can be seen very differently.

While the 1991 Ninth Circuit Court ruling acknowledges that men and women may interpret the same behavior differently, in application this legal understanding is often overshadowed by a grave misunderstanding of the nature of sexual harassment as experienced by its victims. The people doing the judging are in no position to understand the position of those being judged. The powerful make judgments against the powerless.

The dilemma in applying the reasonable person standard to sexual harassment is that a reasonable woman and a reasonable man are likely to differ in their judgment of what is offensive. Men's judgments about what behavior constitutes harassment, and who is to blame are likely to prevail. In terms of the court, what constitutes harassment and what determines the amounts of awards for damages under state law and in the future under federal law, ultimately depend on the perceptions of the judge rather than the victim, and the vestiges of long-standing prejudices do not seem entirely absent from judicial as well as workplace forums.

Rape

Like the crime of rape, sexual harassment is not an issue of lust; it is an issue of power. Sexual harassment must be viewed as the art of a continuum of sexual victimization that ranges from staring and leering to assault and rape. Most sexual harassment starts at the subtle end of the continuum and escalates over time. Each year, 1% of women in the U.S. labor force are sexually assaulted on the job. Yet cultural mythologies consistently blame the victim for sexual abuse and act to keep women in their place. Scholars have identified several similarities in attitudes toward rape and sexual harassment, essentially revealing cultural myths that blame the victim:

1. Women ask for it
   Rape: victims seduce their rapists.
   Sexual harassment: women precipitate harassment by the way they dress and talk.

2. Women say no but mean yes
   Rape: women secretly need and want to be forced into sex. They don't know what they want.
   Sexual harassment: women like the attention.

3. Women lie
   Rape: in most charges of rape, the woman is lying.
   Sexual harassment: women lie about sexual harassment in order to get men they dislike in trouble.

Women who speak about being victims of sexual harassment use words such as humiliating, intimidating, frightening, financially damaging, embarrassing, nerve-wracking, awful, and frustrating. These are not words that are used to describe a situation which one likes.

Historically the rape of a woman was considered to be the infringement of the property rights of man. Sexual harassment is viewed in the same light. The message, as we approach the twenty-first century, is the recognition that changes are needed. We can no longer blame the messenger. We need to understand the message. There is no question that what is referred to as "women's hidden occupational hazard," sexual harassment, is sexual victimization. The fact that sexual harassment exists demonstrates that it must be understood as part of the continuum of violence against women. In a typical sexual harassment case, the female accuser becomes the accused and the victim is twice victimized. This double injury holds true in the case of rape, and now as well in cases of sexual harassment. Underlying the dynamics of the situation is the profound distrust of the woman's word and a serious power differential between the accused and the accuser. Sexual harassment as indicated is the most recent form of victimization of the woman to be redefined as a social rather than a personal problem, following rape and wife abuse.

What actions are being taken? More and more cases are coming to light. There is the understanding that conduct that many men considered **unobjectionable** may very well offend women.

Agenda for Change

Litigation is occurring. Though we do not have a federal equal rights amendment, there are those states who recognize the worth of the E.R.A. As an example the use of male terms to indicate both sexes is slowly being examined. There are those who choose to use gender neutral terms. But sex discrimination is masked when such gender neutral terms are not used. Words are meant to have definitive meaning. "Words are workhorses of law" (Thomas, 1991: p. 116). The state of Washington has a constitution that states that "equality of rights and responsibility under the law shall not be denied or abridged on account of sex." This is a rare law in the nineties.

Women's issues infuse every aspect of social and political thought. Women's basic human rights are inextricably linked to their treatment by and with their participation in today's political world.

What is the agenda for change as we approach the twenty-first century? If the structure of society is found to be corrupt, then we should work to change it. If problems are too big for one person or group to solve, we should come together in cooperation and mutual support. We must do whatever is necessary to fight oppression and alleviate repressive conditions wherever they exist. The struggle of women continues under the law. There is no way to automatically allow both sexes to enjoy the equal protection of the laws unless we are committed to the elimination of all sexual discrimination. The criminal justice system over the years has slowly come to grips with the needed understanding of women and justice. Recent Supreme Court cases have noted that sexual harassment as such creates a hostile environment that defies "a mathematically precise test" and have called for an examination of all the circumstances of a case. As we approach the twenty-first century more and more cases will be heard in the courts where legal procedures and precedent have been established to insure that complainants will receive a fairer hearing than before. Courts will need to allow time for discovery of evidence and the opportunity to hear expert testimony of sexual harassment. Orderly proceedings should be in the offering.

In the 1990s during the Anita Hill/Clarence Thomas hearings there were vast differences between what we knew then about sexual harassment, what we know today, and what we will know for the future. *Then* the general public was unaware of sexual harassment as a legal question. For many the impact was astonishing.

Women are slowly coming out of their shell and are talking about their own painful experiences and how pervasive the problem is. In 1995 women simply asked that claims of sexual harassment be taken seriously—without the prejudicial hyperboles. With the collective efforts of many women, people are reacting to such claims with more intelligence than earlier. Sexual harassment is sex discrimination prohibited by the civil rights laws. Regardless of the movement afoot, when we look at acts of sexual violence against women, i.e., rape, sexual harassment, domestic violence, there will be needed in the twenty-first century efforts demonstrating the improvement of an all out response by the criminal justice system to remedy these situations.

There need to be more mandated services available to all women victims for whatever form of sexual assault occurs. There need to be laws protecting the confidentiality of victims. Victims of all types of sexual assault must be made to feel comfortable in coming forward to press charges. "Sexual assault victims deserve sensitive and fair treatment by police, prosecutors...social workers...the community" (Roberts: 366) and by both employers and the criminal justice system. We still await the day when the promise of reform becomes reality. The twenty-first century is almost here, and still we argue over equality for women.

STUDY QUESTIONS

1. What is it about our criminal justice system that views women differently than men?

2. Can we differentiate between rape, acts of domestic violence, and sexual harassment?

3. How will the twenty-first century view women as victims of crime?

4. Do we need a more formal mechanism for protecting the rights of women victims within the criminal justice system?

5. If you had to propose policies to change the way in which women were viewed by the criminal justice system, what policies would you propose and what would the punishments be, if any?

LEGISLATION

THE EQUAL PAY ACT (1963) prohibits an employer from paying employees in an establishment at a lesser rate than that at which he pays "employees of the opposite sex" where the work is "equal," the performance requires "equal skill, effort and responsibility" and is performed under "similar working conditions."

TITLE IX (1972) provides that no person shall be excluded from participation in, be denied the benefits of, or be subjected to discrimination on the basis of sex under any educational program or activity receiving federal financial assistance. 20 U.S.C. section 1681 (a)

REFERENCES

Faludi, Susan. (1991). *Backlash: The Undeclared War against American Women*. Crown Publishers, Inc.: New York.

MacKinnon, Catharine A. (1979). *Sexual Harassment of Working Women*. Yale University Press: New Haven and London.

Roberts, Albert R. (1993). "Women: Victims of Sexual Assault and Violence," in *It's a Crime: Women and Justice*. (ed. Muraskin and Alleman), Regents/Prentice Hall: New Jersey.

Thomas, Claire Sherman. 1991. *Sex Discrimination*. West Publishers: St. Paul, MN.

CASES

Bundy v. Jackson, 641 F.2d 934 (D.C. Cir 1981).

Continental Can Co., Inc. v. Minnesota, 297 N.W. 2d 241 (Minn. 1980), 242.

E.E.O.C. v. Sage Realty Corp., 507 F. Supp. 599 (D.C.N.Y. 1981), 243.

Ellison v. Brady, 924 F.2d 872 (9th Cir. 1991).

Marauder Savings Bank, FSB v. Vinson, 477 U.S. 57, 106 S. Ct. 2399, 91 L.Ed.2d 49 (1986), 239

Meritor Savings Bank, FSB v. Vinson, 477 U.S. 57, 106 S.Ct. 2399, 91 L.Ed.2d 49 (1986).

Newsday, Inc. v. Long Island Typographical Union, No. 915, 915 F.2d 840 (2nd Cir. 1990), cert. denied Long Island Typographical Union No. 915 v. Newsday, Inc., U.S. 111 S.Ct. 1314, 113 L. Ed. 2d 247 (1991), 195, 214.

Robinson v. Jacksonville Shipyards, Inc., 760 F. Supp. 1486 (M.D. Fla. 1991), 241.

Wagenseller v. Scottsdale Memorial Hosp., 147 Ariz. 370, 710 P.2d 1025 (Ariz. 1985), 194.

CHAPTER 22

JUSTICE FOR INCARCERATED WOMEN WITH HIV IN THE TWENTY-FIRST CENTURY

Mark M. Lanier, Ph.D.

ABSTRACT

As the next century approaches two health issues: Human Immunodeficiency Virus (HIV) and its consequence, Acquired Immunodeficiency Syndrome (AIDS) are posed to create unprecedented administrative, custodial, economic and health care changes within correctional facilities. Most research attention has been directed toward male inmates; however incarcerated females, like females not under custodial care, are among the fastest growing infected group. This chapter outlines the factors driving the increased threat to females. Demographic, epidemiological and social determinants are discussed. Furthermore, unique problems which face females are presented. In addition, a theoretical model—a modification of the AIDS Risk Reduction Model (ARRM)—is described. This heuristic device may help correctional administrators develop reasonable and effective policies. Several policy suggestions are presented which are based on the ARRM.

WOMEN, HIV, AND INCARCERATION

Institutionalized individuals are one of society's most ostracized groups. Much like leper colonies of the eighteenth century today's "correctional" facilities segregate the disempowered, the poor, drug users, and the violent from the rest of society. Also like leper colonies, inhabitants of these institutions face serious medical threats. Contemporary threats include acquired immunodeficiency virus (AIDS), hepatitis, human immunodeficiency virus (HIV), and tuberculosis. Unlike leper colonies, however, most of the inhabitants of modern penal colonies will one day reenter society—some infected with serious, contagious diseases.

Like lepers, in addition to physical separation, the stigma associated with institutionalization further isolates the incarcerated from "mainstream" society. As the unfortunate example of Florida teenager Ryan White illustrates, victims of HIV and AIDS also face considerable stigma and social isolation even when not incarcerated. In addition, in our society women and people of color have a history of being marginalized. When any individual is simultaneously a member of each of these groups, the psychological and physical pressures are immense. Women who belong to high risk groups (drug users, economically disadvantaged, and women of color) are concentrated in correctional institutions.

Medical researchers have the formidable task of identifying a vaccine that prevents the spread of HIV and a treatment that improves the chances of survival for those already infected. Social scientists have the task of developing theory which can be used to guide policy initiatives that slow the spread of HIV. To date, medical breakthroughs have had minimal impact.[1] Social scientists have not fared much better. AIDS and HIV continue to spread through all societal groups. If current trends continue the number of incarcerated people will increase, victims of HIV/AIDS will multiply, and the burdens faced by correctional systems will intensify. In short, the costs in physical, emotional, and fiscal terms will escalate as we enter the twenty-first century unless effective policies are implemented now.

The following discussion focuses on incarcerated women. This population was selected for several reasons. First, high risk groups are concentrated in correctional facilities affording correctional administrators an ideal opportunity to positively influence the at-risk behaviors of this group. Second, heterosexual females comprise the largest growing group to be HIV infected. Third, women who are under correctional supervision have been seriously neglected by researchers and in the AIDS literature. I agree with Young and McHale's statement that, "the problem of the HIV positive woman prisoner is something that it is to be hoped will soon be the subject of more detailed research" (1992, 89). Despite the focus on incarcerated women, the theoretical model and policy suggestions presented are applicable with any at-risk incarcerated group.

This chapter describes the current problems facing these individuals and provides a theoretical model, which if used to shape correctional policy could reduce the occurrence of HIV in the next century and decrease the stigma suffered by those already infected. The policy suggestions would make humane treatment more normative for those incarcerated.

WOMEN WITH HIV AND AIDS

As early as 1987, AIDS has been identified as the eighth leading cause of death among women aged fifteen to forty-four (MMWR, 1990). Currently females are the fastest growing group of people in the United States contracting HIV and AIDS (Davis-Berman and Brown, 1990). Despite this trend, compared to men relatively few women are currently infected. In February, 1993 the Centers for Disease Control (CDC) reported that 6,255 of the 249,199 adult Americans with AIDS were female (HIV/AIDS, 1993). The largest identified risk factors for women are intravenous drug use and sexual activity with male drug injectors. Forty-five percent (2,815) of the known HIV positive women contracted the disease as the result of injecting drugs (HIV/AIDS, 1993). This statistic is alarming when considering that many women in our society inject drugs. It has been estimated that as many as 500 thousand women use intravenous drugs in the United

---

[1]One notable exception has been the drug zidovudine (Retrovir) which has been credited with prolonging and improving lives (Ungvarski and Schmidt, 1992, 37).

States (Wofsky, 1987). Nearly 40% (2,437) of the known women with AIDS were infected through heterosexual contact. Over half (1,321) of these women were involved sexually with drug injecting males. Only 4% have been infected through blood transfusion and 12% have unknown causes of infection (HIV/AIDS, 1993).

AIDS has already been identified as the leading cause of death in some correctional facilities (AIDS: A Demographic profile..., 1986; Florida: AIDS primary cause..., 1989). As the number of cases of HIV and AIDS continues to rise, more correctional systems can expect AIDS to be become a major source of inmates' demise. The exact number of incarcerated females who are HIV positive is unknown.

Incarcerated Women

Nationwide, there are around 70 thousand females who are under correctional supervision and who are held in secured facilities (Bureau of Justice Statistics [BJS], 1992). Most of these women are held in state and federal correctional institutions. There has been an explosion in the number of women sentenced to federal and state facilities since 1980 (BJS, 1992, 634). From 1980 to 1990 the number of females sentenced to federal and state facilities increased from 12,331 per year to 40,484 (BJS, 1992, 636).

There has been a correspondingly large increase in the number of women detained in jails. In 1983 there were 15,330 women incarcerated in jails while by 1988 the number had increased to 28,187 (BJS, 1992, 611). If these trends continue a significantly higher number of women will be under correctional supervision in the twenty-first century.

Most of the women who are incarcerated in correctional facilities are parents and many have used "serious" drugs. Of all women incarcerated in jails in 1989, 71.3% had children under the age of eighteen (BJS, 1992, 626). Also in 1989, 39.3% had used cocaine or crack and 15% had used heroin (BJS, 1992, 629). Thus many incarcerated mothers are at risk for HIV infection.

One corrections officer (who wishes to remain anonymous) at the largest women's facility in Michigan stated that 42 to 44% of the women incarcerated were HIV positive and 20% had symptomatic AIDS (personal correspondence, June 1, 1993). While all women in Michigan correctional facilities are screened for HIV at intake, administrators would not officially confirm or deny his estimation. However, in Massachusetts it has been reported that around 35% of the four hundred women who elected to have the AIDS antibody test in 1989 and 1990 were HIV positive—compared to only 13% of the male inmates in Massachusetts (Waring and Smith, 1990, 1).

In a larger study from 430 correctional facilities that reported the results of HIV antibody testing in 1991 (forty-two states, the District of Columbia and Puerto Rico) 65,724 inmates were HIV positive (HIV Prevention..., 1992). In ten selected federal and state prisons and jails the HIV seroprevalence rate ranged from 2.7% to 14.7% for women (Vlahov et al., 1991). This percentage was higher than the percentage found among male inmates. Males had HIV seropositivity rates from 2.1% to 7.6% (Vlahov et al., 1991, 1129). In fact, in nine of the ten correctional facilities females had higher rates of HIV. Interestingly, unlike men (who had higher rates among inmates over twenty-five years old) age was NOT a predictive factor with female inmates (Vlahov et al., 1991, 1130). Regardless of the actual rate of infection it is apparent that many incarcerated women are perceived (among correctional officers anyway) to be HIV positive, a significant number are HIV positive, and many more are at risk.

UNIQUE PROBLEMS

Incarcerated women and prison officials face many problems related to HIV. For infected women the sophistication and availability of medical care is suspect in some systems. For administrators, the medical expenses associated with caring for HIV inmates are high. For example, New Jersey prison authorities report that the average cost associated with caring for an infected inmate (from diagnosis to death) was $67,000, and that the average length of hospitalization was 102 days. However, this amount is considerably lower than the $140,000 and 160 days of hospitalization which was estimated for the first 100,000 nonincarcerated AIDS patients (Prisons confront dilemma..., 1986).

Biological factors give women a disproportionately high probability of contracting HIV and consequently AIDS compared to men with similar risk behaviors. Women who are most likely to become infected come from socially and economically deprived groups. Therefore, they may also receive inferior medical treatment. Thus, greater risk coupled with insufficient medical care places women at increased risk of premature death due to AIDS.

Medical

According to the findings of several studies, gender-specific diseases also have more serious implications for women who are HIV positive. One study found that among women suffering from cervical cancer those who were HIV positive had a median of ten months until death compared to a median of twenty-three months for women who were not HIV positive (Maiman et al., 1990). It has also been shown that gynecological infections develop much more rapidly in women who are HIV positive (Minkoff and DeHovitz, 1991), such as pelvic inflammatory disease (PID) (Hoegsberg, Abulafia and Sedlis, 1990; Safrin, Dattel, Haver and Sweet, 1990). HIV positive women also appear to have a large number of infections with vaginal candidiasis (Rhoads, et al., 1987). The Centers for Disease Control (CDC) reported[2] that for HIV infected women, "the prevalence of cervical dysplasia on Papanicolaou (Pap) smear for HIV positive women was eight to eleven times greater than the prevalence of dysplasia for women residing in the respective communities" (Risk for Cervical Disease, 1991, 23). Finally, it has also been suggested that, "seropositive women with herpes infection might shed virus more frequently than women not infected with HIV and thereby pose an increased risk of HIV transmission to sexual partners" (Minkoff and DeHovitz, 1991, 2254).

Compounding medical problems. There are also factors which increase both the threat and severity of HIV infection in correctional facilities. According to the editors of the *Journal of the American Medical Association,*

> The recent emergence of multi-drug-resistant TB (tuberculosis) as an important opportunistic infection of HIV infected persons underscores the need for secondary HIV-prevention services in correctional facilities. Persons in correctional institutions are at increased risk for TB because of high prevalences of HIV infection and latent TB, overcrowding, poor venti-

---

[2]The editor did point out that these findings could be associated with other risk factors not identified due to insufficient research methodologies.

lation, and the frequent transfer of inmates within and between institutions (1992, 23).

Tuberculosis (TB), after being controlled for over forty years, is once again posing a major health threat. According to Dixie Snider of the CDC, "(a)t no time in recent history has tuberculosis been of such concern as it is now, and legitimately so, because tuberculosis is out of control in this country" (Altman, 1992). A particularly dangerous strain, resistant to standard antituberculosis drugs (isoniazid, rifampin and strepto-mycin), has been identified in patients in sixteen different states.[3] The recent outbreaks of TB primarily involve HIV positive individuals. However, since TB is spread through airborne droplets others are at risk. Close, prolonged contact (such as is found in correctional facilities) increases risk of infection. In one case, it was reported that more than fifty health care workers were infected from a single patient, though none have yet developed TB (Altman, 1992). However, TB, like HIV, can remain dormant for years. Healthy individuals can harbor the TB bacillus for years without ever being ill. Because of these reasons and due to the concentrations of high risk individuals found in correctional facilities some medical experts are arguing for centering detection and treatment efforts among the incarcerated (DiFerdinando in Altman, 1992).

There is also indication that as a group, incarcerated women generally have more health problems than male prisoners (Waring and Smith, 1990, 5). Concerns with conception are also unique to female populations.

Contraceptive devices. Among all the reported cases of AIDS among women, 85% occurred in women in childbearing years (fifteen to forty-four). Of these, one quarter of the victims are between the ages of twenty and twenty-nine and many were probably infected while teenagers (AIDS in Women, 1991). Thus safe contraceptive devices are a relevant concern for women.

Women who are HIV positive cannot take it for granted that the use of common contraceptive methods are safe for either the woman or her sexual partners. First, Minkoff and DeHovitz stated that, "(t)here are several reasons to be cautious about the use of intrauterine devices...they may render the woman more infectious...The woman herself might be rendered more susceptible to ascending infections and hence PID" (1991, 2255). Second, oral contraceptives have also generated theoretical debate as to whether or not they alter the natural course of HIV disease among women (Minkoff and DeHovitz, 1991; Grossman, 1984).

Psychological Stress

Compared to other infected groups, women who are infected with HIV and/or AIDS may face increased psychological pressures. For example, many economically disadvantaged women are also the primary, and often sole, caretaker for their dependent children. Others are thus financially and emotionally dependent on them. When these women have HIV/AIDS they also have the concern of caring for others while often ill themselves. Incarceration forces a separation and additional stress for the woman who must now rely on others or the state to care for their dependents.

---

[3]Alabama, Arizona, California, Georgia, Florida, Hawaii, Illinois, New Jersey, New York, Pennsylvania, Texas, Virginia, Michigan, Missouri, Utah, and Washington.

Social Stigmata. Groups which are most highly represented among those HIV infected already belong to highly stigmatized groups—women of color and intravenous drug users. While women of color comprise less than 19% of all women in the United States they account for over 72% of all AIDS cases (AIDS in women, 1991, 23). According to Wiener, "(h)istorically, these women have been tangled in a web of poverty, illness, and oppression; by the dictates of racism and poverty, they are disempowered, disenfranchised, and alienated from traditional sources of help and support" (1991). Young and McHale added that, "HIV infection makes visible and explicit and hidden and implicit links between conceptions of disease and criminality. Both are seen as (symbolically or literally) life-threatening. The HIV positive prisoner is a deadly icon of a psychosocial malaise" (1992, 90). Others have also articulated how societal sexism, racism, and classism have effected public perceptions of HIV and women (Anastos and Marte, 1989). McKenzie (1989) argued that HIV positive women's legal rights have also been neglected.

Self-efficacy. Most theoretical models addressing risk reduction practices have included self-efficacy as a central component. Several factors (drug and alcohol use, poverty, cultural norms, gender roles, and sexuality issues) have been identified as decreasing women's self-efficacy (Wermuth et al., 1991, 132). Also according to Wermuth, et al.,

> (w)hen individuals believe they can exercise control over actions and situations that might pose a risk for HIV infection, they are more likely to exercise that control (Bandura, 1989). However, the extent to which this holds true for individuals with less actual control over their material and relational worlds remains to be learned. For example, Mondanaro (1987) points out that women at greatest risk for AIDS are those with the least amount of control over their lives (1991, 133-4).

Of all women in our society those who are incarcerated probably have the LEAST control over their lives. Thus, the thesis that lack of control results in decreased self-efficacy would be more consequential for incarcerated women. (This supposition is especially relevant to the following theoretical model presented here.)

Finally, women who are HIV positive may also not enjoy the widespread and organized support that gay men have. When current or past incarceration is also present stigma may intensify and with current practices support may decrease.

In summary, gender influences social, biological, and treatment consequences of AIDS (Minkoff and DeHovitz, 1991). So far, an overview of the demographics, behaviors and problems facing incarcerated women has been presented. The following section presents a heuristic device which may prove useful for slowing the spread of HIV.

THEORETICAL MODEL

Lacking a cure or preventive vaccine, retardation of further spread of HIV among women in correctional facilities is urgent. One promising theoretical model that may assist by providing a framework is the AIDS Risk Reduction Model (ARRM). This is a variation of the classic Health Belief Model (HBM) which was effective with helping slow the spread of tuberculosis and polio during the 1950s (Becker, 1974). The HBM was first presented as a means to explain behaviors related to preventing illness (Rosenstock, 1974). The HBM focuses on individual's susceptibility, severity, and psychological barriers. Consequently, inhibitions to taking health action are based on perceived benefits and barriers. In other words, the HBM analyzes "an individual's motivation to act as a function of the expectancy of goal attainment in the area of health behavior" (Maiman and Becker, 1974, 348). Thus, the HBM implies that individuals make decisions regarding their health following a *rationally* conducted, cost/benefit analysis. Consequently, health behaviors are a function of people's perceived susceptibility and perceived severity of a health condition, and the perceived benefits and barriers to behavioral change" (Gibson et al., 1991, 63).

Many theoretical extensions and empirical examinations of the traditional Health Belief Model have been presented (for a review of some of the variations see Maiman and Becker, 1974; Rosenstock et al., 1988; also see Feldman and Johnson, 1986 for other theoretical perspectives on AIDS). Conceptual schemes have been developed which may provide insight into factors most susceptible to manipulation in specific health areas. Variations of the HBM have been presented which deal with specific diseases (e.g., tuberculosis, cancer). Recent extensions involve AIDS/HIV prevention (see especially Cleary et al., 1986; Solomon and DeJong, 1986). Consequently, variations of the HBM should, "predict whether someone will adopt behavior to avoid HIV transmission" (Hingson, et al., 1990). This chapter presents a variation which may be particularly useful for incarcerated populations—including women.

The AIDS Risk Reduction Model

The AIDS Risk Reduction Model (ARRM) was first presented by Catania et al., (1990) to help explain motivations for altering sexual practices related to HIV transmission. The ARRM was developed to organize concepts related to the Health Belief Model, decision-making theory, self-efficacy theory, and theories that seek to explain the role of interpersonal processes and emotions in behavior (Gibson et al,. 1991, 62-63). The ARRM is a three-stage model that focuses on social psychological factors that influence risk behaviors. The three distinct stages in the ARRM are *labeling, commitment*, and *enactment*.

The first stage includes "recognition and labeling of one's sexual behaviors as high risk for contracting HIV" (Gibson et al., 1991, 53). This stage is the required first step toward reducing or ceasing at-risk behaviors. Three factors are postulated to necessarily occur during the *labeling* stage:

1. knowledge of sexual activities associated with HIV transmission
2. belief that one is susceptible and
3. belief that being in an HIV positive status is undesirable (Catania et al., 1990, 57).

During this first stage, knowledge is especially critical for providing sufficient motivation for behavioral change since awareness of high-risk behaviors must precede perceived threat. Susceptibility is related to knowledge since awareness that one is engaging in at-risk behaviors would logically succeed identification of these behaviors. Finally, "social networks" are hypothesized to play a dominant role in both acquisitions of knowledge and approval of safe behaviors (Catania et al., 1990, 59).

The second stage is founded on decision-making theory and rational thought. In this step the individual may make a firm commitment to permanent behavioral changes that reduce a risk of HIV exposure. However, the person may also make other choices, such as "remaining undecided, waiting for the problem to rectify itself, or resigning oneself to the problem situation" (Catania et al., 1990, 59). Several factors were postulated to be important to the *commitment* stage. These included aversive emotions and social influences. Furthermore, the perceived benefits of making change (termed "response efficacy"), and self-efficacy are included. Self-efficacy refers to a "person's perceived ability to implement recommended health practices" (Gibson et al., 1991, 63). Each of these factors is related to the individuals practicing "behaviors they believe will yield the greatest overall personal value relative to disvalue" (Catania et al., 1990, 60).

The third and final stage involves actually taking the steps necessary to reduce risk. This final stage is termed *enactment*. The three requisite components of this stage are seeking information, obtaining remedies, and actually changing behavior (Catania, Kegeles and Coates, 1990, 62). Individuals may accept their situation and the consequences of high risk behavior, help themselves, or seek help from others in attempts to modify their at-risk behaviors. Social factors, such as verbal communication skills, reference group norms, and social support are key elements to stage three (Catania et al., 1990, 68).

While the existing model has great value, some data indicate that the ARRM is incomplete. For example, using order probit analyses Gates and Lanier (forthcoming) found that life experiences should also be included as a fundamental component. Also, the assumption that individuals conduct a rational, cost benefit analysis prior to engaging in behavior is suspect—especially for incarcerated populations (see Lanier and McCarthy, 1989a, b). It is therefore proposed that the following changes be made to the ARRM in order for it to have more applicability for incarcerated women.

First, prior histories should be carefully considered. While many incarcerated women belong to high risk groups, they have diverse life experiences. Life experiences play a large role in determining the choices that individuals make regarding health decisions (Gates and Lanier, forthcoming). Their prior history should be included in any treatment model.

Second, the ARRM is founded on a premise of rationality. Not all persons at risk for HIV infection behave rationally. For example, one study found that some individuals who belong to high risk groups do not even acknowledge the existence of HIV (Lanier and McCarthy, 1989a). Others consider the probability of contracting HIV to be very remote and thus do not take precautions. Incarcerated women who abuse illicit drugs may crave the sensation produced by the narcotic so badly that they neglect to take rudimentary precautions (e.g., cleaning needles in chlorine solutions).

In summary, the original HBM was based on preventing behaviors in the 1950s among nonincarcerated populations. It over-relied on the presumed rationality of its target group. As we enter the twenty-first century it is important that theories that were once effective are modified to reflect changing social conditions and mores. The modified ARRM presented here is based on empirical research (Gates and Lanier, 1993) which points out that original ARRM is incomplete for a very diverse modern society. To be more effective with individuals who have not always conducted cost benefit analysis prior to behavior (hence their incarceration) the ARRM must be modified and any policy, educational or preventive measures based on the ARRM must reflect these changes.

POLICY RECOMMENDATIONS

Some incarcerated women face a myriad of social, economic, psychological, and medical problems. Infection, and the threat of infection with HIV and AIDS, create additional stress. Obviously sane, humane and realistic care of women infected with HIV is necessary. However, it is also critical that effective preventive programs are implemented and evaluated. Due to the vast diversity found among incarcerated women no single strategy can be considered effective. A combination of case management, individual counseling, group sessions, role playing, and constant reinforcement while incarcerated needs to be supplemented with post-release treatment. This mixture of strategies may prove effective with women under correctional supervision. The eclectic approach suggested here should be based on a multidisciplinary theoretical model such as the ARRM. The modified ARRM presented here may have great value in helping design programs for incarcerated women.

Case Management

A unique approach based on the modified ARRM would take a case management approach towards treatment and prevention. Each woman would be assigned to a treatment or educational program based on her unique past experiences and practices. For example, women who regularly practiced prostitution could be grouped with similar women for individual counseling and group sessions. The specific program should be devised by experts who are sensitive to each woman's history and (perceived) degree of rationality.

Social Justice for Women has suggested that an interdisciplinary group comprised of clinicians, psychologists, Department of Corrections employees, parole workers, and others be used to collaborate on "medical management, psychosocial services, family counseling, discharge planning,...(and) early consideration for parole" (Waring and Smith, 1990). Such a team-centered approach would be more likely to comprehensively and congruently address the sometimes overlapping problems facing these women.

Counseling

Both groups and individual sessions should be used for educational purposes. Groups sessions have shown some value (Valdiserri et al., 1987) and peer led sessions have great potential. Incarcerated women who are looked up to by the other inmates should be recruited and enticed to lead the group sessions. Peer led sessions may be much more effective with inmates since they may resist the efforts of correctional officials. According to the modified ARRM groups should be formed based on the past experiences of each inmate. For example, "bikers" should be grouped together so that they can relate and share common past risky experiences and jointly develop resistance devices unique to their culture. In part, this grouping based on prior experiences will help identify and perhaps improve existing "social networks" which are a central component of the ARRM.

Role playing should be a major component (e.g., teaching women who practice prostitution how to demand that customers and sexual partners use condoms). The group leaders and those who develop the program should base it on the three distinct stages in the ARRM: labeling, commitment, and enactment. It must be stressed that such programs should be rigorously evaluated by outside, neutral observers.

Health Services

Health services for incarcerated women show great potential. For example, some women who are incarcerated may not have been able to take advantage of comprehensive health services (dental, gynecological, etc.) prior to incarceration. One goal of health educators within the correctional setting is to make inmates aware of community services that are available upon their release. Correctional institutions should conduct mandatory HIV screening at intake (commonly done in many correctional systems) and at six-month intervals for the first eighteen months of incarceration (a less frequent practice).

All women's facilities should also have HIV treatment facilities where drug therapy is provided on a timely basis. It is not improbable that many incarcerated women would also volunteer to participate with testing new HIV and AIDS drugs prior to FDA approval (see Young and McHale (1992, 98) for further discussion of this).

Post-Release Services

Virtually all incarcerated women are released back into the community. Being cognizant of their rights after parole, they should be strongly encouraged to continue participating in counseling sessions, drug therapy, and whatever AIDS/HIV prevention and/or treatment program that was devised for them while under correctional supervision. Many incarcerated individuals could also be monitored with alternative means of control such as community corrections.

ALTERNATIVE SANCTIONS (COMMUNITY CORRECTIONS)

Since most women are not incarcerated for violent offenses and since women's sentences are typically much shorter than men's (BJS, 1990) perhaps it would be more humane and cost effective for women who develop symptomatic AIDS to be released into community corrections. Community corrections offers several benefits. First, community health care services are available. Young and McHale noted that,

> ...a considerable difference does exist in both choice and standard of care in relation to prisoners with HIV.... A HIV positive patient has a far wider choice of care outside prison...he may seek psychotherapeutic care and counseling to bring him to terms with the fact that he has AIDS or is HIV positive. If he has the means, he may also obtain care from "alternative" medical practitioners...(1992, 97).

Courts have also recognized this fact. In November of 1989 a prisoner with AIDS was ordered released from a federal prison because he could not receive adequate medical care (Young and McHale, 1992). Second, more support groups exist in the community. Third, family and friends would be available to assist the woman physically, financially, and emotionally.

McCarthy (personal correspondence, November 24, 1993) also cited four additional factors which should be considered. First, community corrections should be increasingly used due to humanitarian reasons. For one thing, the mortality rate is higher among incarcerated individuals.

Second, from a managerial perspective, community corrections solves many potential problems. One big issue facing correctional administrators is whether or not to segregate HIV infected individuals. Inmate violence against those infected is another related problem. Also detention personnel have been found to be uncomfortable supervising HIV positive offenders (Lurigio, 1989). Community corrections eliminates each of these administrative concerns for inmates who do not pose a threat of violence to community members, and most women are incarcerated for nonviolent offenses.

Third, monetary concerns should be considered. Prisons are designed to be punitive institutions. They are not hospitals. Thus care for critically ill inmates demand replicating (often at an inferior, yet expensive, level) services that are already available through the health care sector. Many institutions cannot afford expensive drugs needed to fight AIDS (such as azdothymidine [AZT]). The National Institute of Justice (NIJ) has noted that many inmates who are eligible for AZT and who need it, are not receiving it while incarcerated (Young and McHale, 1992).

Finally, community corrections is preferable for those with infectious diseases. TB and other infectious diseases are becoming an increasing problem in close custody correctional institutions. Furthermore, "(t)he circumstances and conditions in custody, including overcrowding and lack of privacy, may foster high risk behaviors such as unprotected anal sex, drug injecting, tattooing; and self-injury with consequent blood-spillage" (Dolan et al., 1990). It is also much more likely for inmates, who would otherwise be heterosexual, to engage in homosexual activity (often called "prison homosexuality") while incarcerated. Since condoms are often not provided to inmates, this behavior is even more risky. Incarcerated HIV and AIDS patients thus pose additional problems for other inmates and staff. (See McCarthy and McCarthy, 1991 for additional information on community corrections.)

SUMMARY AND CONCLUSION

As the twenty-first century rapidly approaches, administrators of correctional facilities are going to face increasing problems related to HIV and AIDS. To provide just one example, as more incarcerated women with HIV develop symptomatic AIDS, health care costs will rise dramatically. Current mandatory sentencing requirements and increased sentence lengths for drug offenders mean that more at-risk women will remain under correctional supervision for longer periods of time. The burdens of correctional officers, inmates, medical staff, and society at large will geometrically increase during the twenty-first century unless effective policies are implemented now. Correctional administrators must therefore seriously and rigorously engage in HIV educational and treatment programs. Community corrections should be an increasingly used option. On a positive note, correctional administrators are in an excellent position to reach one high risk group and thus help slow the spread of HIV among the general population. The modified ARRM presented here provides one theoretical basis for developing correctional programs designed to educate and treat women.

STUDY QUESTIONS

1. What is meant by the term "marginalized"? In what ways are incarcerated women with HIV marginalized?

2. Considering current constitutional and legislative guidelines, how could women with HIV who are convicted of a) serious crime and b) minor crime be handled by the justice system? Should they be given different treatment or punishment from nonHIV positive women?

3. AIDS/HIV affects many groups. Why were incarcerated women the focus of this chapter.

4. What are the social, biological, and treatment problems faced by HIV positive inmates?

5. Explain the modified AIDS Risk Reduction Model. How could this theoretical model help slow the spread of HIV?

REFERENCES

Acquired Immunodeficiency Syndrome: A Demographic profile of New York State mortalities 1982-1985. (1986). Albany, NY: New York State Commission of Corrections.

Altman, L.K. (1992). Deadly strain on Tuberculosis is spreading fast, U.S. Finds. *Themes of the Times: Sociology*. The New York Times. New York: Prentice Hall.

Anastos, K. and Marte, C. (1989). Women—the missing persons in the AIDS epidemic. *Health/PAC Bulletin, 19*, 4, 6-13.

Becker, Marshall. (1974). The Health Belief Model and personal health behavior. *Health Education Monographs, 2*, 220-243.

Bureau of Justice Statistics. (1992). *Sourcebook of Criminal Justice Statistics—1991*. Washington, DC: U.S. Department of Justice.

Catania, Joseph, Susan Kegeles and Thomas Coates. (1990). Toward an understanding of risk behavior: An AIDS Risk-Reduction Model, *Health Education Quarterly, 17*, 53-92.

Cleary, Paul, Theresa Rogers, Eleanor Singer, Jerome Avorn, Nancy van Devanter, Samuel Perry and Johanna Pindyck. (1986). Health education about AIDS among Seropositive blood donors. *Health Education Quarterly, 13*,4 317-329.

DiClemente, Ralph, Cherrie Boyer and Edward Morales. (1988). Minorities and AIDS: Knowledge, attitudes, and misperceptions among black and Latino adolescents. *American Journal of Public Health; 78*, 1, 55-57.

DiClemente, Ralph, Jim Zorn and Lydia Temoshok. (1987). The association of gender, ethnicity, and length of residence in the Bay area to adolescent's knowledge and attitudes about Acquired Immunodeficiency Syndrome. *Journal of Applied Social Psychology, 17*, 216-230.

DiClemente, Ralph, Mark Lanier, Patricia Horan and Mark Lodico. (1991). Comparison of AIDS knowledge, attitudes, and behaviors among incarcerated adolescents and a public school sample in San Francisco. *American Journal of Public Health, 81*, 5 628-630.

Dolan, Kate, Martin Donoghoe and Gerry Stimson. (1990). Drug injecting and syringe sharing in custody and in the community: An exploratory survey of HIV risk behaviour. *The Howard Journal, 29*, 3, 177-186.

Feldman, D.A. and T.M. Johnson. (1986). *The social dimensions of AIDS: Methods and theory*. New York: Praeger Press.

Florida: AIDS primary cause of death in prison. (1989). *CDC Weekly*, 2, p. 7.

Gates, Scott and Mark M. Lanier. (1993). Testing the AIDS Risk Reduction Model with high-risk youth. *Journal of Health and Social Behavior* (This is under review).

Gibson, David, Joseph Catania and John Peterson. (1991). Theoretical Background in Sorensen et al. (ed.) *Preventing AIDS*. New York: Guilford.

Grossman, C. (1984). Possible underlying mechanisms of sexual dimorphism in the immune response: fact and hypothesis. *Journal of Steroid Biochemistry*, 34, 241-251.

Hammett, Theodore. (1988). AIDS in correctional facilities: Issues and Options (Bureau of Justice Statistics Report). Washington, DC: National Institute of Justice.

Hingson, Ralph, Lee Strunin, Beth Berlin and Timonthy Heeren. (1990). Beliefs about AIDS, use of alcohol and drugs, and unprotected sex among Massachusetts adolescents. *American Journal of Public Health*, 80, 3, 295-299.

Lanier, Mark and Belinda R. McCarthy. (1989a). AIDS awareness and the impact of AIDS education in juvenile corrections. *Criminal Justice and Behavior*, 16, 4, 395-411, December.

Lanier, Mark and Belinda R. McCarthy. (1989b). Knowledge and concern about AIDS among incarcerated juvenile offenders. *The Prison Journal*, LXVIX, 1, 39-52, Spring-Summer.

Lanier, Mark, Ralph DiClemente and Patricia Horan. (1991). HIV knowledge and behaviors of incarcerated youth: A comparison of high and low risk locales. *Journal of Criminal Justice*, 19, 3, 257-262.

Lurigio, Arthur. (1989). Practitioner's views on AIDS in probation and detention. *Federal Probation*, 53, 4, 16-24.

HIV/AIDS surveillance—year-end edition. (1993). February. Atlanta, GA: Centers for Disease Control.

HIV Prevention in U.S. Correctional System, 1991. (1992). *Journal of the American Medical Association*, 268, 1, 23.

Maiman, Lois and Marshall Becker. (1974). The Health Belief Model: Origins and correlates in psychological theory. *Health Education Monographs*, 2, 4, 337-353.

Maiman, M., Fruchter, R.G., Serur, E., Remy, J.C., Fever, G., and Boyce, J.G. (1990). Human immunodeficiency virus infection and cervical neoplasia. *Gynecological Obstetrics*, 38, 377-382.

Marte, C. and Anastos, K. (1990). Women—The Missing Persons in the AIDS Epidemic: Part II. *Health/PAC Bulletin*, 20, 1, 11-18.

McCarthy, Belinda R. and Bernard J. McCarthy. (1991). *Community-Based Corrections* (2nd ed.). Pacific Grove, CA: Brooks Cole.

McKenzie, N. (1989). The Changing Face of the AIDS Epidemic. *Health/PAC Bulletin*, 19, 4, 3-5.

Minkoff, H. and DeHovitz, J. (1991). Care of Women infected with the Human Immunodeficiency Virus. *Journal of the American Medical Association*, 266, 2253-2258.

AIDS in Women—United States. (1991). *Morbidity and Mortality Weekly Report (MMWR)*, 265, 1, 23-24. Atlanta, GA: Centers for Disease Control.

Prisons confront dilemma of inmates with AIDS. (1986). *Journal of the American Medical Association*, 225, 18, 2399-2404.

Rhoads, J.L., Wright, C., Redfield, R.R., and Burke, D.S. (1987). Chronic vaginal candidiasis in women with human immunodeficiency virus infection. *Journal of the American Medical Association*, 257, 3105-3107.

Richardson, D. (1988). *Women and AIDS*. New York: Methuen.

Risk for Cervical Disease in HIV-Infected Women—New York City. (1991). *Morbidity and Mortality Weekly Report (MMWR)*, *265*, 1, 23-24. Atlanta, GA: Centers for Disease Control.

Rosenstock, Irwin. (1974). The Health Belief Model and Preventive Health Behavior. *Health Education Monographs*, *2*, 4, 355-386.

Rosenstock, Irwin, Victor Strecher and Marshall Becker. (1988). Social learning theory and the Health Belief Model. *Health Education Quarterly*, *15*, 2, 175-183.

Solomon, D., A. Hogan, R. Bouknight and C. Solomon. (1989). Analysis of Michigan Medicaid costs to treat HIV infection. *Public Health Reports*, *105*, 5, 416-424.

Solomon, Mildred and William DeJong. (1986). Recent sexually transmitted disease prevention efforts and their implications for AIDS health education. *Health Education Quarterly*, *13*, 4, 301-316.

Ungvarski, P.J. and Schmidt, J. (1992). AIDS patients under attack. *RN*, *55*, 11, 36-46.

Valdiserri, Ronald, David Lyter, Lawrence Kingsley, Laura Leviton, Janet Schofield, James Huggins, Monto Ho and Charles Rinaldo. (1987). The effect of group education on improving attitudes about AIDS risk reduction. *New York State Journal of Medicine*, *87*, 5, 272-278.

Vlahov, D., Brewer, F., Castro, K., Narkunas, J., Salive, J., Ullrich, J. and Munoz, A. (1991). Prevalence of antibody to HIV-1 among entrants to U.S. Correctional Facilities. *Journal of the American Medical Association*, *265*, 1129-1132.

Waring, N. and Smith, B. (1990). *The AIDS Epidemic: Impact on Women Prisoners in Massachusetts*. Boston, MA: Social Justice for Women.

Wermuth, L., Robbins, R., Choi, K. and Eversley, R. (1991). Reaching and counseling women sexual partners. Chapter in Sorensen, et al., *Preventing AIDS in drug users and their sexual partners*, pp. 130-149, Guilford Press: New York.

Wiener, L.S. (1991). Women and Human Immunodeficiency Virus: A historical and personal psychosocial perspective. *Social Work*, 36, 5, 375-378.

Wofsky, C.B. (1987). Intravenous drug abuse and women's medical issues. *Report of the Surgeon General's Workshop on Children with HIV Infection and Their Families*. Washington, DC: U.S. Department of Health and Human Services.

Young, Alison and Jean McHale. (1992). The dilemmas of the HIV positive prisoner. *The Howard Journal*, 31, 2, 89-104.

CHAPTER 23

WOMEN AS POLICE SUPERVISORS IN THE TWENTY-FIRST CENTURY

A DECADE OF PROMOTIONAL PRACTICES BY GENDER IN THREE MAJOR POLICE AGENCIES

Sean Grennan, Ph.D. and Robert Munoz

ABSTRACT

This chapter researches police promotional practices as they relate to gender in three major urban police agencies: New York City, Chicago, and Los Angeles. The number and percentage of men and women in various police ranks in the years 1981 and 1991 is examined in an effort to ascertain if there has been any significant changes in promotional practices over a ten-year period. It is anticipated that this study will indicate that there has been an ample increase in the number of women in ranking positions within these three police agencies over a ten-year span. Predictions based on this study are made as we look toward the twenty-first century.

INTRODUCTION

As police departments enter into the twenty-first century they must realize that the growing female population is just as competent as anyone in the ever present male contingent. This means that the time has come for women supervisors to be promoted above the ranks of civil service testing, usually captain, into the politically appointed positions from Deputy Inspector to Assistant Chief. Within the past ten years women in policing have gained as much, if not more, administrative experience and command presence as their male counterparts. Yet, a male can become chief of a department at forty-five while a female captain must move from command to command with only the slightest hope of ever being promoted above the rank of deputy inspector.

It is anticipated as women continue to enter law enforcement that their total percentage in policing will reach the 30-35% bracket by the year 2010. As the tables in this research indicate the proportion of women in policing has increased anywhere from 10-14% in the three major police agencies in the United States over a ten-year period. As the number of women in policing continues to increase, men will finally realize that they are in law enforcement to stay and that the women are viable assets to policing. Hopefully, with this future increase will also come the promotions that the women rightfully deserve. Historically, women were confined to non-enforcement duties because the leaders of this male dominated occupation came to the conclusion that women lacked the size and physical strength to perform "rigorous" police work (Dolan and Scariano 1988, 138). The role of women in policing eventually expanded from matron and juvenile duties to include clerical and traffic duties. As the number of women appointed to police departments throughout the United States increased, so did problems related to duty assignment and upward mobility of women in policing. Police agencies were "white male monopolies" steeped in tradition and the notion that a woman supervising males would not ever be considered a remote possibility in most police departments well into the twentieth century. This sexist attitude is not just confined to law enforcement agencies because these same sentiments are very evident in most public and private sector organizations where women have "their place" within an agency. Up until the latter portion of the twentieth century the largest percentage of employment opportunities for women were as telephone operators, nurses, teachers, secretaries and housewives.

WOMEN IN A BLUE COLLAR OCCUPATION

Women who do enter into the working world of men are faced with a great deal of character conflict and sexual harassment. Epstein's research indicates that most of the

TABLE 1

Chicago Police Department

	January 1981				January 1991		
Rank	Male	Female	Total	Rank	Male	Female	Total
PO	8998	478	9476	PO	7179	1437	8616
	95%	5%			83%	17%	
Det	1130	18	1148	Det	1640	100	1740
	98%	2%			94%	6%	
Sgt	1201	3	1204	Sgt	1154	96	1250
	99%	1%			92%	8%	
Lt	300	0	300	Lt	282	14	296
	100%	0%			95%	5%	
Capt	79	0	79	Capt	90	1	91
	100%	0%			99%	1%	
Above Capt	83	2	85	Above Capt	92	2	94
	98%	2%			98%	2%	
Total	11791	501	12292	Total	10437	1650	12087
	96%	4%			86%	14%	

TABLE 2

Los Angeles Police Department

	December 1981				December 1991		
Rank	Male	Female	Total	Rank	Male	Female	Total
PO	4333	197	4530	PO	4596	952	5548
	96%	4%			83%	17%	
Det	1127	71	1198	Det	1313	124	1437
	94%	6%			91%	9%	
Sgt	818	3	821	Sgt	861	29	890
	99%	1%			97%	3%	
Lt	225	2	227	Lt	224	8	232
	99%	1%			97%	3%	
Capt	78	2	80	Capt	66	1	67
	98%	2%			98%	2%	
Above Capt	31	0	31	Above Capt	28	0	28
	100%	0%			100%	0%	
Total	6612	275	6887	Total	7088	1114	8202
	96%	2%			86%	14%	

TABLE 3

New York City Police Department

	July 1980				March 1992		
Rank	Male	Female	Total	Rank	Male	Female	Total
PO	15561	498	16059	PO	15591	2949	18540
	97%	3%			84%	16%	
Det	2812	49	2861	Det	3531	568	4099
	98%	2%			86%	14%	
Sgt	2303	15	2318	Sgt	2617	208	2825
	99%	1%			93%	7%	
Lt	788	4	792	Lt	1079	51	1130
	99%	1%			96%	4%	
Capt	239	0	239	Capt	300	9	309
	100%	0%			97%	3%	
Above Capt	160	2	162	Above Capt	177	1	178
	99%	1%			99%	1%	
Total	21863	568	22431	Total	23295	3786	27081
	97.5%	2.5%			86%	14%	

familiar nurturing attributes such as passivity, nonviolence, and practicality can be uncovered in all individuals but have turned out to be "sexualized and are assumed, asserted, and expected to correlate with sexual differences" (1970, 22).

A female who enters the job market can unquestionably look forward to unavoidable conflict since the desired qualities of a prosperous career (such as competitiveness, aggressiveness, active tenacity, fervent indifference) can be perceived as masculine images (Epstein 1970).

A woman who infiltrates into what is considered a dominant male occupation will definitely be exposed to a status disparity. This female will additionally affront a dominance dilemma. A majority of men have what they consider the prevalent sex status and, in most cases, sex is, without a doubt, the most prominent determination of status; in most situations, a female supervisor is accorded a considerable amount of inferior recognition in comparison to the male police officer. Additionally, most citizens will seek the assistance of a male police officer to substantiate an order given by a female supervisor, or the same female supervisor's orders may be challenged by a male employee who feels that a woman does not belong in a supervisory position in policing. Therefore, the sex of the superior officer has to be considered as a very important factor in establishing the type of reaction that a citizen or a subordinate may have towards a ranking officer. This determination is a significant factor in policing because the image that is put forth by a male police officer leaves absolutely little or no room for females.

Most male police officers feel that the only assignment that female officers can fulfill is as a clerical worker or telephone operator. Historically, a major portion of female police officers were accepting of this assessment. Epstein found that sex and racial status are "central in controlling the choices of most individuals" (1970, 35).

Kanter's research indicates that administrative positions are filled by males; females who are in managerial positions are usually concentrated in what one would consider lower-paying posts. Office work, on the other hand, is an overwhelmingly feminine position; "women are to clerical labor as men are to management" (Millman and Kanter 1976, 39).

Females entering what can be considered a male-dominated occupation experience various dilemmas affiliated with **tokenism**. Woman may be classified into one of the four **stereotyped** roles, which Kanter' has given the self-explanatory labels of *mother, sex object* or *seducers, pet,* or *iron maiden.* The female may also be treated as *average* or *stereotypical* as when a female supervisor performing desk duties is assumed by the public to be a switchboard operator or clerical officer. The result is that the female supervisor may be more likely to adapt to a role as one of the station house cops. This type of personality change will hinder the female officer's ability to establish her competence, due to what can be considered the role defined situation (Kanter 1977 and Grennan 1987a). "Cultures demand that one must do masculine work to be considered a man, and not do it to be a feminine woman" (Epstein 1970, 154). Females infiltrating a masculine *vocation* are thus contrived as deviant and subject to *social faction sanctions* (Epstein 1970).

Remmington's Atlanta research established perhaps the **most stereotypical** opinions and comparable conduct in male officers. "Women do not belong on the streets" was a common commentary made in the presence of female officers and during discussions between male officers. Male officers stated and confirmed a lack of confidence in their female peers. Male officers responded to each and every tumultuous call during the year of observation, and in all cases the male officer took command of each situation. Women officers, in comparison, appeared to fall into a stereotypical mode. Women officers who were questioned as to their choice of partner unanimously agreed they would prefer a male partner. "Most of the women expressed greater trust in the policing capabilities of males" (Remmington 1981, 167).

Price and Gavin relate that the police management hierarchy is rigid and restricted at the top, with a sparse number of middle management and administrative positions. This pyramidical configuration, and the significance placed on crime fighting and a good arrest record as the prime means to promotion, serve "to perpetuate the attitudes about policing being a man's work" (Gavin and Price 1982, 406).

There have been several other studies conducted on the abilities of women to perform in the police role. Milton (1972) examined what the female officers encountered when entering a male dominated work force. Milton found that the majority of men cited the physical strength factor as the major reason they considered unsuitable to perform police tasks. Bloch and Anderson (1974) conducted a one year study that compared eighty-six female to eighty-six male police officers in the NYCPD. This research discovered that men and women officers responded to the same type of calls; that males and females obtained the same results when handling violent or angry individuals; that women were less likely to be charged with conduct unbecoming an officer. Bloch and Anderson concluded that females were just as capable as their male counterparts to perform patrol duties. A study conducted by Sichel et al. (1978) compared the patrol performances of forty-one male and forty-one female NYCPD officers and discovered that both sexes used similar techniques to take control of a situation (e.g., verbally or through the use of force upon the arrival at what would be considered a disruptive or disorderly scene). This report indicated that both sexes were equally likely to draw their weapon or use physical force; that women officers were less likely to try and take command of a situation (e.g., to use the required authority, power or force to take control); that citizens felt female officers were more effective, congenial, and polite than their male counterparts; and that females were less likely to engage in vigorous physical activity (i.e., chasing a suspect on foot, carrying or moving heavy objects, etc.). Grennan (1987b) examined a total of 3701 NYCPD Firearms Discharge/Assault on Officer Reports from 1983 and found that the sex of an officer has no impact on the way that an officer handles a violent confrontation; the sex of an officer does not determine the type of injury that officer receives during a violent encounter; male officers are more likely to use a firearm than their female counterpart; and female officers, alone or with a partner, are more than willing to participate in a violent conflict without any fear of injury or death.

PROMOTIONAL POLICY

Prior to the 1960s the opportunities for upward mobility for women was next to impossible. Advancement for women usually involved an assignment to an investigative unit where, in most cases, the woman was ultimately rewarded with a promotion to detective after an unspecified amount of time in this duty. Then in 1961, after being denied the right to take a promotional examination, Felicia Shpritzer, a New York City police officer, decided to take her protest to court. It wasn't until 1964, after the court had decided in favor of Shpritzer (Shpritzer v. Lang, N.Y.S. 2nd 422, 1963), that the police department agreed to permit women to take the sergeant's test. Shpritzer was promoted to sergeant a short time later. In 1967, Shpritzer and Gertrude Schimmel both passed the lieutenant's test and they became the first females to achieve that rank. In 1971, Schimmel passed the Captain's exam and was the first female promoted to that position. Gertrude Schimmel reached the rank of Deputy Chief before her retirement (Keefe 1981).

Shpritzer and Schimmel were the first of many women to step forward and fight the injustices placed on women by this male monopolized occupation. Yet, the principal obstacle still facing female officers was the lack of acceptance and consideration they obtained from their male counterparts.

LEGAL CONSIDERATIONS

The Civil Rights Act (Title VII) of 1964 was expanded in 1972 with the addition of the Equal Rights Amendment that was extended to include public employees. *Griggs v. Duke Power Co.* 91 S.Ct. 849 (1971) had previously established the opinion that a plaintiff in a work discrimination case need not prove differential intent. The Supreme Court held that, once it is obvious that a job stipulation appears out of proportion in comparison to a group or class of people, the owner or highest ranking supervisor must be able to prove that this precondition is a Bona Fide Occupational Qualification (BFOQ) that is directly associated to the job. Sex cannot be established as a BFOQ merely because many law enforcement agencies had never hired women and there is no possible way to equate the performances of females to males. The Griggs case eliminated just about all of the major standards—height, weight, age, etc.—and reversed almost all actions by plaintiffs and law enforcement. The Supreme Court decision in *Reed v. Reed* 92 S.Ct. 251 (1971) prohibited discrimination on the basis of an individual's sex. A recent court decision *Anne Powers et al., v. Abraham D. Beame et al.*, (341 N.Y.S. 2d437) (1991) cited the following discriminatory practices against women by the NYCPD: women were banned from performing patrol in radio cars, disallowed steady assignments, denied positions in plainclothes and other elite units. Separate examinations for appointment to the police officer position were given until 1974 for men and women. These separate exams were used by the NYCPD to limit to 1-2% the number of women being appointed police officers. This court decision is the outcome of 124 female officers who gathered in 1976 to file complaints against the NYCPD, a police agency that has for years failed to correct any of the past transgressions against female police officers including hiring, assignment, and promotion policy (Murray 1991).

SELECTION AND RECRUITMENT

The 1991 court decision in *Powers v. Beame* 341 NYS 2nd 937 (1991) showed that the NYCPD had used separate examinations for males and females to control the number of women appointed to that department. Fair selection and employment guidelines are necessary to insure that a police agency has a pool of candidates that is representative of the community ethnically, racially, and sexually. In selecting new employees police agencies should use a number of standards in an attempt to appoint the most qualified applicants. The most prominent selection methods include a written and psychological examination, a background investigation, an oral interview, and medical assessment. A recent law enforcement trend has been to lower the difficulty level and adjust passing grades for each racial and ethnic group to allow for more equitable numbers of candidates passing the examination. Lottery systems have also been proposed in which candidates would be randomly selected from a list to insure adequate minority representation.

APPOINTMENT AND PROMOTION BY QUOTA

Public and private agencies have been ordered by the courts (usually under some type of guidelines set forth by a judicial decision) to operate under a "quota system" which calls for a specific percentage of minority members to be present in any group recruited and appointed to an agency. Court ordered quotas may also require that a certain proportion of promotional positions be filled by minorities. These quotas are mandatory and qualifications and test results usually have an inconsequential impact on the promotions. A number of cases involving the legality of quotas have reached the U.S. Supreme Court:

> In 1977, Allen Bakke brought a lawsuit against a California medical school that refused to admit him on the basis that a sufficient number of whites were already enrolled. Bakke charged that this amounted to reverse discrimination! After the case went to the U.S. Supreme Court, he was admitted as a student. The ruling was somewhat ambiguous because on one hand it held that quota systems alone cannot be used to determine enrollment or employment, yet, it still maintained that racial background must be a prime consideration for admission. In the early 1980s, the U.S. Supreme Court held that quota systems could be used. Then in 1987, in a court case involving the Alabama State Police, it was ruled that black officers must receive half the promotions awarded by that agency. Many police officials believe that only future litigation will define the legality or illegality of the quota system (Maguire 1980, 44).

Quotas such as these have resulted in hiring and promotional practices being administered to less qualified individuals. A similar type of decision was handed down against the NYCPD once the results of the 1983 sergeant's test were examined by the courts. A total of 11,593 officers took the examination and only 1.6% of the Blacks and 4.4% of the Hispanics passed this promotional exam. In this case, white females declined to participate in this suit because a sufficient number of these women had excelled in this test. The 1983 test was protested on the basis that it was not sufficiently related to the job performed by a sergeant. Finally in 1985, the City established a quota system that resulted in 20% of sergeants to be promoted being minorities (Mayor's Advisory Committee 1987). One major problem related to the establishment of this promotional policy was that the city actually eliminated the second part of the examination for the minority promotees and dropped the mark on part one to below 60% to meet the 20% quota. These promotions infuriated white officers who had to pass both parts of the examination to be elevated to the rank of sergeant. The minority promotions resulted in a reverse discrimination suit being filed with the city by white officers who passed both parts of the test with higher marks than the minorities who had already been promoted to sergeant. The city recently upheld the suit by the white officers against the 1983 sergeant's test, and these officers were justifiably remunerated. While the rationale for a quota system is to redress past inequities, many male whites view this practice as grossly unfair and amounting to reverse discrimination.

TRADITIONAL METHODS OF PROMOTION

Police officers can be promoted to the rank of detective, sergeant, lieutenant, captain, or higher. However, relatively few police officers advance beyond the rank of police officer during their entire careers. Because of this small percentage, a close look must be given to the validity of the various methods of promotion and, most importantly, how these methods impact upon women.

Merit System

Another path for promotion outside of the supervisory track exists within the NYCPD Detective Bureau. In general, the aspirants for this type of assignment are active precinct patrol officers who compile an impressive arrest record during their assignment to the patrol division. Assignment to investigative duties in the Chicago Police Department (CPD) and the Los Angeles Police Department (LAPD) is accomplished by passing a competitive examination. Approximately 15% of the personnel in these departments are assigned to investigative duties. The problem with the NYCPD system is that the selection system used for the rank of detective is based on job performance and employment records and is frequently riddled with employee charges of nepotism, favoritism, and the "old boy network." It would seem that this would be an ideal mechanism for discrimination, but that is not the case. The most amazing part of this selection method is that women are equally represented in the Detective Bureau in the NYCPD—14%. This does not hold true in either the CPD (6%) or the LAPD (9%) where the percentages of women in the Detective Division are less than the female population in these departments.

Written Examination

The traditional promotional method that has been used by law enforcement agencies is the multiple choice written examination. Two studies conducted on the personnel practices of police departments indicate that there has been very little innovation accomplished in the public sector despite the extraordinary changes within the private sector's advancement process. Many conservative promotional practices, such as the multiple choice written examination, are probably the rule rather than the exception, especially in smaller agencies. One study done by the Educational Testing Services (ETS) dealt with fifteen large cities. Another inquiry done by the Police Foundation/International Association of Chiefs of Police (PF/IACP) included 493 police departments that were large and small but the smaller agencies dominated this study. The following chart illustrates the frequency for each type of promotion selection used by these departments. In most cases, the rating criteria were used in conjunction with other information for final selection:

CHART I

	ETS	PH/IACP
Multiple choice written exams	100%	55%
Oral exam/interview	30%	35%
Education	20%	18%
Promotion potential rating	13%	16%
Performance evaluation/service rating	15%	30%

(Christian and Edwards 1976, 121).

The written examination, consisting of textbook questions with multiple choice answers, is the most traditional and widely used promotional tool (Christian and Edwards 1976, 122). Questions can be written by a committee selected by the agency, another city agency or may even be contracted out to testing services such as the Educational Testing Service of Princeton, New Jersey. In general, the test subjects include law, investigation, patrol and department procedures/policies, supervision and administration, and general intelligence/reading comprehension questions. Several methods may be used to establish the passing grade of the written examination. A standard passing grade may be established such as 75% or the fixed percentage of candidates are deemed to have passed the test.

LITIGATION

The 1973 NYCPD sergeant's and lieutenant's examinations were heavily litigated and resulted in the delays in the rank advancement of numerous officers. This delay resulted in a great deal of racial and ethnic strife within this agency. These promotional tests were the traditional written examinations and consisted exclusively of multiple choice questions (100). A tentative answer key was published immediately after the test, and as is usually the case, most answers were formally protested by many of the aspirants. The sergeant's test was litigated heavily by Blacks, Hispanics, and women and resulted in quotas being imposed on the final list and in the case of women, retroactive seniority being granted to successful candidates as compensatory damages for being denied past promotional opportunities. All but one (#90) of the answers on the lieutenant's test were formally protested and many of these protests suggested three or even four proposed alternate answers, meaning that according to some of the protests, all five selections (A to E) were correct answers. The result of this promotional test was a lieutenant's list that changed three times with some candidates' names and list numbers rising, falling, or just completely dropping off the roster.

One other factor that has complicated the fast rise of women to supervisory ranks in policing has been the constant lawsuits filed against promotional tests. In

New York City, for example, the foundation of most legal challenges to promotional examinations are a result of *Acosta v. Lange* (1963) 13 N.Y.S. 2d 1079, 196 N.E. 2nd 60, 246 N.Y.S. 2nd 404 1963. This court held that if a candidate's answer on a civil service test is "as good as or better than" the answer that the Civil Service Commission has established, the aspirant must be given credit for the answer. This judgment has forced the Civil Service Commission to modify answer keys for promotional tests. This case has managed to virtually remove the previously established judicial protection given to the Civil Service Commission. Since the handing down of the *Acosta* decision, every promotional test answer key has been challenged in the state courts and has, ultimately, resulted in only four sergeants, three lieutenants, and three captains examinations being given by the NYCPD between 1973 and 1993. The CPD has also been faced with test litigation since 1973 with a good portion of the litigation instituted in the *U.S. v. City of Chicago* 73 C. 2080 (1973) evolving around discrimination in promotional practices by the CPD. The court's intervention has led to only two sergeants, lieutenants, and captains examinations being given since 1978. The LAPD, on the other hand, had averaged giving a promotional test for supervisor every two years until recent litigation interfered, and the LAPD is now on the same litigation course as the other two agencies in the study. The results of all this litigation does nothing more than deprive all officers within an agency of the opportunity to move up the ranks.

RANK STRUCTURE

One other aspect that must be remembered when we discuss the rank structure of the three major police agencies in the United States is the fact that the promotional guidelines with the NYCPD indicate that a civil service test is necessary for promotion up to the rank of captain. The appointment to any rank above captain is made at the discretion of the Police commissioner. A very similar method is used by the CPD where a person who passes the lieutenant's test can be, at the discretion of the police chief, appointed to a rank above the position of captain. The LAPD is the only police agency in this study that requires an examination all the way up to the position of police chief. Seeing that the commissioner in NYCPD and chief position in the CPD are held by males it would be conceivable for females in policing to believe that women are being denied the executive positions by a male dominated blue collar occupation.

WOMEN—MOVING UP THE RANKS

Since 1980 women have made progress moving up the ranks of all the police agencies involved in this analysis. The decades of comparison in Tables 1, 2, and 3 indicate that all of three largest police departments in the United States as of late 1991 and early 1992 have a female population of about 14%. This percentage is a considerable change when one considers that in 1980 the NYCPD had a total female population of 2.5%, the 1981 CPD 4%, and the 1981 LAPD 2%. As far as the rank structure is concerned, there has been an increase in women in just about each and every rank of all three police agencies but, once again, these promotions might be considered insignificant because males still dominate the higher positions within these departments. This predominance is a problem that will be overcome sometime within the next twenty years as women continue to ascend the rank structure by passing examinations at higher rates than the female population within their agencies and with promotional test marks that have become, progressively, superior to their male counterparts (Mayor's Advisory Committee 1987, 47). In viewing Tables 1, 2, and 3 we must recall that due to a scarcity of proper testing schedules by all three of these agencies and the constant litigation related to promotional examinations women, as well as men, have not had the proper advancement opportunities.

RECOMMENDATIONS

In viewing this research of the three major police agencies in the United States, one must consider that the increase of women in policing did not begin until the early 1980s. Since then there has been significant growth in the percentage of women entering these police agencies and the females, certainly, have started their movement up the ranks. The major problem that the women have faced evolves around the availability of promotional examination and court litigation. It is a dilemma that must be corrected by all three of these police departments sometime in the near future. If this predicament is not rectified competent officers—female and male—will not have the opportunities for promotion open to them. This problem will, ultimately, create an overabundance of qualified personnel sitting at the bottom of the hierarchy with nowhere to go and no initiative to do any work. If the private sector can create promotional opportunities that are not held up in litigation for years, why can't the public sector review these policies and adapt them to the police advancement examinations? Some contemporary methods of promotion that should be reviewed by police agencies are listed below:

- Oral Interview—an interrogative board that may consist of three to six members who question the candidates. Members of the board can be drawn from the police or any other municipal agency. The questioning of the aspirant can cover a wide spectrum from their personal philosophy to judgments made in police situations with the candidates' response measured accordingly. This process would give an agency the ability to examine an officer in a stressful situation in which the candidate is forced to make immediate decisions (Thibault et al., 1985, 141).

- Assessment Center—The assessment center is a relatively new method of selection in the promotion and evaluation process in the public sector. It was first used by the Germans during World War I and the Americans during World War II. The American Telegraph and Telephone was the first private sector company to use this testing procedure in 1956. The Internal Revenue Service was the first government agency to use the assessment center in 1969 and the Riverside, California Police Department implemented this system in 1970. Since then the FBI, Michigan State Police and the NYCPD have all used this method of selection to test their supervisors. The assessment center consists of five steps. During this process, the candidate is observed, tested, rated, and evaluated by the assessors. The areas of evaluation are:

  1. The in-basket exercise where the candidate may perform tasks involving mail, memos, and directives.
  2. The oral presentation where aspirants present overviews of their work history and personal strengths.

3. The creative writing project which allows the candidate to prepare a special paper and deliver it.

4. Peer group rating where each aspirant ranks his/her peers.

5. The group dialogue where each candidate leads both a group and assigned role discussion (Swank and Conser 1983).

The assessment center method meets EEOC standards and the candidates think that it is a fairer method of selection (Swank and Conser 1983). It also allows for valid evaluation because the candidates are observed doing "hands on" tasks.

- Promotion Potential Ratings—Predicting how well a candidate will perform at the next supervisory level is the goal of a promotion potential rating. This type of classification is more equitably done in conjunction with a performance evaluation system, but it can also be used as a separate type of assessment. In fact, many performance evaluation/efficiency reports have just such a criteria in the body of the form.

- Performance Evaluations—Some police agencies rely heavily on the evaluation of personnel performance for their promotional procedures. Evaluation of personnel is important since it is the only way that police management can maintain records of their police officers' performance and progress. Usually, evaluations are handled by an annual comprehensive report of an officer's performance during a specific rating period. It sometimes is quite detailed and deals with many different types of rating requirements. The following categories comprise most evaluation reports:

1. Quantity of work—amount and completion

2. Quality of work—accuracy, thoroughness, oral expression, neatness

3. Work habits—attendance, punctuality, compliance with department policy

4. Human relations—relationships with peers, community, supervisors, appearance

5. Adaptability—performance in new situations, under stress, and with minimum instructions (Souryal 1985, 76).

- Lateral Entry—This method, as part of the promotional process, is almost nonexistent for the supervisory and managerial ranks in most major police departments. It usually only occurs at the lowest and highest levels of policing. At the top rank, chiefs move from one agency to another, usually in ascending levels to larger, more prestigious organizations.

CONCLUSION

Promotional tests have come under a great deal of scrutiny and often their fairness is decided by costly and protracted litigation. For example, the NY State Division of Human Rights held that grammar questions on a 1978 NYCPD Captain's examination discriminated against Black lieutenants (Lienen 1984). Adverse impact is defined as a "selection rate for any race, sex, or ethnic group which is less than four-fifths (4/5 or 80%) of the rate for the group with the highest rate...(Morris 1978, 65). A federal court in a Chicago ruling decided that a CPD written Sergeant's examination had a discriminating impact upon Blacks and other minorities. The CPD was unable to prove that this test was job-related and was then ordered by the court to make up an entirely new examination.

Few methods of promotion cause as much concern as using racial and gender quotas to achieve equitable rank distribution. Quotas are a stopgap measure and should only be used when no other practical method can be used to correct a disparate impact in promotional procedure. When promotion lists are litigated and the courts enjoin municipalities from using them, very often years can elapse before promotions off a list are finalized. This delay can cause critical management and supervisory shortages that inhibit the day-to-day operations of an agency. In situations such as this, agencies agree to court-imposed gender- and race-related quotas whereby for every white male promoted, a specific number of Blacks, Hispanics, and females have to be promoted in order to resume the promotional process. In many court mandated quota situations, marks are lowered and parts of exams are eliminated and the "quota sergeant" is created by the court's action. This type of systematic process also creates animosity toward the newly promoted supervisors and does little to enhance the self esteem or confidence of the newly promoted minority.

There is a definite need for more upward mobility opportunities for women, but due to the problems caused by litigation, infrequent testing, and the excessive cost of implementing a better method of testing, there is little hope that the future will bring more frequent testing to rectify this situation. As long as the courts continue to interfere in promotional practices of police agencies and to institute rulings such as in *Acosta v. Lange* and *U.S. v. City of Chicago*, the most competent women and men will continue to flounder in the background while a number of incompetents flaunt their advancement.

The future must bring forth promotional testing methods that can defy all challenges and bring to the forefront the most competent female and male supervisors. This innovation must be accompanied by a process that brings equality to women in the ranks that are above the civil service testing procedure (above captain in the NYCPD and the CPD). This equalizing can be easily accomplished through the use of one or a combination of several of the following promotional strategies: an assessment center, oral interviews, and performance valuations. Once the best testing method is put in place and there is no doubt that the technique used is fair and equal, women will finally attain the number of higher ranking positions that should have been offered to them years ago.

STUDY QUESTIONS

1. Historically, what factors led to the hiring of women as members of police organizations?

2. Explain how tokenism applies to women in the police work environment.

3. Discuss the research studies done on women in policing and what, if any, effect these studies have had on the performance of women in policing.

4. Describe several types of promotional practices that might be beneficial to police agencies seeking to avoid Equal Employment Opportunity lawsuits.

REFERENCES

Acosta v. Lange, 13 N.Y.S. 2nd 1079 196. N.E. 2nd 60, 246 N.Y.S. 2nd 404, 1963.

Anne Powers, et al. v. Abraham D. Beame, et al., 341 N.Y.S. 2nd 437 (1991).

Bloch, Peter B. and Deborah Anderson. (1974). *Policewomen on Patrol: Final Report*, Washington, DC: Police Foundation.

Buwalda, Irma W. (1945). "Policewomen: Yesterday, Today and Tomorrow," *Journal of Social Hygiene*, 31, 290-293.

Chicago Police Department. Employment Statistics for 1981 and 1991.

Christian, Kenneth E. and Steven M. Edwards. (1976). *Supervisory Promotional Practices*, New York: Harper and Row.

Crites, Laura. (1973). "Women in Law Enforcement," *Management Information Systems*, 5, 1-16.

Days, Drew S. (1979). "Equalizing Opportunity in Police Departments," *Journal on Intergroup Relations*, V. 8-1.

Dolan, Edward F. and Margaret M. Scariano. (1988). *The Police in American Society*, New York: Franklin Watts.

Drucker, Peter F. (1954). *The Practice of Management*, New York: Harper and Row.

Epstein, Cynthia. (1970). *A Woman's Place*, Berkeley, CA: University of California Press.

Fullwider, Robert K. (1980). *The Reverse Discrimination Controversy*, Totowa, NJ: Rowan and Littlefield.

Gavin, Susan and Barbara Raffel Price. (1979). "A Century of Women in Policing." In Donald O. Schultz, (ed.) *Modern Police Administration*, Houston, Texas: Gulf Publishing Co.

Grennan, Sean A. (1987a). "The Role of Officer Gender During Violent Confrontations with Citizens." (Doctoral Dissertation, Graduate Center, City University of New York). *Dissertation Abstracts International*.

Grennan, Sean A. (1987b). Findings on the Role of Officer Gender in Violent Confrontations with Citizens," *Journal of Police Science and Administration*, 15 no. 1, 78-85.

Grennan, Sean A. (1991). "Are Police Promotional Practices Gender Related?" *Women Police*, Spring, 16-17.

Grennan, Sean A. (1993). "A Perspective on Women in Policing." In Roslyn Muraskin and Ted Alleman, (eds.) *It's a Crime: Women and Justice*, Englewood Cliffs, NJ: Regents/Prentice Hall.

Kanter, Rosabeth. (1977). *Men and Women of the Corporation*, New York: Basic Books.

Keefe, Mary L. (1981). *Overview of Equal Opportunity in Policing for Women*, Washington, DC: National Institute of Justice.

Kohlan, Richard G. (1973). "Police Promotional Procedure in Fifteen Jurisdictions," *Public Personnel Management*, May-June, 167-170.

Lienen, Stephen H. (1984). *Black Police, White Society*, New York: New York University Press.

Los Angeles Police Department. Employment Statistics for 1981 and 1991.

Maguire, Daniel C. (1980). *A New American Justice*, Garden City, NY: Doubleday and Co.

Mayor's Advisory Committee on Police Management and Personnel Police: Final Report. (1987). City of New York.

Millman, Marcia and Rosabeth M. Kanter, (eds.) (1976). *Another Voice*, New York: Octagon Books.

Milton, Catherine. (1972). *Women in Policing*, Washington, DC: Police Foundation.

More, Harry W. Jr. (1975). *Effective Police Administration*, San Jose: Justice Systems Development.

Morris, Frank C. Jr. (1978). *Current Trends in the Use and Misuse of Statistics in Employment Discrimination Litigation*, Washington, DC: Equal Employment Advisory Council.

Nassau County Police Department. (1985). Performance and Awards.

New York City Police Department. Employment Statistics for 1980 and 1992.

Remmington, Patricia. (1981). *Policing: The Occupation and the Introduction of Female Officers*, Washington, DC: University Press of America.

Shpritzer v. Lang, 234 N.Y.S. 2nd 422 (1963).

Sichel, Joyce, Lucy Friedman, Janet Quint, and Michael Smith. (1978). *Women on Patrol: A Pilot Study of Police Performance in New York City*, Washington, DC: Police Foundation.

Smith, Elizabeth S. (1982). *Breakthrough: Women in Law Enforcement*, Rexdale, Ontario: John Wiley and Sons.

Souryal, Sam S. (1985). *Police Organization and Administration*, Cincinnati: Anderson Publishing.

Swank, Calvin J. and James A. Conser. (1983). *The Police Personnel System*, New York: John Wiley.

Thibault, Edward A., Lawrence M. Lynch and F. Bruce McBride. (1985). *Proactive Police Management*, Englewood Cliffs, NJ: Prentice Hall.

U.S. v. City of Chicago, 73 C. 2080 (1973).

PART VIII

CONCLUSION

THE FUTURE

Roslyn Muraskin, Ph.D.

Can we predict the future with any precision? Probably not. What we can predict is that crime will remain with us forever. Perhaps there will be different kinds of crime, but crime remains a factor of life. Regardless if the crime index is down, individual events create the impression that crime is out of control. There are no easy answers or solutions.

We know that we will have sophisticated technology in areas such as corrections and policing. We know that we face a growing aging correctional population—presenting new problems in terms of special care and the health of such inmates. The media continues to focus on the negatives of the criminal justice system—telling us that crime is out of control. We know we are/will be building newer and bigger correctional facilities, knowing that no matter how many cells we have available, they will always be filled. With respect to AIDS with thirty-seven out of one hundred inmates being intravenous drug users, with such a statistic how do we curb the AIDS problem present today and in the future?

There are those, such as George Cole, who refer to the criminal factor as the "PUT" syndrome: we have to put these people someplace; therefore we load up the correctional facilities.

We are told that community policing is the answer, but there are more who say community policing: "let it rest in peace." We hear of boot camps being the answer, but if those participating return to the environments from which they came, then the camps are not the answer. The inmates do return and the result is that boot camps are not fulfilling their original intent.

We know that by the year 2006 the baby boomers of today will be of age to commit criminal acts. Based on demographics, we will have a large amount of individuals involved as defendants in the criminal justice system.

Prediction is a risky business, but we need to review the trends. What we do need in place is the use of high technology (as has been predicted in this text) that can put information in our hands immediately. We need workable policies. "Three strikes and you're out," is not the answer for the future. If we were to multiply the number of felons in each state, we would have correctional facilities with larger populations than some states.

The war on crime has yet to be won. Understanding the past and present should be a catalyst for change. New policies and their implementation *today* is *yesterday's tomorrow* and *tomorrow* is *today's future*. Understanding that crime exists, we must work to bring about a society where crime does not overtake us through the development of hard policies and their implementation.

The violence of youth must be kept in check, not by building bigger and better cells, but through education, alternative programs, and stopping the problems before they begin. Guns are cheap. They are available to the youth of America for as little as $20; guns can even be rented. Gun laws have to be fully enforced and policies have to be directed at their implementation. Violence is a symptom of other problems and we must deal with those symptoms before anything else. Policies are needed that attack the root of the problem. Band aid programs do not work.

The twenty-first century is quickly approaching. Plans are needed to hold crime rates down. Plans are needed to quell the fears of crime. Action is needed. The rhetoric is there. The politicians cry outrage at the crime statistics, but outrage does not accomplish anything unless we see concrete plans and policies being implemented. Crime in the twenty-first century will not go away, unless we are smart enough to plan today. We must have a "vision for change."

PART IX

ABOUT THE AUTHORS

Roslyn Muraskin, Ph.D., is the Associate Dean of the School of Public Service, College of Management at the C.W. Post Campus of Long Island University. She holds the rank of Associate Professor of Criminal Justice at C.W. Post. She is the past President of the Northeastern Association of Criminal Justice Sciences (NEACJS) and is the Director of the Long Island Women's Institute. She received her doctorate in Criminal Justice from the Graduate Center at the City University of New York, and her Master's Degree at New York University. She received her Bachelor's Degree from Queens College.

She is the co-author/editor of *It's a Crime: Women and Justice*, (Prentice Hall, January 1993) and is the editor of *The Justice Professional*, a refereed Journal. She is the author of "Police Work and Juveniles: Revisited" in *Juvenile Justice* (ed. Roberts) 1996. She has reviewed numerous books for leading refereed journals. She is the author/editor of *Issues in Justice: Exploring Policy Issues in the Criminal Justice System* (Wyndham Hall Press, 1990). Her articles include "Mothers and Fetuses: Enter the Fetal Police," (1991), "Issues in Justice: Policy Implications," (1990), "Directions for the Future" in *Ethics in Criminal Justice* (Wyndham Hall, 1990) and "Police Work and Juveniles," (1989). She has written the Forewords for *Critical Issues in Crime and Justice* (Sage, 1994) and *Criminal Justice Today: An Introductory Text for the Twenty-First Century* (first edition, Prentice Hall, 1991). Other publications include *Women's Agenda: Meeting the Challenge to Change* (1992), *The Future of Criminal Justice Education* (1987), *Victims of Crime: Who Cares, A Study of Crime Victims* (1986), *Women: Victims of Domestic Violence, Rape and Criminal Justice* (1985) and *The Suffolk County Police Department: A Managerial Study*. She has presented over thirty papers at Professional Conferences throughout the United States.

In addition she serves as Second Vice-President for the Criminal Justice Educators of New York State (CJEANYS), and is a member of the Academy of Criminal Justice Sciences, American Society of Criminology, the Campus Representative of the American Association of University Women, is a member of the American Correctional Association, American Academy of Political and Social Science, National Women's Association and the Women's Resource Center She was elected to Who's Who Among Teachers and is the founder of the Epsilon Beta Chapter of the National Criminal Justice Honor Society at the C.W. Post Campus.

Her previous work includes Assistant Director of the *Manhattan Bail Project* for the Vera Institute of Justice.

Albert R. Roberts, D.S.W. is a Professor of Criminal Justice and Social Work at the School of Social Work, Rutgers University, New Brunswick, New Jersey. He is chairperson of the Administration of Justice Department at Rutgers University. He previously taught at the Indiana University School of Social Work in Indianapolis, Seton Hall University, the University of New Haven, and Brooklyn College of the City University of New York. He received his doctorate in social work from the University of Maryland School of Social Work with a concentration in social work research and a minor in criminal justice. His M.A. degree is in sociology and criminology from Long Island University, and his B.A. is from the C.W. Post Campus of Long Island University.

He is a lifetime member of the Academy of Criminal Justice Sciences and an active member of the N.A.S.W., the American Correctional Association, and the National Council of Juvenile and Family Court Judges. He is a member of the New Jersey Governor's Juvenile Justice and Delinquency Prevention Commission, as well as the New Jersey Supreme Court's Probation Advisory Board. Dr. Roberts has extensive experience in juvenile and criminal justice research. Over the past two decades, he has served as Project Director or consultant on several research and evaluation projects including: The New Jersey State Law Enforcement planning Agency's Evaluation Projects, Research for Better Schools, Inc., (Philadelphia) Correctional Education Project, the American Correctional Association's National Study on the Utilization of Instructional Technology in corrections, and the National Institute of Justice (N.I.J.) funded study on the Effectiveness of Crisis Intervention with Crime Victims at the Victim Services Agency in New York City.

He serves on the Advisory Board for *The Justice Professional* and is the Editor-in-Chief of the journal *Crisis Intervention Time-Limited Treatment*. He has also authored and edited fifteen books, including *Helping Crime Victims* (Sage, 1990), *Juvenile Justice* (2nd edition, Nelson Hall, 1996), and *Crisis Intervention and Time-Limited Cognitive Therapy* (Sage, 1995). He is the author of *Helping Battered Women: New Perspectives and Remedies*, Oxford University Press, 1996. He has more than 100 publications to his name.

BIOGRAPHIES OF CONTRIBUTORS

Jay S. Albanese, Ph.D. is Professor and Director of the Graduate Program in Criminal Justice Administration at Niagara University. He received his B.A. degree from Niagara University and M.A. and Ph.D. from Rutgers University. He is author of seven books, including *Crime in America: Some Existing and Emerging Issues* (with R. Pursely), *Organized Crime in America*, *Dealing with Delinquency: The Future of Juvenile Justice*, and *White Collar Crime in America*. Dr. Albanese was recipient of the Teaching Excellence and Campus Leadership Award from the Sears Foundation in 1990. He is a Past President of the Northeastern Association of Criminal Justice Sciences and is President of the Academy of Criminal Justice Sciences for 1995-1996.

William G. Archambeault, Ph.D. holds the rank of Professor, School of Social Work, Louisiana State University, Baton Rouge. He was previously chairman of the Department of Criminal Justice at LSU. He has authored numerous works in the area of criminal justice administration, organizational management, the use of computers in criminal justice organizations and the computer assisted monitoring of offenders. His most recent text, *Criminal Justice Administration and Organization Theory: Managing Justice Services into the Twenty-First Century* is to be published by Prentice Hall in 1995. Other books include *Computers in Criminal Justice* (1989) and *Correctional Supervisory Management* (1982). He earned a Ph.D. in Criminology from The Florida State University in 1979.

Charles B. Fields, Ph.D. is an Associate Professor in the Department of Political Science/Criminal Justice at Appalachian State University. He has a B.A. and M.A. in Political Science from Appalachian State University and received his Ph.D. in Criminal Justice from Sam Houston State University in 1984. His most recent articles/reviews have appeared in the *Journal of Criminal Justice, Criminal Justice Policy Review, Quarterly Journal of Ideology, and the Journal of Criminal Law* and the *Journal of Criminal Law and Criminology* among others, and is the author of *Innovative Trends and Specialized Strategies in Community-Based Corrections* (1994—Garland Publishing). He is the immediate Past-President of the Southern Criminal Justice Association and is Region Two Trustee on the Executive Board of the Academy of Criminal Justice Sciences.

Edith Flynn, Ph.D. is a criminologist who has specialized in corrections, criminal justice policy research, personnel management, research and planning, and political crimes and terrorism. She has testified before Congress on corrections policies and has served in leadership positions in the American Society of Criminology, the Society for the Study of Social Problems, the American Correctional Association, and the International Society of Criminology. She received her Ph.D. from the University of Illinois at Urbana. Among her publications are "The Graying of America's Prison Population," in *The Prison Journal* (1994), *Corrections Employee Stress*, Research Monograph (1991), "Neglected Types of Victimization," in *From Crime Policy to Victim Policy*. She is currently working on a major, national research grant from the National Institute of Justice on the problems of managing elderly offender populations in the nation's prisons and jails.

Rosemary L. Gido, Ph.D. is an Assistant Professor in the Administration of Justice Program at Pennsylvania State University. She is the former Director of the Office of Program and Policy Analysis of the New York State Commission of Correction and Work Force Policy Analyst for New State Government. Her research has focused on AIDS in correctional institutions, jails, and intermediate sanctions. She is currently secretary of the Academy of Criminal Justice Sciences Minorities and Women's Section and membership Chair. She is co-editor (with Ted Alleman) of *Correctional Issues: The Practice of Institutional Punishment*.

Joseph J. Grau, Ph.D., received a doctoral degree from the University of Pittsburgh and a Master of Arts from Fordham University. He was Director of the Security Administration Program and served for twenty-eight years as Director of Graduate Studies in the Department of Criminal Justice and Security Administration, School of Public Service/College of Management, Long Island University, C.W. Post Campus. His most recent publications include the Second Edition of the *Criminal and Civil Investigation Handbook* (1994), an authoritative reference book, and "Managing Trade Secrets" focusing on intellectual property rights that appeared in a special edition of the *Legal Studies Forum*. He has organized and chaired conferences such as "Technology and Security Management" and the New York State Legislative Hearings on the "Police Corp and Police Cadet" program.

Sean A. Grennan, Ph.D., is an Associate Professor of Criminal Justice at the C.W. Post Campus of Long Island University. Dr. Grennan received his Ph.D. in Criminal Justice from the Graduate Center of City University of New York. His major areas of research are women in policing, police use of deadly force and organized crime. Dr. Grennan is a twenty-year veteran of N.Y.P.D. and retired with the rank of Detective. He held assignments as investigator in the Queens Homicide Squad and instructor in Advanced Training in the Police Academy.

Kenneth C. Haas, Ph.D. is the Associate Chairperson for the Criminal Justice Program at the University of Delaware. In 1991, he won the University's Excellence-in-Advising Award, and he has won the University's Excellence-in-Teaching Award three times. He specializes in criminal procedure and correctional law. His articles have appeared in law reviews, social science journals, and scholarly books. He is co-editor of *The Dilemmas of Corrections* (1991) and *Challenging Capital Punishment* (1988).

Vincent Henry is a doctoral candidate working on his dissertation in criminal justice at the City University of New York, an Adjunct Professor in the Department of Criminal Justice at the C.W. Post Campus of Long Island University, and a Sergeant assigned to the Special Projects Unit of the New York City Police Department's Office of Management Analysis and Planning. In 1989, he became the first American police officer to win a Fulbright Grant, and spent one year as a Visiting Fellow at Griffith University studying comparative patterns of police corruption and reform. His thirteen-year police career includes assignments in a wide variety of patrol, plainclothes, undercover, investigative and management assignments.

Robert A. Jerin, Ph.D. is an Assistant Professor in the Department of Political Science/Criminal Justice at Appalachian State University. He has a B.S. in Criminal Justice from the University of New Haven, a M.S. in Criminology from Florida State University and received a Ph.D. in Criminal Justice from Sam Houston State University in 1987. He has published in the *American Journal of Police* and his current research includes crime and the media, victim/witness assistance program evaluation and rights of crime victims.

Andrew Karmen, Ph.D. is an associate professor in the Sociology Department of John Jay College of Criminal Justice. He received his Ph.D. in sociology from Columbia University in 1977. He is the author of *Crime Victims: an Introduction to Victimology*, second edition published by Wadsworth (1990), and along with Donal MacNamara edited *Deviants: Victims or Victimizers?* (Sage, 1983). He has written articles about victims' rights, auto thefts, vigilantism, drug abuse, police use of deadly force and the 1950 Rosenberg atom spy case.

Mark M. Lanier, Ph.D. is currently an Assistant Professor in the Department of Criminal Justice and Legal Studies at the University of Central Florida. He received his doctorate from Michigan State University in 1993. His Ph.D. is interdisciplinary with concentrations in psychology, sociology, and criminology. For the past seven years he has been involved with research dealing with AIDS/HIV and the Criminal Justice system. His Masters thesis and two resulting articles were among the first effort to document AIDS knowledge and behavior among adolescents. His work has been published in the *American Journal of Public Health, Journal of Criminal Justice, Criminal Justice and Behavior, Women and Criminal Justice* and other journals. In addition to his interest in AIDS/HIV he has been measuring the impact of community policing in Chicago's Public Housing.

Malcolm L. Lachance-McCullough, M.A. is an Evaluation Specialist in the Prevention Surveys and Evaluation Sections, division of HIV Prevention, AIDS Institute, New York State Department of Health. In 1990, he received his M.S. in Criminology from California State University, Fresno. In 1991, he was awarded an M.A. in Criminal Justice at Albany State University of New York, where he is a fourth year doctoral student. He has conducted research on violent crime, capital punishment sentiment and the fear of crime, correctional health care and HIV/AIDS in both prison and obstetrical settings.

Robert J. Meadows, Ph.D. is an Associate Professor in the Department of Sociology and Criminal Justice at California Lutheran University. Dr. Meadows received his Ph.D. from Claremont Graduate School. His research interests include policing, private security, and legal issues in criminal justice. He is the founder and chair of the Security and Crime Prevention section of the Academy of Criminal Justice Sciences. He is a recognized consultant on police and private security.

Robert Munoz retired from the New York City Police Department as a Sergeant after twenty years of service. He held numerous uniformed police sergeants positions and was also the course coordinator and principal instructor for the Basic Management Orientation Course for Sergeants, the Lieutenants Orientation Course for Lieutenants and the Duty Captains Orientation Course for Captains while assigned to the Advanced and Specialized Training Unit of the New York City Police Academy. He holds a B.S. in Criminal Justice from the New York Institute of Technology and a M.S. degree from Long Island University.

Michael J. Palmiotto, Ph.D. is an Associate Professor of criminal justice at Wichita State University. Professor Palmiotto worked as a police officer in New York State and is the past Director of Criminal Justice and Police Training at the Community College of Beaver County, Monaca Pennsylvania. Professor Palmiotto holds a masters degree from the John Jay College of Criminal Justice and a doctorate from the University of Pittsburgh. His law enforcement interests include civil liabilities, drug enforcement, criminal investigations and community policing. He has published numerous articles and has published a text on criminal investigation.

Kenneth J. Peak, Ph.D., is a professor of criminal justice at the University of Nevada, Reno. He entered municipal policing in 1970 in Kansas, later holding positions as a criminal justice planner, director of a four-state Technical Assistance Institute, director of public safety at two universities, and assistant professor at Wichita State University. In addition to publishing more than 30 book chapters and journal articles, his first textbook, *Policing America: Method, Issues, Challenges* appeared in early 1993, followed by *Justice Administration: Police, Court and Corrections Management*, which appeared in August 1994. He recently co-authored a book on community oriented policing and problem solving, which will appear in 1995.

Harriet Pollack, Ph.D. is Professor Emerita of Constitutional Law at John Jay College of Criminal Justice of the City University of New York. For ten years she was the Chair of the Department of Government and Public Administration at the College. She holds a Ph.D. in Political Science from Columbia University, and has had various articles on Constitutional Law published in periodicals as diverse as the *Saturday Review* (when Norman Cousins was editor) and *Federal Probation*. She was a consultant to the Congressional Commission on Marijuana and Drug Abuse, and is co-author of *Some Sins are Not Crimes* and the third edition of *Criminal Justice: An Overview*. In addition, along with Professor Alexander B. Smith, she co-authored *Civil Liberties and Civil Rights in the United States* (West Publishers).

Donald J. Rebovich, Ph.D. has been Director of Research for the American Prosecutors Research Institute (APRI) since 1990, located in Alexandria, Virginia. In that role Dr. Rebovich has been responsible for the direction of a number of national research programs dedicated to the study of the prosecution of environmental crime, organized crime, domestic violence, and drug-related offenses. Dr. Rebovich's book *Dangerous Ground: The World of Hazardous Waste Crime* (1992) represents the first empirical effort to provide insight into critical characteristics of hazardous waste offenses, offenders and mechanisms used to effectively control these crimes. Before coming to APRI, Dr. Rebovich served for ten years with the Office of the New Jersey Attorney General and was responsible for research and evaluation of environmental and drug crime enforcement initiatives. While with the New Jersey Attorney General's Office, Dr. Rebovich also conducted characteristic of police physical activities, and the use of reasonable force by local police. Dr. Rebovich received his B.S. in Criminal Justice and Psychology from Trenton State College, and received his M.A. and Ph.D. in Criminal Justice from Rutgers University.

Lori Koester Scott, M.C., M.ED is the Administrator of Sex Offender Supervision for Maricopa Adult Probation in Phoenix, Arizona. She received her B.S. in sociology for St. Louis University and a master's in Counseling from Arizona State University. In addition to her specialization in working with sex offenders, she has been a member of the department's planning and programs division, and has worked on implementing legislation to fund and improve community-based treatment programs. A board member and legislative liaison for the Arizona Providers Association for the treatment of Sexual Abusers, she is also a member of several regional and national commissions focusing on improving services to both victims and perpetrators of sexual abuse. She has recently published a chapter on sex offender supervision and treatment in *Critical Issues in Crime and Justice* (1994). A trainer and consultant to probation departments throughout Arizona and other states, she is presently researching the recidivism factors of probationary sex offenders revoked to prison.

Etta F. Morgan-Sharp is an Old Dominion University (Norfolk, VA) President's Graduate Fellow pursuing a doctorate degree at Indiana University of Pennsylvania. Her research interests include: female criminality, gender and racial disparities in the criminal justice system, sentencing reforms, victim impact statements and the serious juvenile offender.

Robert T. Sigler, Ph.D. teaches in the Department of Criminal Justice at the University of Alabama. His research interests include domestic abuse, intimate violence in dating and courtships, justice system employee stress, and community corrections.

Alexander B. Smith, Ph.D., J.D., is Professor Emeritus of Social Psychology at John Jay College of Criminal Justice of the City University of New York. He was the first Dean of Studies and the first chairman of the Division of Social Studies at the College. Before coming to John Jay he was a Case Supervisor, in the Probation Department of the Supreme Court of Kings County, and before that he was a practicing attorney in New York City. He has been a member of the New York Bar since 1931, and a Certified Psychologist in New York State. Since 1963 he has been consultant to the President's Commission of Obscenity and Pornography, the Office of Juvenile Delinquency (Department of Health, Education and Welfare), and the Commission of Marijuana and Drug Abuse. He has written widely in the field of criminal justice having co-authored 14 books (including two monographs) and over 60 articles. His newest books are third editions of *Treating the Criminal Offender* (Plenum) and *Criminal Justice: An Overview* (West).

James M. Tesoriero is an Evaluation Specialist in the Prevention Surveys and Evaluation Section, Division of HIV Prevention, AIDS Institute, New York State Department of Health. He holds a Masters degree in Criminal Justice from Northeastern University and is an advanced doctoral student in Criminology at the University of Albany. His current research interests include measurement of crime, weapons use among juveniles, use of objective risk scales as decision-making instruments, and HIV/AIDS in prison settings.

Michael Welch, Ph.D. received his degree in Sociology from the University of North Texas, Denton. Presently, he is Associate Professor in the Administration of Justice Program at Rutgers University, New Brunswick, New Jersey. Previously, an Associate Professor at St. John's University in Queens, New York, Welch also has correctional experience at the federal, state and local levels. His research interests include corrections and social control. He has published numerous book chapters and articles which have appeared in the *American Journal of Criminal Justice, Journal of Crime and Justice, Dialectical Anthropology*, and the *Journal of Offender Counseling, Services, and Rehabilitation*. He is also the author of *Corrections: A Critical Approach* (McGraw-Hill).

Wayne N. Welsh, Ph.D. is an Assistant Professor of Criminal Justice at Temple University, Philadelphia. His research has examined violent offenders, jail overcrowding, and court-ordered reform of correctional institutions. Recent work has appeared in *Law and Society Review, Law and Policy, Justice Quarterly* and *Criminal Justice and Behavior*. He is currently conducting process and evaluations of nine community-based delinquency prevention programs in Pennsylvania, and he is writing a book about court-ordered jail reforms and organizational change in local justice systems.